# THE ANIMATED MOVIE GUIDE

Jerry Beck

**Contributing Writers**

Martin Goodman
Andrew Leal
W. R. Miller
Fred Patten

CHICAGO
REVIEW
PRESS

An A Cappella Book

Library of Congress Cataloging-in-Publication Data
Beck, Jerry. The animated movie guide / Jerry Beck.— 1st ed. p. cm.
    "An A Cappella book."
    Includes index.
ISBN 1-55652-591-5
    1.  Animated films—Catalogs.  I. Title.
NC1765.B367 2005
016.79143'75—dc22
2005008629

Front cover design: Leslie Cabarga
Interior design: Rattray Design
All images courtesy of Cartoon Research Inc.

Front cover images (clockwise from top left): Photograph from the
motion picture *Shrek* ™ & © 2001 DreamWorks L.L.C. and PDI,
reprinted with permission by DreamWorks Animation; Photograph from
the motion picture *Ghost in the Shell 2* ™ & © 2004 DreamWorks
L.L.C. and PDI, reprinted with permission by DreamWorks Animation;
*Mutant Aliens* © Bill Plympton; *Gulliver's Travels.*

Back cover images (left to right): *Johnny the Giant Killer, Gulliver's
Travels, The Snow Queen*

© 2005 by Jerry Beck
All rights reserved
First edition
Published by A Cappella Books
An Imprint of Chicago Review Press, Incorporated
814 North Franklin Street
Chicago, Illinois 60610
ISBN 1-55652-591-5
Printed in the United States of America
5 4 3 2 1

For Marea

# Contents

# Acknowledgments

This book would not be as complete, as accurate, or as fun without the help of my dedicated friends and enthusiastic colleagues. Here's the part where I get to mention their names and say thanks.

My editor, Yuval Taylor, agreed to take on this project for A Cappella Books and has been generous in extending my deadline several times as well as accommodating my vision for the book.

Helping me keep my sanity through all of this was my wife, Marea Boylan, who assisted me in every phase of the project. Her contributions were numerous. She double-checked facts, typed, and retyped much of the manuscript and had incredible patience with me during this difficult process. Thank you, my love.

One simply cannot write books about animation history without the input, advice, and wisdom of Mark Kausler. He provided me with access to some of the rarest titles cataloged within. On behalf of cartoon historians everywhere, I salute you.

This book also received generous assistance from Leonard Maltin, Howard Green, Amid Amidi, John Canemaker, Will Ryan, Leslie Cabarga, and Michael Barrier. All these guys were there when I needed them—and thus made this book more precise, a better read, and more fun to look at.

The archival resources of Larry Edmunds Bookshop, the Internet Movie Database, Box Office Mojo, the Hollywood Book & Poster Company, *Variety*, the Margaret Herrick Library of the Academy of Motion Picture Arts & Sciences, and Asifa-Hollywood were invaluable.

I don't want to forget Rebecca Poole, Doug Ranney, and Eric Lurio, who were early contributors to my initial filmography.

Sharon Burion compiled many of the film credits and was a first-class research associate on this project. She's a good one.

Stuart Fisher, David Bastian, and Daniel Goldmark were also contributing writers to this volume, each coming through for me when I was facing the dreaded deadline doom. Each provided wisdom, insights, and mighty fine writing.

I'm very proud of my team of contributors, each of whom deserves major credit in helping me make this project a reality. Take a bow, Martin "Dr. Toon" Goodman, Andrew Leal, W. R. Miller, and Fred Patten. Each one was a pleasure to deal with and this book would not be as good without their incredible writing and researching talents.

Thank you all!

Jerry Beck

# Introduction

In November 2004, an unusual event in the history of motion pictures occurred. Three of the top five films of the week, in box-office gross, were animated feature films. *The Incredibles*, *The Polar Express*, and *The SpongeBob SquarePants Movie* were huge blockbuster hits—all at the same time, for three different studios. I love the fact that each film used a different technique (CGI, motion capture, and cel, respectively) and that the subject matter of each (a superhero adventure, a Christmas fairy tale, and a zany cartoon comedy) was just as diverse. Add to it that the biggest moneymaking movie of 2004, *Shrek 2*, was also an animated film, and there can only be one conclusion—the animated feature has come of age.

Narrative fiction animated features have been around since 1926, but the medium's growth in quantity and quality came about only in the last 20 years. Before that, the animated feature was primarily the domain of the Walt Disney Company. Competition from the 1930s through the 1980s followed Disney's superior lead, most without that studio's ambition, style, or heart. Many competing studios simply churned out second-rate children's films, further eroding the development of the medium, and allowing Disney to further dominate the landscape.

Serious competition began to emerge in the late 1980s as a younger generation of animators broke Disney's mold (moldy in more ways than one), expanding the storytelling possibilities, and using the medium in bold new ways by reinventing the tools and techniques themselves.

In 1994, I was working for Nickelodeon Movies developing new ideas for animated features. *The Lion King* had just become the biggest hit in history, and every studio was jumping onto the cartoon feature bandwagon. A question was raised about the grosses for previous animated features and, being the historian I am, I decided to dive into the research.

To my surprise I learned there was very little published on the history of animated features. There were book-length filmographies devoted to animated television series (Hal Erickson's is the best) and animated television specials (George Wollery's is highly recommended), much about Disney features (Leonard Maltin's *The Disney Films* is vital), and theatrical cartoon shorts (see Maltin's *Of Mice & Magic*).

The few tomes that covered animated features did not do it as thoroughly as I would have liked. Bruno Edera's 1976 book (*Full Length Animated Feature Films*) was woefully out of date, incomplete, and filled with problems. Just how many animated features were made? Who made them? Which ones were worth seeing? I needed to know, and decided I had to compile the information myself.

I began collecting data on animated features while at Nick Movies and kept doing it after I left the department. I started a work-in-progress list of titles in chronological order—first on paper, then online as part of my "Cartoon Research" Web site. Doing so allowed me to add new titles as they came to light. I also began, in earnest, keeping close tabs of new animated films as they were released.

I set up criteria for what films to include and exclude, creating a purely subjective list of what qualified for a theatrical release and what an animated feature really is—my opinions, of course, but I think I'm right. First, I decided to start small—just list animated features that were released to movie theaters in the United States. There are literally thousands of animated features from all parts of the globe (though Japan certainly holds the world's record). This was my first line in the sand—limit the list to U.S. releases. If it was a Japanese feature released only to television, bypassing theater showings—titles like *Jack & the Witch* (1967) or *The Little Norse Prince* (1965)—it was excluded. Foreign titles that went direct to video—like Miyazaki's *Kiki's Delivery Service* (1989) or Italy's *The Magic Voyage* (1992)—were also excluded. But if a foreign-made animated film was given a U.S. theatrical release, then it's documented here.

Made-for-television features, such as *The Point* (1971) or *The Flintstones Meet the Jetsons* (1987), were not included on my list. Nor were the dozens of animated films made specifically for home video, from *The Animatrix* (2002) and *Lil' Pimp* (2005) to all the *Land Before Time* movies and numerous Disney "sequels."

An animated feature had to follow in the pattern established by *Snow White and the Seven Dwarfs* (1937). A theatrical release must have played in legitimate movie theaters (college campus showings, museum, and film festival screenings do not count) and should have some residual evidence of its release: distribution accessories such as a movie trailer, a one-sheet poster, a pressbook, presskit, or publicity still photos.

This book contains the most accurate and complete list of U.S. theatrical animated features film ever compiled. It does not include marionette and puppet films like *Thunderbirds Are Go* (1967), *Pufnstuff* (1970), *The Dark Crystal* (1983), Jim Henson Muppet movies, *Thomas and the Magic Railroad* (2000), and *Team America: World Police* (2004). These movies use live-action photography of puppets, models, or people in costumes. In animated films, images are created frame by frame: a new drawing, a separate movement of an object, or a new computer-generated image is created specially for each frame of film. It is not photographed in real time.

Also not listed here are compilation features such as *Hooray for Betty Boop* (1976), *The Speed Racer Show* (1993), and various festivals of animation (package features such as *Fantasia* (1940), *Heavy Metal* (1981), *Robot Carnival* (1991) listed herein contain original animation created specifically for that film)—nor does this list include numerous foreign-animated features that have been dubbed in English and that have appeared on U.S. television, such as *Dot and the Kangaroo* (Australia), *Katy Caterpillar* (Spain), and *The Singing Princess* (Italy). The Disney Channel, in particular, back in the 1980s and '90s showed many foreign-animated features, dubbed in English, that, to date, have appeared nowhere else.

IMAX retreads, such as the television-special-turned-40-minute-featurette *Santa vs. the Snowman* (2002) are also not listed.

This book does not contain listings for films that are primarily live action but have brief animation sequences, bits, and titles. This leaves out *Anchors Aweigh* (1945), *Two Guys from Texas* (1948), *So Dear to My Heart* (1949), *The Pink Panther* (1964), *Monkey Bone* (2001), *The Life Aquatic* (2004), and many others.

Another issue of concern for many is the emerging hybrid film. Movies like *Casper* (1995), *Stuart Little 2* (2002), *Scooby Doo* (2002), and *Garfield: The Movie* (2004) contain computer-generated leading characters. I consider most of these to be live-action movies with "special-effect" creatures. While they contain extraordinary character animation, these films were primarily sold to the public as live-action realizations of famed cartoon characters (not unlike the live-action *Flintstones*, *George of the Jungle*, and *Mr. Magoo* movies). Films like *Cats and Dogs* (2001), *Kangaroo Jack* (2003), and *Racing Stripes* (2005) are gimmick films that manipulate live action in cartoonish ways—I'd no more consider them for this filmography than I would *The Mask* (1994) or *Inspector Gadget* (2001).

Recent hybrids like *Sky Captain and the World of Tomorrow*, the *Lord of the Rings* trilogy, and *Star Wars* Episodes 1, 2, and 3 contain extensive computer-generated scenes and characters; to consider these films as animated features is far-fetched. These films are the heirs to *King Kong* (1933), *The Wizard of Oz* (1939), and *The Thief of Baghdad* (1940). No one has ever considered *Mighty Joe Young* (1949) or *The Seventh Voyage of Sinbad* (1957) to be animated films. These hybrids have always been with us; they are simply live-action films with animated special effects.

I have included some films that may seem, at first, to be breaking my own rules. *Song of the South*? *Who Framed Roger Rabbit*? *The Adventures of Rocky and Bullwinkle*? To me, these are films that were sold to the public as animated films. And they each contain extensive cartoon animation sequences. Thus, how a film was conceived, perceived, and sold was a factor in what I included in this filmography.

Clearly the worlds of live action and animation are blending. And that makes it the perfect time for this book. It's an exciting period for animated features, as they evolve and grow toward new definitions of what animation is, and can be. The recently established Academy Award for Best Animated Feature and exciting new works by traditionally live-action filmmakers (Robert Zemeckis, Richard Linklater) are bringing new prestige to the medium. International animation (Miyazaki, Chomet, and the whole anime genre) is gaining wider acceptance. Independent films (by the likes of Bill Plympton and others) and a variety of animation techniques (CG, cel, clay, stop-motion puppets, motion capture) are proving it's not the technique, it's the story and the storyteller that matter. With all this activity in the medium, it's time to take stock in where we've been, what we've done, and who did what.

Animated features have long been lumped together with the bottom rung of children's fare. My colleagues on this book and I feel that a well-made family film is a film anyone can enjoy, and that the best animated features hold a very important place in the world of film, as well as in pop culture history. Many of the films listed in this book are indeed classic movies deserving of serious study. We urge you to seek out the good ones for a closer look, for their artistic and cinematic aesthetic qualities—or simply for fun.

To do so, we have devised a star rating system and have graded each film accordingly.

---

### STAR RATINGS

0 stars **Pure Torture.** Kiddie-show hell. (Example: *My Little Pony*)

☆ **Poor.** Has some minor saving grace, but otherwise a waste of time and talent. (Example: *Pound Puppies and the Legend of Big Paw*)

☆☆ **Mediocre.** Has redeeming values and artistic possibilities—but not fully realized. (Example: *Osmosis Jones*)

☆☆☆ **Excellent.** Great animation, good story. (Example: *Dumbo*)

☆☆☆☆ **A masterpiece.** A landmark. Perfection. A great film. (Examples: *Snow White and the Seven Dwarfs* and *The Incredibles*)

---

We have done our best to make sure all the titles are correct (yes, *Mad Monster Party?* has a question mark in the title, and *Who Framed Roger Rabbit* does not), that the release dates are accurate, and the key production personnel are acknowledged. Films that do not include MPAA ratings do not include them because they predate that ratings system. This book is by no means finished. It is a work-in-progress that we hope to update and expand in the future, to include many more varieties of animated features (foreign films, direct to video, made for television, compilation festivals, Internet-based, etc.) and those currently in production.

Any feedback, additions, or corrections are welcome and should be e-mailed to jbeck6540@aol.com. Updates will be cataloged on my Web site, www.cartoonresearch.com.

In closing, I hope you have as much fun browsing this book as we did putting it together. Despite 80 years of history, only now is the animated feature emerging as a power player in Hollywood and a true artistic force in film. In the immortal words of Buzz Lightyear, "To infinity and beyond!"

Jerry Beck
Hollywood, California
2005

# Contributors' Biographies

**Jerry Beck** is a noted animation historian who has written numerous articles and several books on the subject. He is also an animation industry executive and producer and has used his expertise to compile classic animation on DVD for the major studios. He has taught at New York University, University of California at Los Angeles, and at the American Film Institute. His books include *Animation Art* (2004), *Looney Tunes: The Ultimate Visual Guide* (2003), *Outlaw Animation* (2003), and *The 50 Greatest Cartoons* (1994). Beck lives in Los Angeles with his wife, Marea Boylan, and maintains an animation history Web site, www.cartoonresearch.com.

**Martin "Dr. Toon" Goodman** makes his home in Indiana, where he works as a counseling psychologist. A lifelong fan and student of American animation, Dr. Goodman has written for *TOON Magazine*, ASIFA International, and *Ani-Mato!* He began writing for the Animation Nerd's Paradise Web site in 1997 and presently writes columns and monthly commentary on animation and culture for Animation World Network. He sincerely believes that any cartoon worth watching is worth seriously writing about.

**Andrew Leal** lives in El Paso, Texas, the hometown of Don Bluth. He serves as webmaster for the Toonjunkies animated feature database, located at Toonhub.com, and is lead contributor to Voicechasers.com. His work has appeared in APAToons, Scarlet Street, the 2004 San Diego Comic-Con Souvenir Book, and the Web publication Graphic Novel Review. Most recently, he contributed to the book *Animation Art*, edited by Jerry Beck, and is currently working on a book proposal covering U.S. propaganda animation during WWII.

**W. R. Miller** has written numerous articles covering the animation industry for publications such as *Starlog, Comics Scene, Comics Buyer's Guide, Animation Magazine, Ani-Mato!,* and *Animation World Magazine.* He has also written for Gerhard Hahn Filmproductions, Berlin; Stretch Films, New York; Cornerstone Animation (Glendale, California); and for Big Idea Productions, Chicago.

**Fred Patten** has written on animation for fan and professional magazines since the late 1970s. He wrote the liner notes for Rhino Entertainment's *The Best of Anime* music CD (1998) and was a contributor to *The World Encyclopedia of Cartoons, 2nd edition*, edited by Maurice Horn (1999), and *Animation in Asia and the Pacific*, edited by John A. Lent (2001). He wrote the entries on Japanese and Chinese animation for *Animation Art*, edited by Jerry Beck (2004). A collection of his writings was recently published: *Watching Anima, Reading Manga* (2004).

# Chronological List
# of Animated Features

1. *The Adventures of Prince Achmed* (9/23/26) UFA. D: Lotte Reiniger.
2. *Snow White and the Seven Dwarfs* (12/21/37) RKO—Walt Disney. D: David Hand.
3. *Gulliver's Travels* (12/22/39) Paramount—Fleischer Studios. D: Dave Fleischer.
4. *Pinocchio* (2/7/40) RKO—Disney. D: Ben Sharpsteen, Hamilton Luske.
5. *Fantasia* (11/13/40) RKO—Disney. D: Samuel Armstrong, James Algar, Bill Roberts, Paul Satterfield, Hamilton Luske, Jim Handley, Ford Beebe, T. Hee, Norman Ferguson, Willfred Jackson.
6. *The Reluctant Dragon* (6/20/41) RKO—Disney. D: Alfred L. Werker, Hamilton Luske, Jim Handley, Ford Beebe, Erwin Verity, Jasper Blystone.
7. *Dumbo* (10/23/41) RKO—Disney. D: Ben Sharpsteen.
8. *Mr. Bug Goes to Town* (12/4/41) Paramount—Fleischer. D: Dave Fleischer.
9. *Bambi* (8/13/42) RKO—Disney. D: David Hand.
10. *Saludos Amigos* (2/6/43) RKO—Disney. D: Bill Roberts, Jack Kinney, Hamilton Luske, Wilfred Jackson.
11. *Victory Through Air Power* (7/17/43) United Artists—Disney. D: H. C. Potter, David Hand.
12. *The Three Caballeros* (2/3/45) RKO—Disney. D: Norman Ferguson.
13. *Make Mine Music* (8/15/46) RKO—Disney. D: Joe Grant.
14. *Song of the South* (11/1/46) RKO—Disney. D: Wilfred Jackson.
15. *Fun and Fancy Free* (9/27/47) RKO—Disney. D: Ben Sharpsteen.
16. *Melody Time* (5/27/48) RKO—Disney. D: Ben Sharpsteen.
17. *The Magic Horse* (4/18/49) Artkino. D: Ivan Ivanov-Vano.
18. *The Adventures of Ichabod and Mr. Toad* (10/5/49) RKO—Disney. D: Ben Sharpsteen, Jack Kinney, Clyde Geronimi, James Algar.
19. *Cinderella* (2/15/50) RKO—Disney. D: Ben Sharpsteen, Wilfred Jackson, Hamilton Luske, Clyde Geronimi.
20. *The Emperor's Nightingale* (5/25/51) New Trends Associates. D: Jiri Trnka.
21. *Alice in Wonderland* (7/28/51) RKO—Disney. D: Ben Sharpsteen, Wilfred Jackson, Hamilton Luske, Clyde Geronimi.
22. *Peter Pan* (2/5/53) RKO—Disney. D: Wilfred Jackson, Hamilton Luske, Clyde Geronimi.
23. *Johnny the Giant Killer* (6/5/53) Lippert Pictures. D: Jean Image, Charles Frank.
24. *Hansel and Gretel* (12/24/54) RKO. D: John Paul.
25. *Animal Farm* (1/5/55) DCA. D: John Halas, Joy Batchelor.
26. *Lady and the Tramp* (6/16/55) Buena Vista—Disney. D: Hamilton Luske, Clyde Geronimi, Wilfred Jackson.
27. *The Adventures of Mr. Wonderbird* (2/1/57) Fine Arts Films. D: Paul Grimault.
28. *Sleeping Beauty* (1/29/59) Buena Vista—Disney. D: Clyde Geronimi.
29. *The Snow Queen* (11/20/59) Universal. D: Lev Atamanov.
30. *1001 Arabian Nights* (12/1/59) Columbia—UPA. D: Jack Kinney.
31. *One Hundred and One Dalmatians* (1/25/61) Buena Vista—Disney. D: Wolfgang Reitherman, Hamilton Luske, Clyde Geronimi.
32. *Magic Boy* (6/22/61) MGM. D: Taiji Yabushita, Akira Okuwara.
33. *Panda and the Magic Serpent* (7/8/61) Globe. D: Taiji Yabushita.
34. *Alakazam the Great* (7/26/61) American International. D: Osamu Tezuka, Taiji Yabushita, Daisaku Shirakawa.
35. *A Midsummer Night's Dream* (12/18/61) Showcorporation. D: Jiri Trinka.
36. *Sinbad, the Sailor* (1962) Signal International. D: Taiji Yabushita.
37. *The Littlest Warrior* (1962) Signal International. D: Taiji Yabushita.
38. *Gay Purr-ee* (10/24/62) Warner Bros.—UPA. D: Abe Levitow.
39. *The Sword in the Stone* (12/25/63) Disney. D: Wolfgang Reitherman.
40. *The Little Prince and the Eight-Headed Dragon* (1/1/64) Columbia. D: Yugo Serikawa.

41. *The Incredible Mr. Limpet* (3/28/64) Warner Bros. D: Arthur Lubin, Bill Tytla.
42. *Of Stars and Men* (5/13/64) Brandon Films Inc. D: John Hubley.
43. *Hey There, It's Yogi Bear!* (6/3/64) Columbia—Hanna-Barbera. D: William Hanna, Joseph Barbera.
44. *The Man from Button Willow* (2/1/65) United Screen Artists. D: David Detiege.
45. *Willy McBean and His Magic Machine* (6/23/65) Mangna Dist. Corp. D: Arthur Rankin Jr.
46. *Pinocchio in Outer Space* (12/22/65) Universal. D: Ray Goossens.
47. *Alice of Wonderland in Paris* (2/5/66) Childhood Productions. D: Gene Deitch.
48. *The Man Called Flintstone* (8/3/66) Columbia—Hanna-Barbera. D: William Hanna, Joseph Barbera.
49. *Gulliver's Travels Beyond the Moon* (7/23/66) Continental. D: Yoshio Kuroda.
50. *The Daydreamer* (7/29/66) Embassy Pictures—Rankin-Bass. D: Jules Bass.
51. *The Jungle Book* (10/18/67) Buena Vista—Disney. D: Wolfgang Reitherman.
52. *The Wacky World of Mother Goose* (12/2/67) Embassy Pictures (Rankin-Bass). D: Jules Bass.
53. *Yellow Submarine* (11/13/68) United Artists. D: George Dunning.
54. *Mad Monster Party?* (3/8/69) Embassy Pictures (Rankin-Bass). D: Jules Bass.
55. *A Boy Named Charlie Brown* (12/4/69) National General—Melendez. D: Bill Melendez.
56. *Santa and the Three Bears* (11/7/70) Ellman Enterprises. D: Tony Benedict.
57. *The Phantom Tollbooth* (11/7/70) MGM. D: Chuck Jones, Abe Levitow, David Monahan.
58. *The Aristocats* (12/11/70) Buena Vista—Disney. D: Wolfgang Reitherman.
59. *The World of Hans Christian Andersen* (3/1/71) United Artists D: Chuck McCann, Al Kilgore, Kimio Yabuki.
60. *Shin-Bone Alley* (6/18/71) Allied Artists. D: John D. Wilson.
61. *Fritz the Cat* (4/12/72) Cinemation Industries. D: Ralph Bakshi.
62. *Cleopatra, Queen of Sex* (4/24/72) Xanadu. D: Eiichi Yamamoto.
63. *Snoopy Come Home* (8/9/72) National General. D: Bill Melendez.
64. *Charlotte's Web* (3/1/73) Paramount. D: Hanna-Barbera.
65. *Marco Polo Jr.* (4/12/73) Premore. D: Eric Porter.
66. *Heavy Traffic* (8/15/73) American International. D: Bakshi.
67. *Robin Hood* (11/8/73) Disney. D: Wolfgang Reitherman.
68. *Fantastic Planet* (12/1/73) New World. D: Rene Laloux.
69. *Journey Back to Oz* (6/19/74) Seymour Borde and Associates (Filmation). D: Hal Sutherland.
70. *Nine Lives of Fritz the Cat* (6/26/74) American International. D: Robert Taylor.
71. *Tubby the Tuba* (4/1/75) Avco-Embassy. D: Alexander Schure.
72. *Aladdin and His Magic Lamp* (7/1/75) Paramount. D: Jean Image.
73. *Coonskin* (8/1/75) Paramount/Bryanston. D: Ralph Bakshi.
74. *Jack and the Beanstalk* (2/13/76) Columbia. D: Gisaburo Sugii, Peter J. Solmo.
75. *Once Upon a Girl* (6/20/76) Producers Releasing Organization. D: Don Jurwich.
76. *Hugo the Hippo* (7/14/76) 20th Century Fox. D: William Feigenbaum and József Gémes.
77. *Once Upon a Time* (10/1/76) G.G. Communications. D: Rolf Kauka, Roberto Gavioli.
78. *Wizards* (3/2/77) 20th Century Fox. D: Ralph Bakshi.
79. *The Many Adventures of Winnie the Pooh* (3/11/77) Disney. D: Wolfgang Reitherman, John Lounsbery.
80. *Raggedy Ann and Andy* (4/1/77) 20th Century Fox. D: Richard Williams.
81. *The Rescuers* (6/22/77) Disney. D: Wolfgang Reitherman, John Lounsbury, Art Stevens.
82. *Dirty Duck* (7/13/77) New World. D: Chuck Swenson.
83. *Allegro Non Troppo* (7/27/77) Specialty Films. D: Bruno Bozzetto.
84. *Race for Your Life, Charlie Brown* (8/24/77) Paramount. D: Bill Melendez.
85. *Metamorphoses* (5/3/78) Sanrio. D: Takashi.
86. *The Mouse and His Child* (5/24/78) Sanrio. D: Fred Wolf, Charles Swenson.
87. *Watership Down* (11/1/78) Avco-Embassy. D: Martin Rosen.
88. *The Lord of the Rings* (11/21/78) United Artists. D: Ralph Bakshi.
89. *Rudolph and Frosty's Christmas in July* (7/1/79) Avco-Embassy. D: Arthur Rankin Jr., Jules Bass.
90. *Nutcracker Fantasy* (7/7/79) Sanrio. D: Takeo Nakamura.
91. *Shame of the Jungle* (9/14/79) International Harmony. D: Picha.
92. *The Bugs Bunny/Road Runner Movie* (9/30/79) Warner Bros. D: Chuck Jones.
93. *Bon Voyage Charlie Brown (and Don't Come Back)* (5/30/80) Paramount. D: Bill Melendez.
94. *I Go Pogo* (8/1/80) 21st Century Distribution. D: Marc Paul Chinoy.
95. *American Pop* (2/13/81) Columbia. D: Ralph Bakshi.
96. *The Fox and the Hound* (7/10/81) Disney. D: Art Stevens, Ted Berman, Richard Rich.
97. *Heavy Metal* (8/7/81) Columbia. D: Gerald Potterton.
98. *Galaxy Express* (8/8/81) New World. D: Taro Rin.
99. *The Looney, Looney, Looney Bugs Bunny Movie* (11/20/81) Warner Bros. D: Friz Freleng.
100. *Grendel Grendel Grendel* (4/1/82) Satori. D: Alexander Stitt.
101. *King Dick* (7/3/82) Aquarius Releasing. D: Cibba.
102. *The Secret of Nimh* (7/3/82) United Artists. D: Don Bluth.
103. *Hey Good Lookin'* (10/1/82) Warner Bros. D: Ralph Bakshi.

104. *Heidi's Song* (11/19/82) Paramount. D: Robert Taylor.
105. *Bugs Bunny's Third Movie: 1001 Rabbit Tales* (11/19/82) Warner Bros. D: Friz Freleng, Dave Detiege.
106. *The Last Unicorn* (11/19/82) Jensen-Farley. D: Arthur Rankin, Jules Bass.
107. *Mighty Mouse in the Great Space Chase* (12/10/82) Filmation. D: Ed Friedman, Lou Kachivas, Marsh Lamore, Gwen Wetzler, Kay Wright, Lou Zukor.
108. *Twice Upon a Time* (8/5/83) Warner Bros. D: John Korty, Charles Swenson.
109. *Daffy Duck's Movie: Fantastic Island* (8/5/83) Warner Bros. D: Friz Freleng.
110. *Fire and Ice* (8/27/83) 20th Century Fox. D: Ralph Bakshi.
111. *The Smurfs and the Magic Flute* (11/25/83) Atlantic. D: Jose Dutillieu.
112. *Plague Dogs* (12/17/83) Self-released. D: Martin Rosen.
113. *The Care Bears Movie* (3/29/85) Samuel Goldwyn. D: Arna Selznick.
114. *The Secret of the Sword* (3/29/85) Atlantic. D: Ed Friedman, Lou Kachivas, Marsh Lamore, Bill Reed, Gwen Wetzler.
115. *Here Come the Littles* (5/24/85) Atlantic. D: Bernard Deyries.
116. *The Black Cauldron* (7/24/85) Disney. D: Ted Berman, Richard Rich.
117. *Rock and Rule* (8/5/85) MGM/UA. D: Clive A. Smith.
118. *Rainbow Brite and the Star Stealer* (11/15/85) Warner Bros. D: Bernard Deyries.
119. *Starchaser: The Legend of Orin* (11/22/85) Atlantic. D: Steven Hahn.
120. *Adventures of Mark Twain* (1/17/86) Atlantic. D: Will Vinton.
121. *Heathcliff the Movie* (1/17/86) Atlantic. D: Bruno Bianchi.
122. *Adventures of the American Rabbit* (2/14/86) Atlantic. D: Fred Wolf, Nobutaka Nishizawa.
123. *Care Bears Movie II: A New Generation* (3/21/86) Columbia. D: Dale Schott.
124. *Gobots: Battle of the Rock Lords* (3/24/86) Atlantic. D: Ray Patterson.
125. *Warriors of the Wind* (4/15/86) New World. D: Hayao Miyazaki.
126. *The Cosmic Eye* (6/6/86) Upfront Releasing. D: Faith Hubley.
127. *My Little Pony: The Movie* (6/20/86) DEG. D: Michael Joens.
128. *The Great Mouse Detective* (7/2/86) Disney. D: John Musker, Ron Clements, Dave Michener, Burny Mattinson.
129. *Robotech: The Movie* (7/25/86) Cannon. D: Carl Macek, Ishiguro Noburo.
130. *Transformers: The Movie* (8/9/86) DEG. D: Nelson Shim.
131. *An American Tail* (11/21/86) Universal. D: Don Bluth.
132. *The Chipmunk Adventure* (5/22/87) Samuel Goldwyn. D: Janice Karman.
133. *The Puppetoon Movie* (6/12/87) Expanded Entertainment. D: Arnold Leibovit.
134. *The Brave Little Toaster* (7/10/87) Hyperion. D: Jerry Rees.
135. *The Care Bears Adventure in Wonderland* (8/7/87) Cineplex Odeon. D: Raymond Jafelice.
136. *Pinocchio and the Emperor of the Night* (12/25/87) New World. D: Hal Sutherland.
137. *Light Years* (1/28/88) Miramax. D: Rene Laloux.
138. *When the Wind Blows* (3/11/88) Kings Road. D: Jimmy T. Murakami.
139. *Pound Puppies and the Legend of Big Paw* (3/18/88) Tri-Star. D: Pierre DeCelles.
140. *Who Framed Roger Rabbit* (6/22/88) Touchstone Pictures. D: Robert Zemeckis, Richard Williams.
141. *Bravestarr: The Legend* (9/17/88) Taurus. D: Tom Tataranowicz.
142. *The Land Before Time* (11/18/88) Universal. D: Don Bluth.
143. *Oliver and Company* (11/18/88) Disney. D: George Scribner.
144. *Laputa: Castle in the Sky* (3/24/89) Streamline D: Hayao Miyazaki.
145. *Twilight of the Cockroaches* (5/5/89) Streamline. D: Hiroaki Yoshida.
146. *Babar: The Movie* (7/28/89) New Line. D: Alan Bunce.
147. *Daffy Duck's Quackbusters* (9/24/89) Warner Bros. D: Greg Ford, Terry Lennon.
148. *The Little Mermaid* (11/15/89) Disney. D: Ron Clements, John Musker.
149. *All Dogs Go to Heaven* (11/17/89) United Artists. D: Don Bluth.
150. *Akira* (12/25/89) Streamline. D: Katsuhiro Otomo.
151. *Jetsons: The Movie* (7/6/90) Universal. D: William Hanna, Joseph Barbera.
152. *DuckTales the Movie: Treasure of the Lost Lamp* (8/3/90) Disney. D: Bob Hathcock.
153. *Lensman* (8/31/90) Streamline. D: Yoshiaki Kawajiri, Kazuyuki Hirokawa.
154. *The Rescuers Down Under* (11/16/90) Disney. D: Hendel Butoy, Mike Gabriel.
155. *The Nutcracker Prince* (11/23/90) Warner Bros. D: Paul Schibli.
156. *Robot Carnival* (1/25/91) Streamline. D: Katsuhiro Otomo, Atsuko Fukushima, Kouji Morimoto, Kiroyuki Kitazume, Mao Lamdo, Hidetoshi Ohmori, Yasuomi Umetsu, Hiroyuki Kitakubo, Takashi Nakamura.
157. *The Castle of Cagliostro* (4/3/91) Streamline. D: Hayao Miyazaki.
158. *Rover Dangerfield* (8/6/91) Warner Bros. D: Jim George, Bob Seeley.
159. *Fist of the Northstar* (9/27/91) Streamline. D: Toyoo Ashida.
160. *Beauty and the Beast* (11/13/91) Disney. D: Gary Trousdale, Kirk Wise.
161. *An American Tale: Fievel Goes West* (11/22/91) Universal. D: Phil Nibbelink, Simon Wells.
162. *Rock*A*Doodle* (4/3/92) Samuel Goldwyn. D: Don Bluth.
163. *Fern Gully: The Last Rainforest* (4/10/92) 20th Century Fox. D: Bill Kroyer.

164. *Barefoot Gen* (7/3/92) Tara. D: Masaki Mori.
165. *Cool World* (7/9/92) Paramount. D: Ralph Bakshi.
166. *Little Nemo: Adventures in Slumberland* (7/24/92) Hemdale. D: Masami Hata, William Hurtz.
167. *Bebe's Kids* (7/31/92) Paramount. D: Bruce Smith.
168. *Freddy as F.R.O.7.* (8/28/92) Miramax. D: Jon Acevski.
169. *The Tune* (9/13/92) October. D: Bill Plympton.
170. *The Professional: Golgo 13* (10/23/92) Streamline. D: Osamu Dezaki.
171. *Aladdin* (11/11/92) Disney. D: John Musker, Ron Clements.
172. *Neo Tokyo/Silent Mobius* (11/20/92) Streamline. D: Rin Taro, Yoshiaki Kawajiri, Katsuhiro Otomo/Michitaka Kikuchi.
173. *Legend of the Overfiend* (3/11/93) Anime 21. D: Hideki Takayama.
174. *Vampire Hunter D* (3/26/93) Streamline. D: Toyoo Ashida.
175. *My Neighbor Totoro* (5/7/93) Troma. D: Hayao Miyazaki.
176. *Happily Ever After* (5/28/93) First National. D: John Howley.
177. *Tom and Jerry: The Movie* (5/28/93) Miramax. D: Phil Roman.
178. *Macross II: Lovers Again* (6/4/93) Tara Teleasing. D: Kenichi Yatagai, Quint Lancaster.
179. *Once Upon a Forest* (6/18/93) 20th Century Fox. D: Charles Grosvenor.
180. *Wicked City* (8/20/93) Streamline Pictures. D: Yoshiaki Kawajiri.
181. *Nightmare Before Christmas* (10/13/93) Disney. D: Henry Selick.
182. *We're Back! A Dinosaurs Story* (11/24/93) Universal. D: Dick Zondag, Ralph Zondag, Phil Nibbelink, Simon Wells.
183. *Batman: Mask of the Phantasm* (12/25/93) Warner Bros. D: Eric Radomski, Bruce Timm.
184. *Megazone 23, Part One* (2/2/94) Streamline Pictures. D: Noburu Ishiguro.
185. *Megazone 23, Part Two* (2/2/94) Streamline Pictures. D: Tosihiro Hirano.
186. *Thumbelina* (3/30/94) Warner Bros. D: Don Bluth, Gary Goldman.
187. *Great Conquest: The Romance of Three Kingdoms* (4/21/94) Streamline Pictures. D: Mashahara Okuwaki.
188. *The Princess and the Goblin* (6/3/94) Hemdale. D: Jozsef Gemes.
189. *The Lion King* (6/15/94) Disney. D: Roger Allers, Rob Minkoff.
190. *A Troll in Central Park* (10/7/94) Warner Bros. D: Don Bluth, Gary Goldman.
191. *The Swan Princess* (11/18/94) New Line. D: Richard Rich.
192. *The Pagemaster* (11/24/94) 20th Century Fox. D: Joe Johnston, Maurice Hunt.
193. *The Wings of Honneamise: Royal Space* (3/10/95) Tara. D: Hiroyuki Yamaga.
194. *A Goofy Movie* (4/7/95) Disney. D: Kevin Lima.
195. *The Pebble and the Penguin* (4/12/95) MGM/UA. D: Don Bluth (uncredited).

196. *Pocahontas* (6/23/95) Disney. D: Eric Goldberg, Mike Gabriel.
197. *Space Adventure Cobra* (8/20/95) Tara. D: Osamu Dezaki.
198. *Arabian Knight* (8/25/95) Miramax. D: Richard Williams.
199. *Toy Story* (11/22/95) Disney. D: John Lasseter.
200. *Gumby the Movie* (12/8/95) Arrow. D: Art Clokey.
201. *Balto* (12/22/95) Universal. D: Simon Wells.
202. *Roujin-Z (Old Man Z)* (1/5/96) Kit Parker Films. D: Hiroyuki Kitabuko.
203. *Ghost in the Shell* (3/29/96) Manga. D: Mamoru Oshii.
204. *All Dogs Go to Heaven 2* (3/29/96) MGM/UA. D: Larry Leker, Paul Sebella.
205. *James and the Giant Peach* (4/12/96) Disney. D: Henry Selick.
206. *Hunchback of Notre Dame* (6/21/96) Disney. D: Kirk Wise, Gary Trousdale.
207. *Tenchi Muyo in Love* (8/16/96) Pioneer. D: Hiroshi Negishi.
208. *Space Jam* (11/15/96) Warner Bros. D: Joe Pytka, Bruce W. Smith, Tony Cervone.
209. *Beavis and Butt-Head Do America* (12/20/96) Paramount. D: Mike Judge, Yvette Kaplan.
210. *Cats Don't Dance* (3/26/97) Warner Bros. D: Mark Dindal.
211. *Hercules* (6/27/97) Disney. D: John Musker, Ron Clements.
212. *Swan Princess II: Escape from Castle Mountain* (7/18/97) Legacy. D: Rich Rich.
213. *Pippi Longstocking* (8/22/97) Legacy. D: Clive Smith.
214. *Aaron's Magic Village* (9/19/97) Avalanche. D: Albert Hanan Kaminski, Buzz Potamkin.
215. *Anastasia* (11/21/97) 20th Century Fox. D: Don Bluth, Gary Goldman.
216. *Quest for Camelot* (5/26/98) Warner Bros. D: Frederik Du Chau.
217. *The Mighty Kong* (5/29/98) Legacy. D: Art Scott.
218. *Mulan* (6/25/98) Disney. D: Barry Cook, Tony Bancroft.
219. *Antz* (10/2/98) DreamWorks. D: Eric Darnell, Tim Johnson.
220. *I Married a Strange Person* (10/28/98) Lion's Gate. D: Bill Plympton.
221. *Rudolph the Red Nosed Reindeer* (11/15/98) Legacy. D: Bill Kowalchuck.
222. *A Bug's Life* (11/20/98) Disney-Pixar. D: John Lasseter, Andrew Stanton.
223. *The Rugrats Movie* (11/25/98) Paramount. D: Norton Virgien, Igor Kovalyov.
224. *The Prince of Egypt* (12/18/98) DreamWorks. D: Brenda Chapman, Steve Hickner, Simon Wells.
225. *The King and I* (3/19/99) Warner Bros. D: Richard Rich.
226. *Doug's 1st Movie* (3/26/99) Disney. D: Maurice Joyce.
227. *Tarzan* (6/18/99) Disney. D: Kevin Lima, Chris Buck.
228. *South Park: Bigger, Longer, and Uncut* (6/30/99) Paramount/Warner Bros. D: Trey Parker.
229. *Iron Giant* (8/6/99) Warner Bros. D: Brad Bird.
230. *Perfect Blue* (10/8/99) Manga. D: Satoshi Kon.

231. *Princess Mononoke* (10/29/99) Miramax. D: Hayao Miyazaki.

232. *Pokémon the First Movie: Mewtwo Strikes Back* (11/12/99) Warner Bros. D: Kunihiko Yuyama.

233. *Toy Story 2* (11/24/99) Disney-Pixar. D: John Lasseter, Ash Brannon, Lee Unkrich.

234. *Fantasia 2000* (12/31/99) Disney. D: Gaetan Brizzi, Paul Brizzi, Hendel Butoy, Francis Glebas, Eric Goldberg, Susan Goldberg, Pixote Hunt.

235. *Sinbad: Beyond the Veil of Mists* (1/28/00) Trimark Pictures. D: Evan Ricks, Alan Jacobs.

236. *The Tigger Movie* (2/11/00) Disney. D: Jun Falkenstein.

237. *Kirikou and the Sorceress* (2/18/00) Artmattan Productions. D: Michael Ocelot.

238. *X* (3/24/00) Manga. D: Rintaro.

239. *The Road to El Dorado* (3/31/00) DreamWorks. D: Eric "Bibo" Bergeron, Don Paul.

240. *Dinosaur* (5/19/00) Disney. D: Ralph Zondag, Eric Leighton.

241. *Titan A.E.* (6/16/00) 20th Century Fox. D: Don Bluth, Gary Goldman.

242. *Chicken Run* (6/21/00) DreamWorks. D: Peter Lord, Nick Park.

243. *The Adventures of Rocky and Bullwinkle* (6/30/00) Universal. D: Des McAnuff.

244. *Pokémon the Movie 2000* (7/21/00) Warner Bros. D: Kunihiko Yuyama.

245. *Digimon: The Movie* (10/6/00) 20th Century Fox. D: Takaaki Yamashita, Hisashi Nayayama, Masahiro Aizawa.

246. *Rugrats in Paris: The Movie* (11/17/00) Paramount. D: Stig Bergqvist, Paul Demeyer.

247. *The Emperor's New Groove* (12/15/00) Disney. D: Mark Dindal.

248. *Recess: School's Out* (2/16/01) Disney. D: Chuck Sheetz.

249. *Pokémon the Movie 3* (4/6/01) Warner Bros. D: Kunihiko Yuyama.

250. *The Trumpet of the Swan* (5/11/01) TriStar Pictures. D: Richard Rich, Terry L. Noss.

251. *Shrek* (5/16/01) DreamWorks. D: Andrew Adamson, Victoria Jensen.

252. *Atlantis: The Lost Empire* (6/8/01) Disney. D: Kirk Wise, Gary Trousdale.

253. *Final Fantasy: The Spirits Within* (7/11/01) Columbia Pictures. D: Hinrobu Sakaguchi.

254. *Jin-Roh: The Wolf Brigade* (8/3/01) Bandai Entertainment. D: Hiroyuki Okiura.

255. *Osmosis Jones* (8/10/01) Warner Bros. D: Piet Kroon, Tom Sito. Live action D: Peter Farrelly, Bobby Farrelly.

256. *Blood: The Last Vampire* (8/18/01) Manga Entertainment. D: Hiroyuki Kitakubo.

257. *Vampire Hunter D: Bloodlust* (10/5/01) Urban Vision. D: Yoshiaki Kawajiri.

258. *Spriggan* (10/12/01) A.D.V. Films. D: Hirotsugu Kawasaki.

259. *Waking Life* (10/19/01) Fox Searchlight. D: Richard Linklater, Bob Sabiston.

260. *Monsters, Inc.* (11/2/01) Disney-Pixar. D: Peter Docter, Lee Unkrich, David Silverman.

261. *Jimmy Neutron, Boy Genius* (12/21/01) Paramount. D: John A. Davis.

262. *Marco Polo: Return to Xanadu* (12/28/01) Tooniversal Co. D: Ron Merk.

263. *Metropolis* (1/25/02) TriStar Pictures. D: Rin Taro.

264. *Escaflowne* (1/25/02) Bandai Entertainment. D: Kazuki Akane.

265. *Return to Neverland* (2/15/02) Disney. D: Robin Budd.

266. *Ice Age* (3/15/02) 20th Century Fox. D: Chris Wedge, Carlos Saldanha.

267. *Mutant Aliens* (4/19/02) Apollo. D: Bill Plympton.

268. *Spirit: Stallion of the Cimarron* (5/24/02) DreamWorks. D: Kelly Asbury, Lorna Cook.

269. *Lilo and Stitch* (6/21/02) Disney. D: Chris Saunders, Dean Debois.

270. *Hey Arnold: The Movie* (6/28/02) Paramount. D: Tuck Tucker.

271. *The Powerpuff Girls* (7/3/02) Warner Bros. D: Craig McCracken.

272. *Spirited Away* (9/20/02) Disney. D: Hayao Miyazaki.

273. *Jonah: A Veggie Tales Movie* (10/4/02) FHE Pictures. D: Phil Vischer, Mike Nawrocki.

274. *Pokémon 4-Ever* (10/11/02) Miramax. D: Kunihiko Yuyama.

275. *Eight Crazy Nights* (11/27/02) Columbia Pictures. D: Seth Kearsley.

276. *Treasure Planet* (11/27/02) Disney. D: Ron Clements, John Musker.

277. *The Wild Thornberrys Movie* (12/20/02) Paramount. D: Jeff McGrath, Cathy Malkasian.

278. *WXIII: Patlabor the Movie 3* (1/10/03) Pioneer. D: Fumihiko Takayama.

279. *The Jungle Book 2* (2/14/03) Disney. D: Steve Trenbirth.

280. *Piglet's Big Movie* (3/21/03) Disney. D: Francis Glebas.

281. *Cowboy Bebop: The Movie* (4/4/03) Sony/Goldwyn. D: Shinichiro Watanabe.

282. *Pokémon Heroes* (05/16/03) Miramax. D: Kunihiko Yuyama, Jim Malone.

283. *Finding Nemo* (5/30/03) Disney-Pixar. D: Andrew Stanton.

284. *Rugrats Go Wild* (6/13/03) Paramount. D: Norton Virgien, John Eng, Kate Boutilier.

285. *Sinbad: Legend of the Seven Seas* (7/2/03) DreamWorks. D: Tim Johnson, Patrick Gilmore.

286. *Sakura Wars: The Movie* (7/18/03) Pioneer. D: Mitsuro Hongo.

287. *Millennium Actress* (9/12/03) Go Fish Pictures (DreamWorks). D: Satoshi Kon.

288. *Brother Bear* (10/24/03) Disney. D: Aaron Blaise and Bob Walker.

289. *Rescue Heroes: The Movie* (10/24/03) Artisan/Family Home Entertainment (Nelvana). D: Ron Pitts.

290. *Looney Tunes: Back in Action* (11/14/03) Warner Bros. D: Joe Dante, Eric Goldberg.

**Aaron's Magic Village** (9/19/97) Avalanche Releasing. 83 mins. Director: Albert Hanan Kaminski. Producers: Dora Benousilio, Peter Volke. Voices: Fyvush Finkel (Narrator), Tommy Michaels (Aaron), Tovah Feldshuh (Aynt Sarah, Zlatch the Goat, Matchmaker), Ronn Carroll (Uncle Shlemiel), Harry Goz (Gronam Ox), Ivy Austin (The Lantuch).

**Consumer Tips:** ☆☆ MPAA Rating: G. Jewish folktale based on a story by Isaac Bashevis Singer.

**Story:** Orphan boy Aaron is sent to live with his aunt and uncle in the tiny village of Chelm, a town blessed with an overdose of foolishness. When a jealous sorcerer, using a Book of Marvels he stole from Chelm, conjures a destructive Golem to destroy the town, it's up to Aaron to use his wits to save his family and friends.

**Comments:** *Aaron's Magic Village* is an adaptation of four fables from Isaac Bashevis Singer's *Stories for Children* and was put into production under the title *The Real Schlemiel*. The resulting film is sincere and has its good moments but is not a great work. Originally, *Aaron's Magic Village* was produced in France as a television project.

To enhance the production, director Kaminski brought in some notable talents, including actors Tovah Feldshuh, Harry Goz, and Fyvush Finkel, well-known composer Michel Legrand (*The Umbrellas of Cherbourg, Summer of '42*), and lyricist Sheldon Harnick (*Fiddler on the Roof*). U.S. animation veteran Buzz Potamkin (*Berenstain Bears*, Hanna-Barbera) provided special animation sequences that enliven the rather pedestrian script and directorial pace. Sadly, the Golem sequence poorly combines computer graphics with traditional hand-drawn cartooning, distracting our attention from the story's continuity.

The film was coproduced by Columbia TriStar Home Video, and given a billboard release in the United States by Avalanche Releasing (a division of Cinepix Film Properties, which later became Lion's Gate Films). (JB)

**Additional Credits:** Screenplay: Albert Hanan Kaminski, Jacqueline Galia Benousilio. Music: Michel Legrand. Lyrics: Sheldon Harnick.

**The Adventures of Ichabod and Mr. Toad** (10/5/49) Disney-RKO. 68 mins. Directors: Jack Kinney, Clyde Geronimi, James Algar. Production supervisor: Ben Sharpsteen. Voices: Bing Crosby (Ichabod), Basil Rathbone (Narrator), Eric Blore (Mr. Toad), Pat O'Malley (Cyril), Claud Allister (Water Rat), John Ployardt (Prosecutor), Collin Campbell (Mole), Campbell Grant (Angus MacBadger), Ollie Wallace (Winky).

**Consumer Tips:** ☆☆☆ Based on *The Legend of Sleepy Hollow* by Washington Irving and *The Wind in the Willows* by Kenneth Grahame.

**Story:** Two classic stories told in vintage Disney style. Basil Rathbone narrates the whimsical adventures of Mr. Toad, an eccentric character with a motor mania, who is put on trial for stealing a car. Bing Crosby relates the tale of Ichabod Crane, a New England school teacher, and his encounter with a legendary Headless Horseman.

**Comments:** *The Adventures of Ichabod and Mr. Toad* was Disney's final package movie of the 1940s. It combines two well-known stories under the theme of "Two Fabulous Characters," which was the original working title of the feature. Both stories reinforce the Disney studio's leadership at the time, in the skills of animation, storytelling, and character animation. *The Wind in the Willows* segment contains some of the funniest bits of cartoon acting and exaggeration—as Toad's motor mania has him going insane with the idea of a wild ride on a road to "nowhere in particular." *The*

*Sleepy Hollow* segment is rich with atmosphere and nuance. Ichabod's encounter with the Headless Horseman (animated by Frank Thomas and John Sibley) is ranked among the finest Disney animation sequences in the studio's history.

The studio was gearing up to tackle a full-length narrative again with its subsequent production of *Cinderella* (1950). These two half-hour-length tales certainly proved the studio was up for the task. The two stories were later released separately as theatrical shorts, as *The Legend of Sleepy Hollow* and *The Madcap Adventures of Mr. Toad*. (JB)

**Additional Credits:** Directing animators: Frank Thomas, Oliver Johnson, Wolfgang Reitherman, Milt Kahl, John Lounsberry, Ward Kimball. Background artists: Ray Huffine, Merle Cox, Art Riley, Brice Mack. Layout artists: Charles Philippi, Tom Codderick, Thor Putnam, Hugh Hennessy, Lance Nolley, Al Zinnen. Effects animators: George Rowley, Jack Boyd. Animators: Fred Moore, John Sibley, Marc Davis, Hal Ambro, Harvey Toombs, Hal King, Hugh Fraser, Don Lusk. Story: Erdman Penner, Winston Hibler, Joe Rinaldi, Ted Sears, Homer Brightman, Harry Reeves. Music/lyrics: Don Raye, Gene DePaul, Frank Churchill, Charles Wolcott, Larry Morey, Ray Gilbert.

©Will Vinton Productions, Inc. & Harbour Town Films, Inc.

**The Adventures of Mark Twain** (1/17/86) Atlantic Releasing. 90 mins. Producer/director: Will Vinton. Voices: James Whitmore (Mark Twain), Chris Ritchie (Tom Sawyer), Gary Krug (Huck Finn), Michele Mariana (Becky), John Morrison (Adam), Carol Edelman (Eve), Dallas McKennon (Jim Smiley), Herb Smith (The Stranger), Marley Stone (Aunt Polly), Wilbur Vincent (The Mysterious Stranger).

**Consumer Tips:** ☆☆☆ MPAA Rating: G. Based on *Tom Sawyer Abroad* by Mark Twain and several of his short stories.

**Story:** Mark Twain takes off for his final adventure, in a riverboat propelled by a balloon, to intercept Halley's Comet and reunite with his late wife. Tom Sawyer, Becky Thatcher, and Huckleberry Finn stow away and are soon enchanted by Twain's most beloved stories.

**Comments:** *The Adventures of Mark Twain* was an ambitious feature-length film by Will Vinton, using his trademark stop-motion Claymation process. The film was three and a half years in the making and was self-financed using profits from his studio's commercial work.

Vinton staked a claim in the industry when his first film, *Closed Mondays* (1974, codirected by Bob Gardiner), won an Oscar for Best Animated Short. That was followed by several subsequent Oscar nominations (*Rip Van Winkle*, 1978, *The Creation*, 1981, *The Great Cognito*, 1982) and several award-winning commercials (*The California Raisins*).

Vinton's wife, Susan Shadburne, researched Mark Twain extensively for the screenplay, using Twain's own words from his autobiography for the character dialogue. Vinton and Shadburne adapted *Tom Sawyer Abroad* as a departure point for the feature-length screenplay and incorporated into the narrative several Twain short stories ("The Diary of Adam and Eve," "The Celebrated Jumping Frog of Calaveras County," "The Mysterious Stranger"). A few of these were created (and later released) as stand-alone shorts. These sequences were undoubtedly produced first, in case funding for the feature-length project failed to materialize.

The film's highlight is James Whitmore's vocal performance as Mark Twain (Whitmore was best known for his signature roles as Harry Truman and Will Rogers). He was filmed while performing his lines, as reference footage for the animators to study. The final character design of Mark Twain in the film is a cross between the actual facial features of Mark Twain and those of the actor Whitmore. (JB)

**Additional Credits:** Screenplay: Susan Shadburne. Executive producer: Hugh Tirrell. Music: Billy Scream. Principal character animation: Barry Bruce, William L. Fiesterman, Tom Gasek,

Mark Gustafson, Craig Bartlett, Bruce McKean. Set design: Joan Gratz, Don Merkt. Claypaint: Joan Gratz. Animators: Don Merkt, Will Vinton, Matt Wuerker. Title layouts: Marilyn Zornado.

## The Adventures of Mr. Wonderbird (2/1/57)

Fine Arts Films. 63 mins. Director: Paul Grimault. Producer: Andre Sarrut. Voices (English dub): Peter Ustinov (Mr. Wonderbird), Claire Bloom (The Shepherdess), Denholm Elliott (The Chimney Sweep), Max Adrian (The King), Alex Clunes (The Blind Man), Cecil Trouncer (The Statue), Philip Stainton (Chief of Police), Harcourt Williams (The Old Begger), Joan Heal (The Killer), Frank Muir (Commentator).

**Consumer Tips:** ☆☆½ Based on Hans Christian Andersen's *Shepherdess and the Chimney-Sweep.*

**Story:** In the kingdom of Upandownia, a cross-eyed tyrant king loves a charming shepherdess who is already in love with a poor chimney sweep. Aided by a wily mockingbird, the lovers escape to the lower city, where the bird instigates a revolt and destroys the royal palace with the help of the king's secret weapon—a giant robot.

**Comments:** A bizarre, but delightful, early animated feature from France. The film was dubbed in England and the English language version received a limited U.S. theatrical release in 1957.

Producer Andre Sarrut and director/cowriter Paul Grimault were well known in France for their animated commercials and short films made through their company Les Gemeaux, founded in 1936. In 1946 they embarked upon a feature-length film production based on Hans Christian Andersen's story *Shepherdess and the Chimney-Sweep.* Years of effort, trial, and error took their toll on the filmmakers—and under pressure from their distributor they were forced to release the film in 1953.

The filmmakers were unhappy with the film. They felt it was incomplete and disowned it, but the critics and public saw it and hailed it as a great surrealist work—and the first true European animated feature.

The film as released is charming, but disjointed. However, the animation is lush and Mr. Wonderbird steals the show with his flowery actions, colorful feathers, and large top hat.

The movie's plot is played out as if a dream. The cross-eyed king has a sumptuous castle in the sky 1,999 floors above his darkened kingdom. The ruler is in love with a shepherdess in one of the paintings in his gallery, and after midnight (just like in several of the old Merrie Melodies cartoons) the paintings come to life. The shepherdess and her lover, the chimney-sweep (in another painting alongside), spend most of the film on the run from the king (a portrait of whom comes to life and disposes of the real king) and the royal policemen (who at one point sprouts bat wings to pursue the pair).

It gets even stranger as the lovers find refuge among the poor, handicapped people of the town, who dwell in the kingdom's lower depths and have never seen the sun, nor birds. Wonderbird leads a revolt that involves dancing lions and the king's giant robot—eventually freeing the townspeople and uniting the shepherdess and the chimney-sweep.

In 1967 Paul Grimault bought back the film's original negative, stripped it of all the footage not his own, and began work on completing the film as he originally envisioned it. He completed the newly revised version in 1979 and began an international release in 1980. It was reviewed in the April 16, 1980 issue of *Variety* under the title *The King and the Mockingbird* with an 87-minute running time. This latter version never had a U.S. theatrical release. (JB)

**Additional Credits:** Screenplay: Jacques Prevert, Paul Gimault. Music/lyrics: Joseph Losma. Executive producer: Anatole de Grunwald. Editor: Gilbert Natot. Sound editor: Ann Chegwidden. Directing animator: Henri Lacam. Animators: Pierre Watrin, Jacques Vausseur. English dub director: Pierre Rouve. Coloring supervisor: Etienne Larouche. This film is also known simply as *Wonderbird* or *Mr. Wonderbird*—as well as *The Curious Mr. Wonderbird, The King and the Bird, The King and Mr. Bird, The King and the Mockingbird*—and under its French title, *La Bergere et Le Ramoneur.*

## The Adventures of Prince Achmed (9/3/26)

UFA. 65 mins. Director: Lotte Reiniger.

**Consumer Tips:** ☆☆☆☆ Based on stories from *The Arabian Nights.* Mild violence and adult situations. This is a silent film, in black and white (though the recent DVD release restores the original color tints). The release date listed above is the original German release date.

©Comenius-Film GmbH

**Story:** Prince Achmed is tricked by a sinister magician into riding a magical horse that will fly him to his doom. Instead, Achmed learns how to control the horse and takes off on a series of adventures in foreign lands. He fights a Fire Mountain Witch, explores China, and woos a princess—and ultimately defeats the magician.

**Comments:** *The Adventures of Prince Achmed* is a very unique film. It is the first animated feature film ever made. It is a silhouette film (stop motion black paper cutouts animated frame by frame against a white backdrop), and it was animated and directed by a woman—rare for any film in 1926. It is an elaborate fantasy, with serious action-adventure sequences and mild sexuality, and it contains some experimental, semiabstract sequences. The film also pioneers an early form of the multi-plane camera, separating foregrounds and backgrounds into layers to give a 3-D effect.

The finished film is a true work of art. Its creator, Lotte Reiniger (1899–1981), became interested in theater and in cutting silhouettes from an early age, building a shadow puppet theater in 1915. She subsequently became excited by the fantasy films of George Méliès and enrolled at the Reinhardt Theater School, where she ended up getting small parts in movies. In 1918, Reiniger joined a group of artists who had just started a studio for experimental films.

In 1923, at the age of 23, Reiniger began work on *The Adventures of Prince Achmed*, more than a decade before Disney's *Snow White and the Seven Dwarfs* (1937). *Prince Achmed* tells its story eloquently, with great style and visual flair. Grey tones and color tints are used effectively to heighten drama. The animation of the lead characters has personality, and special effects (to heighten the magical elements of the story) are wonderfully conceived.

Reiniger cut her figures from cardboard or thin lead, and each limb was cut separately and joined with wire hinges. Walter Ruttman and Berthold Bartosch were experimental animators who created the volcanoes, waves, clouds, and magic fight between the sorcerer and the witch, becoming the world's first effects animators.

Musician Wolfgang Zeller wrote a score for the film concurrently with its production. The original music has been restored to the DVD release.

*The Adventures of Prince Achmed* was completed in 1926, but no film distributor in Germany would take it on. Composer Zeller obtained permission to use a concert hall to stage a premiere showing. The reviews were ecstatic; the *New York Times* ran a huge story on the film preview in July 1926. A theater in Paris picked up the film and played it for almost a year. It slowly began receiving bookings throughout the world.

Its first known U.S. showing was February 21, 1931, at Town Hall in New York. The film's U.S. rights were originally picked up by the University Film Foundation of Harvard, who gave the film a platform release through schools, museums, and specialized art theaters. (JB)

**Additional Credits:** Technical director: Carl Koch. Animators: Walter Ruttman, Berthold Bartosch, Walter Turck, Alexander Kardan. Titles: Edmund Delco. Original music: Wolfgang Zeller.

### The Adventures of Rocky and Bullwinkle
(6/30/00) Universal. 88 mins. Director: Des McAnuff. Producers: Jane Rosenthal, Robert DeNiro. Voices: June Foray (Rocky J. Squirrel, Cartoon Natasha, Narrator's Mother), Keith Scott (Bullwinkle J. Moose, Narrator, Cartoon Fearless Leader, Cartoon Boris, Pottsylvanian TV Announcer), Susan Berman (Weasel). Live action: Rene Russo, Jason Alexander, Piper Perabo, Robert DeNiro, Janeane Garofalo, John Good-

©Universal Studios and Dritte Beteiligung KC & Medien AG and Co., KG

man, Randy Quaid, Kenan Thompson, Kel Mitchell, David Alan Grier, Carl Reiner, Jonathan Winters, Whoopi Goldberg, Billy Crystal.

**Consumer Tips:** ☆☆½ MPAA Rating: PG. Based on the classic television cartoon series by Jay Ward Productions.

**Story:** Former cartoon stars Rocky and Bullwinkle come out of retirement to help the FBI find villains Boris, Natasha, and Fearless Leader, who have jumped from the cartoon world into the real world with a plan to overtake the United States.

**Comments:** *Rocky and His Friends* premiered on ABC in 1959 and went on to become a popular success in prime time and Saturday morning broadcasts—Rocky's companion, Bullwinkle, became a breakout star, and later developed a large cult following. The animation itself was perhaps the cheapest and crudest form of limited animation (farmed out to Mexico years before outsourcing was popular among Hollywood producers). But it was the witty scripts and strong voice acting that won over audiences.

Jane Rosenthal and Robert DeNiro brought the idea of an updated Rocky and Bullwinkle feature film to Universal Pictures and Tiffany Ward (Jay's widow). To develop the project they hired New York playwright Kenneth Lonergan to write the screenplay and Tony award–winning director Des McAnuff to direct the live-action sequences.

This film combines live-action photography with animation (primarily computer-generated images) of the two lead characters. San Francisco–based Wild Brain Inc. provided 11 minutes of traditional hand-drawn cel animation that bookend the film. Industrial Light and Magic handled the computer-generated performances of Rocky and Bullwinkle, taking a year to complete the scenes. David Andrews and Roger Guyett supervised the animation and visual effects.

The film tries hard—maybe too hard—to be funny, to break the fourth wall, and to be cutting edge. Capturing the humor and charm of Ward's low-budget, limited animation on a multimillion-dollar scale may have been an impossible task from the get-go—but the script has its funny moments and the visuals are always interesting. At worst, the film suffers from a post–*Roger Rabbit* déjà vu and never feels as fresh as it wishes it were.

June Foray (the original voice of Rocky and Natasha) provided the vocals for the flying squirrel and is the only actor left from the original cast. Keith Scott, no relation to Bullwinkle voice (and Ward partner) Bill Scott, provided the moose with his lines. Scott also performed as narrator in the film, and was an unofficial moose and squirrel consultant on the project. His book *The Moose That Roared* (St. Martin's Press, 2000) is the definitive Jay Ward Studio history.

Despite the star power of DeNiro, Rene Russo, and Jason Alexander (hot off *Seinfeld*), and numerous cameos (Carl Reiner, Jonathan Winters, Whoopi Goldberg, Billy Crystal, Janeane Garofalo, and others), the film did poorly at the box office, trounced in the summer of 2000 by the likes of *Chicken Run* and *Pokémon 2000*. (JB)

**Additional Credits:** Screenplay: Kenneth Lonergan. Based on characters developed by Jay Ward. Animation producers: Leslie Arvio, Allison P. Brown. Executive producers: Tiffany Ward, David Niksay. Music: Mark Mothersbaugh. Animation supervisor: David Andrews. Animation leads: Jenn Emberly, Julie Lenrie, Julie Nelson, Steve Nichols, Steve Rawlins, Scott Wirtz. Animators: Wolff-Rudiger Bloss, Kyle Clark, Bruce Dahl, Andrew Doucette, Shawn Kelly, Ken King, Greg Kyle, David LaTour, Martin L'Heureux, Victoria Livingstone, Kevin Martel, Neil Michka, Gregory Miller, Chris Minos, Trish Schultz, Dave Sidley, Sharonne Solk, Chi Chung-Tse, Jan Van Buyten, Tim Waddy, John Zidankiewicz. Traditional animation: Wild Brain Inc. Traditional animation supervisor: Phil

Robinson. Animators: Aaron Sorenson, Heiko Drengenberg, Ralph Fernan, John Korellis, Amber MacLean, Marcelo Souza, Yekaterina Tabakh, Dave Thomas, Antonio Toro. Art director: Cindy Ng. Backgrounds: Kristen Borges, Kory Heinzen. Storyboards: Darryl Henley, Carl Aldana, Donna Cline, Tom Jung, Robin Richesson, Hanna Strauss, Pete Von Sholly, Mike Swift.

### The Adventures of the American Rabbit

(2/14/86) Atlantic Releasing. 85 mins. Directors: Fred Wolf, Nobutaka Nishizawa. Producers: Masahura Etoh, Masahissa Saeki, John G. Marshall. Voices: Barry Gordon (Rob, American Rabbit), Bob Arbogast (Theo), Pat Fraley (Tini Meeney), Bob Holt (Rodney), Lew Horn (Dip), Norm Lenzer (Bruno), Kenneth Mars (Vultor, Buzzard), John Mayer (Too Loose), Maitzi Morgan (Lady Pig), Lorenzo Music (Ping Pong), Laurie O'Brien (Bunny O Hare), Hal Smith (Head Jackal), Russi Taylor (Mother), Fred Wolf (Fred Red).

**Consumer Tips:** ☆ MPAA Rating: G. Based on characters created by pop artist Stewart Moskowitz. Stresses good sportsmanship, friendship, loyalty, and nonviolence.

**Story:** Rob the rabbit is told by an old wizard that he's inherited the legacy of a crime-fighting superhero, the American Rabbit. Rob leaves home and works as a pianist in a traveling rock band, but whenever trouble appears—particularly from a jackal motorcycle gang—he transforms into the heroic American Rabbit: his feet become roller skates, his fur morphs into red, white, and blue, and he saves the world from evil.

**Comments:** Based upon painter Stewart Moskowitz's popular *American Rabbit* poster and greeting card artwork of the late 1970s. The roller-skating, stars-and-stripes bunny had no backstory, so Hollywood invented one for this film. Moskowitz found success with a number of prints and posters including *The White Brothers, The Corporation,* and *Chocolate Moose,* some of which were incorporated into the film's screenplay. Moskowitz's work has been especially popular in Japan, where every major company has used one of his characters as their logo—Fuji, Mitsubishi, Panasonic, AT&T Japan. Thus the film found eager backing from Japanese investors, and was coproduced by Toei Doga.

Writer Norman Lenzer (*The Point*) was brought in to write the script (and provides the voice of one of the jackals). This is one of those mid-1980s goodie-goodie family films, a notch better than the pro-social nonviolent Saturday morning network cartoons of the time—but not by much. The occasional rock music by Mark Volman and Howard Kaylan (the Phlorescent Leech and Eddie) enliven the proceedings slightly.

And as far as the super-heroics are concerned, I'd advise sticking with *Mighty Mouse.* Animation critic Charles Solomon summed it up perfectly in his review for the *Los Angeles Times*: "Both the writing and the animation in *The Adventures of the American Rabbit* are so inept that the viewer expects the governor to interrupt the film and declare the theater a disaster area!" (JB)

**Additional Credits:** A Toei Animation Production. Screenplay: Norman Lenzer. Based on the characters created by Stewart Moskowitz. Music/lyrics: Mark Volman, Howard Kaylan, John Hoier. Animation: Shingo Aaraki, Kenji Yokoyama, Yukiyoshi Hane, Yoshitaka Yashima, Shigeo Matoba, Hirohide Shikishima, Ikuo Fudanuki, Katsuyoshi Nakatsuru, Takashi Nashizawa.

**Akira** (12/25/89) Streamline Pictures. 124 mins. Director: Katsuhiro Otomo. Producers: Haruyo Kanesaku, Shunzo Kato, Yutaka Maseba, Ryohei Suzuki, Hiroe Tsukamoto. Voices: Johnny Yong Bosch (Kaneda), Joshua Seth (Tetsuo), Wendee Lee (Kei),

Sandy Fox (Kiyoko), Emily Brown (Kaori), Bambi Darro, Barbara Goodson, Jean Howard, Mona Marshall, Michelle Ruff, Lisa Tarulli.

©Akira Committee

**Consumer Tips:** ☆☆☆☆ MPAA Rating: 1989 Unrated; 2001 R. SF adventure. Based on an award-winning Japanese manga SF novel, *Akira*, by Katsuhiro Otomo.

**Story:** In A.D. 2019 Neo-Tokyo, biker leader Kaneda tries to rescue gang member Tetsuo who has been kidnapped by government agents as a scientific test subject. Tetsuo, who gains mutant powers, runs amok. Several stories are interlinked: Kaneda's mission to protect his biker gang and rule the streets; political power struggles within the Japanese government; the Colonel's desire to control the experiment and keep it from destroying Tokyo again.

**Comments:** Award-winning SF manga author-artist Katsuhiro Otomo had started *Akira* in 1982 as a comic-book SF serial. It became popular enough that he was asked to license it to be made as an animated feature while it was still being published. Otomo had had an unpleasant experience as character designer on a previous anime feature (*Harmegedon*, 1983), and he insisted on retaining so much creative control over *Akira* that he was made its director. *Akira* was so successful that Otomo's career quickly switched from cartoonist to director of both animated and live-action films.

*Akira* was the most expensive animated film produced in Japan at its release (July 1988; production budget nearly U.S. $10 million) and was a major criti-

cal success there and internationally. It is considered one of the greatest animated features of any country, and one of the greatest science-fiction features, animated or live-action. It is one of the seminal titles that introduced Japanese animation to America as worthwhile adult entertainment rather than just kids' cartoons.

*Akira* clicked with America's art-film buffs, college audiences, and the teen "in" crowd. It was active on the fine-art theatrical circuit from its Christmas day 1989 release through the first half of the 1990s, often as a midnight movie alternate to *The Rocky Horror Picture Show*. Its release to video and laser disc during the early 1990s won praise from major film critics, including Siskel and Ebert and *Time* magazine. Its soundtrack by the Geinoh Yamashiro Group was one of the first Japanese movie music CDs released in America.

*Akira* (along with *Blade Runner*) became the model for Japan's intellectual, dystopian SF theatrical features of the 1990s, often made more for the international film festival and American/European market than the Japanese domestic market. *Ghost in the Shell*, *Armitage III*, and Otomo's own *Old Man Z* are leading examples.

The setting of 2019 A.D. Neo-Tokyo (*Akira* opens with the destruction of Tokyo in 1988 by what seems to be a nuclear explosion; Neo-Tokyo is built on its ruins) became a stereotype for every "Neo-Tokyo" or "Mega-Tokyo" depiction of 21st- or 22nd-century Tokyo as a soaring, vast futuristic metropolis, but emphasizing urban decay and lower-class slums as much or more than shiny glamor. These movies have usually been more for the teen and adult action-adventure direct-to-video market (*Bubblegum Crisis*, *Silent Mobius*, *Cyber City Oedo 808*) than for theatrical release. Their video release in America during the 1990s was one of the foundations of the American anime market as a "cool" alternative to domestic superhero comic books and action-adventure movies.

*Akira* was rereleased theatrically with a new English dubbing by Pioneer Entertainment on March 30, 2001. (FP)

**Additional Credits:** Executive producers: James Yosuke Kobayashi, Sawako Noma. Associate producer: Yoshimasa Mizuo. Screenplay: Katsuhiro Otomo, Izo Hashimoto. Designer: Toshiharu Mizutani. Animation director: Takashi Nakamura. Music: Geino Yamashiro. Akira Committee Company Ltd./Tokyo Movie Shinsha Co. Ltd.

©Walt Disney Productions

**Aladdin** (11/11/92) Walt Disney Productions. 90 mins. Directors: Ron Clements, John Musker. Producers: Ron Clements, John Musker. Voices: Scott Weinger (Aladdin speaking), Brad Kane (Aladdin singing), Linda Larkin (Jasmine speaking), Lea Salonga (Jasmine singing), Robin Williams (Genie, Peddler), Jonathan Freeman (Jafar), Gilbert Gottfried (Iago), Douglas Seale (Sultan), Frank Welker (Abu).

**Consumer Tips:** ☆☆☆☆ MPAA Rating: G. Based on the tales *The Thousand and One Nights*. The story of Aladdin and his lamp is given a modern twist through improvisational comedy, musical showstoppers, and saucy animation.

**Story:** A likeable street urchin named Aladdin finds himself duped by the evil vizier Jafar into obtaining a magic lamp whose mercurial genie will grant the owner three wishes. Aladdin ends up with the lamp and uses its power to transform himself into Prince Ali, the better to win the hand of Agrabah's beautiful princess, Jasmine. When the lamp is lost to Jafar, Aladdin must find it within himself to defeat the all-powerful vizier and win the heart of the princess on his own.

**Comments:** Disney's success with fairy and folk tales continued with this outstanding adaptation of Antoine Galland's *The Thousand and One Nights*. *Aladdin* represented the third and final teaming of Howard Ashman and Alan Menken as a songwriting team; although Ashman passed away in 1991, he had written the lyrics to the Broadway-style numbers "Arabian Nights," "Friend Like Me," and "Prince Ali" before his untimely death. Award-winning lyricist Tim Rice stepped in to finish the film. *Aladdin* won the Academy Award for best score and song ("A Whole New World").

The film may have been named for its protagonist, but *Aladdin* was clearly stolen by the character of the Genie. Animator Eric Goldberg and comedian Robin Williams teamed up to provide one of Disney's wildest creations, a large, blue shape-shifting wiseacre visually influenced by the caricatures of *New Yorker* cartoonist, Al Hirschfeld. Goldberg's use of loose, flowing line enabled his creation to rapidly transform in tandem with William's often-improvised patter, and the results are truly hilarious. Their high point was the "Prince Ali" number. Robin Williams was not the only comedian on board; Gilbert Gottfried's irascible but irresistible voicework made the parrot Iago more than just a sidekick to the wicked Jafar.

Aladdin was another Disney hero in a long line of motherless waifs; his mother was originally a central figure in the film and even had a song, "Proud of Your Boy," dedicated to her. When it was decided to focus more on Aladdin, Disney executive Jeffrey Katzenberg allegedly told the writers to "Eighty-six the mother." Other notable changes: Iago the parrot was originally the calm, cool partner in the conspiracy to steal the throne of Agrabah while Jafar was an irrational hothead. *Aladdin* ran into a bit of controversy when the song "Arabian Nights" was contested by the Arab-American Anti-Discrimination Committee, who found the lines "Where they cut off your nose if they don't like your face/ It's barbaric, but hey, it's home!" offensive. The song was redubbed with new lyrics for video release.

*Aladdin* featured the first major character in a Disney film created by computer imaging. Animators Randy Cartwright and Tina Price created a flying carpet that kept its intricate pattern intact in all positions while at the same time giving an appealing performance in pantomime. Another stunning creation generated by computer was the tiger-headed entrance to the Cave of Wonders. *Aladdin* grossed a magical $217 million at the box office and then surpassed that figure in video sales the following year. The movie spawned two direct-to-video releases and a cable television series. If you are fast enough to catch them, other Disney stars take part in the fun: Pinocchio, Sebastian the Crab (*The Little Mermaid*) and the Beast (*Beauty and the Beast*) have brief cameos in the film. (MG)

**Additional Credits:** Screenplay: Ron Clements, John Musker, Ted Elliott, Terry Rossio. Story: Burny Mattinson, Francis Glebas, Rebecca Rees, Roger Allers, Darryll Rooney, David S. Smith, Daan Jippes, Larry Leker, Chris Sanders, Kevin Harkey, James Fujii, Brian Pimental, Sue Nichols, Kevin Hanson, Patrick A. Ventura, Kevin Lima. Music: Alan Menken. Songs: Howard Ashman, Alan Menken and Tim Rice. Supervising animators: Glen Keane, Eric Goldberg, Mark Henn, Andreas Deja, Duncan Marjoribanks, Randy Cartwright, Will Finn, Dave Pruiksma. Animators: Alex Kuperschmidt, David P. Stephan, Tony Fucile, Michael Cedeno, Michael Surrey, Ken Hettig, Anthony DeRosa, Brad Kuha, Mike Swofford, Russ Edmonds, David Burgess, Tom Sito, Rejean Bourdages, Raul Garcia, Joe Haidar, Gilda Palinginis, Broose Johnson, Aaron Blaise, Doug Krohn, Ron Husband, Ken Duncan, Nik Ranieri, Lou Dellarosa, Tim Allen, Ellen Woodbury, Teresa Martin, Michael Show, Rick Farmiloe, Dan M. Wawrzaszek, Tina Price, William Recinos, Brian Ferguson, Tony Bancroft, Tom Bancroft, Barry Temple, Bob Bryan, Larry White, Cynthia Overman, Kathy Zielinski, T. Daniel Hofstedt, Phil Young, Chris Wahl. Visual effects supervisor: Don Paul. Visual effects animators: Dorse Lanpher, David A. Bossert, Ted C. Kierscey, Scott Santoro, Mark Myer, Chris Jenkins, Ed Coffey, Mark Dindal, Christine Harding, Allen Blyth, Kelvin Yasuda.

**Aladdin and His Magic Lamp** (7/1/75) Paramount. 70 mins. Director: Jean Image. Producer: Les Films Jean Image. Voices (original French cast): George Atlas,

©Jean Image

Lucie Dolene, Richard Francoeur, Michel Gudin, Paul Guez, Claire Guibert, Rene Hieronimus, Jean-Pierre Leroux, Lita Recio.

**Consumer Tips:** ☆½ MPAA Rating: G.

**Story:** In order to procure a magic lamp, an evil magician pretends to be the uncle of an innocent urchin named Aladdin. The plan backfires as the lad uses the magic lamp to help his mother and woo a princess. The magician uses another disguise to gain access to the lamp and kidnaps the princess. He is ultimately outwitted by Aladdin—who banishes him into a crystal ball.

**Comments:** French animator Jean Image and his staff of fifty artists produced *Aladin et la Lampe Merveilleuse* within a severe seven-month schedule (April through November) in 1969. Released during 1970 in France, the film was a local success with children and was shown at international film festivals for several years. It eventually found its way to the United States, initially picked up by Paramount Pictures and bundled with several other animated films for a Saturday "Family Matinee" theatrical release in 1975.

Even for the mid-1970s, this is a shoddy-looking film. Cheap television-style animation that is downright crude in several scenes (the climactic fistfight between Aladdin and the evil magician is poorly done by any standard). Colorful is the best I can say for this production. The English dub is also somewhat acceptable—though a monotonous song Aladdin sings (twice) about "My Shiny Piece of Gold" is enough to drive sane adults running to the exit.

It's certainly an improvement over Image's earlier *Johnny the Giant Killer* (1953), but the unexpressive character designs and inconsistent tone will even puzzle the small fry. Aladdin is first introduced as a young boy, but shortly after acquiring the magic lamp he is suddenly of teenage size and seeks to marry the princess. When Aladdin thinks about how to dispose of the evil magician, he imagines sending him to the moon—in a modern NASA-styled spaceship. This sci-fi bit breaks the *Arabian Nights* feel of the film, but at the late point in the film when this occurs, it really doesn't matter anymore.

Avoid at all costs. You've been warned. (JB)

**Additional Credits:** Writer: France Image. Adaptation: France and Jean Image. Animators: Denis Boutin, Guy Lehideux, Marcel Breuil, Ch. el J. Clairfeuille, J. P. Nantis, Alberto Ruiz, J. F. Sornin, Sante Vilani, José Xavier. Voice director: Serge Naduad. Music: Fred Freed. Songs: Christian Sarrel. Also known as *Aladin et la Lampe Merveilleuse.*

©American-International, Inc.

**Alakazam the Great** (7/26/61) American-International Pictures. 84 mins. Directors: Taiji Yabushita, Daisaku Shirakawa, Osamu Tezuka. Producers: Hiroshi Okawa (Japan); Lou Rusoff, Samuel Z. Arkoff, James H. Nicholson (America). Voices: Frankie Avalon (Alakazam, singing voice only), Peter Fernandez (Alakazam), Dodie Stevens (DeeDee), Sterling Holloway (Narrator), Jonathan Winters (Sir Quigley Brokenbottom), Arnold Stang (Lulipopo).

**Consumer Tips:** ☆☆☆½ Fantasy adventure. Based on the Chinese folktale as novelized in the 16th century, adapted as the 1950s Japanese comic strip *My Son Goku.* Also known as *Saiyu-Ki,* 1960 (*The Enchanted Monkey*).

**Story:** Alakazam, a young monkey, uses his bravery to persuade the other monkeys into making him their king. He learns magic, but becomes so vain that he flies to heaven to prove that he is more powerful than King Amo (Buddha). After his defeat, he is sentenced to learn humility as the bodyguard of Prince Amat who is traveling from China to India. Alakazam, with new companions Sir Quigley Brokenbottom and Lulipopo, protects Prince Amat from numerous evil demons.

**Comments:** *Alakazam* was an adaptation of *the Journey to the West/Monkey King* folktale popular throughout the Orient, based upon the actual 7th century A.D. journey by the Chinese monk Tripitaka to India to bring back Buddhist teachings. As built up by popular retellings over the centuries, the priest became a supporting character to his more colorful and dynamic animal-demon bodyguards, usually called Monkey, Pigsy, and Sandy. The legends were given permanent literary form when they were written into a rambling novel during the 1500s by Wu Cheng-en. During the 1950s the main events were turned into a Japanese comic strip by popular cartoonist Osamu Tezuka.

Toei Animation based its animated feature upon that comic strip and named Tezuka as one of the movie's directors. Tezuka later acknowledged that this was a publicity ploy, and the only time he entered the studio was to pose for press photos amidst the animation staff. However, the experience was instrumental in inspiring him to create Japan's first television animation studio a few years later and produce such popular television cartoons as *Astro Boy* and *Kimba the White Lion.* Tezuka remained active as both a cartoonist and an animator for the rest of his life, producing short international film festival award-winners like *Jumping* and *Broken-Down Film.*

*Alakazam the Great* (*Saiyu-Ki*) was the third feature-length release (1960) of Japan's first major animation studio, Toei Animation Co., Ltd. It and the first two were all released in America during June and July 1961 and marketed as Disney-style animated theatrical features. *Alakazam* received the biggest budget and promotion, with an all-star voice cast and original music by popular bandleader Les Baxter. All three failed at the box office, with the result that subsequent Japanese animated theatrical features were only viable in America as children's matinee movies, usually released directly to television and the 16mm rental market, until *Akira* in 1989 made action-adventure anime for teens and adults suitable for art-film release. *Alakazam* has remained available off and on through occasional television screenings and sporadic film rental and home video releases.

Tezuka himself remade his 1950s comic strip as a 1967 animated television series, *The Adventures of Goku.* It was unsold in America because Tezuka's version retained too much of the monkey's original troublemaking juvenile-delinquent personality for American children. *The Monkey King* folktales have been adapted into Chinese and Japanese live-action and animated theatrical features, television series, and comic strips probably more often than any other Oriental legend. (FP)

**Additional Credits:** Screenplay: Lou Rusoff, Lee Kresel (U.S.); Keinosuke Uekusa (Japan). Music: Les Baxter. Animation: Koichi Mori, Yasuo Otsuka, Masao Kumagawa, Akira Daikubara, Hideo Furusawa.

**Alice in a New Wonderland** See *Alice of Wonderland in Paris.*

**Alice in Paris** See *Alice of Wonderland in Paris.*

©Walt Disney Productions

**Alice in Wonderland** (7/28/51) Walt Disney Productions. 75 mins. Directors: Clyde Geronimi, Hamilton Luske, Wilfred Jackson. Voices: Kathryn Beaumont (Alice), Ed Wynn (Mad Hatter), Jerry Colonna (March Hare), Richard Hayden (Caterpillar), Sterling Holloway (Cheshire Cat), Bill Thompson (White Rabbit, Dodo), Pat O'Malley (Walrus, Carpenter, Tweedledee, Tweedledum), Verna Felton (Queen of Hearts), Dink Trout (King of Hearts), Joseph Kearns (Doorknob), Heather Angel (Alice's sister), Larry Grey (Bill the Lizard), Queenie Leonard (Nesting Bird, Flower), Jim Macdonald (Dormouse), Doris Lloyd (Rose), Pinto Colvig (Flamingo), The Mello Men (Card Painters).

**Consumer Tips:** ☆☆½ A well-meaning attempt at capturing the imaginative stories of Lewis Carroll. Walt

Disney himself was not pleased with the results, though some of the animation is wonderfully surreal.

**Story:** A young British girl follows a frantic rabbit into a bizarre world where nonsense is the norm. Virtually every character that Alice meets is completely insane and some are downright dangerous. After considerable frustration and mayhem, Alice discovers that the entire adventure was a dream . . . or in this case, a nightmare.

**Comments:** *Alice* was adapted from Carroll's two novels, *Alice's Adventures in Wonderland* (1865) and *Through the Looking Glass* (1872). Walt Disney had long been captivated by Carroll's works. From 1923 to 1927 Walt produced the live action/animated Alice Comedies, which detailed the adventures of a young girl in a cartoon world. In 1936 Mickey Mouse went *Thru the Mirror* in one of his best shorts, and Disney also considered a live-action film, *Alice*, starring Mary Pickford. Disney purchased the rights to the classic illustrations by Sir John Tenniel in 1931, and the film was more or less in production for almost twenty years.

*Alice* soon became a nightmare for Walt Disney; Carroll's episodic, idiosyncratic story had eighty characters, little narrative flow, and a heroine who mainly reacted to whatever befell her. Scores of writers worked on a treatment, and years passed while the story department went in circles. Walt himself grew frustrated with the film and lost much of his enthusiasm. In an attempt to force the film into shape, over 40 songs were developed to some degree but only 14 made it to the final product, few of them more than a minute long. Disney's five sequence directors finally took control of *Alice* as Walt's interest waned, further fragmenting a disjointed narrative. Audiences were finally left watching a frustrated little girl fight her way through a Technicolor psychiatric ward.

*Alice*, however, is not without merit. Stylist Mary Blair had a field day with the colors and layouts, and this is among her very best efforts. Some sequences, notably the "Unbirthday Party" featuring the Mad Hatter, March Hare, and Dormouse, display excellent comedy, timing, and spirit. "All in a Golden Afternoon," which features a musical recital by living flowers, resembles some of Disney's better *Silly Symphonies* and is an underrated episode in the film. Some of Alice's reaction shots to the general madness are superbly animated (thanks to Ollie Johnston and Marc Davis).

Strong voice work by veteran character actors Ed Wynn and Jerry Colonna as the Mad Hatter and March Hare respectively, complement the manic animation and provide the film's livelier moments. A notable performance by Richard Hayden makes the haughty, hookah-smoking caterpillar a treat, and the show-stealing turn by Sterling Holloway as the Cheshire Cat (coolly animated by Ward Kimball) is the most-remembered by audiences. Unfortunately, with no film to hang them on, these characters and sequences had to stand on their own.

Bill Thompson, who voiced the White Rabbit and the Dodo, was also the voice of Droopy Dog for MGM. Thirteen-year-old Kathryn Beaumont modeled the part of Alice for the animators as well as providing the voice. Speaking of voices, Jim Macdonald must have had an affinity for mice; not only did he voice the Dormouse, he was also the current voice of Mickey Mouse at Disney. The film premiered in London at the Leicester Square Theatre on July 26, 1951. Surprisingly, British critics rather liked the film. Not so in the United States: *Alice* lost $2 million domestically.

French puppeteer Louis Bunin prepared a live-action/stop-motion version of *Alice* and planned to release it on the same day Disney's film opened. Disney sought an 18-month injunction but lost since Carroll's work was in the public domain. Bunin's film opened as planned and bombed, one of Walt's few satisfactions as far as *Alice in Wonderland* was concerned.

*Alice* was rediscovered by the college crowd in the late 1960s and was greatly enjoyed as a "head trip." Although Disney was somewhat concerned about its image, it cashed in by rereleasing the film to theaters in 1974 with a psychedelic poster and press kit. A second rerelease followed in 1981. (MG)

***Additional Credits:*** Story: Winston Hibler, Bill Peet, Joe Rinaldi, Bill Cottrell, Joe Grant, Del Connell, Ted Sears, Erdman Penner, Milt Banta, Dick Kelsey, Dick Huemer, Tom Oreb, John Walbridge. Music: Oliver Wallace. Orchestrations: Joseph S. Dubin. Vocal arrangements: Jud Conlon. Directing animators: Milt Kahl, Ward Kimball, Frank Thomas, Eric Larson, John Lounsbery, Ollie Johnston, Wolfgang Reitherman, Marc Davis, Les Clark, Norman Ferguson. Animators: Hal King, Judge Whitaker, Hal Ambro, Bill Justice, Phil Duncan, Bob Carlson, Don Lusk, Cliff Nordberg, Harvey Toombs, Fred Moore, Marvin Woodward, Hugh Fraser, Charles Nichols. Effects animation: Joshua Meador, Dan McManus, George Rowley, Blaine Gibson. Color styling: John Hench, Mary Blair, Claude Coats, Ken Anderson, Don DaGradi. Layout: MacLaren Stewart, Hugh Hennessey, Tom Codrisk, Don Griffith, Charles Phillipi, Thor Putnam, A. Kendall O'Connor, Lance Nolley. Backgrounds: Ray Huffine, Ralph Hulett, Art Riley, Brice Mack, Dick Anthony, Thelma Witmer.

## Alice of Wonderland in Paris (2/5/66) Childhood Productions. 52 mins. Director: Gene Deitch. Producer: William L. Snyder. Voices: Norma MacMillan (Alice), Allen Swift (Francios; The King), Carl Reiner (Anatole), Howard Morris (Frowning Prince), Lionel Wilson (Minstrel; Royal Mathematician), Trinka Snyder (Princess Lenore), Luce Ennis (Queen).

***Consumer Tips:*** ☆☆½ Though based on Lewis Carroll's *Through the Looking Glass* characters, the film more faithfully adapts several other well-known children's stories: *Anatole* by Eve Titus, *The Frowning Prince* by Crockett Johnson, *Many Moons* by James Thurber, *Madeline and the Gypsies* and *Madeline and the Bad Hat* by Ludwig Bemelmans.

***Story:*** Inspired by reading the story of Madeline, Alice wishes to go to Paris. A beret-wearing mouse named Francois, grandson of the world famous mouse Anatole, gives Alice some magic cheese that shrinks her to a tiny size. Together via bicycle they travel to

©Rembrandt Films

new bridging material, creating a whole new feature film (albeit of short length).

The resulting film, *Alice of Wonderland in Paris*, holds up quite well. The film has a low budget and it shows, but it's a somewhat entertaining mix. There is an original song (sung by Francios), and while the animation isn't quite Disney, it moves more elaborately than it has any right to.

Childhood Productions released the film in the United States, playing Saturday matinees for several weeks. It was released with a companion featurette, the 38-minute live action *White Mane*, a Cannes Film Festival winner about the friendship of a boy and his stallion. (JB)

**Additional Credits:** Music/lyrics: Victor Little, Paul Alter. This film is also known as *Alice in a New Wonderland* and *Alice in Paris*.

**All Dogs Go to Heaven** (11/17/89) United Artists. 85 mins. Director: Don Bluth. Producers: Don Bluth, Gary Goldman, John Pomeroy. Voices: Burt Reynolds (Charlie), Dom DeLuise (Itchy), Judith Barsi (Anne-Marie), Vic Tayback (Carface), Charles Nelson Reilly (Killer), Loni Anderson (Flo), Ken Page (King Gator), Candy Devine (Vera), Melba Moore (Heavenly Whippet), Rob Fuller (Harold).

©Goldcrest Sullivan Bluth Ltd.

**Consumer Tips:** ☆½ MPAA Rating: G. Will appeal mainly to children.

**Story:** Charlie, a rascally mutt, is killed, but finds a way to return to earth and make amends by helping an

Paris, trade famous children's tales, and enjoy cheese tasting.

**Comments:** William Snyder of Rembrandt Films had lured UPA and Terrytoon veteran director Gene Deitch to Prague, Czechoslovakia, in 1959 for a ten-day consulting job. Deitch fell in love with the city, and fell in love with Snyder's animation production manager, Zdenka. He remained based in Prague for the rest of his life.

Snyder got Deitch and his small studio a number of commercial contracts, which included theatrical Tom and Jerry cartoons for MGM, Krazy Kat and Popeye television cartoons for King Features, and a contract with Paramount for a whole series of Nudnik shorts. Deitch was also allowed to indulge in some personal filmmaking, which yielded an Academy Award for *Munro* (1960) and several Oscar nominations (*Self Defense for Cowards*, 1962; *How to Avoid Friendship*, 1964).

Rembrandt Films also made several children's book adaptations for the library and educational film market. These included such titles as *Anatole* by Eve Titus, *The Frowning Prince* by Crockett Johnson, *Many Moons* by James Thurber, and *Madeline and the Gypsies* by Ludwig Bemelmans. By the mid-1960s, Snyder's ambitious plans and financial situation had run into trouble. Hurting for cash, Snyder and Deitch compiled five of these children's films and produced orphan girl. She has the ability to talk to animals, a talent Charlie and his dachshund pal, Itchy, use to play the ponies—in an effort to help the girl find parents.

**Comments:** After the distribution nightmare that kept *The Secret of Nimh* from getting a proper shot at the box office, and the spectacular commercial success and artistic clashes with Steven Spielberg, Don Bluth and his studio were now comfortably set up in Ireland with independent funding from Goldcrest for several feature films. The first movie he produced here was *All Dogs Go to Heaven*. Unfortunately, it was also the first film to reveal the flaws in Don Bluth's storytelling abilities.

On the plus side, the film features the usual superior art direction, layouts, lush color designs, and character animation that Bluth revived successfully in his previous films. It also boasts a fine voice cast, using mainly Burt Reynolds' posse of friends. These include Charles Nelson Reilly, Vic Tayback, then-wife Loni Anderson, and Bluth regular Dom DeLuise.

The problems crop up in the convoluted story about a roguish con-man canine (picture an unlikable version of Disney's Tramp) who dies, tricks his way back to earth, finds an orphan (designed as a little version of Snow White) who is able to talk to animals, and gets involved with gangster dogs, ray guns, and a giant crocodile living in the sewers of New Orleans. Some of the problems could be chalked up to improvisation in the recording booth. "There was almost no direction," recalled Bluth in the film's production notes. "I'd give them a few ideas of what was needed, and then I'd be literally chased from the room. Their ad libs were often better than the original script!"

One musical number, "Let's Make Music Together," sung by King Gator, is a show stopper, literally. All the songs in the film succeed in stopping the story dead in its tracks. However, this one is particularly fun, being a clever take-off on Esther Williams' aquatic spectacles.

*All Dogs Go to Heaven* fared relatively well at the box office, despite Disney's efforts to squash it with an ambush release of *The Little Mermaid* two days earlier. It also spawned a theatrical sequel, a direct-to-video feature (*An All Dogs Christmas Carol*, 1998), and a television series. One unfortunate note, ten-year-old Judith Barsi (voice of Anne-Marie, as well as Ducky in *The Land Before Time*) was shot to death by her father

in July 1988, just days after she completed her work on this film. (JB)

***Additional Credits:*** Screenplay: David Weiss. Codirectors: Dan Kuenster, Gary Goldman. Story: Don Bluth, Ken Cromar, Gary Goldman, Larry Leker, Linda Miller, Monica Parker, John Pomeroy, Guy Schulman, David Steinberg, David N. Weiss. Music: Ralph Burns (songs by Charles Strouse and T. J. Kuenster). Directing animators: John Pomeroy, Linda Miller, Ralph Zondag, Dick Zondag, Lorna Pomeroy-Cook, Jeff Etter, Ken Duncan. Animation: Jeffrey J. Varab, Jean Morel, Cathy Jones, Anne-Marie Bardwell, Silvia Hoefnagels, John Hill, Gary Perkovac, Fernando Moro, Ralf Palmer, Tom Roth, Charlie Bonifacio, Paul Newberry, Alain Costa, David G. Simmons, Michel Gagne, John Power, T. Daniel Hofstedt, Enis Tahsin Ozgur, Jon Hooper. Effects animator: Stephen B. Moore. Layout supervision: Scott Caple, David Goetz. Layouts: Amy Berenz, John Byrne, David Gardner, Kevin Gollaher, Eddie Gribbin, Giorgio Mardegan, Fred Reilly, Mark Swan. Background stylist: Don Moore. Backgrounds: Barry Atkinson, Rick Bentham, Carl Jones, Sunny Apinchapong, David McCamley, Mannix Bennett, Paul M. Kelly. A Sullivan Bluth Studios Ireland Ltd. Production in association with Goldcrest Films.

**All Dogs Go to Heaven 2** (3/29/96) MGM/UA. 82 mins. Directors: Larry Leker, Paul Sebella. Producers: Paul Sebella, Jonathan Dern, Kelly Ward, Mark Young. Voices: Charlie Sheen (Charlie Barkin), Sheena Easton (Sasha LaFleur), Dom DeLuise (Itchy Itchiford), Ernest Borgnine (Carface), George Hearn (Red), Bebe Neuwirth (Annabelle), Adam Wylie (David), Dan Castellaneta (Tall Customs Dog, Angel Dog #1), Wal-

©Metro Goldwyn Mayer Animation, Inc.

lace Shawn (Labrador MC), Jim Cummings (Jingles), Maurice LaMarche (Lost and Found Officer).

**Consumer Tips:** ☆☆½ MPAA Rating: G. Will appeal mainly to children.

**Story:** Deceased dogs Charlie and Itchy, living the high life in pooch heaven, are assigned to retrieve Gabriel's horn, which has fallen back to earth in a bungled burglary. Meanwhile, evil mutt Carface and demonic Red concoct a wild scheme to keep all dogs penned inside Alcatraz.

**Comments:** Much better than *All Dogs 1*, this film has a coherent storyline, better songs, and unique visuals. Charlie Sheen improves upon the vocal characterization created by Burt Reynolds in the first film, and Dom DeLuise gives yet another amusing performance and is the only returning cast member from *All Dogs 1*. Singer/actresses Sheena Easton and Bebe Neuwirth also lend their wonderful voices to the proceedings.

The original *All Dogs* did well enough in theaters and on home video to warrant a sequel (albeit with a lesser budget). With the sequel rights in hand (MGM had fully acquired United Artists' properties and film rights since the original film was released), main character designs already completed, and animator/director Larry Leker (the story artist on the original film) on staff, an *All Dogs* part deux seemed a natural decision.

The film's production was managed by MGM's short-lived, in-house animation division of the 1990s. This division produced mostly television series (i.e., the *Pink Panther*) and direct-to-video movies *(Babes in Toyland)* by outsourcing production. *All Dogs 2* provided employment for hundreds of animators all over the world. Wang Film in Taiwan, Phoenix Animation in Toronto, A-Film in Copenhagen, Dino Animation and Red Rover in London, Bibo Films, and Franck and Franck in Paris—as well as studios in Australia and Ireland—all had a hand in some piece of production for *All Dogs Go to Heaven 2*.

It was an interesting artistic choice to have the backgrounds rendered in a more stylized fashion during the musical numbers. This was the result of input from production designer Deane Taylor, the talented art director of Tim Burton's *The Nightmare Before Christmas*.

*All Dogs Go to Heaven 2* is better than the original, largely because the story follows a logical linear path—something Don Bluth had trouble grasping during his 1990s output. (JB)

**Additional Credits:** Screenplay: Arne Olsen, Kelly Ward, Mark Young. Story: Mark Young, Kelly Ward. Music: Mark Watters. Songs: Barry Mann, Cynthia Weil. Animation director: Tod Waterman. Directing animator: David Feiss. Sequence director: Paul Schibli. Storyboard artists: David Feiss, Larry Scholl, Todd Waterman, Dino Athanassiou, Jasper Moller, Cathy Jones, John Dorman, Thom Enriquez, Andy Knight, Jorgen Lerdam, John Byrne, Sylvia Hoefnagels.

**Allegro Non Troppo** (7/27/77) Specialty Films (Italy). 75 mins. Director/producer: Bruno Bozzetto. Live-action cast: Maurizo Nichetti (The Cartoonist), Maria Luisa Giovannini (The Cleaning Woman), Nestor Garay (The Orchestra Conductor), Maurizio Micheli (The Impresario), Mirella Falco (Old Lady Musician), Osvaldo Salvi (Gorilla), Jolanda Cappi, Franca Mantelli (Old Lady Musicians).

**Consumer Tips:** ☆☆☆☆ MPAA Rating: PG. Not for children. Classical music soundtrack includes Ravel's *Bolero*, Dvorak's *Slavonic Dance #7*, Debussy's *Prelude a L'Apres Midi d'un Faun*, Vivaldi's *Concerto in C*, Sibelius's *Valse Triste* and Stravinsky's *Firebird Suite*.

THE MOVIE FOR THE HEAD SET.

Bruno Bozzetto's
**Allegro Non Troppo**
*(a full-length animated movie)* PG
A Specialty Films Release

©Bruno Bozzetto Film

**Story:** A take-off on Disney's *Fantasia*, bracketed by black and white live action footage of a nebbish animator trying to both visualize the classic music and woo a pretty cleaning lady. The animation sequences include "Evolutionary Fantasy," which illustrates the creation of life from a few drops of Coca-Cola, "The Last Meow," which follows a homeless cat recalling its happy days as a family pet, "From One to Many," which humorously portrays the rise of militarism, "Let It Bee," which follows a bee getting revenge on two lovers in his garden, "A Merry Chase," which follows an aging satyr chasing after several nymphs and his lost youth, and "Paradise Lost," which shows what happens when the serpent himself eats the apple in the Garden of Eden.

**Comments:** The title of *Allegro Non Troppo* refers to a musical tempo that means "fast, but not too fast." The film is a collection of several wonderful short pieces by master Italian animator Bruno Bozzetto. Loosely connected by its use of classical music and slapstick live-action bridging footage, it is an excellent film. Thoroughly entertaining and the homage to Disney's *Fantasia* aside, this is a wholly original and innovative work.

Bozzetto was born in Milan in 1938 and started making films at the age of 17. His short, *Tapum! The History of Arms*, was selected to screen at Cannes in 1958. He studied under Halas and Batchelor in London for a year, and returned to Italy where he balanced commercial work and sharp, satirical, personal films, for which he became best known. Bozzetto's first feature was *West and Soda* (1965), a parody of American Westerns. This was followed by *Vip: My Brother Superman* in 1968, a superhero spoof. Neither film was ever released theatrically in the United States.

His love of U.S. pop culture icons naturally led to poking fun at Disney on his own turf—the animated feature. But Bozzetto's films always had an adult edge and a dark sense of humor and, unlike Disney, some of the segments in *Allegro* are overtly sexual.

*Allegro Non Troppo* is brimming with zany sight gags, exciting visuals, and comic originality. The animation art direction is superb, and the comic timing to the musical beats or to service a joke is masterful. Even the live-action bits have their moments. I love how the orchestra is made up of old women, and the cartoonist is first seen chained up in a dungeon below the stage. Later in the film, the cartoonist transforms himself and his lady love into an animated Prince Charming and Snow White, and they fly off toward a happy ending. Even when the film ends, there is an additional series of outrageous blackout gags: an athlete is sliced apart by the ribbon at the finishing line; a cat flees a mouse only to be crushed by a giant trap; a princess tears a courting prince to pieces; and so on. The live-action segments combine with bits of animation as well: a throwaway gag shows a character inside an animated cel who is sneaking out to steal the conductor's lunch and is inadvertently set on fire.

But such sensory overload doesn't hurt *Allegro Non Troppo* in the least. Although Bozzetto continued to generate great cartoons and win acclaim for his subsequent work (his animated short *Grasshoppers* was nominated for an Academy Award in 1990), *Allegro Non Troppo* has been, and always will be, his crowning achievement. (JB)

**Additional Credits:** Screenplay: Bruno Bozzetto, Guido Manuli, Maurizo Nichetti. Music: Debussy, Dvorak, Ravel, Sibelius, Vivaldi, Stravinsky. Principal animators/designers: Giuseppe Lagana, Walter Cavazzuti, Giovanni Ferrari, Giancarlo Cereda, Giorgio Valentini, Guido Manuli, Paolo Albicocco, Giorgio Forlani. Animators: Edo Cavalli, Roberto Casale, Angelo Beretty, Mirna Masino. Backgrounds: Giancarlo Cereda, Giuseppe Laguna, Paolo Abicocco, Giorgio Forlani. Special animated effects: Luciano Marzetti.

**An American Tail** (11/21/86) Universal Pictures. 80 mins. Director: Don Bluth. Producers: Don Bluth, John Pomeroy, Gary Goldman. Voices: Phillip Glasser (Fievel Mousekowitz), Dom DeLuise (Tiger), Christopher Plummer (Henri), Nehemiah Persoff (Papa Mousekowitz), Gussie Mausheimer (Madeline Kahn), Amy Green (Tanya Mousekowitz), John Finnegan (Warren T. Rat), Cathianne Blore (Bridget), Erica Yohn (Mama Mousekowitz), Neil Ross (Honest John), Will Ryan (Digit).

**Consumer Tips:** ☆☆☆ MPAA Rating: G. Will appeal mainly to children.

**Story:** Young Russian immigrant Fievel Mousekowitz is separated from his family en route to America. Wan-

©Universal City Studios, Inc.

dering around late 19th-century New York, Fievel meets an assortment of characters, including a French pigeon, a friendly vegetarian cat, and a villainous rat. After various adventures, Fievel is reunited with his family.

**Comments:** *An American Tail* was the first animated feature presented by Steven Spielberg. His name was used to sell the film. His influence is felt throughout the story, but his actual role was that of a hands-on executive producer.

This was Don Bluth's second feature-length film production since leaving Disney in a much-publicized exodus in 1979. After *The Secret of Nimh,* Bluth's original financiers backed away from animation. However, his studio continued on, designing and animating the innovative arcade games *Dragon's Lair* and *Space Ace.* In 1985, Don Bluth Productions filed for bankruptcy, and the animation team reorganized as Sullivan Studios.

Bluth's composer on *Nimh,* Jerry Goldsmith, introduced the animator to Steven Spielberg, who had an extreme interest in classic animation (Spielberg has one of the greatest collections of original animation art in Hollywood). The pair agreed to seek out a story that would interest them both.

Writer David Kirschner, a former artist for muppeteer Jim Henson and creator of *Rose Petal Place* for Hallmark Cards and Kenner Toys, pitched the original concept for *An American Tail* to Amblin. It was then presented to Bluth for possible collaboration. The story was worked over by Spielberg, Bluth and his storyboard staff, and screenwriters Tony Geiss and Judy

Freudberg (of *Sesame Street*). The obligatory songs (by Cynthia Weil, Barry Mann, and James Horner) were pretty good. "Somewhere Out There" became a hit; it was nominated for an Academy Award and won a Grammy Award.

The reviews were generally mixed to the positive. Many critics noticed a parallel between the film's story and Art Spiegelman's graphic novel, *Maus,* the Holocaust epic released in book form the same year. Commercial tie-ins with merchandisers Sears and McDonald's gave Disney competition in a field it traditionally dominated. Few religious groups noted a faux pas in the marketing of Christmas ornaments and holiday McDonald's Happy Meals with Fievel, a Jewish mouse.

The grosses were huge. *Tail*'s $47 million domestic gross broke box-office records and beat Disney's *Great Mouse Detective* by over $15 million dollars. This established Spielberg as a player in animated films, solidified Don Bluth's reputation for high quality, and signaled true competition for the Disney studio. (JB)

**Additional Credits:** Writers: Judy Freudberg, Tony Geiss. Executive producers: Steven Spielberg, David Kirschner, Kathleen Kennedy, Frank Marshall. Music: James Horner. Directing animators: John Pomeroy, Dan Kuenster, Linda Miller. Animators: Lorna Pomeroy, Gary Perkovac, Jeff Etter, Ralph Zondag, Skip Jones, Kevin Wurzer, Dave Spafford, Dick Zondag, Dave Molina, Heidi Guedel, Ann Marie Bardwell, Jesse Cosio, Ralph Palmer, T. Daniel Hofstedt. Additional animation: Michael Cedeno, David Concepcion, Jorgen Klubien. Directing effects animator: Dorse A. Lanpher. Character key supervisor: Vera Lanpher. Character key assistants: Terry Shakespeare, Emily Jiuliano, Silvia Hoefnagels, Mark Pudleiner, Jon Hooper, Cathy Jones. Character clean-up: Jan Naylor, Carlos Taveras, Jean Morel. Special effects assistants: Steve Moore, Dave Bossert. Special effects in-betweeners: Joey Mildenberger, Michael Casey, David McCamley, David Tidgwell. Layout supervisor/storyboard assistant: Larry Leker. Layouts: Mark Swan, Mark Swanson. Background stylist: Don Moore. Backgrounds: William Lorencz, Barry Atkinson, David Goetz, Richard Bentham. An Amblin Entertainment Production.

## An American Tail: Fievel Goes West (11/22/91)
Universal Pictures. Directors: Phil Nibbelink, Simon Wells. Producers: Steven Spielberg, Robert Watts. Voices: Phillip Glasser (Fievel), James Stewart (Wylie Burp), Dom DeLuise (Tiger), Cathy Cavadini (Tanya),

©Universal City Studios and Amblin Entertainment

John Cleese (Cat R. Waul), Amy Irving (Miss Kitty), Nehemiah Persoff (Papa Mousekowitz), Erica Yohn (Mama Mousekowitz), Jon Lovitz (Chula), Linda Ronstadt (Vocalist).

**Consumer Tips:** ☆☆½ MPAA Rating: G. Will appeal mainly to children.

**Story:** The Mousekowitz family decides to move west, where villainous Cat R. Waul lures them into his evil schemes. Fievel saves the day by teaming up with a vegetarian cat, Tiger, and over-the-hill canine marshall, Wylie Burp.

**Comments:** After two film successes with Steven Spielberg, Bluth and his studio parted company over creative differences. Both movies (*An American Tail* and *The Land Before Time*) were successful enough to warrant sequels, but Bluth's departure left Spielberg somewhat in the lurch. However, by 1990, Spielberg had collaborated with other animators; he set up *Tiny Toon Adventures* with Warner Bros. Animation and *Who Framed Roger Rabbit* with the Richard Williams Studio.

Production of *An American Tail: Fievel Goes West* led to the opening of a new animation production unit in London: a collaboration of Universal and Amblin named Amblimation. This was large enough to accommodate over 250 directors, animators, ink and paint artists, and others. The studio opened with one film in production (*Fievel Goes West*) and two in development (*We're Back* and an ill-fated adaptation of Andrew Lloyd Webber's *Cats*).

Production on *Fievel Goes West* began in May 1989. Two men were chosen to direct: Simon Wells, the grandson of H. G. Wells and a former storyboard artist with Richard Williams, and Phil Nibbelink, a veteran Disney animator and supervising animator on *Roger Rabbit*.

The resulting film is a visually attractive, family-friendly story, with full flowing animation—perhaps too full flowing. In fact, the over-detail may be the film's weak point. The whole film moves like it's on speed. Great layouts, lush backgrounds, and strong personality animation are sabotaged by the fast timing and overall speedy pace of the film. The movie feels like someone in the projection booth had a finger on the fast-forward button throughout the picture. A sequence with the family river rafting through the sewers of New York could have been fun, but it is ruined due to the fast pace of the scene—the whole film suffers from this problem. Another sore point, no doubt inspired by the success of *Roger Rabbit*, was the "wacky" animation toward the end of the film when Wylie Burp (James Stewart) and Tiger (Dom DeLuise) go "Toon Town" looney after a swig of whiskey.

With a box-office gross of $22 million, it was not enough to continue the *Fievel* films on a theatrical level, but enough to inspire a Saturday morning television series, *Fievel's American Tales* (CBS, 1991) and two direct-to-video sequels: *An American Tail III: The Treasure of Manhattan Island* (1999), and *An American Tail: Mystery of the Night Monster* (2000). (JB)

**Additional Credits:** Story: Charles Swenson. Screenplay: Flint Dille. Based on characters created by David Kirschner. Music: James Horner. Songs: James Horner, Will Jennings. Supervising animators: Nancy Beiman, Kristof Serrand, Rob Stevenhagen. Animation: Bibo E. Bergeron, Raul Garcia, Ceu D'Elia, Phil Morris, Patrick Mate, Rodolphe Guenoden, Roy Meurin, Greg Manwaring, Thierry Schiel, Pete Western, David Bowers, Piet Kroon, Glen Sylvester, Luc Chamberland, Jurgen Richter, Shane Doyle, Daniel Jeanette, Andreas Von Andrian, Ute Von Munchow-Pohl, Nadja Cozic, Eric Bouilette, Jan Van Buyten, Denis Couchon, Paul McDonald, Alain Mandron. Additional animation: Oliver Pont, Quentin Miles, Georges Abolin, Fabio Lignini, Wolf-Ruediger Bloff, Miguel Fuertes, Mark Wolfgang Broecking, Angelos Rouvas, Jean Pilotte, Joe McCaffrey. Art director: Neil Ross. Character design: Uli Meyer. Layout supervisor: Mark Marren. Layouts: Brendan Houghton,

Armen Melkonian, Panagiotis Rappas, Giorgio Mardegan, Tom Humber, Marco Cinello, Antonio Navarro. Background supervisor: Shelley Page. Backgrounds: Gary Sycamore, Rachel Stedman, Sean Eckett, Walter Koessler, Darek Gogol, Mike Rose, Ennio Torresan Jr., Daniel Cacavault, Colin Stimpson, David Womersley. An Amblin Entertainment Production.

**American Pop** (2/13/81) Columbia. 97 mins. Director: Ralph Bakshi. Producer: Martin Ransohoff. Voices: Ron Thompson (Tony Bolinski, Pete), Marya Small (Frankie), Jerry Holland (Louie), Lisa Jane Persky (Bella), Jeffrey Lippa (Zalmie Bolinski), Roz Kelly (Eva Tanguay), Frank DeKova (Crisco), Richard Singer (Benny Bolinski), Elsa Raven (Hannele), Ben Frommer (Nicky Palumbo).

©Columbia Pictures Industries, Inc.

**Consumer Tips:** ☆☆☆ MPAA Rating: R. Suitable for teens and adults.

**Story:** A dark portrait of American popular music, as reflected by four generations of the Bolinsky family. Zalmie Bolinsky enters show business through vaudeville and becomes involved with the mob. His son Benny joins a black jazz band. Benny's boy, Tony, sets out across America and gets involved with a female acid rock singer in San Francisco. Tony's son Pete becomes a drug dealer who gets a shot performing his own songs as a punk rock superstar.

**Comments:** *American Pop* is one of Ralph Bakshi's best films. Once again, Bakshi uses the rotoscope to tell his story (filming live actors and tracing their movements frame by frame to celluloid). He used this technique previously in *Lord of the Rings*, but unlike his *Rings* movie, in this film it works. Instead of a fantasy realm, the backdrops and story are based on reality and history.

The screenplay by Ronni Kern is strong, and Bakshi serves it well. What might have felt rushed in live action works well within 94 minutes of animation. The rotoscope effect softens the gritty reality that Bakshi wants to convey and gives the film a storybook quality that draws viewers into the visuals and storytelling.

The film's scope is epic, thus there are numerous episodes that work fine as short pieces. Many are quite memorable. Tony's meeting and seduction of a Kansas City waitress in a cornfield, and his later relationship with his son, Little Pete, are poignant—something we don't expect from Bakshi.

Critics were harsh on the illogical juxtaposition of songs and styles meant to suggest various moments in the 20th century, but it works in this case, since the animation itself signals an artificial history of 20th-century music, not a literal one. Tunes from George Gershwin, Cole Porter, Bob Dylan, Herbie Hancock, Jimi Hendrix, and Bob Seger evoke each time period perfectly. Music clearance issues kept *American Pop* off the home video market (and virtually out of sight) for 17 years after its release, but it has since been restored, and the film is available on various home video formats.

*American Pop* is a time capsule of American pop music, styles, trends, art, and fashions. Bakshi mixes newsreel footage, still photos, pencil sketches, and references to Andy Warhol, Edward Hopper, and Norman Rockwell to create a compelling original work. (JB)

**Additional Credits:** Executive producers: Richard R. St. Johns, Maggie Abbott. Assistant director: John Sparey. Screenplay: Ronni Kern. Music arrangements/original music: Lee Holdridge. Animators: Lillian Evans, Carl Bell, Craig Armstrong, Debbie Hayes, Steve Gordon, Brenda Banks, Jesus Cortes, James A. Davis, Robert LaDuca, Chrystal Russell, George Scribner, Paul Smith, Tom Tataranowicz, Robert Carr, Xenia. Layout/designs: Louise Zingarelli, Johnnie Vita, Marcia Adams, Barry Jackson. Background assistants: Jeff Skrimstad, Frank Frezzo, Gary Eggleston, Russ Heath. Color models: Janet Cummings.

**Anastasia** (11/21/97) 20th Century Fox. 94 mins. Directors/producers: Don Bluth, Gary Goldman. Voices: Meg Ryan (Anastasia), John Cusack (Dimitri), Kelsey Grammer (Vladimir), Christopher Lloyd (Rasputin), Hank Azaria (Bartok), Bernadette Peters (Sophie), Kirsten Dunst (Young Anastasia), Angela Lansbury (Dowager Empress Marie), Andrea Martin Phlegmenkoff (Old Woman), Liz Callaway (Singing Voice of Anastasia), Lacey Chabert (Singing Voice of Young Anastasia), Jim Cummings (Singing Voice of Rasputin), Jonathan Dokuchitz (Singing Voice of Dimitri).

**Consumer Tips:** ☆☆½ MPAA Rating: G. Will appeal particularly to girls between the ages of 7 and 12. Based on the play by Marcella Maurette.

**Story:** In Czarist Russia of 1916, an orphan named Anya, hoping to find out her true identity, teams up with two rogues, Dimitri and Vladimir, who hope to groom the girl to pass as royalty. However, a powerful magician, Rasputin, returns from the dead to foil plans to continue the Romanov dynasty.

**Comments:** After eight years in Ireland, Don Bluth and Gary Goldman signed a deal to return to the United States to head Fox Animation Studios. In the summer of 1994, they announced a new animation production facility that was to be built in Phoenix, Arizona. It was a $5 million dollar studio meant to house 300 employees.

Three years later, *Anastasia* was the first film to emerge from the studio. It was an animated musical remake of a classic 20th Century Fox property (a 1956 live-action movie starring Ingrid Bergman and Yul Brenner). The film was designed and shot in Cinemascope (still a unique format for animation), suited with songs by Lynn Ahrens and Stephen Flaherty (*Ragtime*), and had a $50 million production budget.

For the most part, Bluth and Goldman were up to the task. The film has heart and several pleasant musical set pieces for the girls, an incredible runaway train action sequence and a magical maniacal villain for the boys, and several comic relief characters for the tots.

It also had Bluth's erratic tone shifts, going from historical drama one moment to light-hearted cartoon fantasy the next, sometimes within the same scene. Still, it is one of Bluth's better films. With an enthusiastic marketing push by Fox, the film grossed $140 million, despite a last-minute ploy by Disney to sink it by rereleasing *The Little Mermaid* (1989) in theaters the week before.

While deciding on the studio's next theatrical feature, Fox had Bluth keep his artists busy on a 67-minute direct-to-video sequel, *Bartok the Magnificent* (1999). This high-quality, fully animated spin-off is actually a bit more entertaining than its big screen predecessor. (JB)

**Additional Credits:** Screenplay: Susan Gauthier, Bruce Graham, Bob Tsudiker, Noni White. Animation adaptation: Eric Tuchman. Based on the play by Marcella Maurette as adapted by Guy Bolton and the screenplay by Arthur Laurents. Music: David Newman. Lyrics: Lyn Ahrens. Song music: Stephen Flaherty. Executive producer: Maureen Donley. Directing animators: Len Simon, Troy Saliba, Sandro Cleuzo, John Hill, Fernando Moro, Paul Newberry. Animators: Edison Goncalves, Dave MacDougall, John Power, Kelly Baigent, Robert Sprathoff, Marco Plantilla, Hugo M. Takahashi, Melvin Silao, Manuel Galiana, Paul J. Kelly, Robert Fox, Allan Fernando, Gabor T. Steisinger, Maximillian Nepomuceno, Glen McIntosh, Joey Paraiso, JoJo Young, Alan Fleming, Celine Kiernan. Character layout/design: Chris Schouten. Production designer: Mike Peraza. Conceptual artist: Suzanne Lemieux Wilson. Pre-production design: John Lakey. Storyboards: Larry Leker, Joe Orrantia, Chip Pace, Jay Schultz, Feran Xalabader.

**Animal Farm** (1/5/55) DCA (Distributors Corporation of America). 75 mins. Directors/producers: John Halas, Joy Batchelor. Voices: Maurice Denham (Napoleon, Snowball, Old Major, Squealer, Sheep, Jones, and all animal sounds), Gordon Heath (Narrator).

BOXER·BENJAMIN

©Distributors Corp. of America

**Consumer Tips:** ☆☆☆ Based on George Orwell's novel. Despite its Disney-styled look, it's not for children.

**Story:** The animals of Farmer Jones' Manor Farm, tired of being treated unfairly, revolt and take over farm. After a while, the pigs have created a dictatorship in which life is worse than before.

**Comments:** Britain's first animated feature has excellent character animation, great designs, layouts, and background art. It also tackles a serious subject—Orwell's classic political satire of government and the corruption of power.

Some changes were made to George Orwell's story, most notably the ending. However, the film still captures most of Orwell's plot and its central themes. Like the novel, the story opens on Manor Farm, where the animals are fearful and unhappy as the drunken Mr. Jones continues to mistreat them while running the farm into the ground. Old Major, the elderly prized pig, gathers the other animals to deliver a call to future revolution, and to remind them of both their grievances and principles, as they must avoid man's vices.

Although the original novel featured conversations or exchanges amongst the different animals, in this film only the pigs engage in lengthy speech, though the sheep do utter the memorable chant, "Four legs good, two legs baaaaad!" Narration is used to cover any other essential exposition points or sum up opinions or exchanges of the other animals. While this technique separates the pigs from the other animals, the other animals are still quite expressive, through the full, realistic animation and through their utterances.

All dialogue and animal sounds were supplied effectively by the versatile Maurice Denham, veteran of British film and BBC radio. Matyas Seiber's score, and particularly the animal's song of revolution, also contributed to the general mood. Orwell's animals symbolize real-life politicians: Napoleon the pig is Stalin, Snowball is Trotsky, and the boar hog, Old Major, is a combination of Marx and Lenin.

Halas and Batchelor's production is handsome and quite well done. The bleak picture of the allegorical socialist farm is not negated by a substituted ending, which was marginally more upbeat yet ambiguous, and fit the overall tone of the film.

Some critics found it too dry for youngsters and too simplistic for adults. Others like Bosley Crowther called it "First rate . . . might well be admired and even envied by Mr. Disney's studio."

It was a triumph for directors John Halas and his wife Joy Batchelor. He was a young animator in Hungary, an apprentice to George Pal. She was a commercial artist and screenwriter. They met in 1938, and in 1940 started

Halas and Batchelor Animation Ltd., the largest and longest lasting of the British animation factories.

It would be over a decade before someone else would attempt an adult-skewed animated feature (Osamu Tezuka in Japan, and Ralph Bakshi in the United States were among the first), but Halas and Batchelor certainly deserve praise for a classy, effective experiment that took animated films in a new direction. The film is a landmark in British animation and still thought-provoking today. (JB)

*Additional Credits:* Story development: Luther Wolff, Borden Mace, Philip Stapp, John Halas, Joy Batchelor. Music: Matyas Seiber. Animation director: John F. Reed. Animators: Edrick Radage, Arthur Humberstone, Ralph Ayres, Hal Whittaker, Frank Moysey. Layout: Geoffrey Martin. Backgrounds: Digby Turpain, Martyn Wright, Bernard Carey. Sound effects: Jack King.

**Antz** (10/2/98) DreamWorks. 83 mins. Directors: Eric Darnell, Tim Johnson. Producers: Brad Lewis, Aron Warner, Patty Wooton. Voices: Woody Allen (Z), Dan Aykroyd (Chip), Anne Bancroft (Queen), Jane Curtin (Muffy), Danny Glover (Barbatus), Gene Hackman (General Mandible), Jennifer Lopez (Azteca), John Mahoney (Drunk Scout), Paul Mazurzky (Psychologist), Sylvester Stallone (Weaver), Sharon Stone (Princess Bala), Christopher Walken (Colonel Cutter).

©DreamWorks L.L.C.

*Consumer Tips:* ☆☆½ MPAA Rating: PG. All-star voice cast.

*Story:* An insignificant ant named Z falls in love with a princess, becomes a war hero, explores the world outside his underground city, and saves his colony from destruction.

*Comments: Antz* was the first animated feature from DreamWorks and its alliance with Pacific Data Images (PDI). It was quite a success, grossing over $90 million in the United States. More importantly, it established DreamWorks as a player in animated features. This film became the blueprint for future DreamWorks releases: script-driven comedies with big name stars in lead voice roles.

*Antz* has its pros and cons, but the good outweighs the bad. On the one hand, the film has a dark look and claustrophobic feel, and the character design is rather drab and unappealing. On the other hand, casting Woody Allen as the neurotic lead character was an inspired choice.

The film begins promisingly enough, as Z (Woody Allen) explains his inferiority complex to his analyst. Meanwhile, he is staring out onto the vast ant colony that is going through its daily routine. This is a stunning opening sequence. We are then introduced to the General (Gene Hackman), who controls the soldiers and worker ants, and is scheming a takeover plot involving digging a strategic tunnel. Z ultimately falls in love with the Ant Princess (Sharon Stone) and joins the Army, where he somehow becomes a war hero. He escapes to the outside world, "Insectopia," and in an action-packed climax, rescues his colony from disaster.

*Antz* fulfills all the requirements expected of a contemporary feature-length animated film, and thus no one will be particularly disappointed. But no one will be particularly surprised either. It's fun to watch, but forgettable.

DreamWorks' adult approach to animated features was refreshing. The first part of *Antz* plays more like a Woody Allen neurosis comedy than any comparable family film. But no character generates much sympathy. For all the stunt casting involved, only Allen, Gene Hackman, and, surprisingly, Stallone's personas really connect with their characters. The computer animation is so slick that the main characters almost feel as if they were live actors in grotesque insect make-up. It's strange to be looking into Z's realistic eyes, his E.T.-like facial features, and his near-perfect dental work.

Much action occurs, but little of it engages the audience, and the film is bland overall. It has no big laughs or comic performances (such as Robin Williams' Genie or Eddie Murphy's Mushu), no dramatic highs that had me cheering (like the climax of *Toy Story*), and no original message of inspiration (as in *Hoppity Goes to Town*). The film holds your full attention for 83 minutes, but it's as hollow as the ants' underground colony. (JB)

**Additional Credits:** Screenplay: Todd Alcott, Chris Weitz, Paul Weitz. Story: Randy Cartwright. Music: Harry Gregson-Williams, John Powell. Director of additional sequences: Laurence Guterman. Supervising animators: Rex Gridnon, Raman Huii. Directing animators: Denis Couchon, Sean Curran, Donnachada Daly. Animation: Edip Agi, Chun Nin Chan, Tim Cheung, Webster Colcord, Raffaella Flipponi, David Griney, Enrique Navarrete Gil, Colin Hennen, Anthony Hodgson, Tim Keon, Justin Kohn, Eric Lessard, Noel McGin Jr., Fred Nilsson, David Rader, Jason A. Reisin, David Spivack, Don Venhaus. A PDI (Pacific Data Images) Production.

**Arabian Knight** (8/25/95) Miramax. 72 mins. Director: Richard Williams. Director, LA Production: Fred Calvert. Producers: Imogene Sutton, Richard Williams, Bette L. Smith, Fred Calvert. Voices: Vincent Price (Zigzag), Matthew Broderick (Tack the Cobbler), Jennifer Beals (Princess Yum Yum), Eric Bogosian (Phido), Toni Collette (The Nurse, The Witch), Jonathan Winters (The Thief), Clive Revill (King Nod), Bobbi Page (Singing Voice of Princess Yum Yum), Kevin Dorsey (Mighty One Eye), Stanley Baxter (Gofer & Slap), Kenneth Williams (Goblet, Tickle).

©The Completion Bond Company

**Consumer Tips:** ☆☆½ MPAA Rating: G. Also known as *The Thief and the Cobbler*.

**Story:** Evil magician Zigzag has eyes for Princess Yum Yum and her father's kingdom, and plots to have them both with the help of a flea-bitten thief and a horde of loutish monsters.

**Comments:** This film has quite a history. Over 30 years in production, *Arabian Knight* began life as a pet project for director Richard Williams in the 1960s and became a legend in the animation industry. Williams began work on the film (then known as *The Thief and the Cobbler*, a title it has reverted back to in video release) with illustrator Errol Le Cain and art designer Roy Naisbitt. They created an elaborate art direction for the film, based on Oriental and Eastern art. Master animators Grim Natwick, Ken Harris, and Art Babbit were also hired, and encouraged to create a cartoon tour-de-force. Vincent Price was hired to voice the villain Zigzag.

Williams tinkered with the film between commercial assignments for 25 years, not attracting financial backing from a major studio until early 1990, shortly after the release of his Oscar-winning work on *Who Framed Roger Rabbit*. Producer Jake Eberts came aboard in 1990, and Warner Bros. agreed to finance and distribute the film.

Expecting to release the film in 1993, Warner Bros. decided to bail out in 1992 when Williams failed to produce a satisfactory version of his film. The Completion Bond Company, a motion picture insurance company, paid Warner Bros. off and took over the film from Williams. They brought the production to Hollywood and attempted to salvage the pieces by creating a Disney-like musical (a la *Aladdin*). Disney, noting the superior animation of Williams, and the *Aladdin*-like similarities, bought the film and released it through its art-house distribution channel, Miramax Films.

The film was a dismal failure, and no wonder. Animator Fred Calvert (*Sesame Street*, *Winky Dink and You*, various television cartoons) was hired, and three mediocre song sequences were added. The thief and the cobbler, silent lead characters in the Williams version, were given voices (Jonathan Winters as the thief and Matthew Broderick as the cobbler) to mouth unnecessary commentary and unfunny mumblings, adding nothing to the film. New sequences tried to match the original Williams footage, but it's pretty easy to tell them apart. The film is a dud in its current incarnation.

Shortly after the film's theatrical release, animators smuggled a copy of Williams' original print out of the production offices and allowed others to see his vision of the film. Roy Disney obtained a copy and became a champion in the effort to restore the Richard Williams version of the film. With Williams' full cooperation, and the backing of Walt Disney Feature Animation, *The Thief and the Cobbler* was being prepared for rerelease. Unfortunately, with Roy Disney's departure from the company and its board of directors, and with the dismantling of Disney's traditional animation department, the current status of *The Thief and the Cobbler*'s restoration is unknown. (JB)

**Additional Credits:** Screenplay: Richard Williams, Margaret French. Additional story/dialogue: Parker Bennett, Terry Runte, Bette L. Smith, Tom Towler, Stephen Zito, Eric Gilliland, Michael Hitchcock, Gary Glasberg. Music: Robert Folk. Additional music/orchestration: Jack Maeby. Songs: Norman Gimbel. Master animator: Ken Harris. Animation supervisors: Neil Boyle, Tim Watts (London), Cynthia Wells (Los Angeles). Lead animators (London): Art Babbitt, Paul Bolger, David Byers-Brown, Denis Deegan, Gary Dunn, Sahin Ersoz, Steven Evangelatos, Margaret Grive, Jurgen Gross, Alyson Hamilton, Emery Hawkins, Dieter Kremer, Holger Leime, Robert Malhers, Mark Naisbitt, Brent O'Dell, Philip Pepper, Dean Roberts, Michael Schilingman, Alan Simpson, Mark Swindall, Venelin Veltchev, Roger Vizard, Andreas Wessel-Therhorn, Alex Williams. Animators (Los Angeles): Becky Bristow, Russell Calabrese, Kimmy Calvert, Jesse Cosio, Jill Culton, Sean Fleming, Frank Garreth, Edison Goncalves, Joe Hawkins, Sylvia Hoefnagels, Jeffrey Johnson, Kevin Johnson, Roy Meurin, Jean Morel, William Nunes, Kevin O'Hara, Kevin O'Neal, Cynthia Overman, Ralf Palmer, Gary Perkovac, Alan Sperling, David Stephan, William C. Waldman II, Shane Zalvin. Special effects supervisor: John M. Cousen (London), Sari Gennis (Los Angeles). An Allied Filmmakers Production.

## The Aristocats

**The Aristocats** (12/24/70) Walt Disney Productions. 78 mins. Director: Wolfgang Reitherman. Producers: Wolfgang Reitherman, Winston Hibler. Voices: Eva Gabor (Duchess), Phil Harris (Thomas O'Malley), Roddy Maude-Roxby (Edgar), Sterling Holloway (Roquefort), Scatman Crothers (Scat Cat), Paul Winchell (Chinese Cat), Lord Tim Hudson (English Cat), Vito Scotti (Italian Cat), Thurl Ravenscroft (Russian Cat), Nancy Kulp (Frou-Frou), Dean Clark

©Walt Disney Productions

(Berlioz), Liz English (Marie), Charles Lane (Georges Hautecourt), Gary Dubin (Toulouse), Hermione Baddeley (Madame Adelaide Bonfamille), Bill Thompson (Uncle Waldo), Monica Evans (Abigail Gabble), Carole Shelley (Amelia Gabble), Pat Buttram (Napoleon), Pete Renoudet (Milkman).

**Consumer Tips:** ☆☆½ MPAA Rating: G. Enjoyable film for younger viewers but not much substance for those used to Disney's meatier animated fare. Professional effort, but a thin story marks this film as a lightweight in the Disney canon.

**Story:** Paris, 1910: A wealthy, aging former star of the opera decides to will her estate and fortune to her pampered cat and her three kittens. After they pass on, her faithful butler is next in line. The bloke doesn't want to wait quite that long, but his nefarious plans are foiled by a resourceful alley cat and a host of his animal friends.

**Comments:** *The Aristocats* is by no means a bad film, but it will never be confused with a classic. Disney's first animated feature of the 1970s was undermined by several factors. Many of the plot elements had already been featured in previous Disney films, notably *101 Dalmatians* and *Lady and the Tramp*. Even the movie's big musical number, "Everybody Wants to Be a Cat" is reminiscent of "I Wanna Be Like You" (from *The Jungle Book*). The studio's practice of modeling major characters on the real-life personas of their voice artists can be traced as far back as *Alice in Wonderland*; while entertaining, this device tended to undercut the development of original personality animation by the talented Disney team. *The Aristocats* is no exception, as Phil Harris and Eva Gabor seem to play themselves rather than cats. There is one genuine piece of personality animation to be found in Marie, Duchess' female kitten. If only the same could be said for most of the other creations.

The movie's villain, Edgar the butler, is by far the weakest to appear in a Disney film; he was originally meant to have a scheming maid named Elvira as a partner-in-crime and it might have been a better film if he had. Finally, Woolie Reitherman's direction brings little heart to the film and few surprises to the audience. Most of the comedy is overly broad and slapstick, with an overabundance of pratfalls and knocks to the noggin (not to mention kicks and bites in the butt). The business concerning two English geese and their tipsy uncle is all but extraneous to the plot and would almost certainly have been cut by Walt in favor of character development. For example, the romance between Duchess the Aristocat and scruffy hero Thomas O'Malley develops almost instantaneously (perhaps to move a slender storyline along with all due speed).

On the plus side, the layouts and backgrounds are uniformly excellent and faithfully evoke old Paree. The animation of grand dame Madame Adelaide Bonfamille is as elegant as any done at Disney, courtesy of master animators Milt Kahl and John Lounsberry.

*The Aristocats* was originally conceived as a two-part live-action feature for the *Wonderful World of Disney* television show (the story was scripted back in 1961). Walt Disney envisioned the special as an animated feature instead and work was picked up on the film after the studio completed *The Jungle Book* in 1967. Maurice Chevalier, a faithful fan of all things Disney, recorded the title song at age 82. Another immortal, Louis Armstrong, was offered the role of O'Malley's comrade Scat Cat but the studio settled on Scatman Crothers when Armstrong was unable to commit to the film.

The story may be set in France, but what diversity! Mme. Bonfamille is Gallic enough, but Duchess, as voiced by Eva Gabor, is as Hungarian as they come. Thomas O'Malley sounds like an American in Paris. The rowdy farm dogs Napoleon and Lafayette seem to have wandered in from Arkansas, and Edgar is decidedly British in tone. Just for fun there are also Italian, Chinese, and Russian cats in Scat's band. Early rushes of the film proved Napoleon and Lafayette to be so entertaining that a second scene featuring the harrying hounds was added. The picture grossed $10 million in America but made $16 million in France, where it was often held over. Does anyone know what an American hippie cat is doing in 1910 Paris? (MG)

**Additional Credits:** Based on a story by Tom McGowan and Tom Rowe. Music: George Bruns. Songs: Richard Sherman, Robert Sherman, Terry Gilkyson, Floyd Huddleston, Al Rinker. Orchestrations: Walter Sheets. Directing animators: Milt Kahl, Oliver M. Johnston, Frank Thomas, John Lounsbury. Backgrounds: Al Dempster, Bill Layne, Ralph Hulett. Layout: Don Griffith, Basil Davidovich, Sylvia Roemer. Effects animators: Don McManus, Dick Lucas. Character animators: Hal King, Eric Cleworth, Fred Hellmich, Eric Larson, Julius Svendsen, Walt Stanchfield, Dave Michner. Story: Larry Clemmons, Vance Gerry, Frank Thomas, Julius Svendsen, Ken Anderson, Eric Cleworth, Ralph Wright. Production design: Ken Anderson. Assistant directors: Ed Hansen, Dan Alguire.

©Walt Disney Productions

**Atlantis: The Lost Empire** (6/3/01) Walt Disney Pictures. 92 mins. Directors: Gary Trousdale, Kirk Wise. Producer: Don Hahn. Voices: Michael J. Fox (Milo James Thatch), Corey Burton (Gaetan "The Mole" Moliere), Claudia Christian (Helga Katrina Sinclair), James Garner (Capt. Lyle Tiberius Rourke), John

Mahoney (Preston B. Whitmore), Phil Morris (Dr. Joshua Strongbear Sweet), Leonard Nimoy (King Kashekim Nedakh), Don Novello (Vincenzo "Vinny" Santorini), Jacqueline Obradors (Audrey Rocio Ramirez), Florence Stanley (Wilhelmina Bertha Packard), David Ogden Stiers (Fenton Q. Harcourt), Cree Summer (Princess Kida Kidagakash), Natalie Storm (Young Kida), Jim Varney (Jebediah Allardyce "Cookie" Farnsworth). Additional voices: Jim Cummings, Patrick Pinney, Steve Barr.

**Consumer Tips:** ☆☆½ MPAA Rating: PG. Commendable adventure epic with marvelous visual effects and a rousing musical score. Inconsistencies in character design and personality, usually rare in a Disney film, hinder the picture and consign it to lesser status among the studio's work.

**Story:** Young historian/linguist Milo Thatch gets his chance to prove that the lost city of Atlantis exists, courtesy of his late grandfather's wealthy friend. An expedition to find the city—and its mysterious but valuable power source—is threatened by the mercenary Captain Rourke and his lieutenant, the sinister Helga. Milo and his colorful crew must join forces with an Atlantean princess to keep the villains from stealing the Heart of Atlantis and dooming the city forever.

**Comments:** Disney's first animated epic of the new millennium carried a budget of close to $100 million. Expectations for the film were boosted by the fact that codirectors Kirk Wise and Gary Trousdale (*Beauty and the Beast*) were joining forces for a second time. An exciting trailer had audiences primed for animated adventure but when the tide finally rolled out on *Atlantis*, the film was left high and dry, grossing only $84 million. *Atlantis* ran into a far bigger Leviathan than the one seen in the movie: DreamWorks' *Shrek* had opened seven weeks earlier and was still drowning the competition when Disney's film came out. Still, competition was not the greatest obstacle *Atlantis* foundered upon; the movie had problems of its own.

The most serious flaws lay in the characters developed for the film. It appeared that assembling an odd-ball cast took precedence over developing their traits, personalities, and, ultimately, their believability. If, for example, we are to accept that "Mole" Moliere is unsurpassed in the expertise of his profession, then he cannot be presented as a psychotic dirtball. If we are to believe that a young female barely out of her teens is hired as master mechanic for a multimillion-dollar expedition, then we need to see her actually *fix* something, preferably of great importance at a crucial point in the film. It is similarly difficult to believe that one of the world's great demolition experts cannot keep his train of thought without trailing off into inanities, that the ship's cook is the reincarnation of Gabby Hayes, or that the too-frowsy communications expert can make gossipy phone calls to her friend from a depth of 100 fathoms. The main characters are reduced, in the end, to their sidebars and idiosyncrasies.

The malady spreads to the animation; it is difficult to watch the film and believe that all the characters exist in the same movie. Outlandish caricature is used for Cookie, Mrs. Packard, "Mole," and Whitmore, while Milo Thatch and Captain Rourke seem to be more clearly defined as human. Princess Kida and Dr. Sweet are presented even more realistically. King Nedakh and Helga (superbly animated with a perpetual sneer by Yoshimichi Tamura) are nearly lifelike. At times when they all appear in the same scene, the effect is jarring.

In the absence of believable characters, the amazing visual set pieces become the film's center. The merging of computer and traditional animation is not as sharp as it would be in later films, but *Atlantis* is a marvelous feast for the eyes. Jim Martin and Mike Mignola designed a mythical world with spectacular results, and twenty-one effects animators bolstered their efforts. The battle with Leviathan, the revelation of Atlantis to the explorers, and the extended sequence featuring Kida's encounter with the Heart of Atlantis are among the true treasures of *The Lost Empire*.

The film may have taken place under the sea, but its connections to deep space were many, courtesy of *Star Trek*. Captain Rourke's middle name is Tiberius, evoking another famous captain. The character Fenton Q. Harcourt is an inversion of Harcourt Fenton, seen in the *Star Trek* episode "Mudd's Women." Mark Okrand, who invented both the Vulcan and Klingon languages, created the Atlantean lingo for the movie, and production designer Jim Martin crafted spaceships for *Star Trek: Deep Space 9*. Last, but by no means least, King Kashekim Nedakh is voiced by Leonard Nimoy, the venerable Mr. Spock himself. Had *Atlantis* taken the time to develop characters as interesting as those aboard the *Enterprise*, the movie may have done much better. (MG)

**Additional Credits:** Screenplay: Tab Murphy. Story: Gary Trousdale, Joss Whedon, Bryce Zabel, Jackie Zabel, Tab Murphy, Kevin Harkey, Chris Ure, Todd Kurosawa, Kelly Wightman, Dean Deblois. Additional screenplay material: David Reynolds. Atlantean language development: Marc Okrand. Music: James Newton Howard. Supervising animators: John Pomeroy, Mike Surrey, Randy Haycock, Russ Emonds, Ron Husband, Yoshimichi Tamura, Anne Marie Bardwell, Dave Pruiksma, Shawn Keller, Anthony DeRosa, Michael Cedeno, Mike "Moe" Merell. Animators: Joe Haidar, Oliver Thomas, Bill Waldman, Ralph Palmer, Jay Jackson, Steven Pierre Gordon, Mario Manjvar, Dougg Williams, Doug Krohn, Robb Pratt, Larry White, Dave Burgess, Danny Galieote, Mark Koetsier, Chris Wahl, Richard Hoppe, Brian Moses Pimental, David Berthier, Kristoff Vergne, Andrea Simonti, Marco Allard, Juanjo Guarnido, Mike D'Isa, Jay N. Davis, Brian Wesley Green, Georges Abolin, Chris Sauve, Bill Recinos, Tom Bancroft, Patrick Delage, Dominique Monferey, Barry Temple, J. C. Tran-Quang-Thieu. Visual effects supervisor: Marlon West. Production designers: Mike Mignola, Matt Codd, Richard Delgado, Jim E. Martin. Art director: David Goetz. Story supervisor: John Sanford. Layout supervisor: Ed Ghertner. Background supervisor: Lisa Keene. Background supervisor (Paris): Joaquin Boyd Morales.

**Babar: The Movie** (7/28/89) New Line Cinema. 70 mins. Director: Alan Bunce. Producers: Michael Hirsh, Patrick Loubert, Clive A. Smith. Voices: Gordon Pinsent (King Babar), Elizabeth Hanna (Queen Celeste, The Old Lady), Lisa Yamanaka (Isabella), Marsha Moreau (Flora), Bobby Becker (Pom), Amos Crawley (Alexander), Gavin Magrath (Boy Babar), Sarah Polley (Young Celeste), Stephen Ouimette (Pompadour), Chris Wiggins (Cornelius).

**Consumer Tips:** ☆☆½ MPAA Rating: G. Based on the characters created by Jean and Laurent de Brunhoff.

©L. de Brunhof Motion Picture

**Story:** King Babar explains to his children the story of how, as a young boy, he and his friend Celeste thwarted a rhinoceros attack that almost destroyed their city.

**Comments:** In 1931, a young Parisian mother, Cecile de Brunhoff, told her young sons a fanciful bedtime story of a little elephant named Babar. The boys, Laurent and Mathieu, persuaded their father, a painter, to create an illustrated book of this charming story.

*Babar* became a huge international success—and father Jean de Brunhoff produced a total of twelve *Babar* children's books before his death in 1937. Ten years later, Laurent de Brunhoff, now an established artist, began authoring an additional 25 titles.

Though considered a children's classic, the screen rights to *Babar* were never made available before 1987. The de Brunhoff family preferred to protect the dignity of the original books and ultimately opted for a French Canadian coproduction deal with Nelvana, the Toronto-based animation studio with international connections and a track record of faithful screen adaptations.

The film itself is no classic, but it's a gentle adventure that *Babar's* younger readers will relate to and parents will approve of. The animation is sufficient, but there is no comparison to Disney's standards.

The movie received generally positive reviews and grossed $1.3 million in limited matinee showings.

A 26-episode television series for HBO followed in 1989 and a feature-length sequel, *Babar King of Elephants*, was released direct-to-video (in the United States) in 1999. (JB)

**Additional Credits:** Executive producers: Michael Hirsh, Patrick Loubert, Clive A. Smith, Stephanie Sperry, Pierre Bertrand Jaume, Yannick Bernard. Screenplay: Peter Sauder, J. D. Smith, John DeKlein, Raymond Jafelice, Alan Bunce. Story: Peter Sauder, Patrick Loubert, Michael Hirsh. Storyboards: Alan Bunce, Raymond Jafelice, Eric Chu, John Flagg, Brian Lee, Arna Selznick, Bob Smith. Music: Milan Kymlicka. Songs: Maribeth Solomon, Phil Balsam. Animation director: John Laurence Collins. Directors (Paris Unit): Paul Brizzi, Gaetan Brizzi. Animators: Greg Court, Mike Fallows, Gerry Fournier, Pierre Grenier, Gary Hurst, Larry Jacobs, Mark Koetsier, Arnie Lipsey, Mike Longden, Rick Marshall, Lynn Reist, Paul Riley, Shawn Seles. Effects animation: Willy Ashworth, Denis Gonzales. Production designer: Ted Bastien. Art directors: Clive Powsey, Carol Bradbury. A Nelvana Production.

**Balto** (12/22/95) Universal Pictures. 74 mins. Director: Simon Wells. Producer: Steve Hickner. Voices: Kevin Bacon (Balto), Bridget Fonda (Jenna), Phil Collins (Muk and Luk), Bob Hoskins (Boris), Jim Cummings (Steele), Robbie Rist (Star), Danny Mann (Kaltag), Jack Angel (Nikki), Juliette Brewer (Rosy), Donald Sinden (Doc). Live-action cast: Miriam Margolyes (Grandma Rosy), Lola Bates-Campbell (Granddaughter).

**Consumer Tips:** ☆☆☆½ MPAA Rating: G. Loosely based on a true story and incidents that occured in Nome, Alaska, 1925.

**Story:** Balto is an outcast Alaskan sled dog half-breed (part husky, part wolf) who is vying for the affection of Jenna, a beautiful husky belonging to a little girl taken ill. When Balto's rival, Steele, gets lost en route bringing medicine to Nome, Balto leads the sled team through various perils to complete the mission.

**Comments:** Set against the Arctic landscape of Alaska during real-life emergencies that befell the territory in 1925 (a diphtheria epidemic and harsh blizzards), which required dog teams to bring in much-needed medicines, *Balto* is an ambitious and well-made story of courage and determination.

The real Balto led a dog team on the final 53-mile leg of a 674-mile "Great Race of Mercy" that saved Nome from the medical disaster. The canine soon became a symbolic champion and toured America as a hero; he even starred in a silent film recreation, *Balto's Race to Nome* (1925). The statue of Balto in New York's Central Park commemorating the event (and appearing in the live-action portion of this film) was dedicated the same year.

Seventy years later, Steven Spielberg produced this animated feature in London using much of the crew assembled for *We're Back! A Dinosaur's Story* (1993). Director Simon Wells was promoted to full director status after stints as supervising animator on *Who Framed Roger Rabbit* (1988) and codirector of *An American Tail II: Fieval Goes West* and *We're Back*.

*Balto* is an exciting, fast-paced, action adventure with heart. The cliffhanging scenes involving cracking ice, ferocious bears, avalanches, and snowstorms are thrilling. The character animation is as good as contemporary Disney. But despite these qualities, and generally favorable reviews, the film failed at the box office (grossing only $11.3 million in the United States) where it was up against a new kid on the block, Pixar's blockbuster debut feature *Toy Story.*

*Balto* was the final film produced by Steven Spielberg's Amblimation studio in London. The principal animation creatives moved on from there to establish DreamWorks' new animation facility in Glendale, California, commencing work on *The Prince of Egypt* (1998). (JB)

**Additional Credits:** Story: Cliff Ruby, Elena Lesser. Screenplay: Cliff Ruby, Elena Lesser, David Steven Cohen, Roger S. H. Schulman. Music: James Horner. Supervising animators: Jeffrey J. Varab, Dick Zondag, Kristof Serrand, Rob Stevenhagen,

©Universal City Studios and Amblin Entertainment

Sahin Ersoz, Rodolphe Guenoden, Nicolas Marlet, William Salazar, David Bowers, Patrick Mate. Animators: Paul Jesper, Sean Leaning, Kevin Spruce, Vladimir Todorov, Arnaud Berthier, Denis Couchon, Emanuela Cozzi, Fabio Lignini, Quentin Miles, Maximilian Graenitz, Jurgen Richter, Andreas Wessel Therhorn, Andreas Von Andrian, Philippe LeBrun, Ken Keys, Jean-Francois Rey, Steve Horrocks, Rune Bennicke, Andreas Simonti, Daniel Jeanette, Erik Schmidt. Additional animation: Cecile Bender, Jan Van Buyten, Mike Eames, Luca Fatoore, Stefan Fjeldmark, Miguel Fuertes, Antony Gray, Keith Greig, Jurgen Gross, Jakob Hjert-Jensen, Jorgen Lerdam, Jane Poole, Andy Schmidt, Oskar Urretabizkaia, Mark Williams. Effects supervisor: Mike Smith. Production designer: Hans Bacher. Storyboard supervisor: Dean Jippes. Storyboards: David Bowers, Rodolphe Gunoden, Fabio Lignini, William Salazar, Harold Sipermann, Dick Zondag. Backgrounds: Steve Albert, Luc DesMarchelier, Julie Gleeson, Natasha Gross, Stephen Hanson, Michael Hirsch, Walter Kossler, Paul Shardlow, Rachel Stedman, Gary Sycamore, Claire Wright. An Amblin Entertainment Production.

**Bambi** (8/13/42) Walt Disney Productions. 69 mins. Director: David Hand. Voices: Bobby Stewart, Donnie Dunagan, Hardy Albright, John Sutherland (Bambi), Cammie King, Ann Gillis (Faline), Paula Winslowe (Bambi's mother), Stanley Alexander, Sterling Holloway, Tim Davis (Flower, Thumper), Peter Behn, Fred Shields (Prince of the Forest), Bill Wright (Friend Owl), Mary Lansing (Aunt Ena, Mrs. Possum), Thelma Boardman (Mrs. Quail), Marjorie Lee (Mrs. Rabbit). Additional voices: Jeanne Christy, Janet Chapman, Bobette Audrey, Marion Darlington, Otis Harlan, Thelma Hubbard, Jack Horner, Babs Nelson, Francesca Santoro, Elouise Wohlwend, Sandra Lee Richards, Dolyn Bramston Cook.

**Consumer Tips:** ☆☆☆☆ MPAA Rating: G. A masterpiece of animation that combines light comedy, tragedy, and even romance while exploring the lives, loves, and travails of forest creatures. The characters are so fully realized that viewers readily laugh—and cry—along with the animals as their lives unfold on screen. Many critics have called *Bambi* Disney's loveliest and most lyrical film. It is certainly Disney's most naturalistic; never again would such attention to detail be seen in Disney animation.

**Story:** Bambi, the newborn prince of the forest, faces the challenges of maturity, responsibility, love, and leadership. Bambi's loyal friends Thumper the rabbit, Flower the skunk, and his future mate Faline will someday look to Bambi to protect them from the predations of man. Can the young prince inherit the mantle of his legendary father and claim his rightful place as scion of the forest?

**Comments:** Rarely has any American studio released an animated film as languid, introspective, and visually beautiful as *Bambi*. Well-developed characters and a mythic story take precedence over relentless action, and *Bambi* is not unlike some of the films directed by the masterful Hayao Miyazaki nearly sixty years later. These very qualities may have accounted for the film's initial lack of success at the box office. America was at war in 1942, and the nation was aflame with a feisty determination to fight and win. Other animation studios were presenting the home front with sassy, spirited cartoons in which the enemy was caricatured, ridiculed, and clobbered with relish. *Bambi* was a quiet, gentle film out of tune with the times despite its undeniable strengths and exceptional beauty. Only through later re-releases did the film attain classic status and finally show a profit.

Walt Disney first took a long look at Felix Salten's book *Bambi: A Life in the Woods* in 1935 and deemed it a fitting project for the studio. However, Walt first had to buy the rights from live-action director Sidney Franklin, who had the same idea. Franklin is duly thanked in the credits and even stayed on to serve as a

©Walt Disney Productions

©Walt Disney Productions

technical advisor. Production on *Bambi* began as early as 1937 and continued in the background as the Disney Studio worked on two other productions, *Pinocchio* and *Fantasia*.

Disney dispatched a camera crew to the woods of Maine where thousands of feet of film were shot in order to help the animation and layout crew form a vision for the film. The state thoughtfully provided a pair of fawns for the animators to study, and the Disney studio soon had its own miniature zoo containing live models of the forest animals. As the story department worked out a treatment, animators Milt Kahl and Frank Thomas designed the animals to look both realistic and appealing, a task so successful that Walt Disney appointed them supervising animators on the film along with Eric Larson and Ollie Johnston. Their favorite scene showed Bambi's attempts to stand up on a frozen pond while Thumper tries to help. Professional skaters Donna Atwood and Jane Reynolds modeled the pratfalls for Kahl and Thomas.

The original book detailed a grim and often bloody odyssey to adulthood for Bambi, but the Disney story team trimmed the death and violence considerably. One exception is the off-screen killing of Bambi's mother by a hunter. This brief scene ranks among the most memorable in the studio's history; audiences responded with sobs of grief at the film's initial show-ing and continue to do so today. *Bambi* nearly became the first animated feature to display a human corpse; at one point the feature included a hunter killed by his own folly, but a test audience was horrified. The scene was among two thousand feet of animation that Disney eventually cut from the film. The movie suffered a real-life tragedy when composer Frank Churchill committed suicide in May 1942, only three months before *Bambi*'s release.

The animals may have been humanized but were a pretty quiet bunch; partway through production Disney complained that the animals talked too much, and ordered drastic cuts in dialogue. The final script contained less than 1,000 words and a mere four songs, none of them sung by the cast. Because the film featured characters that aged over time, the children that voiced the principal characters had to be replaced, often more than once. Thumper needed two voice artists, Flower three, and Bambi himself required no less than four. David Hand directed and later took his act to England in 1944 where he developed an animated series called *Animaland*. Hand's experience with *Bambi* was an undeniable influence on this later work. *Bambi* would be Disney's last full-length animated feature until 1950. The film's prohibitive cost and poor box office (the war had cut off the European market) as well as similar problems with *Pinocchio* and *Fantasia* soured Walt on features for quite some time.

The feature did leave two lasting legacies besides the famous mother scene. For years after *Bambi* was released, Disney animators alerted each other to Walt's presence with the catchphrase "Man is in the forest!" On a wider, more cultural level, the term "Bambi Killer" came into general use as a derogatory reference to hunters. (MG)

***Additional Credits:*** Based on a book by Felix Salten. Story director: Perce Pearce. Story adaption: Larry Morey. Story development: George Stallings, Melvin Shaw, Carl Fallberg, Chuck Couch, Ralph Wright. Music: Frank Churchill, Edward H. Plumb. Orchestrations: Charles Wolcott, Paul J. Smith. Sequence directors: James Algar, Bill Roberts, Norman Wright, Sam Armstrong, Paul Satterfield, Graham Heid. Supervising animators: Franklin Thomas, Milt Kahl, Eric Larson, Oliver M. Johnston Jr. Animators: Fraser Davis, Bill Justice, Bernard Garbutt, Don Lusk, Retta Scott, Kenneth O'Brien, Louis Schmidt, Jack Bradbury, Joshua Meador, Phil Duncan. Art directors: Tom

Codrick, Robert Cormack, Al Zinnen, McLaren Stewart, Lloyd Harting, David Hilberman, John Hubley, Dick Kelsey. Background artists: Merle Cox, Tyrus Wong, Art Riley, Robert McIntosh, Travis Johnson, W. Richard Anthony, Stan Spohn, Ray Huffine, Ed Levitt, Joe Stahley.

**Barefoot Gen** (7/3/92) Tara Releasing. 85 mins. Director: Mori Masaki. Producer: Masao Maruyama, Carl Macek. Voices: Catherine Battistone (Gen Nakaoka), Barbara Goodson (Kimie Nakaoka), Wendee Lee (Shinji Nakaoka, Eiko Nakaoka).

**Consumer Tips:** ☆☆☆½ MPAA Rating: Unrated. War drama/antiwar protest. Based on the autobiographical novel of a cartoonist who lived through the 1945 atomic bombing as a child. Excellent, but not a children's movie despite the child protagonist. It is much too shocking for minors.

**Story:** Six-year-old Gen Nakaoka is a child in 1945 Japan. He is mostly unconcerned with the war until the atomic bomb is dropped. He watches most of his family die and is forced to become "the man of the house" to help his injured mother and newborn sister survive.

**Comments:** *Barefoot Gen* is cartoonist Keiji Nakazawa's reminiscences of the atomic bombing of Hiroshima. The first half-hour establishes young Gen Nakaoka's home life as the Japanese domestic situation becomes increasingly critical. He is happy with his parents, older sister Eiko, and younger brother Shinji. However, food rationing is approaching the starvation level; his sickly pregnant mother Kimie cannot get the medicine she needs; and his father's open scorn for Japan's military government has gotten his family ostracized by their neighbors. Then the atomic bomb is dropped. The family survives the blast, but Gen and his mother are unable to free the others from their collapsed house and listen to their screams as they burn to death. Kimie goes into premature labor, and Gen is the only one who can help her as all other survivors are too busy saving themselves. The last half of the film emphasizes Gen's shock at the gruesomely mutilated walking wounded, and his incomprehension as people start to collapse, apparently unwounded but hair falling out and bleeding from eyes and bowels due to radiation poisoning. Cartoonist

Nakazawa's "cute" art style makes the graphic events especially horrific.

Nakazawa has spent his life promoting his autobiographical *Barefoot Gen (Hadashi no Gen)* through the anti-nuclear peace movement. His manga began serialization in 1972. The cartoon-art novel has been collected into four volumes, continuing far past the events in the movie. The book is even more critical of the Japanese government's arrogant militarism and the people's treatment of Koreans as a slave class. The viewpoint of a six-year-old boy keeps the American military offstage for the most part.

The movie was financed as "Gen Productions," a war protestors' project, and filmed by the Madhouse studio (July 21, 1983). It was shown at antiwar events in Japan and abroad (the first American screening in Los Angeles was on the 40th anniversary of the Hiroshima bombing, August 4, 1985) and at international film festivals. Its American theatrical release in 1992 by Tara Releasing was in Japanese with English subtitles. The dubbed release (Streamline Pictures, July 11, 1995) was on video (later DVD) only. (FP)

**Additional Credits:** Screenplay: Kenji Nakazawa. Character designer/animation director: Kazuo Tomizawa. Music: Kentaro Haneda. Assistant animation director: Nobuko Yuasa. Production companies: Gen Pro, Madhouse.

**Batman: Mask of the Phantasm** (12/25/93) Warner Bros. 76 mins. Directors: Eric Radomski, Bruce Timm. Producers: Benjamin Melniker, Michael Uslan. Voices: Kevin Conroy (Batman/Bruce Wayne), Dana Delaney (Andrea Beaumont), Hart Bochner (Arthur Reeves), Stacy Keach Jr. (Phantasm, Carl Beaumont), Abe Vigoda (Salvatore Valestra), Dick Miller (Chuckie Sol), John P. Ryan (Buzz Bronski), Efrem Zimbalist Jr. (Alfred), Bob Hastings (Commissioner Gordon), Robert Costanzo (Detective Bullock), Mark Hamill (The Joker), Arleen Sorkin (Bambi).

**Consumer Tips:** ☆☆☆ MPAA Rating: PG. Based on the *Batman* comic characters created by Bob Kane.

**Story:** A mysterious phantom is executing aging mobsters and Batman is suspected. Meanwhile, a lost love of Bruce Wayne's returns to his life and the Joker plots to destroy the Caped Crusader.

©Warner Bros.

**Comments:** In the fall of 1992, *Batman: The Animated Series* debuted on the Fox Kids Network. And with it, artist Bruce Timm, writer Paul Dini, and producer Alan Burnett redefined the look and feel of action-adventure cartoons for television. Using a combination of inspirations—one part Max Fleischer 1940s Superman cartoons, two parts the original Bob Kane comic books, a dash of anime and bit of Tim Burton's live-action *Batman* makeover—the team at Warner Bros. Animation came up with an original vision and a television series that stands as a classic.

The voice acting was more realistic, the storylines were dark and gritty, the characters were designed better for animation, the music was moody and miminal.

During that first year of production, Warner Bros. gave the green light to a direct-to-video feature version. Though the Joker plays a large part in the film, producer Burnett decided to make a film removed from the regular gallery of villains on the series—and focus on Bruce Wayne's love life.

A few months into production, Warner Bros. decided to bump *Mask of the Phantasm* up to a theatrical release. This caused director Eric Radomski to quickly reconfigure shots for big screen rectangle ratio instead of the square television format. To open the film up, the producers added additional shots of Gotham City created by computer.

Creatively, the film was a success. But Warner Bros. dumped it in theatrical release on Christmas Day 1993—where it mainly played matinee performances for several weeks, grossing a measly $5.3 million in domestic U.S. release. It was released on home video,

as originally intended, in April 1993 and became a huge hit (garnering two thumbs-up from Siskel and Ebert, who missed it in theatrical release).

Direct-to-video sequels *Batman: Sub Zero* (1998) and *Batman Beyond: Return of the Joker* (2000) were even better films, and the franchise continues on today. (JB)

**Additional Credits:** Executive producer: Tom Ruegger. Screenplay: Alan Burnett, Paul Dini, Martin Pasko, Michael Reaves. Based on the DC Comics character Batman created by Bob Kane. Story: Alan Burnett. Music: Shirley Walker. Sequence directors: Kevin Altieri, Boyd Kirkland, Frank Paur, Dan Riba. Supervising timing director: James T. Walker. Overseas animation supervisor: Ric Machin. Character design: Chen-Yi Chang, Michael Diederich, Craig Kellman, Glen Murakami, Dexter Smith, Bruce W. Timm. Background supervisor: Ted Blackman. Key background design: Troy Adomitis, Robert Haverland, David Karell, Lawrence King, Rae McCarson, Felipe Morell, Jeff Starling, Keith Weesner, Tod Winter. Background styling: Eric Radomski. Background paint: Steve Butz, John Calmette, Russell G. Chang, Charles Pickens. Vehicle/prop design: Trish Burgio, Jonathan Fisher, Shayne Poindexter.

**Beauty and the Beast** (11/15/91) Walt Disney Pictures. 84 mins; restored version 93 mins. Directors: Gary Trousdale, Kirk Wise. Executive producer: Howard Ashman. Voices: Paige O'Hara (Belle), Robby Benson (Beast), Rex Everheart (Maurice), Richard White (Gaston), Jesse Corti (Le Fou), Angela Lansbury (Mrs. Potts), Jerry Orbach (Lumiere), David Ogden Stiers (Cogsworth, Narrator), Bradley Michael Pierce (Chip), Hal Smith (Phillipe), JoAnne Worley (Wardrobe), Mary Kay Bergman (Bimbette), Kath Soucie (Bimbette), Brian Cummings (Stove), Tony Jay (Monsieur D'Arque), Alvin Epstein (Bookseller), Alec Murphy (Baker), Kimmy Robertson (Featherduster), Frank Welker (Footstool, assorted vocal effects).

**Consumer Tips:** ☆☆☆☆ MPAA Rating: G. Exceptional animated film based on the *Contes marins* written by Madame Gabrielle de Villeneuve in 1741, later adapted by Madame Le Prince de Beaumont in 1756.

**Story:** A heartless prince is cursed for his cruelty by being transformed into an ill-tempered, hideous Beast.

©Walt Disney Productions

Only by receiving and giving true love can his plight be resolved, but time is running out. Possible salvation arrives in the form of Belle, a beautiful but unusual girl from a local village. Romance slowly blooms, helped along by the enchanted denizens of the Beast's castle, but love must survive some daunting tests—and tragedies—before the unlikely couple can reverse the spell and find happiness.

**Comments:** Perhaps the greatest screen romance in animation history, and the first animated film to garner an Oscar nomination for Best Picture. The Disney studio was experiencing an artistic and critical revival during the production of *Beauty and the Beast*. Its previous release, *The Little Mermaid*, featured full animation masterfully blended with Broadway-flavored showstoppers by the songwriting team of Howard Ashman and Alan Menken. With *Beauty and the Beast* this combination reached a creative pinnacle and resulted in a film that merited comparison with the finest of its times.

A major reason for success was a return to Disney's former strength, excellent character animation and acting, thanks to a team that had been maturing together since 1985. The Beast starts out as a baleful monster. Belle is pretty and intelligent but is lost in her books and nebulous dreams of escaping village life. When the story throws the pair together, their personalities seem to grow and blossom along with their feelings for each other. The gradual process by which the Beast mellows and Belle discovers her growing tenderness for the monster is believable, sincere, and touching.

At the same time there is a growing tension in the film: the staff of the castle must speed the love affair along if they are ever to reclaim their humanity, and the village is being mobilized to attack the Beast by Gaston, an egocentric muscleman who believes that Belle should be his by right. It is greatly to the credit of Wise, Trousdale, and those who developed the story that Belle, the Beast, and Gaston are fully developed personalities capable of carrying the film on their own. When we realize that the same care has been lavished on a candlestick, a clock, and a teapot, the reason for a Best Picture nomination becomes perfectly clear.

According to Disney animator Ollie Johnston, Walt Disney asked his team to read *Beauty and the Beast* prior to beginning work on *Cinderella*. No evidence of work actually done exists. *Beauty and the Beast* had been a durable entertainment staple for some time. Jean Cocteau directed a classic, poetic live-action version in 1946, and CBS aired a series based on the tale from 1987 to 1990.

The original director was Richard Purdum. He resigned in 1989 after Jeffrey Katzenberg reviewed his story reels and found them to be too far removed from the story Katzenberg was looking for. Howard Ashman did triple duty on *Beauty and the Beast*, serving as producer, contributing heavily to story development, and cowriting the songs. Unfortunately, Ashman did not live to see the film's release; he died on March 14, 1991. One of Ashman and Menken's musical numbers, "Human Again," was cut from the original film, resurrected for the live Broadway version, and eventually restored to the movie for release on a special-edition DVD.

Animator Glen Keane designed the Beast using buffalo, bear, wolf, gorilla, boar, lion, and ibex parts. Animator Andreas Deja originally conceived Gaston as a brute. Deja was asked to make him more handsome to fit the movie's theme of deceptive appearances, and so modeled Gaston on some of the vain, phony men he observed around Los Angeles. Scriptwriter Linda Woolverton was the first woman to pen a finished screenplay for a Disney animated feature. (MG)

**Additional Credits:** Screenplay: Linda Woolverton. Story supervisor: Roger Allers. Story: Brenda Chapman, Burny Mattinson, Brian Pimental, Joe Ranft, Kelly Asbury, Christopher Sanders, Kevin Harkey, Bruce Woodside, Tom Ellery, Robert lence. Executive producer: Howard Ashman. Songs: Howard Ashman, Alan Menken. Original score: Alan Menken. Associate producer: Sarah McArthur. Art director: Brian McEntee. Editor: John Carnochan. Layout supervisor: Ed Ehertner. Background supervisor: Lisa Keene. Cleanup supervisor: Vera Lanpher. Visual effects supervisor: Randy Fullmer. Computer graphics images: Jim Hillin. Supervising animators: Glen Keane, James Baxter, Will Finn, Andreas Deja, Chris Wahl, Nik Raineri, Ruben Aquino, Russ Edmonds, Dave Pruiksma. Animators: Michael Cedeno, Mike Nguyen, Anthony DeRosa, Tom Sito, Joe Haider, Ron Husband, David P. Stephen, Barry Temple, Michael Snow, Tony Bancroft, Phil Young, Dan Boulos, Mark Kausler, Ellen Woodbury, Rick Farmiloe, Lennie Graves, Larry White, Tony Anselmo.

## Beavis and Butt-Head Do America (12/20/96)

Paramount. 70 mins. Director: Mike Judge. Animation director: Yvette Kaplan. Producer: Abby Terkhule. Voices: Mike Judge (Beavis, Butt-Head, Tom Anderson, VanDriessen, Principal McVicker), Bruce Willis (Muddy Grimes), Demi Moore (Dallas Grimes), Robert Stack (Agent Flemming), Cloris Leachman (Old Woman on Airplane and Bus), Jacqueline Barba (Agent Hurly), Pamela Blair (Flight Attendant #1, White House Guide), Eric Bogosian (Ranger at Old Faithful, Press Secretary, Lieutenant at Strategic Air Command), Richard Linklater (Tour Bus Driver), Gail Thomas (Flight Attendant #3, Female Television Reporter), David Letterman (Motley Crue Roadie #1).

**Consumer Tips:** ☆☆☆½ MPAA Rating: PG-13. Based on the MTV series *Beavis and Butt-Head* created by Mike Judge.

©MTV Networks

**Story:** The misadventures of two clueless teenagers, who leave home in search of their beloved television set.

**Comments:** Beavis and Butt-Head were born in 1992 on the kitchen table of musician and part-time comedy writer Mike Judge in Richardson, Texas. Judge had produced two short films (*Frog Baseball* and *Peace Love and Understanding*), crudely drawn and animated all by himself, and submitted them to Spike and Mike's Sick and Twisted Animation Festival, where they played college campuses and art houses and became immediate audience favorites.

This led Beavis and Butt-Head to an appearence on MTV's anthology animation series *Liquid Television*, and a year later, a full-fledged television series was commissioned by MTV. Along with *Ren and Stimpy* and *The Simpsons*, these two brain-dead slackers had suddenly become household words and instant classic cartoon icons.

Geffen Pictures picked up the theatrical motion picture rights, hoping to make a live-action feature out of the animated show. But Judge held out and insisted on an all-animated feature.

When Paramount Pictures became part of the Viacom family in 1995, it was anxious to create some synergy with Viacom sibling MTV, and a Beavis and Butt-Head movie was inevitable. Geffen gave up on a live-action version and handed Judge the controls. And he pulled off the seemingly impossible—*Beavis and Butt-Head Do America* is a hilarious full-length film.

The movie sends the title characters out of their house, and out of their neighborhood, on a cross-country road trip in search of their beloved television set. This leads to one misadventure after another—from Las Vegas to Washington, D.C., ducking an ATF agent (voiced by Robert Stack), rednecks (Demi Moore and Bruce Willis), and various stoned characters (David Letterman) along the way.

The animation is produced on a level just slightly more elaborate than the low-budget television series, with one spectacular, fully animated hallucination sequence directed by Chris Prynoski.

Though it was produced by Paramount and was based on a pair of commercially proven television cartoon stars, the film's feel is closer to an independent film than a big Hollywood franchise.

The film was budgeted at $12 million (though it probably cost less—it certainly looks it) and grossed over $63 million over the Christmas holidays.

Mike Judge has since left *Beavis and Butt-Head* behind at MTV, to produce *King of the Hill* for Fox. (JB)

**Additional Credits:** Executive producers: David Gale, Van Toffler. Coproducer: John Andrews. Line producer: Winnie Chaffee. Screenplay: Mike Judge, Joe Stillman. Sequence directors: Mike De Seve, Miguel Martinez Joffre, Geoffrey Johnson, Tony Kluck, Ray Kosarin, Carol Millican, Brian Mulroney, Ilya Skorupsky, Paul Sparagano. "Hallucination" sequence animation director: Chris Prynoski. Animators: Kimson Albert, Doug Crane, Nick DeMayo, Karen Disher, Geoffrey Johnson, Richard Krantz, Kevin Lofton, Miguel Martinez Joffre, Sue Perrotto. Effects/background animation: John D. Allemand, Peggy Collen, Christopher Paltesy. Art director: Jeff Buckland. Character designers: Karen Hyden, Martin Polansky. Background design: Miriam Katin, Donald Bruce Poynter, Ray daSilva, Freya Tanz, Laura Wakefield. Layout supervisor: Maurice Joyce. Layouts: Kimson Albert, John D. Allemand, Edward Artinian, Kevin Brownie, Ray daSilva, Isauro de la Rosa, Eric Elder, Willy Hartland, Brian Moyer, Guy Moore, Siobhan Mullen, Wayne Arthur Murray, Donald Bruce Poynter, Bill Schwab, Dan Shefelman. Storyboards: Kevin Brownie, Ray daSilva, Tony Eastman, Tony Kluck, Michael LaBash, Guy Moore, Chris Prynoski, John Rice, Dan Shefelman, Ilya Skorupsky, Ted Stearn. An MTV Production.

**Bebe's Kids** (7/31/92) 73 mins. Paramount. Director: Bruce Smith. Producers: Willard Carroll, Thomas L. Wilhite. Voices: Faizon Love (Robin Harris), Nell Carter (Vivian), Myra J. Jamika (Dorothea), Vanessa Bell Calloway (Jamika), Tone Loc (Pee Wee), Wayne Collins (Leon), Jonell Green (LaShawn), Marques Houston (Kahill), Rich Little (President Nixon), John Witherspoon (Card Player #1), Chino "Fats" Williams (Card Player #2), Rodney Winfield (Card Player #3), George Wallace (Card Player #4).

**Consumer Tips:** ☆☆½ MPAA Rating: PG-13. Skewed toward adults, but suitable for kids.

**Story:** Robin takes Jamika, her small son, and three bratty neighbor children, Bebe's kids, to an amusement park.

©Paramount Pictures

**Comments:** *Bebe's Kids* was one of the few theatrical animated features to receive a PG-13 rating, and while that may not be enough in itself to make it more of an "adult" feature, the subject matter was certainly somewhat different from the usual theatrical fair, with no fairy tale accoutrements or funny animals. The film was adapted from a CD with the same name, a recording of the stand-up act of comedian Robin Harris, who died of a heart attack in 1990 at the age of 35.

Producers Reginald Hudlin and Warrington Hudlin were riding a wave of success with such black-oriented crowd pleasers as *House Party* (1990) and *Boomerang* (1992). They had cast Robin Harris in *House Party*, fell in love with his comedy, and fully intended to create a live-action movie around Robin and his characters. When Harris passed away, they kept the film project alive but decided to mount it instead as an animated feature.

Excerpts from Harris's routine and clips of Harris are utilized in the opening of the film, and the central character is an animated caricature of Harris, who relates the film's story in flashback while drowning his sorrows at a seedy bar. The story focuses on Robin's attempts to romance Jamika, a woman he meets at a funeral. He invites her and her son to an amusement park called Fun World. However, the next morning, Robin is greeted not only by Jamika and her son, but by three brats: skinny, pig-tailed LaShawn, gangster rap–attired Kahill, and incongruously deep-voiced toddler Pee Wee (voiced by then-popular rapper Tone Loc).

The threesome belongs to Jamika's unseen friend, Bebe, who left them with Jamika for the day, and they accompany Robin and his sweetheart on their excursion. Needless to say, the three kids run amuck at Fun World (clearly modeled after Disneyland), even going so far as to torture park mascot Rodney Rodent in a brief scene, much to Robin's chagrin.

The entire proceedings in some ways resemble an extended sitcom, but the film was the first to feature predominantly black characters and a rare attempt in animated features to focus on ordinary people. The character designs are stylized and distinctive, yet the animation remains full.

Despite the film's roots in a simple stand-up comedy routine, Robin is actually a fairly engaging character and seems credible as a possible swain to Jamika, apart from being a vehicle for one-liners. However, the film does contain a few extraneous moments, such as an extended rap from Bebe's kids, and a bizarre sequence in which Kahill is put on trial by the park's audio-animatronic figures for damaging one of their own, with a robotic Lincoln as defense attorney and President Nixon figure as the prosecutor.

The film remains engaging and amusing for the most part, and in plot and design, the film stood apart from its competition at the theaters. It grossed a limp $8.4 million in the summer of 1992, but has gone on to find a wider, more receptive audience on home video. (JB)

*Additional Credits:* Screenplay: Reginald Hudlin. Based on characters created by Robin Harris. Music: John Pares. Animation directors: Lennie K. Graves, Chris Buck, Frans Vischer. Animation supervisors (London): Christopher O'Hare, Tony Collingwood. Animators: Stevan Wahl, James Lopez, Colm Duggan, Thomas E. Decker, Stephen Anderson, Raymond Johnson Jr., Jeff Etter, David Simmons, Patrick Gleeson, Arland M. Barron, Gavin Dell, Ernest Keen. Animators (London): Simon Ward-Horner, Duncan Varley, Eric Bouillete, Steve Evangelatos, Al Gaivato, Chuck Gammage, Clive Pallant. Animators (Ohio): Martin Fuller, Jim Kammerud, Thomas Riggin, Dan Root, Brian Smith, Jeff Smith. Effects animation supervisor: Joey Mildenberger. Effects animators: Marlon West, James D. Mansfield, Esther Barr. Production designer: Fred Cline. Principal character design: Bruce Smith. Storyboards: Tom Ellery, Dan Fausett, Raymond Johnson Jr., Phil Mendez, Jim Kammerud, D. Edward Bell Jr. Art director: Doug Walker. Layout supervisors: Dan Fausett, Andrew Austin. Layouts: Marc Christenson, Ken Mimura, Kevyn Wallace, David Dumat, Clint Taylor, Tim Callahan, Gary Mouri, David Gardner. Background supervisor: Lucy Tanashian-Gentry. Backgrounds: David McCamley, Jane Nussbaum, Margette Bonet.

**The Black Cauldron** (7/24/85) Walt Disney Pictures. 80 mins. Directors: Ted Berman, Richard Rich. Producer: Joe Hale. Voices: Grant Bardsley (Taran), Susan Sheridan (Eilonwy), Freddie Jones (Dalben), Nigel Hawthorne (Fflewddur Fflam), Arthur Malet (King Eidilleg), John Byner (Gurgi, Doli), John Hart (Horned King), Phil Fondacaro (Creeper), Eda Reiss Merin (Orddu), Adele Malia-Morey (Orwen), Billie Hayes (Orgoch), John Huston (Narrator), Lindsay Rich, Brandon Call, Gregory Levinson (Fairfolk), Wayne Allwine, Phil Nibbelink, Peter Renaday, Jack Laing, James Almanzar, Steve Hale, Phil Fondacaro (Henchmen).

©Walt Disney Productions

*Consumer Tips:* ☆☆ MPAA Rating: PG. Based on the five books comprising *The Chronicles of Prydain* written by Lloyd Alexander between 1964 and 1968.

*Story:* Taran, a lad of humble origins, is thrust into adventure when his oracular pig sees menacing visions of the terrible Horned King. This tyrant is attempting to secure the legendary Black Cauldron; with it he can raise an invincible army of the undead. With the aid of minstrel Fflewddur Fflam, brave Princess Eilonwy, and a critter named Gurgi, Taran proves his courage in a showdown against ultimate evil and wins the princess's love.

**Comments:** *The Black Cauldron*, begun in 1981, took four years to complete and was the most expensive animated film of its time. While some sources state a $25 million budget, actual production costs were probably closer to $40 million. Almost nothing was going right at Disney while this film was in production; two years before, a contingent of talented young animators led by Don Bluth staged a walkout in the belief that Disney was abandoning its artistic values. In the best tradition of the 1980s the company was beset by hostile takeover bids and survived by bringing in new leadership. Ron Miller was toppled and Roy Disney Jr., Michael Eisner, Frank Wells, and Jeffery Katzenberg tried to right the listing ship. The "Nine Old Men" who had been the guiding hand of Disney animation were down to one, Eric Larson, and the animation department itself was splintered into different units, some of which did not even communicate with others.

Inexperience, corporate turmoil, a lack of veteran leadership, and disorganization turned *The Black Cauldron* into a most unwieldy project, and its failure was probably inevitable. There would eventually be two directors, three assistant directors, and sixteen writers attempting to work Alexander's material into something resembling a film while most of the animators faced a steep learning curve. Despite this sour experience many of them—Ron Clements, John Musker, Reuben Aquino, Andreas Deja, Dave Pruiksma, and Kathy Zielinski—would become key figures in the Disney revival a few years later, A young man named Tim Burton would also go on to greater things. The fact remains, however, that *The Black Cauldron* ended up more of a training experience than a triumphant entry for the "new" Disney animation department.

More's the pity. Much could have been done with *The Chronicles of Prydain*, which reads rather like Tolkien for the junior set. However, it seemed that everywhere a mistake could be made, it was. The abominable Horned King is designed to make him look like a lodge brother on a bad night, and his menace quotient is virtually nil. Apologists for the film present Princess Eilonwy as the prototype of the smart, perky Disney heroine, but in truth she is as underdeveloped as most of the other characters, no more interesting than Alice in *Alice in Wonderland*. The story department argued whether the film should be dark and adult or comical and aimed at a younger audience, leading to a fragmented sense of story; this is especially evidenced in the film's contrived happy ending.

Disney, Wells, Katzenberg, and Eisner sat down to watch the reels already completed and were reportedly aghast with the results, but the film was too far along, and too expensive, for a do-over. The highly anticipated film was trotted out to the theaters where it garnered poor reviews and poorer receipts. Some $21 million came back to Disney in the end, along with a cauldron full of humility. Not to worry: Disney would soon be back.

*The Black Cauldron* was the actual title of one of the *Prydain* books and was written in 1965. Disney was loath to release the film to video and did not do so until 1998, well after most of the classics were on tape. By the time the film was released the animation department had fallen so low that it was moved two miles away to a former warehouse in Glendale while the new management pondered the future. It was rescued by Roy Disney's timely decision to head the animation department himself.

The picture was shot in 70mm, the first Disney animated feature filmed in that format since *Sleeping Beauty*. *The Black Cauldron* featured the first computer-generated images to be used in a Disney animated feature; John Lasseter worked out some minor special effects for the picture. Another first: this film featured the initial use of ATP (animated transfer process), allowing an artist's work to be transferred directly to cels. (MG)

**Additional Credits:** Executive producer: Ron Miller. Music: Elmer Bernstein. Orchestrations: Peter Bernstein. Story: David Jonas, Vance Gerry, Ted Berman, Richard Rich, Al Wilson, Roy Morita, Peter Young, Art Stevens, Joe Hale. Additional dialogue: Rosemary Anne Sisson, Roy Edward Disney. Additional story contributions: Tony Marino, Mel Shaw, Burny Mattinson, John Musker, Ron Clements, Doug Leeler. Animators: Andreas Deja, Phil Nibbelink, Hendel Butoy, Steven Gordon, Dale Baer, Doug Krohn, Ron Husband, Shawn Keller, Jay Jackson, Mike Gabriel, Barry Temple, Phillip Young, Tim Ferriter, Jesse Cosio, Ruben Aquino, Ruben Procopio, Cyndee Whitney, Viki Anderson, George Scribner, David Block, Mark Henn, Charlie Downs, Terry Harrison, Sandra Borgmeyer, David Pacheco. Additional animators: Kathy

Zielinski, Sue DiCicco, Jill Colbert, Richard Hoppe, Kevin Wurzer, Dave Brain, Sylvia Mattinson, Maurice Hunt. Effects animators: Don Paul, Barry Cook, Mark Dindal, Ted Kierscey, Jeff Howard, Kelvin Yasuda, Patricia Peraza, Bruce Woodside, Scott Santoro, Kimberly Knowton, Glenn Chaika, Allen Gonzales. Layout: Don Griffith, Guy Vasilovich, Dan Hansen, Glenn Vilppu, William Frake III. Background: Donald Towns, Brian Sebert, Tia Kratter, John Emerson, Lisa Keene, Andrew Phillipson. Character design: Andreas Deja, Mike Ploog, Phil Nibbelink, Al Wilson, David Jonas. Animation consultant: Eric Larson.

**Blood: The Last Vampire** (8/17/01) Manga Entertainment/Palm Pictures. 48 mins. Director: Hiroyuki Kitakubo. Producers: Mitsuhisa Ishikawa, Yukio Nagasaki, Mamoru Oshii. Voices: Youki Kudoh (Saya), Saemi Nakamura (Nurse Mahiko Caroline Amano), Joe Romersa (Dave), Stuart Robinson (Louis), Rebecca Forstadt (Sharon), Tom Charles (Teacher), Fitz Houston (S.P. #1), Steven Blum (S.P. #2), Paul Carr (School headmaster).

©Production IG / SVW SCGII IG Plus IPA

**Consumer Tips:** ☆☆☆ MPAA Rating: Unrated. Horror SF. Vampires as sci-fi monsters attack a U.S. air base in Japan. They are fought by three secret government agents in a mixture of horror-monster action and film noir gunplay action.

**Story:** A secret war is going on between human defenders and batlike monsters that impersonate humans. Three agents in Japan are assigned to root out vampires infiltrating the Yokota Air Base: two Ameri-can government agents and Saya, a ruthless Japanese girl who exhibits vampire traits herself.

**Comments:** This suspenseful horror film takes advantage of 2001 audiences' familiarity with plots involving massive government cover-ups to leave much frustratingly unexplained. *Blood*, a multiple award-winner at international film festivals (Japanese release November 18, 2000), was used by Tokyo's Production I.G. studio to train its animators in CGI techniques and in drawing realistic Westerners, including black Americans. Veteran director Oshii organized a study group to tutor young animators. They designed *Blood* as a project in three parts, each revealing portions of the human-Chiropteran hidden war: this 48-minute featurette directed by Kitakubo, a novel written by Oshii set in 1969, and a *Blood: Tokyo Battle* video game set in 2000 by teammate Satoru Nakamura. Only the movie has been released in America. (FP)

**Additional Credits:** Screenplay: Kenji Kamiyama, Katsuya Terad. Executive producers: Akira Sato, Ryuzo Shirakawa. Original music: Yoshihiro Ike. Art direction: Yusuke Takeda. Sound editor: Kazuchika Kise. Sound director: Keiichi Momose. Sound rerecording mixer: Jonathan Wales. 3-D CGI: Tokumitsu Kifune, Katsuya Terada. Director of visual concept: Hisashi Ezura. Color designer: Katsue Inoue. Color artist: Kenji Kamiyama. Animation directors: Kazuchika Kise, Hiroyuki Kitakubo. Visual concept director Mamoru Oshi. Animation camera operator: Miki Sakuma. Technical supervisor: Shinji Takagi. Character designer: Katsuya Terada.

**Bon Voyage Charlie Brown (and Don't Come Back)** (5/30/80) Paramount. 75 mins. Director: Bill Melendez. Codirector: Phil Roman. Producer: Lee Mendelson. Voices: Arrin Skelley (Charlie Brown), Laura Planting (Peppermint Patty), Casey Carlson (Marcie), Daniel Anderson (Linus), Analisa Bartolin (Sally Brown), Bill Melendez (Snoopy), Scott Beach (Waiter, Baron, Driver, Tennis Announcer, English Voice, American Male).

**Consumer Tips:** ☆☆ MPAA Rating: G. Based on the *Peanuts* comic strip.

**Story:** The Peanuts gang is sent to France as exchange students, where they learn about French culture and get stranded at a spooky old chateau.

©United Features Syndicate

**Comments:** The final *Peanuts* movie (to date) was a routine affair, with several cute moments of culture clash and a forgettable song sequence ("I Want to Remember This," written and performed by Judy Musen and Ed Bogas).

The chateau that Charlie Brown, Linus, and Snoopy stay in is based on the chateau that Charles Schulz was billeted at for six weeks in World War II.

A follow-up television special, *What Have We Learned, Charlie Brown?* (1983), was created as an epilogue to this movie. The special picks up where this movie leaves off, the gang visiting Omaha Beach in Normandy and Ypres (a World War I battlesite), in tribute to the veterans that fought in both wars.

The problem with the *Peanuts* theatrical features is that they were clearly aimed exclusively at children audiences and Saturday matinees. The prime-time television specials maintained a bit of crossover—appealing to both Schulz adult comic strip readers and kids—but the theatricals were strictly kids' stuff and thus had limited box-office potential.

After *Bon Voyage Charlie Brown*, and a paltry $2 million gross, the *Peanuts* gang said farewell to the movie theaters. *Peanuts* continued its healthy run on television and in newspapers for another 20 years. (JB)

**Additional Credits:** Writer/creator of *Peanuts* characters: Charles M. Schulz. Music: Ed Bogas, Judy Munsen. Cinematography: Nick Vasu. Animation: Sam Jaimes, Hank Smith, Al Pabian, Joe Roman, Ed Newmann, Bill Littlejohn, Bob Carlson, Dale Baer, Spencer Peel, Larry Leichliter, Sergio Bertolli.

**A Boy Named Charlie Brown** (12/4/69) National General Pictures. 85 mins. Director: Bill Melendez. Producers: Lee Mendelson, Bill Melendez. Peter Robbins (Charlie Brown), Pamelyn Ferdin (Lucy), Glenn Gilger (Linus), Andy Pforsich (Schroeder), Sally Dryer (Patty), Ann Altieri (Violet), Erin Sullivan (Sally), Lynda Mendelson (Frieda), Chris DeFaria (Pigpen), Bill Melendez (Snoopy), Hilary Momberger (Sally Brown).

**Consumer Tips:** ☆☆☆ MPAA Rating: G. Based on the *Peanuts* comic strip.

**Story:** Charlie Brown wins the spelling bee and travels to New York for the national contest.

**Comments:** The first of the feature-length movies based on Charles M. Schulz's immortal *Peanuts* comic strip and the best. It has an excellent story, pleasent songs, and perhaps the best animation of Charlie Brown, though that's not saying too much.

Egged-on by others and encouraged by Linus, Charlie Brown volunteers for the school spelling bee. Sucessfully spelling such words as "failure" and "insecure," he proceeds to win both the class bee and the all-school bee. However, Charlie Brown must now bear up to the challenge of the national spelling bee, with Lucy as his manager and Linus's blanket for good luck. After C. B. departs for the competition, Linus and Snoopy soon join him, with Linus anxious to recover his blanket to prevent further fainting spells.

©United Features Syndicate

Though the major plot points focus on Charlie Brown, Linus, Snoopy, and Lucy, several other *Peanuts* regulars from that period (including Frieda and Pigpen) appear in the background. There are also some lovely set pieces, such as the abstract animation accompanying Schroeder's rendition of Beethoven's *Pathetique* Sonata.

Clearly a lot of effort went into making this movie a bigger experience than the comic strip, television specials, and Broadway show adaptations that preceeded it. That said, the film is still a rather simple affair compared to today's animated blockbusters.

Schulz wrote the screenplay (as he did the television specials) and retained a bit of the adult sensibility that charmed readers of the comic strip. Famed poet-composer-singer Rod McKuen was enlisted to pen four songs.

Bill Melendez, a veteran animator from Warner Bros. and the UPA studio, first directed Charlie Brown for Ford Motor commercials in the early 1960s. He started his own company in the mid-1960s with *A Charlie Brown Christmas* as his first production. He has directed of all the Peanuts television specials ever since. Melendez also voices the sounds of Snoopy.

*A Boy Named Charlie Brown* premiered at New York's Radio City Music Hall and was the top-grossing film for the week ending December 17, 1969. The movie was nominated for an Academy Award for Best Music, Original Song Score (it lost to *Let It Be* by the Beatles).

Three theatrical sequels were produced: *Snoopy Come Home, Race for Your Life Charlie Brown*, and *Bon Voyage Charlie Brown*. It should be noted that the video versions of this film are slightly edited: they are missing the scene where Lucy, during Charlie Brown's psychiatric appointment, plays an instant replay of his missed football kick and falling flat on his back, and another scene where Charlie Brown orders room service from his hotel. (JB)

**Additional Credits:** Screenplay: Charles M. Schulz. Original music: Vince Guaraldi. Music/lyrics: Rod McKuen. Musical director: John Scott Trotter. Cinematography: Wally Bulloch, Nick Vasu. Film editing: Robert T. Gillis, Charles McCann. Art department: Ellie Bonnard, Evert Brown, Bernard Gruver, Ruth Kissane, Ed Levitt, Charles McElmurry, Al Shean, Dean Spille. Ink/paint: Celine Miles. Animators: Maggie Bowen, Bob Carlson, Ken Champin, Herman Cohen, Sam Jaimes, Gerry Kane, Faith Kovaleski, Bror Lansing, Bill Littlejohn, Don Lusk, Bob Matz, Barrie Nelson, Spencer Peel, Jay Sarbry, Alan Shean, Frank Smith, Hank Smith, Richard Thompson, Ken O'Brien, Rudy Zamora.

**The Brave Little Toaster** (7/10/87) Hyperion. 80 mins. Director: Jerry Rees. Producers: Donald Kushner, Thomas L. Wilhite. Voices: Deanna Oliver (Toaster), Jon Lovitz (Radio), Tim Stack (Lampy), Thurl Ravenscroft (Kirby), Timothy E. Day (Blanky), Phil Hartman (Air Conditioner), Mindy Sterling (Mother), Joe Ranft (Elmo St. Peters), Judy Toll (Mish-Mash), Wayne Katz (Rob).

©Hyperion-Kushner-Locke

**Consumer Tips:** ☆☆☆ MPAA Rating: G. Based on a novella by Thomas M. Disch.

**Story:** In a country cabin, a group of household appliances are left behind when a beloved family moves to the city. A brave Toaster, a cowardly Lamp, the powerful Vacuum Cleaner, a noisy Radio, and an electric Blanket embark on a perilous journey to reunite with their masters.

**Comments:** *The Brave Little Toaster* is a modest, well-made animated film, made by a group of former Disney artists and executives and many Cal Arts graduates, many of whom would go on to greater things.

Tom Wilhite was a former corporate officer and head of motion picture production for the Walt Disney Company (*Splash* and *Tron* were among his efforts) who left the company with associate Willard Carroll in

1984 to form Hyperion Entertainment. Among their first projects was "Brad Bird's Family Dog" (for Steven Spielberg's television series, *Amazing Stories*).

The film is based on a novella by Thomas M. Disch that was purchased by Disney in 1982 after its publication in *Science Fiction and Fantasy Magazine*. First developed at the Disney studio, the picture was budgeted there at $18 million. When Wilhite left Disney in 1984 he asked then-company president Ron Miller for the project. Disney, together with TDK Corporation and CBS-Fox Home Video, financed the film as an independent production on a budget about one-third of the studio's in-house estimate.

Hyperion's story and character development began in 1986. Jerry Rees, a Disney animator on *The Fox and the Hound* and *Tron* and cowriter of the *Toaster* screenplay with Joe Ranft, was selected to direct. In casting voices Rees relied almost entirely on actors from the Groundlings improvisational group—a group at the time that included Phil Hartman, Jon Lovitz, Tim Stack, and Mindy Sterling. Veteran singer and cartoon voice great Thurl Ravenscroft (Tony the Tiger, the Grinch) was cast as Kirby the vacuum cleaner. Ken O'Connor, the classic Disney artist (dating back to *Snow White*), was hired to color style the production.

The film is a charming fable of a group of inanimate objects (a refreshing change from the usual mice, cats, fairy tales, and comic strips usually the basis for animated features up to this time) abandoned by their owners, who have moved on to the big city. They brave storms and quicksand and an evil repairman who wants them for their spare parts.

Many of the film's personnel went on to bigger and better things, including cowriter Joe Ranft (who became a story supervisor and voice at Pixar), animators Kirk Wise (who codirected Disney's *Beauty and the Beast*), Kevin Lima (who codirected Disney's *A Goofy Movie* and *Tarzan*), effects animator Mark Dindal (who directed *Cats Don't Dance*, *Emperor's New Groove*, and *Chicken Little*), and character designer Rob Minkoff (who directed *Stuart Little* and its sequel).

Director Jerry Rees alas went on to direct a live-action feature, *The Marrying Man* (1991), which bombed and has since been relegated to directing Disney theme park films.

The film was committed to Disney for home video, but no distributor would release the film, as intended, in theaters. Hyperion entered it in film festivals and eventually booked the movie into first-run art theaters across the country, where it won a cult following. It was followed years later by two direct-to-video sequels: *The Brave Little Toaster Goes to Mars* (1998) and *The Brave Little Toaster to the Rescue* (1999). (JB)

**Additional Credits:** Screenplay: Joe Ranft, Jerry Rees. Story: Joe Ranft, Jerry Rees, Brian McEntee. Music: David Newman. Songs: Van Dyke Parks. Directing animators: Joe Ranft, Randy Cartwright, Jerry Rees. Developmental animation: Kevin Lima, Steve Moore, Rebecca Rees, Kirk Wise. Animation: Kevin Lima, Steve Moore, Anne Telnaes, Chris Wahl, Tanya Wilson, Kirk Wise. Color stylist: A. Kendall O'Connor. Storyboard artists: Joe Ranft, Jerry Rees, Darryl Rooney, Alex Mann. Character designers: Kevin Lima, Chris Buck, Mike Giaimo, Dan Haskett, Skip Jones, Rob Minkoff, John Norton. Art director/layout supervisor: Brian McEntee. Layout artists: James Beihold, Kirk Hanson, Tim Hauser, Alex Mann, John Norton, Kevin Richardson, Darrell Rooney, Ann Telnaes, Chris Wahl, Steve Wahl, Tanya Wilson. Effects animation consultant: Mark Dindal. Scene Planning: Glenn Higa, Steve Segal.

**Bravestarr: The Legend** See *Bravestarr: The Movie*.

**Bravestarr: The Movie** (9/17/88) Taurus. 91 mins. Director: Tom Tataranowicz. Producer: Lou Scheimer, Voices: Pat Fraley (Marshall Bravestarr), Charlie Adler (Tex-Hex, Deputy Fuzz), Susan Blu (Judge B. J.), Ed Gilbert (Thirty-Thirty, Shaman), Alan Oppenheimer (Scuzz).

**Consumer Tips:** ☆☆ MPAA Rating: G. Also known as *Bravestarr: The Legend*. Based on a Mattel action figure.

**Story:** A futuristic Western about Marshall Bravestarr, a mystical Native American cowboy/interstellar sheriff, who battles against the evil Stampede (a monster with steer's horns) and his oily henchman, Tex Hex.

**Comments:** The Mattel toy company and Filmation, the television animation studio, found a successful formula with He-Man, an update of the classic Hercules character combined with science fiction and fantasy. Filmation pitched a new idea to Mattel as a follow-up, and *Bravestarr* was the result.

*Bravestarr* was an attempt to combine a Gene Autry–Roy Rogers matinee cowboy with a *Star Wars* sensibility. The television series began airing in 1987. A year later this feature film played limited markets in Saturday matinees. Surprisingly, it's not completely bad.

On the distant planet of New Texas, Marshal Bravestarr uses his superpowers (strength of the bear, speed of the puma, eyes of the hawk, ears of the wolf) to fight for the cause of justice with his talking horse, Thirty-Thirty, and the pint-sized Deputy Fuzz. Thirty-Thirty is an Equestroid with the ability to transform into a humanoid-like form, standing on his rear legs to fight. His advisor was the wise, elderly Shaman who gives our hero his magic powers.

The feature film makes use of computer animation for effects sequences, and several action sequences are effectively staged. The artwork has a pleasing edgier comic book feel missing from the simplistic *He-Man* cartoons.

Unfortunately, *Bravestarr: The Movie*, the television series, and the toy were not successful, and their failure was one of the contributing factors that led to demise of the Filmation studio at this time—ironically just as the animation industry was about to be rejuvenated with the likes of *Roger Rabbit, The Little Mermaid,* and *The Simpsons.* (JB)

**Additional Credits:** Screenplay: Bob Forward, Steve Hayes. Music: Frank W. Becker. Supervising animator: Brett Hisey. A Filmation production.

**Brother Bear** (11/7/03) Walt Disney Productions. 85 mins. Directors: Aaron Blaise, Robert Walker. Producer: Chuck Williams. Voices: Joaquin Phoenix (Kenai), Jeremy Suarez (Koda), Jason Raiz (Denahi), Harold Gould (Old Denahi), D. B. Sweeney (Sitka), Rick Moranis (Rutt), Dave Thomas (Tewk), Joan Copeland (Tanana), Michael Clarke Duncan (Tug), Paul Christie (Ram #1), Daniel Mastrogiorgio (Ram #2), Estelle Harris (Old Lady Bear), Greg Proops (Boy Lover Bear), Pauley Perette (Girl Lover Bear), Darko Cesar (Croatian Bear), Bumper Robinson (Chipmunks).

©Walt Disney Enterprises, Inc.

**Consumer Tips:** ☆☆ MPAA Rating: G. Original tale set in the prehistory of the Pacific Northwest. Breathtaking animation, but tepid story mars one of Disney's last traditional animation efforts.

**Story:** Young Inuit Kenai has just received his totem, "the bear of love," from the village's female shaman. Nevertheless, Kenai goes bear hunting with a vengeance after his beloved older brother Sitka dies while protecting Kenai and another brother, Denahi, from a bear that Kenai has provoked. Kenai kills the bear but the unhappy Great Spirits even the score by transforming the youth into a bear himself. Only by reaching the summit of a sacred mountain can Kenai regain human form. In the process of his quest he befriends a young cub and learns how to see through the eyes of others. After a startling revelation Kenai also learns love, responsibility, and sacrifice.

**Comments:** Not since *Pocahontas* has nature looked as beautiful in a Disney film. The background and layout artists studied the work of landscape artist Albert Bierstadt, a personal favorite of Disney CEO Michael Eisner. The result: marvelous panoramas of primeval earth, vast skies, and achingly blue water rippling with hazy reflections. Especially impressive is the animation during Kenai's transformation scene, where the spirits of dead men and animals canter through the aurora borealis like ghostly cave paintings come to life.

The thin story may have gone over better were the characters more believable. The three brothers sound like modern American teenagers, taunting each other with dialogue that one would hear in a mall rather than in a prehistoric forest. There is little that is likeable about Kenai, the central figure in the story; he whines about his supposedly sacred token, argues with his brothers at every opportunity, and is stupid enough to toss stones at an enormous bear over a trivial incident that was actually due to his own carelessness.

Kenai's foolish actions make him directly responsible for two tragic deaths in the story, and after that he spends most of his existence as a bear gruffly berating the young cub Koda, his only guide to salvation. With such a disagreeable hero at the story's center, the comic relief characters (two addled elk named Rutt and Tewk) have little trouble stealing the show with their faux-Canuck banter. Perhaps they should have written the script.

Another problem is the humanization of the bears. If the point of the story is to have Kenai experience empathy and understanding for another kind, then perhaps the bears should have been more alien, mysterious, and mystical. In the communal storytelling scene most of them come off like stale human comedians; there's an unintelligible Slavic bear, two twitty bears with a sickening crush on each other, and a senile old she-bear that thinks her still-living husband is deceased. They seem to have no relation to the feral bear faced by the brothers earlier. Such are the problems that develop in a film where the plot is set in motion not by some dramatic event, but by a spilled basket of fish. *Brother Bear* may be paint-by-the-numbers, but at least the paint job is worth the price of admission.

For the record:

- Rick Moranis and Dave Thomas reprised their SCTV roles as the wisecracking McKenzie brothers in order to voice the elk brothers Rutt and Tewk. Trample off, eh?
- The film pulls a neat visual trick after Kenai is transformed into a bear: The ratio switches from 1.75:1 to 2.35:1 in order to give the audience a sense of seeing through a bear's eyes.
- Koda must have been an admirer of French painter Georges Seurat; in one scene the cub does a cave painting of *A Sunday Afternoon on the Island of La Grande Jatte* (1886).
- There are 52 voice artists credited in this film.
- The script reportedly went through twelve rewrites; in one of them the cute cub Koda was a full-grown bear named Grizz.
- A lot of effort for nothing: Phil Collins wrote a "transformation song" that was translated into Inuit and then sung by a full Bulgarian choir. It was never used in the film.
- The film grossed $85.2 million at the box office. (MG)

**Additional Credits:** Screenplay: Steve Bencich, Lorne Cameron, Ron J. Friedman, David Hoselton, Tab Murphy. Score: Phil Collins, Mark Mancina. Lyrics: Howard Ashman. Supervising animators: Ruben A. Aquino, Byron Howard, James V. Jackson, Broose Johnson, Alex Kuperschmidt, Anthony Wayne Michaels, Tony Stanley. Story: Nathan Greno, Stevie Wermers-Skelton, Kevin Deters, Woody Woodman, Thom Enriquez, Kevin Harkey, Broose Johnson, John Norton, John Puglisi. Lead animator: Rune Bennicke. Animators: Tom Gately, Jonathan Annand, Gregg Azzopardi, Robert Bryan, Don Crum, Steve Mason, Branko Mihanovic, Jean Claude Tran, John Webber, Ian White. Layout artists: Andrew Hickson, Billy George, Craig Anthony Grasso, Andrew Edward Harkness, Thomas Humber, Richard Carl Livingston, Arman Serrano.

## The Bugs Bunny/Road Runner Movie (9/30/79)

Warner Bros. 92 mins. Director/producer: Chuck Jones. Voices: Mel Blanc (Bugs Bunny, Daffy Duck).

**Consumer Tips:** ☆☆☆ MPAA Rating: G. A Looney Tunes feature compilation film.

**Story:** Bugs Bunny gives us a tour of his mansion and discusses his origins, the topic of humor, and great comic chases. Compilation of classic Warner Bros. cartoons.

©Warner Bros.

**Comments:** In this compilation feature, Bugs Bunny invites the audience into his luxurious carrot-decorated home, where he proceeds to discuss the history of the chase and its frequent use in movies, utilizing old silent film clips. Bugs then very briefly discusses his career and his creators, and introduces several classic cartoon shorts directed by Chuck Jones. These cartoons, which also feature Daffy Duck, Elmer Fudd, Porky Pig, Marvin the Martian, and Pepe LePew, include *Hareway to the Stars* (1958), *Duck Dodgers in the 24 & 1/2 Century* (1953), *Robin Hood Daffy* (1958), *Duck Amuck* (1953), *Rabbit Fire* (1951), *Bully for Bugs* (1953), *Ali Baba Bunny* (1957), *For Scentimental Reasons* (1949), *Long Haired Hare* (1949), *What's Opera Doc* (1957), and *Operation: Rabbit* (1952), and are followed by a 15-minute compilation featuring the Road Runner and Wile E. Coyote, culled from 16 cartoons. The bridging sequences were also directed by Chuck Jones, and former storyman Michael Maltese cowrote the new dialogue with Jones. Most of the old Warner Bros. artistic staff (Maurice Noble, Benny Washam, etc.) contributed as well. Like so many compilation films, the individual shorts are enjoyable without any attempts to connect them. However, some of Jones' best shorts are showcased, and many are amongst the best short cartoons of all time.

This is the first and probably the best Warner Bros. compilation feature (not counting *Bugs Bunny Superstar*, which was largely a documentary with no original animation). Apart from the Road Runner section, most of the shorts are shown more or less in their entirety, albeit shorn of original titles. The bridging animation is somewhat more appealing than usual. The technique of Bugs showing guests around his home while reminiscing about his career is obviously little more than a framing device. In this respect, however, it seems almost less forced than later attempts to slap clips from different cartoons together with new material to somehow form a thin storyline. The fact that the vintage and new material shared the same director also helped (as compared, say, to *Daffy Duck's Fantastic Island*). Bugs himself is aware that he's merely introducing cartoons. The cartoons may be better seen individually and entirely uncut, but this is still a pleasant diversion (and admittedly an inexpensive way for Warner Bros. to release its first Bugs Bunny "feature"). (AL)

**Additional Credits:** "Bugs Bunny at Home" codirector: Phil Monroe. Writers: Michael Maltese, Chuck Jones. Music: Carl Stalling, Milt Franklyn, Dean Elliott. Animation: Phil Monroe, Ben Washam, Ken Harris, Abe Levitow, Dick Thompson, Lloyd Vaughan, Tom Ray. "Bugs Bunny at Home" animators: Virgil Ross, Phil Monroe, Lloyd Vaughan, Manny Perez, Irv Anderson. Production design: Maurice Noble. "Outer Space" by Lloyd Vaughan. "Bugs Bunny at Home" production design: Ray Aragon. "Bugs Bunny at Home" backgrounds: Irv Wyner. A Chuck Jones Production.

## Bugs Bunny's Third Movie: 1001 Rabbit Tales

(11/19/82) Warner Bros. 76 mins. Directors: Friz Freleng, Dave Detiege. Voices: Mel Blanc (Bugs Bunny, Daffy Duck, Sultan Yosemite Sam), Lennie Weinrib (Prince Abadaba), Shep Menken (Old Servant).

**Consumer Tips:** ☆☆ MPAA Rating: G. Compilation of classic Looney Tunes bridged by new framing story.

©Warner Bros.

**Story:** Daffy Duck and Bugs Bunny are rival book salesmen. When Bugs encounters Sultan Sam's bratty Prince Abadaba, he's forced to read him 1001 tales.

**Comments:** For the third Bugs Bunny compilation film, a loose framing story showcases Bugs and Daffy as salesmen for Rambling House publishers. They wind up in the desert, meeting Sultan Yosemite Sam. Sam's bratty nephew, Prince Abadaba (a ringer for Junior from Freleng's 1956 short *A Waggily Tale*, with a similar voice as well), is tired of his old storyteller and wants new bedtime tales. Bugs and Daffy attempt to fill this function, and clips from various old Warner Bros. shorts with a fairy tale theme are utilized, including *Ali Baba Bunny* and *Bewitched Bunny*, as well as the Chuck Jones classic *One Froggy Evening*.

The frame story is a bit forced, and again builds on the later Warner Bros. characterization of Bugs Bunny and Daffy Duck as bitter rivals; some of the classic short excerpts, such as those featuring Speedy Gonzales, feel somewhat out of place. The main plot, setting up Bugs and Daffy as Scherezade figures, owes much to the 1959 short *Hare-abian Nights*, which itself used considerable stock footage and also featured Sam as the sultan. One interesting aspect of this film is that several voice actors who went uncredited in the original shorts are billed in the final credits, under "additional classic voices." For the first time, years after his death, Arthur Q. Bryan receives a credit on a Warner Bros. production, even if it does fail to identify him as the voice of Elmer Fudd. Despite its flaws, the film seems to have been generally well-received by critics, no doubt nostalgic for the original shorts; however, Carrie Rickey, reviewer for the *Village Voice*, remarked that Bugs and Daffy "used to be burrowers, explorers; now they're traveling salesmen imprisoned by the nuclear family." (AL)

**Additional Credits:** Animation: Warren Batchelder, Bob Bransford, Marcia Ferti, Terry Lennon, Bob Matz, Norm McCabe, Tom Ray, Virgil Ross. Music: Rob Walsh, Bill Lava, Milt Franklyn, Carl Stalling.

**A Bug's Life** (11/20/98) Disney-Pixar. 96 mins. Directors: John Lasseter, Andrew Stanton. Producers: Darla K. Anderson, Kevin Reher. Voices: Dave Foley (Flik), Kevin Spacey (Hopper), Julia Louis-Dreyfus (Atta), Hayden Panettiere (Dot), Phyllis Diller (Queen), Richard Kind (Molt), David Hyde Pierce (Slim), Joe Ranft (Heimlich), Denis Leary (Francis), Jonathan Harris (Manny), Madeline Kahn (Gypsy), Bonnie Hunt (Rosie), John Ratzenberger (P. T. Flea), Brad Garrett (Dim), Roddy McDowell (Mr. Soil).

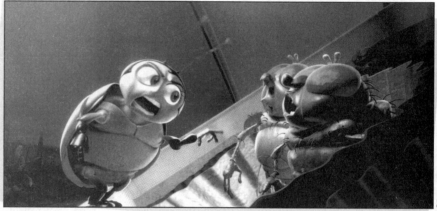

©Disney Enterprises / Pixar Animation Studios

**Consumer Tips:** ☆☆☆ MPAA Rating: G. Pixar's second film.

**Story:** An ant colony, threatened by grasshoppers, enlists the aid of seven defenders—actually flea circus performers mistaken for heroes.

**Comments:** Pixar's follow-up to *Toy Story* proved equally successful, this time focusing on insects rather than toys. The plot reworked the *Ant and the Grasshopper* fable, with a circus motif (always popular in animation) as a prominent side element. The designs of the bugs, while in pastel colors that would not necessarily occur in life—particularly for the ants—were still somewhat closer to real insects than, say, Jiminy Cricket. They still retain very strong elements of caricature, unlike the stars of PDI/DreamWorks' *Antz*, released one month earlier, and a source of mild controversy at the time.

One of the most notable aspects of the film was the use of faux bloopers. Breaking the fourth wall, and parodying "gag reels" often used during the end credits of live-action comedies since the '80s, a set of vignettes presented the insect stars flubbing lines, knocking over scenery, breaking into laughter, and otherwise behaving as film actors rather than animated characters. Several weeks after the film's release, a second set of bloopers was added to encourage return screenings. The fact that such a "blooper reel" could not exist with an animated film, and would have to be deliberately created, only added to the appeal for most. Pixar continued the tradition with *Toy Story 2* and *Monsters, Inc.*, and Disney's feature department borrowed the concept for the more serious *Brother Bear*, with less effective results. *A Bug's Life* was also accompanied by Pixar's new short subject, *Geri's Game*, thus beginning another tradition, as either new or reissued shorts were paired with all subsequent features.

Beyond the gimmicks, however, Pixar's storytelling was effective, and the studio was continuing to prove that it could handle ensemble stories without seemingly tossing in characters purely for merchandising purposes. To date, no official sequel has been produced, unlike *Toy Story* (although Pixar's public separation from Disney has opened the possibility of the latter studio producing a direct-to-video sequel on its own). However, as with the *Toy Story* cast, the characters have been prominently featured in sing-along videos, computer games, and theme park attractions; a 3-D animated show, "It's Tough to Be a Bug," has been featured at both the Animal Kingdom and California Adventure theme parks, and the latter park became host to a slew of *Bug's Life*–themed kiddie rides in late 2002. (AL)

**Additional Credits:** Original story: John Lasseter, Andrew Stanton, Joe Ranft. Screenplay: Andrew Stanton, Donald McEnery, Bob Shaw. Music: Randy Newman. Supervising film editor: Lee Unkrich. Supervising technical directors: William Reeves, Eben Ostby. Production designer: William Cone. Art directors: Tia W. Kratter, Bob Pauley. Supervising animators: Glenn McQueen, Rich Quade. Supervising layout artist: Ewan Johnson. Animation: Michael Berenstein, Dylan Brown, Sandra Christiansen, Scott Clark, Brett Coderre, David Devan, Andrew Gordon, Tim Hittle, John Kahrs, Karen Kiser, Shawn Krause, Bankole Lasekan, Dan Lee, Les Major, Daniel Mason, Billy Merritt, James Ford Murphy, Mark Oftedalk, Michael Parks, Sanjay Patel, Bobby Podesta, Jeff Pratt, Karen Prell, Roger Rose, Andrew Schmidt, Steve Segal, Doug Sheppeck, Alan Sperling, Doug Sweetland, David Tart, J. Warren Trezevant, Mark Walsh, Tasha Wedeen.

**Bustin' Out** See *Coonskin*.

## The Care Bears Adventure in Wonderland

(8/7/87) Cineplex Odeon. 75 mins. Director: Raymond Jafelice. Producers: Michael Hirsh, Patrick Loubert, Clive A. Smith. Voices: Bob Dermer (Grumpy Bear), Eva Almos (Swift Heart Rabbit), Dan Hennessey (Brave Heart Lion, Dum), Jim Henshaw (Tenderheart Bear), Marla Lukofsky (Good Luck Bear), Luba Goy (Lots-a-heart Elephant), Keith Knight (White Rabbit), Tracey Moore (Alice), Colin Fox (Wizard, Dim), John Stocker (Cheshire Cat), Don McManus (Caterpillar), Elizabeth Hanna (Queen of Wonderland), Alan Fawcett (Flamingo), Keith Hampshire (Mad Hatter, Jabberwocky), Alyson Court (Princess).

©Bears in Wonderland, Ltd.

**Consumer Tips:** ☆☆ MPAA Rating: G. Greeting card superstars meet Lewis Carroll's classic characters.

**Story:** The Care Bears return Alice to Wonderland to stand in for a princess who's been kidnapped by an evil wizard.

**Comments:** Third strike and you're out.

The Care Bears were indeed a money machine in the 1980s, and were perhaps the first children's franchise to take advantage of home video; sales of Care Bears merchandise and videotapes were part of this North American marketing phenomenon of the 1980s.

The *Care Bears Adventure in Wonderland* isn't the worst Care Bears epic—*Care Bears II* wins that title. At least the film puts the characters into a new plot line; by placing them in a Wonderland setting, the characters encounter much more imaginative and cartoony visuals. In fact, the film has a mild 1960s psychedelia feel, especially in the initial sequences in Wonderland, with its trippy, laid-back John Sebastian score on the track.

You can almost feel the animators trying to cut loose and go nuts with several bits of zany business, but they are ultimately restricted by the budget and the very polite nature of the Care Bears franchise. On the plus side, the film is fast-moving, and Nelvana's animation staff delivers a few nice sequences of character animation, especially during the Cheshire Cat's song.

Otherwise, it's by the numbers and numbing. Strictly for kids under the age of six. (JB)

**Additional Credits:** Supervising producer: Lenora Hume. Screenplay: Susan Snooks, John DeKlein. Story: Peter Sauder. Music: Trish Cullen. Songs: John Sebastian. Music and lyrics: Maribeth Solomon. Animation director: John Laurence Collins. Storyboard: Raymond Jafelice, Arna Selznick, Sam Dixon, John Van Bruggen, John Flagg, Eric Chu, Tom Nesbitt, Jim Craig. Animators: Robin Budd, Charlie Bonifacio, Ken Stephenson, Shane Doyle, Gary Hurst, Scott Glynn, Andy Bartlett, Greg Court, Gerry Fournier, Michelle Houston, Niall Johnston, Woong Cheon Jang, Shawn Seles, David Simmons, Cynthia Ward, Bill Zeats, Jan Tillcock, Doug Flockhart, Steve Whitehouse.

**The Care Bears Movie** (3/29/85) Samuel Goldwyn. 75 mins. Director: Arna Selznick. Producers: Michael Hirsh, Patrick Loubert, Clive Smith. Voices: Mickey Rooney (Mr. Cherrywood), Jackie Burroughs (The Spirit), Georgia Engel (Love-a-lot Bear), Sunny Bensen Thrasher (Jason), Harry Dean Stanton (Brave Heart Lion), Eva Almos (Friend Bear), Patrice Black (Share Bear, Funshine Bear), Melleny Brown (Birthday Bear), Bobby Dermer (Grumpy Bear).

**Consumer Tips:** ☆☆½ MPAA Rating: G. Best of the bunch. Based on the characters created by American Greetings Corporation.

**Story:** A boy named Nicholas falls under the spell of an evil spirit encased in a magic book, and removes all caring and feeling from the world. The Care Bears sail to the rescue with their cousins from The Forest of Feelings.

©American Greetings Corp.

**Comments:** The Care Bears were created in 1981 by Those Characters from Cleveland, for the greeting card company American Greetings. The Care Bears became a 1980s phenomenon. In 1983, the first of several Care Bears television specials hit the airwaves and related merchandising began. By 1985, a television series by DIC was in syndication, and Nelvana made a deal for a full-length feature film.

After the disastrous distribution experience of their first feature film, *Rock and Rule*, Nelvana bounded back into theatrical territory with this very commercial property. Costing $4 million to produce, it became a surprise hit during the Easter holiday of 1985, grossing over $25 million.

*The Care Bears Movie* is surprisingly good. The story involves the Care Bears, who live among the clouds in "Care-A-Lot," and three children to whom they teach the power of love and friendship through the sharing of feelings. One of the kids falls under the spell of an evil spirit that uses the boy to remove all care and feeling from the world. The Care Bears sail down from their rainbow-colored paradise, join forces with the kids, and do battle to right the wrongs.

It's a simple, serviceable adventure with several standout sequences: a whirlpool that endangers their ship, a tree that comes to life, and a special effects–filled climax. There's no doubt about it, this is a children's film aimed at the under-seven crowd. But it's one of the better animated children's films produced during this period.

Its box-office gross signaled to Hollywood a renewed interest in animated features, albeit for children. This is something *The Secret of Nimh* tried to accomplish but failed to do.

*The Care Bears Movie* was directed by Arna Selznick, who was, at the time, the third woman ever to direct an animated feature (Germany's Lotte Reiniger and England's Joy Batchelor preceded her). Selznick worked her way up at Nelvana, from layout artist on *Rock and Rule* and storyboard supervisor on the *Inspector Gadget* television series, to director on the television special *Strawberry Shortcake and the Baby Without a Name* (1983). She has remained with Nelvana ever since, working on such noted pre-school projects as *Teddy Ruxpin* and *Franklin*. (JB)

**Additional Credits:** Screenplay: Peter Sauder. Executive producers: Carole MacGillvray, Robert Unkel, Jack Chojnacki, Lou Gioia. Associate producers: Paul Pressler, John Bohach, Harvey Levin. Title Song: Carole King. Music producer: Lou Adler. Additional music: Walt Woodward. Songs: John Sebastian. Animation: Lillian Andre, John DeKlein, Ian Freedman, Michelle Houston, Pat Knight, Paul Riley, Lynn Yamazaki, Rejean Bourdages, Chris Delaney, Scott Glynn, Bob Jacques, Beverly Newberg-Lehman, Gian Celestri, Mike Fallows, Jon Hooper, Trevor Keen, Mark Pudleiner, Cynthia Swift, Ralf Zondag.

## The Care Bears Movie II: A New Generation

(3/21/86) Columbia. 77 mins. Director: Dale Schott. Producers: Michael Hirsh, Patrick Loubert, Clive A.

COME HELP THE CARE BEARS SAVE THE KINGDOM OF CARING.

Care Bears Movie II

A NEW GENERATION.
IT'S A WHOLE NEW ADVENTURE.

COLUMBIA PICTURES PRESENTS CARE BEARS MOVIE II: A NEW GENERATION A NELVANA PRODUCTION "NELVANA" PETER SAUDER CAROL PARKS PATRICIA CULLEN MICHAEL HIRSH PATRICK LOUBERT CLIVE A. SMITH DALE SCHOTT

©Columbia Pictures

Smith. Voices: Maxine Miller (True Heart Bear), Pam Hyatt (Noble Heart Horse), Hadley Kay (Dark Heart, The Boy), Cree Summer Francks (Christy), Alyson Court (Dawn), Michael Fantini (John), Chris Wiggins (Great Wishing Star), Dan Hennessey (Brave Heart Lion), Billie Mae Richards (Tender Heart Bear), Eva Almos (Friend Bear), Bob Dermer (Grumpy Bear), Patrice Black (Share & Funshine Bear), Nonnie Griffin (Harmony Bear), Jim Henshaw (Bright Heart Racoon), Melleny Brown (Cheer Bear), Janet Laine Green (Wish Bear), Marla Lukofsky (Playful Heart Monkey), Gloria Figura (Bedtime Bear), Sunny Bensen (Thrasher Camp Champ).

**Consumer Tips:** ½ (half star). MPAA Rating: G.

**Story:** The Care Bears help three awkward summer campers by putting them in charge of the Care Bear Cubs and Care Bear Cousin Cubs. Evil Dark Heart offers the girl, Christy, a chance to become a champion runner and swimmer in return for her help in a plot against the Care Bears.

**Comments:** This film is the story of the origin of the Care Bear Family, introducing the Care Bear Cubs and Care Cousin Cubs, and how they became the champions of caring.

Unfortunately, not many critics cared for the television standard limited animation, uninteresting story, bland songs, and blatant product placement in this film. Strictly for toddlers under age six, the film tries too hard to cram new characters into the plotline. The characters are obviously being introduced to create toy lines.

Dale Schott made his directorial debut on this picture. He served as assistant director on the film's successful predecessor, *The Care Bears Movie*. Prior to that, he worked as assistant director on *Ewoks* (1985), a half-hour animated television series produced by Nelvana for Lucasfilm. He subsequently directed episodes of Nelvana's *Rupert* (1991).

This is the weakest of the Care Bears movies. Avoid at all costs. (JB)

**Additional Credits:** Screenplay: Peter Sauder. Music: Patricia Cullen. Songs: Dean and Carol Parks. Animation director: Charles Bonifacio. Editor: Evan Landis. Production supervisor: Dale Cox. Voice casting: Arlene Berman.

**Castle in the Sky** See *Laputa: Castle in the Sky.*

**The Castle of Cagliostro** (4/3/91) Streamline Pictures—Tokyo Movie Shinsha Co. Ltd. (Japan). 100 mins. Director: Hayao Miyazaki. Producer: Yutaka Fujoka. Voices: Bob Bergen (Arsene Lupin III, Streamline English version), David Hayter (Arsene Lupin III, Manga Video English Dub), Yasuo Yamada (Lupin III, original Japanese dub), Eiko Masuyama (Fujiko Mine), Kiyoshi Kobayashi (Daisuke Jigen), Gorô Naya (Inspector Zenigata), Sumi Shimamoto (Clarisse), Tarô Ishida (Count Cagliostro), Michael McConnohie (Cagliostro, Streamline English version).

©TMS

**Consumer Tips:** ☆☆☆☆ Comedy suspense crime caper. MPAA Rating: 1991, none; 2000, PG-13. Based on the Japanese manga series *Lupin III.*

**Story:** Good-guy international thief Lupin III learns that the world is being flooded with counterfeits of every nation's money. He tracks the bogus bills to the tiny Principality of Cagliostro, in particular the ruler's castle where innocent young Princess Clarisse is imprisoned by the evil regent, her cousin Count Cagliostro. Lupin and his gang switch from trying to cut themselves in on the counterfeiting to rescuing Clarisse from the sinister count.

**Comments:** *The Castle of Cagliostro* is a perfect caper film in almost every respect. It works equally well as a comedy and as a serious suspense thriller, sometimes in the same scene. It features memorable characters and a great jazz score by Yuji Ono. It was the film that first

brought animation writer/character designer/animator/director Hayao Miyazaki to the public's attention.

*Lupin III* began as an adult comedy manga by "Monkey Punch" (Kazuhiko Kato) about the misadventures of the lecherous international jewel thief Lupin III, supposedly the grandson of French author Maurice Leblanc's master criminal Arsene Lupin. The manga was turned into a popular television anime series, *Lupin III,* which ran for 155 episodes from 1977 to 1980. The TMS studio released its first Lupin III feature in 1978. Miyazaki was given carte blanche to write, design, and direct the second feature, *Lupin III: Cagliostro No Shiro* (1979), himself. It is generally acknowledged as a great movie but a very atypical *Lupin III* movie; Lupin is too noble and not egotistical enough. TMS has produced over a dozen *Lupin III* movies since then, as either theatrical or made-for-television releases.

The counterfeit money and Clarisse's rescue are both Maguffins to set up the movie-long battles of wits between Lupin, Count Cagliostro, and Lupin's regular adversary, Interpol Inspector Zenigata. An unacknowledged star is huge, intricately detailed Cagliostro Castle, filled with ancient death traps dating back to the Middle Ages plus new high-tech additions. The intrigue between two intelligent enemies is excellent; the audience never knows what murderous trick will appear next.

TMS considered *The Castle of Cagliostro* a showpiece and exhibited it at international film festivals throughout the 1980s. Miyazaki, who also created the two "grand finale" episodes of the *Lupin III* television series, went on to become Japan's leading film director, animated or live action, and an internationally acclaimed cinematic maestro. Streamline Pictures released *Cagliostro* in the United States theatrically subtitled (April 3, 1991) and dubbed on video (October 15, 1992). A digitally remastered brand-new dubbing by Palm Pictures/Manga Entertainment was released theatrically and on DVD on April 25, 2000. (FP)

**Additional Credits:** Story: Monkey Punch. Screenplay: Hayao Miyazaki, Haruya Yamazaki. Art direction: Yasuo Ohtsuka. Music: Yuji Ohno. Film editing: Mitsutoshi Tsurubuchi. Art direction: Shichirô Kobayashi. Assistant director: Mochitsugu Yoshizawa. Animators: Yasunao Aoki, Nobumasa Arakawa, Hideo Kawauchi, Jôji Manabe, Shôji Maruyama, Masami

Ozaki, Yoko Sakurai, Hideyo Sano, Junko Shimozaki, Masako Shinohara, Atsuko Tanaka, Tsukasa Tannai, Nobuo Tomizawa, Kazuhide Tomonaga, Mikako Ôsato.

**Cats Don't Dance** (3/26/97) Warner Bros. 76 mins. Director: Mark Dindal. Producers: David Kirschner, Paul Gertz. Voices: Scott Bakula (Danny), Jasmine Guy (Sawyer), Natalie Cole (Sawyer singing), Ashley Peldon (Darla Dimple), Lindsay Ridgeway (Darla Dimple singing), Kathy Najimy (Tillie), John Rhys-Davies (Woolie), George Kennedy (L. B. Mammoth), Rene Auberjonois (Flanigan), Hal Holbrook (Cranston), Don Knotts (T. W.), Frank Welker (Farley Wink), David Johansen (Bus Driver).

©Turner Pictures, Inc.

**Consumer Tips:** ☆☆☆½ MPAA Rating: G. Excellent animation, fun story.

**Story:** Danny, a song and dance cat from Indiana, comes to Hollywood in the 1930s and quickly learns that movieland animals are treated like second-class citizens.

**Comments:** The animated equivalent of an old MGM "Let's put on a show" musical, *Cats Don't Dance* deals with the lot of animal actors in Tinseltown.

Danny, a naive young cat from Kokomo, moves to Hollywood in the hopes of hitting it big, and lands a role in the film *Little Ark Angel* alongside Sawyer, a cynical talent agency receptionist, and a gaggle of failed animal actors. However, the vicious child star Darla Dimple is upset at Danny for ad libbing and taking the spotlight away from her and, with the help of her hulk-

ing Erich Von Stroheim–like butler Max, plots to sabotage his efforts to gain an audition for himself and his friends. Meanwhile, Sawyer falls in love with Danny, and finds that her own youthful dreams and hopes are returning.

While many notable animated features had been essentially musicals (and following the success of *The Little Mermaid*, it was difficult to find one that wasn't), this one returns to the form as quintessentially depicted on film. It's not coincidental that the late Gene Kelly (to whom the picture is dedicated) contributed to the choreography of the musical sequences. The film deliberately hearkens back to the heyday of MGM musicals. Even Danny's attire seems to bring to mind Kelly.

The film also subtly examines racism in Hollywood's golden age, substituting animals for black actors. Just as all of the creatures are stuck playing animal parts and most do nothing but purr or bark, so black actors were typecast as mammies, servants, jungle natives, and other menial parts. Even the "stars" (Toto and King Kong, glimpsed in briefly amusing cameos) suffer from the typecasting, as did Hattie McDaniel and others in real life. However, the subtext is not forced.

Also targets of the satire are the likes of fawning directors, pompous agents, and, most particularly, child stars, as represented by the monstrous Shirley Temple takeoff, Darla Dimple. Though Darla comes off as rather obnoxious (and initially put me off the film the first time I saw it), that's the whole point of the joke, and her animation, especially in depicting her mood swings from saccharine princess to devilish brat, is very adeptly handled. Some of the songs, such as the opening number "Our Time Has Come," have more of a modern pop sound, but the delightful "Animal Jam" fits perfectly into the milieu. The caricatures of such Hollywood fixtures as Mae West and Jimmy Durante (by clean-up artist/professional caricaturist Dave Woodman) add to the atmosphere. (AL)

**Additional Credits:** Coproducer: Jim Katz. Screenplay: Roberts Gannaway, Theresa Pettingill, Cliff Ruby, Elana Lesser. Story: Rick Schneider, Mark Dindal, Brian McEntee, Robert Lence, Kelvin Yasuda, David Womersley. Inspired by a story by Sandy Russell Gartin. Additional screenplay material: Joel Paley, Cinco Paul. Music: Steve Goldstein. Songs: Randy Newman, Martin Page, Simon Slimie, Will Jennings. Supervising animators: Jay Jackson, Bob Scott, Lennie K. Graves, Frans Vischer,

Jill Culton, Kevin Johnson, Steve Wahl, Chad Stewart. Animators: Ben Jones, Ernest Keen, Steve Markowski, Mike Polvani, Chad Stewart, Roger Vizard, Dougg Williams, Gavin Dell, Lauren Faust, Steve Garcia, Jon Hooper, Wayne Carlisi, Ralph Fernan, Jeff Johnson, Mike Kunkel, Mauu Bates, Carrie Buell, Yarrow Cheney, Eric "Panama" Koenig, Randy Myers, Mike Stocker, Skip Jones, Dave Kupczyk, Linda Miller, Mike Nguyen. 3-D computer graphics: Corey Hels. Art director: Brian McEntee. Visual development: Dennis Greco, Brian McEntee, Mark Myer, Rick Schneider, Ennio Torresan Jr., David Womersley. Character design: Mark Dindal, Tom Ellery, Brian McEntee, Rick Schneider, Bob Scott, Bruce Smith. Caricature design: Dave Woodman. Storyboard supervisors: Rick Schneider, Mark Dindal. Storyboards: Tony Craig, Jill Culton, Mark Dindal, Tom Ellery, Kevin Johnson, Jason Katz, Eric "Panama" Koenig, Robert Lence, Brian McEntee, Matt O'Callaghan, Theresa Pettengill, Brad Raymond, Darrell Rooney, Larry Scholl, Mark Swan, Frans Vischer, David Womersley, Kelvin Yasuda.

**Charlotte's Web** (3/1/73) Paramount. 94 mins. Directors: Charles A. Nichols, Iwao Takamoto. Producers: William Hanna, Joseph Barbera. Voices: Debbie Reynolds (Charlotte), Paul Lynde (Templeton), Henry Gibson (Wilbur), Rex Allen (Narrator), Martha Scott (Mrs. Arable), Dave Madden (Old Ram), Danny Bonaduce (Avery Arable), Don Messick (Geoffrey, Lamb, Uncle, Bystanders), Herb Vigran (Lurvy), Agnes Moorehead (the Goose), Pamelyn Ferdin (Fern Arable), Joan Gerber (Mrs. Zuckerman, Mrs. Fussy, Old Lady, Operator, Women), Bob Holt (Homer Zuckerman), John Stephenson (Farmer Arable, Judge, Bandleader, Guard), William B. White (Henry Fussy).

©Hanna-Barbera Productions – Sagittarius Production, Inc.

*Consumer Tips:* ☆☆½ MPAA Rating: G. Based on the book by E. B. White.

*Story:* Wilbur the pig gains confidence from the words found spun in Charlotte's spiderweb. With the help of Templeton the rat, Wilbur protects Charlotte's offspring.

*Comments:* This folksy animated adaptation of the E. B. White book (an earlier treatment had been prepared by Gene Deitch) was Hanna-Barbera's third full-length theatrical feature, but the first not to use any of the studio's established characters. Visually, the film's overall style and character design is reminiscent of certain Hanna-Barbera series of the time, such as "These Are the Days," but the background and movement are generally more fluid, and the design of the animal characters is appealing. The script by Earl Hamner Jr., later to create *The Waltons*, and narration by Rex Allen, veteran of numerous Disney animal epics, creates a laid-back, nostalgic tone. The film's pleasant flow is occasionally spliced with touches of realism, as in Wilbur's fear of death, as well as ripe cynicism in the character of Templeton the rat. Indeed, though many of the film's songs by the prolific Sherman Brothers are fairly catchy and enjoyable, Templeton's ode to gluttony, "A Fair Is a Veritable Smorgasbord," stands out. Though much of White's imagery and language is inevitably excised, the central plot and themes remain the same, and Charlotte's death at the end, though it fails to take full advantage of the medium, is still quite affecting. The voices are generally fine, with Paul Lynde relishing the role of Templeton, and Hanna-Barbera stalwarts Don Messick, John Stephenson, and Joan Gerber in multiple roles. The death of Charlotte, however, ranks alongside Old Yeller's shooting as one of the most famous tragic moments in family films.

Following its initial release, *Charlotte's Web* became a staple of Saturday matinees and "Summer Movie Camp" programs for years. Rather belatedly, in an apparent attempt to cash in on the direct-to-video craze, Paramount released a sequel in 2003. Not surprisingly, none of the original cast or crew was retained. (AL)

*Additional Credits:* Executive producer: Edgar Bronfman. Story: Earl Hamner Jr. Music: Richard M. Sherman, Robert M.

Sherman. Key animators: Hal Ambro, Ed Barge, Lars Galonius, Dick Lundy, Irv Spence. Animators: Ed Aardal, Lee Dyer, Bob Gow, George Kreisl, Don Patterson, Carlo Vinci, O. E. Callahan, Hugh Fraser, Volus Jones, Ed Parks, Ray Patterson, Xenia. Art directors: Bob Singer, Ray Aragon, Paul Julian. Layouts: Mo Gollub, Jerry Eisenberg, John Ahern, Jack Huber, Gary Hoffman, Alex Ignatiev, David High, Mike Arens, Don Morgan, Lew Ott, Ric Gonzales, Goerge Wheeler, Leo Swenson. Background supervisor: F. Montealegre. Backgrounds: Lorraine Andrina, Ferdinand Arce, Lyle Bendes, Venetia Epler, Ronald Erickson, Martin Forte, Bob Gentle, Al Gmuer, Joseph Griffith Jr., Gino Guidice, Richard Khim, Tom Knowles, Gary Niblett, Rolando Oliva, Eric Semones, Jeanette Toews, Peter Van Elk.

**Chicken Run** (6/21/00) DreamWorks. 85 mins. Directors: Peter Lord, Nick Park. Producers: Peter Lord, David Sproxton, Nick Park. Voices: Mel Gibson (Rocky), Julia Sawalha (Ginger), Miranda Richardson (Mrs. Tweedy), Benjamin Whitrow (Fowler), Tony Haygarth (Mr. Tweedy), Phil Daniels (Fetcher), Lynn Ferguson (Mac), Jane Horrocks (Babs), Timothy Spall (Nick), Imelda Staunton (Bunty), John Sharian (Circus Man).

©DreamWorks/Aardman

**Consumer Tips:** ☆☆☆ MPAA Rating: G.

**Story:** The chickens of Tweedy's Egg Farm try to escape their captivity, and Mrs. Tweedy's new Chicken-Pot-Pie-Machine, with the help of a "flying hen" named Rocky.

**Comments:** Following the international success of its shorts and featurettes, especially the three *Wallace and Gromit* shorts, Britain's Aardman Studios partnered with DreamWorks in a relationship somewhat similar to that of Pixar and Disney, or more appropriately Pacific Data Images (PDI) and DreamWorks. The film, directed by *Wallace* creators Nick Park and Peter Lord, was a surprise hit ($105.5 million U.S. gross), appealing to a wide range of audiences. The basic theme, of a group of animals trying to avoid both imprisonment and death, is a fairly common motif in British films, from *Animal Farm* and *Watership Down* to *The Plague Dogs*. However, *Chicken Run*, while still emphasizing the reality of the chickens' plight, takes a far more comedic approach. The film satirizes a slew of POW and escape films, with allusions to everything from *Stalag 17* and *The Great Escape* to *Hogan's Heroes*, with a couple of *Star Trek* references and an *ET* homage tossed in for good measure (the latter presumably contributions from DreamWorks staffers). All this aside, however, unlike the following year's *Shrek*, the core story is not overwhelmed by the cultural references.

For Aardman's first feature film, the crew list was expanded considerably, beyond the handful used on a typical short and featurette, including several storyboard artists and storymen borrowed from DreamWorks, much as Disney feature artists often consulted or assisted on Pixar films. Notable animators on the film included Steve Box (who worked on the penguin scenes in *The Wrong Trousers*) and from the United States, Vinton veterans Teresa Drilling and Tom Gasek. Mel Gibson, who had previously turned in a fairly bland performance as John Smith in Disney's *Pocahontas*, did a fine job voicing the cocky American rooster. Although the cast was fairly large, the characters were carefully individualized, fitting both the cliché types of the genres and standing as personalities of their own, rather than just filling space. Apart from Gibson, most voices were provided by veteran British stage and film thespians, not name actors (at least in the States) but stalwart performers. The film was also unusual in that the studio made extensive use of plasticine for the characters, rather than clay, and even went so far as to create large-scale figures for Mr. and Mrs. Tweedy in order to properly represent character scale (something that had never been done with *Wallace and Gromit*). However, Aardman's trademark beady eyes were still in place, and such motifs as frightening modern machinery and Mr. Tweedy's somewhat oafish good-nature, reminiscent of Wallace, helped tie the feature to Park and Lord's earlier films. The film proved surprisingly successful, appealing to adults, children, and critics alike, and once again suggested that stop-motion animation was not a dead medium. However, Aardman's initially planned follow-up, an adaptation of *The Tortoise and the Hare*, quickly experienced production difficulties and has been delayed, with a feature-length *Wallace and Gromit* feature planned for 2005 instead. (AL)

**Additional Credits:** Executive producers: Jake Eberts, Jeffrey Katzenberg, Michael Rose. Original story: Peter Lord, Nick Park. Screenplay: Karey Kirkpatrick. Additional dialogue: Mark Burton, John O'Farrell. Music: John Powell, Harry Gregson-Williams. Supervising animator: Loyd Price. Key animators: Merlin Crossingham, Sergio Delfino, Suzy Fagan, Guionne Leroy, Dave Osmand, Darren Robbie, Jason Spencer-Galsworthy. Animators: Jay Grace, Will Hodge, Seamus Malone, John Pinfield, Andy Symanowski, Ian Whitlock, Douglas Calder, Stefano Cassini. Additional key animators: Teresa Drilling, Jeff Newitt, Chris Sadler, Steve Box, Tom Gasek. Additional animators: Terry Brain, Gary Cureton, Mike Cottee, Tobias Fouracre, Mike Booth. Storyboard supervisor: David Bowers. Storyboards: Michael Salter, Rejean Bourdages, Dan Lane, Martin Asbury, David Soren. Additional story: Kelly Asbury, Cody Cameron, Randy Cartwright, Brenda Chapman, Jurgen Gross, Vicki Jenson, Robert Koo, Sergei Kouchnerov, Damien Neary, Simon Wells, Catherine Yuh. Script consultant: Peter Aitkin. Production designer: Phil Lewis. Art director: Tim Farrington. Additional production designer: Roger Hall. Graphic artist: John Davey. Model production designer: Jan Sanger. An Aardman Production released through DreamWorks Pictures in association with Pathe.

## The Chipmunk Adventure (5/22/87) Samuel Goldwyn. 76 mins. Director: Janice Karman. Producer: Ross Bagdasarian. Voices: Ross Bagdasarian (David Seville, Alvin Seville, Simon), Janice Karman (Theodore, Brittany Miller, Jeanette Miller, Eleanor Miller), Dody Goodman (Miss Rebecca Miller), Anthony De Longis (Klaus Furschtien), Susan Tyrrell (Claudia Furschtien), Frank Welker (Sophie, Arab Prince, Additional Voices), Nancy Cartwright (Arabian Prince), Philip L. Clarke, Ken Sansom, George Poulos, Charles Adler (Additional Voices).

**Consumer Tips:** ☆☆ MPAA Rating: G.

**Story:** The Chipmunks and their female counterparts, The Chipettes, are sent on a race around the world by two con artists who use the singers to smuggle diamonds hidden within chipmunk dolls.

**Comments:** *The Chipmunk Adventure* is typical of animated features from the mid-1980s: a routine storyline peppered with moments of exciting animation, based on a strong, presold juvenile property.

*Alvin and the Chipmunks* were created by songwriter Ross Bagdasarian Sr. in 1958. Bagdasarian, with his cousin William Saroyan, previously cowrote the hit song, "Come on a My House," for Rosemary Clooney in 1951. Bagdasarian later devised a studio technique for recording voices at various high-pitched levels. Under the pseudonym of David Seville, he produced a hit record, "Witch Doctor," in 1958 with his sped-up "Chipmunks" voices. At Christmas, a second disc was released, "The Chipmunk Song," which became a number one hit by New Year's Day.

This led to a string of Chipmunk hit records for Bagdasarian as well as several Grammy Awards. In 1961, CBS ordered a prime-time television series, *The*

*Alvin Show*, from Format Films. Reruns of this show in subsequent years made the Chipmunks a Saturday morning staple throughout the 1960s.

Bagdasarian Sr. died in 1972, and many thought the Chipmunks were gone for good. Not quite. In 1980, Ross Bagdasarian Jr. decided to revive the franchise by releasing an album, *Chipmunk Punk*. To everyone's surprise it went gold, reviving Alvin and the Chipmunks as both a rock-and-roll novelty and Saturday morning superstars. In 1981, the Chipmunks returned in a new prime-time television special, *A Chipmunk Christmas*, directed by Chuck Jones. This led to several more specials and finally a return to a weekly series on NBC in 1983.

*The Chipmunk Adventure* was an elaborate, big budget film. Alvin, Simon, and Theodore never looked so good. The character animation and production values are superb, and the story promises a lot of adventure but unfortunately fails to deliver. The missing ingredients are excitement and danger, which would have made this tale more memorable and less mediocre.

The backgrounds, supervised by Disney and Don Bluth veteran Ron Dias, are gorgeous. Some animation sequences in the middle of the film, particularly the musical numbers "The Girls of Rock and Roll" and "Getting Lucky," are very good. This is where many ex-Disney and ex-Don Bluth animators get to show off some stuff.

But the film is ultimately ordinary. It's a shame to see so many talented people involved in a mediocre project. There is a thank you credit at the end of the film to Disney legendary animators Frank Thomas and Ollie Johnson. Unfortunately, their inspiration is nowhere to be seen. (JB)

**Additional Credits:** Screenplay: Janice Karman, Ross Bagdasarian. Music and lyrics: Randy Edelman. Associate producer: Gwendolyn Sue Shakespear. Production executive: Hope London. Production supervisor: Rocky Stoloff. Directing animators: Skip Jones, Don Spencer, Andrew Gaskill, Mitch Rochon, Becky Bristrow. Color stylist: Ron Dias. Chipmunk and Chipettes design: Sandra. Character designer: Louise Zingerelli. Production designer: Carol Holman Grosvenor.

**Cinderella** (2/15/50) Walt Disney Pictures. 74 mins. Directors: Wilfred Jackson, Hamilton Luske, Clyde Geronimi. Production supervisor: Ben Sharpsteen. Voices: Ilene Woods (Cinderella), Verna Felton (Fairy Godmother), Eleanor Audley (Lady Tremaine), Rhoda Williams (Drizella), Lucille Bliss (Anastasia), William Phipps (Prince Charming), Mike Douglas (singing voice of Prince), Luis Van Rooten (King, Grand Duke), James Macdonald (Gus, Jaq, Bruno), June Foray (Lucifer), Betty Lou Gerson (Narrator), Helen Siebert, Lucille Williams, Clint McCauley, June Sullivan (Mice).

©Walt Disney Productions

**Consumer Tips:** ☆☆☆ MPAA Rating: G. Adapted from the fairy tale written by Charles Perrault (1628–1703) during the late 1600s.

**Story:** When a handsome prince hosts a ball in order to find a bride, the most select ladies of the land look forward to attending. Lovely Cinderella, however, cannot; she is kept a virtual slave by her cruel stepmother Lady Tremaine and two mean stepsisters. By dint of her kind heart Cinderella finds allies in the form of helpful mice, but the greatest help comes from her fairy godmother, whose magic allows Cinderella to go to the ball—as long as she is home by midnight. Even though Cinderella wins the prince's heart, Lady Tremaine is determined to see that all ends unhappily ever after. True love triumphs in an exciting climax, thanks to a very familiar glass slipper.

**Comments:** *Cinderella* marked Disney's return to full-length animated features, ending an eight-year hiatus. Money was still tight following the war years, so Walt and company had to produce a sure, profitable winner as cheaply as possible. One way to do so was to return to what worked before: adapting one of the most popular fairy tales of all time. Another method of keeping costs down was to film the feature extensively in live-action beforehand, and then animate from the timing, movement, and poses found in the footage and stills. There would be very little freehand experimentation, but the scrapping of animation would be kept to a minimum. Animator Marc Davis stated in an interview that he believed some 90 percent of *Cinderella* had been shot in live-action prior to and during production.

The liveliest parts of the film, however, were not based on live action. Animator Ward Kimball, the wildest of Disney's "Nine Old Men," was entrusted with the animation of Gus and Jaq (Cinderella's valiant mouse buddies) and Lucifer (Lady Tremaine's lazy but dangerous house cat). They face off several times in the movie and are central to the movie's most thrilling scene, Cinderella's rescue after Lady Tremaine has locked her away on high. There is nothing vaguely naturalistic about Kimball's creatures, and it might have been horrifying if there were, considering the many close shaves the mice must endure. Kimball's manic animation and riveting sense of timing almost give the sense that his characters belong in an entirely different film.

Not that *Cinderella* is less than the sum of its parts. The movie boasts many fine scenes that leave an impression even after a single viewing. In one of them, the mice and their animal allies construct a gown for Cinderella; Lady Tremaine (expertly animated by Frank Thomas) has promised the hapless girl that she can attend the ball if she can find attire more suitable than her dowdy housedress. When Cinderella displays the gown to Tremaine and the ugly stepsisters, the girls recognize the material as scraps from their old clothing—thanks to Lady Tremaine's sharp eye—and demand they be returned, literally ripping the dress off Cinderella's back. The camera lingers on Lady Tremaine's smug, sadistic smirk. The cruelty and pathos of this scene is almost painful to watch. The other features of the story, including the magical transformation of common animals and a pumpkin into Cinderella's exquisite coach and retinue, are technically excellent. In the end, Walt Disney got his wish: The film was a rousing success, easily recouping its modest costs. Full-length glory had returned to the Disney studio.

*Cinderella* was an old favorite at Disney; one of Walt's earliest works was a 1922 "Laugh-O-Gram" fea-

turing the tale. A Silly Symphony was reportedly planned in 1933. The first attempts at a movie script surfaced in 1940. Walt was not alone in his affinity for the tale: 38 different versions of the story have been filmed, the earliest one in 1898.

*Cinderella* turned a $2.9 million budget into an eventual $85 million in profit, but the box-office gross was not the whole story; for the first time, Disney made a huge profit from the film's soundtrack. The newly formed Walt Disney Music Company retained all rights (and the copyright) to songs used in its films. The wisdom of this strategy became evident when "Bibbity Bobbity Boo" became a hit. The luminous particles that accompany the Fairy Godmother's magic spell so enthralled Walt Disney that he asked his effects team to put more of it in the scene. The effect was known forever after as "Disney Dust." (MG)

©Walt Disney Productions

**Additional Credits:** Directing animators: Eric Larson, Milt Kahl, Frank Thomas, John Lounsbery, Wolfgang Reitherman, Ward Kimball, Ollie Johnston, Marc Davis, Les Clark, Norm Ferguson. Character animators: Don Lusk, Hugh Fraser, Fred Moore, Judge Whitaker, Marvin Woodward, George Nichols, Phil Duncan, Hal King, Harvey Toombs, Cliff Nordberg, Hal Ambro, Ken O'Brien. Story: Bill Peet, Ted Sears, Homer Brightman, Kenneth Anderson, Erdman Penner, Winston Hibler, Harry Reeves, Joe Rinaldi. Songs: Mack David, Jerry Livingston, Al Hoffman. Orchestrations: Joseph Dubin. Background artists: Brice Mack, Ralph Hulett, Dick Anthony, Art Riley, Ray Huffine, Merle Cox, Thelma Witner. Layout artists: Mac Stewart, Tom Codrick, Lance Nolley, Don Griffith, Kendall O'Connor, Hugh Hennesy, Charles Philippi, Thor Putnam. Effects animators: George Rowley, Josh Meador, Jack Boyd.

**Cleopatra, Queen of Sex** (4/24/72) Xanadu Productions—Mushi Pro (Japan). 100 mins. Directors: Eiichi Yamamoto, Osamu Tezuka. Producer: Yoneyama Abiko. Voices: Nakayama Chinatsu (Cleopatra), Hana Takamura (Ceasar), Nabe Osami (Antonius), Yoshimura Miko (Libya), Hatsui Kotoe (Apollodrius), Yanagiya Tsubame (Lupa), Tsukamoto Nobuo (Ionius), Imai Kazuko (Carpania), Abe Susumu (Cabagonis), Kato Yoshio (Chief Tarabach), Nozawa Nachi (Octavian).

©Mushi

**Consumer Tips:** ☆☆☆☆ SF/fantasy adventure. MPAA Rating: none (advertised as X-rated). An erotic fantasy/comedy based on the legend of Cleopatra as a great beauty and lover.

**Story:** In the future three friends argue over whether Cleopatra was really as great a lover as her legend. They time travel to ancient Egypt to find out for themselves. Egypt is a burlesque parody of actual history, and deliberate anachronisms (Julius Caesar's chariot is a horse-drawn Edsel automobile) are mixed with *Playboy*-style bawdy erotic humor.

**Comments:** The plot follows multiple stories: Cleopatra's winning of freedom from the Egyptians who try to make her their puppet; her seduction of the Roman leaders Caesar and later Marc Anthony (and attempted seduction of Octavian, who turns out to be homosexual); the lovers Ionius' and Lybia's efforts to escape slavery together; and Lupa's comedic attempts at bestiality with Cleopatra.

Osamu Tezuka was determined to make an intelligent erotic comedy for adults in the style of *Playboy* magazine, to prove that animation was not just for children. *Cleopatra* contains "guest appearance" parodies of many popular Japanese cartoon characters, and the "living lips" animation process of America's Clutch Cargo television series. The art design is grotesque (Caesar is blond with bright green skin), and there are many deliberately jarring anachronisms such as showing Caesar's assassination as a stylized kabuki play. *Cleopatra* was intended to be in intellectual good taste. Tezuka later claimed that he was outraged that the American version was retitled *Cleopatra, Queen of Sex* and presented as X-rated pornography and was delighted to learn that American audiences had demanded their money back because of its lack of raw sex. The Japanese release on September 11, 1970, was 112 minutes; the American was cut to 100 minutes by eliminating some of the non-erotic scenes.

*Cleopatra* is frenetically undisciplined, barraging the adult audience with quickly changing art styles and mood swings from slapstick humor to tender romance to tense suspense. It is usually very funny, undeniably clever, and totally unique in a good way. (FP)

**Additional Credits:** Screenplay: Shigemi Satoyoshi. Designer: Ko Kojima. Animation: Kazuko Nakamura, Gisaburo Sugii, Yoshiaki Kawajiri. Music: Isao Tomita. Animation opening credits: Nakamura Kazuko, Hata Masami, Akabori Mikiharu, Kamiguchi Teruto, Sugii Gisaburo, Shimamura Tatsuo, Furusawa Hideo, Kishita Renzo. Animation closing credits: Kitano Hideaki, Shindo Mitsuo, Sasakado Nobuyoshi, Ogawa Takao, Watanabe Keiko, Ushigoe Noritomo, Kobayashi Junji, Tanizawa Yutaka, Kamiri Kazuya, Ushigoe Kazuo, Arata Masatoshi, Satsuki Ikuo, Yoshimura Masaki, Kiguchi Jun, Kimura Ichiro, Ebizawa Sachio, Ashida Toyoo, Nobe Hayao, Asado Sumiko, Horigoe Shintaro, Kawajiri Yoshiaki, Yamamori Hiroaki, Iijima Atsushi, Tada Sachiko, Kato Shin'ichi, Shindo Miyuki, Matsuda Nobuo, Ishikuro Atsushi, Ozaki Mitsuo, Kanako Kensuke, Matsumoto Yutaka, Yoshino Yasuko, Negishi Mineo. Backgrounds: Nishimura Kumiko, Kawanabe Hiroji, Hirabayashi Shigeru, and others.

**Clifford's Really Big Movie** (2/20/04) Warner Bros. 73 mins. Director: Robert Ramirez. Producer: Deborah Forte. Voices: John Ritter (Clifford the Big Red Dog), Wayne Brady (Shackelford), Grey DeLisle

(Emily Elizabeth), Jenna Elfman (Dorothy), John Goodman (George Wolfsbottom), Jess Harnell (Dirk), Kel Mitchell (T-Bone), Judge Reinhold (Larry), Kath Soucie (Jetta, Madison), Cree Summer (Cleo), Wilmer Valderrama (Rodrigo), Earl Boen (Mr. Bleakman), Ernie Hudson (P. T.).

**Consumer Tips:** ☆☆☆ MPAA Rating: G. Based on the books and PBS series created by Norman Bridwell.

**Story:** Clifford, concerned that his owner can't afford to feed a dog his size, leaves home in search of financial aid. He ends up as the star attraction at a ramshackle carnival of performing animals, wins a dog food talent contest, and is kidnapped by a millionaire's daughter who collects the world's biggest things.

**Comments:** In 1962, author and illustrator Norman Bridwell found himself having to support a wife and infant daughter. He picked up extra money as a freelance artist, illustrating picture books. Bridwell chose to write a story about an illustration he had made of a little girl modeled after his young daughter, and a VERY big dog. Bridwell wanted to name the dog Tiny, but his wife suggested the name Clifford, after an imaginary play friend from her own childhood. Bridwell named the little girl in his book after his own daughter, Emily Elizabeth. Three weeks after submitting his story and illustrations to Scholastic Books, the publishers called with an offer to publish his work. Forty titles and sixty million copies later, *Clifford the Big Red Dog* made the canine a well-known and beloved character to the preschool set.

In 2000, a PBS animated series debuted based on the books. John Ritter voiced the lead role of Clifford, and the series was an immediate success. Deciding to make a full-length theatrical film two years later, Scholastic Entertainment made all the right moves. Robert Ramirez, who had directed Cartoon Network's *Johnny Bravo* and helmed DreamWorks' direct-to-video feature *Joseph: King of Dreams* (2000), was hired to oversee the production. Ramirez wrote the script with comedy writer Rhett Reese (*The Joe Schmo Show*), and it is filled with clever touches.

The result is a very pleasant, fully animated feature that is perfect for young kids and entirely watchable for parents. The animation is full at times, and the produc-

tion values are first-rate. Warner Home Video coproduced the film with Scholastic Entertainment. With Hollywood having jitters about traditional hand-drawn animation at the box office, it was decided to give the film a limited platform release to reduce marketing costs. It opened on February 20 in New York, Atlanta, Minneapolis, Phoenix, and Austin. The studio added nine more markets on April 23, including Los Angeles. The box-office gross was a dissappointing $2.8 million, but the DVD sales were as big as Clifford—through the roof. (JB)

**Additional Credits:** Screenplay: Robert C. Ramirez, Rhett Reese. Coproducers: Martha Atwater, Jef Kaminsky. Supervising producer: Liz Young. Consulting producers: Mike Young, Bill Schultz. Line producer: Chris Henderson. Associate producer: Kathleen Zuelch. Animation director: Murray Debus. Original music: Jody Gray. Songs: Jody Gray, David Steven Cohen. Film editor: Monte Bramer. Casting: Mary Hidalgo. Art direction: Michael Humphries. Unit director: Steve Trenbirth. Voice director: Susan Blu. Character designer: Phil Mendez. Storyboard artists: Ray Claffey, Sahin Ersoz, Skip Jones, Dan Kuenster, Lane Luras, Alex Mann, John D. Williamson. Layout: David Rodriquez, Will Weston, Brian Woods.

**Cool World** (7/9/92) Paramount. 102 mins. Director: Ralph Bakshi. Producer: Frank Mancuso Jr. Cast: Kim Basinger (Holli Would), Gabrielle Byrne (Jack Deebs), Brad Pitt (Detective Frank Harris), Michele Abrams (Jennifer Malley), Deidre O'Connell (Isabel Malley), Janni Brenn-Lowen (Mom Harris), Carrie Hamilton (Comic Bookstore Cashier), Stephen Worth

©Paramount Pictures

(Store Patron), Frank Sinatra Jr. (Himself). Voices: Maurice LaMarche (Doc Whiskers, Mash, Interrogator, Drunk Bar Patron, Super Jack), Joey Camen (Interrogator, Slash, Holli's Door), Michael David Lally (Sparks), Jenine Jennings (Craps Bunny), Gregory Snegoff (Bash), Candi Milo (Bob, Lonette), Charlie Adler (Nails), Patrick Pinney (Bouncer).

**Consumer Tips:** ☆½ MPAA Rating: PG-13. For adults and Bakshi completists only.

**Story:** Burnt-out cartoonist Jack Deebs mentally withdraws into his cartoon creation, the Cool World, where a sexy "doodle" named Holli Would uses him to become human.

**Comments:** Producer Frank Mancuso Jr. approached Ralph Bakshi shortly after the release of *Who Framed Roger Rabbit* (1988) to discuss a film about "a man creating a world and then becoming trapped in it." Unfortunately, what could have been a cool R-rated variation on *Roger Rabbit* wound up as a complete mess.

Bakshi's final feature film has a great premise, a great cast, and the best animation he's ever been involved with. Regretably, the movie is a pointless rehash of many of Ralph's favorite themes, and the story literally goes nowhere.

The "Cool World" itself is a nightmare version of "Toon Town." The characters are totally unlikeable, unappealing, and depressing. Animated sex and violence is Bakshi's specialty, but a key sex scene between the live-action Deebs and the cartoon Holli was severely curtailed to receive a PG-13 rating, undoubtedly diminishing its effectiveness. The idea of a man descending into his own personal cartoon hell is a great one, but here it is wasted.

So, is it all bad? The film does move along at a fast pace and some of the animation is fun, particularly a sequence at the end when Deebs turns into a superhero. Fans of cartoonist Milton Knight and background painter Barry Jackson will enjoy their contributions. Otherwise this is a huge misfire.

Grossing a mere $14 million in the U.S. market, *Cool World* was a small world, after all. (JB)

**Additional Credits:** Screenplay: Michael Grais, Mark Victor. Music: Mark Isham. Additional music: John Dickson. Music

director: Allan Wilson. Supervising animator: Bruce Woodside. Animators: George Bakes, Anne Marie Bardwell, Paul Bolger, James Davis, Michael R. Gerard, Steve Gordon, Ronald P. Hughart, Mike Kazaleh, Gregory A. Manwaring, Jules Marino, Bill Melendez, Roy Meurin, James Murphy, Samuel W. Nicholson, Dana O'Connor, Alan Sperling, Greg Tiernan, Kenneth D. Walker. Background character animation: Milton Knight, Mark S. O'Hare. Effects animation creative supervisor: Lee Crowe. Effects animators: Craig Clark, Pat Clark, Phil Cummings, Mike D'Isa, Al Holter, Joey Mildenberger, Juli Murphy, Conrad Vernon, Dan Wanket. Animation layout/design: Greg Hill, Dave Wasson. Character layout/design: Louise Zingarelli. Backgrounds: Patricia Doktor, Brad Hicks, Ian Miller, Charles Pickens. Art director: David James Bomba. Animation consultant: Silvia Pompei.

**Coonskin** (8/1/75) Bryanston. 83 mins. Director: Ralph Bakshi. Producer: Albert S. Ruddy. Voices: Barry White (Brother Bear, Samson), Charles Gordone (Preacher, Brother Fox), Scatman Crothers (Pappy), Philip Thomas (Brother Rabbit, Randy), Danny Rees (Clown), Buddy Douglas (Referee), Jim Moore (Mime).

©Bakshi Productions

**Consumer Tips:** ☆☆ MPAA Rating: R. Alternate titles *Street Fight* and *Bustin' Out*.

**Story:** Two escaped convicts, hiding from authorities, listen to Pappy (Scatman Crothers) tell stories of cartoon characters Brother Rabbit, Brother Bear, and Brother Fox (told with animation) that resemble a violent, inner-city update of *Song of the South*.

**Comments:** *Coonskin* was Ralph Bakshi's third feature film, following *Fritz the Cat* and *Heavy Traffic*. It was perhaps his most ambitious and notorious project. Combining live action and animation, the film is an inner-city variation on Disney's *Song of the South* (1946), with Brother Rabbit, Brother Fox, and Brother Bear personified as escaped convicts in live action, versus the Mafia in Harlem.

The film takes aim at everyone, including blacks, whites, women, homosexuals, crime, and the whole United States (personified by a red, white, and blue blonde bimbo named "Miss America"). Bakshi tried to bite off a lot in his newfound role as a radical animator-turned-social commentator. The film is not as edgy as his previous features, and the filmmaking (particularly the live-action sequences) leaves a lot to be desired.

This was Bakshi's first feature to be backed by a major studio (Paramount, where Bakshi had run its cartoon short subjects division in 1967) and by a major producer, Albert S. Ruddy (*The Godfather*). It was to be the first of a multipicture deal made by Paramount's president Frank Yablans with Bakshi and Ruddy. It cost $1.6 million to produce.

Its depiction of black caricatures in cartoon form was very offensive to the black community. Particularly vocal were the members of CORE (Congress of Racial Equality), who disrupted a Q&A session following an advance screening at New York's Museum of Modern Art.

While the film was in production, Yablans left Paramount, and Barry Diller was president when the MoMA incident occured in March of 1975. A month later, independent distributor Bryanston took over the distribution arrangements. Paramount dumped it and its deal with Bakshi and Ruddy. Their second film, *The American Chronicles*, which was in development at the time, also got canned.

The *L.A. Times, New York Times, Variety*, Gene Shalit on NBC, and the *Wall Street Journal* all gave the film rave reviews. However, Bryanston's weak distribution efforts, and the controversy surrounding the film, kept it out of most markets. Bryanston tried rereleasing the film in black theaters as *Bustin' Out*, but it languished. In an interview in the March 1976 issue of *Action*, a Directors Guild of America publication, Bakshi remarked, "Sure, *Coonskin* was a disaster. The picture itself was the best thing I've done. At least it provoked some discussion about animation. That's been the problem with animation. After Walt Disney,

it's been nowhere." *Coonskin* is currently available on home video under the title *Street Fight*. (JB)

**Additional Credits:** Screenplay: Ralph Bakshi. Music: Chico Hamilton. Songs: Ralph Bakshi, Scatman Crothers, Grover Washington. Assistant director: James Roden. Sequence animators: Irven Spence, Charlie Downs, Ambrozi Paliwoda, John E. Walker, Xeni. Animation: Thomas A. Ray, Edward J. Barge, Fred C. Hellmich, Bob Carlson, John Sparey, Lars Calonius, Raymond Patterson. Layout design: Don Morgan, John Sparey, Charlie Downs. Stills: Ralph Bakshi, Johnny Vita. Background assistants: Ira Turek, Rene Garcia.

## The Cosmic Eye (6/6/86) Upfront Releasing. 72 mins. Director/producer/designer: Faith Hubley. Voices: Dizzy Gillespie (Father Time, Musican), Sam Hubley (Musician), Linda Atkinson (Musican), Maureen Stapleton (Mother Earth), Jack Warden (Rocko).

**Consumer Tips:** ☆☆½ MPAA Rating: Unrated. An art film with elements that children may enjoy—or that may bore them to tears.

**Story:** Three space creatures observe the follies of earth through sequences from animated shorts created by John and Faith Hubley.

**Comments:** Following the death of her husband and creative collaborator, John Hubley, in 1977, Faith Hubley made it her mission to complete one independent film each year for the rest of her life. She turned to larger themes and more abstract images in her solo work. Most of her films don't have linear storylines. Instead, they draw on her interest in mythology to present ideas and themes, celebrating the wonders of life and the art of indigenous peoples.

In January 1985, Faith announced she would take seven of her existing short films and combine them with new footage to create a feature film. This was to be submitted to the first Hiroshima International Film Festival, to be held in August of that year.

This highly erratic and abstract animated feature lacks a solid narrative but is fascinating to watch, both for Faith Hubley's ambitious attempt at personal feature filmmaking and for the excerpts of some of her greatest works (as well as her husband's), including *Moonbird* (1959), *A Windy Day* (1968), and *Cockaboody* (1974).

Faith Hubley's work has been honored in the Cannes, Venice, and London film festivals. She made 25 solo films by the time of her death in 2001. *The Cosmic Eye* was her only solo feature. (JB)

**Additional Credits:** Associate producer: Emily Hubley. Production supervisors: Janet Benn, Ida Greenberg. Composers: Benny Carter, Elizabeth Swados, Dizzy Gillespie, Conrad Cummings, William Russo. Animators: Fred Burns, William Littlejohn, Emily Hubley, Robert Cannon, Ed Smith, Georgia Hubley, Tissa David, Phil Duncan, Katherine Woddell. Rendering artists: Janet Benn, Elizabeth Sackler Berner, Constance D'Antuono.

## Cowboy Bebop: The Movie (4/4/03) Sony Pictures and Destination Films/Samuel Goldwyn Films—Sunrise (Japan). 116 mins. Director: Shinichiro Watanabe. Producers: Kazuhiko Ikeguchi, Haruyo Kanesaku, Yutaka Maseba, Masahiko Minami. Voices: Beau Billingslea (Jet Black—English version), Steven Blum (Spike Spiegel, English version), Kôichi Yamadera (Spike Spiegel, Japanese version), Unshô Ishizuka (Jet Black, Japanese version), Megumi Hayashibara (Faye Valentine, Japanese version), Gara Takashima, (Julia, Japanese version), Norio Wakamoto (Vicious, Japanese version).

**Consumer Tips:** ☆☆☆½ MPAA Rating: R. SF suspense thriller. Based on the Japanese television anime series *Cowboy Bebop*.

**Story:** In A.D. 2071 the solar system has been colonized. A loose society has legalized bounty hunters to hunt interplanetary criminals. The spaceship Bebop, crewed by a team of these "cowboys," is on Mars when its capital city is devastated by a terrorist. The Bebop gang hunts him for the huge reward offered. But the terrorist is more deadly than expected. What's worse, sinister government and corporate agents are ready to kill anyone who learns too much about the terrorist and his mystery weapon.

**Comments:** *Cowboy Bebop* was developed by the Sunrise studio as an adult action-comedy 26-episode television series in 1998. Director Watanabe went crazy designing a chaotic sci-fi "Wild West" society that was his tribute to his favorite martial-arts movies, spaghetti Westerns, 1970s Blaxploitation movies, conspiracy-coverup thrillers, and more. High-quality cartoon animation for character-oriented scenes was blended with cutting-edge computer graphics for the deep-space scenes.

These elements were anchored in a human-interest serial about the likeable although deeply flawed five-man cast and their futuristic world. The original crew of the Bebop were Spike Spiegel, a cool young martial-artist wannabe, and Jet Black, a beefy ex-interplanetary policeman. They gradually picked up Faye Valentine, a sexy femme fatale and compulsive gambler; "Radical Ed," a runaway child genius who was clearly psychotic but had computer skills they needed; and Ein, an apparently normal Welsh corgi with hinted-at super-canine intelligence. The adults casually smoked, got drunk, and bantered in clever dialogue loaded with mature innuendo.

*Cowboy Bebop* was such a critical and popular success that there was never any doubt that there would be a movie. *Cowboy Bebop: Tengoku No Tobira (Knockin' on Heaven's Door)* is set entirely in Mars' Alba City, the largest city off Earth. Many people do not believe it was actually released in Japan on September 1, 2001, eleven days before the 9/11 terrorist attack on America, because it looks like an imitation of that event and its aftermath.

The suspenseful plot is well developed. Some audience familiarity with the main characters is expected. Each of the Bebop crew gets a solo scene, but the focus is upon Spike's tracking down of the enigmatic Vincent Volaju and the revelation of his motive. There are two lengthy, excellently choreographed martial-arts battles between Spike and Vincent that demonstrate Spike's prowess that is only hinted at in the television series. Both the general NYC background and its "Morocco Street" Arabic ghetto are richly detailed, based upon the animators' visits to those locations to collect reference art.

The movie, shown with subtitles at the 2002 Anime Expo, was voted the 2001 Best Japanese Anime Theatrical Release. The English dub premiered at the Big Apple Anime Fest in NYC on August 30, 2002. It got an art-theater release in 17 cities beginning April 4, 2003, and a DVD release by Sony Pictures/Tristar on June 24, 2003. (FP)

**Additional Credits:** Screenplay: Marc Handler (English version), Akihiko Inari, Sadayuki Murai, Keiko Nobumoto, Dai

Sato, Shinichirô Watanabe, Ryota Yamaguchi, Michiko Yokote. Coproducers: Jerry Chu, Osamu Maseba, Charles McCarter. Original music: Yôko Kanno. Cinematography: Yoichi Ogami. Film editing: Tomoaki Tsurubuchi. Art direction: Jun'ichi Higashi. Set decoration: Isamu Imakake. Set design: Isamu Imakake. Sound director: Katsuyoshi Kobayashi. Sound rerecording mixer: Mike Verta (dubbed version).

**The Curious Mr. Wonderbird** See *The Adventures of Mr. Wonderbird*

**Daffy Duck's Movie: Fantastic Island** (8/5/83) Warner Bros. 78 mins. Director/producer: Friz Freleng. Voices: Mel Blanc (Daffy Duck, Speedy Gonzales, Yosemite Sam, Bugs Bunny, Tasmanian Devil, Porky Pig, Foghorn Leghorn), June Foray (Granny, Miss Prissy), Les Tremayne (Spirit of the Well).

©Warner Bros.

**Consumer Tips:** ☆☆ MPAA Rating: G. A compilation of classic Looney Tunes.

**Story:** Daffy Duck and Speedy Gonzales, stranded on a deserted island, find a treasure map that leads to a magical wishing well.

**Comments:** This is the final film in the Freleng compilation trilogy. This time, the bridging sequences are a lame take-off on the 1970s television show *Fantasy Island*, with Daffy in the Ricardo Montalban role (Mr. Rourke) and Speedy as an enthusiastic Tattoo stand-in.

As routine as this sounds, it's the best plot of Freleng's three feature-length narratives, cleverly having the classic cartoons as visions in a wishing well, making the

transitions from new to old footage play a bit easier. The subplot of Pirate Sam and the Tasmanian Devil hunting for treasure on the same island adds to the fun.

Classic Looney Tunes reused in this film include Freleng's "Buccaneer Bunny" (1948, with Bugs Bunny), "Greedy for Tweety" (1957, with Tweety and Sylvester), "Tree for Two" (1952, with Spike and Chester), "Curtain Razor" (1949, with Porky Pig), "A Mouse Divided" (1953, with Sylvester), "From Hare to Heir" (1960, with Sam and Bugs), Robert McKimson's "Stupor Duck" (1956, with Daffy Duck), "Banty Raids" (1963, with Foghorn Leghorn), and Chuck Jones' "Louvre Come Back to Me" (1962, with Pepe LePew). (JB)

***Additional Credits:*** Screenplay: John Dunn, David Detiege, Friz Freleng. Music: Milt Franklyn, Carl Stalling. Sequence directors: David Detiege, Friz Freleng, Phil Monroe. Animation: Brenda Banks, Warren Batchelder, Bob Bransford, Brad Case, Terrence Lennon, Bob Matz, Norm McCabe, Sam Nicholson, Derry Ray, Richard Thompson. Classic cartoon effects animation: Harry Love. Production design and layout: Bob Givens, Michael Mitchell. Backgrounds: Richard H. Thomas.

**Daffy Duck's Quackbusters** (9/24/89) Warner Bros. 72 mins. Directors/story: Greg Ford, Terry Lennon. Producers: Steven S. Greene, Kathleen Helppie-Shipley. Voices: Mel Blanc (Daffy Duck, Bugs Bunny, Sylvester the Cat, Tweety, J. P. Cubish, Monsters), Mel Torme (Singing Voice of Daffy Duck), Roy Firestone (Zed Koppell, Lawyer), B. J. Ward (Thelma, Operator), Ben Frommer (Count Bloodcount), Julie Bennett (Emily and Agatha).

©Warner Bros.

**Consumer Tips:** ☆☆½ MPAA Rating: G. A compilation of classic Looney Tunes.

**Story:** Street salesman Daffy Duck inherits a million dollars from the estate of J. B. Cubish, then sets up a ghost-busting service with pals Bugs Bunny and Porky Pig for the purposes of destroying Cubish's ghost—who is trying to take away the inheritance.

**Comments:** *Daffy Duck's Quackbusters* is the most satisfying of the five Warner Bros. cartoon pastiche features. It cleverly links several classic Looney Tunes with a "spooky" theme, and brings together some of the most talented younger generation of animators (Beiman, Kausler, Haskett, Van Citters, etc.) with a remaining few of the old guard (Norm McCabe, Richard Thomas).

Noted animation historian and producer Greg Ford joined the staff at Warner Bros. Animation in 1985. He teamed with director Terry Lennon on several theatrical shorts, television specials, and this feature compilation movie. Exploring the vaults at Warner Bros., Ford found master tapes of the Milt Franklyn and Carl Stalling musical recording sessions for several Looney Tunes in the 1950s. This material would be the basis of the two-volume CD set of *The Carl Stalling Project*, coproduced with Hal Willner. The original music cues on these master tapes were used to score scenes in *Quackbusters* and helped bridge the new material with the classic cartoons.

Unfortunately, Mel Blanc's voice was far from its prime, so it's easy to spot the newer parts based on his vocal performances. This film, along with character voices in *Who Framed Roger Rabbit*, marked his last performances in the roles of Daffy Duck and Bugs Bunny.

Classic cartoons used in this production include excerpts from Chucks Jones' "Daffy Dilly" (1948), "Water Water Every Hare" (1952, with Bugs Bunny), "Claws for Alarm" (1954, with Porky and Sylvester), "The Abominable Snow Rabbit" (1961), "Transylvania 6-5000" (1963), "Punch Trunk" (1953), "Jumpin' Jupiter" (1955), Friz Freleng's "Hyde and Go Tweet" (1960, with Tweety and Sylvester), Robert McKimson's "The Prize Pest" (1951), and a Ford Lennon original, "The Duxorcist" (1987). (JB)

**Additional Credits:** Classic music: Carl Stalling, Milt Franklyn, Bill Lava (music coordinated by Hal Willner).

Sequence directors: Chuck Jones, Friz Freleng, Robert McKimson. Animation: Brenda Banks, Nancy Beiman, Daniel Haskett, Mark Kausler, Norm McCabe, Rebecca Rees, Darryl Van Citters, Frans Vischer. Production design/layout: Bob Givens. Backgrounds: Richard H. Thomas, Alan Bodner.

**The Daydreamer** (7/29/66) Embassy Pictures. 98 mins. Director: Jules Bass. Producer: Arthur Rankin Jr. Cast: Paul O'Keefe (Hans Christian Andersen), Jack Gilford (Papa Andersen), Ray Bolger (The Pieman), Margaret Hamilton (Mrs. Klopplebobbler), Robert Harter (Big Claus). Voices: Cyril Ritchard (The Sandman), Hayley Mills (The Little Mermaid), Burl Ives (Father Neptune), Tallulah Bankhead (The Sea Witch), Terry-Thomas (First Tailor), Victor Borge (Second Tailor), Ed Wynn (The Emperor), Patty Duke (Thumbelina), Boris Karloff (The Rat), Sessue Hayakawa (The Mole), Robert Goulet (The Singer).

©Rankin-Bass

**Consumer Tips:** ☆☆½ Rankin-Bass strike again!

**Story:** A boy dreams himself into a fairy-tale world (of stop-motion animated puppets) where he meets many Hans Christian Andersen characters, such as Thumbelina, the Ugly Duckling, and the Little Mermaid.

**Comments:** *The Daydreamer*, the second theatrical feature produced by Rankin-Bass, was one of the studio's early forays into an all-star cast that went beyond a headlining narrator, a la Burl Ives (here cast as King Neptune) for *Rudolph the Red-Nosed Reindeer*. The episodic movie features Paul O'Keefe, then late of *The Patty Duke Show* (whose star is also in the film), as a rather callow young Hans Christian Andersen, in both live-action and stop-motion "Animagic" segments (the former were directed by former juvenile actor Ezra Stone, radio's Henry Aldrich). In some ways, the film plays like a sketch television show, with young Hans appearing in each story, in dream form, surrounded by celebrity guests as the various fairy tale figures. As with the Rankin-Bass television specials, most of these were designed to at least slightly invoke the original performer (Ed Wynn's emperor with fluttery eyes, Terry-Thomas's gap-toothed tailor, etc.), and the star voices, combined with the stories as written, provide a ready-made yet surprisingly effective template for characterization. To add the final Hollywood touch to the film, the inimitable Al Hirschfeld was hired to pen caricatures of the stars, in and out of character, for use both in rather ingenious main titles (as the puppet character pops up beside the caricature) and in publicity materials. The songs by Maury Laws and Jules Bass are typically adept, if largely forgettable, with the exception of a jauntily gloomy tune sung by the mole (played by dramatic actor Sessue Hayakawa, of all people) and a chorus of bats as he attempts to woo Thumbelina.

O'Keefe's Hans is largely dull and somewhat bratty in both live action and animation (often spurring on the tragic endings of the original tales!), but the fairy tales themselves are mostly engaging. The voice cast alone makes the film worth seeing at least once. Rankin-Bass would repeatedly return to the works of Andersen for television. (AL)

**Additional Credits:** Writer: Arthur Rankin Jr. Based on the stories of Hans Christian Andersen. Additional dialogue: Romeo Muller. Music: Maury Laws. Cinematography: Daniel Cavelli, Tad Mochinaga. Art direction: Maurice Gordon. Costume design: Oleg Cassini. Assistant director: Kizo Nagashima. Recording supervisor: Bernard Cowan. Stager "animagic" sequences: Don Duga. Technician "animagic": Tad Mochinaga. Stager live-action sequences: Ezra Stone.

**Digimon: The Movie** (10/6/00) 20th Century Fox. 85 mins. Directors: Takaaki Yamashita, Hisashi Nayayama, Masahiro Aizawa. Producers: Seki Hiromi, Terri-Lei O'Malley. Voices: Lara Jill Miller (Kari), Joshua Seth (Tai), Bob Papenbrook (Red Greymon), Doug Erholtz (T. K.), David Lodge (Parrotmon), Dorothy Melendrez (Mrs. Kamiya), Michael Sorich (Big Agumon, Gar-

gomon, Miko), Peggy O'Neal (Botamon), Colleen O'Shaughnessey (Sora), Brianne Siddall (Koromon), and additional voices: Mona Marshall, Michael Lindsay, Michael Reisz, Wendee Lee, Mike Reynolds, Kirk Thornton, Laura Summer, Edie Mirman, Dave Mallow, Robert Axelrod.

**Consumer Tips:** ☆☆½ MPAA Rating: PG. Juvenile fantasy. Based on the television series *Digimon: Digital Monsters*, itself based on the video game.

**Story:** A group of 10- to 12-year-old children at summer camp are transported to a computer world where they meet digital monsters (Digimon) resembling cute miniature dinosaurs. Each Digimon bonds to the child who matches its personality. The kids and their Digipartners must fight Digimon corrupted by computer viruses who would endanger the real world. The movie is a compilation of three short adventures.

**Comments:** The huge commercial success of Japan's kid-friendly *Pocket Monsters* (*Pokémon*) quickly spawned imitations. *Digimon Adventures* was the most successful as a television cartoon (March 1999). It became *Digimon: Digital Monsters* on the Fox Kids Network in August 1999.

The main story differences are that Pokémon is set entirely in a fantasy world, while the children in *Digimon* travel back and forth between the real world and the Digiworld. The *Pokémon* fantasy animals are basically non-speaking pets, while the Digimon talk and accompany their human pals as equals. The *Digimon* stories are more action-oriented, climaxing in landscape-destroying (but bloodless) battles between good and evil (or sick) Digimon while the kids root for their Digipartners.

All game-based animated titles rely upon as many characters as possible to maximize toy marketing potential. *Digimon*'s original cast is seven children and their Digipartners: Taichi "Tai" Kamiya (Digipartner: Koromon), Sora Takenouchi (Digipartner: Yokomon), Yamato "Matt" Ishida (Tsunomon), Takeru "T. K." Takaishi (Tokomon), Koushiro "Izzy" Izumi (Motimon), Mimi Tachikawa (Tanemon), and Joe Kido (Bukamon). Each Digimon can evolve into several larger forms, each of which has a special power. For example, Bukamon can become Gomamon, Ikkikimon, and Zudomon; and Gomamon can talk to fish. These original characters meet many new friends and adversaries; an important newcomer for the movie is Kari, Tai's eight-year-old sister.

When the first two *Pokémon* features were huge theatrical hits, Fox wanted to duplicate their success with a Digimon feature. There was none; however, Toei Animation produces a theatrical Toei Animation Fair every spring and summer of two to four theatrical-quality featurettes to showcase its most popular television cartoons. The three most recent had included *A Digimon Adventure*. These were edited together to make *Digimon: The Movie* for American theatrical release.

*A Digimon Adventure* (released March 4, 1999, in Japan) is set four years before the television series. When Tai was seven and Kari was four, a Digi-egg appears on their family's computer screen. It hatches into a Digimon large enough for Kari to ride on. When an evil Digimon appears through a dimensional warp, Kari's Digimon fights to protect her. The other "Digidestined" kids are shown watching the fight from their bedroom windows, but they dismiss it as a dream.

*Digimon: Our War Game* (released March 4, 2000, in Japan) is a transition story between the television series' first and second seasons. The kids have returned from summer camp and gone back to their individual homes. When Izzy discovers a new, evil Digi-egg hatching, he must e-mail the team to send their Digimon into their computers to fight it before it infects every nation's military computers with a virus that will launch all their missiles and start a war.

In *Digimon: Hurricane Touchtown/The Golden Digimentals* (released July 8, 2000, in Japan), an American boy, Willis, had two Digipartners, Chocomon and Gumimon. Chocomon got a virus that maddened it. T. K. and Kari, visiting America years later, meet Willis and Gumimon who are still trying to subdue Chocomon. The latter is too strong, so T. K. and Kari summon their pals from Japan to join the effort. Chocomon tries to cure himself by turning back time to before he was infected, but this would turn all the kids into infants.

These three stories are united through voiceover dialogue by Kari. The original running times were 20, 40, and 60 minutes, respectively, so something was lost in their compression to a total of 85 minutes. (FP)

**Additional Credits:** Executive producers: Yasushi Mitsui, Makoto Shibazaki, Tan Takaiwa, Teruo Tamamura, Tsutomu Tomari, Makoto Toriyama, Makoto Yamashina. Screenplay/English voice direction: Jeff Nimoy, Bob Buchholz. Music: Udi Harpaz, Amotz Plessner. Original concept/chararter design: Akiyoshi Hongo. Cinematography: Shigeru Ando. Film editing: Gary Friedman, Douglas Purgason. Production management: Kimberly S. Moreau. Assistant directors: Yuriko Kado, Tatsuya Nagamine, Tetsuya Sato, Masafumi Tanaka. Visual effects: Omar McClinton, John R. McConnell. Computer graphics producer: Toyokazu Hattori. A Toei Animation Co., Ltd. Production.

**Dinosaur** (5/19/00) Disney. 82 mins. Directors: Ralph Zondag and Eric Leighton. Producer: Pam Marsden. Voices: D. B. Sweeney (Aladar), Alfre Woodard (Plio), Hayden Panettiere (Suri), Ossie Davis (Yar), Max Cassella (Zini), Julianna Margulies (Neera), Samuel E. Wright (Kron), Peter Siragusa (Bruton), Joan Plowright (Baylene), Della Reese (Eema).

**Consumer Tips:** ☆☆½ MPAA Rating: PG.

**Story:** An iguanodon named Aladar is raised on an island by a family of lemurs. When meteors destroy their island, they join a group of lost dinosaurs on a trek through the desert to locate a hidden nesting ground.

**Comments:** *Dinosaur* was hailed as Disney's first computer-animated feature. The film attempted to distinguish itself by an admittedly appealing blend of computer-animated characters and lush, live-action

©Walt Disney Productions

backdrops. The movie was also part of the studio's attempt to move away from its image as a producer of cuddly fairy tale musicals. The principal characters were enormous prehistoric beasts, and the plot dealt with natural disasters and survival of the fittest, as exemplified by several characters' deaths and brutal fight scenes. A sweeping epic score with occasional choral vocals replaced musical comedy routines. Though the obvious parallel was Don Bluth's more child-friendly *Land Before Time*, *Dinosaur* owes more to *Bambi*, with its coming-of-age motif, romance, and physical challenges for herd leadership. The Rites of Spring sequence from *Fantasia* is also indirectly evoked in several of the fight scenes. These scenes are often quite riveting. However, the characterization of the antagonist herd leaders, for example, is underdeveloped, and the lemurs for the most part serve only to offer sage advice and voice-over commentary to place the film's story in context, provide a fluffy distraction, and crack one-liners. Also, even more than other dinosaur films, it's somewhat difficult to appreciate the happy ending when it is clearly implied that utter extinction is still impending.

As with Disney's other recent attempts to break away from public perception and appeal to teenagers and adults as much if not more than to kids, the film failed to do as well as expected at the box office. The effects house reorganized for the film as the Secret Lab was soon largely dismantled (although the name did appear on subsequent features such as *Return to Neverland* and the live-action/CGI film *Reign of Fire*). The crew consisted of a mixture of traditional animators, computer animators, and stop-motion specialists, and numerous paleontology experts, dinosaur illustrators (notably James Gurney of the *Dinotopia* books), and sculptors were called in.

The film did fairly well at the box office ($136.5 million U.S. gross) but was considered a failure because it didn't recoup its mammoth production costs. Four years later, and following innumerable financial and structural shifts, Disney is once again returning to computer animation, although with upcoming entries such as *Chicken Little*, the studio appears to be returning to cuddly comedy. (AL)

**Additional Credits:** Screenplay: John Harrison, Robert Nelson Jacobs. Original screenplay: Walon Green. Story: Thom Enriquez, John Harrison, Robert Nelson Jacobs, Ralph Zondag. Director of story: Thom Enriquez. Story artists: Darryl Kidder, Roy Meurin, Frank Nissen, Ray Shenusay, Dick Zondag. Additional story: Julius Aguimatang, Kurt Anderson, Jim Capobianco, Ricardo Delgado, Robert Gibbs, Francis Glebas, Ben Gluck, Kirk Hanson, Doug Henderson, Fred Lucky, Floyd Norman, Tom Sito, Michael Spooner, Tamara Lusher Stocker, Oliver Thomas, Peter Von Sholly. Workbook supervisor: David Womersley. Music: James Newton Howard. Supervising animators: Mark Anthony Austin, Trey Thomas, Tom Roth, Bill Fletcher, Larry White, Eamonn Butler, Joel Fletcher, Dick Zondag, Michael Belzer, Gregory William Griffith, Atsushi Sato. Animators: Jason Anastas, Darrin Butts, Jay N. Davis, Chad Ferron, Amy McNamara, Eric Strand, Greg Maguire, Sean Mahoney, Luci Napier, Peter Lepeniotis, Christopher Oakley, Les Major, Yuriko Senoo, Alex Tysowsky, Sheryl Sardina Sackett, Henry Sato Jr., Doug Bennett, Jason Ryan, Rebecca Wilson Bresee, Sandra Maria Groeneveld, Tony Smeed, Owen Klatte, Brian Wesley Green, James Michael Crossley, Angie Glocka, Bobby Beck, Stephen A. Buckley, Kent Burton, Chris Hurtt, Don Waller, Paul Wood, Tom Gurney, Ethan Marak, Neil Richmond. Art director: Christy Maltese. Visual development/character design: Ricardo Delgado, Ian S. Gooding, Mark Hallett, Doug Henderson, David Krentz. Sculptors: Michael Floyd Jones, Gary Staab. Additional visual development: Barry Atkinson, Jim Aupperle, Hans Bacher, John Bindon, Justin Brandstater, Marek Buchwald, Brooks Campbell, Peter Clarke, Guy Deel, Paul Felix, Brian Franczak, Mike Gabriel, Jean Gillmore, Darek Gogol, Eric Goldberg, Valerie Grineau, Carlos Huerte, Caroline Hu, Terry Isaac, Buck Lewis, Rick Maki, Serge Michaels, Craig Mullins, Peter Oedekoven, Tina Price, Craig Paul, William Stout, Christophe Vacher, Marcelo Vignali.

**Dirty Duck** (7/13/77) New World. 75 mins. Director: Chuck Swenson. Producer: Jerry Good. Voices: Mark Volman (Willard), Cynthia Adler, Aynsley Dunbar, Walker Edmiston, Janet Ferguson, Jerry D. Good, Howard Kaylan, Janet Lee, Jim Pons, Don Preston, Robert Ridgeley, Lurene Tuttle.

©New World Pictures Inc.

**Consumer Tips:** ☆☆ MPAA Rating: X. Adults only. Not based on the underground comix character by the same name. Also known as *Down and Dirty Duck.*

**Story:** Uptight Willard Eisenbaum inherits a large lewd-talking duck who convinces him that sex will straighten him out.

**Comments:** In 1973, Hollywood-based independent animator Charles Swenson took "B" movie producer Roger Corman up on an offer to produce a low-budget knock off of *Fritz the Cat.* The budget was so low, the film was christened "Cheap," in honor of the penny-pinching producer. In order to keep "Cheap" cheap, Swenson did almost everything himself (except the voices and music). The production was completed in 1974 and reviewed in *Variety* at that time, but the film wasn't widely released until 1977.

The resultant work, *Dirty Duck,* is raunchier than *Fritz the Cat,* and quite crude in other ways—particularly in character designs. The unappealing rushed, squiggly Jules Feiffer–esque characters often make you wonder how a film like this could have been produced. The main plot concerns a human insurance investigator, a mild-mannered sort, with a wild imagination and overt sexual fantasies, who meets a talking duck. This film depicts their travels around the country looking for the meaning of life. There is no reason the duck should be a duck other than to give the film a catchy title.

As noted, even the title seems to have been an afterthought. Bobby London created a *Dirty Duck* underground comic strip in 1971, and it was picked up by *National Lampoon* in 1972. By the time this film came out, London's *Duck* was picked up by *Playboy* magazine, where it still runs today. This film has nothing to do with London's character.

Howard Kaylan and Mark Volman of the Turtles and Frank Zappa's Mothers of Invention (also known as the Fluorescent Leach and Eddie) perform the songs and voice the main characters.

Swenson managed to make an interesting picture despite his budget, cleverly animating over still photos and clip art. He captures the feeling of underground comics of the time, and predates edgy homegrown animation efforts such as *Beavis and Butt-Head* and the first *South Park* film.

Swenson moved onto direct bigger and better things, including *The Mouse and His Child* (1977), *Twice Upon a Time* (1983), and television series such as *Rugrats* (1991) and *Mike, Lu and Og* (1999). (JB)

**Additional Credits:** A Murakami Wolf Production. Music written/performed: Mark Volman and Howard Kaylan (Flo and Eddie).

**Doug's 1st Movie** (3/26/99) Disney. 81 mins. Director: Maurice Joyce. Producers: Jim Jenkins, David Campbell, Melanie Grisanti, Jack Spillum. Voices: Thomas McHugh (Doug Funnie, Lincoln), Fred Newman (Skeeter, Mr. Dink, Porkchop, Ned, Vocal Effects), Chris Phillips (Roger Klotz, Boomer, Larry, Mr. Chiminy), Constance Schulman (Patti Mayonaisse), Frank Welker (Herman Melville), Doug Preis (Mr. Funnie, Mr. Bluff, Willie, Chalky, Bluff Agent #1), Guy Hadley (Guy Graham), Alice Playten (Beebe Bluff, Elmo), Eddie Korbich (Al & Moo Sleech, Robocrusher), David O'Brien (Stentorian Announcer).

**Consumer Tips:** ☆ MPAA Rating: G. Don't let the Disney name fool you.

**Story:** Youngster Doug finds himself caught between saving the endangered "monster" of polluted Lucky

Duck Lake and his burning desire to take girlfriend Patti to the school dance.

**Comments:** Writer, director, and animator Jim Jinkins developed the character Doug Funnie from a series of doodles he made in 1984. He used the character's image as part of a series of "Cartoon Express" bumpers he designed for the USA Network in the mid-1980s. Joining Nickelodeon as an on-camera performer and artist on such early Nick programs as *Pinwheel* and *Hocus Focus*, Jenkins developed his *Doug* further under Nick President Gerry Laybourne's watch. The character made his debut in August 1991 as one of the first three original Nicktoons series. Jenkins teamed with producer David Campbell to form Jumbo Pictures and produced the show out of New York City.

*Doug* was not as much a sensation as *Rugrats* and *Ren and Stimpy* (which all debuted the same day), but he had his loyal followers. When Gerry Laybourne moved to Disney in 1996, she had Disney acquire Jumbo Pictures, and Disney's *Doug* premiered that fall on ABC Saturday morning. *Doug's* popularity grew and *Doug's 1st Movie*, though clearly designed for home video sell-through, was released to movie theaters.

This is possibly the sorriest animated feature to bear the Disney imprint. The animation (mainly farmed out to Korea) and the simplistic character design are a far cry from the lessons of Disney's "Nine Old Men." The film grossed a modest $19.4 million at U.S. box offices. On the plus side, the story is quite adequate and fans of the television series should enjoy themselves.

Parents may welcome the pro-social values, but the rest of us will be bored. An in-joke fantasy sequence has Doug's nemesis Roger imagining he's in a scene not unlike Marv Newland's *Bambi Meets Godzilla*. Luckily, Doug's 2nd and 3rd movies have failed to materialize. (JB)

*Additional Credits:* Writer: Ken Scarborough. Based on characters created by Jim Jinkins. Music: Mark Watters. Songs: Dan Sawyer, Fred Newman, Krysten Osborne, Linda Garvey, William Squier, Jeffrey Lodin. Storyboard supervisor: Siobhan Mullen. Storyboard coordinator: Deidre Stammers. Storyboard artists: Liz Rathke, Barking Bullfrog Cartoon Company, Jean Charles Finck, Victor Glasko, Tapani Knuutila, Jean Lajeunesse. Animation production: Plus One Animation, Inc. Supervising director: Choon-Man Lee. Animation directors: Hon-Gil Oh, Hyeon-Deok Ma, Soeng-Chean Shin, Joon-Bok Kim. NY additional animation: Mick Foran, Ray daSilva. A Jumbo Pictures Production.

### DuckTales the Movie: The Treasure of the Lost Lamp

(8/3/90) Walt Disney Pictures. 74 mins. Director/producer: Bob Hathcock. Voices: Alan Young (Scrooge McDuck), Russi Taylor (Huey, Dewy, Louie, Webbigail Vanderquack), Rip Taylor (Genie), Christopher Lloyd (Merlock), Richard Libertini (Dijon), Joan Gerber (Mrs. Beakley), Chuck McCann (Duckworth), Terence McGovern (Launchpad McQuack), June Foray (Mrs. Featherby), Charlie Adler, Steve Bulen, Jack Angel, Sherry Lynn, Mickie T. McGowan, Patrick Pinney, Frank Welker (Additional Voices).

**Consumer Tips:** ☆ MPAA Rating: G. The first Disney movie to be spun off from a television series.

**Story:** Archaeologist/Jillionaire Scrooge McDuck has spent 40 years tracking down the treasure of Collie Baba. With the help of Pilot Launchpad McQuack, nephews Huey, Dewey, and Louie, and little Webbigail Vanderquack, Scrooge finally succeeds. The dastardly Merlock is after the treasure as well, since it contains a magic lamp and genie. A comic henchman, Dijon, aids Merlock. The lamp changes hands many times in a series of thefts and mishaps, but Scrooge and the *DuckTales* gang emerge triumphant. The overworked young genie is transformed into a human boy by Scrooge's wish and all ends well.

**Comments:** The entire *DuckTales* franchise dates back to one Carl Barks, a Disney artist who spent his career producing comic books for the studio's coffers. Barks created Scrooge McDuck in 1947 and teamed him with Donald Duck's nephews; the books were very popular and today sell for exorbitant prices. Barks stopped drawing in 1967 but left behind a legacy of very stylish ducks having the kinds of adventures that every young reader could envy. In 1987 Disney decided to make a series for its new television channel based on Barks's stories and characters. *DuckTales* ran for three successful seasons before the decision to make a movie; Disney's overseas animation studio in Paris did the bulk of the work.

When a movie is made from a television series, it should be a rule of thumb that the film has something novel to offer, something that goes beyond the ordinary series or at least illuminates the backstory in a new light. *DuckTales the Movie* does neither. It is much the same as watching three consecutive half-hours of the series, with the exception of slightly better production values such as extra modeling (the use of shadows on characters and objects). The only interesting idea in this film is having a genie that is no older than the nephews. The discovery of the treasure is straight out of *Indiana Jones*, long stretches of the movie are taken up with the nephews and Webbigail making foolish wishes, and there are too many plot reversals that one can see coming from miles away.

One of the most irritating themes is the empathy we are supposed to feel for Scrooge McDuck at several points during the film. He feels cheated and humiliated because he has lost the treasure and has to face his peers at the Archeological Society. It's hard to feel sorry for someone who owns most of North America and greedily thinks of wishing for more at one point. Collie Baba's treasure, shown several times in the movie, could not fill even a corner of Scrooge's enormous swimming pool of coins and gems. The poor duck.

Merlock is not a particularly interesting villain, even with Christopher Lloyd's voice. His lackey Dijon resembles a poor cousin of Wile E. Coyote. Dijon is a cowering fool straight out of the "Yes, Sahib" school of desert movie clichés. He spends a lot of time stuffing loot down his pants; by the third time, the joke wears pretty thin.

Just for the record:

- The nephews' mother is Aunt Dumbella.
- Union rep needed: the poor genie has no less than seven masters in this film and has to grant wishes to all of them.
- What's a nice girl like you doing in a film like this? June Foray, the *grande dame* of animation's voice artists, is featured as Scrooge's secretary Mrs. Featherly. (MG)

**Additional Credits:** Screenplay: Alan Burnett. Music: David Newman. Sequence directors: Paul Brizzi, Gaetan Brizzi, Clive Pallant, Matias Marcos Rodric, Vincent Woodcock. Animation: Gary Andrews, James Baker, Javier Gutierez Blas, Eric Bouillette, Moran Caouissin, Caron Creed, Caroline Cruikshank, Roberto Corilli, Sylvain Deboissy, Joe Ekers, Mark Eoche Duval, Pierre Fassal, Al Gaivoto, Manolo Galiana, Bruno Gaumetou, Dina Gellert-Nielsen, Arnold Gransac, Teddy Hall, Peter Hausner, Francisco Alaminos Hodar, Daniel Jeannette, Nicolas Marlet, Bob McKnight, Ramon Modiano, Sean Newton, Brent Odell, Catherine Poulain, Jean-Christopher Roger, Pascal Ropars, Larry Ruppel, Stephane Sainte-Foi, Alberto Conejo Sanz, Anna Saunders, Ventura R. Vallejo, Jan Van Buyten, Duncan Varley, Simon Ward-Horner, Johnny Zeuten.

**Dumbo** (10/23/41) Walt Disney Pictures. 64 mins. Supervising director: Ben Sharpsteen. Voices: John McLeish (Narrator), Ed Brophy (Timothy Mouse), Margaret Wright (Casey Jr.), Sterling Holloway (Stork), Herman Bing (Ringmaster), Verna Felton, Sarah Selby,

©Walt Disney Productions

Dorothy Scott, Noreen Gamill (Elephants), Billy Sheets (Joe, Clown), Billy Bletcher (Clown), Cliff Edwards, Jin Carmichael, Hall Johnson Choir (Crows), Malcolm Hutton (Skinny), The King's Men (Circus Roustabouts), Harold Manley, Tony Neil, Charles Stubbs (Boys).

**Consumer Tips:** ☆☆☆ MPAA Rating: G. Adapted from *Dumbo the Flying Elephant* by Helen Aberson and Harold Pearl.

**Story:** The stork brings joy to circus elephant Mrs. Jumbo, but her sweet new baby has ears so enormous that other circus members treat little Dumbo like a freak. So do humans, leading to Mrs. Jumbo's imprisonment as a "mad elephant" when she tries to protect her son from hecklers. Abused and scorned, the tiny elephant's only friend is brash Timothy Mouse. Things take a soaring turn for the better when Dumbo discovers that his much-maligned ears enable him to fly.

**Comments:** It may be hard to recall today, but *Pinocchio, Bambi,* and *Fantasia* were initially box-office failures. With the studio's financial situation in a precarious state, Disney needed a film that was both quick and inexpensive to produce, the better to recoup much-needed profits. *Dumbo* not only met both goals, it also became one of Disney's most beloved films. A strong, direct story and an emphasis on simplicity made the film a joy to work on for animators who had struggled with verisimilitude for the past three films.

*Dumbo* features bright colors, very few special effects, minimal use of multiplane cameras, and a relaxed sense of design. The circus animals could easily fit into any *Silly Symphony,* including the key character Timothy Mouse. Any comparison to the forest creatures seen in *Bambi* is an exercise in contrast.

Story men Joe Grant and Dick Huemer, if the legends are correct, found the story in a cereal box; it was a little scroll given away as a "prize." The first screen treatment began in 1939, and Grant and Huemer kept Walt Disney interested by presenting the story to their boss chapter by chapter. The film was approved, the first in which Disney delegated virtually all the work to his staff. Distracted by financial woes and dealing with the ugly stirrings of the labor strike that would cripple the studio, Walt gave the reins to Ben Sharpsteen and lessened his own involvement in the film. By this time the Disney animators and writers were a seasoned bunch who, if asked, could definitely do more with less. Out of an $800,000 budget they crafted an endearing film filled with pathos, charm, and, yes, flying elephants.

*Dumbo*'s strengths lay in economy of storytelling backed by strong character animation. Bill Tytla animated Dumbo with an eye on the innocence and emotions of childhood; he focused his animation by observing his own baby daughter rather than an elephant. Then Tytla went a step further and began animating from his own feelings and actions as a parent. The celebrated "trunk touching" scene, in which a despairing Dumbo visits his imprisoned mother, is the culmination of Tytla's keen eye and expert draftsmanship: When Mrs. Jumbo's trunk (the only part of her that is visible in the scene) waves farewell to Dumbo, the animation is so heartfelt that it seems like a character in its own right.

Another favorite scene is the surrealistic "Pink Elephants on Parade" sequence animated by Howard Swift and Hicks Lokey. Dumbo and Timothy accidentally become intoxicated and begin to hallucinate; a fantastic array of stylized elephants put on a lively display of multicolored mayhem. Transforming at will, morphing into different shapes, sizes, and objects, the elephants give a musical concert and dance recital amidst a rapid series of unexpected cuts, fades, and zooms. This is animated fantasy—and unfettered imagination—at its finest.

Some latter-day critics find the black crows that set up the film *denouement* to be stereotypical and racially offensive, but in truth they are good-natured characters, easily the liveliest ones in the film. Animator Ward Kimball was warming up for the raucous three-bird circus he would animate in *The Three Caballeros* a few years later, and his crows get the film's best musical number, "When I See an Elephant Fly."

The movie's original title was "Dumbo of the Circus." From start to finish, production took only 17 months. Walt Kelly assisted Ward Kimball with the animation of the crows. This was Kelly's last film at Disney; he went on to create the comic strip *Pogo.*

Steven Spielberg paid tribute to *Dumbo* in his film *1941.* One of the movie's characters, General Joseph Stillwell (Robert Stack), is seen in a movie theater weeping at the "trunk touching" scene.

At only 64 minutes, this is by far the shortest Disney feature. Additional scenes were contemplated to flesh the film out for theaters, but Walt estimated that another ten minutes of animation could have cost up to $500,000. For the record, Dumbo's actual name is Jumbo Jr. (MG)

**Additional Credits:** Screen story: Joe Grant, Dick Huemer. Story development: Bill Peet, Aurie Bataglia, Joe Rinaldi, George Stallings, Webb Smith. Music: Oliver Wallace, Frank Churchill, Ned Washington. Orchestrations: Edward Plumb. Sequence directors: Norman Ferguson, Wilfred Jackson, Bill Roberts, Jack Kinney, Sam Armstrong. Animation directors: Vladimir Tytla, Fred Moore, Ward Kimball, John Lounsbery, Art Babbitt, Wolfgang Reitherman. Animators: Hugh Fraser, Harvey Toombs, Milt Neil, Hicks Lokey, Howard Swift, Don Towsley, Les Clark, Claude Smith, Berny Wolf, Ray Patterson, Jack Campbell, Grant Simmons, Walt Kelly, Joshua Meador, Don Patterson, Bill Shull, Cy Young, Art Palmer. Character designs: John P. Miller, Martin Provensen, John Walbridge, James Bodrero, Maurice Noble, Elmer Plummer. Art directors: Herb Ryman, Ken O'Connor, Terrell Stapp, Don DaGradi, Al Zinnen, Ernest Nordli, Dick Kelsey, Charles Payzant. Backgrounds: Claude Coats, Albert Dempster, John Hench, Gerald Neivus, Ray Lochrem, Joe Stahley.

**Eight Crazy Nights** (11/27/02) Columbia Pictures. 86 mins. Director: Seth Kearsley. Producers: Adam Sandler, Jack Giarrupto, Allen Covert. Voices: Adam Sandler (Davey Stone, Whitey Duvall, Eleanore Duvall, Deer),

Jackie Titone (Jennifer), Austin Stout (Benjamin), Kevin Nealon (Mayor Stewey Dewey), Rob Schneider (Chinese Waiter, Narrator), Norm Crosby (Judge), Jon Lovitz (Tom Baltezor). Additional voices: Tyra Banks, Blake Clark, Peter Dante, Ellen Albertini Dow, Kevin Farley, Lari Friedman, Tom Kenny, Cole Sprouse, Dylan Sprouse, Carl Weathers, Jamie Alcroft, Brooks Arthur, James Barbour, Allen Covert, J. D. Donaruma, Archie Hahn, Todd Holland, Lainie Kazan.

©Columbia Pictures

**Consumer Tips:** ☆½ MPAA Rating: PG-13.

**Story:** Adam Sandler animated musical comedy about a former local basketball champ who is given a second chance at redemption by aiding an old dwarf during the Hanukkah holidays.

**Comments:** *Eight Crazy Nights* is one of those films that could just as easily have been done in live action, both in terms of content and visual style. The film seems to owe more to its star and producer Adam Sandler than to its animation crew. Along with *Rover Dangerfield* and *Bebe's Kids* (posthumously based on the routines of Robin Harris), *Eight Crazy Nights* essentially presents a comedian's shtick and style in animated form. However, the film has a much weaker story than the former; the attempts to meld holiday sentiment with gross-out humor and bizarre and often pathetic characters—including an utterly unlikable lead character—fall flat. The film essentially feels like a mere exercise in ego for Sandler, who voices his animated alter ego; he also vocalizes the two cheerful grotesques, Whitey and Eleanore, who take the character in, using rather painfully contrived tones for both. Side characters similarly seem like little more than pegs for either cliché bonding situations (the love interest and her son) or for Sandler's fellow *Saturday Night Live* veterans (Rob Schneider as a stereotyped Chinese restaurant owner, Kevin Nealon as the smug mayor, etc.). *Eight Crazy Nights* is one of the few holiday movies, animated or otherwise, to address Jewish culture, but this is played mostly for cheap laughs mixed with schmaltz and strange commercialism. The many musical numbers are rather forgettable, with the possible exception of Sandler's third version of his "Chanukah Song," played over the closing titles.

Though distributed through Columbia Pictures, the animation staff was comprised of mostly displaced Warner Bros., Bluth, and DreamWorks veterans, with additional work farmed out to no less than three animation houses (A-Film in Denmark, Yowza in Canada, and Anvil Animation in Nebraska).

The U.S. box-office gross was only $23.4 million—poor for both an Adam Sandler film and an animated feature. Ultimately, *Eight Crazy Nights* found its niche amongst Sandler fans rather than animation buffs. (AL)

***Additional Credits:*** Screenplay: Brooks Arthur, Allen Covert, Brad Isaacs, Adam Sandler. Music: Ray Ellis, Marc Ellis, Teddy Castelucci. Character animation supervisor: Stephan Franck. Supervising animators: Steve Cunningham, Ralph Fernan, Holger Leige, Melina Sydney Padua. Animators: David R. Boudrea, Ken Boyer, Dave Brewster, Steven E. Gordon, Adam Henry, Bo Johannesson, Jae H. Kim, Eric Koenig, Craig Maras, James Parris, Wendy Perdue, Scott T. Peterson, Shane Prigmore, Michael Swofford, Jim Vanderkeyl, John D. Williamson, Kevin Wurzer. Animating assistants: Richard Bazley, Adam Burke, Paul Newberry. Digital effects animation: Richard Baneham, Damon Robert Crowe, Rick Echevarria, Kevin Oakley, Ryan Woodward. CGI supervisor: Christian Bouyer. CGI animators: Karl Fornander, Jeff Siergey, Kolja Erman. Additional animation supervisors: Jesper Moller (A-Film), Roger Chiasson, Len Simon (Anvil Animation). Additional animators: Valentin Amador, Line Korsgaard Andersen, Meelis Arulepp, Svetlana Bezdomnikova, Padraig Collins, Sahin Ersoz, Stefan Fjeldmark, Gabriell Genoche, Don Hander, Michael Helmuth Hansen, Gabe Hordos, Juna Jose Bravo, Christian Kuntz, Martin Madsen, Vittorio Pirajno, Evelin Temmin. Production designer: Perry Andelin Blake. Art director/layout supervisor: Phillip A. Cruden. Story artists: Steve Fonti, Jennifer Graves, Douglas McCarthy, James Tidwell, Hank

Tucker. Additional story: Julius Aguimatang, Rick Del Carmen, Lane Lueras, Aurian Redson, Armando Neito Soto III, Perry Zombolas. Character design supervisor: Fil Barlow. Character designs: Devin Crane, Helen Maier, Christopher Shannon Tindle. Backgrounds: Bari Greenberg, Robert Lowden, Brian Sebern, Don Vanderbeck, Micki Zurcher. Digital background supervisor: Dennis Venizelos. Digital backgrounds: David Bailey, Chris C. Duncan, Craig Kelly, Mary Locatell, Brian Sebern, Jesse Silver, Micki Zurcher.

## The Emperor's New Groove (12/10/00) Walt Disney Pictures. 78 mins. Director: Mark Dindal. Producer: Randy Fullmer. Voices: David Spade (Kuzco), John Goodman (Pacha), Eartha Kitt (Yzma), Patrick Warburton (Kronk), Wendie Malick (ChiCha), Kellyann Kelso (Chaca), Eli Russell Linnerty (Tipo), Bob Bergen (Bucky), Tom Jones (Theme Song Guy), Patti Deutsch (Waitress), John Fiedler (Old Man).

©Walt Disney Productions

***Consumer Tips:*** ☆☆☆ MPAA Rating: G. Hilarious film with verbal and sight gags aplenty and fine voice work by an enthusiastic cast.

***Story:*** Egotistical Emperor Kuzco owns all of ancient Central America, but that's not enough; he wants to level the village headed by gentle llama herder Pacha in order to build a summer playhouse. Behind Kuzco's back, his no-good "advisor" Yzma (aided by her incredibly stupid boy-toy Kronk) plans to poison him and claim the throne. Kronk fouls up the plot and Kuzco is turned into a llama instead. The now-humbled Emperor ends up depending on Pacha to help restore him to humanity—in more ways than one.

**Comments:** *The Emperor's New Groove* is the funniest animated film to come out of the Disney studio to date. A great deal of the comedy comes from devices alien to traditional Disney storytelling. Characters address the audience at will or even interrupt the film in order to scribble on it; situations are set up not so much to advance the plot as to add to its silliness; throwaway lines and quick innuendos abound; and the characters are so unrelentingly cartoony that any pretense at realism would have thrown the film out of balance. In one sequence where Yzma and Kronk pursue Kuzco and Pacha, the chase is shown as dotted lines on a stylized map; when the camera cuts to the action, the dotted lines are actually painted on the ground for Yzma to follow, and Kronk is generating more of them as he runs. The film begins with a flash-forward of llama Kuzco sitting miserably in the rain as his voice-over begins the tale. When that point is eventually reached in the story, Kuzco tells his own voice-over to shut up since the audience has seen it all in the movie anyway.

Critics have likened the humor in *The Emperor's New Groove* to that found in Chuck Jones' cartoons at Warner Bros. While some comic devices and gags are similar to Jones', the film owes most of its flavor to the animated offerings and sitcoms being produced for television. In fact, David Spade and Wendie Malick were stars of the snippy sitcom *Just Shoot Me*. The terminal silliness of shows such as *Pinky and the Brain* and *Freakazoid!* are echoed in *Groove*, a film that is very much a product of its times. The place may be Mesoamerica, but the dialogue is straight out of prime-time television 2000. In truth, producer Randy Fullmer and director Mark Dindal had nothing to lose: *The Emperor's New Groove* was born from total disaster and built on the wreckage of a completely different film.

The film was originally titled *Kingdom in the Sun*, then *Kingdom of the Sun*, and was to be a dramatic retelling of "The Price and the Pauper," Inca style. As production went on it was apparent that there were serious flaws in the film, mainly that it was not in the least entertaining. The story seemed to be built more around six songs written by the rock artist Sting than its characters, and after a disastrous test screening of the finished footage, producer Randy Fullmer huddled with his writers and did something that had not been done since *Pinocchio*: The entire film was dismantled and reconceived as a laugh-a-minute comedy. Sting remained on the project while codirector Roger Allers dropped out and animator Andreas Deja left to work on the film that became *Lilo and Stitch*.

As with *Pinocchio*, the revisions led to a much better film. The voice actors were given free reign to camp it up, and Spade, Warburton, and Kitt put an already funny screenplay into comic hyperdrive. A scene set in an Incan fast-food restaurant shows the trio in top form at top speed and is a true gem. *The Emperor's New Groove* is an anomaly in the canon of Disney films, but it is also a delightful flurry of goofy gags well worth repeated viewings. (MG)

**Additional Credits:** Story: Chris Williams, Mark Dindal. Screenplay: David Reynolds. Original story: Roger Allers, Matthew Jacobs. Music score: John Debney. Songs: Sting, David Hartley. Supervising animators: Nik Ranieri, Bruce W. Smith, Dale Baer, Tony Bancroft. Supervising animator (Paris unit): Dominique Monferey. Lead animators: Doug Frankel, James Lopez, Brian Ferguson, Sandro Lucio Cleuzo. Animators: Tim Allen, James Baker, Jennifer Cardon Klein, Jerry Yo Ching, Sang-Ju Kim, Mark Mitchell, Joe Oh, Jamie Oliff, Marc Pudleiner, Marc Smith, Andreas Wessel-Therhorn, Phil Young, Jared Beckstrand, Tom Gately, David Hancock, Clay Katin, Bert Klein, Theresa Wiseman, Anthony Ho Wong, Robert Espanto Domingo, Chad Stewart, Stevan Wahl, David Block, Bob Davies, Michael Stocker, Pierre Alary, Patrick Delage, Eric Delbecq, Marc Eoche Duval, Thierry Goulard, Borja Montoro Cavero, Catherine Poulain, J. C. Ttan-Quang-Thieu. Additional animation: Hendel Butoy, Mark Henn. Visual effects supervisor: Mauro Maressa. Art director: Colin Stimpson. Coart director: Thomas Cardone. Story supervisor: Stephen Anderson. Story artists: Don Hall, John Norton, Jeff R. Ranjo, Stevie Wermer, Kelly Wightman, Chris Williams. Character design: Joseph C. Moshier. Production design: Paul Felix. Layout supervisor: Jean Christophe Poulain. Layout stylists: Kevin Nelson, Rob Ruppel. Background supervisor: Natalie Franscioni-Karp.

**The Emperor's Nightingale** (5/25/51) New Trends Associates. 75 mins. Director: Jiri Trnka. Producer: Jiri Trnka, William L. Snyder. Live-action director: Milos Makovec. Voices: Boris Karloff (Narrator), Helena Patockova (The Girl), Jaromir Sobotoa (The Boy).

**Consumer Tips:** ☆☆☆ Based on the story by Hans Christian Andersen.

©Rembrandt Productions

**Story:** A little boy (in live action) dreams of his toys come to life. His dream, told with stop-motion animated puppets, concerns a Chinese emperor who enjoys the song, and friendship, of a nightingale.

**Comments:** By 1948, when the film was first produced (under the title *Cisaruv Slavík*), Czechoslovakian animator Jiri Trnka had established himself in Europe as an exceptional stop-motion animator, having previous experience working as a stage puppeteer in the 1930s and as an animator for traditional cel works, while also maintaining a busy side-career as an illustrator. The versatile Trnka even delved into live-action set design, with the stage opera *Raduz and Mubulena* in 1940 and a later live-action film with a similar title, *The Emperor and the Golem* (1955). *The Emperor's Nightingale* was his first feature-length production, and the best remembered. Trnka's choice of a Hans Christian Andersen fable about a mechanical bird was ideally suited in some ways to stop-motion animation, and begets a motif in the film. A live-action prologue, featuring two Czech child actors, sets the mood, as an ill boy imagines the narrative. As in such classic film fantasies as *Wizard of Oz*, elements of this prologue, notably the young child's playthings, find their counterparts in the fairy tale that makes up the bulk of the film (a toy monkey reworked into an aged and fussy professor is a particular delight). This device also compensates for the limits of the puppet figures, as they are intended to be seen as dreamlike toys. The music by long-time Trnka collaborator Vaclav Trojan establishes the mood, but the leisurely pacing and emphasis on charming, pantomimed set pieces may cause one's attention to wander. However, the ingenuity and charm of this early stop-motion feature is ingratiating.

Trnka followed *Emperor's Nightingale* with two subsequent, more ambitious features: *Old Czech Legends* (1953), dramatizing several epics from Czechoslovakian folklore, and *A Midsummer Night's Dream* (1959), which was later dubbed into English with a cast of Shakespeareans and released in the United States around 1960. *Emperor's Nightingale* remains the most readily accessible of his works, however. The English version of *Emperor's Nightingale* featured new narration by Boris Karloff, marking the horror actor's first foray into animation. He would later contribute to the Rankin-Bass features *The Daydreamer* and *Mad Monster Party*, the Terrytoons short *The Juggler of Our Lady* (1958), and most memorably, the perennial television special *How the Grinch Stole Christmas*. (AL)

**Additional Credits:** Screenplay: Jirí Brdecka, Jiri Trnka. English narrative: Phyllis McGinley. Original music: Václav Trojan. Cinematography: Ferdinand Pecenka.

**Escaflowne** (1/25/02) Bandai Entertainment. 96 mins. Director: Kazuki Akane. Producers: Masahiko Minami, Minoru Takanashi, Masuo Ueda, Toyoyuki Yokohama. Voices: Trevor Devall (Shesta), Brian Dobson (Nukushi), Michael Dobson (Dryden), Paul Dobson (Folken), Brian Drummond (Allen), Andrew Francis (Dilandau), Mayumi Iizuka (Sora), Willow Johnson (Yukari), Terry Klassen (Mole Man), Hisako Kyôda (Old Woman).

**Consumer Tips:** ☆☆ MPAA Rating: PG-13. SF/fantasy romantic adventure. Based on the Japanese television series *The Vision of Escaflowne*.

**Story:** High school student Hitomi Kanzaki, subject to severe depression, is frightened by the responsibilities of growing up. She is transported to the parallel world of Gaea where medieval kingdoms fight wars in airships and aerial suits of armor. Hitomi is hailed as the Wing Goddess who can empower the legendary Escaflowne armor needed by young King Van to defeat his country's enemies. But Escaflowne is powered by Hitomi's emotions, and her self-doubts may cause it to destroy Gaea.

**Comments:** *Tenku No Escaflowne* (literally "heavenly Escaflowne" but translated to English as *The Vision of Escaflowne*) was a 26-episode television series by the Sunrise studio (April 2, 1996 to September 24, 1996), taking the boys'-adventure sci-fi formula of adolescent heroes in "giant robot" transformable battle suits and turning it into a girls' romantic fantasy. Hitomi Kanzaki, a high school student popular with her friends for telling their futures with tarot cards, is transported to the alternate world of Gaea where our earth looms in its sky like a huge moon. Gaea is designed around medieval Europe and Celtic spiritual themes. There are kingdoms of humans and exotic cat- and wolf-people fighting wars with sword-wielding knights on horseback and in flying suits of armor powered by "magic." Hitomi at first only wants to return to Tokyo, but the longer she is in Gaea, the more emotionally attached she becomes to its handsome tragic heroes; notably young King Van of Fanelia whose land has been overrun by the brutal Zaibach empire and who secretly doubts his competence to liberate it; Sir Allen of Asturia who is ordered by his own king to break his oaths of friendship to Van; and Van's brother Folken, apparently a noble traitor who is forced to betray Fanelia to Zaibach for honorable reasons. There are hints that Gaea's magic is an unknown technology controlled by psychic powers and that Hitomi's affinity to seeing flashes of the future indicates that she may have the greatest psychic strength on the planet. This makes her a target of Zaibach, whose emperor wants to either kidnap and control her or kill her.

The television series was tremendously popular, and fans in Japan demanded a movie. *Escaflowne* (called *Escaflowne: A Girl in Gaea* in Japanese publicity; June 24, 2000) is a condensation of the story in impressively higher-quality animation, but with a much darker emotional tone. Hitomi is changed from an adolescent excited by thoughts of her first romantic encounters to a solitary girl subject to such fits of depression that she wishes she could "disappear from the world." Her wish transports her to Gaea (now modeled upon ancient China and Japan rather than Europe), where the conquering Black Dragon empire has just overrun the kingdom of Fanelia.

*Escaflowne* (called *Escaflowne: The Movie* in American publicity) is visually beautiful but grim, violent, and depressing. The television serial's condensation into 96 minutes robs the story of most of its depth. What shallow personalities the main characters have are emotionally tortured and seriously disturbed, making it difficult for audiences to care for any of them. (FP)

**Additional Credits:** Screenplay: Kazuki Sekine, Ryota Yamaguchi. English adaptation producer: Charles McCarter. Screenplay adaptation: Robert Chomiak. Animation director/character designer: Nobuteru Yuki. Original music: Yôko Kanno, Hajime Mizoguchi, Inon Zur. Creator: Shôji Kawamorim, Hajime Yatate. Video post-production: Leland Miller.

## The Extraordinary Adventures of the Mouse and His Child See *The Mouse and His Child.*

**Fantasia** (11/13/40) Walt Disney Pictures. 120 mins. Production supervisor: Ben Sharpsteen. Directors: Samuel Armstrong ("Toccata and Fugue," "The Nutcracker Suite"), James Algar ("The Sorcerer's Apprentice"), Bill Roberts ("Rite of Spring"), Hamilton Luske ("The Pastoral Symphony"), T. Hee ("Dance of the Hours"), Wilfred Jackson ("Night on Bald Mountain," "Ave Maria"). Voices: Deems Taylor (Narrator), Walt Disney (Mickey Mouse), Leopold Stokowski (Conductor).

©Walt Disney Productions

**Consumer Tips:** ☆☆☆☆ MPAA Rating: G. A landmark film in animation history, *Fantasia* is an ambitious attempt to fuse classical music, animation, and state-of-the-art technology into what Walt Disney hoped would represent a new form of entertainment.

**Story:** *Fantasia* is composed of seven unrelated animated vignettes, all structured around popular pieces of classical music.

**Comments:** Originally titled "The Concert Feature," *Fantasia* grew out of a proposed two-reel Mickey Mouse short based on Paul Dukas' 1897 composition *The Sorcerer's Apprentice.* Walt Disney met Leopold Stokowski, the colorful conductor of the Philadelphia Orchestra, by chance in a restaurant in 1937 and discussed the short with him. The maestro readily pledged his cooperation. As "Apprentice" developed, however, its cost escalated to over $125,000, which would be impossible to recoup as a theatrical short. Disney decided at that point to expand the original idea and include several pieces of animation set to classical music. Stokowski and Disney finally settled on the following selections after eliminating several others: *Toccata and Fugue in D Minor* (J. S. Bach), *The Nutcracker Suite* (Piotr Ilyich Tchaikovsky), *Rite of Spring* (Igor Stravinsky), *The Pastoral Symphony* (Ludwig van Beethoven), *Dance of the Hours* (Amilcare Ponchielli), and a medley of *Night on Bald Mountain* (Modest Moussorgsky) and *Ave Maria* (Franz Schubert) joined the Dukas piece.

*Fantasia's* strengths and flaws are best examined within each section. The "Toccata and Fugue" was intended to be an abstract piece but the most daring animation does not appear until the Fugue section. While interesting, there is always the feeling that the animation team headed by Cy Young is restrained by having to tie images to the concept of an orchestra playing classical music. Only late in the Fugue do the images break into pure abstraction, and by then the piece is over.

"The Nutcracker Suite," consisting of eight brief movements heard in Tchaikovsky's ballet, represents Disney animation acknowledging its past as it faced the future. Much of this segment resembles Disney's own *Silly Symphonies* of the 1930s, particularly "The Dance of the Sugar Plum Fairy," "Dance of the Reed Flutes," and "Waltz of the Flowers." The difference lies in stronger drawing, animation, and layout, not to mention an army of special effects artists. Lacking modern computer-generated tools, the effects team dressed up "The Nutcracker Suite" with airbrush, stipple, the application of paint to both sides of a cel, diaphanous paint, and every other trick of the trade known to animation. Still, most people remember not the effects but a charming sequence in which Chinese mushrooms perform a sedate dance constantly thrown out of rhythm by the smallest mushroom, Hop Low. It would become animator Art Babbitt's signature piece.

The short that started it all, "The Sorcerer's Apprentice," is actually the heart of *Fantasia.* It is ironic that the segment starring Mickey Mouse as a wayward wizard-in-training most honestly expresses what *Fantasia* was intended to do: entertain audiences with a seamless blend of animated action and popular classical music. Mickey is bored with his chores, appropriates his master's magical hat, brings a broom to life to take over the job of fetching water, and quickly loses control of things. Lacking the knowledge to stop the mayhem, Mickey makes things worse until the sorcerer awakens and fixes the mess with one sweeping gesture. Mickey was redesigned for "apprentice" by animator Fred Moore; for the first time Mickey would have eyes with pupils as well as a body that could accommodate more realistic movement. Moore teamed with animators Les Clark, Bill Tytla, and Preston Blair to create a mini-masterpiece.

The animation could not have fit Dukas' piece better. Stokowski and the Disney animators enjoyed a synergistic creativity present nowhere else in the film. When one views the scene where Mickey commands the broom to life and the one where he dreams he is atop a mountain commanding the heavens and seas it is difficult to believe that Paul Dukas did not actually work at the Disney studio in 1940. "The Sorcerer's Apprentice" is a deceptively simple, brilliantly executed vignette that gave *Fantasia* its defining symbol; Mickey Mouse, clad in a blue peaked hat bedecked with stars and crescent moons.

"Rite of Spring" details the origin of the planet earth and its development up to the extinction of the dinosaurs. Like the Stravinsky score, much of it brims with vivid primeval power. The birth of our planet, awash in violent volcanic eruptions and swaths of boiling lava, is followed by the evolution of life from single-celled organisms to mighty saurians. Woolie Reitherman toiled long and hard to animate the spectacular struggle between a Tyrannosaurus rex and a stegosaurus as a thunderstorm rages, the highlight of this majestic segment.

After a brief diversion featuring a short jazz improv and an animated soundtrack, *Fantasia* seriously falters for the first time. "The Pastoral Symphony" started out as a study of classical Greek myths set to the music of Pierne's *Cydalise et le Chevre-pied*. Disney decided that the music was inferior to Beethoven's for the purposes of animating his mythological travelogue. The result was a misfire, not least because "The Pastoral Symphony" features gods who make Goofy seem bright, twee cherubs, too-cute centaurs and centaurettes that are animated poorly, and backgrounds far too grand for such cartoonish twaddle. The music had to be cropped to fit the action, infuriating purists. At least one layout artist attempted to convince Disney that the animation called for the stylization found in Greek art of the period, but Disney would have none of it. This segment is generally regarded as the film's poorest.

There is a rebound with "Dance of the Hours," an endearingly silly ballet performed by hippos, ostriches, elephants, and alligators—the most ungainly animals possible to cast as a dance troupe. Played for laughs and dead-on in its parody of ballet, "Hours" features John Lounsberry's stellar work on Ben Ali Gator, the lusty leader of a balletic crew of crocs. Famous ballerinas of the era, including the great Irina Baranova, posed for the artists, who by all accounts greatly enjoyed working on this delightful sequence.

*Fantasia*'s finale begins with "Night on Bald Mountain." Animator Bill Tytla had done yeoman's work at Disney, hitting his stride while animating on *Snow White*. This sequence of *Fantasia* cemented Tytla's reputation as one of the greatest living animators of his era. The story of "Bald Mountain" is summed up as the wakening of Tchernobog, the Slovonic god of evil, who presides over a hellish Witches' Sabbath on Walpurgis Night. Designer Kay Neilsen designed a terrifying horned god for the sequence but it was Tytla who brought him to life. Seldom have the powers of darkness and evil been so vividly represented on screen. Tchernobog, his stark musculature seemingly carved from the mountain's stone, grins evilly as demons, witches, ghosts, and incubi swarm about him or dance in his massive palms. Every gesture and pose the dark god strikes is imbued with naked power, and even as church bells force him back into an unwilling repose, Tchernobog is never truly defeated. As with all evil, he will someday return. "Bald Mountain" then segues into "Ave Maria," which completes the victory of the holy over evil. A procession of pilgrims seen in long shot serenely pass through a foggy wood, candles in hand as the hymn is sung. Dawn then breaks, filling the sky with light and the world with hope.

*Fantasia* was produced for $2,280,000; the music alone accounted for $400,000 of the cost. The movie did not break even until its third release in 1956.

For the record:

- Production of this film took three full years.
- One byproduct of *Fantasia* was the invention of stereophonic sound by Bill Garity and the Disney engineers. The multichannel process was called Fantasound.
- Disney also envisioned filming the "Toccata and Fugue" in 3-D and filling the air with floral fragrances and incense during "The Nutcracker Suite" and "Ave Maria," respectively.
- The sorcerer was modeled on Disney and was named Yen Sid—spell it backwards.
- The Chinese mushrooms were originally Chinese lizards.
- Due to technical problems with "Ave Maria," the film was finished only one day before its premiere.
- Mickey reprised his role as the Sorcerer's Apprentice in a direct-to-video release called *Mickey's House of Villains* in 2004.
- Hyacinth Hippo and the enchanted brooms had cameos in the 1988 film *Who Framed Roger Rabbit*.
- Disney planned to update the film every year with new segments but never followed up; his nephew Roy Jr. updated the film for the first time 34 years after Walt's death. (MG)

**Additional Credits:** Story directors: Joe Grant, Dick Huemer. "Toccata and Fugue in D Minor" music: Johan Sebastian Bach. Story: Lee Blair, Elmer Plummer, Phil Dike. Animators: Cy Young, Art Palmer, Daniel McManus, George Rowley, Edwin Aardal, Joshua Meador, Cornett Wood. Art director: Robert Cormack. Backgrounds: Joe Stanley, John Hench, Nino Carbe. "The Nutcracker Suite" music: Peter Ilich Tchaikovsky. Story: Sylvia Moberly-Holland, Norman Wright, Albert Heath, Bianca Majolie, Graham Heid. Animators: Arthur Babbitt, Les Clark, Don Lusk, Cy Young, Robert Stokes. Character designers: John Walbridge, Elmer Plummer, Ethel Kulsar. Art directors: Robert Cormack, Al Zinnen, Curtiss D. Perkins, Arthur Byram, Bruce Bushman. Backgrounds: John Hench, Ethel Kulsar, Nino Carbe. "The Sorcerer's Apprentice" music: Paul Dukas. Story: Perce

Pearce, Carl Fallberg. Animation supervisors: Fred Moore, Vladimir Tytla. Animators: Les Clark, Riley Thomson, Marvin Woodward, Preston Blair, Edward Love, Ugo D Orsi, George Rowley, Cornett Wood. Art directors: Tom Codrick, Charles Phillipi, Zack Schwartz. Backgrounds: Claude Coats, Stan Spohn, Albert Dempster, Eric Hansen. "The Rite of Spring" music: Igor Stravinsky. Story development/research: William Martin, Leo Thiele, Robert Sterner, John Fraser McLeish. Animation supervisors: Wolfgang Reitherman, Joshua Meador. Animators: Philip Duncan, John McManus, Paul Busch, Art Palmer, Don Tobin, Edwin Aardal, Paul B. Kossoff. Art direction: McLaren Stewart, Dick Kelsey, John Hubley. Backgrounds: Ed Starr, Brice Mack, Edward Levitt. "Pastoral Symphony" music: Ludwig von Beethoven. Story development/research: Otto Englander, Webb Smith, Erdman Penner, Joseph Sabo, Bill Peet, George Stallings. Animation supervisors: Fred Moore, Ward Kimball, Eric Larson, Arthur Babbitt, Oliver M. Johnston Jr., Don Towsley. Animators: Berny Wolf, Jack Campbell, John Bradbury, James Moore, Milt Neil, Bill Justice, John Elliotte, Walt Kelly, Don Lusk, Lynn Karp, Murray McClellan, Robert W. Youngquist, Harry Hamsel. Art directors: Hugh Hennesy, Kenneth Anderson, J. Gordon Legg, Herbert Ryman, Yale Gracey, Lance Nolley. Backgrounds: Claude Coats, Ray Huffine, W. Richard Anthony, Arthur Riley, Gerald Nevius, Roy Forkum. "Dance of the Hours" music: Amilcare Ponchielli. Supervising animator: Norman Ferguson. Animators: John Lounsbery, Howard Swift, Preston Blair, Hugh Fraser, Harvey Toombs, Norman Tate, Hicks Lokey, Art Elliott, Grant Simmons, Ray Patterson, Frank Grundeen. Character designs: Martin Provensen, James Brodrero, Duke Russell, Earl Hurd. Art directors: Kendall O'Connor, Harold Doughty, Ernest Nordli. Backgrounds: Albert Dempster, Charles Conner. "Night on Bald Mountain" music: Modest Moussorgsky. "Ave Maria" music: Franz Schubert. Story development: Campbell Grant, Arthur Heinemann, Phil Dike. Supervising animator: Vladimir Tytla. Animation: John McManus, William N. Schull, Robert W. Carlson Jr., Lester Novros, Don Patterson. Effects animation: Joshua Meador, Miles E. Pike, John F. Reed, Daniel MacManus. Art directors: Kay Nielsen, Terrell Stapp, Charles Payzant, Thor Putnam. Backgrounds: Merle Cox, Ray Lockrem, Robert Storms, W. Richard Anthony.

**Fantasia/2000** (12/17/99) Walt Disney Pictures. 74 mins. Directors: Pixote Hunt ("Symphony No. 5"), Hendel Butoy ("Pines of Rome," "Piano Concerto No. 2, Allegro, Opus 102"), Eric Goldberg ("Rhapsody in Blue," "Carnival of the Animals"), James Algar ("The Sorcerer's Apprentice"), Frances Glebas ("Pomp and

©Walt Disney Productions

Circumstance, Marches 1, 2, 3, and 4"), Gaetan and Paul Brizzi ("Firebird Suite—1919 Version"). Producer: Don Ernst. Voices: Wayne Allwine (Mickey Mouse), Tony Anselmo (Donald Duck), Russi Taylor (Daisy Duck). "Pomp and Circumstance" featured soprano: Kathleen Battle. "Pomp and Circumstance" choral: Chicago Symphony Chorus. Guest appearances: Leopold Stokowski, Bette Midler, Steve Martin, Penn and Teller, Itzhak Perlman, Quicy Jones, James Earl Jones, Angela Lansbury.

**Consumer Tips:** ☆☆☆½ MPAA Rating: G. The long-awaited continuation of Walt Disney's 1940 *magnum opus* features eight more animated vignettes set to popular and classical music.

**Story:** Like the original *Fantasia*, there is no cohesive narrative. A new addition: guest stars now introduce each segment. A venerable holdover: "The Sorcerer's Apprentice" from the 1940 film, cleaned up and restored to pristine perfection.

**Comments:** Roy Disney Jr. teamed with conductor James Levine of the Metropolitan Opera to fulfill one of the few dreams Walt Disney never attained: the updating of the 1940 classic *Fantasia*. Under the working title "Fantasia Continued" the following selections were chosen to join "The Sorcerer's Apprentice": "Symphony No. 5" (Ludwig van Beethoven), "Pines of Rome" (Ottorino Respighi), "Rhapsody in Blue" (George Gershwin), "Piano Concerto No. 2, Allegro,

©Walt Disney Productions

Opus 102" (Dmitri Shostakovich), "Carnival of the Animals" (Camille Saint-Saens), "Pomp and Circumstance—Marches 1, 2, 3, and 4" (Sir Edward Elgar), and "Firebird Suite—1919 Version" (Igor Stravinsky).

This time the Disney animators and effects crew possessed an awesome array of computer technology and used it to maximum effect. From digital paint to a "particle generator" that allowed the animation of up to a million separate points of light, the technical wonders of *Fantasia/2000* pervaded every frame. "Piano Concerto No. 2" was, in fact, mostly computer generated.

"Symphony No. 5" is a counterpart to the original film's "Toccata and Fugue in D Minor." Both open their respective versions of *Fantasia* and both feature pure abstraction. "Symphony No. 5" is superior, however, in that it does not focus on the orchestra and anchors its images in a loose but identifiable story.

"Pines of Rome" is an amazing fantasy in which a cosmic anomaly gives computer-generated whales the power to fly to the very edge of space itself. Unforgettable images include a pod of whales steadily ascending through the atmosphere in unison until they burst through the clouds to leap with joy. The segment is somewhat weakened by focusing on one young whale for much of its length, especially since the artists have imbued him with cartoon-like eyes and eyebrows that do not fit with his three-dimensional design.

Animator Eric Goldberg had been working on an independent short based on George Gershwin's "Rhapsody in Blue" while at Disney. Goldberg's concept of merging Gershwin's music with the flowing line of car-

icaturist Al Hirschfeld and the urban bustle of New York City circa 1930 made this short especially creative, and Roy Disney asked that the 12-minute piece be included in the new *Fantasia*. At the same time the production known as "Kingdom of the Sun" went into hiatus while being rewritten as *The Emperor's New Groove*. The artists were diverted to Goldberg's project, enabling him to finish it in nine months. Goldberg's wife Susan was art director for the sequence and turned in an incredible job matching color to mood and music simultaneously. "Rhapsody" tells the story of four lives intersecting in the big city and is one of the most sophisticated and smoothest animated shorts of all time.

"Piano Concerto No. 2" is adapted from Hans Christian Andersen's *The Steadfast Tin Soldier* and is notable for the extensive computer animation used in the sequence. The story is unremarkable but some of the effects, such as the computer-generated ballerina, are uncanny.

Eric and Susan Goldberg struck again in the "Carnival of the Animals" sequence, which is simply two minutes of pure, energetic fun. Six dignified flamingoes are constantly embarrassed by a seventh, who slings a yo-yo around at breakneck speed. Master animator and director Chuck Jones had always impressed Goldberg, and many of the facial expressions that cross the birds' beaks reflect Jones' influence. Susan Goldberg, meanwhile, came up with a bright watercolor palette for the sequence, and it is one of *Fantasia/2000*'s triumphs.

"The Sorcerer's Apprentice" follows and remains as much a masterwork as it was in 1940. Immediately afterwards, Donald Duck is featured as Noah's assistant in "Pomp and Circumstance." Director Francis Glebas went for the 1940s style of animation that suited Donald best, and the result is an energetic, beautifully animated—but not particularly outstanding—Donald Duck short.

*Fantasia/2000* concludes like its predecessor; a display of raw elemental power is resolved into a message of hope. Nature's messenger, in the form of a great elk, awakens a lovely vernal sprite. She proceeds to bring lush, green life to the land until she encounters a volcanic mountain where nothing will grow. Within its crater lies the fearsome firebird, who roars to life at the sprite's curious touch. The firebird pursues the hapless sprite, destroying the entire landscape in a maelstrom of fire and lava before he corners and consumes his quarry.

The elk sifts through the ashes of the ruined land until he finds the dejected sprite in a pile of ashes and gently urges her back to her duty. Her tears produce plants where they strike the ground, and the sprite, rejuvenated once more, regenerates the entire forest.

"Firebird" is the most lyrical and beautiful segment of the film, swelling and stirring with the force of Stravinsky's music. The vernal sprite was animated in 2-D and then enhanced with computer effects to produce a supernatural beauty in her appearance and movement. The firebird was animated in 2-D as well but his flaming grandeur was composed of hand-drawn effects, making him a rougher, more primal counterpoint to the sprite. The effects animation, featuring Disney's spectacular particle generator, are first-rate throughout.

It is difficult, and perhaps futile, to compare the two *Fantasia*s, except to say that the second version contains more narrative in its sequences. Both films bear the Disney imprimatur, but in truth they are two different films made by different teams using different technology. Both share the same general concept but execute it in a different spirit. Walt Disney put his studio on the line with a bold experiment; Roy Disney was simply building on what had gone before, and *Fantasia/2000* is a far more relaxed, comfortable film as a result.

*Fantasia 2000* was actually released in the last month of 1999. It was the first feature film to be shown in the large-format IMAX process. The film played exclusively in the giant-screen IMAX theaters for a few months, usually to large crowds, before moving to general release.

For the record:

- The yo-yo flipping flamingo's name is "Punkin."
- A caricature of George Gershwin, animated by Eric Goldberg, appears in the "Rhapsody in Blue" segment as does trade journalist/Disney historian John Culhane.
- Steve Martin, Bette Midler, James Earl Jones, and Angela Lansbury all had voice parts in Disney films at one time or another. (MG)

**Additional Credits:** Executive producer: Roy E. Disney. Supervising animation director: Hendel Butoy. Conductor: James Levine, with the Chicago Symphony Orchestra. Special musical arrangements: Bruce Coughlin. Music consultant: Chris Montan. Artistic coordinator/visual effects supervisor: David A. Bossert. Layout supervisor: Mitchell Guintu Bernal. Background supervisor: Dean Gordon. Clean-up supervisor: Alex Topete. CGI supervisors: Steve Goldberg, Shyh-Chyuan Huang, Susan Thayer, Mary Jane "MJ" Turner. "Symphony No. 5" music: Ludwig van Beethoven. Animators: Wayne Carlisli, Raul Garcia. Story development: Kelvin Yasuda. "Pines of Rome" music: Ottorino Respigini. Art directors: Dean Gordon, William Perkins. Story development: James Fuji, Francis Glebas (original concept: Brenda Chapman, Christopher Sanders). Animation: Linda Bel, Darrin Butts, Darko Cesar, Sasha Dorogov, Sergei Kouchnerov, Andrea Losch, Teresa Martin, Branko Mihanovic, William Recinos, William Wright. Visual development: Francis Glebas, Kelvin Yasuda. Character design: Tina Price, Rick Maki. "Rhapsody in Blue" music: George Gershwin (Conductor/supervisor: Bruce Broughton. Piano: Ralph Grierson). Story: Eric Goldberg. Animation: Tim Allen, James Baker, Jared Beckstrand, Nancy Beiman, Jerry Yu Ching, Andreas Deja, Robert Espanto Domingo, Brian Ferguson, Douglas Frankel, Thomas Gateley David Hancock, Sang-Jin Kim, Bert Klein, Joe Oh, Jamie Oliff, Mark Pudleiner, Michael Show, Marc Smith, Chad Stewart, Michael Stocker, Andreas Wessel-Therhorn, Theresa Wiseman, Anthony Ho Wong, Ellen Woodbury, Phil Young, Eric Goldberg. Visual effects: Mauro Maressa. Assistant head of effects: Marlon West. Effects animators: Colbert Fennelly, Michael Cadwallader Jones, Dorse A. Lanpher, Dan Lund, David J. Mildenberger. Art director: Susan McKinsey Goldberg. Artistic consultant: Al Hirschfeld. Layout: Rasoul Azadani. Layout journeymen: Douglas Walker, Antonio Navarro, Jeffrey Purves. Backgrounds: Natalie Franscioni-Karp. Background journeymen: Gregory C. Miller, Tom Woodington. Blue sketch: Bill Davis. "Piano Concerto No. 2, Allegro, Opus 102" music: Dmitri Shostakovich (Piano: Yefim Brinfman). Story development: James Capobianco, Roy Meurin (based on the story "The Steadfast Tin Soldier" by Hans Christian Andersen). Animation: Tim Allen, Doug Bennett, Eamonn Butler, Darrin Butts, Sandro Cleuzo, Steve Hunter, Ron Husband, Mark Kausler, Sang-Jin Kim, David Kuhn, Roy Meurin, Gregory G. Miller, Neil Richmond, Jason Ryan, Henry Sato Jr. Art director: Michael Humphries. Visual development: Hans Bacher, Guy Deel, Caroline Hu. Character design: Sergei Kouchnerov, Gary J. Perkovac, Nik Ranieri. Ballet choreography: Kendra McCool. "Carnival of the Animals (Le Carnaval des Animaux)" music: Camille Saint-Saens. Story and animation: Eric Goldberg. Art director: Susan McKinsey Goldberg. Original concept: Joe Grant. Conceptual storyboard: Vance

Gerry, David Cutler. Watercolorists: Jill A. Petrilak, Emily Jiu-liano, Fara Rose, Mary Jo Ayers, Christina Stocks, Jennifer Phillips. "Pomp and Circumstance—Marches 1, 2, 3, & 4" music: Sir Edward Elgar (arranged by Peter Schickele). Story development: Robert Gibbs, Todd Kurosawa, Don Dougherty, Terry Naughton, Patrick Ventura, Stevie Wermers. Lead animator: Tim Allen. Animators: Doug Bennett, Tim George, Mark Kausler, Sang-Jin Kim, Roy Meurin, Gregory G. Miller. Art director: Daniel Cooper. Visual development: William Frake III, Darek Gogol. Character design: Jeffrey R. Ranjo, Peter Clarke. "Firebird Suite—1919 Version" music: Igor Stravinsky. Directors/designers/story: Paul Brizzi and Gaetan Brizzi. Lead animators: Anthony DeRosa, Ron Husband, John Pomeroy. Animators: Tim Allen, Sandro Cleuzo, David Hancock, Sang-Jin Kim, Gregory G. Miller, Joe Oh, David Alan Zaboski. Art director: Carl Jones. Concept for "Death and ReBirth of the Forest": Elena Driskill. Visual development: Kelvin Yasuda. "Host Sequences" director: Don Hahn. Writers: Don Hahn, Irene Mecchi, David Reynolds (story development by Kirk Hanson). Character animator: Andreas Deja. Design: Pixote Hunt. Visual effects supervisor: Richard Hollander.

**Fantastic Planet** (12/1/73) New World Pictures. 72 mins. Director: Rene Laloux. Producers: Simon Damiani, Ande Valio-Cavglione. English voices: Barry Bostwick (Terr), Marvin Miller (Chief of the Oms, Master Kon), Olan Soule (Master Taj), Cynthia Adler, Nora Heflin, Hal Smith (Master Sihn, Om Sorceror), Mark Gruner, Monika Ramirez, Janet Waldo (Hollow Log Chief, Traag Child).

**Consumer Tips:** ☆☆½ MPAA Rating: PG.

©Les Films Armorial-Paris

**Story:** On the planet Ygam, giant androids—the Draags—face resistance from the humanoid Oms.

**Comments:** The late animator/director Rene Laloux, who passed away in March 2004, was a distinctive figure in French animation, producing often-hypnotic science-fiction epics. *Fantastic Planet* is the perfect example of this, and both the English and French titles (*Le Planete Sauvage*) appropriately describe the film. The tale of clashes between humans (here called Oms) and giant, intelligent alien beings known as Traags, is populated by an ecosystem of strange plants and animals. Sexual symbolism abounds, often overtly, as the aliens gain intellectual and erotic stimulus through meditation in rather unusual ways. Yet the film does not come across as exploitational or intentionally bawdy. The emphasis is less on fluid, lively character animation than on visuals that resemble moving illustrations. The dialogue was redubbed into English by an able crew including radio veterans Olan Soule and Marvin Miller, and relative newcomer Barry Bostwick as the protagonist. However, spoken dialogue is minimal, with narration filling in most of the gaps. The presumably allegorical narrative, containing a cautionary message about self-destruction, is trumped by the surreal and compelling visuals, creating a harsh world full of cruelty and savagery. In one scene, a newly hatched creature is licked maternally by another creature, only to immediately be consumed. The domestic humans are dressed in bizarre, prissy costumes and used in dogfights. In many ways, the film is far more "adult" than subsequent films that actively tried to be so.

The film was in some ways a coproduction with Czechoslovakia, initially utilizing the studio of Czech puppet animator Jiri Trnka. Laloux's subsequent films, *The Time Masters* (1981) and *Light Years* (1988), were also released in the United States—the latter of which boasted an English-language script by Isaac Asimov. In general, though, both seem to have attracted less interest and attention than *Fantastic Planet*, and have fallen into obscurity. (AL)

**Additional Credits:** Writers: Rene Laloux, Roland Topor (based on the novel Ems En Serie by Stefan Wul). English script: Stephen Hayes. Original artwork: Roland Topor. Music: Alain Gorogeur. Character graphics: Josef Kabrt. Set graphics: Josef Vana. Animation: Jindrick Barta, Zdena Bartova, Bohumil Sedja, Zdenek Sob, Karel Strebl, Jiri Vokoum. A Les Films Armorial/Service De Recherche Ortif Production.

## Ferngully . . . The Last Rainforest (4/10/92) 20th

Century Fox. 74 mins. Director: Bill Kroyer. Producers: Peter Faiman, Wayne Young, Jim Cox, Brian Rosen, Richard Harper. Voices: Tim Curry (Hexxus), Samantha Mathis (Crysta), Christian Slater (Pips), Jonathan Ward (Zak), Grace Zabriskie (Magi Lune), Robin Williams (Batty Koda), Geoffrey Blake (Ralph), Robert Pastorelli (Tony), Tommy Chong (Stump), Cheech Marin (Root), Tone Loc (The Goanna), Townsend Coleman (Knotty), Brian Cummings (Ock), Kathleen Freeman (Elder #1).

©FAI Film Pty. Ltd.

**Consumer Tips:** ☆☆☆ MPAA Rating: G. Based on the stories of "FernGully" by Diana Young.

**Story:** Evil spirit Hexxus, imprisoned in an enchanted tree, is released by workers leveling a rain forest. One of the crew, Zak, is reduced to pixie size by a winged sprite, Crysta. With the help of the fairy kingdom, and a burnt-out laboratory escapee, Batty, the battle commences against the forces of evil.

**Comments:** Australian author Diana Young began writing *FernGully* stories for children in 1980. Producers Peter Faiman and Wayne Young (*Crocodile Dundee*) began developing *FernGully* as an animated film in 1982, designing the film to assist in the effort of preserving the Australian rain forest. The producers sought cooperation from Greenpeace, the Rainforest Foundation, the Sierra Club, and the Smithsonian Institution.

All of these organizations received a piece of the profits from the final film.

20th Century Fox, with its own eye on Disney and Spielberg's success with animated features, decided to pick up the project. It brought in screenwriter Jim Cox (*The Rescuers Down Under* and *Oliver and Company*) to write and coproduce.

Bill Kroyer (*Tron*) was signed to direct. In an old Van Nuys brewery, a studio was set up to create a feature film that could compete with Disney and Spielberg (animation and various other production functions were farmed out to Toronto, London, Copenhagen, and Korea). The end result is *FernGully . . . the Last Rainforest*, which is a delightfully lush animated feature.

In February of 1990, animation director Tony Fucile (*The Little Mermaid*) and art director Victoria Jenson (subsequently the codirector of *Shrek*), joined Kroyer and key personnel on a trip to the Australian rain forest. There they photographed, researched, sketched, painted, and were inspired by what would become the film's setting. Kroyer created an "artist-run studio" where everyone was encouraged to offer input.

The voice cast was excellent—particularly the choice of Robin Williams (just before his turn as the genie in *Aladdin*) as the brain-damaged Batty Koda. It's too bad he's a bit restrained here and is not as loose as he would be with his Disney role. Cheech and Chong as the Beetle Boys, Tim Curry as evil Hexxus, and Tone Loc as a threatening, rap-singing lizard also make memorable impressions.

The film grossed a decent $24.6 million in the spring of 1992 and spawned a direct-to-video sequel, *FernGully 2: The Magical Rescue*, in 1997. Bill Kroyer went on to develop the feature film *Quest for Camelot* (1998) for Warner Bros., then left that project to direct the CG-starring characters (for Rhythm and Hues) in such hybrid features as *Cats and Dogs* (2001), *Scooby Doo* (2002), and *Garfield the Movie* (2004). (JB)

**Additional Credits:** Screenplay: Jim Cox. Music: Alan Silvestri. Music supervision: Tim Sexton, Becky Mancuso. Animation director: Tony Fucile. Sequence directors: Bret Haaland, Tim Hauser, Dan Jeup, Susan Kroyer. Supervising animators: Stephen Franck (A-Film), Dave Brewster, Greg Manwaring (Kroyer Films). Animation supervisor: Tim Hauser. Computer animation supervisor: Mark Pompain. Leading character animators: Doug Frankel, David Brewster, Chrystal Klabunde, Jeffrey James Varab, Kathy Zielinski, John Allen Armstrong, Dan Kuenster, Chuck Gammage, Stefan Fjeldmark. Animators: Jesse Cosio, Anne Marie Bardwell, Wendy Perdue, Bret Haaland, Mike Cachuela, Ken Bruce, Tony Fucile, Susan Kroyer, Greg Manwaring, Dan Jeup, Mike Genz, Rob Schedlowich, Roy Meurin, Chris Sauve, Susan M. Zytka, Ralph Eggleston, Mark Sevier, Greg Hill, John Collins, Hana Kukal, Jamie Oliff, Bob Scott, John Eddings, Roger Chiasson, Charlie Bonifacio, Doug Bennett, Bibo Bergeron, Ulrich W. Meyer, Glen Sylvester, David Bowers, Steve Markowski. Additional animators: Albanassios Vakalis, Kevin Johnson, Robert Gibbs, Dave Kupczyk, Rick Villeneuve, Shane Zalvin, Gary Andrews, Kevin Wurzer, Linda Miller, Mark Koetsier, Chris Mitchell, Kamoon Song, Teddy Hall, Larry Whitaker, Deke Wightman, Skip Jones, Brian Mitchell, Adam Kuhlman. Special effects animation director/title designer: Sari Gennis. Assistant effects supervisor/designer: Brett G. Cook. Principal effects animators: John Allen Armstrong, Al Holter, Lisze Beckhold, Kim Knowlton, Phil Cummings, Craig Littell-Herrick, Brett Hisey, Sallie McHenry, Kathleen Quaife-Hodge.

## Final Fantasy: The Spirits Within (7/11/01)

Columbia Pictures. 106 mins. Director: Hironubu Sakaguchi. Producers: Jun Aida, Chris Lee. Voices: Ming-Na (Dr. Aki Ross), Alec Baldwin (Captain Gray Edwards), Ving Rhames (Ryan), Steve Buscemi (Neil), Peri Gilpin (Jane), Donald Sutherland (Dr. Sid), James Woods (General Hein), Keith David (Council Member #1), Jean Simmons (Council Member #2), Matt McKenzie (Major Elliott), John DiMaggio (BFW Soldier #1).

©Square Pictures

**Consumer Tips:** ☆☆½ MPAA Rating: PG.

**Story:** Scientists try to save the earth from spiritual enemy forces and a corrupt government military leader.

**Comments:** Noted Japanese video game manufacturer Square had achieved great success with its "Final Fantasy" games, which increasingly used sophisticated computer animation. Having established a U.S. sidearm, with a staff based in Hawaii, the company ventured into feature films. *Final Fantasy: The Spirits Within* is more of a straight science-fiction epic compared to the sword and sorcery-themed games, the primary connection beyond the production company and title being an emphasis on "Gaia," a concept that planets have their own spirits within. The computer animation, using motion-capture performers, was realistic and highly detailed. However, taken away from the PC and onto a theater or even television screen, the effect can often be unnerving. The plot is a rather convoluted blend of spiritual theories and alien battles and explosions. The score by Elliot Goldenthal is often haunting, and the central concept and depiction of CG souls literally being dragged out of bodies is disturbing. However, the film lacks a clear focus and emotional foundation. The characters are types and the voices, including Alec Baldwin as the male lead, are largely generic and add little to the characterization. The effects set pieces are more interesting than the cast.

Despite the computer artistry and articles suggesting that the "photo-realistic performers" could eventually replace on-camera actors, the film's theatrical release proved rather short-lived, grossing a limp $32 million in U.S. box-office receipts.

The studio did go on to produce an animated short as part of *The Animatrix* sequels, *Final Flight of the Osiris*, in 2003, which was screened theatrically with the movie *Dreamcatcher*. Despite the short's success, Square has since abandoned all future film animation projects. Oddly enough, the company recently achieved one of its biggest successes through a collaboration with Disney, a game blending "Final Fantasy" characters and the familiar Disney stars, called "Kingdom Hearts," with a sequel currently in the works. (AL)

**Additional Credits:** Screenplay: Al Reinert, Jeff Vinntar. Additional dialogue: Jack Fletcher. Music: Elliot Goldenthal.

Animation director: Andy Jones. Sequence supervisors: Eiji Fujii, Hiroyuki Hayashida, Kenichi Isaka, Takumi Kimura, Claude Precourt, Steve Preeg, Teru "Yosh" Yoshida. Lead character animators: Roy Sato, Toby M. Haruno, Ben Rush, Christopher Erin Walsh, Jay Randall, Alice Kaiserian, Louis Lefebvre, Matthew T. Hackett, Timothy Heath. Lead animator: Jongbo Kim. Animators: Robin Akin, Walton Burgwyn, Kelly Hartigan Goldstein, Yoshinobu Inano, Yung Sheng Jong, Michael Kitchen, Nanji Nishida, Kunhiko Noguchi, Jeff Schu, Eric Weiss, Kazuyoshi Yaginuma, Cindy Yamauchi. Voice director/motion capture director: Jack Fletcher. Original character design: Shuko Murase. Lead character artist: Steven Eric Giesler. Character artists: Francisco A. Cortina, Veronique Garcia, Koichi Iwatsuka, Tatsuya Kosaka, Rene Morel, Jeremy Ray. Cloth simulation artists: Patricia Pawlak, Cheryl Rye. Storyboards: John Fox, Trevor Goring, Raymond Harvie, Tim Holtrop, Ed Klautky, Shinsaku Kozumo, Mark Moretti, Akira Ohuro, Masao Okuba, Marc Vena, Masahito Yamashita.

**Finding Nemo** (5/30/03) Disney-Pixar. 100 mins. Director: Andrew Stanton. Producer: Graham Walters. Codirector: Lee Unkrich. Voices: Albert Brooks (Marlin), Ellen DeGeneres (Dory), Alexander Gould (Nemo), Willem Dafoe (Gill), Brad Garrett (Bloat), Allison Janney (Peach), Austin Pendleton (Gurgle), Stephen Root (Bubbles), Vicki Lewis (Deb & Flo), Joe Ranft (Jacques), Geoffrey Rush (Nigel), Andrew Stanton (Crush), Elizabeth Perkins (Coral), Barry Humphries (Bruce), Eric Bana (Anchor), John Ratzenberger (Fish School).

**Consumer Tips:** ☆☆☆☆ MPAA Rating: G. Academy Award Winner for Best Animated Feature.

**Story:** A father fish searches the ocean for his lost son, who has been caught and is held captive in a dentist office aquarium.

**Comments:** Pixar's fourth film, *Finding Nemo*, became one of the surprise box-office hits of summer 2003, ultimately grossing $339,714,978 domestically. However, several critics pointed out that the film failed to break new ground, again functioning as a buddy/quest movie with an ensemble cast. But if Pixar failed to break new ground, it remained as skilled as ever in retreading and polishing old ground. The central

©Disney / Pixar

theme of family loss, hammered home in the film's opening moments, is surprisingly affecting, and the characters Marlin encounters are well delineated in their own right, even when playing off of types, from the surfer turtles to the school of fish obsessed with visual art. As with most Pixar films, the use of recognizable voice talent is handled fairly well, with mostly distinctive performers who add to the characterization, and is in fact somewhat less distracting than Billy Crystal's comic patter in *Monsters, Inc.* Ellen DeGeneres's performance as the absentminded Dory led to critical acclaim and an Annie award for outstanding voice acting. Since much of the film takes place in the waters off Australia, authentic Aussie actors played key supporting roles, including Barry Humphries, famed for his Dame Edna characterization, as the amiably menacing shark Bruce. The fact that fish could be brought to animation as engaging and sympathic figures surprised many, and the father/son relationship is extremely real and touching.

As a change of pace from Pixar's tradition of "blooper reels," the closing credits feature "encore" appearances by almost the entire cast of characters, swimming alongside the list of names. A title card reading "In Memory of Glenn McQueen" appears briefly, in tribute to the longtime Pixar directing animator, who died suddenly in the fall of 2002. In the spring of 2004, *Finding Nemo* received the Academy Award for Best Animated Feature, beating out indie favorite *The Triplets of Belleville*. (AL)

*Additional Credits:* Executive producer: John Lassetter. Story: Andrew Stanton. Screenplay: Andrew Stanton, Bob Peterson, David Reynolds. Music: Thomas Newman. Supervising technical director: Oren Jacob. Supervising animator: Dylan Brown. CG supervisors: Brian Green, Lisa Forssell, Danielle Feinberg, David Eisenmann, Jesse Hollander, Steve May, Michael Fong, Anthony A. Apodaca, Michael Lorenzen. Directing animators: Alan Barillaro, Mark Walsh. Animators: Carlos Baena, Bobby "Boom" Beck, Misha Berenstein, Ben Catmull, Scott Clark, Brett Coderre, Tim Crawfurd, David DeVan, Doug Dooley, Ike Feldman, Andrew Gordon, Stephen Gregory, Travis Hathaway, Jimmy Hayward, Steven Clay Hunter, Rob Jensen, Nancy Kato, Karen Kiser, Shawn P. Krause, Wendell Lee, Angus MacLane, Matt Majers, Daniel Mason, Dale McBeath, Amy McNamara, Jon Mead, Billy Merritt, Cameron Miyasaki, Dave Mullins, James Ford Murphy, Roderigo Blaas Nacle, Peter Nash, Victor Navone, Bret Parker, Michael Parks, Bobby Podesta, Brett Pulliam, Rich Quade, Roger Rose, Gini Cruz Santos, Andy Schmidt, Doug Sheppeck, Ross Stevenson, Patty Kihm Stevenson, Doug Sweetland, David Tart, J. Warren Trezevant, Michael Venturini, Tasha Weeden, Adam Wood, Kureha Yakoo, Ron Zorman.

**Fire and Ice** (8/27/83) 20th Century Fox. 81 mins. Director: Ralph Bakshi. Producers: Ralph Bakshi, Frank Frazetta. Voices: Susan Tyrrell (Juliana), Maggie Roswell (Teegra), William Ostrander (Larn, Taro), Steve Sandor (Darkwolf), Stephen Mendel (Nekron), Leo Gordon (Jarol), Elizabeth Lloyd Shaw (Roleil), Mickey Morton (Otwa), Clare Nono (Tutor), Big Yank (Monga).

**Consumer Tips:** ☆☆ MPAA Rating: PG.

**Story:** Heroes Larn and Darkwolf rescue a fire princess who was kidnapped by Nekron, an evil ice king.

**Comments:** *Fire and Ice* continues Ralph Bakshi's explorations into fantasy, this time inspired by (and in collaboration with) famed illustrator Frank Frazetta. As predicted by Frazetta's involvement, the movie is essentially a "sword and sandal" epic; the film's reliance on live-action reference for rotoscope is hinted by the fact that the performers for such, only a few of whom also provided their voices, receive star billing in the opening credits. The plot is standard, with most of the genre's types (noble barbarian leader, evil sorceror, manipulative mother, etc.) carefully represented within a battle between natural elements, as indicated by the title. As with *American Pop*, often the performer overshadows the animator, as with character actor Leo Gordon, who served as voice and model for the good king. Interestingly, however, the comic-book style adventure was scripted by two veterans of the field, Marvel scribes Roy Thomas and Gerry Conway, both of whom had worked on the "Conan" comic-books. The archetypes are simply that: types. Certain moments, such as a savage lizard creature suddenly consuming wanderers, stand out, but overall the narrative is as slim as those in the movie's live-action counterparts.

*Fire and Ice* might be considered the last entry in Bakshi's fantasy cycle, along with *Wizards* and *Lord of the Rings*. However, *Fire and Ice* uses a less folkloric and mythic form of fantasy, recalling nothing so much as a more graphic episode of Filmation's *He-Man* series. Frazetta's art had previously been adapted for animation by Richard Williams in 1978, as a commercial for Jovan cologne. (And in an interview with Milton Gray for *Funnyworld*, Williams dismissed the concept of Frazetta's work being used in a feature film as "a disaster. It's tough to sustain for 30 seconds, it takes forever.") Thus, *Fire and Ice* essentially stands as a footnote to the spate of barbarian films that followed in the wake of Arnold Schwarzenegger's appearance as Conan. (AL)

*Additional Credits:* Executive producers: John W. Hyde, Richard R. St.Johns. Screenplay: Roy Thomas, Gerry Conway. Characters created by Ralph Bakshi and Frank Frazetta. Music composer/conductor: William Kraft. Orchestrations: Angela

Morley. Animators: Brenda Banks, Carl A. Bell, Bryan Berry, Lillian Evans, Steve Gordon, Debbie Hayes, David Hoover, Charles Howell, Adam Kuhlman, Mauro Maressa, Russell Mooney, Jack Ozark, William Recinos, Mitch Rochon, Tom Tataranowicz, Bruce Woodside. Assistant animators: Kathleen Castillo, Derek Eversfield, Warren Greenwood, Todd Hoff, Michael Kaweski, William Knoll, Hope London, Sharon Murray, Chris Peterson, Brian Ray, Leticia Ruiz, Janice Stocks, Susan Sugita, Marilyn Taylor, Michael Wolf. Costume designer: Frank Frazetta. Production supervisor: Michael Svayko. Layout: John Sparey, Michael Svayko. Background layout: Tim Callahan. Backgrounds: James Gurney, Thomas Kinkade. Color models: Janet Cummings.

**Fist of the North Star** (9/27/91) Streamline Pictures. 110 mins. Director: Toyoo Ashida. Producer: Shôji Kishimoto. Voices: John Vickery (Ken), Jeff Corey (Ryûken), Barbara Goodson (Alei), Catherine Battistone (Old Woman), Michael McConnohie (Shin), Steve Bulen (Wise Man), Michael Forest (Jackel), Wendee Lee (Pillage Victim), Dave Mallow (Hart), Tony Oliver (Bat), Holly Sidell (Lynn), Gregory Snegoff (Ray, Uygle), Melodee Spevack (Julia), Doug Stone (Torture Victim), Kirk Thornton (Head Banger), Tom Wyner (Thugmeister).

©Toei Animation Co. Ltd.

***Consumer Tips:*** ☆☆ MPAA Rating: Not rated. SF martial-arts extravaganza. Based on the Japanese television series, based in turn on the manga series *Fist of the North Star.*

***Story:*** In the year 199X, the world has become a desolate desert after nuclear Armageddon destroys it. A few emaciated survivors huddle in tiny farm towns around the few oases in the global desert. They are preyed upon by brutal biker gangs and hulking mutants. Kenshiro, heir to the mystically powerful North Star martial arts school, is a lone avenger who wanders from town to town looking for his kidnapped fiancee, incidentally saving each town from the sadistic villains preventing its survivors from rebuilding civilization.

***Comments:*** *Fist of the North Star* is either a shallow, stupid rip-off of *The Road Warrior* and martial-arts video games, or a clever parody that exaggerates the violence and story implausibilities to a hilariously inoffensive level. The manga, by "Buronson" (a pseudonym evoking action star Charles Bronson) and Tetsu Hara, began in 1983, putting its "199X" at most 17 years in the future; yet a whole generation of 500- to 1,000-lb. mutants has had time to mature. The oceans have evaporated; cities are skeletal ruins; the only food is grown in tiny struggling farms; but the biker gangs are well-fed musclemen and there is always plenty of fuel for their finely-tuned choppers. Ken is a burlesque exaggeration of martial-arts star Bruce Lee, with seven scars in the pattern of the Big Dipper on his chest. (The Japanese title, *Hokuto No Ken*, is a pun. "Hokuto" is the Big Dipper or North Star constellation, while "Ken" is both the nickname for Kenshiro and the word for "fist".)

Ken's North Star technique is so deadly that he can punch his opponents' bodies at pressure points that cause them to self-destruct in timed releases. The audience's favorite action routine is a villain's taunt that Ken's blows only tickled him, Ken coolly replies, "You're already dead!", and the shocked villain's head messily explodes or his body doubles in half to break its back. Ken's continuing adversaries, including Shin of the rival Southern Cross martial-arts school, Jaggi, and Raoh, have their own techniques, such as hands that can slice and dice opponents like a chain saw. These scenes are shown in arty slow motion against abstract backgrounds of pastel colors. Spurting blood looks more like sparkle glitter. The dialogue is a pastiche of the super-macho taunts of the combatants in "Street Fighter"-type video games.

The 1983 manga was turned into a television series of 109 episodes, immediately followed by *Hokuto No Ken 2* for 42 more episodes (October 11, 1984 to February 18, 1988). It features endless variants of the small town terrorized by a bandit gang, and the wandering cowboy or samurai hero who either defends it or liberates it. Ken and his two tagalong child companions—barely adolescent Bat (after Bat Masterson), who thinks the fighting is cool until he experiences it firsthand, and the timid young girl, Lynne—face biker gangs, commando teams left over after the nuclear war setting themselves up as feudal lords, and mutants indistinguishable from comic-book super-villains. Ken is looking for his fiancee, Julia, who has been kidnapped by his rival, Shin, who is trying to set up a Roman empire–style kingdom. As Ken gets closer, he also must combat increasingly powerful ninja killers sent by Shin.

This summarizes the first 49 television episodes. The motion picture (Japan, March 8, 1986) is a reprise in theatrical-quality animation highlighting the most popular battles from this story-arc. The result is a series of equally dramatic battles against different adversaries without any buildup establishing who they are. The movie includes all the action without any of the television episodes' character development or motivation. Despite generally negative reviews as nothing but mindless violence, the movie was popular enough to generate a U.S./Australian live-action remake in 1995. (FP)

**Additional Credits:** Screenplay: Susumu Takahisa. Original music: Katsuhisa Hattori, Tsuyoshi Ujiki. Cinematography: Tamio Hosoda. Film editor: Masaaki Hanai. Art director: Shiko Tanaka. Animation director: Masami Suda. English dub producer: Carl Macek. Production manager: Jerry Beck. Assistant directors: Masahiro Hosoda, Junnen Umezawa. Production planner: Ken Ariga. Production coordinator: Tsuneichi Murakami. Toei Animation Co., Ltd.

**The Fox and the Hound** (7/10/81) Walt Disney Productions. 83 mins. Directors: Art Stevens, Ted Berman, Richard Rich. Producers: Woolie Reitherman, Art Stevens. Voices: Mickey Rooney (Tod), Keith Mitchell (Young Tod), Kurt Russell (Copper), Corey Feldman (Young Copper), Pearl Bailey (Big Mama), Pat Buttram (Chief), Sandy Duncan (Vixey), Jeanette Nolan (Widow Tweed), Jack Albertson (Amos Slade), Paul Winchell (Boomer), Dick Bakalyan (Dinky), John McIntire (Badger), John Fiedler (Porcupine).

**Consumer Tips:** ☆☆ MPAA Rating: G. Adapted from the 1967 novel *The Fox and the Hound* by Daniel P. Mannix.

©Walt Disney Productions

**Story:** A motherly owl named Big Mama rescues an orphaned fox cub. Big Mama deposits the cub with a kindly widow who takes him in and names him Tod. Down the road lives a hunter who has just purchased a new puppy, Copper, with the intention of having his number-one hound, Chief, teach Copper the art of hunting. Tod and Copper meet and become fast friends until the puppy goes on an extended hunting trip and returns as a well-trained enemy. Does friendship triumph or does cruel nature take its course?

**Comments:** *The Fox and the Hound* began with high hopes; CEO Ron Miller had hired a slew of new animators, writers, and directorial talent and was hoping that they would cut their teeth on this film. The "Nine Old Men" of Walt Disney's heyday were either dead or on the verge of retirement; *The Fox and the Hound* marked the last time the legendary team of Ollie Johnston and Frank Thomas would work on a film, and coproducer Woolie Reitherman was on his final assignment.

It is perhaps unavoidable that the end of any era happens with upheaval. Reitherman, Stevens, and Miller quarreled over key sections of the film, with Miller backing the younger Stevens and his neophyte crew. Reitherman, for his part, had perhaps the better sense of story but lacked the trust in the young animation team. In the end Stevens prevailed and the team went forward using designs and layouts set by veterans Johnston and Thomas.

Or at least most of them did. In the midst of production a highly touted young animator named Don

Bluth announced that Disney animation had gone stale and ventured too far from its days of glory. Bluth declared his intention to form a studio dedicated to the old ideals and walked out, taking seven other animators and four assistant animators with him. It was a punch to the gut for both Ron Miller and *The Fox and the Hound*. The film had been scheduled for release during Christmas 1980; Miller had to hire new artists while others did double duty, and the movie did not premiere until July 1981.

In the end, it was much ado about nothing: *The Fox and the Hound* is average Disney fare best suited for youngsters. The significance of the film lies in the fact that it began the long and ultimately fruitful gestation period of the Disney revival. In just eight years the studio would reclaim ascendancy in the realm of animated features, and few would remember where it all started. For those looking for highlights, *The Fox and the Hound* features excellent voice work by Pearl Bailey as Mother Owl, and there is a magnificent job turned in by young Glen Keane, who animated a violent melee between Copper, Tod, and an enormous bear. Keane was so intent on perfecting his animation that he had a small, flexible bear skeleton made to ensure he got the drawing right. His dedication would pay off in less than a decade.

In the original book every main character is dead by the end of the story except for Slade, who is well on the way to an alcoholic demise. *The Fox and the Hound* almost featured the first on-screen death of a main character (Chief, who falls from a railroad trestle), but coproducer Art Stevens nixed the idea. (MG)

**Additional Credits:** Executive producer: Ron Miller. Story: Larry Clemons, Ted Berman, Peter Young, Steve Hulett, David Michener, Burny Mattinson, Earl Kress, Vance Gerry. Supervising animators: Randy Cartwright, Cliff Nordberg, Frank Thomas, Glen Keane, Ron Clements, Ollie Johnston. Musical score: Buddy Baker. Animators: Ed Gombert, Dale Oliver, Ron Husband, David Block, Chris Buck, Hendel S. Butoy, Darrell Van Citters, Phillip Young, John Musker, Jerry Rees, Dick Lucas, Jeffery J. Varab, Chuck Harvey, Phil Nibbelink, Michael Cedeno. Layout artists: Dan Hansen, Sylvia Roemer, Michael Peraza Jr., Glenn V. Vilppu, Guy Vasilovich, Joe Hale. Film editors: James Koford, James Melton. Art direction: Don Griffith. Production managers: Don A. Duckwall, Edward Hansen. Assistant directors: Don Hahn, Mark A. Hester, Terry

L. Noss. Background artists: Daniela Bielecka, Brian Cebern, Kathleen Swain. Effects animators: Jack Boyd, Ted Kierscey, Don C. Paul.

**Freddie as F. R. O. 7.** (8/28/92) Miramax. 72 mins. Director: Jon Acevski. Producers: Norman Priggen, Jon Acevski. Voices: Ben Kingsley (Freddie), James Earl Jones (Narrator), Jenny Agutter (Daffers), Brian Blessed (El Supremo), Nigel Hawthorne (Brigadier G), Sir Michael Hordern (King), Jonathan Pryce (Trilby), Prunella Scales (Queen), John Sessions (Scotty), Billie Whitelaw (Messina).

©Hollywood Motion Pictures of London, Ltd.

**Consumer Tips:** 0 (zero stars) MPAA Rating: PG. Don't bother.

**Story:** Secret agent Freddy the frog battles against evil Aunt Messina and her partner El Supremo, who plot to take over the world.

**Comments:** This movie is an illustration on how NOT to make an animated film. It has an awful script, boring visuals, pedestrian animation, dull colors, stupid ideas, terrible songs, music, and background score . . . need I go on?

*Freddie as F.R.0.7* (also known simply as *Freddie the Frog*) has an incredible voice cast (Ben Kingsley! Jonathan Pryce! James Earl Jones!) and occasional bits of effects animation worth watching. But the whole film is off-putting from the first frame.

It begins with a depressing love ballad and moves into a badly told medieval fairy tale about a prince who is transformed into a frog. Said frog grows up into Freddie, a super-secret agent in the modern world, who fights off his futuristic enemies and their science-fiction devices with only his wits (and a few magical powers). None of it makes much sense.

Ben Kingsley decided to enact his voice-over part in a pseudo–French accent (sounding much like Peter Sellers's Inspector Clouseau), and the director designed him as a clone of Disney's Mr. Toad. The story is simply a mess.

The film cost about $18 million and bombed at the U.S. and British box offices, grossing only $1.1 million in the states. London-based Hollywood Road Film Productions went out of business shortly after the film's release. A sequel, *Freddie Goes to Washington*, was in production, with 12 minutes of footage produced at the time of the shutdown.

With luck, the world will be spared that 12 minutes. (JB)

**Additional Credits:** Screenplay: John Acevski, David Ashton. Animation director: Tony Guy. Music: David Dundas, Rick Wentworth. Lyrics: Don Black, Asia, David Ashton, Boy George, John Acevski, Holly Johnson. Art Director: Paul Shadlow. Character designer: Richard Fawdry. Special effects director: Peter Chiang. Sequence directors: Dave Unwin, Bill Hajee, Roberty Casle, Richard Eawdry, Stephen Weston, Alain Maindron. Storyboard director: Denis Rich. Coordinating animators: Edoardo Cavalli, Ramon Modiano, Kevin Malloy, Gary McCarver, Gaston Marzio, Alan Simpson. Animators: Philippe Rejaundry, David Stone, Paul Stone, Dave Osborne, Mike Pfeil, Keiko Masuda, Keith Greig, Bruno LeFloch, Arthur Button, Ronaldo Canfora.

**Freddie the Frog** See *Freddie as F.R.O.7.*

**Fritz the Cat** (4/12/72) Cinemation Industries. 78 mins. Director: Ralph Bakshi. Producer: Steve Krantz. Voices: Skip Hinnant (Fritz), Rosetta LeNoire (Big Bertha), Phil Seuling (Pig Cop #1 "Ralph"), Ralph Bakshi (Pig Cop 2), John McCurry.

**Consumer Tips:** ☆☆☆ MPAA Rating: X; rating later changed to R. Based on comics by R. Crumb.

©Aurica Finance Co. N.V.

**Story:** Fritz, an NYU college student, explores sex, drugs, and race relations in the late 1960s. In the course of his episodic adventures, Fritz makes love to three girls in a bathtub, is chased by two "pig" policemen, causes a riot in Harlem, and joins a radical motorcycle gang out West.

**Comments:** Ralph Bakshi's explosive first feature is an enjoyable animated time capsule, capturing the feelings of the 1960s youth movement and of underground comics from the period.

Bakshi started as a teenager at the Terrytoons studio (Mighty Mouse, Heckle and Jeckle, et al.) in the 1950s. He slowly worked his way up, from inker to in-betweener to animator and then director. He emerged in the late 1960s, when alternative comic books began to surface. These comics influenced his ultimate direction in animation.

Bakshi joined animator Steve Krantz in 1968, helping bail Krantz out of numerous production problems with the low-budget television cartoons *Rocket Robin Hood* and *Spiderman*. Bakshi and Krantz soon found themselves in agreement on the idea of doing something for the almost nonexistent adult animation field. In 1969, Krantz discovered *Fritz the Cat*, which was then-recently collected in a trade paperback. Krantz and Bakshi quickly agreed this was material on which they wanted to base an adult cartoon. They contacted Robert Crumb and bought the movie rights.

Krantz found a small-time distributor, Cinemation Industries, and a new rock music label, Fantasy

Records, to put up the initial funds for production. The film was made on a budget of less than a million dollars. Bakshi hired all the remaining "old hands" of New York animation he could—animators he had worked with previously at Terrytoons and Paramount. These included Jim Tyer, John Gentilella, Nick Tafuri, Martin Taras, Larry Riley, and Cliff Augustine. Production commenced in early 1970.

Sections of the film were preplanned to play as stand-alone short subjects. Thus, they would have something to help recoup their investment if funding dried up. But that didn't happen. For a year and a half, Bakshi sweated out the production of footage in New York. Afterwards, he shifted his production headquarters to Los Angeles, where he completed the film. There he hired additional qualified animators, including veterans like Norm McCabe, Manuel Perez, Virgil Ross, Dick Lundy, Jim Davis, Ted Bonnicksen, and Rod Scribner.

The film was completed in early 1972. *Fritz the Cat* screened at New York's Museum of Modern Art, where it won rave reviews from the New York film critics. The film got an expected X rating from the MPAA for its numerous sex scenes, language, and drug use, but this gave *Fritz* its notoriety and press. *Playboy* did an illustrated preview.

*Fritz* was a huge box-office success. It was followed by a sequel two years later, *The Nine Lives of Fritz the Cat*, directed by Robert Taylor. Crumb has since disowned *Fritz the Cat*, killing off the character in *The People Comics #1* (1972). Bakshi moved on to other projects; his next film, *Heavy Traffic* (1973), would prove to be his best. (JB)

**Additional Credits:** Screenplay: Ralph Bakshi. Characters created by R. Crumb. Music: Ed Bogas, Ray Shanklin. Animators: John Gentilella, Martin Taras, Lawrence Riley, Clifford Augustine, Norman McCabe, John Sparey, Manuel Perez, Cosmo Anzilotti, Virgil Ross, Milton Gray, Richard Lundy, John Walker, Edwin Aardal, James Davis, Theodore Bonnicksen, Rod Scribner, Jim Tyer, Robert Maxfield, Nicholas Tafuri. Layout: Cosmo Anzilotti, John Sparey, James Davis. Second layout: Lewis Ott Jr., John Walker, Theodore Bonnickson, Richard Lundy. Backgrounds: Johnny Vita, Ira Turek. Second background: Michael Lloyd. Cinematography: Ted C. Bemiller, Gene Borghi. Film editing: Renn Reynolds. Production management: Bob Revell. Special effects: Susan Cary, Helen Jordan, Irene Sandberg. Visual effects: Ellie Zika.

**Fun and Fancy Free** (9/27/47) Walt Disney Pictures. 73 mins. Directors: Jack Kinney, Bill Roberts, Hamilton Luske (Animation), William Morgan (Live-Action). Voices: Jim Macdonald (Lumpjaw, Mickey Mouse), Cliff Edwards (Jiminy Cricket), Clarence Nash (Donald Duck), Pinto Colvig (Goofy), Billy Gilbert (Willie the Giant), Anita Gordon (Singing Harp), Edgar Bergen (Narrator), Dinah Shore (Narrator). Additional voices: the King's Men, the Starlighters, the Dinning Sisters.

©Walt Disney Productions

**Consumer Tips:** ☆☆½ *Bongo* is based on a story by Sinclair Lewis. *Mickey and the Beanstalk* is based on the popular fairy tale *Jack and the Beanstalk.*

**Story:** Jiminy Cricket, late of *Pinocchio*, is the link between two featurettes. *Bongo* is the story of an escaped circus bear who finds his true love and happiness in the wild. *Mickey and the Beanstalk* is a story related to little Luana Patten (*Song of the South*) on her birthday by ventriloquist Edgar Bergen and his two dummies, Charlie McCarthy and Mortimer Snerd. They serve as the live-action narrators to the animated story starring Mickey Mouse, Donald Duck, and Goofy.

**Comments:** Jiminy Cricket is in fine form here, making one wonder why Disney sat him on the shelf for so long. The jocular cricket cheers up a pair of despondent dolls by playing Dinah Shore's recording of "Bongo" on a phonograph; we see the animation once the record starts to spin. This featurette was once considered for full-length screen treatment but it is difficult to see how that might have been accomplished. *Bongo* is a very thin but still entertaining tale featuring energetic animation and one tongue-in-cheek scene filled with enough romantic kitsch to sicken Cupid himself.

As Bongo and girlfriend Lulubelle fall in love, two cute but goofy "valentine bears" construct an ongoing special-effects fantasy on the wing (as it were) featuring every known cliché in the Book of Love. There was a very similar scene planned in *Snow White and the Seven Dwarfs* for the heroine and Prince Charming, complete with a "love tree" filled with heart-shaped fruit and other such nonsense. Perhaps the Disney animators were doing a parody or paying homage to the cutting-room floor.

Jiminy sees an invitation to Luanna Patten's birthday party across the street and hops over to attend. Edgar Bergen and his famous dummies, Charlie McCarthy and Mortimer Snerd, have the floor for a retelling of "Jack and the Beanstalk" now starring Mickey Mouse, Donald Duck, and Goofy. This trio was often teamed up in Disney shorts of the mid- to late 1930s. In truth, this is not one of their finest collaborations. There are surprisingly few gags, mainly because Bergen, McCarthy, and Snerd are providing the laughs. As Bergen narrates the tale offscreen, the two puppets make snide, critical, or stupid remarks during the action, some of which are genuinely funny. It's like watching an eerie precursor to the cult television show of the late 1990s, *Mystery Science Theater 3000.*

There is one funny scene, almost certainly directed by Jack Kinney, in which Goofy battles a giant slab of Jello, and serious animation students would do well to watch the timing in the scene where the beanstalk carries our heroes' cottage up to the giant's lair. Willie the Giant is an unexpected pleasure, and it is probably no coincidence that he was used to provide the entertaining ending to the film. *Fun and Fancy Free* is pleasant enough to pass the time with, but can never be considered a significant work in the Disney catalogue.

For the record:

- Jiminy Cricket enters singing "I'm a Happy-Go-Lucky Fellow," a song he was originally slated to sing in *Pinocchio.* (It must be old-home week for veterans of that film; Cleo the goldfish makes an appearance as well.)
- It is often reported that this film marked the final time Walt Disney was the voice of Mickey Mouse,

but in fact Jim Macdonald had already taken over the job. (MG)

**Additional Credits:** Production supervisor: Ben Sharpsteen. Story: Homer Brightman, Harry Reeves, Ted Sears, Lance Nolley, Alton Dedini, Tom Oreb. "Bongo" based on an original story by Sinclair Lewis. Musical director: Charles Wolcott. Music score: Paul J. Smith, Oliver Wallace, Eliot Daniel. Directing animators: Ward Kimball, Les Clark, John Lounsbery, Fred Moore, Wolfgang Reitherman. Animation: Hugh Fraser, Phil Duncan, Judge Whitaker, Art Babbitt, John Sibley, Marc Davis, Harvey Toombs, Hal King, Ken O'Brien, Jack Campbell. Effects animation: George Rowley, Jack Boyd. Layouts: Don DaGradi, Al Zinnen, Ken O'Connor, Hugh Hennesey, John Hench, Glenn Scott. Backgrounds: Ed Starr, Claude Coats, Art Riley, Brice Mack, Ray Huffine, Ralph Hulett. Special processes: Ub Iwerks.

**Galaxy Express** (8/8/81) New World Pictures. 91 mins. Director: Rintaro. Producer: Roger Corman. Voices: Masako Nozawa (Tetsurô Hoshino), Reiko Tajima (Queen Emeralda), Makio Inoue (Captain Harlock), Tatsuya Jô (Narrator), Kaneta Kimotsuki (Conductor), Masako Ikeda (Maetel), Yôko Asagama (Claire), Miyoko Asô (Tochirô's Mother), Toshiko Fujita (Shadow), Banjô Ginga (Captain of the Guard), Yasuo Hisamatsu (Antares), Yoshiko Kimiya (Queen Promethium), Kei Tomiyama (Tochirô Ôyama).

**Consumer Tips:** ☆☆ MPAA Rating: PG. SF adventure. Based on the popular Japanese animated television series *Galaxy Express 999*, an adaptation of the manga series by Leiji Matsumoto.

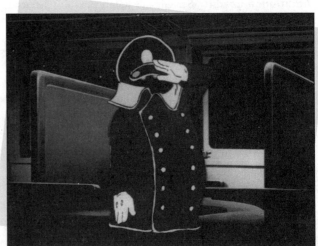

©New World Pictures

**Story:** In the distant future mankind has spread throughout the galaxy. The rich have their brains transplanted into immortal metal bodies. Joey Smith, a young boy, dreams of getting a mechanical body. A mysterious beautiful woman, Maetel, offers to accompany him on Galaxy Express 999 to Andromeda where mechanical bodies are given away free. At each planet they stop at, Joey has an adventure that shows him that eternal life is not so great. At the climax, he decides to keep his natural body.

**Comments:** *Galaxy Express* can be taken as both sci-fi space opera aboard a high-tech spaceship disguised as an old-fashioned passenger train traveling from planet to planet, and as an allegorical fantasy about traveling from youth to adulthood with stops at planets that are each metaphors for a decision in life that an adolescent must make.

*Galaxy Express* was a hit in Japan on its release on August 4, 1979, but it failed in America for several reasons. The concept of an old-fashioned railroad train chugging through the galaxy was considered ridiculous. (Matsumoto acknowledged it as his tribute to the Japanese literary classic fantasy *Night on the Galactic Railroad* by Kenji Miyazawa.) It was a condensed remake by Toei Animation Co., Ltd. in high-quality theatrical animation of the first year of the 1978–1981 113-episode *Galaxy Express 999* television series, flashing through the highlights of the most popular episodes. The individual action scenes are too brief to be meaningful to American viewers unfamiliar with the television series. This was made even worse by cutting the Japanese 129-minute running time to 91 minutes. The movie feels shallow and choppy as a result.

This was the first anime theatrical release in America after the establishment of anime fandom, and the fans reviled it for producer Roger Corman's poor-quality voices and silly name changes such as Joey "Hana-cana-boba-camanda" Smith for Tetsuro Hoshino; Captain Warlock (a campy pseudo–John Wayne voice) for Captain Harlock; and Sundown McMoon for Tochiro Oyama. There were complaints at the time about the obvious error of renaming Maeter as Maetel since "maeter" is Latin for "mother" and she is obviously a mother-surrogate for Joey; however, American licensees have since adopted Maetel as the correct spelling. The symphonic disco score by

Nozomi Aoki is lovely but quickly dated the movie to the late 1970s. (FP)

**Additional Credits:** Screenplay: Kon Ichikawa, Shiro Ishimori, Leiji Matsumoto. Original music: Nozomu Aoki, Yukihide Takekawa. Cinematography: Masatoshi Fukui, Toshio Katayama. Film editing (U.S. version): R. J. Kizer, Skip Schoolnik. Production design: Tadao Kubota, Takamura Mukuo. Animators: Tomeko Horikawa, Yoshinobu Ineno, Yoshinori Kanada, Reiko Kuwahara, Jôji Manabe, Shigeo Matoba, Hiroshi Oikawa, Rintaro, Kazuhide Tomonaga, Emiko Tsukima, Kôichi Tsunoda.

**Gay Purr-ee** (10/24/62) Warner Bros. 86 mins. Director: Abe Levitow. Producer: Henry G. Saperstein. Voices: Judy Garland (Mewsette), Robert Goulet (Jaune Tom), Red Buttons (Robespierre), Paul Frees (Meowrice, Railway Cat, Bartender Cat), Hermione Gingold (Mme. Rubens-Chatte), Morey Amsterdam (Narrator, Mariner), Mel Blanc (Bulldog, Driver, Mice Sounds), Joan Gardner (Jeanette), Julie Bennett (Marie).

©Warner Bros.

**Consumer Tips:** ☆☆½ MPAA Rating: G. Artsy and entertaining.

**Story:** A French farm cat runs away to Paris where she becomes the toast of the town and inspiration to the great artists (Cezanne, Monet, Van Gogh, Picasso, etc.).

**Comments:** Romance between French cats is examined in this film. Mewsette, voiced by Judy Garland in one of her last roles, grows dissatisfied with her farmlife after hearing her mistress's sister extolling the virtues of Paris. She leaves her mouser boyfriend Jaune Tom, and falls into the clutches of the urbane "money cat" Meowrice. While Mewsette is being tutored by Mme. Rubens-Chatte, Meowrice actually plans to sell her as a mail-order bride to a wealthy American cat. Jaune Tom and his pint-sized friend Robespierre travel to Paris to find Mewsette, but they too are conned by Meowrice and wind up on a ship to Alaska. Eventually, despite these setbacks, love conquers all.

The second animated film produced by UPA (now owned by Henry Saperstein, though most of the original artists had departed), *Gay Purr-ee* reflects not only the stylistic roots of UPA's shorts but also the sensibilities of story writer Chuck Jones. The characters' eyes seem reminiscent on many occasions of the more stylized faces in the later Jones' films (albeit minus the cutesy eyelashes), and the animation crew included Jones' veterans Ben Washam and Ken Harris. However, as artist/Warner animation buff Greg Duffell points out, there are some moments when the animation is on a television level or worse. Overall, the strong design sense helps overcome those moments, as does the voice cast, particularly Red Buttons and Paul Frees, who makes a wonderfully suave villain. Tellingly, one of the best moments in the film is not even animated, consisting of a series of still paintings demonstrating how various contemporary French painters would have depicted Mewsette. Still, there's a greater sense of actual French atmosphere here than in Disney's later *The Aristocats*, thanks again to the production design, especially the lavishly stylized backgrounds. While not as memorable as such UPA shorts as *Rooty Toot Toot* or *The Tell-Tale Heart*, the film is still a good effort and has been unjustly underrated over the years. (AL)

***Additional Credits:*** Story: Dorothy and Chuck Jones. Additional dialogue: Ralph Wright. Associate producer: Lee Orgel. Production manager: Earl Jonas. Music: Harold Arlen. Lyrics: E. Y. Harburg. Music arranger/conductor: Mort Lindsay. Sequence director: Steve Clark. Animators: Ben Washam, Phil Duncan, Hal Ambro, Ray Patterson, Grant Simmons, Irv Spence, Don Lusk, Hank Smith, Harvey Toombs, Volus Jones, Ken Harris, Art Davis, Fred Madison. Art director: Victor Haboush. Production design: Robert Singer, Richard Ung,

Corny Cole, Ray Aragon, Ed Levitt, Ernest Nordli. Color styling: Gloria Wood, Robert Inman, Don Peters, Phil Norman, Richard Kelsey. A UPA Production.

**Ghost in the Shell** (3/29/96) Palm Pictures/Manga Entertainment. 81 mins. Director: Mamoru Oshii. Producers: Shigeru Watanabe, Laurence Guinness, Yoshimasa Mizuo, Ken Iyadomi, Mitsuhisa Ishikawa. Voices: Abe Lasser (Puppet Master), William Frederick (Aramaki), Simon Prescott (Nakamura), Richard Epcar (Bateau), Christopher Joyce (Togusa), Henry Douglas Grey (Minister), Michael Sorich (Ishikawa), Phil Williams (Dr. Willis), Steve Bulen (Section 9 Staff Cyberneticist, Coroner).

©Shirow Masamune / KODANSHA IG, ITNDOTD

***Consumer Tips:*** ☆☆☆ MPAA Rating: R. Sci-fi suspense thriller. Based on the Japanese sci-fi manga novel *Ghost in the Shell*.

***Story:*** In the near future, it is hard to tell the difference between Artificial Intelligences and real people. The police's Section 9 must catch a computer terrorist that turns out to be an Artificial Intelligence that wants its own body. Major Kusanagi, who is little more than a brain in a cyborg body herself, must decide whether to destroy the Puppet Master or support its claim to life.

***Comments:*** *Kokaku Kidotai* (*Ghost in the Shell*) was a critically acclaimed cyberpunk sci-fi manga novel by Masamune Shirow (Japan 1989–90). Thirty years in the future, computer technology has integrated the world so completely that separate nations barely exist.

Bodies can be connected to cybernetic bioenhancements, including skull-jacks to allow people to plug their brains directly into the Internet. The detective team of the Japanese nationalized police's Section 9, in charge of computer crimes, is developed through several stories that are clever blends of action scenes; the exposure of intellectual crimes involving computer hacking and corporate or international espionage; Asimovian speculation on the expanding possibilities of Artificial Intelligence, both in robot bodies and in pure electronic form; and at what point an A.I. should be considered as much a "real person" as someone born in a flesh body. The central character is Section 9's top detective, Major Motoko Kusanagi, who appears to be an attractive woman but who is morosely aware that she is little more than a mind, a ghost, in an artificial shell built and owned by the government.

Production I.G, a new Japanese animation studio specializing in CGI animation, picked *Ghost in the Shell* to showcase itself in a big way. Director Oshii used the story involving a computer hacker known as the Puppet Master. In A.D. 2029, Section 9 (personified through Aramaki, Section 9's "old man" department head; Kusanagi, its top field agent, who looks like a young woman but whose body can unfold into more mechanical attachments than a Swiss knife; and Bateau, her partner, who looks like beefy muscle but is as cynically intelligent as she is and whose body is still about half natural) is attracted by surreptitious attempts to implant false memories into people's minds when they use their brain-Internet connections. The investigation is interrupted by violent terrorism and attempted infiltration of the Japanese government's computers.

The movie is intelligent and visually spectacular. Oshii changed the setting from a futuristic Tokyo to a *Blade Runner*-ized anonymous Asiatic metropolis based more upon Hong Kong. Its main flaw is its pacing. Dynamic action scenes are followed by lengthy "talking heads" scenes necessary to explain the technological and political background to the audience.

Manga Entertainment obtained American rights by cofinancing its production. *Ghost in the Shell* was released on November 18, 1995, in Japan and March 29, 1996, in America. It was intended primarily for international film festival exhibition and home-video sales. Its Palm Pictures limited theatrical release (only one theater per city) grossed only $515,905, but it won film festival awards and topped *Billboard* magazine's video sales charts during August 1996. It was acknowledged by the Wachowski Brothers as one of their inspirations for *The Matrix*. (FP)

**Additional Credits:** Screenplay: Kazunori Itô. English translator: Paul C. Halbert. ADR script: Mary Mason, Quint Lancaster. Associate producers: Laurence Guinness, Makoto Ibuki, Yasushi Sukeof, Hiroshi Yamazaki. Executive producers: Andy Frain, Teruo Miyahara, Takashi Mogi. Original music: Brian Eno, Kenji Kawai. Cinematography: Hisao Shirai. Film editing: Shuichi Kakesu. Production design: Takashi Watabe. Art direction: Hiromasa Ogura. Production management: Ryuji Mitsumoto. Special effects: Mutsu Murakami. Key animation supervisors: Kazuchika Kise, Hiroyuki Okiura. Animation director: Toshihiko Nishikubo. Animators: Masahiro Andô, Koichi Arai, Shinji Arakawa, Hisashi Eguchi, Toyoaki Emura, Hideki Hamazu, Takashi Hashimoto, Kazuya Hoshi, Tashiyuki Inoue, Akiharu Ishii, Mitsuo Iso, Yoshiyuki Itô, Kumiko Kawana, Hiroshi Kawasaki, Kazuchika Kise, Kôji Komurakata, Yasushi Muraki, Yasuhiro Ohshima, Tensai Okamura, Hiroyuki Okiura, Tetsuhito Saitô, Mamoru Sasaki, Atsushi Takeuchi, Yuichi Tanaka, Manabu Tanzawa, Miyako Yatsu, Masayuki Yoshiwara.

## Ghost in the Shell 2: Innocence (9/17/04) Go Fish Pictures. 99 mins. Director: Mamoru Oshii. Producers: Mitsuhisa Ishikawa, Toshio Suzuki. Voices: Akio Otsuka (Batou), Atsuko Tanaka (Motoko Kusanagi), Loichi Yamadera (Togusa), Naoto Takenaka (Kim), Tamio Oki (Aramaki), Yutaki Nakano (Ishikawa), Yoshiko Sakakibara (Haraway), Sumi Mutoh (Mysterious Young Girl).

**Consumer Tips:** ☆☆☆☆ MPAA Rating: PG-13. SF intellectual thriller. A sequel to *Ghost in the Shell*.

**Story:** In A.D. 2032, Detective Batou investigates the killings of men by female pleasure androids that go murderously defective. Clues suggest sabotage of the androids, organized crime involvement, and a cover-up by the megapowerful manufacturer. Batou and his partner Togusa have electronically enhanced brains, and the villains have a virus that can flood their minds with false memories until they can no longer be sure what reality is.

**Comments:** Several years after the success of *Ghost in the Shell*, Production I.G planned a double sequel. The television series, *Ghost in the Shell: Stand Alone Complex*, consisted of 26 episodes broadcast on a pay-per-view channel between October 1, 2002, and October 1, 2003. The theatrical sequel, *Ghost in the Shell 2: Innocence*, was scheduled for early 2004. The television series, directed by Kenji Kamiyama, was a futuristic police procedural drama featuring the detectives of Section 9 investigating intellectual crimes involving computers and Artificial Intelligences. It was so popular that a second, 52-episode series, *Ghost in the Shell: Stand Alone Complex—2nd Gig* began on January 1, 2004.

*Kokaku Kidotai (Ghost in the Shell) 2: Innocence* (March 6, 2004), written and directed by Oshii, is the true sequel to the 1995 movie. Set three years after Kusanagi's disappearance, it stars her former partner Batou, who has replaced her as Section 9's top detective, and his new partner, Togusa.

*Innocence* is impressively, cerebrally intelligent, but deliberately emotionless. Batou's body has been 50 percent or more replaced by natural-looking prosthetics that are super-strong and contain hidden weaponry. Togusa, Section 9's rookie, is nervous about getting the artificial upgrades that will improve his job performance. Togusa is happily married with a young daughter, while Batou is a bachelor whose only affection is for his pet basset hound. The audience is left to wonder whether affection and old-fashioned feelings can exist where people are increasingly mechanizing themselves and plugging their minds directly into the Internet. Aside from the brief allusions to Togusa's home life, the only emotional friendship shown is at the climax in the intellectual respect between Batou and Kusanagi. (FP)

**Additional Credits:** Screenplay: Mamoru Oshii. Original music: Kenji Kawai. Animation director: Toshihiko Nishikubo. Character designer: Hiroyuki Okiura. Production designer: Yohei Taneda. Supervising animators: Kazuchika Kise, Tetsuya Nishio. Art director: Shuichi Hirata. Visual effects supervisor: Hisahi Ezura.

## GoBots: Battle of the Rock Lords (3/21/86)

Atlantic. 73 mins. Director: Ray Patterson. Producer: Kay Wright. Voices: Margot Kidder (Solitaire), Roddy McDowell (Nuggit), Michael Nouri (Boulder), Telly Savalas (Magmar), Arthur Bughardt (Turbo), Ike Eisenmann (Nick), Bernard Erhard (Cy-Kill), Marilyn Lightstone (Crasher), Morgan Paul (Matt), Lou Richards (Leader-1), Leslie Speights (A. J.), Frank Welker (Scooter).

©Hanna-Barbera Productions and Tonka Corporation

**Consumer Tips:** ☆ MPAA Rating: G. Based on the GoBots Tonka Toys. Strictly for little boys.

**Story:** The transforming GoBots come to the aid of the Rock People who are fighting against the evil Rock Lord and a group of GoBot Renegades.

**Comments:** 1985 was the year that giant transforming robots, led by *The Transformers*, hit their zenith as the latest craze, sweeping the minds and money of American kids. There were many spin-offs and imitations by U.S. toy companies and animation producers. One of them was the GoBots, created by Tonka Toys, which was turned into a television cartoon by Hanna-Barbera.

Premiering in 1984, 65 episodes of *Challenge of the GoBots* were sold to local television stations as a weekday afternoon series. The series followed the noble guardian GoBots, a race of robots who can transform into vehicles. They pursue the evil Renegades, who scheme to enslave the earth and use its resources to conquer their home planet, GoBotron, and the galaxy. A year later, the decision was made to produce a feature-length film.

The *GoBots* movie introduces a new race of creature (and a new line of action figures): the Rock

Lords, living mineral creatures that can change from stone to humanoid shape. The Rock Lords are voiced by mid-level celebrities: Telly Savalas (Kojak), Margot Kidder (Lois Lane), Roddy McDowell (The Bookworm), and Michael Nouri (err . . . remember him from *Flashdance*?).

The production values of the movie are only a notch better than that of the syndicated series. The animation is flat and limited, and is a far cry from the stylish anime that inspired this giant robot craze. The story is a standard retread of *Star Wars*, with the peaceful Rock Lords calling upon friendly GoBots for help with their war against sinister Rock Lords (who have teamed up with evil GoBot Renegades). They encounter various Rock Lord dinosaurs, ray guns, spaceships, and numerous forgettable characters.

The makers of *GoBots: Battle of the Rock Lords* should be stoned—and maybe they were. (JB)

**Additional Credits:** Executive producers: William Hanna, Joseph Barbera. Screenplay: Jeff Segal. Storyboard artists: Rich Chidlaw, Ric Estrada, Tony Sgroi, Bob Taylor. Story consultant: Kelly Ward. Musical director: Hoyt Curtin. Directing animators: Don Lusk, Alan Zaslove. Assistant directors: Bob Goe, Don Patterson. Coexecutive producer: Joe Taritero. Supervising animation director: Paul Sabella. Background supervisor: Al Gmuer. Background color key: Bill Proctor, Michael Humphries, Fernando Arce, Jeff Richie, Bonnie Goodknight, Matin Forte. Layout supervisior: Charles Grosvenor. Production supervisor: Janine Dawson. Sound direction: Alvy Dorman, Phil Flad C.A.S. A Hanna-Barbera production. Produced in Association with Cuckoo's Nest, Wang Film Productions Co. Ltd.

**The Golden Laws** (12/5/04) IRH Press Co. 110 mins. Director: Takaaki Ishiyama. Producers: Seikyo Oda, Kujyou Ogawa, Naifumi Sato.

**Consumer Tips:** ☆☆ MPAA Rating: Unrated. SF adventure/religious tract. Based on *The Golden Laws*, one of the holy books from Japan's Institute for Research in Human Happiness (IRH).

**Story:** Satoru, a 25th-century boy, and Alisa, a 30th-century girl, time travel into the past to witness key events in the lives of the holy leaders of ancient Greece (Hermes and Aphrodite), Egypt (Prometheus), India (Buddha and Manjusri), Israel (Moses and Jesus Christ), and China (Tien-tai Chih-i), which lead to the writing of the Golden Laws, the basis of the perfect society of the future.

**Comments:** Kofuku-no-Kagaku, a religion officially translated as the Institute for Research in Human Happiness, was created in 1986 when businessman Ryuho Okawa realized that he was the current incarnation of El Cantare (God), whose previous incarnations include many of the great leaders of history back to Atlantis and humanity's migration to Earth from Venus.

The IRH is roughly analogous to Scientology as a new faith. By the mid-1990s the IRH had grown large enough in Japan, Hawaii, and the West Coast of North America to commission Toei Animation Co. to produce animated theatrical features dramatizing its teachings. *The Golden Laws: El Cantare's History (Ougon no Hou: El Kantare no Rekishikan)*, the third of these, is the first to achieve a theatrical release in America although *Hermes: Winds of Love* (1997) and *The Laws of the Sun* (2000) had limited screenings at the IRH's meditation centers and on some university campuses and *Hermes* had a video release.

*The Golden Laws* is more youth oriented and is comparable to animated television and home-video dramatizations of the Bible in which modern Christian children travel to the past to personally observe dramatic moments such as Noah's Flood.

*The Golden Laws* combines traditional animation by Toei Animation Co. with effects by Colorado FX. It premiered in Japan on October 11, 2003, and was in Japan's box office top ten for four weeks. It played in Los Angeles from December 5 to 11, 2003, and has had art-theater releases around America since then. It was reviewed in the *Los Angeles Times* as "a well-meaning but tedious and heavily didactic spiritual odyssey." (FP)

**Additional Credits:** Executive producer: Ryuho Okawa. Visual director: Isamu Imakake. Animation creators: Masami Suda, Keizo Shimizu, Yukiyoshi Hane, Marisuke Eguchi. Visual effects creative director: Yumiko Awaya. Visual effects: Visual Magic Nice and Day, Colorado FX, Sim EX Digital Studio. Visual effects supervisor: Norihiko Ito. Music: Yuichi Mizusawa. Editor: Masahi Furukawa.

©Walt Disney Productions

**A Goofy Movie** (4/7/95) Walt Disney Pictures. 78 mins. Director: Kevin Lima. Producer: Dan Rounds. Voices: Bill Farmer (Goofy), Jason Marsden (Max), Kellie Martin (Roxanne), Jim Cummings (Pete), Rob Paulsen (P. J.), Wallace Shawn (Principal Mazur), Jenna von Oy (Stacey), Frank Welker (Bigfoot), Kevin Lima (Lesters), Jo Anne Worley (Miss Maples), Florence Stanley (Waitress), Herscel Sparber (Security Guard), Pat Buttram (Hillbilly Emcee), Klee Bragger (Tourist boy), Wayne Allwine (Mickey Mouse).

**Consumer Tips:** ☆☆½ MPAA Rating: G. A movie featuring the characters from Disney Channel's television series *Goof Troop*.

**Story:** Goofy's son Max is constantly embarrassed by his un-hip dad and is desperate to hook up with high-school cutie Roxanne. His impersonation of the hip-hop star Powerline does the trick but lands him in detention. Fearing that the lad is out of control, Goofy decides to take Max on a cross-country fishing vacation—days before his big date with Roxanne. Max lies to his girl and tells her they are going onstage in Los Angeles with Powerline, then lies to his dad by changing the road map. After some harrowing adventures and father-son bonding, all turns out well.

**Comments:** *A Goofy Movie* is *Goof Troop* writ large, and perhaps a bit better. As with most television-to-movie adaptations, the production values are a tad more extravagant. *A Goofy Movie* is a pleasant time-filler with some good moments. The opening musical number celebrating the last day of school is spirited and filled with lively characters, and the scene where Goofy takes Max to Lester's Possum Park is the funniest one in the film. Bill Farmer, as always, turns in a fine job as Goofy, which is a good thing since this is a dialogue-heavy film.

The road trip takes up most of the movie and turns out much like you would expect, with Max and Goofy eventually rediscovering their relationship. The scene where the pair crash Powerline's concert is contrived and unlikely, but this is, after all, a goofy movie. Director Lima livens things up with such devices as an encounter with Bigfoot. There are also some offbeat touches like a bevy of nuns who turn up every time Max and Goofy stop, and a weird motel that seems to have been designed by SpongeBob SquarePants. Fans of the television show and younger kids will find this movie fun, though less goofy than one might expect.

Mickey Mouse, Donald Duck, and Bambi all have cameos in the film. Goofy's car keys dangle from a Disney logo fob. Disney's studio in Paris did most of the animation after the Burbank facility storyboarded and designed the film.

The film was a modest surprise at the box office, grossing $35.3 million, and spawned an excellent direct-to-video sequel, *An Extremely Goofy Movie* in 2000. (MG)

**Additional Credits:** Story: Jymn Magon. Screenplay: Jymn Magon, Chris Matheson, Brian Pimental. Storyboard: Chris Ure, Viki Anderson, Jim Kammerud, Hank Tucker, Steve Moore, Andy Gaskill, Enrique May, John Norton, Carole Holliday, Darrell Rooney, Frans Vischer. Associate producer: Patrick Reagan. Original music: Carter Burwell. Songs: Patrick DeRemer, Jack Feldman, Roy Freedland, Tom Snow. Film editing: Gregory Perler. Production design: Fred Warter. Art direction: Wendell Luebbe, Larry Leker. Supervising animators: Nancy Beiman, Matias Marcos, Stephane Sainte-Foi, Dominique Monfery.

**Great Conquest: The Romance of Three Kingdoms** (4/21/94) Streamline Pictures. 118 mins. Director: Tomoharu Katsumata. Producers: Yusuke Okada, Takamasa Yoshinari. Voices: Pat Morita (Narrator).

**Consumer Tips:** ☆☆½ MPAA Rating: Not rated. Chinese historical drama. Based on the Chinese literary classic *The Romance of Three Kingdoms*.

©Enoki Films

**Story:** By A.D. 220, weak kings were no longer able to hold China's first united kingdom together. China split into three rival kingdoms that constantly tried to conquer each other, while hordes of bandits pillaged the helpless peasants. Finally, three brave friends resolved to establish a new united kingdom and restore peace to all China.

**Comments:** China was united into a single empire in 206 B.C. under the Han dynasty. Later, Han rulers grew too weak to stop powerful lords and generals from seizing power. The Yellow Turban Rebellion in A.D. 184 marked the beginning of general social breakdown. In A.D. 220 a powerful general forced the last Han emperor to abdicate in favor of the general's son. Other generals refused to recognize this and proclaimed their own dynasties. China split into the kingdoms of Wu, Shu-han, and Wei, which fought among each other until one briefly conquered the other two in A.D. 280 China suffered through civil wars for several more centuries, but 220 to 280 is considered the Three Kingdoms period when three separate kings fought each other for the legacy of the Han dynasty.

Oral retellings over centuries exaggerated the rival kings and their generals and advisors into larger-than-life heroes and villains, aided by gods and demons. Around the 13th century, scholars started to document these tales. Luo Guanzhong's version, written between 1330 and 1400, is China's first attempt at accurate history as distinct from overdramatized storytelling, trying to separate and discard the mythological additions.

The hero of Luo's history is Liu Pei, the son of a minor official distantly related to the Han dynasty, who proclaimed the Shu-han kingdom in 221. Liu Pei is portrayed as an honorable young scholar and natural leader who is dismayed by the chaos into which China has fallen. He and his two friends, Kuan Yu and Chang Fei, pledge to aid each other in raising armies, fighting to rebuild the Chinese nation, and restoring justice to the people.

*The Romance of Three Kingdoms* has been an inspiration for popular Chinese drama for centuries. In Japan, there were three animated television movie specials, aired as *San Go Kushi* on January 4, 1982, March 20, 1985, and August 22, 1986, and a 47-episode television serial that ran from October 18, 1991, to September 29, 1992.

The animated two-part theatrical feature (February 1, 1992, and March 20, 1993, combined for the American release), commissioned from Toei Animation Co., Ltd., is visually the most spectacular of the animated versions. It is full of mighty cavalry charges, individual sword battles between mounted warriors, sieges of walled cities, dramatic royal proclamations, betrayals, agonizing decisions by loyal junior officers whether to obey incompetent superiors, military victories and reversals, and more. But the flashing back and forth to show three kingdoms' interlocking political intrigues and military histories over about a decade, with all the lookalike nobles, ministers, and warriors, grows too confusing. The story ends abruptly after Liu Pei's first few victories, with the implication that of course the educated audience knows what ultimately happened to his quest. (FP)

**Additional Credits:** Story: Takamasa Yoshinari, Shoji Yazawa. Screenplay: Kazuo Kasahara. Music: Seiji Yokoyama. Associate producers: Toyotaro Ogino, Tomoharu Katsumata. Executive in charge of production: Matsusi Kishimoto. Production design: Takamura Mukuo. Art directors: Takamura Mukuo, Tadao Kubota. Character design/animation director: Koichi Tsunoda. Directors of photography: Toshiharu Takei, Yoichi Takashima. Editor: Yutaka Chitose, Masaaki Hanai. Production supervisor: Toshio Masuda.

**The Great Mouse Detective** (7/2/86) Walt Disney Pictures. 74 mins. Directors: Ron Clements, John Musker, Dave Michener, Burny Mattinson. Producer:

Burny Mattinson. Voices: Barrie Ingham (Basil, Bartholomew), Val Bettin (Dr. Dawson, thug, guard), Vincent Price (Professor Ratigan), Susanne Pollatschek (Olivia), Alan Young (Hiram Flaversham), Candy Candido (Fidget), Ellen FitzHugh (Barmaid), Shani Wallis (Lady Mouse), Eve Brenner (Queen Moustoria), Diana Chesney (Mrs. Judson), Basil Rathbone (Sherlock Holmes), Laurie Main (Dr. Watson), Wayne Allwine, Tony Anselmo, Walker Edmiston (thugs, guards).

©Walt Disney Productions

**Consumer Tips:** ☆☆☆ MPAA Rating: G. Adapted from the book *Basil of Baker Street* by Eve Titus, the first of a series of books featuring the rodent detective.

**Story:** The great mouse detective Basil and his new assistant Dr. Dawson are pitted against the dastardly Professor Ratigan and his assistant Fidget the bat when Ratigan forces toymaker Hiram Flaversham to construct a robotic Queen Moustoria. On the night of the Queen's Diamond Jubilee she is to be kidnapped and replaced with the robot, who will hand all power over to Ratigan. With the help of Dr. Dawson, Flaversham's young daughter Olivia, and Sherlock Holmes's faithful dog, Toby, Basil quashes the plot and defeats his archfoe at last.

**Comments:** This is a film made by a team on the cusp of greatness. The directors, writers, and animators who would restore Disney to the premiere position among animation studios was almost totally in place, including Jeffrey Katzenberg, whose input helped shape the film. As such, *The Great Mouse Detective* is an impor-

tant transitional film in Disney's recent history. It is also great fun to watch, although the animation falters in places and some of the backgrounds involving other characters are little more than still paintings. The movie is notable for the first extended sequence in an animated film involving computer-generated imagery. The finale is a battle between Basil and Ratigan inside Big Ben; the mice are traditionally animated but the gears and cogs (which move in perspective) are all CGI. Considering this was state of the art in 1986, the combination comes off surprisingly well.

The script, with input from 10 writers, is a strong one and as a result there are no dead spots in the film; it seems shorter than its 74-minute running time. A weak character or two hampers many animated films, including Disney's, but such is not the case with *The Great Mouse Detective*. Solid character animation brightens the film and makes it believable. The struggle between Basil and Ratigan is not simply one of good versus evil; it is also a battle between two enormous egos. Caught in Ratigan's dreadful deathtrap, Basil simply gives up. This is not because he is defeated or resigned to his fate but because he has been outsmarted. Ratigan's inflated pretensions will not allow him to be called a rat by his henchmen, even though that's what he plainly is. *The Great Mouse Detective* is an underrated film in the Disney canon, probably because it, along with *Oliver and Company* (1988), was the last of its kind. In just a year or two Disney would be changing the design and scope of its animated features, but that does not mean that *The Great Mouse Detective* should be overlooked.

For the record:

- The film was originally called "Basil of Baker Street" after the book of the same name, but it was thought that the title sounded "too British." It finally wound up being called *The Great Mouse Detective* but was reissued in 1992 as *Adventures of the Great Mouse Detective*. In England, the feature was called *Basil—The Great Mouse Detective*.
- Bill the Lizard must have left Alice's Wonderland to take up a life of crime, as he is now in Ratigan's gang. (One would think that there were plenty of chimneys to sweep in 1897 London!)
- Dumbo makes a cameo appearance in the film as a bubble-blowing toy.

• Oh, for shame: there are several instances of tobacco smoking, alcohol consumption, and intoxication in this film.

Henry Mancini wrote the musical score except for the sultry dancehall number "Let Me Be Good to You," which was written and recorded by Melissa Manchester. (MG)

**Additional Credits:** Story adaptation: Pete Young, Vance Gerry, Steve Hulett, Ron Clements, John Musker, Bruce M. Morria, Matthew O'Callaghan, Burny Mattinson, Dave Michener, Melvin Shaw. Music: Henry Mancini. Supervising animators: Mark Henn, Glen Keane, Robert Minkoff, Hendel Butoy. Animators: Matthew O'Callaghan, Mike Gabriel, Ruben A. Aquino, Jay Jackson, Kathy Zielinski, Doug Krohn, Phil Nibbelink, Andreas Deja, Phil Young, Shawn Keller, Ron Husband, Joseph Lanzisero, Rick Farmiloe, Dave Pruiksma, Sandra Borgmeyer, Cyndee Whitney, Barry Temple, David Block, Ed Gombert, Steven E. Gordon. Effects animators: Ted C. Kierscey, Kelvin Yasuda, Dave Bossert, Patricia Peraza, Mark Dindal. Art director: Guy Vasilovich. Layout: Dan Hansen, David A. Dunnet, Karen A. Keller, Gil DiCicco, Michael A. Peraza Jr., Edward L. Ghertner. Color styling: Jim Coleman. Backgrounds: Donald A. Towns, Tia Kratter, Andrew Phillipson, Phillip Phillipson. Animation consultant: Eric Larson.

## Grendel, Grendel, Grendel (4/1/82) Satori Productions. 90 mins. Director: Alexander Stitt. Producer: Phillip Adams. Voices: Peter Ustinov (Grendel), Keith Mitchell (Beowulf), Arthur Dignam (King Hrothgar), Julie McKenna (King's Mistress), Ed Rosser, Ric Stone, Bobby Bright, Ernie Bourne, Alison Bird, Barry Hill.

**Consumer Tips:** ☆☆ MPAA Rating: Unrated. Too talky for kids. Too cerebral for adults. Based on the novel *Grendel* by John Gardner.

**Story:** Humorous story, told from the point of view of a 12-foot, sophisticated monster, whom we observe pondering his existence, taunting the king's warriors, and challenging the hero, Beowulf.

**Comments:** John Gardner was a noted novelist, professor of medieval literature, and scholar of ancient languages. He published his critically acclaimed novel, *Grendel*, in 1971. The book was modern retelling of the eighth-century Anglo-Saxon epic *Beowulf* from the point of view of the villain of the story.

Australian filmmaker Alexander Stitt, noted for his animated commercials, titles, and designs, acquired the film rights to Gardner's novel in 1978. Work on the animated adaptation commenced at Stitt's Melbourne Al et al. Studios in 1979, as a coproduction with film producer Phillip Adams, under the banner of Animation Australia. The budget was reportedly between $560,000 and $680,000. *Grendel Grendel Grendel* was completed in 1981, but given its formal U.S. release in the spring of 1982.

The film generally succeeds as a fractured fairy tale for grown-ups. Musical numbers were added to pad the length, but they slowed the pace of the narrative. The film's limited animation, highly stylized graphic design, and dialogue-heavy, literate screenplay kept the film restricted to art theaters in urban centers.

Critics were generally enchanted with this intelligent, colorful, and witty film. *Grendel, Grendel, Grendel* was a true departure for feature animation in a year when Hollywood was serving up the likes of *The Fox and the Hound, Heavy Metal,* and *The Looney Looney Looney Bugs Bunny Movie.* (JB)

**Additional Credits:** Screenplay/design: Alexander Stitt. Animation director: Frank Hellard. Animators: Frank Hellard, David Atkinson, Ralph Peverill, Gus McLaren, Anne Jolliffe, Alexander Stitt. Production supervisor: Maggie Geddes. Music: Bruce Smeaton. Painters: Maggie Geddes, Marilyn Davies, Denis Pryor, Suzan Harris, Janet Arup, Chris Neely, Sally Anne Rozario. Graphics: David Dalgarno. Animation Australia Pty. Ltd.

## Gulliver's Travels (12/22/39) Paramount—Fleischer Studios. 74 mins. Director: Dave Fleischer. Producer: Max Fleischer. Voices: Sam Parker (Gulliver), Jessica Dragonette (Princess Glory), Lanny Ross (Prince David), Pinto Colvig (Gabby), Jack Mercer (King Little), Tedd Pierce (King Bombo).

**Consumer Tips:** ☆☆☆½ MPAA Rating: Unrated. Musical adventure. For all ages. A classic story based on the famous book by Jonathan Swift.

**Story:** Shipwreck survivor Gulliver washes up at the kingdom of Lilliput, where he is a giant to the tiny inhabitants of the land. Gulliver befriends the king and town crier, Gabby, unites Princess Glory to Prince David, and helps prevent a war between two fueding nations.

**Comments:** *Gulliver's Travels* was the first attempt by a rival Hollywood studio (Paramount) to cash in on Disney's success with animated features. Max Fleischer was Disney's greatest rival during the 1930s, when his characters (Popeye, Betty Boop, etc.) became as popular, or more popular, than Mickey Mouse and Donald Duck. In addition, his pioneering use of innovative technical processes (three-dimensional backgrounds, sound, color, etc.) broke new ground in animation, usually before Walt tried them out himself.

It should be noted that this was not Max Fleischer's first attempt at making a feature film. In 1923, Fleischer produced a pair of one-hour documentaries (mainly live action with bits of animation) of *The Einstein Theory of Relativity* and *Darwin's Theory of Evolution*. In 1936, the studio began a series of annual extra-length Popeye two-reelers (18 minutes in length), billed as *Popeye Color Features* and sold to theaters as such. *Gulliver*, however, was the studio's first true animated feature-length film.

Paramount moved Fleischer's animation studio from New York City to a state-of-the-art facility in Miami to escape problems with New York's film production unions. For the production of this film, 200 employees (mainly animators and artists) relocated from Fleischer's New York location and were joined by over 150 artists recruited from Hollywood and Miami.

One of the talents recruited from Hollywood was Pinto Colvig, the voice of Disney's Goofy, who came aboard *Gulliver* to vocalize the character of Gabby, the town crier. Gabby was later spun off into his own series of twelve short subjects. Likewise, various supporting characters had their shot at subsequent solo stardom in sequels in separate short subjets: Twinkletoes the pigeon, and villians Snoop, Sneak, and Snitch.

Colvig hung around Fleischer studios long enough to voice several characters in Fleischer's other series. These included several appearances in Popeye cartoons (sometimes as Bluto), as the Camel in *Raggedy Ann and Raggedy Andy* (1940), and as Mr. Creeper in Fleischer's second feature, *Mr. Bug Goes to Town* (1942).

©Fleischer Studios

Popeye was briefly considered for the lead role of Gulliver, but that was abandoned when it was decided to use Max Fleischer's 1917 invention, the rotoscope—a device used to trace live-action photography to drawings. All of the shots of *Gulliver* were taken from live action of actor Sam Parker—a very effective use of the process—which also helped speed production of the film. A standout sequence has King Little dancing with Gulliver's realistically rotoscoped fingers, to a swinging rendition of "Bluebirds in the Moonlight."

The main music in the film was provided by Paramount's Famous Music songwriters Leo Robin and Ralph Rainger (who penned "Please," "Love in Bloom," "Blue Hawaii," and "Thanks for the Memories"). Some of the tunes, including "All's Well" and "It's a Hap-Hap-Happy Day," became hits. The most enduring song, "It's a Hap-Hap-Happy Day," was written by Fleischer staff musicians Sammy Timberg, Winston Sharples, and Al Neiberg.

Although much of Swift's social satire is gone, the film's antiwar message is delivered in an entertaining way. Falling a bit short of the Disney standard, *Gulliver's Travels* is a most enjoyable film, and was a modest success at the box office. This gave Paramount the confidence to allow the Fleischer studio to start a second feature, *Mr. Bug Goes to Town* (1942). *Gulliver's Travels* stands as one of Max Fleischer's considerable achievements, an underrated classic of Hollywood animation. (JB)

**Additional Credits:** Screenplay: Dan Gordon, Cal Howard, Tedd Pierce, I. Sparber, Edward Seward. Based on the novel *Gulliver's Travels* by Jonathan Swift. Music/lyrics: Ralph Rainger,

Leo Robin. Atmospheric music written/conducted: Victor Young. Song, "It's a Hap-Hap-Happy Day" by Sammy Timberg, Al Neiberg, Winston Sharples. Directors of animation: Seymour Kneitel, Willard Bowsky, Tom Palmer, Grim Natwick, William Henning, Roland Crandall, Tom Johnson, Robert Leffingwell, Frank Kelling, Winfield Hoskins, Orestes Calpini.

**Gulliver's Travels Beyond the Moon** (7/23/66) Continental—Toei Animation Co., Ltd. (Japan). 78 mins. Director: Yoshio Kuroda. Producer: Okawa Hiroshi. Voices: Sakamoto Kyu (Boy Ted), Miyaguchi Seiji (Professor Gulliver), Robert Harter (Professor Gulliver—English version), Hori Junko (Mack the Stray Dog), Herb Duncan (Pug—English version), Honma Chiyoko (Queen of the Purple Star), Darla Hood (Princess—English version), Ozawa Akio (Doll General), Oizumi Ko (King of the Purple Planet), Imanishi Masao (Robot of the Blue Planet), Ito Makiko (Island Crow).

©Continental Distribution

**Consumer Tips:** ☆☆½ MPAA Rating: Not rated. Children's sci-fi/fantasy light adventure. Inspired by Jonathan Swift's *Gulliver's Travels*.

**Story:** Ricky, a homeless child, is inspired by a movie about the adventures of the heroic explorer Gulliver. The boy, a toy soldier named "the Colonel," and Pug the stray puppy meet the real Gulliver, now a scientist building a spaceship to explore the Milky Way. They travel to the Star of Hope where they save a kingdom of dolls from evil robots.

**Comments:** *Gulliver No Uchu Ryoko* (Japan, March 20, 1965) was one of Toei Animation's first theatrical features to abandon its original formula of movies based upon traditional Oriental folk tales, following its failure to achieve international box-office success. The story that mixes the modern juvenile popularity of space-travel adventures with the classic story of *Gulliver's Travels* to exotic lands and the imagery of Hans Christian Andersen's tales featuring 19th-century toys and dolls is clearly designed to appeal to European and American audiences.

Ricky ("Ted" in Japan) is "a homeless waif" in the style of Andersen's Little Match Girl; not quite freezing to death but very despondent. He is eight or ten years old and lives in alleys. It is perfectly natural for him to meet a talking puppy, Pug (Mack), and a live 19th-century-style toy soldier. It is also natural for him to see a movie about *Gullliver's Travels* and coincidentally meet the real Gulliver immediately afterwards. Gulliver (still wearing 18th-century-style clothes) is now an elderly scientist, Dr. Gulliver, building a spaceship with only the assistance of Sylvester, his faithful crow assistant (just "Crow" in Japan). They invite the boy, toy soldier, and puppy to join them as their crew.

*Gulliver's Travels Beyond the Moon* was designed in the style of a typical American children's animated feature, with five great happy songs. For the American release, the music and songs were written by the husband-wife team of Milton and Anne Delugg, veteran composers of movie, television, radio, and nightclub music.

The movie is inoffensive for young children, but its lighthearted plot has no suspense. The attempt to mix sci-fi with talking dolls would probably be considered by anyone over 10 as an insult to their intelligence. It did no better at the American box office than Toei's previous features with Oriental stories. (FP)

**Additional Credits:** Screenplay: Sekizawa Shinichi. Animation supervisor: Hideo Furusawa. Original songs/music: Milton and Anne DeLugg. Art director: Yokoi Saburo. Planning: Ono Sawahiro, Hatano Yoshifumi. Supervisors: Yamamoto Sanae, Yabushita Taiji. Director's assistants: Shidara Hiroshi, Yamaguchi Yasuo. Photography: Shinozaki Fumio, Hayashi Akio. Recording: Ishii Sachio. Effects: Iwafuji Ryuzo. Editing: Inaba Ikuzo. Key animation: Otsuka Yasuo, Nagasawa Makoto, Takeuchi Tomekichi, Oda Katsuya, Kikuchi Sadao, Ota Akemi, Matsubara Akinori, Mori Yasuji. Backgrounds: Sugimoto Eiko, Endo Shigeyoshi, Dota Isamu, Tsuji Tadanao.

**Gumby: The Movie** (12/8/95) Arrow. 90 mins. Director: Art Clokey. Producers: Art Clokey, Gloria Clokey. Voices: Art Clokey (Gumby, Claybert, Fatbuckle, Kapp), Charles Farrington (Pokey, Prickle, Gumbo), Gloria Clokey (Goo), Manny LaCarrubba (Thinbuckle), Alice Young (Ginger), Janet MacDuff (Gumba), Patti Morse (Tara), Bonnie Randolph (Lowbelly, Farm Lady), Ozzie Ahlers (Radio Announcer).

**Consumer Tips:** ☆☆ MPAA Rating: G.

**Story:** Episodic tale begins when Gumby's dog is kidnapped by the evil Blockheads. The bad guys soon replace all of Gumby's pals with robotic clones. Gumby battles the baddies through various storybook settings, including a *Star Wars* spoof.

**Comments:** Gumby was television's first stop-motion star, introduced on Howdy Doody in the late 1950s, and indeed for many is still synonymous with "clay animation" or "stop motion." Creator Art Clokey's foray into feature films came seven years after a syndicated Gumby revival series. The new series redubbed and rescored the original episodes, and added new installments. Returning characters such as Goo were heavily redesigned for series and film, and Gumby's parents, fixtures of the earliest shorts, became more prominent. The rock motif used in the film also first surfaced in the 1980s series. The movie was something of a family affair, with Clokey and his wife Gloria voicing several characters, Gloria penning script and song lyrics, and daughter Holly Harman building puppets and sets. As with the original series, the plot is simplistic and secondary to surreal set pieces, such as Pokey, Goo, and Prickle accidentally forming one solid mass, or the climatic music video involving multiple Pokeys. Animators included veterans of the newer television series who would go on to work on *Nightmare Before Christmas*, such as Mike Belzer and Angie Glocka, as well as veteran Peter Kleinow, who had worked with George Pal in the 1950s, and whose association with Clokey stretched back to the original series.

The film works best as either a study in nostalgia or a study in surrealism. After this film, Gumby's career became dormant again. However, recent DVD releases of the series may help to rekindle interest, and as an iconic character, Gumby shall probably continue to resurface. (AL)

**Additional Credits:** Screenplay: Art Clokey, Gloria Clokey. Storyboards/script: Art Clokey. Music: Jerry Gerber, Marco Ambroaio. Songs: Ozzie Ahlers. Lyrics: Gloria Clokey. Trimensional animators: Stephen Buckley, Tony Laudati, Dan Mason, Ken Willard, Mike Belzer, Art Clokey, Angie Glocka, Kurt Hanson, Peter Kleinow, Harry Walton. Animated effects: Tom Rubalcava. Animation assistants: Tansy Brooks, Dan Mason, Dennis Yasukawa. Animation consultant: John R. Dilworth. Set breakdown: Gloria Clokey, Holly Harman. Model sculpturing: Tom Rubalcava. Model construction: Dennis Yasukawa, Earle Murphy. Puppets/costumes: Cora Craig, Tom Rubalcava, Gloria Clokey, Janet McDuff, Holly Harman, Mindy Breede-Harman. Sets/backgrounds: Holly Harman, Bonnie Liebhold, Dennis Yasukawa, Janet MacDuff, Dan Morgan, Mary Bradley. Character molds: Cora Craig, Tom Rubalcava. Armature construction: Kurt Hanson.

**Hansel and Gretel** (10/10/54) RKO. 72 mins. Director: John Paul. Producer: Michael Myerberg. Voices: Constance Brigham (Hansel and Gretel), Anna Russell (Rosina Rubylips the Witch), Mildred Dunnock (Mother), Frank Rogier (Father), Delbert Anderson (Sandman), Helen Boatright (Dew Fairy), Apollo Boys' Choir (Angels, Children and Chorus).

©Michael Myerberg Productions

**Consumer Tips:** ☆☆½ MPAA Rating: Unrated. Delightful stop-motion puppet version of *Hansel and Gretel*, based on the Grimm fairy tale and the Englebert Humperdinck opera.

**Story:** You know the story: a witch tricks two children into a candy house and attempts to eat them. Kids push witch into oven and escape death.

**Comments:** This visually inventive stop-motion puppet film is quite entertaining, despite less-than-perfect animation.

*Hansel and Gretel* was the brainchild of Broadway producer Michael Myerberg, whose roots in classical music date back to his earlier career managing Leopold Stokowski. Myerberg persuaded Stokowski to go to Hollywood in the late 1930s, and appear in films like Universal's *100 Men and a Girl* (1936).

It was during his work with Stokowski on Walt Disney's *Fantasia* (1940) that Myerberg became enchanted with the ability of animation to translate music visually. Teaming up with artist James Russell Summers, Myerberg financed the creation of articulated puppets dubbed "Kinemins." Studio publicity tried to pass these models off as dolls that acted and emoted via a mysterious electronically operated process. However, they were actually standard stop-motion armatures, hand-animated before the camera on a frame-by-frame basis. According to studio publicity, it took 15 years and $600,000 worth of experiments to create the "Kinemins."

Regardless of the hype, the puppets are very attractive and expressive, and they performed well on elaborate miniature sets designed by Evalds Dajevskis. The production was filmed in a small studio on Manhattan's Lower East Side (on Second Street between Avenues B and C).

Myerberg hired noted Irish poet and playwright, Padraic Colum, to adapt *Hansel and Gretel* into a screenplay, weaving it into the score of the 1893 Humperdinck opera. The voices were cast from various New York stage and opera companies. Anna Russell (as the witch), Frank Rogier (father), and Constance Brigham (as both Hansel and Gretel) were well known and versatile Broadway performers. Milldred Dunnock (mother) had a long, illustrious career on both stage and screen.

Myerberg opened the film himself, without a distributor, in October 1954 at New York's Broadway Theater. Excellent reviews and grosses convinced RKO to pick the film up for Christmas release.

RKO was familiar with distributing animated features, but was on the verge of losing its lucrative Disney contract (Disney set up its own distribution company, Buena Vista, at this time). Thus RKO put a lot of muscle into the release of this film. *Hansel and Gretel* recieved promotion and merchandising worthy of a Disney classic: $10 million worth of tie-ins with Nabisco crackers, Mars candy, clothing, fabrics, figurines, and an extensive toy line, which was quickly put in place for the 1954 Christmas holidays.

Myerberg told *Variety* in 1972 that RKO originally grossed $1.3 million on the film. Myerberg himself rereleased the film in 1965, through New Trends Associates. He made headlines at the time by taking Saturday matinee distributor Childhood Productions to court, to block their release of a live-action German-made *Hansel and Gretel*.

Alas, for all his good intentions, Myerberg's *Hansel and Gretel* film does not have the heart and charm of a Disney classic, or of a George Pal Puppetoon, for that matter. The operatic tone was too highbrow for the kids, and the herky-jerky puppet movements were a far cry from the warmth of Disney's hand-drawn, personality-driven character animation.

The film found its place in subsequent classroom screenings and later on home video. It is no Disney film, but is a worthy animated effort with much to enjoy. (JB)

**Additional Credits:** Original play: Adelheid Wette. Story adaptation: Padraic Colum. Film editor: James R. Barclay. Production manager: William F. Rodgers. Music: Engelbert Humperdinck. Musical conductor: Franz Allers. Director of photography: Martin Munkacs. Animation: Joseph Horstmann, Inez Anderson, Daniel Diamond, Ralph Emory, Hobart Rosen, Don Sahlin, Teddy Shapard, Nathalie Schulz. Costume designers: Ida Venedicktow. Character designs: James Summers. Sets: Evalds Dajevskis. Chief engineer: Anthony Pete Ianuzzi. Creator of special effects: Herbert Schaffer.

**Happily Ever After** (5/28/93) First National Film Corp. 74 mins. Director: John Howley. Producer: Lou Scheimer. Voices: Irene Cara (Snow White), Edward Asner (Scowl), Carol Channing (Muddy), Dom DeLuise (Looking Glass), Phyllis Diller (Mother Nature), Zsa Zsa Gabor (Blossom), Linda Gary (Critterina, Marina), Jonathan Harris (Sunflower), Sally Kellerman (Sunburn), Michael Horton (Prince), Tracey Ullman (Moonbeamm, Thunderella), Malcolm McDowell (Lord Maliss), Frank Welker (Batso).

©Filmation Associates

*Consumer Tips:* **0** (zero stars) MPAA Rating: G. Loosely based on the Brothers Grimm fairy tale. Also known as *Snow White and the Seven Dwarfelles, Snow White in the Land of Doom,* and *Snow White: The Adventure Continues.*

*Story:* Snow White and her prince are pursued by an evil king who wants revenge on those who caused the death of his sister (the queen). For help, Snow White returns to the Seven Dwarfs, but finds their cottage occupied by seven Dwarfelles (female cousins).

*Comments:* Filmation's swan song production is a slow-moving, old-fashioned, artless "sequel" to the Disney classic *Snow White and the Seven Dwarfs.* It's awful.

During its salad days of the 1980s, Saturday morning cartoon factory Filmation announced an ambitious plan to create a series of feature-length films that were direct sequels to Disney animated features. Only their Pinocchio (1987's *Pinocchio and the Emperor of the Night*) and Snow White productions were ever completed.

At least the Pinocchio film contained a smidgen of ambition and enthusiasm. In contrast, *Happily Ever After* has a hurried look, as if everyone had to finish their work before the doors to the studio were locked forever.

The convoluted story of *Happily Ever After* is a rehash of the Disney version of *Snow White*, minus the wit, charm, and heart. It presents forgettable songs, a wasted all-star voice cast, mundane action, and mediocre animation. It is a total snooze.

The film grossed a dismal $3.2 million, and shortly thereafter Filmation and the film disappeared completely . . . and animation fans lived happily ever after. (JB)

*Additional Credits:* Screenplay: Martha Moran, Robby London. Music composed/performed by: Frank M. Becker. Music supervisor: Erika Scheimer. Sequence directors: Gian Celestri, Kamoon Song, Larry White. Associate producers: John Grusd, Robby London, Erika Scheimer. Film editing: Joe Gall, Jeffrey C. Patch. Casting: Cheryl Bascom. Assistant production controller: David Bumler. Assistant to producer: Joyce Loeb. A Filmation production.

## Heathcliff: The Movie (1/17/86) Atlantic. 73 mins.
Director: Bruno Bianchi. Producers: Jean Chalopin, Denys Heroux. Voices: Mel Blanc (Heathcliff), Donna Christie, Peter Cullen, Jeannie Elias, Stan Jones, Marilyn Lightstone, Danny Mann, Derek McGrath, Marilyn Schreffler, Danny Wells, Ted Zeigler.

©Atlantic Entertainment Group

*Consumer Tips:* ☆ MPAA Rating: G. Based on the comic strip by George Gately.

*Story:* Heathcliff, the cat, entertains his nephews with stories of his greatest adventures.

*Comments:* This "movie" is a complete sham and a total cheat. It is really a compilation of several television episodes, bridged with new footage of Heathcliffe recounting his exploits to his three bored nephews on a rainy day. The new footage is awful—even his nephews try to escape listening to Heathcliff's many recycled adventures. The reused material includes the time Heathcliff appeared in a cat food commercial, the story of when he beat up the neighborhood bulldog, the time he turned over a new leaf, the day he tackled the wrestling champ, the time he helped his ex-con father, the week he enrolled in an obedience school, and the time he took on the mob run by "the Catfather."

George Gately's comic strip kitty first appeared in 1973 and leaped into an ABC animated series in 1980, produced by Ruby Spears. Andy Heyward's DiC took over production chores with an all-new syndicated show in 1984. Mel Blanc, as the voice of Heathcliff, was the series' saving grace. Otherwise, the television show and this feature film had nothing to offer, save from being an early credit for John Kricfalusi.

*Heathcliff: The Movie* was released as part of Atlantic Pictures' ambitious Clubhouse Pictures initiative. Inspired by its huge-grossing release of *Smurfs and the Magic Flute*, Atlantic picked up every animated film in sight for a series of Saturday matinee releases in 1986. Most of the films tanked, and deservedly so. *Heathcliff* grossed a dismal $2.6 million, and has been haunting the video rental shelves ever since. (JB)

**Additional Credits:** Executive producers: Jean Chalopin, Andy Heyward, Tesuo Katayana. Head writer: Alan Swayze. Post-production supervisor: W. R. Kowalchuck Jr. Animation coordinator: Don Spencer. Original music: Shuki Levy, Haim Saban. Heathcliff creator: George Gately. Cats and Co. creator: Jean Chalopin, Bruno Bianchi. Development: Jean Chalopin. Development assistant: Alan Swayze, Chuck Lorre. Cats and Co. character designs: Bruno Bianchi, Christian Choquet, Byron Vaughns. Design assistants: Stephan Marttiniere, Jean Maxime-Perramon, John Kricfalusi, Lynne Naylor, Kit Harper. Senior storyboard artists: Zlatko Grigc, Andre Knight, David Marshall. Production coordination: Shiro Aono, Dick Brown, Mitsuya Fujimoto, W. R. Kowalchuck Jr., Victor Villegas, James Wang.

**Heavy Metal** (8/7/81) Columbia. 90 mins. Director: Gerald Potterton. Producer: Ivan Reitman. Voices: Don Francks (Grimaldi), Caroline Semple (Grimaldi's Student), Richard Romanus (Harry Canyon), Susan Roman (Girl, Satellite), Al Waxman (Rudnick), Harvey Atkin (Alien), John Candy (Dan, Den, Desk Sergeant, Robot), Marilyn Lightstone (Queen, Whore), John Vernon (Prosecutor), Eugene Levy (Captain Lincoln F. Sternn, Edsel, Male Reporter), Joe Flaherty (Lawyer Charlie, General), Rodger Bumpass (Hanover

*©Columbia Pictures Industries, Inc.*

Fiste, Dr. Anrak), Douglas Kenney (Regolian), Harold Ramis (Zeke).

**Consumer Tips:** ☆☆☆ MPAA Rating: R. Based on graphic stories in *Heavy Metal* magazine.

**Story:** A compilation of science-fiction stories based on the *Heavy Metal* comic book. Includes Taarna, Den, and Harry Canyon.

**Comments:** *Heavy Metal* was an outgrowth of the popular comic magazine of the same name, featuring graphic science-fiction and fantasy tales. An anthology film, the movie functions in some ways as a post-pubescent *Fantasia* with rock music (by Blue Öyster Cult, Grand Funk Railroad, Sammy Hagar, and Devo, whose "Working in a Coal Mine" appropriately underscores the closing credits) in place of classical symphonies. The seven segments that make up the film are loosely strung together by linking narration involving a mystical rock, which somehow sets the various tales into motion. Although Ivan Reitman produced and Canadian animator Gerald Potterton was the overall director, the sequences were farmed out across the United States, Canada, and Britain, with Halas and Batchelor ("Soft Landing" and "So Beautiful, So Dangerous") and Atkinson-Film Arts ("Harry Canyon," "B-17") handling two segments apiece. However, the film overall has the predictable

1980s animation look, especially in terms of paint and gloss. Numerous artists and writers who had worked for the magazine, including Richard Corben, Neal Adams, and Angus McKie, contributed to the film. One of the best-remembered segments, "Den" was a direct adaptation of a popular Corben tale. A bevy of mostly Canadian actors/comedians (especially *SCTV* alums) supplied voices for the segments, with John Candy's portrayals of Den and a neurotic, sex-crazed robot in another segment as particular highlights. Other performers, such as Harvey Atkin, Susan Roman, and Marilyn Lightstone, ironically became staples of Nelvana's series based on children's books. The final segment, "Taarna," while arguably the most exploitive of teenage fantasies, featuring a nubile Amazon warrior, is also the least reliant on dialogue (a rotoscope model was used for the lead character).

Receiving an R rating, each segment is highlighted by violence, nudity, and sex, which, in addition to the soundtrack, allowed the movie to develop something of a cult following through frequent cable broadcasts, and even inspired a belated sequel (linked only by name and magazine roots), *Heavy Metal 2000*. Due to its graphic content, the film has often been mislabeled as a Bakshi production by Blockbuster Video and others. (AL)

**Additional Credits:** Screenplay: Dan Goldberg, Len Blum (based on original art and stories by Richard Corben, Angus McKie, Dan O'Bannon, Thomas Warkentin, and Berni Wrightson). Music: Elmer Bernstein. Songs performed by Black Sabbath, Blue Oyster Cult, Cheap Trick, Devo, Donald Fagin, Don Felder, Grand Funk Railroad, Sammy Hagar, Journey, Nazareth, Stevie Nicks, and Riggs and Trust. Main title animation: Jay Teitzell, John LePrevost, Dale Heisstad. Production designer: Michael Gross. "Soft Landing" producer: John Coates, T. V. Cartoons. Sequence director: Jimmy T. Murikami. Story: Dan O'Bannon. Original art: Thomas Warkentin. Animation: Joanne Fryer, Hilary Audus. Assistant animators: Andrew Breen, Mike Lodge. "Grimaldi" producer: John Halas. Sequence director/animation director: Harold Whitaker. Animators: Harold Whitaker, Roger Mainwood, John Perkins, Euen Frizzell. Assistant animators: Julie Krasniewicz, Les Orton, Hugh Workman. "Harry Canyon" producers: Vic Atkinson, W. H. Stevens Jr., Atkinson Film-Arts. Director: Pino Van Lamsweerde. Story: Goldberg and Blum. Animation: Doug Crane, Ray da Silva, Peter Miller, Fabio Pacifico, Greg Reyna, Norm Roen, Chris

Schouten, Sebastian, Ken Stephenson, Stephen Weston. Assistant animators: Jim Cleland, Dan Graia, Ian Freedman, Steve Rabatich, Helen Wenzelbach, Robin White. Storyboard/design: Juan Gimenez. "Den" producer: John Coates, Jerry Hibbert, and Votetone Ltd. Sequence director: Jack Stokes. Story/art: Richard Corben. Animators: Hilary Audus, Bob Balser, Bobbie Clennel, Rich Cox, Douglas Crane, Michael Dudok de Witt, Richard Fawdry, Joanne Fryer, Jerry Hibbert, Mike Hibbert, Dick Horn, Dave Livesy, Reg Lodge, Alistair McIlwain, John Perkins, Edrick Radage, Jack Stokes, Mike Williams. Assistant animators: Hester Cobleniz, Kurt Conner, John Cox, Helga Eglison, Gaston Mauzo, Phillip Norwood, Corimor Poore, Phil Scarrold, Pat Schaverton, Paul Stone, Rosemary Webb. Art director: Pat Gavin. Layouts: David Elvin, Ted Pettingell, Paul Shardlow. "Captain Sternn" producer: Boxcar Animation Studios. Directors: Paul Sabella, Julian Szuchopa. Story/art: Berni Wrightson. Key animators: Shivan Ramsaran, Paul Sabella, Julian Szuchopa, Gary Mooney. Assistant animators: Paul McGarry, Susan Kapigian. "B-17" producer: Vic Atkinson, W. H. Stevens Jr., Atkinson Film-Arts. Sequence director: Barrie Nelson. Story: Dan O'Bannon. Animators: Vic Atkinson, Jeff Hale, Fred Hellmich, Ruth Kissane, Bill Littlejohn, Spencer Peel, Norm Roen, Sebastian, Bill Perkins. Assistant animators: Jim Cleland, Ian Freedman, Steve Rabatich. Storyboard director: Lee Mishkin. "So Beautiful and So Dangerous" producer: Halas and Batchelor Animation. Sequence director: John Halas. Animation director: Brian Larkin. Story/art: Angus McKie. Animators: Brian Larkin, Harold Whitaker, Roger Mainwood, John Cousen, Borge Ring. Assistant animators: Paul Lowen, Julie Krasniewicz, Gaston Marzlo, Mike Salter, Les Orton, Hugh Workman. Storyboards/layouts: Brian Larkin, Harold Whitaker. "Taarna" Director: John Bruno. Story: Goldberg, Blum. Key animators: Jose Abel, Gary Mooney, Ernesto Lopez, Sean Newton, Milt Gray, Zdenco Gasparovic, Dan Thompson, Mitch Rochon. Animators: Charlie Downs, William Recinos, George Ungar, George Scribner, Mauro Maressa, Russ Mooney, Malcolm Draper, Arnie Wong, Trell W. Yocum, Michael Stribling, Norton Virgien, Spencer Peel, Ruth Kissane, Norm Drew, Alvaro Gaivoto, Danny Antonucci, Colin Baker, Michael Bannon, Roger Chiasson, David Feiss, Mike Longden, Daniel DeCelles. Assistant animation supervisors: Retta Davidson, Renee Holt. Assistant animators: Grace Stanzell, Joseph Gilland, Daniel DeCelles, Michael Leggad, Marilyn Taylor, Jean Sariut, Vicky Winiz, Lynn Yamasaki, Cathy Castillo, John Cox, Sharon Murray, Alasmic Maronsiki, Marik Schwarcz, Anne Chevalier, Belinda Olafert, Michael Lemie, Kevin Brownie, Scott Claus, Marie-Christiane Mathiew, Christiane Bissamette, Marelle Sarfull, Danny Turado, Richard Max Tremblay, Marie Faucher, Anne E. Peterson, Louise Robinson, Richard Villeneuve, Jane Jurasek Cullie, Elizabeth Lewis Steele, Wayne Mullins, Bernie Mircault, Irene Rappaport, Koutila A. Taponi, Kunio Shingamuta, Phyllis Blumenfeld, Lureline Weatherly, Susan Sugita, Leticia Ruiz, Ron Stangl, Ronald Wong, Mary Ann Tucker, Richard Coleman, Michael Wolf, Christopher Chu, Roderick Miles Maki, Sue Marale, Neal Warner, Paul Growell, Judith Niver, Marshall Toomey, Phillip Phillipson, Michael Kayeski. Storyboards: Kurt Conner, John Dorman, Sherman Labby, Hank Tucker, Jeffrey Gatrall.

**Heavy Traffic** (8/15/73) American International. 76 mins. Director: Ralph Bakshi. Producer: Steve Krantz. Voices: Joseph Kaufman (Michael), Beverly Hope Atkinson (Carole), Frank De Kova (Angie), Terri Haven (Ida), Mary Dean Lauria (Molly), Jacqueline Mills (Rosalyn), Lillian Adams (Rosa), Jim Bates, Jamie Farr, Robert Easton, Charles Gordone, Candy Candido, Helene Winston.

©American International Pictures, Inc.

**Consumer Tips:** ☆☆☆ MPAA Rating: X.

**Story:** Young cartoonist living in Brooklyn tries to survive his battling parents and assorted characters at the local bar.

**Comments:** Ralph Bakshi's second animated feature (precipitated by a split with producer Steve Krantz, which would only be fully realized after the film's release) is, like *Fritz the Cat*, a tale of sex and drugs. Unlike Fritz, however, the characters are all humans (or heavily caricatured facsimiles, at least), and live

backdrops and performers are incorporated, notably in the closing epilogue. The fact that the film's protagonist is an aspiring underground cartoonist is one of many indicators of the degree to which Bakshi's personal life was incorporated. The film presents a gritty, often chaotic view of a New York populated by Mafiosi, prostitutes, transvestites, and feckless young thugs (running themes in Bakshi's films; the Godfather here is essentially a warm-up for the even more grotesque creature in Bakshi's next movie, *Coonskin*). Characters stream in and out of Michael's life, with his squabbling Italian gangster mother and shrewish Jewish mother as focal points. A sequence involving an eccentric pigeon-chasing black man, Crazy Moe (voiced by playwright Charles Gordone, also used in *Coonskin*) is surprisingly philosophical, beneath the vulgarity. As with *Fritz*, Bakshi used a mixture of New York veterans (Martin Taras and Nicholas Tafuri), Hollywood veterans (Lloyd Vaughan, Irv Spence), and relative up-and-comers (including Milt Gray and Mark Kausler, the latter animating a rough-hewn adaptation of the song "Maybelline"). As with most of Bakshi's other films, the subject matter and approach to storytelling can be difficult for viewers to accept. Sequences such as a pitch for a comic book in which God is shot to death, leaving an aging publisher in shock, were and are undoubtedly a change from what one expects in animation, and with a certain intellectual point beyond the titillation and revulsion. Along with *Fritz* (and the Bakshi-less sequel, *The Nine Lives of Fritz the Cat*), *Heavy Traffic* was recently released on DVD as part of MGM's "Avant-Garde" line, to fascinate or repulse future generations. (AL)

**Additional Credits:** Screenplay: Ralph Bakshi. Original score: Ray Shanklin, Ed Bogas. Cinematography: Ted C. Bemiller, Gregg Heschong. Film editing: Donald W. Ernst, A.C.E. Layout: John Sparey, Ric Gonzalez, Robert Taylor, D. Morgan, Al Shean, Al Wilson. Background photography: John Vita, Ralph Bakshi. Backgrounds drawn by: Ira Turek. Background Artists: John Vita, Bill Butler. Background assisting: Matt Golden, Joseph Griffith. Fantasy animation: Mark Kausler. Animators: Bob Bransford, Ed De Mattia, Milt Gray, Volus Jones, Bob Maxfield, Manny Perez, Tom Ray, Lloyd Vaughn, Carlo Vinci, J. E. Walker Sr., Bob Bemiller, Irv Spence, Manny Gould, Barney Posner, Fred Hellmich, Nick Tafuri, Martin Taras, Dave Tendlar, Alex Ignatiev.

©Hanna-Barbera Productions

**Heidi's Song** (11/19/82) Paramount. 94 mins. Director: Robert Taylor. Producers: William Hanna, Joseph Barbera. Voices: Lorne Greene (Grandfather), Sammy Davis Jr. (Head Ratte), Margery Gray (Heidi), Michael Bell (Willie), Peter Cullen (Gruffle), Roger DeWitt (Peter), Richard Erdman (Herr Sessman), Fritz Feld (Sebastian), Pamelyn Ferdin (Klara), Joan Gerber (Fraulein Rottenmeie), Virginia Gregg (Aunt Dete), Janet Waldo (Tinette), Frank Welker (Schnoodle, Hootie), Michael Winslow (Mountain).

**Consumer Tips:** ☆☆ MPAA Rating: G. Based on the novel *Heidi* by Johanna Spyri.

**Story:** Heidi bonds with her gruff grandfather and the animals of the mountain, then moves to the city to become a companion to Clara, who is confined to a wheelchair. A wicked housekeeper locks Heidi in the cellar, but with the help of some swingin' cellar rats and her mountain friends, she returns to her grandfather.

**Comments:** Presented in the format of a contemporary musical, *Heidi's Song* is unfortunately a very lackluster family film. Hanna-Barbera tried awfully hard to create an animation classic. They forced a number of Disney film cliches into the framework of the original Johanna Spyri novel, but unfortunately, years of cheapjack television Saturday morning cartooning won't rub off, and *Heidi's Song* becomes a major chore to sit through.

Robert Taylor was formerly associated with Ralph Bakshi and was the director of *The Nine Lives of Fritz*

*the Cat* (1974). He couldn't resist adding his own bizarre touches to this film, such as a "Nightmare Ballet," where Heidi first encounters the creatures of the forest, and a Las Vegas musical sequence, "Ode to a Rat"—led by Sammy Davis Jr., no less—which seems to go on forever.

Old-time songwriters Sammy Cahn and Burton Lane provide 15 songs, each of which stop the story dead in its tracks. The best we can say about this production is that the animation is reasonably well done, by a team of veteran artists including Irv Spence (who did the Sammy Davis rat), Hal Ambro (who primarily did the grandfather voiced by Lorne Greene), and background painter Paul Julian.

The film grossed $5.1 million in U.S. theatrical release at the time. (JB)

**Additional Credits:** Screenplay: Joseph Barbera, Jameson Brewer, Robert Taylor. Music: Hoyt S. Curtin. Songs: Sammy Cahn, Burton Lane. Associate producer: Iwao Takamoto. Production supervisor: Jayne Barbera. Special scheduling: Art Scott. Supervising animators: Hal Ambro, Charlie Downs. Character animators: Irv Spence, Bob Bachman, Ed Barge, Jessie Cosio, John Freeman, Ernesto Lopez, Duncan Marjoribanks, Spencer Peel, Manny Perez, Mitch Rochon, George Scribner, Robert Taylor, Mauro Maressa, Sean Newton, Margaret Nichols, John Walker, Ken Walker. Art director: Paul Julian. Character design: Iwao Takamoto. Key layout: Moe Gollub, Tony Sgroi, Marty Strudler, Dick Ung. Background supervisor: Al Gumer.

**Hercules** (6/27/97) Walt Disney Pictures. 86 mins. Directors: Ron Clements, John Musker. Producers: Alice Dewey, Ron Clements, John Musker. Voices: Tate Donovan (Hercules), Josh Keaton (Young Hercules speaking), Roger Bart (Young Hercules singing), Susan Egan (Megara), Danny DeVito (Philoctetes), James Woods (Hades), Matt Frewer (Panic), Bobcat Goldwaithe (Pain), Cheryl Freeman (Melpomene), Vanesse Thomas (Clio), Lillias White (Calliope), La Chanze (Terpsichore), Roz Ryan (Thalia), Paddi Edwards (Atropos), Carole Shelley (Lachesis), Amanda Plummer (Clotho), Mary Kay Bergman (Athena), Samantha Eggar (Hera), Rip Torn (Zeus), Keith David (Apollo), Paul Shaffer (Hermes), Bug Hall (Child Panic), Kellen Hathaway (Child Pain), Hal Holbrook (Amphitryon), Barbara Barrie (Alcmene), Charlton Heston (Narrator), Corey Burton (Rock Titan, Tornado Titan), Patrick Pinney (Cyclops, Hephaestus, Ice Titan).

©Walt Disney Productions

**Consumer Tips:** ☆☆☆ MPAA Rating: G. Loosely based on the Greek myths of Hercules. Average fare uplifted by stunning art direction.

**Story:** Hades, Lord of the Underworld, forever plots to usurp the throne of Zeus. His best chance is to take out Zeus' newborn son, Hercules, but a botched murder attempt leaves Hercules only a demigod. Hercules must prove himself to be a true hero on earth if he is to reclaim his godly birthright in Olympus and so trains diligently under the guidance of satyr Philoctetes. Unfortunately, Hades isn't finished with Hercules yet. Key to Hades' trap: the beautiful Megara, who has sold her soul to the dark lord.

**Comments:** If originality was the goal of *Hercules*, the team of Musker and Clements were batting .500. The story is nothing that Disney hadn't been doing since 1989: there's the hero who sings an "I Want" number about his strivings as he faces the challenges of finding The Hero Within; a beautiful love interest who sings a romantic number about her awakening feelings; hip, anachronistic humor; a sleazy villain who gets his comeuppance; comic sidekicks; and, of course, an ending far happier than the one experienced by the mythical Hercules. In the final analysis *Hercules* has clever moments but is too bound by its narrative constraints. The movie may be formulaic, but there are some clever concepts that make *Hercules* worth a look.

Foremost among these is the casting of James Woods as Hades. Musker and Clements noticed that recent Disney villains were somewhat British in voice and they wanted a different sound. Woods came up with a fast-talking cross between a Hollywood schmoozer and a corporate raider, ad-libbing his way through what was reportedly a hilarious audition. This is one film where the villain steals the show. Another terrific idea was recasting the Greek Muses as a lively R&B-gospel quintet resembling the cast of *Dreamgirls*. This idea was perfectly congruent with Disney's recent bent toward Broadway in its animated features, and the movie positively bounces whenever the Muses are on screen. There are some nice swipes at the cult of sports stars and their myriad endorsements, but Hercules himself is not very interesting as a character. He is most appealing as a gawky, clueless teenager (a fact astutely recognized by Disney when it decided to make a television series based on the film).

The best decision made prior to the film's production was the hiring of Gerald Scarfe as production designer. Scarfe was a famous—and infamous—British caricaturist whose work was nearly always controversial. American audiences knew him best for his animation design in the film version of Pink Floyd's *The Wall*. Both Musker and Clements were fans of Scarfe's art, and he became the first production designer hired from outside the studio. Scarfe's elongated faces, hatchet-sharp features, and razored rows of teeth were incorporated into the softer Disney style with tremendous success. Some of Scarfe's designs went directly to screen: His later concept art of Pain and Panic, Hades' fumbling imps, are identical to the characters on screen, as is the final animation of Hades himself. Scarfe never did come up with an attractive Megara, but his concept art inspired animator Ken Duncan's sassy, beautiful version of Hercules' lady love.

For the record:

- *Hercules* was so heavily promoted that merchandise was in the Disney stores before the film came out, in concert with a series of mall tours.
- The computer-generated Hydra in the film needed 24,000 separate animation controls to coordinate its thirty heads.
- All is forgiven: Gerald Scarfe once made an independent animated film that showed Mickey Mouse smoking pot.
- The final fate of villain Scar (*The Lion King*) is revealed if one can catch it.

• Susan Egan (Megara) also portrayed Belle in the Broadway stage production of *Beauty and the Beast*. (MG)

**Additional Credits:** Screenplay: Ron Clements, John Musker, Donald McEnery, Bob Shaw, Irene Mecchi. Story supervisor: Barry Johnson. Story: Laan Kalyon, Kelly Wrightman, Randy Cartwright, John Ramirez, Jeff Snow, Vance Gerry, Kirk Hanson, Tamara Lusher-Stocker, Francis Glebas, Mark Kennedy, Bruce M. Morris, Don Dougherty, Thom Enriquez. Music: Alan Menken. Lyrics: David Zippel. Production stylist: Sue C. Nichols. Layout supervisor: Rasoul Azadani. Background supervisor: Thomas Cardone. Visual effects supervisor: Mauro Maressa. Computer graphics imagery supervisor: Roger L. Gould. Animation: Andreas Deja, Georges Abolin, Patrick Delage, Sahin Ersoz, Tom Gately, Gilda Palinginis Kouros, Doug Krohn, Jean Morel, Marc Smith, Bill Waldman, Andreas Wessel-Therhorn, Eric Goldberg, Caroline Cruikshank, Raul Garcia, Teddy Hall, Richard Hoppe, Bert Klein, Teresa Martin, Tom Roth, Theresa Wiseman, Nik Raineri, James Baker, Bolhem Bouchiba, Roger Chiasson, Eric Delbecq, Juanjo Guarnido, Dave Kuhn, Jamie Oliff, Sergio Pablos, Mike Polvani, Ken Duncan, Jared Beckstrand, Bob Bryan, Joe Oh, Catherine Poulain, Mark Pudleiner, William Recinos, Stephane Sainte-Foi, Yoshimichi Tamura, Ellen Woodbury, David Block, Steven P. Gordon, Kent Hammerstrom, David Hancock, Jefferey Johnson, Mike Kunkel, Enis Tahsin Ozgur, Randy R. Haydock, Michael Cedeno, Danny Galieote, Michael Stocker, Eric Walls, Anthony Ho Wong, Anthony DeRosa, Robert Espanto Domingo, Borja Montoro, Michael Snow, Adam Dykstra, T. Daniel Hofstedt, Jay Jackson, Dan O'Sullivan, James Lopez, Brian Ferguson, Marc Eoche Duval, Dominique Monfery, David Berthier, Thierry Goulard, Ron Husband, Richard Bazley, Sang-Jin Kim, Nancy Beiman, Oskar Urretabizkaia, Michael Swafford, Chris Bailey, Jean-Luc Ballestar, Dave Kupczyk, David Alan Zaboski.

**Here Come the Littles** (5/24/85) Atlantic. 75 mins. Director: Bernard Deyriès. Producers: Jean Chalopin, Andy Heyward, Tetsuo Katayama. Voices: Gregg Berger (William Little), Bettina Bush (Lucy Little), Donovan Freburg (Tom Little), Pat Fraley (Slick), Robert David Hall (Dinky Little), Jimmy Keegan (Henry Bigg), Mona Marshall (Mrs. Evans), Alvy Moore (Grandpa Little), Patricia Parris (Helen Little), Hal Smith (Uncle Augustus), B. J. Ward (Ashely).

©D.I.C.

**Consumer Tips:** ☆ MPAA Rating: G. Based on a series of books by Jon Peterson.

**Story:** The Littles, tiny people who live inside the walls, help youngster Henry Bigg when he is left in the cruel care of his wicked Uncle Augustus.

**Comments:** A feature-length version of a television series, based on a series of books by Jon Peterson, *Here Come the Littles* is animated in the same bland style of the 1983 television version. The premise involves little elfin characters who live inside the walls of a house. The television series tackled many pro-social kid's issues, and the movie version follows suit.

This time the Littles try to rescue siblings Tom and Lucy, who get trapped inside a suitcase. They give aid to young Henry Bigg, who is sent to live with his abusive evil uncle. The film raises issues of homelessness, the loss of parents, and the importance of family and friends, in a mild, one-dimensional way.

*Here Come the Littles* grossed $6.5 million in the United States in limited Saturday matinee release. (JB)

**Additional Credits:** Screenplay: Woody Kling. Voice recording director: Wally Burr. Post-production executive: William Kowalchuck Jr. Supervising sound editor: Robert S. Birchard. Animation directors: Tsukasa Tannai, Yoshinobu Michihata. Key animators: Masako Hinohara, Koichi Maruyama, Atsuko Tanaka, Keiko Hara, Chie Uratani, Yoko Sukaura, Yayoi Kobayashi, Masanori Ono, Masai Endo, Makiko Tutaki. Assistant director: Sunao Katabunchi. Associate producer: Koji Takeuchi. Camera: Hajime Hasegawa, Kenichi Kobayashi.

Original music: Shuki Levy, Haim Saban. Editor: Masatoshi Tsurbushi. Art director: Mutsuo Koeski.

## Hey Arnold! The Movie (6/28/02) Paramount. 75 mins.

Director: Tuck Tucker. Producers: Craig Bartlett, Albie Hecht. Voices: Spencer Klein (Arnold), Francesca Marie Smith (Helga Geraldine Pataki, Deep Voice), Jamil Walker Smith (Gerald Martin Johanssen, Rasta Guy), Dan Castellaneta (Grandpa "Steely" Phil, Nick Vermicelli), Tress MacNeille (Grandma Gertie "Pookie," Mayor Dixie, Red), Paul Sorvino (Scheck), Jennifer Jason Leigh (Bridget), Christopher Lloyd (Coroner), Vincent Schiavelli (Mr. Bailey), Maurice LaMarche (Big Bob Pataki, Head of Security), Kath Soucie (Miriam Pataki, Reporter), Christopher Walberg (Stinky Peterson), Elizabeth Ashley (Mrs. Vitello), Craig Bartlett (Brainy, Murray, Grubby, Monkeyman).

©Paramount Pictures

**Consumer Tips:** ☆ MPAA Rating: PG. Based on the Nickelodeon television series.

**Story:** Arnold and his friends try to track down a document declaring his town a historical landmark in an effort to stop a greedy corporation from razing his neighborhood.

**Comments:** Craig Bartlett began his animation career at Will Vinton's Claymation studio in Portland, Oregon. He moved to Los Angeles to work on *Pee Wee's Playhouse* (the "Penny" cartoons) and in his spare time developed his own character, Arnold. He started making clay animation shorts starring Arnold in 1988, and drew several Arnold comic strips, which appeared in

*The Simpsons* comics magazine (Bartlett was then married to Matt Groening's sister, Lisa). After writing several episodes of *Rugrats*, Bartlett pitched Arnold to Nickelodeon in 1994. It became a weekly series in 1995, known as *Hey Arnold*.

For several years, *Hey Arnold* was the most popular cartoon on Nickelodeon. When Nick renewed Bartlett's contract in 1998 and greenlit the fourth season, his deal included the development of an Arnold feature film. Shortly after the completion of the fifth season, Craig and his animation crew began to conceive a direct-to-video feature film, *Arnold Saves the Neighborhood*. However, something funny happened on the way to the video store shelves: the success of Nickelodeon's theatrical *Rugrats* movies gave Paramount cause to consider releasing the Arnold feature to theaters.

*Arnold Saves the Neighborhood* quickly became *Hey Arnold! The Movie*. It was never meant to be seen in a movie theater. The blow-up to 35mm looks hasty, and the film has a low-budget feel. Compared to the lavish *Rugrats* theatricals, the movie looks particularly cheesy.

Critics may have complained about the flat character design and cheap production values, but they liked the story of kids' empowerment. After five years, the characters themselves had proven to be quite strong.

Paul Sorvino and Jennifer Jason Leigh give effective performances in their guest roles. The box-office gross topped out at $12.6 million, which was chump change compared to Nickelodeon's *Rugrats* and *Jimmy Neutron* features. *Hey Arnold! The Movie* isn't much of a movie, particularly for adults, but should feel a lot better on home video, and the kids will probably enjoy it. (JB)

**Additional Credits:** Executive producers: Marjorie Cohn, Julia Pistor. Coproducer: Joseph Purdy. Coexecutive producer: Steve Viksten. Screenplay: Craig Bartlett, Steve Viksten. Original music: Jim Lang. Film editing: Christopher Hink. Production designer: Guy Vasilovich. Art direction: Christine Kolosov. Production manager: Kelly Crews. Executive in charge of production: Lolee Aries. Storyboard artist: Carson Kugler. Supervising sound editor: Timothy Borquez. Sound rerecording mixer: Eric Freeman. Supervising art editor: William Griggs. Foley artist: Monett Holderer. CG visual effects animator: David Wigforss. Background designer: Charles Garcia. Digital background coordinator: Steven Kellams. Animation directors: Christine Kolosov, Frank Weiss. Story editor: Michelle Lamoreaux.

©Warner Bros., Inc.

**Hey Good Lookin'** (10/1/82) Warner Bros. 76 mins. Director/producer: Ralph Bakshi. Voices: Richard Romanus (Vinnie), David Proval (Crazy Shapiro), Jesse Welles (Eva), Tina Bowman (Rozzie), Angelo Grisanti (Solly), Philip Michael Thomas (Chaplain), Frank DeKova (Old Vinnie), Candy Candido (Sal), Ed Peck (Italian Man), Juno Dawson (Waitress), Martin Garner (Yonkel), Terri Haven (Alice), Allen Joseph (Max).

**Consumer Tips:** ☆☆ MPAA Rating: R.

**Story:** Brooklyn, 1953. A serio-comic look at teenage life, focusing on Vinnie, the definitive greaser; his nutty Jewish pal, nicknamed Crazy; the neighborhood sex symbol, Roz; and her overweight girlfriend, Eva.

**Comments:** Ralph Bakshi clearly had a desire to direct live action. Both *Heavy Traffic* and *Coonskin* included prolonged live-action sequences. *Hey Good Lookin'* was Bakshi's attempt to fictionalize another aspect of his 1950s youth, and he conceived it as a film that would combine cartoon characters and live action extensively.

It was an ambitious concept to be sure, but it failed to work. "The illusion I attempted to create was that of a completely live-action film," Bakshi told the Director's Guild magazine, *Action*, in 1976. "Making it work almost drove us crazy."

Filmed for less than $2 million, Bakshi filmed four weeks of live-action seqences with Hollywood actors (including screen tough guy Mike Mazurki). The previews were disasterous, and after the failure of *Coon-*

*skin*, Warner Bros. was nervous about Bakshi's penchant for offending blacks, Italians, Jews, and women, as well as his cartoon visualizations of sex and nudity. The film was temporarily shelved.

A few years later, after the success of Bakshi's subsequent films, *Wizards* (1977), *Lord of the Rings* (1978), and *American Pop* (1981), Warner Bros. renewed its enthusiasm for *Hey Good Lookin'*. It was decided to strip the film of its live action and replace those scenes with completely animated characters and backgrounds.

The beginning of the film is quite promising, with a garbage can discussing life on the streets with some garbage. This is an example of what Bakshi did best—using the medium of animation to comment on society. Unfortunately, he doesn't do it enough in this film. There is a wildly imaginative fantasy sequence during the climax, when the character named Crazy starts hallucinating during a rooftop shooting spree. This scene almost justifies the whole film. But otherwise, this is a rehash of ideas better explored in *Coonskin, Heavy Traffic*, and *Fritz the Cat*.

*Hey Good Lookin'* is one of Bakshi's least-known efforts. It opened in New York during October 1982, and was released in Los Angeles in January 1983. (JB)

**Additional Credits:** Executive producer: Ronald Kauffman. Screenplay: Ralph Bakshi. Music: John Madara, Ric Sandler. Animators: Brenda Banks, Carl Bell, Bob Carlson, John Gentilella, Steve Gordon, Manny Perez, Virgil Ross, John Sparey, Irven Spence, Tom Tataranowicz, John E. Walker Sr., Robert Taylor. Layout: John Sparey, David Jonas, Don Morgan. Backgrounds: Rene Garcia, Matthew Golden, Johnny Vita.

**Hey There, It's Yogi Bear!** (6/3/64) Columbia. 89 mins. Directors/producers: William Hanna, Joseph Barbera. Voices: Daws Butler (Yogi Bear), Don Messick (Boo-Boo, Ranger Smith), Julie Bennett (Cindy Bear), Mel Blanc (Grifter), J. Pat O'Malley (Snively), Hal Smith (Corn Pone).

**Consumer Tips:** ☆☆½ MPAA Rating: Unrated. Based on the television series.

**Story:** Ranger Smith ships Yogi to the San Diego Zoo, but Yogi substitutes another bear and remains at Jellystone. Cindy runs off to find Yogi, and they all wind up in the circus.

©Hanna-Barbera Productions, Inc.

**Comments:** *Hey There, It's Yogi Bear!* marked the entrance of Hanna-Barbera into the world of animated theatrical features, but was also the first feature-length theatrical release based on a television property. In retrospect, this may not seem like a legacy to be proud of, as the new trend resulted in a number of inferior films. However, *Hey There, It's Yogi Bear!* is one of the best films of its kind, and a marked improvement over the television series in terms of animation quality, and even in chracterization. The film opens in Jellystone Park in spring and relates the adventures of Yogi who, despite the usual protestations from Boo Boo, attempts to filch "pic-a-nick goodies" by various means and is repeatedly foiled by the ranger. An ultimatum to the ranger does not result in the removal of the "Do Not Feed the Bears" signs but, rather, the planned departure of Yogi to the San Diego Zoo. Yogi cons the hick bear Corn Pone into taking his place, but Cindy, prostrate at the news of Yogi's departure, manages to get herself shipped to the zoo as well, only it turns out to be the St. Louis Zoo. Cindy winds up lost en route, and the rest of the film follows Yogi and Boo Boo as they venture outside the park to rescue Cindy, while Ranger Smith worries about how to deal with the absences of all three bears. Further complications involve Cindy's run-in with a pair of broken-down, crooked circus operators and their nasty dog Mugger, and run-ins with a rural sheriff and an incident at a barn dance, culminating in the three bears getting stuck on the frame of an under-construction high-rise in New York City.

The plot involves a number of incidents but is surprisingly well-structured. The film as a whole, while longer than the average cartoon episode, holds together surprisingly well. The animation and character designs, while still below the standard of the Disney classics or even Hanna-Barbera's own Tom and Jerry shorts, are much more fluid, and the redesigned appearances of Cindy Bear and Ranger Smith are much cleaner and more appealing, and would define their subsequent television appearances. The backgrounds, designed by such veterans as Warner Bros. layout men Richard H. Thomas and Bob Gribboek, are colorful, even lush, for the forest sequences. The song sequences are amiable enough and don't bog the proceedings down much. A few seeming plot inconsistencies or loose ends occur (at the film's end, Ranger Smith announces his promotion to chief ranger, despite referring to himself as "chief ranger" earlier in the film). However, beyond this, the character relationships between Yogi and Boo Boo, the Ranger, and especially Cindy benefit from the expanded running time, and Cindy finally comes into her own as a character. The supporting characters created for the film are for the most part pleasant and well-rendered, from the seedy Chizzling Brothers and the rambunctious train bears to the old country lady who partners with Yogi for a square dance. The stand-out of these is undoubtedly Mugger, the nasty, growling, snickering circus dog. Mugger's laugh (provided by Don Messick, though Mel Blanc seems to have done part of the growling) and even his general appearance led to the development of more than one television character: first Precious Pupp in 1965 and, more memorably, Muttley in 1966. The voice cast is superb, and for once the animation can almost compare to the characterizations of Daws Butler and Don Messick (who also played a multitude of minor bits in the film); the film also marks one of character actor J. Pat O'Malley's few non-Disney vocal roles. If not quite a classic, *Hey There, It's Yogi Bear!* is certainly more watchable than many other animated films produced in the 1960s, or most of Hanna-Barbera's subsequent attempts at features. The film continues to enjoy a certain popularity at summer or holiday matinees for children. (AL)

**Additional Credits:** Associate producer: Alex Lovy. Writers: Joseph Barbera, Warren Foster, William Hanna. Music: Marty Paich. Songs: Ray Gilbert, Doug Goodwin. Animation director:

Charles A. Nichols. Story sketches: Dan Gordon. Animators: Don Lusk, Irv Spence, George Kreisl, Ray Patterson, Jerry Hathcock, Grant Simmons, Fred Wolf, Don Patterson, Gerry Chiniquy, Ken Harris, George Goepper, Edwin Aardal, Ed Parks, Kenneth Muse, Harry Holt. Layouts: Richard Bickenbach, Iwao Takamoto, William Perez, Jacques V. Rupp, Willie Ito, Tony Sordi, Ernest Nordli, Jerry Eisenberg, Zigamond Jableski, Bruce Bushman. Backgrounds: F. Montealegre, Richard H. Thomas, Art Lozzi, Ron Dias, Dick Kelsey, Fernando Arce, Don Peters, Bob Abrams, Dick Ung, Robert Gentile, Tom O'Loughlin, Bob Givens, Curtiss D. Perkins.

**Home on the Range** (4/2/04) Walt Disney Pictures. 76 mins. Directors: Will Finn, John Sanford. Producer: Alice Dewey Goldstone. Voices: Roseanne Barr (Maggie), Judi Dench (Mrs. Caloway), Jennifer Tilly (Grace), Randy Quaid (Almeda Slim), Cuba Gooding Jr. (Buck), Charles Haid (Lucky Jack), Anne Richards (Annie), Richard Riehle (Sheriff Sam Brown), Sam J. Levine (The Willie Brothers), Joe Flaherty (Jeb), Charlie Dell (Ollie), Steve Buscemi (Mr. Wesley), Charles Dennis (Rico), Lance LeGault (Junior), Estelle Harris (Audrey), Mark Waltons (Barry and Bob), Dennis Weaver (Abner), Marshall Efron (Larry), Bobby Block (Piggy), Keaton Savage and Ross Simanteris (Little Pigs), Patrick Warburton (Patrick), Carole Cook (Pearl Gesner), G. W. Bailey (Rusty).

©Walt Disney Enterprises, Inc.

**Consumer Tips:** ☆☆ MPAA Rating: PG. A lively original adventure mainly for the younger set.

**Story:** Cattle rustler Almeda Slim can hypnotize cattle with his yodeling. Slim cleans out ranches in this unorthodox manner, the better to buy them up when they foreclose. One of his victims is show cow Maggie, whose owner has to sell her to the Patch of Heaven farm in the wake of foreclosure. Maggie meets bovine stable mates in the form of bossy Mrs. Caloway and bubble-headed Grace. When foreclosure threatens this farm too, the cows decide to capture Almeda Slim and use the reward to save the farm. They meet obstacles in the form of would-be hero stallion Buck and bounty hunter Rico (who is working both sides of the law). With courage, determination, and the help of a wily jackrabbit, the cows win out and the Patch of Heaven is saved.

**Comments:** *Home on the Range* has ended, for the time being, production of 2-D animation at Disney. The animation department was closed after the film was made, and after 67 years Disney animators laid their pencils down. This decision was made well before the film was released, and working on it must have been a poignant experience for all involved. These sad facts did little, however, to dampen the high spirits of the movie. *Home on the Range* will not captivate many adults, but it is a very good kids' picture, full of cowboys, goofy characters, and wild chases. There is also a healthy dose of cartoon violence and slapstick fighting in the film, but nothing that the kids will want to emulate.

The visual style used in *Home on the Range* is unusual for Disney; the film bears a strong resemblance to the work that designer Ed Benedict did for master director Tex Avery at MGM during the 1950s. Benedict was a major aficionado of the graphic arts, and his stylized, deliberately two-dimensional artwork influenced this movie to a large degree. *Home on the Range* is animated in such flat style that it could figuratively slip under the door with inches to spare. Even the computer-animated objects come out looking like 2-D. The characters have no shadowing on them, nor do their features recall anything resembling real animals. Some of them, like Ollie, seem more like cutouts. Maggie, Mrs. Caloway, and Grace sport greatly exaggerated features to make up for their lack of dimensionality, yet somehow the whole thing works, even when the characters are placed against naturalistic backgrounds.

There is an all-star voice cast, something that Disney once eschewed. They all do a fine job, even governor Anne Richards of Texas. Roseanne Barr has the

Hugo the Hippo **115**

requisite brassiness needed for Maggie, Judi Dench is very entertaining as Mrs. Caloway, and Cuba Gooding Jr., in the role of Buck, does an understated version of Eddie Murphy's typical shtick to better effect.

Even for those who aren't fans of country music, there are fine offerings by Bonnie Raitt, k.d. lang, and Tim McGraw added to a faux Copland score by Alan Menken. Almeda Slim's yodeling number (in which Randy Quaid does his own yodeling) is fun to watch, especially when the hypnotized longhorns turn different day-glo colors to the beat and prance in marching band formation. The sequence is the film's imaginative high point, but it doesn't last long enough to make the same sort of impact as "Pink Elephants on Parade" does in *Dumbo*.

*Home on the Range* was reportedly budgeted at $110 million and it's hard to see where all that money went, since the animation was so simple and the crew bereft of all big-name veterans save Mark Henn. The film made back less than half its cost at the box office. It took 67 years for Disney to turn 180 degrees. Its first feature was taken from a European fairy tale and presented highly realistic work with human characters. Its final feature was an American Western developed from an original script that presented highly stylized talking cows. It was a finish that Walt Disney certainly never could have foreseen. (MG)

**Additional Credits:** Original music: Alan Menken. Casting: Matthew Jon Beck. Production design: David Cutler. Lead layout artist: Craig Elliott. Key layout artist: Karen A. Keller. Effects animator: Mauro Maressa. Effects key assistant: Joseph C. Pepe. Animators: Tim Allen, Dale Baer, James Baker, Tony Bancroft, Dan Boulos, Chris Buck, Andreas Deja, Frank Dietz, Russ Edmonds, Will Finn, Steven E. Gordon, Mark Henn, Jay Jackson, Shawn Keller, James Lopez, Duncan Marjoribanks, Mark Pudleiner, Chris Sauve, Bruce W. Smith, Marc Smith, Michael Stocker, Michael Surrey, Barry Temple, Andreas Wessel-Therhorn, Dougg Williams, Ellen Woodbury, Phillip Young.

**Hoppity Goes to Town** See *Mr. Bug Goes to Town.*

**The Horse from Button Willow** See *The Man from Button Willow.*

**Hugo the Hippo** (7/14/76) 20th Century Fox. 90 mins. Producer: Robert Halmi. Director: Bill Feigen-

baum. Voices: Burl Ives (Narrator), Robert Morley (The Sultan), Paul Lynde (Aban-Khan), Ronnie Cox (Jorma), Percy Rodriguez (Jorma's Father), Jesse Emmette (Royal Magician), Len Maxwell (Judge, Grown-Up), Frank Welker, Nancy Wible, Jerry Hausner (Special Voice Effects), Marie Osmond, Jimmy Osmond (Vocalists).

©Twentieth Century Fox Film Corporation

**Consumer Tips:** ☆☆½ MPAA Rating: G.

**Story:** Loyal hippos are left to starve after saving the kingdom from shark attack. Little Hugo is arrested, but ultimately brings harmony between the species.

**Comments:** "Color, creatures, music, sound like you've never seen or heard before. It's the wildest trip ever animated. It's a treat for the whole family. It's PHANTASMAGORICAL!" That's the way the one-sheet poster described this animated feature. Dark, bizarre, and surreal would also be good words to describe it.

Robert Halmi was a freelance journalist and staff photographer for *Life* magazine. He began developing the script for *Hugo the Hippo* based on a real-life incident he witnessed in Zanzibar. Halmi, who is Hungarian, said he did not pick Pannonia's studio to do the production because of loyalty to his homeland (Halmi had in fact been evicted from the country due to his involvement with the underground during the Stalinist regime), but because of dissatisfaction with the poor work coming out of Hollywood at the time.

Produced in 1973 by Hungary's Pannonia Film studio, *Hugo the Hippo* is voiced by several well-known

U.S. celebrities and was distributed in 1976 by 20th Century Fox. Fox picked it up as part of a three-picture deal with Brut Productions (including a pair of Elliot Gould films, *Whiffs* and *I Will I Will . . . For Now*).

The Pannonia studio was established in 1959. It became internationally known for a variety of high-quality children's films and serious artistic short subjects. The artistic shorts, aimed toward adult audiences, were well recieved and began winning awards at various international festivals in the 1960s. Hungarian animation, like the animated films from Zagreb and Estonia, were dark, sarcastic reflections of everyday life under Communist rule. By the late 1960s, political reforms ended the state-run programs that supported the studio, and thus Pannonia had to find new ways to market its films internationally, and create a more commercially acceptable product.

*Hugo the Hippo* found funding from French fragrance maker Faberge (under its Brut Productions label). The movie took two years to produce and cost a little over $1 million. The final product is not the light, upbeat family film it appears on the surface.

The first part of the movie brings Hugo and his hippo brethren to the island of Zanzibar to help rid the harbor of sharks. After they accomplish their mission, the sultan decides to shoot them all—all except Hugo, that is. From this point, the film takes on a harsh, cynical tone. Although Hugo is the main character around which everything in the plot revolves, little is done to develop his personality or show what he's thinking. In fact, he's the least animated character in the movie.

This was Pannonia's first feature to have international distribution. It did not fare well at the U.S. box office. But the film's trippy 1960s art direction and full animation make watching it a worthwhile experience for animation buffs. However, parents and children beware! (JB)

*Additional Credits:* Screenplay: Thomas Baum. Music: Bert Keyes, Robert Larimer. Animation director: Joszef Gemes. Design: Graham Percy. Animation: Kati Banki, Zsuka Dekany, Edit Hernadi, Ivan Jenkovsky, Mikloa Kaim, Edit Szalai, Andras Szemenyei, Csba Szorady, Sarolta Toth. A Brut/Hungarofilm Pannonia Filmstudio Production.

## The Hunchback of Notre Dame (7/21/96) Walt Disney Pictures. 91 mins. Directors: Gary Trousdale,

Kirk Wise. Producer: Don Hahn. Voices: Tom Hulce (Quasimodo), Demi Moore (Esmerelda, speaking), Heidi Mollenhauser (Esmerelda, singing), Kevin Kline (Captain Phoebus), Tony Jay (Judge Frollo), Jason Alexander (Hugo), Charles Kimbrough (Victor), Mary Wickes (Laverne), Jane Withers (additional Laverne dialogue), Paul Kandel (Clopin), David Ogden Stiers (Archdeacon), Mary Kay Bergman (Quasimodo's mother), Corey Burton, Bill Fagerbakke (Guards), Jim Cummings, Patrick Pinney (Guards, Gypsies), Gary Trousdale (Old Heretic), Frank Welker (Baby Bird).

©Walt Disney Productions

**Consumer Tips:** ☆☆☆ MPAA Rating: G. Based on the 1831 novel *The Hunchback of Notre Dame* by Victor Hugo.

**Story:** Ugly, misshapen Quasimodo has been taken in as a child by the cruel Judge Frollo. He is the bell-ringer—and virtual captive—of Notre Dame cathedral; his only friends are three stone gargoyles. Quasimodo is humiliated at the Festival of Fools but rescued by the beautiful gypsy Esmerelda, who is also the object of Frollo's lust. Quasimodo falls in love with Esmerelda, but so does handsome Captain Pheobus, whom Frollo has brought to Paris to eliminate all gypsies. Phoebus and Esmerelda find each other. Quasimodo finds liberation from his cruel master and, more importantly, the realization that he is not a monster after all.

**Comments:** Those familiar with Hugo's novel may look askance at the above synopsis. Dozens of liberties are taken with the original work, but some of the darker themes, such as Frollo's sexual obsessions, remain intact. Trousdale and Wise had previously made Disney's most adult-oriented film of the 1990s, *Beauty and the Beast*, and in *Hunchback* they would depict ethnic cleansing, emotional abuse, and the gratuitous murder of Quasimodo's mother at Frollo's hands. Michael Eisner insisted that the studio take a gamble and got his wish. No Disney film had ever featured a musical number (performed here by Frollo) based on pure sexual desire. Esmerelda, the subject of that number, will not be in the Disney Princess collection anytime soon, either. Sexy, voluptuous, and the object of much lusting by the three male leads, there is little innocence about Esmerelda, although her heart is kind.

Yet Trousdale and Wise pull it off, for the most part. The Disney version of Quasimodo is a far cry from the barely human brute of Hugo's novel. He is creative, kind, and unbowed after years of Frollo's denigrations. This change is essential to the film's success, since Quasimodo is needed to provide the romantic tension, heroism, and selfless actions that make him the dramatic equal of Esmerelda and Captain Phoebus. Tom Hulce gave Quasimodo the voice of an unsure adolescent, making him even more sympathetic. Transforming Quasimodo into a downtrodden underdog also throws Frollo's evil into greater contrast and thus makes the film's ending more believable.

One of the surest moves made by the writers was to have a narrator, Clopin the gypsy, tell the background to the story in the musical number that opens the film. With no time wasted setting up the story, there is time to develop the complexities that Quasimodo, Esmerelda, and Frollo all display as the movie unfolds. The worst slip was the inclusion of Quasimodo's gargoyle friends, Victor, Hugo, and Laverne. Writer Tab Murphy noted that in the novel Quasimodo talked to his bells, so the three characters were written into the script. The gargoyles only come to life when alone with Quasimodo and mostly provide silly comic relief and cheerleading, the last thing such a mature script needed.

Worth noting is the breathtaking evocation of Notre Dame and Paris, a masterwork created by art director David Goetz, artistic coordinator Randy Fullmer, and all those who worked long hours on background and layout. As Quasimodo sings "Out There" high above the streets of Paris, dizzying sweeps, pans, and zooms display a city in all its vitality. The cathedral itself, with its cyclopean stained-glass window, is virtually a character in the film. Dark and foreboding interiors predominate when Esmerelda is imprisoned inside, but in other scenes Notre Dame is brilliantly lit in tawny splendor.

Although *Hunchback* was not the financial success Disney hoped it would be, it is a very solid film that ventures into territory seldom explored at the studio. Beneath its exterior one can almost feel the creators longing to make an even more mature version, one free of silly gargoyle sidekicks or considerations of marketing and licensing characters. If any studio could have taken that risk in 1996, it would have been Disney, but audiences hoping for more daring sophistication would have to wait. If nothing else, *Hunchback* is at least the best movie Demi Moore has done to date.

For the record:

- *The Hunchback of Notre Dame* had been filmed in live action in 1923, 1939, 1956, and 1982. This is the only musical version.
- The three gargoyles were originally to be named Chaney, Laughton, and Quinn, after the actors who previously portrayed Quasimodo.
- Seen in the streets of Paris: Belle (*Beauty and the Beast*), Aladdin's magic carpet, and Pumbaa (*The Lion King*).
- In the novel Frollo is a priest, but the writers changed him to a judge to avoid offending religious sensibilities.
- *Hunchback* features a computer animation program that made it possible to animate large crowds in constant, independent motion. The siege of the cathedral at the film's finale showcases this stunning technical software. (MG)

***Additional Credits:*** Story: Tab Murphy. Screenplay: Tab Murphy, Irene Mecchi, Bob Tzudiker, Noni White, Jonathan Roberts. Music: Alan Menken. Songs: Alan Menken, Stephen Schwartz. Sequence directors: Paul Brizzi, Gaetan Brizzi. Supervising animators: James Baxter, Tony Fucile, Kathy Zielinski, Russ Edmonds, Michael Surrey, David Pruiksma, Will Finn, Ron Husband, David Burgess. Animators: Christopher Bradley, Tom Finney, Doug Frankel, Tom Gately, Shawn E. Keller, Ralf Palmer, John Ripa, Stephane Sainte-Foi, Christopher Suave, Yoshimichi Tamura, Eric Walls, Anthony Ho-Wong, Phil Young, Anne Marie Bardwell, Jared Beckstrand, Bolhem Bouchiba, David Brewster, Robert Espanto Domingo, Mark Koetsier, Gilda

Kouros, Doug Krohn, Dave Kupczyk, Mark Pudleiner, Bill Waldman, Travis Blaise, Roger Chiasson, Patrick Delage, Steven Pierre Gordon, Dominique Monferey, Sergio Pablos, William Recinos, Chris Wahl, Robert Bryan, Michael Cedeno, Marc Eoche Duval, Bradley Kuha, David A. Zaboski, Danny Galieote, Rejean Bourdages, David Hancock, T. Daniel Hofstedt, Jamie Oliff, Larry White, Kent Hammerstrom, Sylvain Deboissy, Sasha Dorogov, Raul Garcia, Teresa Martin, Jean Morel, Daniel O'Sullivan, Catherine Poulain, Gregory Griffith, Mike Moe Merell. Additional animation: Ruben A. Aquino, Georges Abolin, Tony Bancroft, Charlie Bonifacio, Robert Casale, Alain Costa, Ken Hettig, James Young Jackson, Duncan Marjoribanks, Roy Meurin, Gary Perkovac, Carol Seidl, Pres Antonio Romanillos, Ellen Woodbury. Effects supervisors: Christopher Jenkins, Mike Smith. Supervising effects animators: Tom Hush, Dorse Lanpher, Bruce Mallier. Effects animators: Allen Blyth, Ed Coffey, Thierry Chaffoin, Mark Cumberton, Peter DeMund, Joseph Gilland, Troy A. Gustafson, Dan Lund, David (Joey) Mildenberger, Paul Smith, Marlon West. CGI supervisor: Hiram Bhakta Joshi. Art director: David Goetz. Story supervisor: Will Finn. Character design/visual development: James Baxter, Anne Marie Bardwell, Geefwee Boedoe, Thom Enriquez, Peter DeSeve, Vance Gerry, Ed Ghertner, Jean Gillmore, Joe Grant, Darek Gogol, Lisa Keene, Shawn E. Keller, Rick Maki, Joseph Mosher, Sue C. Nichols, Tony Fucile, Rowland B. Wilson. Story: Kevin Harkey, Gaetan Brizzi, Paul Brizzi, Edward Gombert, Brenda Chapman, Jeff Snow, Jim Capobianco, Denis Rich, Burny Mattinson, John Sanford, Kelly Wightman, James Fujii, Geefwee Boedoe, Floyd Norman, Francis Glebas, Kirk Hanson, Christine Blue, Sue C. Nichols. Layout Supervisors: Ed Ghertner, Daniel St. Pierre. Key layout/workbook: Fred Craig, Tom Shannon, Scott Caple, Lorenzo Martinez, Samuel Piehl. Background supervisors: Lisa Keene, Doug Ball. Backgrounds: Gregory Alexander Drolette, Don Moore, Colin Stimpson, Mikyung Joung-Raynis, Michael Humphries, Pierre Buloff, Joaquin Royo Morales, Allison Belliveau-Proulx, Dominick R. Domingo, Christophe Vacher, Olivier Besson, William Lorencz, Maryann Thomas, David McCamley, Debbie DuBois, Brooks Campbell, Patricia Palmer-Phillipson, Justin Brandstater, George Taylor, Patricia Millerau, Jean-Paul Fernandez, Tom Woodington, Brad Hicks, Serge Michaels, Jennifer Ando.

**Ice Age** (3/15/02) 20th Century Fox. 80 mins. Director: Chris Wedge. Codirector: Carlos Saldanha. Producer: Lori Forte. Voices: Ray Romano (Manfred), John Leguizamo (Sid), Denis Leary (Diego), Goran Visnjic (Soto), Jack Black (Zeke), Tara Strong (Roshan), Cedric the Entertainer (Rhino), Stephen Root (Rhino), Diedrich Bader (Sabretooth Tiger), Chris Wedge (Scrat).

©Twentieth Century Fox Film Corporation

**Consumer Tips:** ☆☆☆ MPAA Rating: PG. Nominated for Academy Award—Best Animated Feature.

**Story:** In prehistoric times, an unlikely trio consisting of a sloth, a mammoth, and a sabre-toothed tiger trek across a frozen tundra to return a human child to its tribe.

**Comments:** The second animated feature to be released in 2002, *Ice Age* centers on the exploits of assorted prehistoric animals during the titular era. While large herds of creatures are migrating due to changing weather conditions, Sid, a hyperactive sloth who is left behind, is befriended (loosely speaking) by a moody loner mastadon named Manfred. The pair stumble upon a human baby, lost and separated from his tribe when a pack of sabre-toothed tigers attack his mother. Sid persuades the mastadon to seek out the human tribe and return the child, only to be joined by Diego, a sly sabre-toothed tiger who offers to assist them with his tracking skills. Diego has actually been ordered by pack leader Soto to bring him the child. Despite their differences, the three animals and the child form a bond in the wilderness. A parallel subplot, intertwined with the main story, involves a prehistoric squirrel, Scrat, and his quest to hold on to and open a nut.

*Ice Age* is the first feature film from commercial and video game studio Blue Sky (which also produced the Oscar-winning short "Bunny"). The focus on the film is on comedy, with rapid one-liners, sight gags, and slapstick action, particularly in a frantic sequence involving a flock of zanily militaristic dodos. The animation of the animal characters is smooth and benefits from pleasantly cartoonish character designs from New Yorker cartoonist Peter DeSeve (who also contributed to *Monsters, Inc.*). The humans, too, are caricatured (reminiscent of the designs in *Prince of Egypt*, which DeSeve also worked on), but their movements are rather stiff, looking more like toy action figures than cartoon characters. The story itself veers towards the saccharine, with the heartfelt search for the baby's family. Despite the obviously calculated nature of the child's inclusion, however, there is something quite endearing in his gradual attempts to walk. The film, like so many in recent memory, is dominated by celebrity voice casting, which in some ways works against the film, though not as strongly as in other films. John Leguizamo's sloth is rather irritating at times, a fact that works given the character's purpose as a well-meaning annoyance, but still grates. Ray Romano's monotone, however, is effective in telegraphing Manfred's moodiness. Denis Leary's Diego comes across as oddly flat. Many of the incidental roles are filled by recent sitcom actors or production personnel. Possibly the best, if most irrelevant, aspect of the film is Scrat's quest, which, while hilarious, is also strongly remniscent of the works of the late Chuck Jones. This isn't merely because of the frustration humor that is the hallmark of the Road Runner/Coyote cartoons, but because Jones dealt with the same situation—a squirrel attempting to crack open a nut—in the 1953 short *Much Ado About Nuttin.* A follow-up short starring Scrat, *Goin' Nutty*, received a 2004 Oscar nomination for best short. *Ice Age* grossed $175.6 million in U.S. box-office receipts. (AL)

**Additional Credits:** Executive producer: Chris Meledandri. Story: Michael J. Wilson. Screenplay: Michael Berg, Michael J. Wilson, Peter Ackerman. Music: David Newman. Sequence directors: Mark Baldo, Jan Carle. Lead animators: James Bresnahan, Michael Thurmeier. Animators: Nina Bafaro, Floyd Bishop Jr., Thomas Bisogno, James Campbell, Jaime Andres Castaneda, Galen T. Chu, Nick Craven, Marcelo Fernandes DeMoura, Everett Downing Jr., Aaron J. Hartline, James Hundertmark, Jeffrey K. Joe, Kompin Kemgunird, Dean Kalman Lennert, Rodrigo Blaas, Simi Nallasetg, Dana O'Connor, David S. Peng, Andreas Procopiou, Mika Ripatti, Scott Robideau, David J. Smith, David B. Vallone, Joshua West. Production Designer: Brian McEntee. Character design: Peter DeSeve. Environmental design: Peter Clarke. Head of story: Yvette Kaplan. Story artists: Enrico Casarosa, William H. Frake III, Tony Kluck, Moroni, Kevin O'Brien, Wilbert Plijnaar, Dan Shefelman, Ilya Skorupsky. Additional story: James Bresnahan, Galen T. Chu, Doug Compton, Xeth Feinberg, Jeff Siergey, Michael Thurmeier. Story consultants: David Silberman, Jon Vitti.

**I Go Pogo** (8/01/80) 21st Century Distribution. 82 mins. Director/producer: Marc Paul Chinoy. Voices: Skip Hinnant (Pogo Possum), Jonathan Winters (Porky Pine, Mole, Wiley Katt), Vincent Price (The Deacon Mushrat), Ruth Buzzi (Mam'zelle Hepsibah, Miz Beaver), Stan Freberg (Albert Alligator), Jimmy Breslin (P. T. Bridgeport), Arnold Stang (Churchy La Femme), Bob McFadden (Howland Owl, Bothered Bat), Len Maxwell (Bewitched Bat, Seminole Sam, Narrator), Bob Kaliban (Bewildered Bat), Marcia Savella (Miz Bettle), Muke Schultz (Freemount Bug).

©Estate of Walt Kelly

**Consumer Tips:** ☆☆ MPAA Rating: G. Based on Walt Kelly's famed comic strip of the 1950s and 1960s. Also known as *Pogo for President*.

**Story:** Pogo finds himself reluctantly recruited to run for the nation's highest office, president of the United States.

**Comments:** The third animated adaptation of Walt Kelly's *Pogo* (following Chuck Jones' *Pogo's Special Birthday Special* and Kelly's own, unfinished *We Have Met the Enemy and He Is Us*), *I Go Pogo* attempts to use stop-motion animation to portray the classic comic-strip characters. The results are decidedly mixed. The lovingly detailed sets, recreating the Okefenokee swamp in three dimensions, are extremely effective in capturing the ambiance of Kelly's world. The figures themselves, however (adapted by two of the three Chiodo Bros, of *Killer Klowns from Outer Space* fame), have generally been simplified, and Pogo in particular lacks the range of expression and detail of his print counterpart.

The translation of two-dimensional comic-strip characters into three dimensions has always been problematic. Depictions as toys or statues, at least, are merely decorative and not intended to convey the illusion of life. Indeed, some of the more effective moments display the swamp critters in silhouette, or ambling down roads in long shots. The basic premise is taken from the many serial stories in which a reluctant Pogo somehow is being championed as a candidate, and at times the film does succeed in capturing at least elements of the original strip's humor (Fremont Bug's "'es Fine;" "If Pogo's for president, who's for vice?"). The political satire is more general, however, and the characters are far more one-dimensional than in the strips, with Deacon Mushrat reduced to a generic greedy villain, P. T. Bridgeport a mere con man, and Wiley Catt taking on the sinister aspects of his cousin, Simple J. Malarkey. Unlike another adaptation of a politically slanted rural comic strip, *Li'l Abner* (1959), no introduction is provided regarding these folks' rich backgrounds and eccentricities. The predominantly New York voice cast feels out of place delivering Southern-fried dialogue (columnist Jimmy Breslin as a Runyonesque P. T. Bridgeport is particularly miscast). The less said about the jarring synthesized songs, the better. The movie does have its simpler, quieter moments, such as conversations between Pogo and Porky, which while never quite plumbing the philosophical or linguistic depths of Kelly's work, are rather satisfying by themselves.

On the whole, though hard-core stop-motion enthusiasts and Kelly completists would probably enjoy the film, the experiment serves as something of a cautionary tale, as studios rush to convert beloved animated and comic-strip icons into computer-animated goldmines. (AL)

**Additional Credits:** Executive producer: Kerry H. Stowall. Associate producers: Selby Kelly, Pete Kelly. Writer: Marc Paul Chinoy. Music: Gary Baker, Thom Flora. Directing animator/character adaptation: Stephen Chiodo. Art direction/production design: Charles Chiodo. Senior animators: Diedre A. Knowlton, Stephen Oakes. Animators: Kim Blanchette, R. Kent Burton, Louise Campbell, Justin Kohn, Ruth Schwartz. Voice casting/director: Ed Graham.

**I Married a Strange Person** (10/28/98) Lion's Gate. 72 mins. Director/producer: Bill Plympton. Voices: Tom Larson (Grant Boyer), Richard Spore (Larson P. Giles), Chris Cooke (Col. Ferguson), Ruth Ray (Mom), J. B. Adams (Dad), John Russo Jr. (Bud Sweeny), Jennifer Senko (Smiley), Etta Valeska (Sex Video Model), Bill Martone (Announcer).

©Bill Plympton

**Consumer Tips:** ☆☆☆ MPAA Rating: R.

**Story:** A man develops supernatural powers that make anything he imagines become reality.

**Comments:** Bill Plympton's second full-length animated feature (not counting the compilation feature *Mondo Plympton*), *I Married a Strange Person* showcases Plympton's penchant for distortion in even more bizarre ways than *The Tune*. The movie is also more joyously perverse (Plympton's short *How to Have Sex* is highlighted). While the transmutations in *The Tune* went unexplained, here the chaos is engineered by a lobe appearing on the neck of a young husband, leading to such classic Plympton moments as the giant grass blade that attacks a neighbor, and a sour father-in-law's facial features turning into musical instruments, which proceed to play jazz. Sex and violence also dominate these incidents, such as Keri changing to accommodate Grant's fantasies, while various household items mirror increased stages of sexual excitement. The comedian Solly Jim's act, consisting of lopping off and tossing various body parts, is particularly gory, and the climax is marred to some extent by the blood. Unlike the two men in the "Push Comes to Shove" sequence featured in *The Tune*, these violent acts obviously lead to death.

The satire on multimedia corporations and the extents to which they pry into our private lives is clever, while also accompanied by intentionally silly television show concepts such as "Amoeba Wrestling." Maureen McElheron's songs, so integral to *The Tune*, feel more like irrelevant interruptions here. While colored pencils have been replaced by paint to color the cels, the vibrantly rough feel of the animation itself, and the line shadings and edges, are retained. Live reference was used for most of the characters, yet the film manages to avoid the rotoscoped look. The fact that the director appears to once again have been the sole animator is singularly impressive, and the film, while bizarre and certainly not for the squeamish, is in many ways more engaging than certain films from another leading animation auteur, Ralph Bakshi.

A pair of fornicating birds runs into a satellite dish, sending it off-kilter and zapping recently married businessman Grant Boyer, causing a lobe to develop on the back of his neck. This lobe causes strange things to occur, as Grant's thoughts and fantasies come to life, much to the dismay of his voluptuous wife, Keri. Grant's powers affect everyone from his in-laws to his gardening neighbor, who calls a talk show and recommends booking Grant. While Grant's marriage is disintegrating, he finds himself thrust into the spotlight on national television, which brings his strange powers to the attention of first Solly Jim, a washed-up comedian, and then more importantly, Larson P. Giles, head of militaristic multimedia empire Smile Corp. Giles dispatches his militaristic yet oafish aide Col. Ferguson to bring Grant to him, while Keri continues to

wonder what's wrong with her husband. As Grant and his lobe are caught in a struggle between Giles, Ferguson, and Solly Jim, the conflict grows increasingly bizarre and violent. (AL)

***Additional Credits:*** Writer and animator: Bill Plympton. Music: Maureen McElheron. Art supervisors: Signe Baumane, Sophie Hogarth. Background props: Greg Pair, Graham Blythe, Jim Wilson; Photographs: Greg Pair, Graham Blythe, Pam Gurnan, Elizabeth Geddes. A PlympCorp Production in association with Italtoons released through Lions Gate Films.

## The Incredible Mr. Limpet (3/28/64) Warner Bros. 102 mins. Director (live action): Arthur Lubin. Director (animation): Bill Tytla. Producer: John C. Rose. Cast: Don Knotts (Henry Limpet), Carole Cook (Bessie Limpet), Jack Weston (George Stickle), Andrew Duggan (Commander Harlock), Larry Keating (Admiral Spewter), Oscar Beregi (Nazi Admiral Doemitz), Charles Meredith (Admiral Fourstar).

©Warner Brothers, Inc.

***Consumer Tips:*** ☆☆☆ Fine family film.

***Story:*** During World War II, meek 4-F Henry Limpet (Don Knotts) falls in the ocean and is transformed into a fish. He aids the Allies' war effort as a secret weapon below the waves.

***Comments:*** In live action, a 1940s sad sack Flatbush office clerk (played by television comedian Don Knotts, in his first top-billed film role), disappointed over being declared 4-F, is obsessed with fish and, after falling off of a Coney Island pier, turns into one. In an engaging plot twist, the new fish decides to assist the U.S. Navy in spotting U-boats.

The fantastic premise is carried off surprisingly well, in a manner palatable for younger viewers and adults as well. The live-action sequences with Knotts are well handled, and character actor Jack Weston makes an agreeable foil as Limpet's sailor buddy; a crotchety crab (voiced by Paul Frees, in his only job for a Warner-produced animated product) serves the same purpose in the animated segments. Though Knott's starring role becomes a voiceover part early in the film, his performance is surprisingly warm. The design of the Limpet fish is nicely streamlined, while the bags under the eyes and the accentuated lips caricature aspects of Knotts' real-life appearance. There is even a certain amount of genuine suspense in the scenes in which a Russian sound-tracking torpedo targets Limpet.

*The Incredible Mr. Limpet* contains the last animation produced by the legendary Warner Bros. cartoon department, the same studio responsible for Bugs Bunny, the Road Runner, and Tweety. Veteran Disney animator Vladimir Tytla (his only assignment at Warner Bros.) was brought in from the East Coast to supervise production but, due to illness, Robert McKimson and Hawley Pratt had to take over much of the work on the film. At the completion of this film, the studio was disbanded. Director Arthur Lubin, in addition to years of comedy experience ranging from Abbott and Costello films such as *Buck Privates* and *Hold that Ghost* to many of the more amusing episodes of television's *Maverick*, was also something of an expert at talking animal pictures, having helmed most of the Francis the Talking Mule films as well as many episodes of *Mr. Ed.* As another trivia note, actress Carole Cook, playing the fierce Mrs. Limpet, returned to animation in 2003, voicing Grace the farm owner in Disney's *Home on the Range.*

In recent years, early plans by Warner Bros. to remake the film circulated, at one point with Mike Judge directing, but the project has been in limbo since the original star, Jim Carrey, backed out, and despite brief rumors of Mike Myers as the new Mr. Limpet, it's unlikely to see the light of day. Thus the charm and whimsy of the original film remain untarnished. (AL)

**Additional Credits:** Screenplay: Jameson Brewer, John C. Rose. Adaptation: Joe DiMona (from the novel *Mr. Limpet* by Theodore Pratt). Story development: John Dunn. Music: Frank Perkins. Songs: Sammy Fain, Harold Adamson. Associate directors: Gerry Chiniquy, Hawley Pratt. Sequence director: Robert McKimson. Animators: Art Babbitt, Ken Harris. Production design: Maurice Noble, Pratt. Background styling: Don Peters. Art director: LeRoy Deane.

## The Incredibles (11/5/04) Disney/Pixar. 115 mins.

Director: Brad Bird. Producer: John Walker. Voices: Craig T. Nelson (Bob Parr, Mr. Incredible), Holly Hunter (Helen Parr, Elastigirl), Samuel L. Jackson (Lucius Best, Frozone), Jason Lee (Buddy Pine, Syndrome), Sarah Vowell (Violet Parr), Spencer Fox (Dash Parr), Brad Bird (Edna "E" Mode), Elizabeth Pena (Mirage), Wallace Shawn (Gilbert Huph), John Ratzenberger (The Underminer), Maeve Andrews, Eli Fucile (Jack Jack), Jean Sincere (Mrs. Hogenson), Bud Luckey (Rick Dicker), Bret Parker (Kari), Teddy Newton (Newsreel Narrator), Michael Bird (Tony Rydinger), Kimberly Adair Clark (Honey), Dominique Louis (Bomb Voyage), Wayne Canney (Principal).

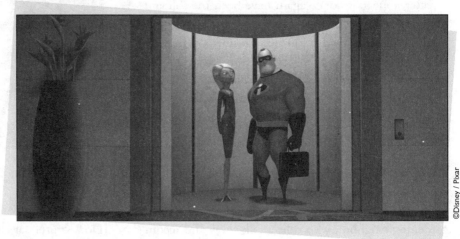

©Disney / Pixar

**Consumer Tips:** ☆☆☆☆ MPAA Rating: PG.

**Story:** A family of superheroes, ordered to hide their superpowers and shed their masked identities, are forced to come out of retirement to save the world— an adventure that bonds their relationship.

**Comments:** *The Incredibles*, Brad Bird's highly anticipated second feature, delves into much the same territory as *The Iron Giant*, examining a range of issues including middle-aged discontent, family responsibilities, oppressive workplace bureaucracy, loss of self-identity, and mortality. Whereas *The Iron Giant* pretended to be Superman, protagonist Bob "Mr. Incredible" Parr is a super man, coping with hiding his (and his family's) powers in a world where the folks one saves can turn around and sue. Whereas Pixar's previous hit *Finding Nemo* was very episodic, Bird's script is carefully constructed, as Mr. Incredible's return to crime fighting (or so he thinks) and subsequent adventures are cross-cut with his family's situations. The sitcom-style "suspected infidelity" subplot for wife Helen/Elastigirl is a bit cliche, but provides a converging point.

Characterization overall is superb. The family bonds and struggles amongst Bob, Helen, and the kids are deftly handled. Compared to *Iron Giant*, which had no true villain, Syndrome is a complex, rather disturbing creation, and a reflection on the distortions of obsession and deluded hero worship; the extent to which the film reveals his past atrocities is frankly chilling. The supporting roles all make strong impressions, as voice, design, and animation meld together. Little gestures, such as Bob's boss Mr. Huph methodically aligning the pencils on his desk, speak volumes about the personality, and each character has its own unique walk. The true scene-stealer is Edna "E" Mode, the superhero costume designer loosely modeled after Edith Head and voiced by Bird himself (her cape monologue alone makes the film).

Unlike the more or less concurrent *Shark Tale*, *The Incredibles* took a more unique approach to voices. Though fairly well-known, Craig T. Nelson and Holly Hunter were used not for name value, but because their qualities suited the superpowered husband and wife (indeed, only Samuel L. Jackson, as family friend Frozone, really had marquee value at the time). Instead of a teen starlet, NPR commentator/author Sarah Vowell was cast as daughter Violet. The vast majority of the remaining roles, down to the one-line bits, were filled by Pixar folk, which, in addition to Bird, included Bud Luckey, director of the short "Boundin'," which accompanied the film, as a government liaison; animator Bret Parker as a harried babysitter; character designer Teddy Newton, narrating the newsreel that explains the backstory; and Bird's sons Michael and Nicholas, as Violet's school crush and an awestruck neighbor boy respectively.

Frank Thomas and Ollie Johnston, last seen in *Iron Giant*, again have cameo roles (and receive "special thanks" credits along with Matthew Robbins, Bird's cowriter for the 1987 live film *batteries not included*). Their appearance is more tangential this time, but the pair praising the Parr family for doing things "old school" seems like a nod of approval for Pixar and Brad Bird. No matter what the method, good storytelling and complex characters shine through. (AL)

**Additional Credits:** Screenplay: Brad Bird. Executive producer: John Lasseter. Associate producer: Kori Rae. Assistant producer: Katherine Sarafian. Music: Michael Giacchino. Story supervisor: Mark Andrews. Cinematography: Andrew Jimenez, Patrick Lin, Janet Lucroy. Character designer: Tony Fucile, Teddy Newton. Supervising animators: Tony Fucile, Steven Clay Hunter, Alan Barillaro. Film editor: Stephen Schaffer. Production designer: Lou Romano. Animators: Carlos Baena, Bobby Beck, Michael Berenstein, Rodrigo Blaas Nacle, Bolhem Bouchiva, Dylan Brown, Adame Burke, Scott Clark, Brett Coderre, Tim Crawfurd, David Devan, Doug Dooley, Ike Feldman, Doug Frankel, Andrew Gordon, Stephen Gregory, Travis Hathway, Timothy Hittle, Daniel Holland, John Kahrs, Nancy Kato, Patty Kihm Stevenson, Karen Kiser, Shawn Krause, Wendell Lee, Angus MacLane, Matt Majers, Michael Makarewicz, Daniel Maso, Dale McBeath, Amy McNamara, Jon Mead, Paul Mendoza, Billy Merritt, Cameron Miyasaki, Dave Mullins, James Ford Murphy, Victor Navone, Dan Nguyen, Alex Orrelle, Bret Parker, Michael Parks, Sanjay Patel, Bobby Podesta, Brett Pulliam, Richard Quade, Roberet H. Russ, Gini Cruz Santos, Andrew L. Schmidt, Bob Scott, Doug Sheppeck, David Earl Smith, Peter Sohn, Ross Stevenson, Michael Stocker, Doug Sweetland, J. Warren Trezevant, Michael Venturini, Mark A. Walsh, Michael Wu, Kurehla Yokoo, Ron Zorman.

**The Iron Giant** (8/6/99) Warner Brothers. 86 mins. Director: Brad Bird. Producers: Allison Abbate, Des McAnuff. Voices: Eli Marienthal (Hogarth Hughes), Vin Diesel (The Iron Giant), Christopher MacDonald (Kent Mansley), Harry Connick Jr. (Dean McCoppen), Jennifer Aniston (Annie Hughes), John Mahoney (General Rogard), M. Emmet Walsh (Earl Stutz), James Gammon (Foreman Marv Loach, Floyd

Turbeaux), Cloris Leachman (Mrs. Tensedge). Additional Voices: Bill Farmer (B-Movie Scientist), Ollie Johnston (Train Engineer), Frank Thomas (Frank the Train Brakeman).

©Warner Brothers, Entertainment, Inc.

**Consumer Tips:** ☆☆☆☆ MPAA Rating: G. Based on a novel by Ted Hughes.

**Story:** A giant robot from outer space crashes to earth and is befriended by a lonely little boy.

**Comments:** *The Iron Giant* is probably the most significant animated feature to come out in the late 1990s. Its critical acclaim and success on video (compared to rather poor box office), plus numerous Annie Awards, might have been factors in the establishment, two years later, of an Academy Award category for animated features. It was also the debut film for veteran film animator and television director Brad Bird (*The Simpsons, Family Dog*), an auspicious first outing. Adapted from British author Ted Hughes' 1968 children's tale of a boy and a metal man, the movie recasts the fable as a Cold War adventure in New England, complete with government paranoia, a beatnik artist, and "Duck and Cover" classroom films. The titular character, created through CG animation shaded to blend remarkably well with the drawn characters, is essentially a being searching for its purpose and morality, uttering the telling phrase "I am not a gun." The boy, Hogarth (here given the surname Hughes in honor of the original author, who died during production), is neither unduly cloying nor an obnoxious brat (child actor Eli Marienthal netted an Annie Award for

best voice acting). There are no stereotyped villains here: the giant is destructive in a childish, unintentional way; government agent Kent Mansley is somewhat justifiably alarmed by the robot's implications; and the army troops are just following orders.

Effects animation (particularly effective in the opening shots of Maine's coast) and character animation complement rather than compete with each other, and in the case of the giant (animated chiefly by Steve Markowski), are combined. The many visual, playful gags with the giant, spoofs of 1950s movies and television, and witty dialogue exchanges keep the film mostly upbeat without undercutting the dramatic moments or the poignance of the giant's final act. Though a few celebrities are used in the cast (singer Harry Connick Jr. as the understanding beat artist, *Friends* star Jennifer Aniston as Hogarth's mother), they actually suit the roles, and the film doesn't allow one-liners to control the story. In-jokes abound, from vintage Chipmunk doppelgangers the Nutty Squirrels on the soundtrack to visual and vocal cameos by "Nine Old Men" members Ollie Johnston and the late Frank Thomas (as train engineers, referencing Ollie's hobby). Another pair of animation vets, designers Victor Haboush and Ray Aragon, contributed to the film's look. Despite receiving great critical acclaim, the film's box-office performance was underwhelming, grossing $23.10 million. A shaky, uncertain marketing campaign was probably a factor, as the film was more complex and adult than the average fare, but also somewhat more violent. However, since its video release, the movie has garnered an almost cult-like following. Director Bird subsequently left Warner Bros. for Pixar, to write and direct *The Incredibles*. (AL)

**Additional Credits:** Screenplay: Tim McCanlies. Screen story: Brad Bird. Based on the book *The Iron Man* by Ted Hughes. Music: Michael Kamen. Head of animation: Tony Fucile. Supervising animators: Richard Bazley, General Rogard, Bob Davies, Stephan Franck, Tony Fucile, Gregory S. E. Manwaring, Steven Markowski, Mike Nguyen, Wendy Perdue, Christopher Sauve, Dean Wellings. Animation: Richard Baneham, Adam Burke, Jennifer Cardon, Mike Chavez, Richard Curtis, Ruth Daly, Marcelo Fernandes DeMoura, Jeff Etter, Lauren Faust, Ralph Fernan, Steve Garcia, Lennie K. Graves, Russell Hall, Adam Henry, Ken Hettig, Kevin Johnson, Ben Jones, Ernest Keen, Jae H. Kim, Holger Leihe, Lane Lueras, Craig R. Maras, Roy Meurin, Randy

Myers, Melina Sydney Padua, Scott T. Petersen, Andrew Schmidt, Sean Springer, Mike Swofford, Derek Thompson, Craig Valde, Jim Vander Keyl, Roger Vizard, Alex Williams, Mark A. Williams, John D. Williams. CGI animation: Richard Baneham, Grace Blanco, Brad Booker, Andrew D. Brownlow, Yarrow Cheney, Minhee Choe, Stephane Cros, Adam Dotson, Bruce Edwards, Mark R. R. Farquar, Ron Hughart, Yair Kantor, Les Major, Mike Murphy, Susan L. Oslin, Glenn Storm, Vincent Truitner. Effects head: Allen Foster. Effects animation: John Bermudes, Jesse M. Cosio, John Dillon, Rick Echevarria, Marc Ellis, Michel Gagne, Earl A. Hibbert, Brett Hisey, John MacFarlane, Kevin M. O'Neil, Volker Pajatsch, David Pritchard, Gary Sole, Ryan Woodward. Additional animation: Joanne Coughlin, Devin Crane, Jean Cullen De Moura, Phil Langone, Brian Larsen, Boowon Lee, Michael Mullen, Shane Prigmore, Eddie Rosas, Andy Shuhler, Michael Shannon, Kyung S. Shin, Peter Sohn, Stephen Steinbach, Michael Venturini. Production designer: Mark Whiting. Story head: Jeffrey Lynch. Storyboard artists: Dean Wellins, Mark Andrews, Kevin O'Brien, Viki Anderson, Piet Kroon, Fergal Reilly. Additional story: Teddy Newton, Stephen G. Lumley, Harry A. Sabin Jr., Moroni, Ron Hughart, Brian Kindregan. Visual development/character design: Tony Fucile, Ray Aragon, Victor J. Haboush, Lou Romano, Laura L. Corsiglia, Dominique R. Louis, Teddy Newton. Iron Giant designers: Joe Johnston, Mark Whiting, Hiroki Itokazu, Teddy T. Yang, Steven Markowski. Layout/workbook head: William H. Frake III. Layout/workbook: James P. Alles, Teresa Coffey-Wellins, Frederick J. Gardner III, Louis Gonzales, Karen Hamrock. Background head: Dennis Venizelos. Backgrounds: Christopher Brock, Ruben Chavez, William Dely, Dennis Durrell, James Finn, Greg Gibbons, Anie Guenther, Joel Parod, Craig Robertson, Jonathan Salt, Nadia Vurbenova, Wei M. Zhao.

**Jack and the Beanstalk** (2/13/76) Columbia Pictures. 82 mins. Directors: Gisaburo Sugii (Japan), Peter J. Solmo (U.S.). Producer: Katsumi Furukawa. Voices (U.S.): Billie Lou Watt (Jack, Madame Hecuba), Corinne Orr (Princess Margaret).

*Consumer Tips:* ☆☆☆☆ MPAA Rating: G. Fantasy adventure. Based on the English folktale. A successful Japanese emulation of American animated fairy tale theatrical cartoon features with many delightful songs.

*Story:* Jack, a young farmboy, sells a cow for a handful of magic beans. They grow up to a castle in the clouds where Jack and his dog Crosby find that an evil

©Columbia Pictures Industries, Inc.

witch has enchanted Princess Margaret and is about to force her to marry the giant ogre Tulip. Jack, Crosby, and the princess's loyal servants, who have been enchanted into mice, rescue her.

*Comments:* After Japan's Mushi Pro studio collapsed into bankruptcy in 1973, director Gisaburo Sugii and many of its animators (veterans of Mushi's 1970 *Cleopatra*) started a new studio, Group TAC. *Jack and the Beanstalk* (*Jack to Mame no Ki*), funded by the *Nippon Herald* as a family feature and released July 20, 1974, in Japan, was deliberately aimed to break into the American theatrical feature market. Group TAC used its experience from *Cleopatra* to design a fast-paced feature that would please adults with clever dialogue and suspense, and children with cute animals.

Jack is an irresponsibly carefree boy of 12 to 14 who plays all day with his old hound dog Crosby while his harried mother worries about losing their farm. When Jack is sent to sell their cow, he trades her to a con-artist traveling showman for a handful of "magic beans." The beans grow into a huge beanstalk at night that lifts the sleeping Jack and Crosby and carries them to a cloud-land dominated by a huge castle inhabited by only three people: beautiful but dazed Princess Margaret; a huge ogre she calls "handsome Prince Tulip," whom she is about to marry; and Tulip's mother, the sinister Madame Hecuba (Mrs. Noire). Margaret and Hecuba invite Jack to stay for the wedding, though it is obvious that Hecuba plans to eat him.

The movie is full of witty dialogue. The spritely songs advance the plot, with many subtle touches such as the wedding eve "No One's Happier Than I," which shows Margaret's, Tulip's, and Hecuba's thoughts: Margaret, bespelled, sees Tulip as a handsome, loving prince; Tulip is a giant childish sadistic bully but he really does love Margaret in his own way; while Hecuba plans to kill them both as soon as they are wed because Tulip is becoming too independent.

*Jack and the Beanstalk* was produced for Columbia Pictures by the New York veteran voice-dubbers who produced *Astro Boy, Gigantor, Kimba,* and *Speed Racer* for television during the 1960s. It was briefly released and disappeared almost immediately despite excellent reviews. A fan claimed that a Columbia executive admitted off-the-record that it had been made as a tax writeoff, and had been pulled from theaters as soon as it looked like it might actually make money. It was frequently seen during the 1980s on HBO and was an early Columbia home-video release. (FP)

**Additional Credits:** Screenplay: Shuji Hirami. Executive producer: Mikio Nakada. Art directors: Takao Kodama, Yoshiyuki Uchida, Koji Abe, Shiro Fujimoto. Music coordinator: Yuh Aku. Editor: Masashi Furukawa. Sound effects: Mitsuru Kashiwabara. Animators: Shigeru, Yamaoto, Yasuo Maeda, Teruhito Kamiguchi, Takateru Miwa, Kazuko Nakamura, Toshio Hirata, Kanji Akabori, Sadao Ysukioka.

**James and the Giant Peach** (4/12/96) Disney. 80 mins. Director: Henry Selick. Producers: Tim Burton, Denise DiNovi. Voices: Paul Terry (James), Joanna Lumley (Aunt Spiker), Miriam Margolyes (Aunt Sponge), Pete Postlethwaite (Old Man, Narrator), Simon Callow (Grasshopper), Richard Dreyfuss (Centipede), Susan Sarandon (Miss Spider), Jane Leeves (Mrs. Ladybug), David Thewlis (Earthworm).

**Consumer Tips:** ☆☆½ MPAA Rating: G. Partial live action/stop-motion puppets. Based on the book by Roald Dahl.

**Story:** Young orphan boy, forced to live with two eccentric aunts, escapes to take a journey on a giant peach. He is accompanied by a variety of talking insects on his adventure at sea and in New York City.

**Comments:** Roald Dahl's fantasy works, though long popular with children, have always had serious under-

©Walt Disney Productions

currents (the 1971 film, *Willy Wonka and the Chocolate Factory,* retained much of that), and much of that is retained, at least initially, in *James and the Giant Peach.* Fresh from the success of *The Nightmare Before Christmas,* Disney ventured into stop-motion animation a second time, retaining *Nightmare* director Henry Selick and much of the same crew. The lighthearted score by Pixar stalwart Randy Newman adds an entirely different flavor to the proceedings, though, and this time Tim Burton functioned solely as producer, with little if any creative involvement. This was actually Disney's second brush with Dahl; during World War II, the British author penned a manuscript about gremlins, the scourge of pilots, which Disney spent a lengthy period struggling to adapt as a feature (by fall 1943, the project was abandoned, though gremlins were used on insignia and in a Disney children's book).

*James and the Giant Peach* opens rather bleakly, with live-action sequences showing how James was orphaned and essentially became the kept servant of his vicious, greedy aunts Spiker and Sponge (well-played by British comediennes Joanna Lumley and Miriam Margolyes). His situation changes, however, when magic "tongues" from a strange old man cause the titular fruit to grow on a barren tree. The model effects for this scene are particularly superb, and indeed when the movie shifts from live action to stop motion, there is a momentary loss of momentum. The shift occurs when James bites into and enters the giant peach, encountering a motley group of giant arthropods, representing various class systems.

At this point, the movie becomes completely episodic, as the peach and its passengers drift across the ocean or fly through the air (James' dream destination being New York City), and also turns into a comedy of manners, as the aristocratic old British grasshopper clashes with the brash, American centipede, amongst other character conflicts. These character interactions are generally more enjoyable than the perils that the crew face, including a mechanical shark and an undersea crew of skeleton pirates. Both were inventions for the film, and the latter incident offers a cameo from *Nightmare*'s Jack Skellington as the pirate captain, complete with skeletal parrot.

The filmmakers made a few crucial alterations, such as sparing the evil aunts (satisfyingly crushed to death by the peach in the original tale). The movie does retain much of Dahl's tone, though, even incorporating his lyrics into the song numbers. An intriguing nightmare sequence, using paper cut-outs of the aunts, is also included. Overall, though less visually distinct than *Nightmare*, the film retains enough of Dahl's bite for most adults, while the fantasy elements of talking insects and giant fruit have a natural appeal to children. Following *James*, Selick faded from view, resurfacing with the rather ill-fated *Monkeybone* (2001) and stop-motion animation inserts for *The Life Aquatic with Steve Zissou* (2004). (AL)

**Additional Credits:** Screenplay: Karey Kirkpatrick, Jonathan Roberts, Steve Bloom. Based on the novel by Roald Dahl. Music, songs written/performed: Randy Newman. Animation supervisor: Paul Berry. Animators: Anthony Scott, Michael Belzer, Timothy Hittle, Trey Thomas, Justin Kohn, Christopher Gilligan, Richard C. Zimmerman, Stephen A. Buckley, Guionne Leroy, Michael W. Johnson, Josephine T. Huang, Daniel K. Mason, Paul Berry, Kent Burton, Tom St. Amand, Webster Colcord, Chuck Duke. Additional animators: Owen Klatte, Sue Pugh, Paul W. Jessel, Tom Gibbons, D. Sean Burns, Jerold Howard. Computer animation supervisors: Jerome Chen, Harry Walton. Lighting/lead computer animator: Louis Cetorelli. Computer animators: Allen Edwards, Arnaud Hervas, Alex Sokoloff, David Vallone, Peter Warner. Cut-out animation: Tim Myers, Owen Klatte. Cel effects supervisor/lead effects animator: Sari Gennis. Effects animators: Anthony Stacchi, Mike Smith, Joseph Gilland, Stuart Canin, Arnold Belnick, Maria Newman. Storyboard supervisors: Kelly Asbury, Joe Ranft. Art directors: Bill Boes, Kendal Cronkhite. Storyboards: Michael Cachuela, Jorgen Klubien, Peter Von Sholly, Mike Mitchall. Cut-out character designer: James Stimson. Cut-out production artist: Chance Lane.

**Jetsons: The Movie** (7/6/90) Universal. 81 mins. Directors/producers: William Hanna, Joseph Barbera. Voices: George O. Hanlon (George Jetson), Mel Blanc (Mr. Spaceley), Penny Singleton (Jane Jetson), Tiffany (Judy Jetson), Patric Zimmerman (Elroy Jetson), Don Messick (Astro), Jean Vander Pyl (Rosie the Robot), Ronnie Schell (Rudy 2), Patti Deutsch (Lucy 2), Dana Hill (Teddy 2), Russi Taylor (Fergie Furbelow), Paul Kreppel (Apollo Blue), Rick Dees (Rocket Rick).

©Universal City Studios, Inc.

**Consumer Tips:** ☆☆½ MPAA Rating: G. Futuristic comedy-adventure.

**Story:** In the late 21st century, someone is sabotaging the Spacely Sprocket and Spindle Orbiting Ore Asteroid Manufacturing Plant, Unlimited. Mr. Spacely promotes George Jetson to vice president and sends him and his family to the asteroid to get production to resume. Unknown to George, the mining operation is destroying the homes of the cute-and-cuddly Grungies, who live within the asteroid. George soon gets involved with a sabotage mystery, while Judy falls under the spell of rock-and-roll idol, Apollo Blue.

**Comments:** In this movie, a main problem is solved when George Jetson convinces Mr. Spacely to hire the Grungies as cheap labor to process space ore. Ironically, Hanna-Barbera hired Wang Film Productions Co., Inc./Cuckoo's Nest Studios in Taiwan as cheap labor to produce a mediocre movie.

*Jetsons: The Movie* was dedicated to George O'Hanlon and Mel Blanc. Both veteran actors had passed away during production, and O'Hanlon actually passed away during a recording session. Jeff Bergman completed O'Hanlon's lines and rerecorded dialogue underperformed by O'Hanlon and Blanc.

Patric Zimmerman voiced Elroy because Daws Butler had died in May 1988. Penny Singleton reprised Jane Jetson; Don Messick reprised the loveable mutt, Astro; and Jean Vander Pyl voiced Rosie the Robot.

Janet Waldo had recorded Judy Jetson, but Universal wanted to promote pop singer Tiffany (Tiffany Renee Darwish), who rose to fame in late 1987 with her hit singles "I Think We're Alone Now" and "Could've Been." Tiffany replaced Waldo.

"I was totally crushed," Waldo told Kyle Counts of the *Los Angeles Times* (July 8, 1990). "I originated the character, and I feel very sentimental about Judy. If they had recast the whole show, there wouldn't have been any problem at all. But the fact that my part was the only one that was changed just threw me. I felt it was very disloyal (of Hanna and Barbera)."

Said Bill Hanna, "I can understand how Janet feels. It was purely a business decision, based on the thought that Tiffany would bring in more dollars at the box office."

By the time *Jetsons: The Movie* made it to theaters (July 1990, delayed from the previous Christmas), Tiffany had become just a pop music footnote.

Said Joe Barbera in his autobiography, *My Life in Toons,* "The folks putting up the money have a very natural urge to take over everything. When I at last had had enough of it, I walked out on the production, and I can't really say much more about the movie, because I've never had the heart to go see it. . . . *The Jetsons* was not a happy experience."

*Jetsons: The Movie,* which earned $23 million at the box office, turned out to be the last theatrical release from Hanna-Barbera. Joe Barbera had to enlist the services of Film Roman for his next feature, *Tom and Jerry: The Movie.* Dennis Marks wrote both features.

The main plot basically rehashes *Star Trek*'s "Devil in the Dark" episode, in which miners disrupt the environment of the native life forms, then exploit them as cheap labor. The Grungies, with their wide eyes, furry bodies, diminutive size, and tribal society, resemble George Lucas's Ewoks.

The film's opening reprised the television show's opening, with two notable exceptions: Jane no longer grabs George's wallet to go shopping, and the family

flies in a computer-generated environment. The original conveyed a vaster amount of speed and excitement, compared to the lethargic and lifeless CG of the film.

Animation-wise, the characters move as if they were made of rubber, in stark contrast to the hard-edged CG surroundings. The timing is actually snappier, and more vibrant, in the original television series. (WRM)

***Additional Credits:*** Writer: Dennis Marks. Music: John Debney. Supervising director: Iawo Takamoto. Animation directors: David Michener, Ray Patterson. Assistant animation supervisor: Joanna Romersa. Key animators: Frank Andrina, Oliver Lefty Callahan, David Feiss, Don MacKinnon, Irv Spence. Animators: Robert Alvarez, Brad Case, David Concepcion, Jesse Cosio, Charlie Downs, Robert Coe, Dan Hunn, Glenn Kennedy, Ernesto Lopez, Ed Love, Istvan Majorosi, Jon McClenehan, Mark Christanssen, Mike Bennett, Barry Anderson, Brenda Banks, Andre Knutson, Bob Tyler, Leon Dawson, Bill Nunes, Simon O'Leary, Joanna Romersa, Carl Urbano, Allen Wilzbach, Berny Wolf, Chris Houser, Raul Stibal, Kevin Petrilak, Gabby Payn, Phil Cummings, Lee Mishkin, Kathy Castillo. Production design: Al Gmuer. Storyboard artists: Don Sheppard, Alex Lovy, Chris Otsuki, Kay Wright, Jim Willoughby, Don Jurwich, Scott Jeralds. Layout director: Deane Taylor. Layout supervisor: John Ahern. Computer animation: deGraf/Wahrman Inc. CG vehicles by Kroyer Films. Film sequence ("You and Me") by Kurtz and Friends.

**Jimmy Neutron, Boy Genius** (12/21/01) Paramount. 83 mins. Director: John A. Davis. Producers: Steve Oedekerk, John A. Davis, Albie Hecht. Voices: Debi Derryberry (James "Jimmy" Isaac Neutron), Carolyn Lawrence (Cindy Vortex), Rob Paulsen (Carl Wheezer, Carl's Mom and Dad, Kid in Classroom, Kid), Megan Cavanagh (Judy Neutron, VOX), Mark De Carlo (Hugh Neutron, Pilot, Arena Guard), Jeffrey Garcia (Sheen Estevez), Andrea Martin (Mrs. Fowl), Candi Milo (Nick Dean, Britanny, PJ), Crystal Scales (Libby), Martin Short (Ooblar), Patrick Stewart (King Goobot), Jim Cummings (Ultra Lord, Mission Control), David L. Lander (Yokian Guard, Gus), Bob Goen (Newscaster), Mary Hart (Newscaster).

***Consumer Tips:*** ☆☆½ MPAA Rating: G. Nominated for an Academy Award as Best Animated Feature.

**Story:** When a 10-year-old inventor inadvertently causes alien invaders to kidnap all neighborhood parents, he and his classmates travel through space and mount a rescue.

**Comments:** Jimmy Neutron started life as a 40-second short "Runaway Rocket Boy" by John A. Davis of Dallas, Texas-based DNA Productions. That film was later expanded into "The Adventures of Johnny Quasar." The concept was picked up by Nickelodeon and it was decided to launch the character first in a feature film, and then have a series spun off of that.

Nick attached writer/producer Steve Oedekerk, who had previously written the Jim Carrey *Ace Ventura* movies and had an affinity toward animated films, to spearhead the project. The resultant feature film is a very entertaining package. Its retro production design is delightful and the climactic sequences in outer space are dazzling and funny.

*Jimmy Neutron: Boy Genius* is Nickelodeon's sixth movie released through Paramount, and its first CG-animated film. Its target audience: kids 8 and younger.

In 2002, *Jimmy Neutron* was nominated for Academy Award—Best Animated Feature, for a Golden Satellite Award—Best Motion Picture, Animated or Mixed Media, and for two Golden Reel Awards by the Motion Picture Sounds Editors, USA.

Nickelodeon premiered *The Adventures of Jimmy Neutron: Boy Genius* (the television series) in September 2002. The show won an Annie award for Outstanding Achievement in an Animated Television Production Produced for Children.

*Jimmy Neutron* demonstrates that it is possible to make a well-crafted G-rated film outside of Hollywood and still be a financial success. Its total U.S. box-office gross was $80,920,948. (WRM)

**Additional Credits:** Executive producers: Julia Pistor, Keith Alcorn. Screenplay: Joan A. Davis, David N. Weiss, J. David Stern, Steve Oedekerk. Story: John A. Davis, Steve Oedekerk. Music: John Debney. Sequence directors: Russell Calabrese, John Eng, Raul Garcia, Robert LaDuca. Directors of animation: Keith Alcorn, John A. Davis. Animation supervisors: Paul C. Allen, Renata Dos Anjos, Mike Gasaway, Bryan Hillestad, Troy Saliba. Animators: Kirby Atkins, Jourdan S. Biziou, Brad Blevins, David Lee Brehm, Brian Capshaw, Ray Chase, Andrea Kay Davis, Ryan Davis, Matthew Russell, Sam Fleming, Michael Gargiulo, Tom

Grevera, Tim Hatcher, Moses L. Hood, Thomas Judd, Ted Loo, Rena Mintzas, Deanna Molinaro, Travis (Jesus) Neal, Brett Paton, Tom Saville, Carl Schembri, Mark Thielen, Michael C. Walling, Aaron Werntz. Vehicle animation supervisor: Matthew Russell. Vehicle animators: Dave Adams, Craig Hamilton Nisbet, August Wartenberg. Secondary animation lead: Cheryl Ray. Secondary animators: Sean Ermey, Joseph J. Johnston, Ben Williams. Lip sync animators: Keith Alcorn, Paul Clearhout, Nick Gibbons. Additional animators: John Sore, Michael Kimmel, Tim Pyle. Production design: Fred Cline. Art director/storyboard supervisor: James Beihold. Character designs: Keith Alcorn. Additional character designs: Paul Claerhout.

**Jin-Roh: The Wolf Brigade** (8/3/01) Bandai Entertainment. 98 mins. Director: Hiroyuki Okiura. Producers: Tsutomu Sugita, Hidekazu Terakawa (Japan), Satoshi Kanuma, Toshifumi Yoshida (U.S.). Voices: Yoshiktsu Fujiki, Michael Dobson (Kazuki Fuse), Sumi Mutoh, Moneca Stori (Kei Amamiya), Hiroyuki Kinoshita, Colin Murdoch (Atsushi Henmi), Yukio Hirota, Dale Wilson (Bunmei Hiroto), Yukihiro Yoshida, Michael Kopsa (Hajime Handa), Yoshisada Sakaguchi, Doug Abrahams (Hachiro Tobe, Narrator).

**Consumer Tips:** ☆☆☆☆ MPAA Rating: Not rated. SF political thriller. A drama of intrigue in a fictional 1950s Japan between urban terrorists and two government police organizations that are also plotting against each other.

**Story:** Kazuki Fuse, a rookie in the Special Force Unit of Tokyo's Capital Police, hesitates to shoot a schoolgirl terrorist, allowing her to detonate a suicide bomb. Later Fuse meets her innocent sister, Kei, and a romance develops. This plays into the hands of Tokyo's regular police, longtime rivals of the Capital Police, who plan to turn Fuze's "love affair with a terrorist girl" into a scandal that could force the Capital Police to disband. And Kei may really be a terrorist, after all.

**Comments:** *Jin-Roh's* story was a well-publicized script by Mamoru Oshii, acclaimed director of *Patlabor* and *Ghost in the Shell* for animation studio Production I.G., who assigned it to Hiroyuki Okiura, his young protégé on the latter. Oshii's fondness for dramas of intrigue and interservice rivalry among political and military organizations is well-established. *Jin-Roh* is set in a fictional late 1950s Japan that fought and lost World War II and was occupied for 10 years by Germany rather than the United States. The result is a Tokyo whose vehicles, military uniforms and weapons, and police organizations show a Germanic rather than American influence.

In the real world, 1950s leftist terrorism in Japan was successfully ended by the regular police and the improvement of the economic situation. In *Jin-Roh*, terrorism is so severe that a separate Capital Police is created just to combat it. The CP's paramilitary Special Force Unit is administered through a Public Security Division. The entire Capital Police is considered an unnecessary duplicate by the resentful "local" (regular) Tokyo police.

Kazuki Fuse, a new member of the Special Force Unit, seems emotionally confused. He wants to find out why members of "the Sect" are fanatics willing to die for their cause. This wins the admiration of Kei, the sister of "Red Riding Hood" terrorist Nanami, who died in a suicide explosion.

Henmi, Fuse's pal in basic training who transferred to Public Security's administrative staff, shows sympathy while most other Special Force patrolmen consider Fuse weak. Tobe, the tough drill-sergeant head of the academy's training program, keeps emphasizing that they are wolves only disguised as men, and whenever wolves try to live with men, one or the other dies. Kei seems to unconsciously echo this by pointing out Nanami's obsession with the Red Riding Hood folktale (much grimmer in its original Germanic version than in the cleaned-up children's version).

*Jin-Roh* was one of Japan's theatrical features designed more for international film festival exhibition and award consideration than for general release. It was first shown at a festival in France in 1999 and was not released in Japan until June 3, 2000. (FP)

**Additional Credits:** Story/screenplay: Mamoru Oshii. English script: Kevin Mckeown, Robert Chomiak. Music: Hajime Mizoguchi. Character designs: Hiroyuki Okiura, Tetsuya Nishio. Animation director: Kenji Kamiyama.

**Johnny the Giant Killer** (6/5/53) Lippert Pictures. 62 mins. Director and producer: Jean Image, Charles Frank. A Jean Image Films Production. No voice actors credited.

©Jean Image Films

**Consumer Tips:** 0 (zero stars) MPAA Rating: Unrated.

**Story:** A group of boys explore a castle and are captured by a giant. Johnny escapes, becomes allies with a swarm of bees, and helps the boys escape.

**Comments:** Produced in 18 months with a low budget and small staff, Hungarian-born cartoonist Jean Image (Imre Hajdu, 1911–89) managed to produce France's first animated feature, *The Intrepid Jeannot* (*Jeannot L'Intrepide*) in 1950. The film went on to win the Grand Prix for children's films at the 1951 Venice Film Festival and was eventually released in the United States (by B-Movie studio Lippert Pictures) in 1953, as *Johnny the Giant Killer*. It was one of the very first foreign animated features to hit the states, and one of the first non-Disney cel-animated full-length movies.

The character designs are poor, the animation is terrible, and the storytelling is atrocious. Yet I can't say you won't find this film entertaining in a Mystery Science Theater, "so-bad-it's-good" way. Nevertheless, as poor as the film is (the cheapest American cartoons of the day were far superior to this on every technical level), it still boasts the novelty of Technicolor, and the musical score is quite lively.

René Cloërec (1911–1995), the film's musical director, had previously written songs for Edith Piaf and scored the French classic *Devil in the Flesh* (1949). Doing the music for France's first animated feature must have seemed like an honor. "In live action films, particularly dramas, music is used to highlight certain moments," Cloërec was quoted at the time. "A dramatic picture may have as little as three minutes of music. But in animation, music runs all the way through the picture."

The film has since drifted into obscurity (as it should), save for the fact that it was never copyrighted and is easily found for sale, lingering in cheap video bins around the world. (JB)

**Additional Credits:** English-language screenplay: Paul Colline, Charles Frank, Nesta MacDonald. Story: Eraine. Music: René Cloërec. Cinematography: Kostia Tchikine. Sound: René Sarazin. Backgrounds: Pierre Baudin, Saint-Joyerie, Amidie Tardivon, Serge Tessanech. Chief animator: Albert Chapeaux. Animators: Denis Boutin, Marcel Breuil, Albert Champeaux, O'Klein.

## Jonah: A VeggieTales Movie

**Jonah: A VeggieTales Movie** (10/4/02) FHE Pictures. 82 mins. Directors: Mike Nawrocki, Phil Vischer. Producer: Ameake Owens. Voices: Phil Vischer (Archibald Asparagus, Jonah, Twippo, Bob the Tomato, Mr. Lunt, Pirate Lunt, Percy Pea, Phillipe Pea, Pa Grape, Pirate Pa, Nezzer, King Twistomer, Cockney Pea #2), Mike Nawrocki (Larry the Cucumber, Pirate Larry, Jean Claude Pea, Cockney Pea #1, Self-Help Tape Voice, Jerry Gourd, Whooping BBQ Pea), Tim Hodge (Khalil), Lisa Vischer (Junior Asparagus), Dan Anderson (Dad Asparagus), Kristin Blegen (Laura Carrot), Shelby Vischer (Annie), Jim Poole (Scooter, Townsperson), Ron Smith (City Official, Crazy Jopponian), Sarah Catherine Brooks (Message from the Lord Choir).

**Consumer Tips:** ☆☆☆ MPAA Rating: G.

**Story:** The VeggieTales gang learns a lesson in compassion and mercy in the story of Jonah, the messenger of God, who is swallowed by a whale—then given a second chance to deliver his message to the wayward people of Nineveh.

**Comments:** The VeggieTales characters from Big Idea Productions were one of the few truly successful direct-to-video animation franchises not based on preexisting characters. The series, created by Minnesota Bible college expunges Phil Vischer and Mike Nawrocki (neither of whom had prior animation experience), began in 1992. To some extent marking a return to the 1930s animated shorts in which food products or kitchenware came to life, these limbless refugees from the produce counter proved surprisingly endearing and popular, demonstrating that videos focusing on moral lessons and Bible stories need not be relegated to Christian bookstores. *Jonah* represented the studio's first (and only) foray into theatrical features, and one of the few Biblically based animated films to hit the big-screen.

*Jonah* is a much looser and less sweeping tale than DreamWorks' *Prince of Egypt*, however. Casting Archibald Asparagus, one of the video series' regulars, as the titular prophet, and incorporating a woodworm sidekick and a crew of incompetent pirates, the movie takes a decidedly whimsical approach. Despite its evangelical roots, and despite a moral emphasizing "following God," the movie is surprisingly accessible. The veggies themselves are an endearing lot, and the computer-animated whale is reasonably impressive. The lack of any body movement, aside from occasional bouncing, must have been quite a challenge for the animators, but they met it surprisingly well. Best of all, the movie never takes itself too seriously, as evidenced by the closing ballad, "The Song over the Credits," in which Larry the Cucumber proudly warbles the fact that it "has nothing to do with the movie you just saw." The in-house voice talent roster, including creators Vischer and Nawrocki in multiple roles and former Disney storyboard artist Tim Hodge as Kalill the worm, turns in sterling, if self-consciously cartoony, performances.

Despite the series' popularity, the Biblical themes and certain perceptions of *Jonah* as a pure "kiddie" film proved limiting. Jonah raked in a mere $25.5 million theatrically. Coupled with other financial setbacks, including a lawsuit upon switching video distributors, the film's poor performance forced Big Idea out of business. The company and characters were sold to Classic Media, the firm that also owns the rights to Mr. Magoo, Casper, and Bullwinkle, in December 2003, and has recently succeeded in selling the series to international markets. Stateside, however, it seems that the veggies have temporarily been put in the freezer. (WRM)

*Additional Credits:* Exective producers: Terry Botwick, Dan Philips, Phil Vischer. Writers: Phil Vischer, Mike Nawrocki. Story: Tim Hodge. Music/songs: Kurt Heinecke, David Mullen, Mike Nawrocki, Phil Vischer. Art director: Joseph Sapulich. Production manager: Jennifer Combs. Animation director: Marc Vulcano. Animators: Andy Arnett, Justin Barett, Tom Danen, Thom Falter, Joe Gorski, Christopher Hickman, Amber Rudolph, Nathan Tungseth, Danny Wawrzaszek.

## Journey Back to Oz (6/19/74) Filmation—Seymour Borde. 102 mins. Director: Hal Sutherland. Producers: Lou Scheimer, Norm Prescott. Voices: Liza Minelli (Dorothy), Milton Berle (Lion), Herschel Bernardi (Woodenhead), Paul Ford (Uncle Henry), Margaret Hamilton (Aunt Em), Jack E. Leonard (Sing post), Paul Lynde (Pumpkinhead), Ethel Merman (Mombi), Mickey Rooney (Scarecrow), Rise Stevens (Glinda), Danny Thomas (Tin Man), Mel Blanc (Crow), also Larry Storch and Dallas McKennon.

©Filmation Associates

**Consumer Tips:** ☆☆½ MPAA Rating: G. Musical Fantasy. For all ages. Based on Frank Baum's *Oz* characters.

**Story:** A cyclone brings Dorothy and Toto back to Oz, where her friend, the Scarecrow, now king of Emerald City, is warring with evil witch Mombi. Pumpkinhead and Woodenhead, a horse, join Dorothy in saving Oz.

**Comments:** The project for this film began in the early 1960s with partners Fred Ladd and Norm Prescott, who conceived and produced *Pinocchio in Outer Space* (1965). They spent a year with famed animator Preston Blair, producing the first six minutes

with an untried studio in Yugoslavia, which proved disastrous. Blair drew the production storyboards for the project and left it in Prescott's hands.

Prescott and Lou Scheimer formed Filmation in 1964 and found success in television animation series (*Superman, Archie*, et al.). *Journey Back to Oz* was finally put into production in 1970. The all-star soundtrack was recorded in 1962, when Liza Minelli was 15 years old. Peter Lawford was originally recorded for the Scarecrow, but was replaced by Mickey Rooney because Lawford's English accent wasn't right for the part. Danny Thomas's dialogue as the Tin Man is replaced in parts by Larry Storch because the Thomas tracks deteriorated during the time between recording and production. This was Filmation's first feature-length film, and was financed with money through parent company Teleprompter. Filmation distributed the film itself in 1974 by renting theaters, paying for all advertising, and collecting 100 percent of the box-office receipts (this method is called "four wall distribution" because the producer rents the four walls and pays for every seat of the theater).

The film is far superior to Filmation's usual television fare, but poor by any other feature film standard. The voice work is good, but there are far too many songs. On the plus side, there are some excellent fantasy sequences and imaginative background designs. Produced during a low point in American animation history, *Journey Back to Oz* sadly represents the state of the art in the mid-1970s. (JB)

*Additional Credits:* Associate producers: Fred Ladd, Preston Blair. Story: Fred Ladd, Norman Prescott. Songs: Sammy Cahn, James Van Heusen. Songs arranged/conducted by: Walter Scharf. Sequence directors: Rudy Larriva, Don Towsley. Supervising animator: Ambi Paliwoda. Animators: Bob Bransford, Bob Carlson, Jim Davis, Ed Friedman, Otto Feuer, Fred Grable, LaVerne Harding, Lou Kachivas, Les Kaluza, Anatole Kirsanoff, George Kreisi, Paul Krukowski, Bill Nunes, Jack Ozark, Manny Perez, Vigil Raddatz, Bill Reed, Virgil Ross, George Rowley, Ed Solomon, Ralph Sommerville, Reuben Timmens, Lou Zukor. Production manager: Rock Benedict. Art director: Don Christensen. Layout: Alberto DeMello, Kay Wright, Don Bluth, Dale Baer, Herb Hazelton, C.L. Hartman.

## The Jungle Book (10/18/67) Walt Disney Pictures. 78 mins. Director: Wolfgang Reitherman. Voices: Phil

Harris (Baloo), Sterling Holloway (Kaa), Louis Prima (King Louie), Sebastian Cabot (Bagheera), George Sanders (Shere Khan), Bruce Reitherman (Mowgli), J. Pat O'Malley (Col. Hathi, Buzzie), John Abbott (Akela), Ben Wright (Rama), Chad Stewart (Flaps), Digby Wolfe (Ziggy), Lord Tim Hudson (Dizzy), Verna Felton, Clint Howard (Elephants), Darleen Carr (Girl), Hal Smith, Leo De Lyon, Bill Skiles, Pete Henderson (Additional Voices).

©Walt Disney Productions

**Consumer Tips:** ☆☆☆ Adapted from *The Jungle Books* (1894–95) by Rudyard Kipling.

**Story:** Bagheera the panther finds an orphaned "man-cub" and leaves him in the care of wolves. The wolves raise young Mowgli, as he is called, but when the dreaded tiger Shere Khan returns to the area, the wolves decide to send the boy back to his own kind. Shere Khan hates man for possessing both guns and fire, and will surely kill Mowgli at the first opportunity. Bagheera escorts a reluctant Mowgli back to the "man-village" but is interrupted by the irrepressible bear Baloo, who decides (with Mowgli's agreement) that the boy would make a fine bear. After some misadventures Baloo agrees that Mowgli belongs with his own kind, but Shere Khan shows up to take matters into his own paws. Mowgli wins out and then abandons the jungle upon seeing a comely young girl from the "man village."

**Comments:** No serious reader of Kipling would recognize much of his Mowgli stories in the film, but serious animation fans may not care all that much. *The Jungle Book* is an exuberant movie that boasts winning

characters and has few lags. Some Disney fans and historians point to this film as the beginning of Disney's decline due to the fact that writer Bill Peet built his characters around the personalities that voiced them. Peet quit the movie, in fact, due to an argument over Bagheera's voice. Traditional Disney films designed the characters first and then found voices, so that the characters were pure creations of the designers and animators. Peet believed that Phil Harris' personality *was* Baloo the bear, and for the next decade Disney films featured characters that resembled their voice artists.

Whether or not he usurped the animators, Phil Harris turns in a fine job. The original Baloo of Kipling's story was a sage old bruin entrusted with teaching Mowgli "the Law of the Jungle." In this movie he becomes "that shiftless jungle bum," but he's a bum with a lot of heart, one of animation's best party animals. Baloo is central to the story, which basically covers the journey from the jungle to the man-village. Along the way Baloo and Mowgli contend with swingin' scat-singer King Louie the orangutan, who tries to be-bop the secret of fire from Mowgli; Sterling Holloway's sinister but fumbling python Kaa; and a troop of silly elephants led by Colonel Hathi, formerly of the Maharajah's Fifth Pachyderm Brigade. Helping the pair out are four Liverpudian vultures patterned on the Beatles. Shere Khan is simply one of the best villains in animal form Disney ever created (thanks to George Sanders' excellent voice work and Milt Kahl's keen animation). It's too bad that he has so little screen time; nearly half the movie goes by before we ever see him.

Much is made of the fact that this was the last movie that Walt Disney was directly involved in, but with Reitherman in charge and Milt Kahl, Ollie Johnston, Frank Thomas, and John Lounsberry as supervising animators, Walt did not give all that much input in any case. Walt Disney would pass away in December of 1966, nearly a year before *The Jungle Book* was released. He did not live to see its success, which was considerable: the movie made $13 million, killer play in 1966 dollars. Popular with critics and loved by audiences, this film is nearly the last hurrah for Disney's "Nine Old Men." Without Walt, the old order was soon to change, bringing with it a period of malaise and uncertainty about the future.

The Fab Four vultures talk like the Beatles, but they sing barbershop quartet. Kaa was Sterling Holloway's only role as a Disney villain. George Sanders, the voice of Shere Khan, was so jaded that when he was given a drawing of Shere Khan autographed by Disney, he handed it back saying, "What am I to do with it? This is absurd." Sanders committed suicide not long afterwards, leaving behind a note reading, "I'm so bored." Louis Prima, on the other hand, enjoyed his role as King Louie so much that he became upset when not cast in later Disney pictures. *The Jungle Book* was the first Disney film for which a sequel was planned. It didn't happen, though, for another three decades. (MG)

***Additional Credits:*** Story: Larry Clemmons, Ralph Wright, Ken Anderson, Vance Gerry. Inspired by the Rudyard Kipling "Mowgli" stories. Music: George Bruns. Songs: Robert B. Sherman, Richard M. Sherman, Terry Gilkyson. Directing animators: Milt Kahl, Ollie Johnston, Frank Thomas, John Lounsbery. Background styling: Al Dempster. Background artists: Bill Layne, Ralph Hulett, Art Riley, Thelma Witmer, Frank Armitage. Layout director: Don Griffith. Layout artists: Basil Davidovich, Tom Codrick, Dale Barnhart, Sylvia Roemer. Effects animation: Dan MacManus. Animators: Hal King, Eric Cleworth, Eric Larson, Fred Hellmich, Walt Stranchfield, John Ewing, Dick Lucas.

**The Jungle Book 2** (4/9/03) Walt Disney Pictures. 72 mins. Director: Steve Trenbirth. Producers: Mary Thorne, Christopher Chase. Voices: Haley Joel Osmont (Mowgli), John Goodman (Baloo), Mae Whitman (Shanti), Bob Joles (Bagheera), Tony Jay (Shere Khan), Connor Funk (Ranjan), Jim Cummings (Kaa, Col. Hathi), John Rhys-Davies (Ranjan's Father),

©Walt Disney Enterprises, Inc.

Phil Collins (Lucky the Vulture), Bobby Edner, J. Grant Albrecht (Additional Voices).

***Consumer Tips:*** ☆ MPAA Rating: G. Loosely based on the books by Rudyard Kipling.

***Story:*** Mowgli is dissatisfied with village life; although he has a family and a cute girlfriend (Shanti, the girl seen in the conclusion of the first film) he longs for the jungle and old friend Baloo the Bear. Baloo pays a long-awaited visit, but so does the angry tiger Shere Khan, who wants revenge on the "man-cub." Baloo and Mowgli flee into the jungle and are followed by Shanti and kid brother Ranjan. All eventually face a showdown with Shere Khan and discover their true places in life.

***Comments:*** *The Jungle Book 2* was originally intended as a direct-to-video release. With the original movie on moratorium and money to be made, Disney decided to see whether this sequel would fly on the big screen. It is not often that an animated film is without at least one or two redeeming features, but *The Jungle Book 2* strives mightily to achieve this dubious goal. There is virtually nothing to hang a story on; half-hour television episodes typically carry at least a minor subplot, but this film cannot even approach such complexity. Mowgli goes into the jungle, takes up with Baloo, faces Shere Khan, wins, and goes home realizing his place is with humans.

Considerable meddling is done with the original characters. Shanti, a submissive, very traditional female in her brief appearance in the first film is now a midriff-baring, spunky-tough heroine of the type that Disney was stamping out like cookies by 2003. Shere Khan has lost almost all of his emotional complexity and now simply stalks around in a bad mood, nursing his grudge. Kaa may as well not even be in the film; his role is little more than a rehash of his earlier schtick with Shere Kahn. Bagheera has gone from a sophisticated moralist to a bit player who has no part in any of the action (such as it exists). One of the more lively characters from the last film, King Louie, is now splitsville with no further explanation. The truth is, Disney simply did not want to pay the estate of Louis Prima for depicting the bandleader's likeness. One new character, Ranjan, is so annoying that one wishes Shere Khan had been just a bit hungrier.

The animation is competent but consists of the stock facial expression found in Disney animated features of the period. One can almost see Disney's young, second-string animators hitting their "pause" buttons to catch the expressions in *Aladdin* while they worked on this film. One musical number, "Wild," is virtually stolen from similar numbers in *The Lion King* and *The Little Mermaid*. Still, it's a welcome break from no less than three reprises of "The Bare Necessities." Haley Joel Osmont does Mowgli's speaking and singing voice, which works well enough for this film, but other voice work is surprisingly weak. John Goodman cannot match Phil Harris's evocation of Baloo, and Jim Cumming's imitation of the late Sterling Holloway's Kaa is noticeably off. This is especially disappointing since Cummings has done fine work taking over for Holloway in Disney's Winnie the Pooh films.

*The Jungle Book 2* is for small children and for those who must have a complete Disney feature collection; the latter may do well to keep it in its original packaging. (MG)

**Additional Credits:** Supervising animators: Kevin Peaty, Kelly Baigent, Simon Ashton. Animation supervisor: Bob Baxter. Senior animators: Davide Benvenuti, Andrew Brooks, Bernard Derriman, Adam Murphu, Myke Sutherland, Jozef Szekeres, Marc Wasik, Robert Fox, Ian Harrowell, Andries Maritz, Manny Banados, Lianne Hughes, Alexis Staderman. Animators: Warwick Gilbert, Hike Howie, Charlie Lee, Kathie O'Rourke, Donn Pattenden, Gie Santos, Rizaldy Valencia, Marco Zanoni, Deborah Cameron, Manuk Chang, Lily Dell, Alan Lam, David Mah, Toby Schwarz, Jocelyn Sy, Donald Walker, Kevin Wotton, Michael Badman, Donna Brockopp, Noel Cleary, Randy Glusac, Rowena Hamlyn-Aspden, Robert Mason, John Power, Allan Fernando.

**The King and I** (3/19/99) Warner Bros. 90 mins. Director: Richard Rich. Producers: James G. Robinson, Arthur Rankin, Peter Bakalian. Voices: Miranda Richardson (Anna Leanowens, speaking), Christiane Nell (Anna, singing), Martin Vidnovic (The King of Siam), Ian Richardson (The Kralahome), Darrell Hammond (Master Little), Allen D. Hong (Prince Chulalangkorn), David Burnham (Prince Chulalangkorn—singing), Armi Arrabee (Tuptim), Tracy Venner Warren (Tuptim—singing), Adam Wylie (Louis Leanowens).

©Morgan Creek Productions, Inc.

**Consumer Tips:** ☆ MPAA Rating: G. Based on the Rodgers and Hammerstein musical.

**Story:** An animated version of the Rogers and Hammerstein Broadway musical. Anna, a British school teacher, arrives in Siam to teach the king's children but finds her dealings with his highness her greatest challenge.

**Comments:** This movie is an animated version of the famous Richard Rodgers and Oscar Hammerstein stage and screen musical, *The King and I*. This musical was one of the most highly regarded stage productions in the history of theater. Unfortunately, the fine source material was wasted in this poorly animated remake.

This film tries hard to remain loyal to the original stage production, and uses the animated likenesses of the original Broadway cast (including Yul Brenner and Gertrude Lawrence). That's about the best thing you can say in its defense.

There were a number of people and companies that helped bring this ill-conceived project to life. Morgan Creek Productions is an independent movie company that has had a long affiliation with Warner Bros. Rankin/Bass Productions held the animation rights to the property, and thought that the Rodgers and Hammerstein musical would be a marvelous animated film, in the mold of the currently successful Disney features, *Beauty and the Beast, Aladdin,* and others.

Nest Entertainment, a studio run by animation veteran Richard Rich (*The Fox and the Hound, The Swan Princess*), was selected to bring that Disney magic to this material. He failed miserably. In fact, Rogers and Hammerstein's estate took the producers to court over the final product—a film they are ashamed of.

Reviews by the press were mainly negative, and box-office attendance was limited; the film grossed only $11.9 million in its theatrical run. "Et cetera, et cetera. . . ." (SF)

*Additional Credits:* Music: Richard Rodgers. Lyrics: Oscar Hammerstein II. Arranger/orchestrator/conductor: William Kidd. Screenplay: Peter Bakalian, Jacqueline Feather, David Seidler. Adaptation: Arthur Rankin. Supervising animators: Patrick Gleeson, Colm Duggan. Animation: Steven E. Gordon, Nassos Vakalis, Chrystal S. Klabunde, John Celestri, Chris DeRochie, Craig R. Maras, Steven Burke, Michael Coppieters, Elana Kravels, Mark Bykor, Jesse M. Cosio, James A. Davis, Tom Decker, Jeff Etter, Mark Fisher, Heidi Guedel, Leon Joosen, Juliana Korsborn, Larry Leker, Bookwan Lin, Kymaghee Lin, Les McCaulla, Kem McDonald, Stan P. Mullen, Cynthia Overman, Greg Ramsey, Todd Shaffer, Kyan Shin, Kanoon Song, Susan M. Zytka, John D. Suggs, Todd Waterman, Larry Whitaker Jr., Frank Gabriel, Kez Wilson, Deborah Abbott, Dan Abraham, Conrad Winterlich, Siddhartka B. Akearne, Alan T. Pickett, Gabriel Valles, Manuel Carrasco, Celine Kiernan, Noel Kieran, Jacques Muller, Sam Fleming, Warren Ling, Marcela F. DeMoura, Nile Santillan, John D. Williamson, Robert K. Skedlovitch, Bradley M. Forbush, G. Sem, Richard Bauchon.

**The King and the Mockingbird** See *The Adventures of Mr. Wonderbird.*

**The King and Mr. Bird** See *The Adventures of Mr. Wonderbird.*

**The King and the Bird** See *The Adventures of Mr. Wonderbird.*

**Lady and the Tramp** (6/22/55) Walt Disney Pictures. 76 mins. Directors: Hamilton Luske, Glyde Geronimi, Wilfred Jackson. Voices: Barbara Luddy (Lady), Larry Roberts (Tramp), Bill Thompson (Bull, Daschsie, Jock, Joe), Peggy Lee (Darling, Si, Am, Peg), Bill Baucom (Trusty), Lee Millar (Jim Dear, Dogcatcher), Verna Felton (Aunt Sarah), Dallas McKennon (Toughie, Professor, Pedro), Stan Freberg (Beaver, Pet Store Clerk), The Mello Men (Pound Dogs), George Givot (Tony), Alan Reed (Boris).

©Walt Disney Productions

**Consumer Tips:** ☆☆☆ MPAA Rating: Unrated. Disney's first animated feature that was not based on a published story or fairy tale; the book actually came afterwards.

**Story:** Jim Dear gives his wife Darling a cocker spaniel puppy named Lady. Lady is a bit sheltered and naive, protected by her trusted friends Jock the Scottie and Trusty the old bloodhound. She finds out that a Darling baby is on the way and is confused when the rascally Tramp, a disreputable mongrel, avers that the baby will replace Lady for the couple's affections. When Aunt Sarah and her two cruel Siamese cats come to babysit, Lady is blamed for the cats' mischief and flees. She is aided by Tramp, who wines and dines the pretty spaniel but also gets her confined to the dog pound. Lady returns home just as a rat attacks the baby. Tramp shows up and kills the rat, but Aunt Sarah believes he and Lady are the culprits. Tramp is hauled off by the dogcatcher but saved by Jock and Trusty. The dead rat is discovered; Lady and Tramp marry at the Darling house and have a litter of pups.

**Comments:** *Lady and the Tramp* may have begun as early as 1937; writers Joe Grant and Dick Huemer were toying with the idea of a canine romance and had a finished treatment by 1943. Around the same time, Walt Disney discovered a short story by Ward Greene about a carefree mongrel. Disney contacted Greene and had him expand the tale into a short book called *Happy Dan the Whistling Dog and Miss Patsy the Beautiful Spaniel.* Elements of the story were revised and wedded to Grant and Huemer's work, resulting in Disney's first original feature.

The movie was not a critical success, and to this day Disney fans argue passionately about its place in the studio's works. History has been kinder to the film, and it remains a charming piece of animated whimsy that fans of all ages enjoy. Every character is likable to some degree, with the exception of the rat. Even the sinister Siamese cats (Si and Am, of course) are highly entertaining in their villainy. They also sing a great duet in the bargain. Unlike later features where the protagonists fall in love at first sight before facing obstacles, the romance between Lady and Tramp takes time to develop, and the romantic tryst culminating in the famous spaghetti kiss is more realistic and touching as a result.

The animators and performers working on the film provide many of the high points. John Lounsberry animated Tony and Joe, owners of Tramp's favorite Italian restaurant, to perfection. Garlic, oregano, and *amore* fairly roll off the soundtrack as they sing the enchanting "Bella Notte" to the romantic couple. Eric Larson turned torch singer Peggy Lee into a raffish pooch. Her hip-swinging number "He's a Tramp" is one of the most memorable moments in the movie. Woolie Reitherman animated the vicious rat and much of the fight scene with Tramp. Reitherman studied live rats for weeks as he animated, trying to capture their most repulsive qualities. The battle amid thunder and flashes of lightning is as powerful as the similar fight between dinosaurs that Reitherman animated in *Fantasia* (1940).

Along with romance and danger there is also comedy; Stan Freberg is excellent as a bemused whistle-voiced beaver, and the euthanasia of Nutsy in the dog pound is actually played for laughs. Writer Ed Penner did the scene as a send-up of live-action prison movies, using every "last mile" cliche he could dig up. Some of the dialogue between Lady and Tramp recalls patter heard in the romantic screwball comedies of the 1930s. Whether *Lady and the Tramp* is one of Disney's best films can be argued indefinitely. What really matters is that *Lady and the Tramp* is entertaining, warm, funny, and engaging on its own terms. It also features some of Disney's most trusted animators near the top of their form while making it look easy.

For the record:

- Tramp was nearly named "Rags" or "Bozo." The cats were originally named "Nip" and "Tuck."
- Trusty was to be killed while saving Tramp, but Peggy Lee cried at the scene and begged Walt Disney not to traumatize children. Walt gave in.
- The picture took nearly 10 years to get to the screen.
- The rat was originally a comic character called Herman.
- Peg was originally named "Mame," but that was the nickname of President Eisenhower's wife; the dog was renamed to avoid the appearance of mocking her.
- *Lady and the Tramp* was the first animated feature to be made in CinemaScope, a forerunner of widescreen.
- Lady and Tramp's son, Scamp, went on to a long career in comic books before starring in the direct-to-video sequel nearly fifty years later. (MG)

**Additional Credits:** Story: Erdman Penner, Joe Rinaldi, Ralph Wright, Don DaGradi. Based on a story by Ward Greene. Music: Oliver Wallace. Songs: Peggy Lee, Sonny Burke. Directing animators: Milt Kahl, Frank Thomas, Ollie Johnston, John Lounsbery, Wolfgang Reitherman, Eric Larson, Hal King, Les Clark. Animation: George Nicholas, Hal Ambro, Ken O'Brien, Jerry Hatchcock, Eric Cleworth, Marvin Woodward, Ed Aardal, John Sibley, Harvey Toombs, Cliff Nordberg, Don Lusk, George Kreisl, Hugh Fraser, John Freeman, Jack Campbell, Bob Carlson. Effects animators: George Rowley, Daniel MacManus. Layouts: Ken Anderson, Tom Codrick, Al Zinnen, A. Kendall O'Connor, Hugh Hennesy, Lance Nolley, Jacques Rupp, McLaren Stewart, Don Griffith, Thor Putnam, Colin Campbell, Victor Haboush, Bill Boche. Backgrounds: Claude Coats, Dick Anthony, Ralph Hulett, Al Dempster, Thelma Witmer, Eyvind Earle, Jimi Trout, Ray Huffine, Brice Mack.

**The Land Before Time** (11/18/88) Universal. 66 mins. Director: Don Bluth. Producers: Don Bluth, Gary Goldman, John Pomeroy. Voices: Pat Hingle (Narrator, Rooter), Gabriel Damon (Littlefoot), Helen Shaver (Littlefoot's Mother), Candy Huston (Cera), Judith Barsi (Ducky), Will Ryan (Petrie), Burke Byrnes (Daddy Topps), Bill Erwin (Grandfather).

**Consumer Tips:** ☆☆☆½ MPAA Rating: G.

©Universal City Studios Inc.

**Story:** A baby apatasaurus named Littlefoot, separated from his family after his mother dies, must find his way to the Great Valley or become extinct. To survive, he has to join forces with other dinosaurs who normally don't get along.

**Comments:** When luminaries such as Steven Spielberg, George Lucas, and Don Bluth join forces to make a film about awesome dinosaurs, what can possibly go wrong?

In an interview with Ernest Tucker in the *Chicago Sun-Times* (November 12, 1989), Bluth said that even though he directed and produced the film, "I didn't have a free enough hand. I pushed a lot of themes—searching for the Great Valley, and the only time you're going to find it is when you get along with others. We could have simply said we're telling a story about a little dinosaur trying to find his mom and dad without actually focusing on very real issues."

Even Gary Goldman admitted, "It dipped down into what we call pabulum and it was directed, after the fact, to an age group of four- to six- or seven-year olds and it eliminated some of the things that we found exciting" (*The Animated Films of Don Bluth* by John Cawley, 1991, p. 115).

Bluth's artists animated a ferocious sharp-toothed Tyrannosaurus attacking Littlefoot and Cera and battling Littlefoot's mom, culminating in her death. Disregarding the hard labor in bringing these scenes to life, executive producer Steven Spielberg demanded the sequence be cut and the kids' screams toned down. According to Bluth in *Toon Talk* (January 2001), Spielberg said, "It's too scary. We'll have kids crying in the lobby, and a lot of angry parents. You don't want that." Over 10 minutes of material—including 19 scenes already in color—were chopped from the print. Five years later, Spielberg directed *Jurassic Park*, with hungry dinosaurs threatening children.

Littlefoot was originally called "Thunderfoot," until it was discovered a children's book had a triceratops with the same name. Cera, the triceratops with attitude, had undergone a gender change from a male called "Bambo." Petrie, the pterodactyl who was afraid to fly, had a larger role in the story as comic relief, but Ducky, a lively "Big Mouth" anatosaurus, stole the show, thanks to a delightful performance by Judith Barsi (which lead to her voicing the heroine of *All Dogs Go to Heaven*). Spike, the perpetually hungry stegosaurus, was Don Bluth's favorite character, "a pure soul, simple, accommodating, and eager to please," inspired by Cubby, his pet Chowhound.

Because the film was slightly over an hour, Universal added a short: the first segment of Brad Bird's *Family Dog*.

The smash success of *An American Tail* shook Disney out of its complacency. Disney released *Oliver and Co.* on the same day as *Land*, but *Land* had the top-grossing opening weekend for an animated feature at $7,526,000. Oliver grossed just over $4 million. For the next four weeks, the dinosaurs stomped their cat-and-dog competition. Determined not to be upstaged by Bluth again, Michael Eisner kept his film in theaters longer, to ensure *Oliver* would ultimately outgross *Land*. Ironically, *Land* wound up showing on the Disney Channel.

*The Land Before Time* ultimately grossed $72 million worldwide, and it spawned the most successful American direct-to-video series. To date 11 sequels have generated over $250 million in sales. In the tenth installment, subtitled *The Great Longneck Migration*, Littlefoot finds his missing father, Bron, who as a youth was also called "Littlefoot."

One of the directing animators, Ralph Zondag, would later codirect *We're Back! A Dinosaur's Story* for Spielberg. He also codirected Disney's *Dinosaur*, which was essentially a CG remake of *The Land Before Time*.

Bluth and Spielberg parted company after *Land*. Bluth found a new sponsor with Goldcrest International, lining up a three-picture deal starting with *All*

*Dogs Go to Heaven*. Spielberg continued with *Who Framed Roger Rabbit* and *An American Tail II: Fievel Goes West*, and he entered the television animation arena with *Tiny Toon Adventures*.

With allusions to Disney's "Rite of Spring" sequence from *Fantasia* and *Dumbo*, *The Land Before Time* is basically a prehistoric *Bambi*, complete with a survival-of-the-fittest theme, homage to the newborn by the neighborhood predators, and the mother meeting an untimely death. *Land* awes with some wonderful animation, gorgeous backgrounds, and music fit for an epic, but the effect is ruined by shoddy editing, a wimpy hero, annoying sidekicks, slow pacing, and a lackluster story.

It's inconsistent. Sometimes the dinosaurs behave like the fascinating creatures they really were (as when Mama Littlefoot slowly turns her long neck to speak to her son; an impressive moment). Other times, they behave like Saturday-morning caricatures.

Predictably, the movie has a character who sacrifices his life, but it turns out he isn't really dead. You've seen it before in *Lady and the Tramp* (Trusty), *Jungle Book* (Baloo), *Peter Pan* (Tinkerbell), and *The Black Cauldron* (Gurgi). At least in *Land*, the comical sidekick is so annoying he deserves to stay dead.

Despite the film's flaws, *The Land Before Time* has achieved enormous success as a franchise, and did exactly what Spielberg and Lucas wanted: entertain its preschool audience. (WRM)

*Additional Credits:* Executive producers: Steven Spielberg, George Lucas, Kathleen Kennedy, Peter Marshall. Screenplay: Stu Krieger. Story: Judy Freudberg, Tony Geiss. Music: James Horner. Vocalist: Diana Ross. Directing animators: John Pomeroy, Linda Miller, Ralph Zondag, Dan Kuenster, Lorna Pomeroy, Dick Zondag. Animation: Anne Marie Bardwell, Victoria Brewster, Colm Duggan, Ken Duncan, Jeff Etter, Mark Fisher, Michel Gagné, Raul Garcia, Patrick Gleeson, Ken Hammerstorm, T. Daniel Hofstedt, Jon Hooper, Skip Jones, Jean Morel, Paul Newberry, Ralf Palmer, Gary Perkovac, John Power. Additional animation: Charlie Bonifacio, Wendy Perdue, Jesse Cosio, Mark Pudleiner, John Hill, David Simmons, Silvia Hoefnagels, Konrad Winterlich, Fernando Moro, Kevin Wurzer. Special effects directing animator: Dorse A. Lanpher. Effects animators: Kathleen Quaife-Hodge, Steve Moore, Tom Hush, Don Paul, Diann Landau, Bob Simmons, David Tidgwell. Storyboard: Don Bluth, Larry Leker, Dan Kuenster. Layout supervisor: David Goetz. Layouts: Rick Bentham, Mark Swan, Mark Swanson, Richard Fawdry. Background stylist: Don Moore. Backgrounds: Barry Atkinson, Carl Jones, Sunny Apinchapong, Mannix Bennett, David McCamley. Key color stylists: Carmen Oliver, Susan Vanderhorst. Color stylists: Laurie Curran, Violet McKenna, Donal Freeney, Suzanne O'Reilly. Special effects painting: Shirley (Sam) Mapes.

**Laputa: Castle in the Sky** (3/24/89) Streamline Pictures. 124 mins. Director: Hayao Miyazaki. Producer: Isao Takahata. Voices: Mayumi Tanaka (Pazu), James Van Der Beek (Pazu, 2003 English version). Keiko Yokozawa (Sheeta), Anna Paquin (Sheeta, 2003 English version), Kotoe Hatsui (Dola), Cloris Leachman (Dola, 2003 English version), Mark Hamill (Col. Muska, 2003 English version).

©Tokuma Shoten

*Consumer Tips:* ☆☆☆☆ MPAA Rating: Not rated. SF/fantasy adventure. A Jules Verne–type adventure set in a mythical 19th century with huge airships and a city floating in the sky powered by a levitation stone, inspired by the "Laputa" section of Jonathan Swift's *Gulliver's Travels*.

*Story:* Sheeta, an orphaned farm girl, is seized by government agents. Their airship is attacked by a family of sky pirates. Sheeta escapes in the confusion, but falls off the ship. She is saved when her heirloom pendant carries her gently to earth, where she is found by Pazu, a miner boy. They realize that everyone is after Sheeta's pendant, a mysterious stone with levitation powers, which is a clue to the legendary lost flying city of Laputa.

**Comments:** *Laputa* was the third feature to bring public attention to writer/character designer/director Hayao Miyazaki, and the first produced by his Studio Ghibli. It is an almost-perfect boy's adventure film in the style of Verne's *The Clipper of the Clouds*, with 19th century–style aerial battleships and pirates, a heroic barely adolescent hero and heroine, and an exotic ancient flying city full of wealth (sought by the pirates) powered by a lost technology (sought by the military/ political villains). Laputa turns out to be an awesome lost civilization that almost steals the show from the human characters.

Miyazaki's 1984 independently produced *Nausicaä* did well enough that financier Tokuma Publishing established Miyazaki and his production crew as a per-manent studio, Studio Ghibli. *Tenko no Shiro: Laputa*, released August 2, 1986, was the first feature under the Ghibli name. It was first shown in America at the Sec-ond Los Angeles International Animation Celebration in July 1987. Tokuma commissioned an English dub to make Laputa available as an in-flight movie for Japan Air Lines' trans-Pacific flights. This dub was also licensed to Streamline Pictures for theatrical release for a year starting in March 1989. In 1996 Tokuma licensed all of Miyazaki's Studio Ghibli features to the Walt Disney Company, which released *Laputa* in a new dub and titled just *Castle in the Sky*. The Disney ver-sion was premiered at the New York International Chil-dren's Film Festival in February 2000, and released directly to video on April 15, 2003. (FP)

**Additional Credits:** Screenplay: Hayao Miyazaki. Original music: Joe Hisaishi. Executive producer: Yasuyoshi Tokuma. Asso-ciate executive producers: Tatsumi Yamashita, Hideo Ogata. Film editing: Yoshihiro Kasahara, Hayao Miyazaki, Takeshi Seyama. Art direction: Toshio Nozaki, Nizou Yamamoto. Animators: Toyoaki Emura, Masaaki Endo, Tadashi Fukuda, Makiko Futaki, Megumi Kagawa, Yoshinori Kanada, Toshio Kawaguchi, Kazuhiro Kinoshita, Kazuyuki Kobayashi, Katsuya Kondô, Kitaro Kosaka, Mahiro Maeda, Noriko Moritomo, Osamu Nabeshima, Yasuhiro Nakura, Shinji Otsuka, Michiyo Sakuraim, Masako Shinohara, Tsukasa Tannai, Kazuhide Tomonaga, Atsuko Ôtani.

**The Last Unicorn** (11/19/82) Jensen-Farley (Japan). 85 mins. Directors/producers: Arthur Rankin Jr., Jules Bass. Voices: Alan Arkin (Schmendrick the Magician), Jeff Bridges (Prince Lir), Mia Farrow (the Last Uni-corn, Lady Almathea), Tammy Grimes (Molly Grue), Robert Klein (the Butterfly), Angela Lansbury (Mommy Fortuna), Christopher Lee (King Haggard), Keenan Wynn (Captain Cully), Paul Frees (the Talking Cat, Mabruk, Living Tree), Rene Auberjonois (the Speaking Skull).

©Rankin-Bass Productions

**Consumer Tips:** ☆☆½ MPAA Rating: G. Based on the book by Peter S. Beagle.

**Story:** The last unicorn is captured and put in a car-nival. Schmendrick the magician helps her escape and joins her in the quest for others of her species.

**Comments:** Arthur Rankin was looking for material in the vein of *Lord of the Rings,* and stumbled accross *The Last Unicorn*, a novel with a cult following. It was written by Peter S. Beagle, an author who had recently written the screenplay for Ralph Bakshi's *The Lord of the Rings.*

With funding from Britian's ITC Films, Rankin-Bass secured both the book and the author, and began plans to create a theatrical feature film of this fantasy adventure. Jules Bass approached songwriter Jimmy

Webb ("By the Time I Get to Pheonix," "Up, Up, and Away") about doing the score. Luckily, Webb had been a fan of the book and he quickly accepted.

Animation production was set up with Rankin-Bass' studio in Japan. No effort was spared to engage a big-name voice cast. In addition to the players listed, various diverse talents played smaller roles, such as eccentic performance artist Brother Theodore and veteran Hanna-Barbera voice man Don Messick.

The film's Japanese production design and animation give the film an anime feel. Regrettably, the creators sacrificed full character animation for spectacular visuals, special effects, and action sequences. On the whole, however, the film works. It tells its story well, with ample adventure, humor, and romance. For its modest budget, *The Last Unicorn* did pretty well at the box office (grossing $6.5 million at the time) and received good reviews. It is one of Rankin-Bass' best efforts and is well worth a look. (SF)

*Additional Credits:* Writer: Peter S. Beagle, based on his novel. Music/lyrics: Jimmy Webb. Associate producers: Martin Starger, Michael Chase Walker. Animation coordinator: Toru Hara. Continuity animation: Gut Kubo. Backgrounds: Minouru Nishaa, Kazusuke Yoshihara, Mitsuo Iwasaki. Character designer: Lester Abrams. Additional storyboard sequences: Don Duga. Key animators: Yoshiko Sasaki, Masahiro Yoshida, Kayoko Sakano, Fukuo Suzuki, Ioru Hala, Guy Kubo.

## Legend of the Overfiend (3/11/93) Anime 21.

108 mins. Director: Hideki Takayama. Producer: Yoshinobu Nishizaki, Yasuhito Yamaki. Voices: Bick Balse (Ozaki), Danny Bush (Tatsuo Nagumo), Christopher Courage (Amano Jyaku), Rebel Joy (Akemi), Lucy Morales (Megumi Amano), Rose Palmer (Kuroko) Bill Timoney (Niki).

*Consumer Tips:* ☆☆ MPAA Rating: NC-17. Adult fantasy adventure.

*Story:* There are three parallel worlds: our human world, the world of man-beasts (peaceful and lusty), and the world of demons (constant, brutal rape-orgies). A legend states that after 3,000 years, a godlike "Overfiend" will arise to unite all three into a single world of peace and love. Amanojaku has been on Earth for 300 years awaiting this Overfiend, but when he is

born, he brings slaughter and devastation to all three dimensions.

*Comments:* This was the title that established the anime catchphrase "tentacle rape."

The rise of Japan's direct-to-video market in 1984 led to many short animated pornographic videos by mostly pseudonymous animators. *Legend of the Overfiend* (*Chojin Densetsu Urotsukidoji*) was the first to be presented as a serious adult literary SF/fantasy by acknowledged creators: an adaptation of an adult manga series of novels by Toshio Maeda, produced by West Cape Corporation (Space Battleship Yamato).

A voiceover prologue explains that there are three parallel-dimension worlds: those of humans (ningenkai), of half-demons or man-beasts (jujunkai), and of true demons (makai). Our world is the only one ignorant of the others. The half-demons have supernatural powers like the true demons, but also a peaceful civilization like humans. They are strongly erotic and freely copulate unashamedly like animals. The demons are brutal and spend all their time in sadistic rape-dominance grapples. There is a legend that after 3,000 years, a Chojin or "god above all gods" will be born into the body of a human who will unite all three worlds into a single perfect and peaceful society. The half-demons look forward to this while the demons want to prevent it.

*Legend of the Overfiend* was released in Japan in three half-hour direct-to-video volumes: "Birth of the Overfiend" on January 27, 1987; "Curse of the Overfiend," March 21, 1988; and "Final Inferno," April 10, 1989, totalling 134 minutes. The feature was also a video release in Japan. The English-language theatrical release was first shown at an anime film festival in London in October 1992, and was popular during the mid-1990s as an art-theater and campus midnight-movie feature. *Urotsukidoji II: Legend of the Demon Womb* (two video volumes) continued the adaptation of Maeda's manga novels showing the battles between the uneasy alliance (with many betrayals) of humans, half-demons, and demons against the Chojin in its lair in Osaka Castle. I and II sold well enough in America and Britain to finance the completion of animating the series with *Urotsukidoji III: Return of the Overfiend* (four volumes), and *IV: Inferno Road* (three volumes).

*Legend of the Overfiend* has sparked critical debate over whether its plot has genuine adult intellectual merit or is a mere excuse for wallowing in brutal sadomasochistic rape and mass violence. The few intelligent sexual questions raised are not answered by the lengthy torture/copulation orgies. The animation is of standard quality for a 1980s direct-to-video production, which is poor by theatrical standards. (FP)

**Additional Credits:** Screenplay: Shô Aikawa, Michael Lawrence, Toshio Maeda. Music: Masamichi Amano. Art direction: Shigemi Ikeda. Sound director: Yasunori Honda. Post-production supervisor (U.S. version): Ron Kalish. Character designers: Eitaro Tono, Akihiko Yamashita, Dan Kongoji. Animation directors: Shiro Kasami, Dan Kongoji, Mari Mizuta.

**Lensman** (8/31/90) Streamline (Japan). 107 mins. Director: Yoshiaki Kawajiri, Kazuyuki Hirokawa. Voices: Kerrigan Mahan (Kimball Kinnison), Steve Kramer (Worsel), Alexandra Kenworthy (Lens), Michael McConnohie (Van Buskirk), Edie Mirman (Clarisse), Robert Axelrod (Sol), Michael Forest (Adm. Haines), Milton James (Zuiik), Dave Mallow (Thorndyke), Mike Reynolds (Gary Kinnison), Gregory Snegoff (Adm. Haynes), Doug Stone (Lekesly), Tom Wyner (Lord Helmuth).

©E.E. "Doc" Smith / MK Company

**Consumer Tips:** ☆☆☆ MPAA Rating: PG-13. SF adventure. Based on the *Lensman* SF novels by Edward E. Smith, Ph.D., written during the 1930s and 1940s.

**Story:** In the 25th century humanity has spread throughout the galaxy. Kim Kinnison, a teenager on a colony planet, is entrusted by a dying Galactic Patrol agent to deliver the plans of an alien invasion to Patrol HQ. Kim and his friend Buskirk flee toward earth barely ahead of the evil Boskone empire's warfleet, having adventures at several planets on the way.

**Comments:** *Star Wars* was extremely popular during the late 1970s and early '80s, and the Japanese animation industry made two imitations based upon George Lucas' acknowledged boyhood inspirations for *Star Wars*. One was Edmond Hamilton's 1940s Captain Future pulp novels, which Toei Animation Co. adapted into a 1978–79 television series. The other was E. E. "Doc" Smith's six Lensman novels written during the 1930s and '40s. MK Productions used these as the basis for the 1984 Lensman feature, followed immediately by the 25-episode *Lensman: Galactic Patrol* television anime series.

Smith's story was rewritten into a close imitation of *Star Wars*. Kimball Kinnison, a veteran Galactic Patrol "Lensman" agent (roughly a futuristic James Bond secret agent), becomes an enthusiastic but naive teenager. Buskirk, his father's burly friend who owns a spaceship, becomes a friendly Chewbacca-like large furry humanoid. The extra-galactic evil Boskone aliens remain totally inhuman but act like Darth Vader-stand-ins; Boskone's leader Helmuth breathes heavily and kills each of his generals who fail to catch Kim and Buskirk. The Galactic Patrol's unique Lens badge becomes a mystic device that gives Kim great powers similar to "the Force." Kinnison's tough female partner in Smith's stories, Clarissa MacDougall, becomes a simpering Princess Leia imitation who merely postures bravely before needing to be rescued by Kim. Worsel, another Galactic Patrolman from a planet of huge reptilian aliens allied to earth, is redesigned to be much more humanoid so he can accompany Kim as a close friend. Sol, an imitation-R2D2 cute little robot, was a completely new character.

*Lensman* was reviled by science-fiction purists in both Japan and America for oversimplifying Smith's novels and turning them into an imitation of *Star Wars*. Further controversy was generated by Smith's daughter, who conducted a one-woman war charging that the movie was made without her permission and an unauthorized violation of her father's copyrights. Apparently Smith had sold his American publisher all rights, which enabled the American publisher to license the series to a Japanese publisher, which relicensed the movie and television rights to MK Productions without needing any further permission from Smith's estate. *The Galactic Patrol* television series received such poor ratings that it was concluded after 25 episodes rather than the originally announced 39.

However, most audiences who saw *Lensman* without comparing it to Smith's novels enjoyed it as a fast-paced galactic adventure in the *Star Wars* vein without being too close to a *Star Wars* imitation. The use of the mystic Lens badges brought several favorable comparisons to the Green Lantern comic-book series, and some comic-book fans recommended it as a Green Lantern movie. It was the first production to gain attention for the Madhouse animation studio and director Yoshiaki Kawajiri, and the second Japanese animated feature (after 1983's *Golgo 13*) to blend computer graphics with cel animation. It received an American publicity premiere (subtitled) at the 1984 World Science Fiction Convention in Los Angeles but was not generally released until 1990. (FP)

**Additional Credits:** Screenplay: Soji Yoshikawa. Music: Akira Inoue. English version producer: Carl Macek. Production manager: Jerry Beck. Model maker: Carter Burwell. Digital artist: Theresa Ellis. Animators: Hiroyuki Kitakubo, Kôji Morimoto.

**Light Years** (1/28/88) Miramax (French). 83 mins. Directors: Rene Laloux, Harvey Weinstein. Producers: Bob Weinstein, Henry Rollin, Jean-Claude Delnyre. Voices: Glenn Close (Queen Ambisextra), Jennifer Grey (Altelle), Christopher Plummer (Metamorphosis), John Shea (Sylvain), Penn Jillette (Chief of the Deformed), David Johansen (Shaol), Terrence Mann (The Collective Voice), Charles Busch (Gemmen), Bridget Fonda (Historian, Head #2), Sheila McCarthy (Council Spokeswoman, Head #4), Paul Shaffer (Opeflow), Teller (Octum), Earl Hyman (Maxum, Chief of the Deformed), Earl Hammond (Blaminhoe), Alexander Marshall (Apod, Metal Men), Dennis Predovic (Head #3, Metal Men), Chip Bolcik (Head #1, Metal Men), Kevin O'Rourke, Ray Owens (The Metal Men), Jill Haworth (Announcer).

**Consumer Tips:** ☆ MPAA Rating: PG.

**Story:** In the future, a war breaks out between the genetically perfect, who dwell on the surface, and the deformed mutations ruled by a super-brain, who live underground.

**Comments:** Rene Laloux (*Fantastic Planet*) produced *Gandahar* in France, where it met with critical and public acceptance. It cost $5.5 million to produce. Harvey Weinstein picked the film up for U.S. distribution, through his company Miramax, at the 1987 Cannes Film Festival.

Weinstein went about turning *Gandahar* into a saleable American film—at least for discerning adults who might frequent art houses and college campus screenings. The first thing he did was to hire noted science fiction author Isaac Asimov to adapt the screenplay into in English and change the title of the film to *Light Years*.

Next he hired an all-star cast to read the script into a microphone. Unfortunately, the resultant dub is a dud. The animation is amateurish, the storyline weak, and the sci-fi mumbo jumbo attributed to Asimov is ludicrous.

Weinstein thought he had a cutting edge sci-fi comic book, but he ended up with a turkey—a space turkey. It ultimately grossed $370,698 in the United States. Hardly worth the effort. (JB)

**Additional Credits:** Adaptation: Isaac Asimov. Original French screenplay: Raphael Cluzel. Adaptation: Rene Laloux (from the novel *Metal Men Against Gandahar* by Jean-Pierre Andrevan). Music: Gabriel Yared, Bob Jewett, Jack Maeby. Animation: Philippe Caza.

**Lilo and Stitch** (6/16/02) Walt Disney Pictures. 84 mins. Directors/writers: Dean DeBlois, Chris Sanders. Producer: Clark Spencer. Voices: Daveigh Chase (Lilo), Chris Sanders (Stitch), Tia Carrere (Nani), David Ogden Stiers (Dr. Jumba Jookiba), Kevin McDonald (Agent Pleakley), Ving Rhames (Cobra Bubbles), Zoe Caldwell (Grand Councilwoman of the United Galactic Federation), Jason Scott Lee (David Kawena), Kevin Michael Richardson (Captain Gantu), Susan Hegarty (Animal Rescue Lady), Amy Hill (Mrs. Hasagawa).

**Consumer Tips:** ☆☆☆☆ MPAA Rating: PG. Wonderful original story by Chris Sanders about a lonely girl, her alien pet, and . . . Elvis?

©Walt Disney Enterprises, Inc.

**Story:** A tragic accident takes the parents of young woman Nani and her Elvis-worshipping kid sister Lilo. Money is scarce and social worker Cobra Bubbles is threatening to take custody of Lilo when things get even more complicated; an escaped alien creature, Experiment 626, crash-lands near their Hawaiian home. Lilo adopts the destructive puppy-sized beastie and names it Stitch, but she certainly doesn't tame it. Troubles increase when the Galactic Federation sends the creator of Experiment 626, Dr. Jookiba, to earth to retrieve the monster. Special Agent Pleakley is sent along to ensure Jookiba's success. Out to destroy them all is Captain Gantu, an overzealous enforcer of the Federation. Science fiction, nonstop action, and an unexpected development make for a wild finish as Lilo, Nani, and Stitch become *ohana*—family.

**Comments:** If one were to conceive a film set in Hawaii as a science-fiction/surfing/family/fairy tale movie with an Elvis Presley soundtrack, one might think it would be some feat to integrate all those ideas into an 84-minute script. Perhaps that's why the hero's name is Stitch. *Lilo and Stitch* is a wonderful film in which all these elements blend to tell the tale of a family repaired and faith rewarded. Even aliens in permanent exile can find the joys of belonging among the warm sands and blue seas of Hawaii.

Chris Sanders and Dean DeBlois set this film up perfectly from the extended opening scene depicting Stitch's ferocity and cunning to the sequence where we meet Lilo and her harried older sister-cum-guardian. The directors make the effort to draw clear parallels between the nasty little alien and the maladjusted young girl. When the two finally meet we have insight into both of them and can believe the changes they undergo through their relationship. The audience feels for Lilo when she is on the verge of being taken into the custody of social worker Cobra Bubbles, and is just as tearful when Stitch is shown in a long down shot crying in the woods, waiting for a family that will never come.

There is, perhaps, a bit too much foreshadowing and symbolism in the film, giving it pretensions that it does not really need: Lilo names her alien "dog" Stitch, and that is just what he does in bringing the hapless family together. Stitch has markings that clearly resemble angels on the rear of his head and back. The social worker Cobra Bubbles (Ving Rhames' own vocal and visual parody of the crime boss he portrayed in *Pulp Fiction*) has a name suggesting both danger and playfulness, roles that he fulfills in that order during the picture. Still, these are minor quibbles.

The art direction under Jeff Dutton is superb, with Disney's first full use of watercolor backgrounds since *Dumbo* in 1941. Rather than use fashion-doll figures for Lilo and Nani, Andreas Deja and Stephanie Sainte-Foi approximate Hawaiian physiognomy and give the girls more realistic builds. This results in authentic, appealing character designs as lovely as any created by Disney. Special mention should be made of the digital animation; supervisor Ron Bekuirs produces some fantastic starship designs, and the climactic battle between Captain Gantu's cruiser and Jookiba's ship is especially well done.

What truly makes *Lilo and Stitch* a great film is the gradual coming together of a special family, one that appeared to be damaged beyond all repair. Stitch makes things much worse before they get better, but in the end he proves to be a magical creature. His destructive programming is gradually subsumed by love and loyalty, and in the end he changes every major character in the film for the better. There is not one false emotional note or cliched manipulation along the way, and few films, let alone animated ones, can make such a claim. Audiences agreed and returned to Disney in droves; on an $80 million budget *Lilo and Stitch* brought in $146 million at the box office.

For the record:

- Chris Sanders created Stitch in 1986, 16 years before the film was made.
- The movie was originally to be set in Kansas.
- There are cameos by Mulan, Dumbo, and the dog pound gang from *Lady and the Tramp.* Captain Gantu's crew on his first ship contains alien versions of Winnie the Pooh and friends.
- There are seven Elvis songs in the film (two of them cover versions).
- There wasn't much promotion for *Lilo and Stitch,* but one gimmick was a beauty: Theatrical trailers for the film had Stitch invading mock trailers for *The Little Mermaid, Beauty and the Beast, Aladdin,* and *The Lion King.* The little alien wreaks hilarious havoc in each one. (MG)

©Walt Disney Productions

***Additional Credits:*** Executive producer: Don Hahn. Story: Ed Gombert, Chris Williams. Additional story: John Sanford, Roger Allers. Music: Alan Silvestri. Supervising animators: Alex Kuperschmidt, Andreas Deja, Stephane Sainte Foi, Byron Howard, Bolhem Bouchiba, Ruben A. Aquino. Lead animators: James Young Jackson, Theodore Anthony Lee Ty, Dominic M. Carola, Mark Henn. Animators: Jonathan Annand, Michael Benet, Travis Blaise, Robert O. Corley, Sasha Dorogov, Ian White, Gregg A. Azzopardi, Darko Cesar, Trey Finney, Branko Mihanovic, Philip Morris, Carol Seidl, John Webber, Jason Boose, Bob Bryan, John Hurst, Anthony Wayne Michaels, J. C. Tran-Quang-Thieu, Dominic M. Carola, David Berthier, Charles Bonifacio, Steve Mason, Tony Stanley, Rune Brandt Bennicke, Barry Temple, D. M. Wawrzaszek, David W. Zach. Computer animation supervisor: Eric Gauglione. Digital production animation supervisor: Rob Bekuhrs. Digital production animators: Sandra Maria Groeneveld, Darlene Hadrika, Jason William Wolbert, James Michael Crossley. Art director: Ric Sluiter. Production designer: Paul Felix. Visual development: Jim Martin, Marcello Vignali, Sue Nichols. Character designs: Chris Sanders, Byron Howard.

**The Lion King** (6/15/94) Walt Disney Pictures. 88 mins. Directors: Roger Allers, Rob Minkoff. Producer: Don Hahn. Voices: Matthew Broderick (Simba), Jonathan Taylor Thomas (Young Simba), James Earl Jones (Mufasa), Jeremy Irons (Scar), Moira Kelly (Nala), Niketa Calame (Young Nala), Rowan Atkinson (Zasu), Robert Guillaume (Rafiki), Whoopi Goldberg (Shenzi), Cheech Marin (Banzai), Jim Cummings (Ed), Nathan Lane (Timon), Ernie Sabella (Pumbaa), Madge Sinclair (Sarabi).

***Consumer Tips:*** ☆☆☆☆ MPAA Rating: G. The apotheosis of the modern Disney formula and one of the top-grossing animated films of all time.

***Story:*** Lion King Mufasa takes delight in his young son, Simba. Mufasa's dastardly brother Scar sees the cub as an obstacle to the throne. Scar joins forces with hyenas, murders Mufasa, and makes it appear that Simba is at fault. The guilt-ridden cub flees into exile and meets up with carefree meerkat Timon and flatulent warthog Pumbaa. After several years Simba's old girlfriend Nala finds him and implores Simba to return to the pride, which is perishing under Scar's misrule. Baboon shaman Rafiki, who reveals the truth to Simba, aids Nala. Simba returns to face his uncle in a showdown and earns the mantle of Lion King.

***Comments:*** *The Lion King* is a mythic tale that encapsulates the hero's journey: a hero is called to find himself and save his people by dint of a harrowing series of trials that test his mettle to the utmost. The journey is fraught with danger but forces both natural and supernatural aid for the hero. The hero's triumph restores order to man and nature, and in the process timeless legends are born. The Disney crew took this concept, allegedly forwarded by Jeffrey Katzenberg, and in 1989 developed a script for a film called "King of the Jungle." The art crew visited West Africa in 1991 for inspiration, and directors George Scribner and Roger Allers teamed with writer Linda Woolverton to develop the story.

Rob Minkoff replaced Scribner when it was felt that the story lacked lightness and humor. After several false starts a working script was developed, but two other figures also shaped the film considerably. Broadway lyricist Sir Tim Rice suggested that pop star Elton John be recruited, and together they wrote five songs that added to, rather than simply accented, the script. Composer Hans Zimmer won an Oscar for his African-flavored score, a masterwork that was composed in a mere 65 days. *The Lion King* also benefits from excellent artistic direction. Andy Gaskill, Chris Sanders, and Randy Fullmer conjure up African savannah, jungle, and wasteland with equal aplomb.

Disney summoned up the most impressive list of actors ever to grace an animated feature. James Earl Jones is a powerful yet warm Mufasa, scion of the jungle. Broadway stars Nathan Lane and Ernie Sabella camp it up wonderfully as Timon and Pumbaa, Simba's pals in exile. Robert Guillaume, Matthew Broderick, and Rowan Atkinson all contribute solid work, and the hyena trio of Whoopi Goldberg, Cheech Marin, and Jim Cummings are over the top in their depiction of dastardly scavengers. Jeremy Irons's oily villain Scar is by turns sardonic and savage, and nearly steals the picture thanks to Andreas Deja's flawless animation. Was Scar villainous? His number "Be Prepared" was designed after the Nazi propaganda documentaries of Leni Riefenstahl, with Scar cast as Adolf Hitler. The fact that Scar commits an actual, on-screen murder makes him especially despicable and dangerous. Scar kills Mufasa by dropping him into a wildebeest stampede, and it was hotly debated whether or not to show the dead lion in the aftermath. Allers and Minkoff went with it, adding an emotional resonance to a story that is, after all, about the circle of life and death in the jungle.

*The Lion King* is a film about growing up, accepting responsibility, and maturing. In one early scene young Simba steps into a footprint left by Mufasa and is daunted by its size. He knows all too well that someday he will have to fill his father's place and his duties. The film imparts these themes to young viewers through a solid story, lively music, and memorable characters. Adults who understand these concepts will still be wowed by the lush visuals, showstopper tunes, and entertaining acting. It is hardly amazing that *The Lion King* made nearly $300 million dollars and spawned two direct-to-video sequels, a Broadway production, and a television spinoff series.

After the success of the film, fans of Japanese manga artist Ozama Tekuza assailed Disney. Tekuza created a character named "Kimba" in 1950 for his comic book *The Jungle Emporer*. The young lion starred in an animated series called *Jungle Tatei*, and a later version of the series appeared in America under the title *Kimba the White Lion*. A number of characters, plot devices, and situations in *Kimba* bore a resemblance to those found in *The Lion King*. Rabid anime fans known as *otaku* claimed plagiarism; Allers and Minkoff denied ever seeing the television series, which the *otaku* found laughable. Tekuza's estate asked Disney to at least acknowledge Tekuza's influence but neither they nor the *otaku* got their wish. To this day conventions sell T-shirts featuring Simba looking into a mirror and seeing Kimba on the other side. (MG)

**Additional Credits:** Executive producers: Thomas Schumacher, Sarah McArthur. Screenplay: Irene Mecchi, Jonathan Roberts, Linda Woolverton. Story: Burny Mattinson, Barry Johnson, Lorna Cook, Thom Enriquez, Andy Gaskill, Gary Trousdale, Jim Capobianco, Kevin Harkey, Jorgen Klubien, Chris Sanders, Tom Sito, Larry Leker, Joe Ranft, Rick Maki, Ed Gombert, Francis Glebas, Mark Kausler. Music: Hans Zimmer. Songs: Elton John, Tim Rice. Supervising animators: Mark Henn, Ruben Aquino, Tony Fucile, Andreas Deja, Anthony DeRosa, Aaron Blaise, Tony Bancroft, Michael Surrey, James Baxter, Ellen Woodbury, Russ Edmonds, David Burgess, Alex Kupershmidt. Animators: Tom Bancroft, Broose Johnson, T. Daniel Hofstedt, Danny Wawrzaszek, Randy Haycock, Joe Ekers, Michael Cedeno, Dale Baer, Lorna Cook, Phil Young, Chris Wahl, Brad Kuha, Doug Frankel, Jean Morel, Mark Koetsier, Alex Williams, Bob Bryan, Gilda Palinginis, Ron Husband, Tim Allen, Dave Pruiksma, Brian Ferguson, James Lopez, Mike Show, Randy Cartwright, Barry Temple, Michael Swofford, Rejean Bourdages, Gregory S. Manwaring, Ken Boyer, Lou Dellarosa, Larry White, Gregory Griffith, Linda Bel, Chris Bailey, Ken Duncan, Raul Garcia, Ken Stephan. Visual effects supervisor: Scott Santoro. CGI supervisor: Scott F. Johnston. Art director: Andy Gaskill. Story supervisor: Brenda Chapman. Layout supervisor: Dan St. Pierre. Layout: Mitchell Berrnal, Jennifer Chao-Lin Yuan, Fred Craig, Guy Deel, Jeff Dickson, Ed Ghertner, Tom Humber, Lorenzo Martinez, Tom Shannon, Allen Tam, Tanya Wilson. Background supervisor: Doug Ball. Backgrounds: Gregory Alexander Drolette, Don Moore, Kathy

Alteri, Serge Michaels, Debbie DuBois, Sunny Apinchapong, Michael Humphries, Natalie Franscioni-Karp, Philip Phillipson, Barry Atkinson, Dan Cooper, Kevin Turcotte, Thomas Woodington, David McCamley, Dominick R. Domingo, Charles Vollmer, Barry R. Kooser, Patricia Palmer-Phillipson, Brooks Campbell, Richard Slutter.

**Little Dick, the Mighty Midget** See *King Dick*.

**The Little Mermaid** (11/17/89) Walt Disney Pictures. 82 mins. Directors: John Musker, Ron Clements. Producers: Howard Ashman, John Musker. Voices: Jodi Benson (Ariel), Christopher Daniel Barnes (Eric), Samuel E. Wright (Sebastian), Ben Wright (Grimsby), Rene Auberjonois (Louie), Pat Carroll (Ursula), Kenneth Mars (Triton), Buddy Hackett (Scuttle), Jason Martin (Flounder), Paddi Edwards (Flotsam and Jetsam), Edie McClurg (Carlotta), Will Ryan (Seahorse).

©Walt Disney Productions

***Consumer Tips:*** ✮✮✮✮ MPAA Rating: G. Based on the 1837 fairy tale by Hans Christian Andersen. Disney returned to feature animation supremacy with this outstanding film.

***Story:*** Young Ariel is the daughter of King Triton and should be happy amongst her fellow merpeople, but she's intensely curious about the surface world and its inhabitants. Neither her father's warnings nor the watchful eye of Triton's court composer Sebastian can deter her from going above the waves and falling in love with handsome seafaring prince, Eric. Ariel's chance to win his heart comes in the form of a deal with the devil—in this case the evil sea witch Ursula, who plans to use Ariel to steal Triton's throne. Only love can save the day, but Ursula has foreseen that threat to her plans. A desperate Ariel and her prince must defeat Ursula at the height of her evil powers or all is lost.

***Comments:*** *The Little Mermaid* was not fully responsible for the revival of the Disney film in the 1990s; the success of *Who Framed Roger Rabbit* (1988) was at least as instrumental in sparking America's new love affair with animated features. What *The Little Mermaid* did achieve was an ingenious integration of Broadway theater with Disney tradition. This film is a hybrid of exceptional character animation, classic fairy tale, and the modern American stage musical. Irresistible to kids and sophisticated enough for any adult, *The Little Mermaid* made $84 million, restored Disney animation to supremacy, and defined the formula that would dominate the studio's films for the next decade.

There was no doubt that the Disney creative team was ready for such a breakthrough. Directing animators Glen Keane, Ruben Aquino, Andreas Deja, Mark Henn, Duncan Marjoribanks, and Matthew O'Callaghan, along with rising stars like Rob Minkoff and David Pruiksma, had trained together over several films and were worthy successors to the "Nine Old Men." Jeffrey Katzenberg imported the Broadway songwriting team of Howard Ashman and Alan Menken, late of *The Little Shop of Horrors*, to create musical synergy with the animation department. The beneficiary of all that talent was an idea that Ron Musker forwarded after he wrapped up his work on *The Great Mouse Detective* in 1985: a musical version of Hans Christian Andersen's "The Little Mermaid."

This idea was not new; Disney had proposed it during the 1940s but the concept never came to fruition. Ron Clements and John Musker revived the story as a musical. Ashman and Menken became major collaborators; one of Ashman's best ideas was to turn a stuffy English crab named Clarence into a Jamaican songster, the better to add contemporary reggae and calypso music to the script. Their influence was felt in other ways as well; the film actually opens with a stage production, and there is no doubt that the cool number "Under the Sea" was meant to be a showstopper. The visuals team under the direction of Mark Dindal pulled out all the stops; over 80 percent of *The Little Mermaid* contains one special effect or another, and at times several simultaneously.

The star of the feature is beautiful Ariel, a 16-year-old mermaid. Spirited, curious, and hopelessly romantic, Ariel is one of animation's most believable heroines. Ashman and Menken followed Broadway conventions in giving her a classic "I Want" number that tells us of her hopes. In Ariel's case, it is to go among the surface dwellers, a dream that her father the king strictly forbids. The song "Part of Your World" (sung by Jodi Benson) captures Ariel's yearning so intensely that when she extends her hand toward the surface we long to reach out with her. It is a tribute to Mark Henn and Glen Keane, who animated most of Ariel's scenes, that she retains every aspect of her personality even when mute—a condition she endures for more than a third of the film.

The other star is the villainess, the hefty sea witch Ursula. After several unsatisfying designs for the proposed character, Rob Minkoff sketched a caricature of the 300-pound transvestite Divine. The actor had starred in several of John Waters's controversial films, and Minkoff probably had *Pink Flamingoes* in mind as he sketched. Animator Reuben Aquino thought it hilarious and grafted the image onto an obese octopus. The result was the greatest villainess since Cruella DeVil. Stage veteran Pat Carroll completed the character with a campy, theatrical vocal performance that enchants every bit as much as it repulses.

There are some weaknesses in the film. Although Buddy Hackett's performance as Scuttle the seagull is excellent, the character seems to be a relic of an earlier Disney style. The same can be said for Carlotta, Prince Eric's housemaid. Sharp audiences may note when different animators are handling Ariel from one scene to the next, and despite brilliant animation overall, there are some isolated weak moments, such as a long shot of Ariel perched on a rock as she sings a reprise to "Part of Your World." These are easily disregarded as one becomes emotionally involved with the charming story. In some ways Disney would never surpass this feature, which rightfully takes its place among the studio's best.

For the record:

- One aspect of the 1940s project was carried over to the new film when the Disney archives found some of Kay Nielsen's stunning concept art and integrated it into the backgrounds.
- Mickey, Donald, and Goofy can be quickly glimpsed taking their seats during Triton's entrance to his daughter's recital.
- The Disney art department developed a new shade of color named "Ariel" for the film. It can be seen in Ariel's tail fins. (MG)

**Additional Credits:** Screenplay: Ron Clements, John Musker. Story: Roger Allers. Adapted from the fairytale by Hans Christian Andersen. Music: Alan Menken. Songs: Howard Ashman, Alan Menken, Robby Merkin. Directing animators: Mark Henn, Glen Keane, Duncan Marjoribanks, Ruben Aquino, Andreas Deja, Matthew O'Callaghan. Animation: Michael Cedeno, Rick Farmiloe, Shawn E. Keller, David Pruiksma, Dan Jeup, Phil Young, Anthony DeRosa, David Cutler, Nik Ranieri, Dave Spafford, Jay Jackson, Barry Temple, James Baxter, Kathy Zielinski, Jorgen Klubien, Chris Bailey, Tony Fucile, Chris Wahl, Chuck Harvey, Tom Sito, Will Finn, Doug Krohn, Leon Joosen, Russ Edmonds, David P. Stephen, Ellen Woodbury, Ron Husband, David A. Pacheco, Tony Anselmo, Rob Minkoff. Visual effects supervisor: Mark Dindal. Art director: Michael A. Peraza Jr., Donald A. Towns. Background supervisor: Donald A. Towns. Layout supervisor: David A. Dunnet. Layouts: Rasoual Azadani, James Baihold, Fred Cline, Lorenzo A. Martinez, Bill Perkins, Daniel St. Pierre. Backgrounds: Kathy Alteri, Doug Ball, Jim Coleman, Greg Drolette, Dennis Durrell, Dean Gordon, Lisa L. Keene, Tia Kratter, Christy Maltese, Andrew Richard Phillipson, Phillip Phillipson, Craig Robertson, Brian Sebern, Robert Edward Stanton.

## Little Nemo: Adventures in Slumberland

(7/24/92) Hemdale (Japan). 85 mins. Directors: Masami Hata, Mansanori Hata, William Hurtz. Producers: Yutaka Fujioka, Barry Glasser, Eiji Katayama, Shunzo Kato. Voices: Gabriel Damon (Little Nemo), Mickey Rooney (Flip), Rene Auberjonois (Professor Genius), Danny Mann (Icarus), Laura Mooney (Princess Camilla), Bernard Erhard (King Morpheus), William E. Martin (The Nightmare King), Alan Oppenheimer (Oomp), Michael Bell (Oompy), Sidney Miller (Oompe), Neil Ross (Oompa), John Stephenson (Oompo, Dirigible Captain), Jennifer Darling (Nemo's Mother), Greg Burson (Nemo's Father, Flap), Sherry Lynn (Bon Bon), Guy Christopher (Courtier, Cop), Nancy Cartwright (Page), Ellen Ger-

©Hemdale Pictures Corporation

stell (Page), Tress MacNeille (Elevator Creature), Gregg Berger (Equestrian Master), June Foray (Librarian).

**Consumer Tips:** ☆☆☆ MPAA Rating: G. Based on the comic strip by Winsor McCay.

**Story:** Little Nemo, hero of his dream world, Slumberland, accidentally unleashes the evil Nightmare King. Together with his companions, Icarus his flying squirrel, Professor Genius, and a trickster named Flip, Nemo travels to Nightmare Land to rescue King Morpheus and win the hand of lovely Princess Camille.

**Comments:** Comic/animation legend Winsor McCay's landmark strip, which first graced newspaper pages in 1905, had already been adapted multiple times: in 1908 as a musical, in 1911 as an animated film by McCay himself for use in his vaudeville act, and in 1990 as a Nintendo game. The latter particularly seems to have influenced (or been influenced by) this pleasant feature. Most of McCay's cast have been retained, foremost the mischievous Flip, with slight alterations (Dr. Pill is now Professor Genius, the princess now has a first name, and Impy the cannibal, from McCay's earlier *Jungle Imps* strip, has been replaced by the goblin Oomps, no doubt to be PC).

The biggest change is that while Nemo's strip dreams had no basis in reality, an early scene in which Nemo watches a circus parade provides real-life counterparts for all of the principals. Additionally, a flying squirrel pet for Nemo is included as a kid-friendly side-

kick (or as an improbable homage to Jay Ward's Rocky, whose voice, June Foray, has a tiny bit here). Though the main cast could have come from any 1990s Japanese outsourced television cartoon, McCay's designs surface unexpectedly in certain of the background animals and characters (etiquette teachers taken straight from the first strip). Fun, unexpected salutes to Winsor's other creations crop up (Nemo's mother asks if he's been "sneaking pies again," a la *Dreams of the Rarebit Fiend*, and Gertie the Dinosaur is seen swaying along to band music).

The first half of the film, like the early months of McCay's strip, introduces Nemo to Slumberland and its denizens (especially the princess). However, while the strip was content to have its stars explore a different Slumberland region in each tale, the film incorporates magical items and somewhat cliched threats from nightmares to provide slight conflict. The movie is thus considerably uneven, further hindered by surprisingly limp songs from the Sherman Brothers (only the teachers' ensemble number has any life).

More impressive (and often more interesting) than the film itself is the diverse crew behind it. McCay historian/animator John Canemaker (credited with visual development) stated in a 2002 interview with John Grant, "I don't think there's anybody in animation who *didn't* work on *Nemo*! It was ten years in production." Apart from the Shermans, the roster included UPA veteran William Hurtz, codirecting with Japan's Masami Hata; Ray Bradbury, who worked on the adaptation; future *Harry Potter* director Chris Columbus, who scripted; and in various capacities, Warners designer Paul Julian, fantasy illustrators Brian Froud and Moebius Giraus, and such Disney vets as Ken Anderson, Dave Hilberman, *Parent Trap* director David Swift, and Frank Thomas and Ollie Johnston. The latter presumably contributed the sequence in which King Morpheus, much jollier than his regal strip counterpart, tinkers with his model train in full engineer regalia. *Little Nemo* is still a pleasant enough diversion for family audiences, but comic and animation buffs would probably have as much fun just gazing at the names in the credits. (AL)

**Additional Credits:** Screenplay: Chris Columbus, Richard Outten. Story: Jean Moebius Giraud, Yutaka Fujioka (based on the comic strip by Winsor McCay). Concept for the screen:

Ray Bradbury. Music: Thomas Chase, Steve Rucker. Songs: Richard M. Sherman, Robert B. Sherman. Vocalist: Melissa Manchester. Animation directors: Kazuhide Tomonaga, Nobuo Tomizawa. Story consultants: Frank Thomas, Oliver Johnston, Dave Hilberman, Koji Shinizu, Robert Towne. Concept design: Jean Moebius Giraud. Design development: Brian Froud, Paul Julian, Kazuhike Tomonaga, Ken Mundie, Corny Cole, Nobuo Tomizawa. Visual image development: John Canemaker. Story sketch: Ken Anderson, Yasuo Otsuko, Leo Salkin, Boyd Kirkland, Marty Murphy, Tomonaga Tomizawa, Lee Mishkin, Milt Schaefer, Bob Taylor, Roy Wilson. Storyboards: Masami Hata, Tomizawa, Tomasa, Yasuo Otsuka. Background design: Ray Aragon, Dean Gordon, Carol Police, Fred Warter. Voice director: David Swift. Choreography: Michael Peters.

**The Little Prince and the Eight-Headed Dragon** (1/1/64) Columbia Pictures. 85 mins. Director: Yugo Serikawa. No voices credited.

**Consumer Tips:** ☆☆☆ MPAA Rating: Not rated. Fantasy Adventure. Based on Japanese mythology. The exploits of the troublemaking god Susano and the heroic knight Yamato Takeru are combined into the episodic adventures of an impishly hotheaded but basically well-meaning young boy-prince.

**Story:** Little Prince Susano's mother dies, but his father just tells him that she has "gone away." Susano sets out with his pet rabbit to find her in the lands of enchantment, each ruled by one of his siblings or cousins. In each he has an adventure such as fighting a giant fish or a fire monster, and he gains a new magical weapon or a new companion. The climax is his rescue of Princess Kushinada from Orochi, the eight-headed dragon.

**Comments:** *Wanpaku Ohji no Orochi Taiji* (more literally "The Bratty Prince and the Giant Snake," produced by Toei Animation Co. (and released in Japan on March 24, 1963), is a conflation of tales of the gods and heroes of Japan's past, first recorded in *Nihon Shoki* (*Tales of Japan*) in A.D. 712. Hell-raising Susano was roughly the equivalent of Norse mythology's Loki, the god of chaos. A handsome, brave, and invincible warrior, he was best known for drunkenness, brawling, fighting with his divine brothers and sisters, and bedeviling helpless mortals with disasters just for the fun of it. Yamato Takeru, contrarily, was a prince who was supposedly cursed to bring bad luck and death to all around him. He had to constantly do heroic deeds to prove the falsity of this. His greatest battle was with the eight-headed dragon. The movie adds a sequence from Greek mythology based on Bellerophon's taming of the flying horse Pegasus and using it to slay the Chimera.

Prince Susano (Susanoo or Susanoh) is recast as a child about eight years old, and the brave but terribly spoiled heir of one of the kingdoms of the lands of enchantment. He loves his mother and is distraught when she disappears. His royal father does not tell him that she has died; just that she had to go away and can never return. (Technically true, since in mythology death just means that she has been forcibly relocated to the Underworld.) Susano, irate that nobody seems interested in rescuing her, stomps off with his loyal pet black rabbit Red Nose (Aka-hana) to bring her home himself.

Advertised by Columbia as being "in Magicolor and Wonderscope," *The Little Prince and the Eight-Headed Dragon* was one of the last Japanese features to hew to the Disney formula of a classic fairy tale featuring heroes surrounded by cute forest animals. It is notable for its dynamic, stylized art design by animation director Yasuji Mori. (FP)

**Additional Credits:** Screenplay: Ichiro Ikeda, Kei Lijima. Animation: Sanae Yamamoto, Yasuji Mori, Hideo Furusawa.

Music: Akira Ifukube. Codirectors: Isao Takahata, Kimio Yabuki. A Toei Animation Production.

**The Littlest Warrior** (3/1/62) Signal International (Japan). 70 mins. Director: Taiji Yabushita. Producer: Isamu Takahashi. Voices: Yoshiko Sakuma (Anjue), Kinya Kitaoji (Zooshio).

**Consumer Tips:** ☆☆ MPAA Rating: Unrated. Japanese Heian-era historical fantasy. Based on the Japanese literary classic *Sansho Dayu* (*Sansho the Bailiff*) by Ogai Mori, aka *The Orphan Brother* (*Anju to Zushio-Maru*, 1961).

**Story:** In 11th-century Japan, an evil palace official has an honest governor falsely imprisoned. His wife and two children, Zooshio (brother) and Anjue (sister), are forced to flee. The family is captured by bandits who sell them as slaves to Dayu, a brutal local chieftain. Zooshio and his animal friends escape, while Anjue falls into a lake and is transformed into a mermaid. Zooshio reaches the palace, where he is adopted by a kindly official. After growing up to become a hero who saves villagers from a monster, Zooshio is appointed to his father's former governorship. He conquers the evil Dayu and releases all the slaves, including his mother.

**Comments:** *The Littlest Warrior* (aka *The Orphan Brother*, Japanese title *Anju to Zushio-maru*) was the

fourth of Toei Animation's annual theatrical features (released July 19, 1961; 83 minutes) based on the Disney formula of a famous folktale or literary classic, with plenty of cute animals gamboling around the human stars. It was the first based upon a modern literary tale, the short novel *Sansho the Bailiff* by Ogai Mori (1862–1922), one of Japan's first modern authors. This story was also the subject of one of Japan's first live-action cinematic classics, *Sansho the Bailiff*, directed by Kenji Mizoguchi (Daiei, 1954).

The story seems an unlikely choice for the Disney formula because it is a relentless tragedy. It contains no fantasy elements. The father dies in prison, the mother is sold into prostitution, and Anjue deliberately drowns herself to escape torture for helping Zooshio to escape. By the time Zooshio is in a position to rescue his family, they are all dead.

Toei turned this into a children's feature by substituting a mood of suspense and adventure for the despondent misery. Zooshio is given several animal companions and made into a hero who conquers fantasy monsters rather than an honest governor who arrests bandits and corrupt minor officials.

The movie adds several juvenile scenes such as Dayu trying to force the dog, bear cub, and mouse to become circus performers who can be sold for a big profit. Despite this, *The Littlest Warrior* seems the most slowly paced of Toei's early features; much too slow for Western audiences. (FP)

**Additional Credits:** Screenplay: Sumie Tanaka. Cinematography: Shinkichi Otsuka. Music: Tadashi Kishimo. Animation director: Sanae Yamamoto. Design: Akira Okuwara, Yasuji Mori. Animators: Akira Daikuhara, Hideo Furusawa, Masao Kumagawa, Daikichiro Kusube, Yasuji Mori, Yasuo Ôtsuka.

**The Looney Looney Looney Bugs Bunny Movie**
(11/20/81) Warner Bros. 80 mins. Director: Friz Freleng. Producer: Friz Freleng. Voices: Mel Blanc (Bugs Bunny, Yosemite Sam, Gerry the Idgit Dragon, Daffy Duck, Sylvester, Tweety Pie, Porky Pig, Speedy Gonzales, Pepe Le Pew, additional characters), June Foray (Granny), Stan Freberg (Big Bad Wolf, Three Little Bops, Singing Narrator), Ralph James (Narrator), Frank Welker (Lawyer, Interviewing Dog), Frank Nelson.

**Consumer Tips:** ☆☆½ MPAA Rating: G.

©Warner Bros.

**Story:** In three parts: Yosemite Sam does the devil's bidding, Bugs Bunny rescues Tweety from gangsters Rocky and Mugsy, and Bugs hosts a Hollywood award show.

**Comments:** Warner Bros. decided to reestablish its classic animation department because of several factors: the success of Chuck Jones' feature-length *Bugs Bunny/Road Runner Movie* (1979), the recent availability of Looney Tunes veteran Friz Freleng, who had just closed his DePatie Freleng animation studio in 1980, and the success of several prime-time holiday-themed Looney Tunes television specials. Looney Tunes were suddenly profitable again.

Friz rejoined Warner Bros. and set about creating a series of compilation features, which involved creating about 20 minutes of new animation to bridge existing scenes from the classic cartoon library. The full title of the first film is *Friz Freleng's Looney Looney Looney Bugs Bunny Movie.* The first one was set up like three separate half-hour specials, with three separate plotlines (almost to hedge their bet).

The format was similar to the "cheater" short cartoons they produced in the late 1950s and 1960s when budgets were tight, and were not unlike the format of prime-time *The Bugs Bunny Show* (1960–62). In fact, the first segment of this feature—the premise of Yosemite Sam in Hades, who was forced to bring Bugs Bunny to the devil—is a remake itself. It was first done as a segment of *The Bugs Bunny Show*, entitled *Satan's Waitin'* (1961), then again in 1963 as a separate Merrie Melodies short, *Devil's Feud Cake.*

The second segment of the film was a variation of Freleng's 1953 short, *Catty Cornered.* The third segment is the film's most original, and best. A spoof of television award shows, it features most of the film's alloted new footage—and surprise, it's pretty good.

*Friz Freleng's Looney Looney Looney Bugs Bunny Movie* is one of the best of these makeshift features. Clips from classic cartoons include lengthy excerpts from *The Three Little Bops, Show Biz Bugs, Golden Yeggs, High Diving Hare,* and Friz's 1958 Oscar-winner, *Bugs Bunny, Knighty Knight Bugs.* (JB)

**Additional Credits:** Story: Friz Freleng, David Detiege, John Dunn, Phil Monroe, Gerry Chinquy. Music: Milt Franklyn, William Lava, Carl W. Stalling, Robert J. Walsh, Don McGinnis, Shorty Rogers. Production designer: Corny Cole. Sequence directors: David Detiege, Phil Monroe. Animators: Warren Batchelder, Charles Downs, Marcia Fertig, Bob Matz, Manuel Perez, Vigil Ross, Lloyd Vaughan, Arthur Davis, Ted Bonnicksen, Pete Burness. Layout artists: Hawley Pratt, Peter Alvarado, Robert Givens, Michael Mitchell. Backgrounds: Paul Julian, Tom O'Louglin, Richard H. Thomson, Irving Wyner.

**Looney Tunes: Back in Action** (11/14/03) Warner Bros. 92 mins. Director (live action): Joe Dante. Director (animation): Eric Goldberg. Producers: Paula Weinstein, Bernie Goldmann. Live-action cast: Brendan Fraser (DJ Drake, Himself), Jenna Elfman (Kate Houghton), Timothy Dalton (Damien Drake), Joan Cusack (Mother), Heather Locklear (Dusty Tails), Steve Martin (Mr. Chairman). Voices: Joe Alaskey (Bugs Bunny, Daffy Duck, Beaky Buzzard, Sylvester, Ma Bear), Jeff Glen Bennett (Yosemite Sam, Foghorn Leghorn, Nasty Canasta), Billy West (Elmer Fudd, Peter Lorre), Eric Goldberg (Tweety Bird, Marvin the Martian, Speedy Gonzales), Bruce Lanoil (Pepe LePew), June Foray (Granny), Bob Bergen (Porky Pig), Brendan Fraser (Tazmanian Devil, Tazmanian She-Devil), Casey Kasem (Shaggy), Frank Welker (Scooby Doo), Danny Chambers (Cottontail Smith), Stan Freberg (Baby Bear), Will Ryan (Papa Bear), Danny Mann (Robo Dog, Spy Car), Mel Blanc (Gremlin Car—archival recordings of "The Maxwell" from The Jack Benny Program).

**Consumer Tips:** ☆☆☆ MPAA Rating: PG.

©Warner Bros. Entertainment

**Story:** Bugs Bunny helps a Warner Bros. executive find Daffy Duck, whom she fired from the lot. But Daffy is off on an adventure with a fired Warner Bros. studio security guard—whose famous father has been kidnapped by the evil ACME corporation.

**Comments:** Following the appearance of the Looney Tunes characters in 1996's *Space Jam* as backups to Michael Jordan, the characters attempt to retake center stage in yet another live-action/animation blend, but one that generally makes sure its animated stars have equal time. The loose plot focuses on two strands of the buddy movie, as Daffy and a fired studio guard, DJ (Brendan Fraser), search for DJ's father, and Bugs and a studio exec (Jenna Elfman) try to track them down. This ultimately pits the characters against the flamboyant head of the omnipresent ACME corporation (Steve Martin, giving a very bizarre performance). This loose framework actually works surprisingly well, however, allowing for much inventiveness and slapstick.

Live-action director Joe Dante, collaborating with former Disney animation director Eric Goldberg, has paid homage to old Hollywood in general and Warner Bros. in particular in many of his films (notably *Gremlins* and *Matinee*), and here he does so with a vengeance. Indeed, at times the in-jokes and visual gags flow too quickly and heavily, and are easily lost amidst the garish live-action backdrops and noisy soundtrack. The film also feels slightly schizophrenic, as Dante's homages (scores of Looney Tunes stars in a commissary with a framed Chuck Jones portrait, a lab filled with 1950s B-movie monsters) coexist with somewhat more

smug, hip in-jokes and product placements, likely the result of studio interference (such as an advance promotion for *Scooby Doo 2*; DJ being Fraser the actor's stunt double and complaining about what a jerk he is; and a Las Vegas sequence spotlighting name casinos and NASCAR driver Jeff Gordon).

Animated set pieces abound. A Louvre chase, with Bugs, Elmer, and Daffy melding into famous paintings, is brilliant, as is an opening tribute to Jones's "Rabbit Season" shorts. This Bugs melds the suave, cool rabbit of the later Jones and Freleng shorts with the early, more lunatic rabbit of Avery and Clampett (highlighted by Bugs recreating the Psycho shower scene). Daffy Duck, like Bugs, is a blend of early and late Daffy, both greedy coward and insane "darned fool duck," and somehow he seems almost more whole than either incarnation. Most of the other characters, instead of being crammed in as "friends/teammates" a la *Space Jam* are accorded either supporting roles as antagonists in different set pieces or showy cameos. Only Elmer Fudd is rather weak, as his dual roles as actor playing an antagonist on-screen and a genuine villain pursuing Bugs and Daffy to aid the evil ACME head. This seems contradictory to his classic screen characterization as well-meaning (if hunting-inclined) simpleton.

The live-action cast is mostly serviceable, with some particularly fun tongue-in-cheek portrayals by Timothy Dalton, Joan Cusack, and Heather Locklear, oddly enough. The voices are mostly fine evocations of the originals, with Joe Alaskey doing outstanding work as Bugs and Daffy, a rarity since Mel's passing. Though the film failed to recreate the originals, as many fans had hoped, and was generally a box-office disappointment (making little over $20 million), it's arguably the finest feature-length appearance by Bugs and friends. (AL)

**Additional Credits:** Executive producers: Chris DeFaria, Larry Doyle. Animation producer: Allison Abbate. Screenplay: Larry Doyle. Music: Jerry Goldsmith, John Debney. Lead animators: David Brewster, Anthony DeRosa, Bert Klein, Frank Molieri, Jeff Siergey. Animators: James Baker, Arland Barron, Richard Bazley, Robert Casale, Crystal Chesney, Caroline Cruikshank, Gavin Dell, Mike D'Isa, Brian Ferguson, Danny Galieote, Joe Haidar, T. Daniel Hofstedt, Jon Hooper, Chris Hubbard, Ron Husband, Mark Kausler, Ernest Keen, Shawn Keller, Dave Kuhn, Erik Kuska, Craig Maras, Gaston Marzio, Robert L. McKnight II, Mario Menjivar, Jamie Oliff, Wendy

Perdue, Kevin Petrilak, Robb Pratt, Shane Prigmore, Tom Roth, Harry Sabin, Chris Sauve, Tom Sito, Beth Sleven, Derek L. Thompson, Chris Wahl, Bill Waldman, Eric Walls, Andreas Wessel-Therhorn, Matt Williams, Alexander Williams, Theresa Wiseman, Phil Young, David Alan Zaboski. Effects animators: Lynette Charters, Noe Garcia, John MacFarlane, Jorge Hiram Ramos. CG Animation/modeling: Mike Amron, William Ball, Kieron Lo Cheuk-Chi, Steve Cummings, Thomas Dickins, Adam Dotson, Karl Fornander, Corey Hels, Jennifer Kim Jongo, Didier Levy, Thanh "John" Nguyen, Neil Rubenstein, Osama Takehiro, Michael Teperson, Jerry Weil, Genevieve Yee. Storyboards: Chris Aguirre, Bob Camp. Danelle Davenport, Kurt Dumas, Eric Goldberg, Christopher Headrick, T. J. House, Tom Jung, Mark Kausler, Hank Mayo, John McIntyre, Steve Moore, Felipe Morell, Len Morganti, John Ramirez, Eric Ramsey, Peter Shin, Jeff Siergey, Tom Sito, David Smith, Guy Vasilovich, Johnny Williamson. Layout artists: Karen Hamrock, Julio Leon, Doug Walker, Jennifer Yuan. Backgrounds: Miguel Gill, Carl Jones, Craig Kelly, Philip Phillipson, Dennis Venizelos. Animation art directors: John Kleber, Paul Sonski. Technical consultants: David Barclay, Bruce Lanoil. Animation consultant: David Silverman. Robo dog CG animation consultant: Jeff Lew.

**The Lord of the Rings** (11/21/78) United Artists. 133 mins. Director: Ralph Bakshi. Producer: Saul Zaentz. Voices: Christopher Guard (Frodo), William Squire (Gandalf), Michael Scholes (Samwise), John Hurt (Aragon), Simon Chandler (Merry), Dominic Guard (Pippin), Norman Bird (Bilbo), Michael Graham-Cox (Boromir), Anthony Daniels (Legolas), David Buck (Gimli), Peter Wood Thorpe (Gollum), Fraser Kerr (Sauron), Phillip Stone (Theoden), Michael Deacon (Wormtongue), Andre Morell (Elrond), Alan Tilvern (Innkeeper), Annette Crosbie (Galadriel), John Westbrook (Treebeard). Live-action reference/rotoscope cast: Sharon Baird (Frodo), John A. Neris (Gandalf), Paul Gale, Michael Lee Gogin, Billy Barty (Bilbo, Samwise), Donn Whyte, Trey Wilson, Albert Grimele, Patty Maloney, Jeri Lea Ray, Felix Silla, Mike Clifford, Larry Larsen, Art Hern, David Dotson, Tommy Madden, Gary Jensen, Aesop Aquarian, Santy Josol, Stan Barrett, John L., Herb Braha, Sam Laws, Hank Calia, Terry Leonard, Frank Delfino, Peter Looney, Russ Earnest, Dennis Madalone, Louis Elias, Buck Maffei, Eddy Fay, Jerry Maren, Carmen Filpi, Harry Monty, Ruth Gay, Frank

©Saul Zaentz Production Company

Morson, Lenny Gear, Walt Robles, Harriett Gibson, Mic Rodgers, Bob Haney, Angelo Rossitto, Chuck Hayward, Pete Risch, Eddy Hice, Jack Verbois, Loren Janes, Gregg Walker.

**Consumer Tips:** ☆☆½ MPAA Rating: PG. A film designed for adults but appropriate for kids and families.

**Story:** In the mythical realm of Middle Earth, a hobbit named Frodo undertakes a quest to protect a magic ring from the hands of Dark Lord Sauron. Accompanied by the Wizard Gandalf and assorted warriors, elves, and gnomes, the pair encounters and overcomes many forces of evil.

**Comments:** Veteran animation director Ralph Bakshi was the first filmmaker to attempt to bring to the screen J. R. R. Tolkien's epic masterpiece, *The Lord of the Rings*. Bakshi's movie covers the first 1½ books of the trilogy. The film is considered to be a flawed but inspired interpretation of the classic story.

Tolkien's *The Lord of the Rings* has been hugely popular since its publication in the 1950s. This trilogy (and the rest of Tolkien's works) has enjoyed four waves of popularity since being published: in the 1950s as an underground phenomenon; in the 1960s as a symbol of the mass peace movement, with its vision of a world that valued honor, loyalty, and integrity; in the 1970s; and in the early 21st century, with the release of Peter Jackson's three live-action films of *The Lord of the Rings*.

Walt Disney held the film rights to *The Lord of the Rings* for 10 years, passing it on to United Artists in 1968. At UA, Stanley Kubrick and John Boorman each tried, unsuccessfully, to adapt the novels into a screenplay. In the mid-1970s, Ralph Bakshi burst onto the animated feature scene in the United States with the X-rated *Fritz the Cat* and *Heavy Traffic*, the controversial *Coonskin*, and the commercially successful *Wizards*. Subsequently, he lobbied UA to let him make an animated film of *The Lord of the Rings*.

UA brought in Saul Zaentz, who was a friend of Bakshi's and had helped him initiate and produce *Fritz the Cat*. Zaentz was soon to win a Best Picture Academy Award for another bestselling novel that languished in Hollywood for years before being produced, *One Flew over the Cuckoo's Nest*. (He won an additional Best Picture Oscar for *Amadeus* nearly a decade later.)

It was courageous of Bakshi and Zaentz to undertake the ultra-complex *The Lord of the Rings*, risking the wrath of the trilogy's countless fans if their interpretation of the classic was not to their liking. To prevent this, Bakshi and Zaentz talked extensively with members of Tolkien's family and with his British publishers. They attempted to make the screenplay as faithful to the Tolkien novels as possible. The early versions of the screenplay were written by Tolkien scholar, Chris Conkling. Final revisions were written by fantasy/nonfiction author Peter S. Beagle (who later created the book and animated film, *The Last Unicorn*).

With a unique creative vision, Bakshi decided to first film a live-action version of the screenplay and then transform it into animation by painting cels over the film frames. Thus, live action was the foundation of the film's animation. This technique is called "rotoscoping" and was invented by Max Fleischer in 1917.

Up to that point, animated films had not depicted extensive battle scenes with hundreds of characters. By using the rotoscope, Bakshi could trace highly complex scenes from live-action footage and transform them into animation, thereby taking advantage of the complexity live-action film can capture without incurring the exorbitant costs of producing a live-action film.

Bakshi later used rotoscope in *American Pop* and *Fire and Ice*. In a review from *Cue*, William Wolf wrote of *The Lord of the Rings*, "the spectacular epic scenes have the quality of paintings come to life." Indeed, Bakshi designed the film to be a sequence of "moving paintings," including backgrounds influenced by Brueghel, Rembrandt, Winslow Homer, and Wyeth.

The first half of Bakshi's *The Lord of the Rings* is the best. The plot is detailed well, and rotoscoping results in character movements that are realistic and nuanced, and facial expressions that are amazingly subtle. In the second half, however, the plot becomes difficult to understand for viewers not well-acquainted with the books; the film focuses on the highlights of the plot, ignoring important background and exposition. Also, the extensive battle sequences are disorienting and do not show clearly who is winning. Perhaps the biggest drawback of the film, Bakshi mixes beautiful rotoscope footage with ugly color overlays of high-contrast, live-action film. The result is a confusing and unaesthetic experience for the viewer. Did he do this because it was an artistic choice or because of budget constraints? As if this weren't enough, the movie ends abruptly in the middle of Tolkien's second of three books, although the film was advertised as Tolkien's complete *Lord of the Rings*. In 1980, Rankin-Bass produced an animated film of the third novel in the trilogy, *The Return of the King*, for television, a year and a half after Bakshi's film.

*The Lord of the Rings* cost $4 million to make and earned $30.5 million at the box office. Therefore, it was successful financially, though not a huge hit. The film received mixed reviews from critics and audiences. Frank Barrow, from the *Hollywood Reporter*, said "*The Lord of the Rings* is undoubtedly the most adventuresome animated feature ever made . . . daring and unusual in concept. . . ." Joseph Gelmis of *Newsday* wrote, "The film's principal reward is a visual experience unlike anything that other animation features are doing at the moment." As artistically inspired as this film is in many ways, many Tolkein loyalists intensely dislike Bakshi's version of *The Lord of the Rings*, deploring what they consider the cheap-looking effects and the missing ending.

Bakshi's animated feature influenced Peter Jackson, the director of the live-action *The Lord of the Rings* films. Bakshi's film was Jackson's first exposure to Tolkien's classic, which prompted him to buy the trilogy of books. This resulted in Jackson becoming a lifelong fan of the classic. (Marea Boylan)

**Additional Credits:** Screenplay: Chris Conkling, Peter S. Beagle. Based on the stories by J. R. R. Tolkien. Music: Leonard

Roseman, Paul Kont. Key animators: Craig Armstrong, Dale Baer, Brenda Banks, Carl Bell, Jesus Cortes, Lillian Evans, Frank Gonzales, Steven Gordon, Sean Joyce, Lenord Robinson, Chrystal Russell, Paul Smith, Irven Spence, Hank Tucker, Edward Wexler, Bruce Woodside, James A. Davis. Animators: Sam Jaimes, Manny Perez, Joe Roman, Phil Roman, Martin Taras. Effects animators: Stan Green, Nino Carbe, Christopher Andrew. Layout artists: Dale Baer, Louise Zingarelli, Mentor Huebner, David Jonas, Mike Ploog, Kevin Hanna. Background artists: Barry Jackson, Johnnie Vita, Marcia Adams, Edwin B. Hirth III, Carol Kieffer.

**Lupin III: Castle of Cagliostro** See *The Castle of Cagliostro*.

**Macross II: Lovers Again** (6/4/93) Tara Releasing. 134 mins. Directors: Kenichi Yatagai, Quint Lancaster. Producers: Shinichi Iguchi, Hiroaki Inoue, Hiroshi Kakoi, Hirotake Kanda, Keiji Kusano. Voices (English version): Jonathan Charles (Hibiki), Raymond Garcia (Marduk), Tom Fahn (Marduk Commander), Debra Jean Rogers (Ishtar), Steven Blum (Lord Feff, Maj. Nexx), Hal Cleaveland (Exxegran), Bill Kestin (Lord Emperor Ingues), Trish Ledoux (Wendy Ryder).

**Consumer Tips:** ☆☆ MPAA Rating: Unrated. SF adventure. A sequel to the 1982–83 anime television series *Super-Dimension Fortress Macross*.

**Story:** Eighty years after the Zentraedi-human space war, the descendants of the Zentraedi defected to earth live in harmony. The U.N. Spacy, the military force that defeated the Zentraedi, has become the world government. When a new hostile faction of Zentraedi, the Marduk, attack earth again, the government is confident that its pop-music defenses will work again. But 17-year-old reporter Hibiki Kanzaki learns from young Marduk singer Ishtar that the Marduk now have their own musical weapons. Hibiki enlightens Ishtar into preferring earth's peace and love society to her militaristic own, but the reactionary U.N. Spacy command refuses to listen to them. Hibiki, Ishtar, and teen Spacy fighter pilot Sylvie Gena take their own steps to broadcast the truth to both the earth and Marduk armies.

**Comments:** *Super-Dimensional Fortress Macross (Chôjikû Yôsai Macross)* was an unexpected television hit in both Japan and America. Originally scheduled for 27 episodes, the story was expanded to 36 episodes (October 1982 to June 1983). In America Macross was edited into the first and most popular third of the *Robotech* television series (March 1985). In 2009 earth is attacked by a battle fleet of giant humanoid Zentraedi aliens. The Zentraedi have been mentally conditioned over centuries into a militaristic race lacking any culture. Their weapons are superior to any of earth's, but their soldiers are emotionally confused and panicked by broadcasts of earth music, especially pop songs by idol singer Lynn Minmay. *Macross* ends with most of the surviving Zentraedi rejecting their militaristic culture and "micronizing" themselves to settle on earth as peaceful immigrants to help the humans rebuild the ravaged planet.

*Macross*'s fans demanded a sequel, which was held up due to disagreements between the title's several rights holders. Finally Big West, the financier of the original series, did not want to pass up *Macross*'s 10th anniversary and unilaterally commissioned *Chôjikû Yôsai Macross II: Lovers Again* as a six half-hour episode, direct-to-video series, released monthly (except for July) from May through November 1992. The series was licensed in the United States by U.S. Renditions, which edited this compilation for theatrical distribution (through Tara Releasing) in June 1993, titled *Super Dimensional Fortress Macross II: Lovers Again* but with posters titled *Macross II: The Movie*. U.S. Renditions' video release was in three volumes of two episodes each in August 1992, January 1993, and January 1994. Manga Entertainment has subsequently released the movie compilation under the *Macross II: The Movie* title on video beginning in October 1995.

*Macross II* is a fast-moving story, but extremely simplistic wish-fulfillment about how a 17-year-old ace television news reporter, a 17-year-old female ace fighter pilot, and an exotically beautiful alien priestess (about 17 years old) can stop a cataclysmic war ordered by militaristic adults just by preaching peace and love. It features attractive character design by Haruhiko Mikimoto, the original *Macross* designer. But it was made without any participation by the original writers. As a result, when the rights conflict was resolved shortly afterwards and several further Macross series were made (*Macross Plus*, *Macross 7*, *Macross 7 Dynamite*, and *Macross Zero*), *Macross II* was written out of the official comprehensive future history. (FP)

**Additional Credits:** Executive producers: Katsushi Murakami, Hirohiko Suekichi, Minoru Takanashi, Eiji Takî, Yoshiaki Ônishi. Music: Shirô Sagisu. Cinematography: Kazuhiro Konishi. Art direction: Hidenori Nakahata. ADR direction and script: Raymond Garcia. Character designer: Haruhiko Mikimoto. Mechanical design supervisor: Koichi Ohata. Concept designer: Takashi Watabe.

**Mad Monster Party?** (3/8/69) Embassy Pictures— Rankin-Bass. 94 mins. Director: Jules Bass. Producer: Arthur Rankin Jr. Voices: Boris Karloff (Baron Boris von Frankenstein), Phyllis Diller (Monster's Mate), Gale Garnett (Francesca), Allen Swift (Felix Flankin, Dracula, Yetch, Invisible Man, Dr. Jekyll & Mr. Hyde, Mr. Cronkite, Chef Machiavelli, Hunchback of Notre Dame, Werewolf Howls). Vocalist: Ethel Ennis.

©Rankin-Bass Productions

**Consumer Tips:** ☆☆☆ MPAA Rating: Unrated.

**Story:** Baron Von Frankenstein invites all monsters to his castle for a party to announce his new discovery and his retirement. His nephew and heir, Felix Flankin, falls in love with Frankenstein's sexy assistant.

**Comments:** *Mad Monster Party?* was Rankin-Bass's third theatrical film. The general look of the stop-motion animation and the backgrounds seem to be essentially the same as those of any other cheery Rankin-Bass holiday special, and a few of the song numbers (notably "Stay One Step Ahead") feel like refugees from *Rudolph the Red-Nosed Reindeer* and the like. However, the character designs, script, voices, and even the opening song sequence all suggest that this is something other than an average Rankin-Bass production. The film opens with Baron Von Frankenstein (who is both voiced by Boris Karloff and designed to look like a caricature of him as well) succeeding in his experiments to develop a formula that can destroy matter. The baron proceeds to invite the various famous film monsters to a gathering. At this point, the opening credit roll begins in earnest, accompanied by the eerie yet offbeat and jazzy title tune, overlapping images of the various monsters receiving their invitations, and punctuated by odd sound effects ("Eek!" "Phew!" "Yikes," etc.), which also manifest onscreen. The baron's long-lost nephew, Felix, a bespectacled nebbish whose voice is styled after Jimmy Stewart, is also among the guests, a fact that enrages the baron's sultry assistant Francesca. The various monsters, as well as Felix, arrive, and while the baron tries to convince Felix to be his successor, certain parties try to do away with him (notably Francesca, Dracula, the monster, and his mate, the latter voiced by and patterned after Phyllis Diller, adding to the eeriness).

Several set pieces, ancillary to the plot, provide some of the film's most memorable moments. These include a catfight between Francesca and the mate in which they strip each other down to their lingerie, a lengthy food fight amongst the monsters, and a sequence in which the Peter Lorre–type assistant Yetch discusses the dinner menu with the mad Chef Machiavelli, with Allen Swift providing over-the-top voice performances for both characters. The deliberate vocal and physical mimickry of older film stars seems to suggest that the film was targeted more for adults (certainly the catfight scene would make one think so). Yet this offbeat film (with key contributions by *Mad* magazine veterans Jack Davis and Harvey Kurtzman) usually wound up at kiddie matinees. Interest has increased in recent years, however, and decent prints of the film have recently resurfaced. For the record, the film was produced between 1966 and 1967, but its first actual release seems to have come in 1969 in New York. (AL)

**Additional Credits:** Executive producer: Joseph E. Levine. Associate producer: Larry Roemer. Assistant director: Kizo Nagashima. Screenplay: Len Korobkin, Harvey Kurtzman. Story: Arthur Rankin Jr. Music/lyrics: Maury Laws, Jules Bass. Storyboard artists: Jack Davis, Don Duga. Character design:

Jack Davis. Animagic technician: Tad Mochinaga. Continuity design: Don Duga.

**Magic Boy** (6/22/61) MGM. 82 mins. Directors: Taiji Yabushita, Akira Okuwara. Producer: Sanae Yamamoto. Voices: Teruo Miyazaki (Sarutobi Sasuke), Katsuo Nakamura (Yukimura Sanada), Hiroko Sakura-machi (Oyû), Tomoko Matsushima (Okei-chan), Kenji Usuda (Master Tozawa Hakuun), Harue Akagi (Omon Yayamata), Yoshio Yoshida (Gonkurô the Mountain Storm).

©Metro-Goldwyn-Mayer, Inc.

**Consumer Tips:** ☆☆☆ MPAA Rating: Unrated. Fantasy adventure.

**Story:** In medieval Japan, Sasuke is a peasant boy living happily in the forest with his older sister and many animal friends. An evil witch begins to plague the region with her magic and a ruthless bandit gang that she controls. After the witch kills one of Sasuke's animal friends, he runs away to learn magic to defeat her. While he is gone, a handsome prince who has come to fight the witch meets and falls in love with Sasuke's sister. The witch orders the prince and Sasuke's sister killed. Sasuke returns just in time to defeat the witch and save them.

**Comments:** *Magic Boy* (*Shonen Sarutobi Sasuke*; literally "Sasuke the Ninja Boy") was the second theatrical feature of the new Toei Animation Co., released December 25, 1959. It continued Toei's effort to duplicate the Disney formula of presenting a traditional folktale with songs and plenty of cute animals,

although this was an original story in the style of folk legends about ninja as peasants during the sixteenth to eighteenth centuries who trained in battle skills to a supernatural degree.

Interestingly, MGM left most of the original songs from the Japanese soundtrack with their Japanese lyrics. MGM's publicity falsely said that the movie's Japanese title was "The Adventures of the Little Samurai," preferring to identify Sasuke with the public image of Japan's samurai (heroic knights), rather than with ninja (sinister spies and assassins). (FP)

**Additional Credits:** Screenplay: Toppei Marsumura. Story: Kazuo Dan, Dohei Muramatsu. Director of animation: Sanae Yamamoto. Music: Satoshi Funemura. U.S. version title song: Fred Spielman, Janice Torre. Title song sung by Danny Valentino. Cinematography: Mitsuaki Ishikawa, Seigo Otsuka. Film editor: Shintarô Miyamoto. Art direction: Seigo Shindo. Character design: Akira Okuwara, Hideo Furusawa. Animation: Taku Sugiyama, Gisaburo Sugli, Notio Hikone, Masatake Kita, Shuji Konno, Daikichiro Kusube, Kazuko Nakamura, Reiko Okuyama, Chikao Tera.

**The Magic Horse** (4/18/49) Artkino (Russian). 60 mins. Director: Ivan Ivanov-Vano. Producer: C. B. Wismar. Voices (1977 dub): Jim Backus (King), Hans Conried (Red-Haired Groom), Erin Moran (Zip the Pony), Johnny Whitaker (Ivan).

**Consumer Tips:** ☆☆☆ MPAA Rating: Unrated. This is based on classic Russian folktales.

©Soyuzmultfilm Studios

**Story:** A magical flying horse takes young Ivan to a castle where he captures a firebird, becomes a prime minister, wins a princess, and foils a king.

**Comments:** *The Magic Horse* is a delightful animated film from Russia. A bit dated in terms of animation quality, the film has charms and an elaborate animation style that is a pleasure to watch. The narrative moves at a fast pace, and there is something of interest to see in every scene.

*The Magic Horse* is based on a classic Russian folktale. This was the first feature-length animated film from the Soviet Union to be released in the United States. In fact, it was the first foreign animated feature since *The Adventures of Prince Achmed* (1926) to find commercial distribution in the United States. It was also the first animated alternative to Disney feature animation since Fleischer's *Mr. Bug Goes to Town* in 1942.

*The Magic Horse* was produced at the Soyuzmultfilm Studios in Moscow, commencing production at the end of World War II. After two years in production and over 150,000 drawings and color sketches created, the finished movie had its Russian premiere in 1947. Some of the sequences are quite spectacular, with most of the animation produced "on ones" (24 drawings per second). It made Ivan Ivanov-Vano a major figure in international animation.

This film was first released in the United States in 1949 with subtitles, limiting its distribution to art theaters catering to audiences interested in foreign films. Reviewers of the day were impressed with the film's artistic qualities. The *New York Times* called it "thoroughly charming," and the *Los Angeles Times* said it was "enchanting."

In the 1950s, *The Magic Horse* was dubbed in English for non-theatrical showings (churches, schools, museums). Redubbed in 1977, it was released to video as *The Magic Pony*. It was also known as *Over the Rainbow* and *The Little Humped Back Horse*. (JB)

**Additional Credits:** Screenplay: George Malko. Based on the Russian folktale adapted by Peter Yershow. Music: Tom Ed Williams. Animation: Lev Milchin, V. Rodzhero, I. Troyanova, A. Bewlyakov.

**Make Mine Music** (8/15/46) Walt Disney Pictures. 75 mins. Directors: Jack Kinney, Clyde Geronimi,

©Walt Disney Productions

Hamilton Luske, Bob Cormack, Josh Meador. Voices: Pinto Colvig (Animal Sounds), Nelson Eddy (Willie the Operatic Whale). Narrators, singers, live actors: Nelson Eddy, Dinah Shore, the Andrews Sisters, Benny Goodman, Sterling Holloway, Jerry Colonna, Tania Riabouchinska, Andy Russell, The Pied Pipers, David Lichine, The Ken Darby Chorus, The King's Men.

**Consumer Tips:** ☆☆ MPAA Rating : Unrated. *Make Mine Music* is an anthology of animated shorts.

**Story:** Ten short features of variable quality are presented: "After You're Gone," "All the Cats Join In," "Blue Bayou," "Casey at the Bat," "Johnny Fedora and Alice Bluebonnet," "The Martins and the Coys," "Peter and the Wolf," "Two Silhouettes," "The Whale Who Wanted to Sing at the Met," and "Without You."

**Comments:** Watching Disney's older films can be like stepping back in time, but very few of them have become dated. *Make Mine Music* is a decided exception. This film depicts a post-war popular culture that no longer exists, and modern viewers must take it as such. With the exception of some of the animated segments there is little for today's younger viewers to relate to. *Make Mine Music* is a relic of Disney's America, a film more suited for cultural historians than audiences.

Animation historians, however, may take note that "Blue Bayou" was originally intended for *Fantasia* and was to be animated to Debussy's *Clair de lune*. It's a pretty mood piece in which nothing much happens, and its themes were stated to better effect in other segments of *Fantasia*. Also considered for *Fantasia* was "Peter and the Wolf." The 1936 composition by Prokofiev was not used for that film, but the short surfaced in *Make Mine Music* using narration by Sterling Holloway. The segment is marred by terminal cuteness except for the jarring incongruity of a wolf that is terrifying enough to scare young viewers.

"After You've Gone" and "All the Cats Join In" are the best of the musical pieces and both benefit from the lively music of the Benny Goodman Orchestra. The former segment features animated musical instruments going through their paces, with good use of color and timing. The latter segment is a favorite of many Disney fans: teenagers that echo Fred Moore's character designs cavort down at the malt shop in a delightful romp. An unseen artist animates some of the short on the wing, and there's a good laugh when one of the teenage girls reprimands him for drawing her hips too broad. Still, Benny Goodman's music belongs to another time, teenagers are no longer "cats," and the malt shop is now a piece of history.

Even the segments "Casey at the Bat" and "The Martins and the Coys" invoke American nostalgia. "Casey" is designed and animated in "Gay Nineties" style to good effect and is better on its own terms than the other segment depicting feuding hillbillies. The best idea in "The Martins and the Coys" is having deceased combatants ascend into the clouds where they act as a backwoods Greek chorus/cheerleading section; the rest of the short is undistinguished. Worse can be said for "Johnny Fedora and Alice Bluebonnet," a soppy musical fantasy about sentient hats. This segment recalls efforts by the Fleischer Studio to copy Disney's shorts during the previous decade.

The high point of *Make Mine Music* is "The Whale Who Wanted to Sing at the Met," the only segment that holds up credibly today. Willie the Whale is blessed with several multi-octave voices. Professor Tetti Tatti concludes that Willie must have swallowed some opera singers and hunts the whale down. Tatti has the poor whale harpooned in the belief he is performing a rescue. Willie's concerts continue, however, to SRO crowds in heaven. This synopsis does not do justice to the visuals, which combine engaging animation with deliberately silly character design. Nelson Eddy spoke and sang every word in the short, from "Shortnin' Bread" to the arias of "Pagliacci." To view the extended

sequence where Willie imagines his operatic performances is to engage in pure fantasy; it is the saving grace of an otherwise mediocre film. (MG)

**Additional Credits:** Production supervisor: Joe Grant. Story: Homer Brightman, Dick Huemer, Dick Kinney, John Walbridge, Tom Oreb, Dick Shaw, Eric Gurney, Sylvia Holland, T. Hee, Dick Kelsey, Jesse Marsh, Roy Williams, Ed Penner, James Bodrero, Cap Palmer, Erwin Graham. Music director: Charles Wolcott. Music associates: Ken Darby, Oliver Wallace, Edward H. Plumb. Songs: Ray Gilbert, Eliot Daniel, Allie Wrubel, Bobby Worth. Animation: Les Clark, Ward Kimball, Milt Kahl, John Sibley, Eric Larson, John Lounsbery, Oliver M. Johnston Jr., Fred Moore, Hugh Fraser, Judge Whitaker, Harvey Toombs, Tom Massey, Phil Duncan, Hal Ambro, Jack Campbell, Cliff Nordberg, Bill Justice, Al Bertino, John McManus, Ken O. Brien. Effects animation: George Rowley, Jack Boyd, Andy Engman, Brad Case, Don Patterson. Uncredited animators: Harry Hamse, Milt Neil, Noel Tucker, Karl Van Leuven, Cy Young. Art supervisors: Mary Blair, Elmer Plummer, John Hench. Background artists: Claude Coats, Art Riley, Ralph Hulett, Merle Cox, Ray Huffine, Albert Dempster, Thelma Witmer, Jim Trout. Layout artists: A. Kendall O'Connor, Hugh Hennesy, Al Zinnen, Ed Benedict, Charles Phillipi, Donald DaGradi, Lance Nolley.

**The Man Called Flintstone** (8/3/66) Columbia. 87 mins. Directors/producers: William Hanna, Joseph Barbera. Voices: Alan Reed (Fred Flintstone, speaking), Mel Blanc (Barney Rubble, Dino), Jean Vander Pyl (Wilma Flintstone), Gerry Johnson (Betty Rubble), Paul Frees (Rock Slag), Harvey Korman (Chief Mount-

more, Green Goose, Triple X), June Foray (Tanya Malichite), Henry Corden (Fred Flinstone, singing), Don Messick (Ali), Janet Waldo, John Stephenson (Additional Voices), Russi Taylor (Cave Mouse, uncredited), Louis Prima (Vocalist).

**Consumer Tips:** ☆☆½ MPAA rating: Unrated. Based on the Hanna-Barbera television series.

**Story:** Fred Flintstone, the exact double of secret agent Rock Slag, is asked to take his place in dangerous situations around the world.

**Comments:** The Flintstones made their big-screen debut in Hanna-Barbera's second animated feature, which began production under the working title, *That Man Flintstone*. As *Hey There, It's Yogi Bear* was a fairly natural extension of the themes and stories of the original series, *A Man Called Flintstone* follows the then-current trend of spoofing spy films and shows in general, and James Bond in particular. *Get Smart* was a television hit at the time, and here Agent Rock Slag, though voiced by Paul Frees, has a wry Don Adams-ish delivery.

Several *Flintstones* television episodes had already dealt with spy organizations, and Fred's resemblance to Rock Slag seems borrowed from yet another television episode, as well as numerous sitcoms and films. Though Barney is featured prominently as Fred's sidekick, the other regulars are relegated to supporting roles or cameos. The animation is generally only slightly above that of the television series, compared to the almost lush look of the Yogi Bear movie. However, a more stylized approach is used for several song sequences, notably "Spy Type Guy," with a string of spy vignettes, and "When We Are Grown Up," in which children's dreams are rendered in UPA-esque graphics. The latter, along with another song featuring Pebbles and Bamm Bamm, while fairly charming, are irrelevant diversions that seem to pander to the kiddie audience more than any other parts of the film.

The voices from the show's last season reprise their roles (Bea Benaderet having been replaced by Gerry Johnson as Betty), with the inimitable Alan Reed in fine voice as Fred Flintstone. Mel Blanc is fine as Barney, as well as in several other bits, and the guest roles are filled by several HB regulars, including Paul Frees

and Don Messick, demonstrating their versatility with more than six roles apiece. Harvey Korman, who played the rather annoying Great Gazoo in the last episodes of *The Flintstones*, is heard as Fred's government supervisor.

Although its television roots are all too evident, *A Man Called Flintstone* is still a fun little movie. The best gag occurs before anything even starts, in fact, with Wilma in place of Columbia's standard torchbearer for the opening logo. (AL)

**Additional Credits:** Story: R. S. (Ray) Allen, Harvey Bullock. Story material: William Hanna, Joseph Barbera, Warren Foster, Alex Lovy. Music: Marty Paich, Ted Nichols. Art direction: Bill Perez. Special effects: Brooke Linden. Animation director: Charles A. Nichols. Animation: Edwin Aardal, Ed Barge, Hugh Fraser, George Germanetti, George Goepper, Jerry Hathcock, Bill Keil, George Kreisl, Hicks Lokey, Richard Lundy, Don Lusk, Kenneth Muse, George Nicholas, Ed Parks, John Sparey, Irven Spence, Carlo Vinci, Allen Wilzbach. Assistant animators: Sam Jaimes, Charlotte Huffine, Frank Carr, Tom Ferriter, Richard Gonzales, Jack Carr, Bill Carr, Joe Roman, Grace Stanzell, Jack Kerns, John Boersma, Joan Orbison, William Pratt, Jim Brummett, Rae McSmoden, Tony Love, Pat Combs, Veve Risto, Dennis Sills. Layout artists: Richard Bickenbach, Lance Nolley, Iwao Takamoto, Jerry Eisenberg, Bob Singer, Homer Jonas, Bruce Bushman, Jack Huber, Brad Case, Walter Clinton, Steve Nakagawa. Background design: F. Montealgre, Paul Julian, Robert Gentle, Art Lozzi, Ron Dias, Janet Brown, Tom Knowles, Fernando Arce, Rene Garcia, Richard Khim, Don Watson.

**The Man from Button Willow** (2/1/65) United Screen Artists. 81 mins. Director: David Detiege. Producer: Phyllis Bounds Detiege. Voices: Dale Robertson (Justin Eagle), Edgar Buchanan (Sorry), Barbara Jean Wong (Stormy), Howard Keel (Vocalist), Herschel Bernardi (The Captain, Saloon Man #1), Ross Martin (Andy Svenson), Shep Menken (Shanghai Kelly, Chinese Singer, Saloon Man #3, Conductor), Clarence Nash (Senator Freeman, Mountain Lion), Verna Felton (Mrs. Pomeroy, Mother, Lady on Trolley), Pinto Colvig (Abner Hawkins, Animal Sounds, Man on Trolley, Laughing Saloon Man), Cliff Edwards (Doc, Whip), Thurl Ravenscroft (Reverend, Saloon Man #2), John Hiedstand (Old Salt, Montgomerey Blaine), Edward Platt (The Man in the Black Cape), Buck Black (News Boy, Boy).

©United Screen Arts

**Consumer Tips:** ☆ MPAA Rating: G.

**Story:** In this animated Western, a government agent named Justin Eagle is sent out to track down a missing U.S. senator and battle a gang planning to blackmail the railroad company.

**Comments:** *The Man from Button Willow* is something of a departure from most animated features of the 1960s, since it is neither a musical nor a comedy, but a serious action drama based on intrigue and espionage.

The story is a classic "B-Western," though it is animated in the stiff television style of the era (like *Jonny Quest*). In fact, this film looks as if it were made as a television pilot, with just enough padded material to bring it to feature length.

The padded material featured a four-year-old Asian girl, her pets, a comical dog, skunk, and pony, and their antics around the ranch. This material is clichéd and awful.

Actor Dale Robertson, who starred for six and half years on NBC's *Tales of Wells Fargo,* plays the lead character, Justin Eagle. The character is drawn to look exactly like Robertson (Robertson also cowrote and recorded the film's theme song).

In fact, according to the film's pressbook, Robertson created the idea for the picture, wrote the original story, and "financed the project to the tune of one million dollars." Significantly, Robertson was also the chairman of the board of United Screen Artists, the original distributor of this film.

*The Man from Button Willow* is a real curiosity but a dull, sluggish film. It will be of interest mainly to fans of Dale Robertson, and to animation buffs who are studying the obscure works of cult Hollywood animators Ben Washam, Ken Hultgren, and John Dunn. If you are not in one of those camps, I'd advise you to hit the trail. (JB)

**Additional Credits:** Writer: Dave Detiege. Music: George Stoll, Robert Van Eps. Songs: Phil Bounds, Dale Robertson, George Bruns, Mel Henke. Animation: Morris Gollub, Ken Hultgren, Don Towsley, Don Lusk, John Sparey, Ed Friedman, Amby Paliwoda, Harry Holt, Stan Green, John Dunn, Walt Clinton, Gil Turner, Ben Washam, George Rowley.

## The Many Adventures of Winnie the Pooh

(3/11/77) Disney. 74 mins. Directors: Wolfgang Reitherman, John Lounsbery. Producer: Wolfgang Reitherman. Voices: Sebastian Cabot (Narrator), Sterling Holloway (Winnie the Pooh), Paul Winchell (Tigger), Junius Matthews (Rabbit), John Fiedler (Piglet), Ralph Wright (Eeyore), Barbara Luddy (Kanga), Hal Smith (Owl), Howard Morris (Gopher), Clint Howard (Roo), Bruce Reitherman (Christopher Robin).

©Walt Disney Productions

**Consumer Tips:** ☆☆☆ MPAA Rating: G. Based on the books *Winnie the Pooh* and *The House at Pooh Corner* by A. A. Milne.

**Story:** Pooh tries to get honey from a beehive, has a blustery day, and meets the irrepressible Tigger. This film is made up of three *Pooh* featurettes with 10 minutes of new animation.

**Comments:** It has been said that Winnie the Pooh's rise in popularity began with the release of this feature, *The Many Adventures of Winnie the Pooh.* This resulted in Pooh becoming Disney's second most licensed character in its stable, behind Mickey Mouse.

Walt Disney originally optioned the rights to make an animated film of Winnie the Pooh in 1961. The first film produced, "Winnie the Pooh and the Honey Tree" (1966), was the last animated short produced by Walt Disney before he died. The second film, "Winnie the Pooh and the Blustery Day" (1968), won an Academy Award for Best Cartoon Short. And the third, "Winnie the Pooh and Tigger Too" (1974), was a big hit and also nominated for an Oscar.

*The Many Adventures of Winnie the Pooh* is a feature-length compilation of these first three short subjects, bridged by bits of new animation by Disney's new guard. These young animators included Don Bluth, Gary Goldman, and John Pomeroy.

One of the new segments at the end of the film depicts the parting of Christopher Robin and Pooh. It is based on the final chapter in *The House at Pooh Corner.* Despite that scene being the final one in the story, this film would be followed by numerous *Winnie the Pooh* television episodes, theatrical shorts, direct-to-video features, and further theatrical movies in the years to come. (JB)

**Additional Credits:** Story: Larry Clemmons, Vance Gerry, Ken Anderson, Ted Berman, Ralph Wright, Xavier Atencio, Julius Svendsen, Eric Cleworth. "Blustery Day" story supervisor: Winston Hibler. Music/lyrics: Richard M. Sherman, Robert B. Sherman. Animators: Hal King, Milt Kahl, Ollie Johnston, Art Stevens, Cliff Nordberg, Eric Larson, Gary Goldman, Burny Mattinson, John Pomeroy, Chuck Williams, Richard Sebast, John Lounsbery, Frank Thomas, Eric Cleworth, John Sibley, Don Bluth, Walt Stanchfield, Hal Ambro, Dale Baer, Fred Hellmich, Bill Keil, Andrew Gaskill. Layout artists: Don Griffith, Basil Davidovich, Dale Barnhart, Joe Hale, Sylvia Roemer. Background artists: Al Dempster, Art Riley, Bill Layne, Ann Guenther.

**Megazone 23, Part One** (2/2/94) Streamline Pictures (Japan). 80 mins. Director: Noburu Ishiguro. Voices: Masato Kubota (Shôgo Yahagi), Mîna Tominaga (Tomomi Murashita), Mayumi Shô (Mai Yumekanô), Kaneto Shiozawa (B. D.), Hitoshi Takagi (Coco), Kiyoshi Kobayashi (Eigen Yumekanô), Yûji Mitsuya (Môrii), Katsumi Toriumi (Chonbo).

**Consumer Tips:** ☆☆☆ MPAA Rating: Unrated. SF adventure. A teenage biker in modern (1980s) Tokyo gets involved in a government conspiracy and learns that Tokyo is really an artificial satellite fleeing a world-destroying menace 500 years in the future.

**Story:** Shogo Yahagi is a carefree older teen hanging out with his biker pals and crusing for girls. His accidental acquisition of a military prototype motorcycle with incredible abilities gets him marked for assassination by government agents for knowing too much, but his use of the super-cycle saves him. The cycle leads him to an unsuspected giant computer underneath Tokyo, where he discovers that he is really in a giant artificial satellite circling a war-destroyed earth, and that the automated weapons that killed everyone on earth are closing in.

**Comments:** *Megazone 23, Part I* is an anime landmark that is still well worth watching. It was the first direct-to-video anime to become a big hit, and confirmed the new Original Anime Video (OAV) market as a viable alternative to the theatrical and television markets for the animation industry. Produced by the Artland and Artmic animation studios, it was released to video on March 5, 1985, and theatrically on March 23. It had popular music (one of the main characters, Eve Tokimaturi, is an idol singer who is revealed to be an A.I. simulation created by the Bahamut super-computer) and attractive character design by Haruhiko Mikimoto, the designer of the then mega-popular Macross characters. It took advantage of the OAV market's freedom from television censorship to include adult themes. Shogo and his girlfriend Yui are clearly sleeping together, and she sees nothing wrong with sleeping with producers to break into show business. It is full of genuine consumer products to create a startling verisimitude: cans of Coca-Cola and Heineken beer, packs of Camel and Lucky Strike cigarettes, Suzuki cycles, and a McDonald's. The government's "men in black" assassins are shown as more realistically ruthless than was common for animation at the time (comparable to violent live-action adult movies).

*Megazone 23, Part 1* ends on a cliffhanger because the story is too long for a single movie. Its success led to the story's completion a year later in *Megazone 23, Part 2*. The movie's visual similarity to *Macross* due to the character design by Mikimoto led to its adaptation in America as the little-seen *Robotech: The Movie* in 1986. (FP)

**Comments:** Screenplay: Hiroyuki Hoshiyama. Animation director and character designer: Toshihiro Hirano. Cinematography: Kenichi Yoshizaka. Art direction: Mitsuki Nakamura. Color key: Hiromi Anzai. Sound director: Yasunori Honda. Animators: Kiyotoshi Aoi, Yoshiharu Fukushima, Yoko Kadokami, Narumi Kakinouchi, Hiroyuki Kitazume, Toru Miyoshi, Sadami Morikawa, Hiroaki Okami, Haruhiko Sato, Hideaki Shimada, Yasuomi Umetsu, Masahito Yamashita, Nobuteru Yuuki.

## Megazone 23, Part Two (Tell Me the Secret)

(2/2/94) Streamline Pictures. 85 mins. Director: Ichirô Itano. Producer: Toru Miura. Voices: Vic Mignogna (Shougo Yahagi), Alison Shipp (Yui Takanaka), Phil Ross (Admiral), Kurt Stoll (Morley), John Swasey (Coco), John Tyson (Eigen), Mike Vance (Nakao).

**Consumer Tips:** ☆☆ MPAA Rating: Unrated. SF adventure. The sequel to *Megazone 23, Part I*. A biker gang rebels against an oppressive police-state government while automated weapons from a forgotten war threaten all humanity.

**Story:** Shogo Yahagi and his girlfriend Yui Takanaka have sought refuge with a biker gang to escape the military government imposed by Colonel B. D., while the military is preparing to defend Tokyo (*Megazone 23*) from the automated doomsday weapons that destroyed earth 500 years ago. Shogo is told by the Bahamut super-computer that it is ready to return humanity to the restored earth, if he can protect it from B. D.'s computer technicians that are trying to gain control of its programming.

**Comments:** This completion of the story begun in *Megazone 23, Part I* appeared a year later in Japan. It was given a limited theatrical release on April 26, 1986, and its main OAV release on May 30. It is so different from *Part I* as to suggest that its producers did not really expect *Part I* to be successful, and had to assemble a new creative team to finish the story.

The most obvious difference is a totally different character design by Yasuomi Umetsu that completely changes the appearance of the main cast (except for Eve Tokimaturi, the idol singer; the credits make a point of noting that Haruhiko Mikimoto's character design for her has been retained). The story emphasis is on a new subplot pitting Shogo and the Hells' Angels-like "Trash" biker gang (not his biker friends in the first movie) against Tokyo's Police Department, which has been turned into a repressive military force under Lieutenant Shiratori, B. D.'s civilian deputy who is a fanatical law and order martinet. B. D.'s attention has been diverted from Shogo by his need to supervise the defense of Megazone 23 against the automated weapons that destroyed earth 500 years ago and which are finally breaking through the Megazone's defenses. These two plots are practically two separate stories for the first half of the movie. Then the climax happens so fast that the movie ends as a confused jumble. The fadeout shows Shogo and Yui looking out over an Edenic earth, and being joined by their Trash friends who only have flesh wounds rather than the fatal wounds seen in the previous action sequences.

*Megazone 23, Part II* is action packed, but most of the action consists of the battles between the clownishly costumed and punk-hairstyled bikers (with names like Rakko, Guts, Garam, and Dumpi) against the professionally militaristic police. The movie emphasizes an anarchistic good-buddy brotherhood among the bikers, which might make them sympathetic towards Shogo and Yui but does not convincingly justify their willingness to die in suicidal charges (which are negated by the movie's fadeout) against the police so Shogo can get back his motorcycle and see Eve. *Part II* is so different from *Part I* that it does not really feel like a conclusion of the same story.

In 1989, a two-part *Megazone 23, Part 3* was produced in Japan as an OAV release that was never released theatrically. It is set over 1,000 years later and is an unnecessary sequel to the original story. (FP)

**Additional Credits:** Screenplay: Hiroyuki Hoshiyama. Animation designer: Yasuomi Umetsu. Mechanical designer: Shinji Aramaki. Cinematography: Kenichi Yoshizaka. Art direction: Mitsuki Nakamura. Color key: Hiromi Anzai. Sound director: Yasunori Honda. Animators: Kiyotoshi Aoi, Yoshiharu Fukushima, Yoko Kadokami, Narumi Kakinouchi, Hiroyuki Kitazume, Toru Miyoshi, Sadami Morikawa, Hiroaki Okami, Haruhiko Sato, Hideaki Shimada, Yasuomi Umetsu, Masahito Yamashita, Nobuteru Yuuki.

**Melody Time** (5/27/48) Walt Disney Pictures. 75 mins. Directors: Clyde Geronimi, Wilfred Jackson, Jack Kinney, Hamilton Luske. Voices: Pinto Colvig (Aracuan Bird), Buddy Clark (Master of Ceremonies). Live actors/musicians: Ethel Smith, Luana Patten, Bobby Driscoll, Roy Rogers, Trigger, Bob Nolan and the Sons of the Pioneers, Frances Langford, Fred War-

©Walt Disney Productions

ing and his Pennsylvanians, Freddy Martin and his Orchestra, Dennis Day, the Andrews Sisters.

**Consumer Tips:** ☆☆ MPAA Rating: Unrated. Odds and ends from a studio gearing up for revival.

**Story:** *Melody Time* is a compilation of seven short animated features: "Once Upon a Wintertime," "Bumble Boogie," "Johnny Appleseed," "Little Toot," "Trees," "Blame it on the Samba," and "Pecos Bill."

**Comments:** *Melody Time* was the last of Disney's postwar anthology features, and by this time the formula was tired. Less than half the shorts are of any interest, and one can almost feel the animators pushing for something more creative to do. Like its earlier counterpart, *Make Mine Music*, much of the film feels dated today, such as the live segment with Roy Rogers and the Sons of the Pioneers. It is difficult to watch this film and recall that these were the same great artists and animators who produced *Pinocchio* only eight years before. While *Melody Time* has a few good visual moments, it must be considered a vast underachievement by the Disney studio.

Of note are the exceptional designs and palettes of Mary Blair, Disney's star stylist. Her work is especially evident in the "Wintertime" and "Johnny Appleseed" segments. The former short features flat, stylized backgrounds while the look of the latter is adapted from both Impressionist painting and the folk art of Grandma Moses. Look past the animated characters for the true treat. Ward Kimball's broad, slapstick treatment of the Pecos Bill legend is worth a look for the impressive montage of Bill's legendary feats.

"Bumble Boogie," in which a tiny bee is terrorized by musical symbols and instruments come to life, is Disney's best piece of surrealism since the "Pink Elephants on Parade" sequence in *Dumbo*. Watch the bee change colors and outlines from one moment to the next as the backgrounds seamlessly dissolve, change, or morph around him, all in time to Jack Fina's manic interpretation of *Flight of the Bumblebee*.

The only other fun to be found is watching Donald Duck, Jose Carioca, and the Aracuan Bird reprise their roles from *The Three Caballeros* in "Blame it on the Samba." The short is part live action and features Ethel Smith on the organ. While Donald and Jose dance away, the Aracuan Bird (winningly animated by Eric Larson) plays tricks on the poor organist, at one point blowing her instrument up with dynamite. Ub Iwerks turned in his usual stellar special effects for this sequence. The rest of *Melody Time*, sad to say, is rather forgettable.

For the record:

- What you can get away with: Ward Kimball snuck a risqué joke into "Pecos Bill" under Walt Disney's nose; when Pecos Bill kisses Slue Foot Sue his guns rise straight up from their holsters and start firing by themselves. (Perhaps Roy Rogers was covering the eyes of Bobby Driscoll and Luana Patten during this scene.)

- What you can't get away with: in the original film Pecos Bill lights up a cigarette by using a bolt of lightning; the scene is still missing, even on the "Gold Collection" DVD. (MG)

**Additional Credits:** Production supervisor: Ben Sharpsteen. Animators: Eric Larson, Ward Kimball, Oliver Johnston, Les Clark, John Lounsberry, Milt Kahl. Story: Winston Hibler, Harry Reeves, Ken Anderson, Erdman Penner, Homer Brightman, Ted Sears, Joe Rinaldi, Art Scott, Bob Moore, Bill Cottrell, Jesse Marsh, John Walbridge. Story "Little Toot": Hardie Gramatky. Musical direction: Eliot Daniel, Ken Darby. Directing animators: Eric Larson, Ward Kimball, Milt Kahl, Oliver M. Johnston Jr., John Lounsbery, Les Clark. Animation: Harvey Toombs, Ed Aardal, Cliff Nordberg, John Sibley, Ken O'Brien, Judge Whitaker, Marvin Woodward, Hal King, Don Lusk, Rudy Larriva, Bob Cannon, Hal Ambro. Effects animation: George Rowly, Jack Boyd, Joshua Meador, Hal McManus. Background artists: Art Riley, Brice Mack, Ralph Hulett, Ray Huffine, Merle Cox, Dick Anthony. Uncredited backgrounds: Berk Anthony, John Hench. Layout artists: Hugh Hennesy, A. Kendall O'Connor, Al Zinnen, Don Griffith, McLaren Stewart, Lance Nolley, Robert Cormack, Thor Putnam, Donald DaGradi. Color/styling: Mary Blair, Claude Coats, Dick Kelsey.

**Metamorphoses** (5/3/78) Sanrio (U.S.-Japan). 89 mins. Director: Takashi. Producers: Terry Ogisu, Hrio Tsugawa, Takashi. Voices: Norman Corwin (Narrator), Peter Ustinov (Narrator).

**Consumer Tips:** ☆☆ MPAA Rating: PG. Musical fantasy. Five Greco-Roman myths from the *Metamor-*

©Sanrio Communications, Inc.

*phoses* by Ovid are integrated into one wordless musical storyline, unified by the same boy and girl who represent all humanity.

**Story:** In this attempt to create a modern, rock-music version of *Fantasia*, five ancient tales of humans and gods as written into literary form by the Roman poet Ovid are presented with the same allegorical young boy and girl playing the main characters. The five are "Actaeon," "Orpheus and Eurydice," "The House of Envy," "Perseus," and "Phaethon."

**Comments:** In the late 1970s, the Japanese gift company Sanrio Ltd. (best known in America for its "Hello Kitty" character) announced that, with the decline of the Disney studio following Walt Disney's death, it would enter the American theatrical animated film business. Sanrio produced two features in America for American release, *Metamorphoses* and *The Mouse and His Child*, and distributed in America the stop-motion *Nutcracker Fantasy* produced in Japan, before withdrawing. Some Sanrio theatrical features produced in Japan in the early 1980s were shown on television and released to home video in America.

*Metamorphoses* could easily be mistaken as a parody of elitist, intellectual "thea-tah" at its most high brow. It was intended to be a modern *Fantasia* with all-original symphonic rock-music performances by such prestigious popular composers as Joan Baez, Mick Jagger and the Rolling Stones, and the Pointer Sisters. A studio was assembled in Hollywood and staffed with over

170 veteran animators, who spent three years producing its lush full animation for 70mm release.

*Metamorphoses* closed almost immediately after its premiere. In addition to the bad reviews, many of its animators claimed that they had pointed out problems with the film during production and were ignored. The music was written first with no guidelines to the composers except length, and much of it is inappropriate to the mood of the scenarios. The action is all in pantomime, and some of it is not clear enough for audiences to follow the story. Some viewers were confused by the constant reappearances of the boy and girl as the lead characters—the same in appearance but in changing roles. And some just did not enjoy the basic tales that expose the capriciousness and casual cruelty of the gods.

*Metamorphoses* was withdrawn, recut to 82 minutes, and rereleased a year later in May 1979 retitled *Winds of Change* (other titles this film was released under were *Star of Orpheus* and *Orpheus of the Stars*). The original deafening music is replaced by a score by Alec R. Costandinos as background to a new "hip" voiceover narration (written by Norman Corwin and performed by Peter Ustinov), which makes fun of the action as much as it explains it. The order of the sequences is now Perseus, Actaeon, Envy, Orpheus, and Phaethon. The boy is now named Wondermaker, the girl is identified as the different girls in the separate myths, and a couple of the gods reverse their Greek and Roman names; Hades is called Pluto and Apollo is called Helios. It does not help much. (FP)

**Additional Credits:** Story: Takashi. Based on Ovid's *Metamorphoses*. Music: Bob Randles. Sequence directors: Jerry Eisenberg, Richard Huebner, Sadao Miyamoto, Amby Paliwoda, Ray Patterson, Manny Perez, George Singer, Stan Walsh. Animators: Edwin Aardal, John Ahern, Mikaharu Akabori, Robert Carlson, Brad Case, Marija Dail, Edward DeMattia, Joan Drake, Edgar Friedman, Edwardo Fuentes, Morris Gollub, Fred Grable, Masami Hata, Fred Hellmich, Ernesto Lopez, Daniel Noonan, Ken O'Brian, Jack Ozark, William Pratt, Thomas Ray, Virgil Ross, Glenn Schmitz, Martha Swanson, Reuben Timmins, James Walker, John Walker, Shigeru Yamamoto, Rudolfo Zamora. Visual effects: Elrene Cowan. Production designers: Paul Julian, Ray Aragon, Kuni Fukai, Rebecca Ortega Mills, Akira Uno. Layout artist: Michael G. Ploog. Background artist: Ron Dias.

**Metropolis** (1/25/02) TriStar (Japan). 107 mins. Director: Rintaro. Producers: Yutaka Maseba, Tasao Maruyama, Iwao Yamaki. Voices: Rebecca Forstadt (Tima), Brianne Siddall (Kenichi, Fifi), Michael Reisz (Rock), Jamieson K. Price (Duke Red), Tony Pope (Shunsaku Ban), Dave Mallow (Pero), Simon Prescott (Dr. Laughton), Doug Stone (Dr. Ponkotsu), Steve McGowan (President Boon), William Knight (Notarlin), Dan Woren (Skunk), Steve Blum (Lamp), Robert Axelrod (Ham and Egg), Peter Spellos (Mayor Lyon), Scott Weinger (Atlas), Barbara Goodson (Enmy).

©Tri Star Pictures

**Consumer Tips:** ☆☆☆☆ MPAA Rating: PG-13. SF drama.

**Story:** A detective and his young nephew come to Metropolis, the most powerful city in the future, searching for a criminal scientist. They become mired in a complex social situation involving a magnate's attempt to control the economy of the world and Metropolis's government, the president's attempt to sabotage the magnate's political power, a class struggle between humans and robot workers, and a young girl who is unknowingly a super-powerful but dangerously unstable robot.

**Comments:** Osamu Tezuka (1928–1989) was a leader in creating Japan's comic book industry in the 1940s and '50s and animation industry in the 1950s and '60s. One of his first major works was *Metropolis* (1949), a cartoon novel inspired by the 1926 German SF movie but with an original story. This animated feature, produced by Madhouse and released in Japan on May 26,

2001, was produced as a tribute to him, written and directed by two of Japan's currently most prestigious animation directors and writers. It retains Tezuka's American 1920s/'30s animation art style and has music in the style of period American jazz and swing, but is in spectacular color and displays cutting-edge cel and CGI animation technology.

Tezuka was well-known for using the same characters in almost all of his cartoon works, as though they were actors playing different roles. This technique is featured in *Metropolis*. Ban is usually called Higeoyaji (Old Man Moustache), known as Mr. Pompus in *Astro Boy* and *Kimba the White Lion*. Pero appeared as a tragic robot in *Astro Boy*. Some minor characters recognizable to fans of Tezuka's work include the supervisor of Metropolis' power and sewage zones (Hamegg), Boone's political advisor (Acetylene Lamp), and the General of Metropolis' military forces (Skunk). (FP)

**Additional Credits:** Screenplay: Katsuhiro Otomo. English dubbing script (uncredited): Marc Handler, Mary Elizabeth McGlynn. Based on the manga by Osamu Tezuka. Music: Toshiyuki Honda. Character design/chief key animation supervisor: Yasuhrio Nakura. Animation supervisors: Shigeo Akahori, Kunihiko Sakurai, Shigeru Fujita. Assistant animation supervisors: Shigeto Tsuji, Toshio Hirata. Animators: Kazuo Komatsubaro, Kumiko Kawana, Norimoto Tokura, Manuba Ohashi, Yasushi Muraki, Masami Ozone, Tetsuro Kaku, Mahiro Ando, Takuo Noda, Nobumasa Shinkawa, Masanaru Tada, Hiromi Nioka, Shinji Hashimoto, Katsuay Yamada, Hiroshi Oikawa, Hitoshi Ueda, Kaichi Honma, Tsutoma Awada, Masaaki Endo, Hiroshi Shimizu, El Inue, Shinsaku Saaki, Satoshi Iriyoshi, Morifumi Naka, Shigeto Tsuji, Kunihiko Namada, Masaru Kitao, Kahoru Hirata, Hiroyuki Kasugai, Toshiya Nidome, Yasuhiro Endo, Kazuhiko Udagawa, Hiroshi Wagatsuma, Takashi Saijou, Jyuji Mizumura, Akira Watanabe, Masateru Yoshimura, Hiroshi Uchida, Masayoshi Nishida, Atsuya Mura, Miyuki Katayama, Mieko Hosoi, Yuko Iwaso, Hiroki Kawasoe, Seiji Tanda, Hiroyuki Okura, Hiroshi Hamasaki, Hirotsugo Kawasaki, Yutaka Minowa, Kitaro Kousaka, Yoshiaki Kawajii, Shigero Fujita, Shigeo Akahori, Hiromitsu Morita, Toshio Hirata, Yoshinori Kana. Art director/CGI art director: Shuichi Hirata. CGI technical director: Tsuneo Maeda. Storyboard artist: Katsuhiro Otomo.

## A Midsummer Night's Dream (12/18/61) Showcorporation (Czech). 74 mins. Director: Jiri Trnka. Producers: Erna Kmínkovç, Jaroslav Mozis. Voices: Richard Burton (Narrator), Jack Gwillim (Oberon), Barbara Jefford (Titania), Roger Shepherd (Puck), Michael Meacham (Demetrius), Tom Criddle (Lysander), Anne Bell (Hermia), Barbara Leigh-Hunt (Helena), Alec McCowen (Bottom), Hugh Manning (Theseus), Joss Ackland (Quince), Laura Graham (Hippolyta), Stephen Moore (Flute), John Warner (Egeus).

**Consumer Tips:** ☆☆☆ MPAA Rating: Unrated. Based on the play by William Shakespeare.

**Story:** Shakespeare's play enacted by stop-motion puppets.

**Comments:** Jiri Trnka's *A Midsummer Night's Dream* is a marvelous blend of color, music, and artistry, and is a unique experience for theater and Shakespeare buffs, as well as animation enthusiasts.

Trnka, the great Czech artist and stop-motion animator, had long desired to make a feature film of *A Midsummer Night's Dream*. His goal, beyond making the film with animated puppets, was to make a silent film, eliminating all of Shakespeare's dialogue from his senario. He invented pantomime cheoreography to convey the thoughts and actions of the performers.

Filmed in Cinemascope, *A Midsummer Night's Dream* was released in Czechoslovakia in 1959. It won the Cannes Festival Grand Prix prize that year. Unfortunately, that version of the film never came to the United States.

Playwright Howard Sackler was recruited to help make this art film more saleable in the United States and in other English-speaking countries. To this end, Shakespeare's dialogue was added to the soundtrack, and the film was cut to 74 minutes. An English voice cast was recruited from London's Old Vic repertory theater, all except Richard Burton. He recorded his lines in New York between performances in *Camelot*, in which he was currently starring on Broadway.

The film was showcased at special reserved seat performances in the big cities around the country, and was included in *Time* magazine's Annual Ten Best List in 1961, under foreign films. (JB)

**Additional Credits:** Story: Jiri Trnka, Jiri Brdecka, Josef Kainar, Howard Sackler. Based on the play by William Shakespeare. Text direction/adaption: Howard Sackler. Dialogue production supervisor: Len Appelson. Music composer/conductor: Vaclav Trojan. Art direction: Jiri Trnka. Choreography: Ladislaw Fialka. Cinematographer: Jiri Vojta. Editor: Armond Lebowitz. Art director: Albert Brenner. Scultures: Jaroslav Kulhanek. Costumes: Karinska. Animation: Jan Adams, Vlasta Jurajdovç, Jan Karpas, Stanislav Lçtal, Bretislav Pojar, Bohuslav Srçmek.

**Millennium Actress** (9/12/03) Go Fish Pictures (DreamWorks). 87 mins. Director: Satoshi Kon. Producer: Taro Maki. Voices: Miyoko Shôji (Chiyoko Fujiwara, 70s), Mami Koyama (Chiyoko Fujiwara, 20–40s), Fumiko Orikasa (Chiyoko Fujiwara, 10–20s), Shôzô Îzuka (Genya Tachibana), Shouko Tsuda (Eiko Shimao), Hirotaka Suzuoki (Junichi Ootaki), Hisako Kyôda (Mother), Kan Tokumaru (Senior Manager of Ginei), Tomie Kataoka (Mino), Masamichi Sato (Genya), Masaya Onosaka (Kyoji Ida).

©Go Fish Pictures

**Consumer Tips:** ☆☆☆☆ MPAA Rating: PG. Romantic melodrama.

**Story:** Genya Tachibana, a documentary filmmaker, is hired to make a biography of Chiyoko Fujiwara, a legendary movie star from the late 1930s to the 1960s, but a recluse since then. Fujiwara surprisingly allows herself to be personally interviewed. She is such a vivid conversationalist that Tachibana and his cameraman are drawn into her memories as she relives her greatest roles as well as her personal life.

**Comments:** Writer/director Satoshi Kon's second feature is structurally similar to James Cameron's *Titanic*.

An elderly woman reminisces about her past so vividly that her listeners are drawn along with her into a story in which the historical events are background to her tragic romance. Chiyoko's big roles are in obvious pastiches of Japan's major theatrical features from the late 1930s to the late 1960s, so *Millennium Actress* also serves as a fictionalized history of the Japanese cinematic industry from its co-option by the military government on the eve of World War II to make propaganda films to its evolution into a major producer of domestic and international features by the early 1970s.

The major difference is that middle-aged Tachibana and his wiseguy young cameraman, Kyoji Ida, find themselves literally alongside Chiyoko in her past. They are buffeted by the crowds in crowd scenes; they have to leap out of the way of galloping horses in samurai dramas; sometimes they find themselves as extras in her movies. It is gradually revealed that Tachibana began his career as an assistant at Chiyoko's studio just before her final films, and that he hero-worshipped her then and still does. Although he is embarrassed about prying, he hopes to learn why she unexpectedly retired thirty years earlier. Chiyoko's story leads through films recognizable as pastiches of Japan's greatest movies from *Throne of Blood* to *Godzilla*; from the movie industry's devastation at the end of World War II to its slow regrowth.

*Millennium Actress* (*Sennen Joyu*), animated at the Madhouse studio, was not generally released in Japan until September 14, 2002, almost a year after it began winning awards at international film festivals around the world. It was the first American release for DreamWorks's Go Fish Pictures, a specialized art film distribution division. In limited release, its U.S. box-office gross was a mere $37,285. (FP)

**Additional Credits:** Writers: Satoshi Kon, Sadayuki Murai. Original music: Susumu Hirasawa. Cinematography: Hisao Shirai. Editor: Satoshi Terauchi. Art director: Nobutaka Ike. Sound director: Masafumi Mima.

**Monsters, Inc.** (11/2/01) Disney-Pixar. 92 mins. Director: Peter Docter. Codirectors: Lee Unkrich, David Silverman. Producer: Darla K. Anderson. Voices: John Goodman (James P. "Sulley" Sullivan), Billy Crystal (Mike Wazowski), Mary Gibbs (Boo), Steve

©Disney / Pixar

Buscemi (Randall Boggs), James Coburn (Henry J. Waternoose), Jennifer Tilly (Celia), Bob Peterson (Roz), John Ratzenberger (Yeti), Frank Oz (Fungus), Daniel Gerson (Needleman, Smitty), Steve Susskind (Floor Manager), Bonnie Hunt (Flint), Jeff Pidgeon (Bile), Sam Black (George).

**Consumer Tips:** ☆☆☆½ MPAA Rating G. Comedy-adventure. According to a disclaimer, "No monsters were harmed in the making of this movie."

**Story:** In Monstropolis, the local power plant, Monsters, Inc., generates power by scaring children in our dimension. When a little girl named Mary (nicknamed "Boo") wanders into their world, she is befriended by two blue-collar scare-inducers, James P. "Sully" Sullivan (a furry blue beast) and Mike Wazowski (a wisecracking eyeball). Together they unravel a mysterious plot and return the girl to her bedroom while trying to hide her from the other monsters.

**Comments:** Fantastic family entertainment that doesn't condescend.

With each release, Pixar's reputation as purveyor of high-quality animation and solid storytelling continues to grow. The CG studio's fourth motion picture skewed younger but grossed higher than its predecessors. The film's opening day was the biggest debut for an animated film, at $62,577,067. *Monsters, Inc.* eventually earned a U.S. box-office gross of $255,745,941. Not bad for a film budgeted at around $115 million in an era when traditional animation studio executives were blaming artists for escalating production costs. (By contrast, *The Iron Giant* cost around $48 million.)

*Monsters, Inc.* has charm, spectacle, and heart. Its eye-popping visuals, innovative character animation, and attention to detail have always distiguished Pixar's product from its competitors'. Note the references to stop-motion animator Ray Harryhausen in the film (in the restaurant sequence) and the homage to the classic 1952 Chuck Jones cartoon, *Feed the Kitty* (in the scenes where Scully thinks he has lost Boo in a garbage compressor).

Pixar made a special trailer that played in front of *Harry Potter and the Sorcerer's Stone*, which was in simultaneous release with *Monsters*. Mike and Sulley played a game of charades, calling attention to *Potter* and then to themselves, noting that *Monsters, Inc.* is "Now playing at a theater near you—really, really near you—like, right next door." Another draw to *Monsters* was the exclusive trailer to *Star Wars Episode IV: The Phantom Menace*.

Although it lost out to *Shrek* the first year Oscars were given to Best Animated Feature, *Monsters, Inc.* won three Academy Awards: Best Music, Best Original Score and Original Song (Randy Newman for "If I Didn't Have You"), and Best Sound Effects Editing (Gary Rydstrom and Michael Silvers). It also won a prize in the 2002 ASCAP Film and Television Music Awards, an Annie Award for Outstanding Character Animation, and a BAFTA Childrens' Award for Best Feature Film.

For the record:

- Here's an example of the integrity of executive producer John Lasseter. In 2003, when *Monsters, Inc.* was eligible for the Annie Awards, Lasseter arranged for Hayao Miyazaki's *Spirited Away* to be entered, even though it would compete against his own film. *Spirited Away* won four major Annies that year. (WRM)

**Additional Credits:** Executive producers: John Lasseter, Andrew Stanton. Screenplay: Andrew Stanton, Daniel Gerson. Additional screenplay material: Robert Baird, Rhett Reese, Jonathan Roberts. Original story: Pete Docter, Jill Culton, Jeff Pidgeon, Ralph Eggleston. Music: Randy Newman. Supervising animators: Glenn McQueen, Rich Quade. Directing animators:

Doug Sweetland, Scott Clark. Animators: Kyle Balda, Alan Barillaro, Stephen Barnes, Bobby Beck, Michael Berenstein, Dylan Brown, Brett Coderre, Tim Crawfurd, Ricardo Curtis, Dave DeVan, Doug Dooley, Ike Feldman, Andrew Gordon, Stephen Gregory, Jimmy Hayward, John Kahrs, Nancy Kato, Karen Kiser, Shawn P. Krause, Wendell Lee, Angus MacLane, Dan Mason, Amy McNamara, Jon Mead, Billy Merritt, Dave Mullins, James Ford Murphy, Peter Nash, Victor Navone, Bret Parker, Michael Parks, Sanjay Patel, Bobby Podesta, Jeff Pratt, Bret Pulliam, Roger Rose, Robert H. Russ, Gini Cruz Santos, Andy Schmidt, Alan Sperling, Patty Kihm Stevenson, Ross Stevenson, David Tart, J. Warren Trezevant, Mike Venturini, Tasha Weeden, Adam Wood, Kureha Yokoo, Ron Zorman. Fix animator: Paul Mendoza. Main titles design/animation director: GeeFwee Boedoe. Main title animator: Patrick Siemer. Art directors: Tia W. Kratter, Dominique Louis. Story supervisor: Bob Peterson. Additional story material by Peterson, David Silverman, Joe Ranft. Development story supervisor: Jill Culton. Story artists: Max Brace, Jim Capobianco, David Fulp, Rob Gibbs, Jason Katz, Bud Luckey, Matthew Luhn, Ted Mathot, Ken Mitchroney, Sanjay Patel, Jeff Pidgeon, Joe Ranft, Bob Scott, David Skelly, Nathan Stanton. Additional storyboarding: GeeFwee Boedoe, Joseph "Rocket" Ekers, Jorgen Klubien, Angus MacLane, Ricky Vega Nierva, Floyd Norman, Jan Pinkava. Layout supervisor: Ewan Johnson. Lead layout artist: Patrick Lin. Senior layout artist: Craig Good. Layouts: Robert Anderson, Cortney Armitage, Louis Gonzales, Sungyeon Joh Jongo, Jeremy Lasky, Mark Sanford, Gabriel Schlumberger, Shin Yun, Sylvia Wong. Sequence supervisors: Steve May, Mark T. Henne, Guido Quaroni, Michael Lorenzen, Jack Paulus, Brad Winemiller. Character design: Ricky Vega Nierva. Additional character design: Bob Pauley, Dan Lee. Visual development: GeeFwee Boedoe, Ralph Eggleston, Ricky Vega Nierva, Jill Culton, Lou Romano, Nicolas Marlet, Carter Goodrich, Peter de Seve, Dave Gordon, Oscar Grillo, Kevin Hawkes, Bud Luckey, J. Otto Seibold, Lane Smith, Chris Ure.

**The Mouse and His Child** (5/24/78) Sanrio. 83 mins. Directors: Fred Wolf, Charles Swenson. Producer: Walt deFaria. Voices: Peter Ustinov (Manny), Cloris Leachman (Eutrepe), Sally Kellerman (Seal), Andy Devine (Frog), Alan Barman (Mouse), Marcy Swenson (Mouse Child), Neville Brand (Iggy), Regis Cordic (Clock, Hawk), Joan Gerber (Elephant), Mel Leven (The Paper People), John Carradine (The Tramp).

**Consumer Tips:** ☆☆ MPAA Rating: G.

©deFaria / Lockhart / Sanrio Productions

**Story:** A windup toy mouse and his child, cast from an elegant toy store into the street, try to become self-winding and self-reliant. They experience many adventures, make friends with a fortune-telling frog, a plush pink elephant, and a tin seal, and find an enemy in Manny Rat.

**Comments:** This animated film is based on a novel by Russell Hoban, a television art director turned children's book author. His novel, *The Extraordinary Adventures of the Mouse and His Child*, was picked up for development by Sanrio, the Japanese gift retailer responsible for the character Hello Kitty and its ubiquitous merchandise.

Sanrio decided to expand into motion pictures in the 1970s—and quickly became a Hollywood player when its experimental release of John Korty's live-action film, *Who Are the De Bolts and Where Did They Get Nineteen Kids*, won an Oscar for Best Documentary.

Producers Walt DeFaria and Warren Lockhart became Sanrio's point men Hollywood. Both had experience with family entertainment properties, particularly with Charles Schulz and various live-action *Peanuts* specials. The pair produced the Emmy- and Peabody-award-winning Hallmark Hall of Fame family special, *The Borrowers* (1973).

Screenwriter Carol Monpere also worked on *The Borrowers*, as script editor. She was an associate producer and cowriter of a number of NBC television specials aimed at children and later went on to write and direct an acclaimed television movie, *Pink Lightning* (1991).

DeFaria and Lockhart contracted with Murakami-Wolf, a well-known independent animation studio in

Hollywood, to develop the Hoban's book into a feature film. Directors Swenson (*Dirty Duck*, 1975) and Wolf (*The Point*, 1971) were cutting-edge animators who were expanding their studio and moving toward more mainstream projects.

With *The Mouse and His Child* they produced an acceptable, but bland, animated feature. It's got moments of brilliance—and large sections of incoherence. There is an uncomfortable feel to the picture caused by the fact that the two leading characters are bound to each other (connected by their hands) like Siamese twins. Kids will not mind and should be able to follow the narrative without too much trouble. The all-star voice cast makes it tolerable for adults.

Though the film was advertised and known as *The Mouse and His Child*, the film's full on-screen title is *The Extraordinary Adventures of the Mouse and His Child*. (SF)

**Additional Credits:** Executive producers: Warren Lockhart, Shintarô Tsuji. Writer: Carol Mon Pere. Music: Roger Kellaway. Lyricist: Gene Lees. Animators: Fred Wolf, Charles Swenson, Dave Brain, Vince Davis, Gary Mooney, Mike Sanger, Lu Guarnier, Willie Pyle, Frank Zamboni. Assistant animators: Brad Frost, Barry Temple. Production design: Vincent Davis, Sam Kirson, Bob Mitchell, Alan Shean.

## Mr. Bug Goes to Town

**Mr. Bug Goes to Town** (12/4/41) Paramount. 77 mins. Director: Dave Fleischer. Producer: Max Fleischer. Voices: Kenny Gardner (Dick Dickens), Gwen Williams (Mary Dickens), Jack Mercer (Mr. Bumble, Swat the Fly), Tedd Pierce (C. Bagley Beetle), Carl Meyer (Smack the Mosquito), Stan Freed (Hoppity), Pauline Loth (Honey Bee), Pinto Colvig (Jeepers Creepers), Margie Hines (Mrs. Ladybug), Mae Questel (Buzz), Guinn "Big Boy" Williams (Narrator), The Four Marshals, The Royal Guards.

**Consumer Tips:** ☆☆☆ MPAA Rating: Unrated. Also known as *Hoppity Goes to Town*.

**Story:** A community of insects, who inhabit the site of a skyscraper under construction, must move.

**Comments:** The Fleischers' second (and final) animated feature, *Mr. Bug Goes to Town* was in many ways derivative of popular live-action romantic comedies of

©Paramount Pictures, Inc.

the period, particularly the Capra films (*Mr. Deeds Goes to Town, Mr. Smith Goes to Washington,* etc.). Even the title proclaims that fact (the film was later renamed *Hoppity Goes to Town*, and has been released on video under that title). The bug village that the film centers around, threatened by human encroachment, is populated by film archetypes. Hoppity is an "Aw shucks" Jimmy Stewart/Gary Cooper type; the villain C. Bagley Beetle is a ruthless business type of the sort played by Edward Arnold (though visually he resembles Gene Lockheart); Honey Bee is a generic debutante, etc.

The simple, folksy love story is often quite charming in the telling, but even at a mere 77 minutes, the movie feels too long at times. The animation is in many ways better than that in *Gulliver's Travels*, without rotoscoping. The urban scenic designs are impressive, though, and a pseudo-Gershwin background score by Leigh Harline is quite engaging. This is in counterpoint to the songs (by future *Flintstones* guest Hoagy Carmichael, Frank Loesser, and resident Fleischer composer Sammy Timberg), which are even more irritatingly infectious than certain Gulliver tunes, particularly the monotonous "Boy Oh Boy." But the film definitely has its moments, and the interplay between Mr. Beetle and his henchmen Smack and Swat (the latter voiced by Jack Mercer in his Felix the Cat tones) is especially fun. The romance is dull, however, and a side-plot involving a struggling human songwriter almost feels like another movie entirely, trying to break out.

Today, *Mr. Bug* is notable mainly for two reasons. One, it was the first animated film to include a voice

Ever since the blockbuster box-office success of *Snow White and the Seven Dwarfs* in 1937, animated features have delighted movie-going audiences of all ages. For the first 30 years, the medium was dominated by Disney and competing animated features were merely considered novelties or Saturday matinee fodder. *Yellow Submarine* (1968) and *Fritz the Cat* (1972) broke the mold and opened the door to new possibilities. The emergence of anime and computer graphics, the revitalization of Disney, plus serious competition from DreamWorks and Don Bluth led to an animated feature boom in the 1990s. Animated features continue to dominate box-office ticket sales today. The following gallery of color stills and promotional materials provides a glimpse into the rich history of the medium and the way these films were marketed to the public.

*The Blue Fairy attends to Pinocchio's dilemma in Disney's second full-length feature,* Pinocchio *(1940).*

©Walt Disney Productions

**GULLIVER'S TRAVELS**

*Paramount's answer to Disney success, Max Fleischer's* Gulliver's Travels *(1939).*

©Fleischer Studios

Some of the first animated films to compete with Disney in the 1950s were from Europe. Johnny the Giant Killer (1953) was from France.

©Jean Image Films

An early stop-motion feature, filmed in New York, Hansel and Gretel (1954).

©Michael Myerberg Productions

The Snow Queen (1959) was produced in Russia. Universal added a live-action prologue starring television host Art Linkletter. Dave Fleischer supervised the English-language production.

©Universal International

The first cel-animated feature to compete with Disney since the 1940s was UPA's 1001 Arabian Nights (1959).

©Columbia Pictures Corp.

1001 Arabian Nights (1959) was a fine example of UPA's groundbreaking design and filmmaking style that defied Disney's school of cartoons. ©Columbia Pictures Corp.

The Wacky World of Mother Goose (1967) was one of several animated features from Rankin-Bass Productions.

©Embassy Pictures Corp.

The first anime features were based on Asian legends and folktales. Still, they had plenty of color, comedy, and action.

Magic Boy (1961) was the very first Japanese animated feature released in the United States—by MGM no less!

©Metro-Goldwyn-Mayer, Inc.

Alakazam the Great (1961) tried to mask its Asian origins with an all-star voice cast.

©American-International, Inc.

Panda and the Magic Serpent (1961) (also known as The White Snake Enchantress) was released in Japan in 1958 and was the first modern Japanese animation film.

©Globe Releasing Corp.

The Little Prince and the Eight-Headed Dragon *(1964) combined a simple yet stylized look with action-packed adventure.*

©Columbia Pictures Corp.

BLAST OFF WITH
GULLIVER
AND HIS FRIENDS—
—To a colorful world
of fantasy and song...

THE PRINCESS

RICKY

PUG

THE KING

THE COLONEL

ALL NEW!
ALL
EXCITING!

THE ROBOT

GULLIVER

WALTER READE-STERLING presents

Gulliver's Travels
Beyond The Moon
in COLOR

Music by MILTON DELUGG · Lyrics by ANNE DELUGG CONTINENTAL

YOU'LL SING THESE 5
GREAT HAPPY SONGS!
"THINK TALL"
"DEEDLE DE DUM"
"GULLIVER'S MARCH"
"SONG
OF THE EARTH"
"ROBOT'S MARCH"
AVAILABLE ON MAINSTREAM RECORDS

Gulliver's Travels Beyond the Moon *(1966) was one of the first Japanese animated features to abandon Asian folktales as subject matter and to update a literary classic as a sci-fi fantasy.*

©Continental Distribution

The 1960s brought a spate of animated features designed to lure kids to Saturday morning movie matinees. New ideas and designs crept into various productions—but the films were still squeaky clean and G-rated.

(Top) Hey There, It's Yogi Bear (1964) was Hanna-Barbera's first full-length feature—and a noble effort to transform the television cartoon icon into a movie star.
©Hanna-Barbera Productions, Inc.

The Man Called Flintstone (1966) brought the Bedrock buddies to the big screen in a secret agent caper.
©Hanna-Barbera Productions, Inc.

The Man from Button Willow (1965) allowed television cowboy star Dale Robertson a chance to get animated in this highly unusual, and dull, comedy adventure. ©United Screen Arts

Pinocchio in Outer Space *(1965) was produced in Belgium and was the creation of producers Norm Prescott (Filmation) and Fred Ladd (Gigantor).* ©Swallow Ltd.

Yellow Submarine *(1968) appealed to all ages thanks to the participation, albeit limited, of the Beatles.* ©Subafilms Ltd.

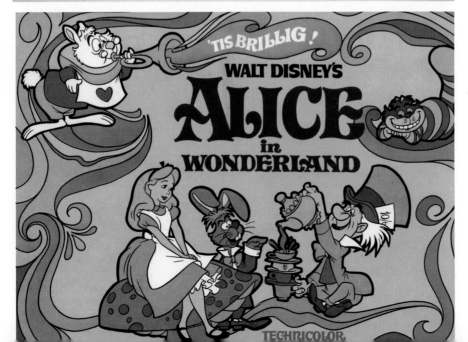

Alice in Wonderland *(1951) was reissued in the late 1960s with this groovy psychedelic ad campaign.* ©Walt Disney Productions

Charles Schulz's comic strip, *Peanuts*, became an overnight sensation after Bill Melendez's first television special, *A Charlie Brown Christmas*, aired in 1965. After a series of successful television specials, a feature-length movie was called for, and Charlie Brown conquered the big screen as well.

Charlie Brown and the 'Peanuts' Gang in their First Movie!

"A Boy Named Charlie Brown"

A LEE MENDELSON · BILL MELENDEZ PRODUCTION Directed by BILL MELENDEZ and Written by CHARLES M. SCHULZ
Produced by LEE MENDELSON and BILL MELENDEZ · Music and Lyrics by ROD McKUEN · Original Music Score by VINCE GUARALDI
Musical Director JOHN SCOTT TROTTER TECHNICOLOR® · A NATIONAL GENERAL PICTURES RELEASE [G] · A CINEMA CENTER FILMS PRESENTATION

*(Top)* A Boy Named Charlie Brown *(1969), the first Peanuts movie, was a huge hit and inspired several sequels.*

©United Features Syndicate

SNOOPY, COME HOME!

INTRODUCING WOODSTOCK THE NEWEST MEMBER OF THE PEANUTS GANG

"Snoopy, Come Home"

A CINEMA CENTER FILMS PRESENTATION
A LEE MENDELSON-BILL MELENDEZ PRODUCTION · CREATED AND WRITTEN BY CHARLES SCHULZ
PRODUCED BY LEE MENDELSON AND BILL MELENDEZ · DIRECTED BY BILL MELENDEZ
MUSIC AND LYRICS BY RICHARD M. AND ROBERT B. SHERMAN · TECHNICOLOR® · A NATIONAL GENERAL PICTURES RELEASE
[G] GENERAL AUDIENCES

7                                                              72/59

Snoopy, Come Home *(1972) put the spotlight on Charlie Brown's dog.*

©United Features Syndicate

Bon Voyage, Charlie Brown (and Don't Come Back) *(1980) was the final theatrical Peanuts feature to date. Unlike the comic strip and television specials, these feature films were aimed exclusively at a children's audience.*

©United Features Syndicate.

Paramount Pictures Presents
A Lee Mendelson-Bill Melendez Production of

BON VOYAGE CHARLIE BROWN (AND DON'T COME BACK!)

Written and Created by Charles M. Schulz  Produced by Lee Mendelson and Bill Melendez  Music by Ed Bogas and Judy Munsen
Directed by Bill Melendez  In Color  A Paramount Release

IT'S
SOPHISTICATED
ENOUGH
FOR KIDS,
SIMPLE
ENOUGH
FOR ADULTS!

carol channing as mehitabel
eddie bracken as archy

sing!
dance!
enchant!
in

SHINBONE ALLEY

THE WONDERFUL REAL ROMANCE OF ARCHY AND MEHITABEL

emanuel l. wolf presents an allied artists film "shinbone alley" • carol channing as mehitabel • eddie bracken is archy • screenplay by joe darion • based on the famous 'archy and mehitabel' stories by don marquis • produced by preston m. fleet • music by george kleinsinger • directed by john d. wilson • color • released by allied artists

G SUGGESTED FOR GENERAL AUDIENCES

(Top) Shinbone Alley (1970) adapted the "Archy and Mehitabel" stories of Don Marquis into a unique animated feature film. ©Allied Arists

© 1974 American International Pictures, Inc.

LITHO. IN U.S.A.

"THE NINE LIVES of FRITZ THE CAT"

74/22

The Nine Lives of Fritz the Cat (1974) was an R-rated sequel to the X-rated blockbuster, sans Ralph Bakshi. Robert Taylor directed. ©American International Pictures, Inc.

It's classic encounters of the funniest kind!

PEPE LE PEW

CHUCK JONES'
THE BUGS BUNNY/
ROAD RUNNER
MOVIE

STARRING BUGS BUNNY • ROAD RUNNER • WILE E. COYOTE
PRODUCED AND DIRECTED BY CHUCK JONES
WRITTEN BY MICHAEL MALTESE AND CHUCK JONES
PRODUCTION DESIGN BY MAURICE NOBLE
VOCAL CHARACTERIZATION BY MEL BLANC

G GENERAL AUDIENCES

RELEASED BY WARNER BROS. INC.
A WARNER COMMUNICATIONS COMPANY

© Copyright 1979 Warner Bros. Inc. All Rights Reserved.

The Bugs Bunny/Road Runner Movie (1979) was a feature-length compilation of old and new Chuck Jones cartoons. Its success paved the way for several other Looney Tunes movies. ©Warner Bros. Inc.

**Ralph Bakshi changed the face of animated features in the 1970s with his X-rated, adult-oriented subject matter and his attempt to animate elaborate sword and sorcery subjects.**

*Ralph Bakshi began his career at the Terrytoons studio in the 1950s and '60s, where he worked his way up the ranks from inker (on Heckle and Jeckle cartoons) to director (on Deputy Dawg) to creator (Sad Cat, The Mighty Heroes).*

©Paramount Pictures Corporation

*(Left) Heavy Traffic (1973) is considered Bakshi's best film. A follow-up to Fritz the Cat, this semi-autobiographical film pulled no punches.*

©American International Pictures, Inc.

*(Bottom left) Coonskin (1975) caused a sensation in preview screenings and prompted Paramount to drop its distribution plans. Small distributor Bryanston eventually released it.* ©Bakshi Productions

*(Bottom right) Coonskin (1975) was an inner-city update of the Uncle Remus tales. Brother Bear (voiced by Barry White) and Brother Rabbit (Phillip Michael Thomas) are now urban gangsters.* ©Bakshi Productions

Wizards (1977) was an original fantasy inspired by Tolkien, Vaughn Bode, and E. C. Comics science fiction.

©20th Century Fox Film Corporation

Lord of the Rings (1978) used the rotoscope to trace live actors—giving the film a realism that wowed critics.

©The Saul Zaentz Production Company

J.R.R. Tolkien's
"the **Lord** of the **Rings**"

DOLBY STEREO    A Fantasy Films Presentation    Released thru United Artists A Transamerica Company    PG

Cool World (1992), Bakshi's last feature, starring Brad Pitt and Kim Basinger, was essentially an R-rated variation on Who Framed Roger Rabbit.

©Paramount Pictures Corporation

The 1980s was a decade of experimentation and rediscovery. New ideas were tried, but most failed. But a return to classic Disney style brought success and a renewed interest in the medium.

TWICE UPON A TIME

A LADD COMPANY RELEASE
THRU WARNER BROS.
A WARNER COMMUNICATIONS COMPANY
8201

*(Top)* Twice Upon a Time *(1983) was an ambitious effort that tried to create a new animated art form using backlit cut-outs. The film was clever and creative—but no one went to see it.*

©Korty Films and The Ladd Company

Heavy Metal *(1981), based on stories from the popular comics magazine, was an R-rated rock 'n' roll cult favorite.*

©Columbia Pictures Industries, Inc.

HEAVY METAL

Rock & Rule *(1985) has won a following despite the best efforts of its distributors to keep it off the market.*

©The Canada Trust Company

ROCK & RULE

CHEAP TRICK    EARTH, WIND & FIRE
DEBBIE HARRY    LOU REED    IGGY POP

The Secret of NIMH (1982) was the first feature film from Disney renegade Don Bluth's own studio. Stunning art and character animation harkened back to Disney's golden age, but the story was disjointed. ©Mrs. Brisby, Ltd.

An American Tail (1986) brought Bluth together with Steven Spielberg. The result: a box-office smash.

©Universal City Studios

Anastasia (1997) was Bluth's biggest film of the 1990s. 20th Century Fox was determined to grab a piece of Disney's market share with this effort—and almost did!

©20th Century-Fox Film Corp.

**Reviving classic cartoon stars of the past and placing them into contemporary feature films is an old Hollywood trick.**

The Chipmunk Adventure (1989) took Alvin, Simon, and Theodore to the big screen and placed them in a colorful adventure.

©Bagdasarian Productions

The Adventures of Rocky and Bullwinkle (2000) combined computer animation, drawn animation, and live action in an ambitious effort to pay homage to the Jay Ward classics.

©Universal City Studios and Dritte Beteiligung KC & Medien AG + Co.KG.

Looney Tunes: Back in Action (2003) had big stars, great animation, and the perfect director—cartoon buff Joe Dante.

©2003 Warner Bros. Entertainment

Beavis and Butt-Head Do America *(1996)*
*was a pleasant surprise. A funny, well-made*
*feature film starring the two slackers from*
*Mike Judge's MTV series.*
©MTV Networks

Finding Nemo *(2003) won an*
*Academy Award for Best Animated*
*Feature.*
©Disney/Pixar

Shrek 2 *(2004) was the highest*
*grossing film of 2004.*
©DreamWorks Animation

Japanese animated films (aka anime) are not only popular with young people and teenagers, but the style of filmmaking has influenced American animators and live-action filmmakers. Hollywood studios were late in recognizing this trend, though nearly every one of them, at this point, has released several anime feature films.

Akira (1989) was the groundbreaking cyberpunk epic that forced mainstream U.S. media to take notice.
©Akira Committee

(Above left) Ghost in the Shell 2: Innocence (2004) is sophisticated and action packed—two traits that make anime appealing to its fan base.
©Shirow-Masamune/Kodansha IG

(Above right) Warriors of the Wind (1984) was the title for the severely cut U.S. version of Hayao Miyazaki's fantasy masterpiece Nausicaä and the Valley of the Wind.
©New World Pictures

(Right) Digimon: The Movie (2000), like the Pokémon and Yu-Gi-Oh movies, was a spin-off of a megasuccessful television series.
©Toei, FFP, FKEP, and FKIP

cast list, comparable to those used in live-action films. These players were mostly in-house folks like Mercer and storymen Carl Meyer and Tedd Pierce (wonderfully oily as Beetle). Singer Kenny Gardner, later to join Guy Lombardo, is featured as the songwriter. The larger distinction is that this was the film that led to the ouster of the Fleischer Brothers due to its poor box office, as Paramount assembled a new studio team headed by Fleischer alums (notably Max's son-in-law Seymour Kneitel), with the studio renamed Famous officially taking over in 1942. Thus *Mr. Bug* in many ways marks the end of an era, for the later Famous shorts, starring Casper, Baby Huey, and the like, were seldom as surreal or inventive, technically and visually, as the classic Boops and Popeyes. Surprisingly, when *Bug's Life* and *Antz* were both hits in 1998, nobody bothered to reissue *Mr. Bug*. (AL)

**Additional Credits:** Story: Dave Fleischer, Dan Gordon, Ted Pierce, Isadore Sparber, William Turner, Carl Meyer, Graham Place, Bob Wickersham, Cal Howard. Music director: Leigh Harline. Music/lyrics: Hoagy Carmichael, Frank Loesser, Sammy Timberg. Directing animators: Willard Bowsky, Myron Waldman, Thomas Johnson, David Tendlar, James Culhane, H. C. Ellison, Stan Quackenbush, Graham Place, Al Eugste. Animation: Bob Wickersham, Abner Kneitel, Irving Spector, Louis Zukor, Nelson Demorest, Harold Walker, Joseph D'Igalo, Sam Stimson, Thomas Golden, Reuben Grossman, Lod Rossner, Gordon Sheehan, Dick Williams, Hal Seeger, Winfield Hoskins, George Waiss, Anthony DiPadla, John Walworth. Scenics: Robert Little, Shane Miller, Hemia Calpini, Eddie Bowlds, Anton Loeb, Robert Connovale, Marjorie Young.

**Mulan** (6/19/98) Walt Disney Pictures. 88 mins. Directors: Barry Cook, Tony Bancroft. Producer: Pam Coats. Voices: Ming Na Wen (Mulan), Lea Salonga (Mulan singing), Soon Teck Oh (Fa Zhou), Freda Foh Shen (Fa Li), Eddie Murphy (Mushu), B. D. Wong (Shang), Donny Osmond (Shang singing), Gedde Watanabe (Ling), Jerry S. Tondo (Chein-Po), Harvey Fierstein (Yao), Miguel Ferrer (Shan-Yu), James Hong (Chi Fu), Pat Morita (The Emperor), George Takei (First Ancestor), June Foray (Grandmother Fa).

**Consumer Tips:** ☆☆☆ MPAA Rating: G. *Mulan* is based on a venerable Chinese legend that may have some basis in historical fact.

©Walt Disney Productions

**Story:** When Mongol hordes led by Shan-Yu invade China, the lame war hero Fa Zhou is recalled to duty. In order to save Fa Zhou's life, his daughter Mulan disguises herself as a man and reports in his place. The ancestors of the Fa family send her protection in the form of Mushu, a small dragon of less-than-heroic stature. Mulan proves her cunning in battle but is wounded, exposing her secret. Captain Li Shang banishes the girl but Mulan carries on, using her brains to save the emperor and China from Shan-Yu. Mulan also wins the heart of the handsome Captain Shang and becomes the pride of her family.

**Comments:** The character Mulan represented the apex of the Disney heroine. Although Mulan mangles a tea ceremony so badly that the village matchmaker dismisses her in exasperation, she is intelligent and brave enough to stand the charge of a Mongol army. Several times in the film Mulan must battle her way back from humiliation or defeat, and never takes the easy way in doing so. The heroine wins the audience over in a brilliantly staged scene filmed entirely without dialogue. Mulan slices the hair from her head with a sword, dons her father's armor, and steels herself for the sacrifice she will make in order to protect her father from certain death. Mark Henn animated Mulan in a simple but sure style that extended the Disney tradition of strong personality animation. Mulan is on screen for nearly the entire film and never once falters as a consistent character.

What sets Mulan apart from other valorous Disney heroines? None of the others engage in such perilous combat or come as close to sacrificing their lives for a greater ideal. Mulan initially joins the Imperial Army in order to protect her father, but after witnessing the devastation visited on a hapless village by the Mongols—there are no survivors—Mulan realizes that much more is at stake. In this revealing scene Mulan reaches down into the snow to pick up a small rag doll that once belonged to a child. She then places the doll next to a general's grave where it lies forlornly in close-up, a symbol of who Mulan used to be before experiencing the horrors of war. With these acts Mulan is subtly but unmistakably transformed into the warrior who will avenge this terrible atrocity.

It is this scene and the next that mark *Mulan* as an exceptional war film. CGI supervisor Eric Guaglione was responsible for one of animation's best battle scenes to date. The Mongol band that destroyed the village is nearby, and they descend on Captain Shang's outmanned company with sweeping ferocity. Computer software animated the charging army using a program similar to the one that created the wildebeest stampede in *The Lion King*. The Mongol charge down a mountain slope is seen from the view of Mulan and her helpless comrades, and the fear and awe they feel carries directly to the audience, thanks to this powerful display of computer animation.

*Mulan* has only one failing, but it puts a considerable dent in the film. The subject matter is serious, but the 13 people who worked on the story apparently felt a need to interject brash comedy; this was an unfortunate choice. Eddie Murphy's Mushu is simply the wrong character in the wrong film. Mushu's rapid-fire wisecracks (and the subplot concerning his desire to prove himself worthy to the Fa ancestors) detract from the narrative and provide unnecessary comic relief in a film that may have been stronger without it. Worse, the revered ancestors are a bunch of comical, squabbling fools that throw a most undignified party at the film's end. Directors Cook and Bancroft had a strong story to begin with; had they resisted the urge to go for laughs *Mulan* could have been one of the most unique films in the Disney canon. (MG)

**Additional Credits:** Screenplay: Rita Hsiao, Christopher Sanders, Philip La Zebnik, Raymond Singer, Eugenia Bostwick Singer. Based on a story by Robert D. San Souci. Music: Jerry Goldsmith. Songs: Matthew Wilder, David Zippel. Supervising animators: Mark Henn, Ruben A. Aquino, Tom Bancroft, Aaron Blaise, Broose Johnson, Pres Antonio Romanillos, Alex Kuperschmidt, Jeffrey J. Varab, Barry Temple, T. Daniel Hofstedt, Rob Bekuhrs. Lead animators: Brian Ferguson, Shawn Keller. Animation: Anthony Wayne Michaels, James Young Jackson, Rune Brandt Bennice, Carol Seidl, Tom Gately, Elliot M. Bour, Robert Espanto Domingo, Mark Pudleiner, Joe Haidar, Marcelo Fernandes De Moora, Craig R. Maras, Philip Morris, Theodore Anthony Leely, Bill Waldman, Charles Bonfacio, Dominic M. Carola, Jamie Oliff, Robert O. Corley, James Baker, John Webber, Byron Howard, Christopher Bradley, Ian White, Michael Benet, Daniel M. Wawrzazek, Bert Klein, Dave Kupczyk, Travis Blaise, Tony Stanley, Trey Finn, Anthony Ho Wong, Sasha Dorogov, Branko Mihanovic, Darko Cesar, Todd Waterman, Jerry Yu Ching, Sandra Maria Groeneveld, Chad Ferron. Visual effects supervisors: David Tidgwell, David "Joey" Mildenberger. Story supervisor: Christopher Sanders. Cohead of story: Dean DeBlois. Story: John Sanford, Tim Hodge, Burny Mattinson, Barry Johnson, Ed Gombert, Chris Williams, Julius L. Aguimatang, Lorna Cook, Thom Enriquez, Joe Grant, Floyd Norman. Production design: Hans Bacher. Art director: Ric Sluiter. Character design supervisor: Chen Yi-Chang. Character design/visual development: Sai Ping Lok, Robh Ruppel, Paul Felix, Alex Nino, Marcelo Vigrali, Richard P. Chavez, John Puglisi, Jean Gillmore, Caroline K. Hu, Sue Nichols, Peter DeSeve. Layout supervisor: Robert Walker. Background supervisor: Robert E. Stanton, Sunny Apinchapong.

**Mutant Aliens** (4/19/02) Apollo. 83 mins. Director/producer: Bill Plympton. Voices: Dan McComas (Earl Jensen), Francine Lobis (Josie Jensen, Squeeze Rod Voice), Matthew Brown (Darby, Tomkins), George Casden (Dr. Frubar, President), Jay Cavanaugh (Boris, NASA Technician, Alien Voices), Amy Allison (Secretary), Kevin Kolack (Preacher), Vera Beren (Signe Bullwinkel), Bill Plympton (Guard), Thea Button (Young Josie), Silkie O'Ishi (Alien Voices), Samantha Ridgway (Computer Access Voice).

**Consumer Tips:** ☆☆☆ MPAA Rating: R.

**Story:** An astronaut stranded in space returns to earth, with space creatures, looking for revenge.

**Comments:** For his third feature film, Bill Plympton delves even further into body humor and sexual themes, and yet this does not overshadow the basic

© Bill Plympton

narrative. The plot focuses on the return of embittered astronaut Earl Jensen, abandoned for 20 years in space, to wreak revenge with his mutant alien friends, with Plympton taking potshots at advertising, religion, and presidential press conferences along the way.

The odd juxtaposition of fanciful transformations and cute ideas with brutal violence and strange sex, which by now is something of a Plympton trademark, is particularly prominent here. Rather adorable-looking pig, hamster, and caterpillar creatures, amongst others, attack and disembowel bystanders. The scenes in which the aliens are the result of Earl's bestiality fetish is either so repulsive as to be funny, or so funny as to be repulsive. (Naturally, for all of these reasons, the movie is not for the kiddies.) On the other end, however, Earl's tale of his time with the nose people is a wonderful piece of visual whimsy, and surprisingly touching. Other attempts at romance and emotional bonds between characters in the film fall flat in a way that the pairing of a spaceman and a busty nose queen does not.

Longtime Plympton composer Maureen McElheron's primary contributions this time were a rather haunting score and "Can't Drag Race with Jesus" (with Hank Bones), a revivalist song picturing Christ as a champion racer and rock star. As with other Plympton films, this sequence had previously been released as a stand-alone short to help raise funds for the final film. Though certainly not for family audiences, the movie

is a fun ride, and a reminder of how uninhibited (for better or worse) animation can be when produced outside the traditional studio system. (AL)

**Additional Credits:** Associate producer: John Holderried. Writer/animator: Bill Plympton. Music: Hank Bones, Maureen McElheron. Art supervisors: Jennifer Senko, Delphine Burrus, Signe Baumane. Models: Paul Zoanowicz. Shadows: Tom Herpich.

**My Little Pony: The Movie** (6/20/86) DEG (DeLaurentis Entertainment Group). 89 mins. Director: Michael Joens. Producers: Joe Bacal, Tom Griffin, Michael Joens. Voices: Danny DeVito (Grundle King), Madeline Kahn (Droggle), Cloris Leachman (Hydia), Rhea Perlman (Reeka), Tony Randall (The Moochick), Tammy Amerson (Megan), Jon Bauman (The Smooze), Alice Playten (Baby Lickety Split, Bushwoolie #1), Charlie Adler (Spike, Woodland Creature), Michael Bell (Grundle), Sheryl Bernstein (Buttons, Woodland Creature, Bushwoolie), Susan Blu (Lofty, Grundle, Bushwoolie), Nancy Cartwright (Gusty, Bushwoolie #4).

©Sunbow Productions, Inc. and Hasbro, Inc.

**Consumer Tips:** 0 (no stars). MPAA Rating: G.

**Story:** A trio of wicked witches hatches a plot to turn peaceful Ponyland into a dark and dreary wasteland.

Ponies Lickety Split, Wind Whistler, and North Star team up with the furry Grundles and children Megan, Molly, and Danny to take on the witches and a purple goose named Snooze.

**Comments:** Pure torture. In 1984, Sunbow Productions Inc. licensed the right to use the popular My Little Pony characters from the toy manufacturer Hasbro, Inc. With Marvel Productions Ltd. (the animation arm of Marvel Comics), they produced two half-hour animated television specials starring the ponies. Both television programs were a hit. This was enough to convince Sunbow and Marvel to produce a movie based on the toy ponies.

My Little Pony: The Movie was animated in Japan and Korea for Sunbow/Marvel. The mechanical stilted animation did not help endear the ponies to anyone but the most ardent five-year-old fans of the series. I hope Danny DeVito, Madeline Kahn, Cloris Leachman, and Tony Randall had fun in the recording booth—because none of it came through to the audience. This film is everyone's worst nightmare of what "kid's flick" is—and should be required viewing by anyone wanting to learn how *not* to make a family film.

Although a lone film critic, Daniel Neman in the Richmond *News Leader*, was quoted, "*My Little Pony: The Movie* is . . . an animated movie for children that is worth seeing," the movie was not received with enthusiasm by most critics. Charles Solomon of the *Los Angeles Times* wrote that *My Little Pony* represented a gigantic Hasbro commercial disguised as an animated feature for children. It was a meandering series of formula adventures, and "the real theme song of *My Little Pony* is the ring of the cash register, as Hasbro attempts to turn unwitting young viewers into customers. The sugary cuteness of the Little Ponies masks a corporate greed as cold and sharp as a razor blade." (SF)

**Additional Credits:** Executive producers: Margaret Loesch, Lee Gunther. Supervising producer: Jay Bacal. Writers: George Arthur Bloom. Associate story consultant: Buzz Dixon. Music: Rob Walsh. Songs: Tommy Goodman. Lyrics: Barry Herman. Theme song: Spencer Michilin, Ford Kinder. Supervising animators: Pierre DeCelles, Michael Fallows, Ray Lee. Animation directors: Brad Case, Joan Case, Gerry Chiniquy, Charlie Downs, Bill Exter, Milton Gray, Songpil Kim, Heungsun Kim, Margaret Nichols, Karen Peterson, Tom Ray, Bob Shellhorn, Bob Treat, Greg Vanzo, Gwen Wetzler, Jaeho Hong, Nak Jong Kim, Michihiro Kanayama, Akinori Matsubara. Storyboard artists: Boyd Kirkland, Debra Pugh.

**My Neighbor Totoro** (5/7/93) 50th Street Films (Troma). 86 mins. Director: Hayao Miyazaki. Voices: Noriko Hidaka (Satsuki), Chika Sakamoto (Mei), Shigesato Itoi (Tatsuo Kusakabe), Sumi Shimamoto (Yasuko Kusakabe), Tanie Kitabayashi (Kanta no obâsan), Hitoshi Takagi (Totoro), Yûko Maruyama (Kanta no okâsan), Machiko Washio (Teacher), Reiko Suzuki (Furoi on'na no hito), Masashi Hirose (Kanta no otôsan), Toshiyuki Amagasa (Kanta), Shigeru Chiba (Kusakari-Otoko), Lisa Michelson (Satsuki, Troma and English version), Cheryl Chase (Mei, Troma and English version).

©Nibariki / Tokuma Shoten

**Consumer Tips:** ☆☆☆☆ MPAA Rating: G. Children's fantasy.

**Story:** Satsuki Kusakabe and her little sister Mei move with their college teacher father to the Japanese countryside to be near their mother, who is ill in a hospital. Both girls are fascinated by the growing crops and nearby forest, and meet a giant but friendly nature spirit that only innocent children can see. When Mei runs away to visit her mother in the hospital and becomes lost, the Totoro helps Satsuki to find her sister.

**Comments:** *My Neighbor Totoro* (*Tonari no Totoro*) was the first theatrical feature by Japan's acclaimed writer/artist/director Hayao Miyazaki to be seen by the American general public. Although anime fans had long been devotees of his films, none had been released before in America (not counting the negligible release of *Warriors of the Wind* as a minor children's video in the mid-1980s). *My Neighbor Totoro* was seen less in its 1993 limited theatrical release than in its Fox Video Family Feature release in July 1994. Named a "Pick of the Year" by popular critics Siskel and Ebert, the video was a strong seller for years afterward.

Acknowledged by Miyazaki (born in 1941) as a semiautobiographical fantasy, *Totoro* is set around the mid-1950s when Japan's recovery from World War II–era economic devastation meant that urban growth was about to cover the agricultural countryside near big cities. College professor Kusakabe is moving with his daughters Satsuki (ten) and Mei (four) to an old house in the countryside so they can be near their mother, who is sick in the Shichikokuyama Hospital (this detail will be meaningless to children, but it's a famous tuberculosis sanatorium near Tokyo where Miyazaki's mother spent several years). The ebullient little girls dash about the old farmhouse into which they are moving, and encounter their first traditional Japanese nature spirits: tiny "soot sprites" hiding in dark corners.

Mei, fascinated by butterflies and tadpoles in a little brook, sees a small furry creature and chases it into the woods where it enters a hollow tree. Mei follows and drops into an underground sunny glade inhabited by a huge sleeping duplicate of the creature, a sort of cat/bear/gorilla. Mei dubs this "a Totoro, just like in my picture book" (Miyazaki has said this was supposed to be a childish mispronunciation of "troll") and treats him like a giant plush toy, crawling onto his belly and falling asleep.

An emergency message from the hospital panics the girls into thinking that their mother is dying. Mei runs away to try to go to the hospital, and becomes lost. While granny and the neighboring farmers search the countryside, Satsuki calls on Totoro to help them. Totoro summons the Catbus, which takes them to Mei, and then takes both children to the hospital where they see that their mother is all right.

*My Neighbor Totoro*, released April 16, 1988, in Japan, was dubbed the next year by Streamline Pictures for use by Japan Air Lines as an in-flight movie on trans-Pacific flights. It was not released in America until 1993. It has been called one of the most perfect family films ever made, able to be appreciated equally by young girls, by boys who usually prefer more dramatic fantasy, and by adults seeing it on their own. It is easily understandable by foreign audiences with no personal knowledge of Japanese rural life in the 1950s. Miyazaki wanted to document and pay tribute to the passing of Japan's traditional agricultural lifestyle and beliefs. The Totoro is his original combination of many of the separate nature spirits from Japan's mythology into a representative essence of all of them. (FP)

***Additional Credits:*** Executive producer: Yasuyoshi Tokuma. Based on the book by Hayao Miyazaki. Music: Joe Hisaishi. Lyricists: Hayao Miyazaki, Kieko Nakagawa, Severin Browne. Animation director: Yoshiharu Sato. Animators: Masaaki Endo, Makiko Futaki, Yoshinori Kanada, Toshio Kawaguchi, Katsuya Kondo, Shinji Otsuka, Masako Shinohara, Hideko Tagawa, Makoto Tanaka, Tsukasa Tannai, Hiromi Yamakawa. Producer (U.S.): Carl Macek.

**Nausicaä of the Valley of the Wind** See *Warriors of the Wind.*

**Neo-Tokyo/Silent Möbius** (11/20/92) Streamline Pictures. 50 mins. Directors: (Neo-Tokyo) Rintaro, Yoshiaki Kawajiri, Katsuhiro Otomo; (Silent Möbius) Michitaka Kikuchi. Producer: Haruki Kadokawa. Voices: (Neo-Tokyo) Robert Axelrod (Tsutomu Sugioka), Cheryl Chase (Sachi), Barbara Goodson (Mother), Steve Kramer (Chief Technician, Boat Pilot),

©Kadakowa Films

Michael McConnohie (Reporter), Jeff Winkless (Robot 444-1), Tom Wyner (Tech, Boss). (Silent Mobius) Iona Morris (Katsumi), Alexandra Kenworthy (Miyuka), Joyce Kurtz (Kiddy), Jeff Winkless (Lucifer Hawke), Wendee Lee (Nami), Melora Harte (Rally), Barbara Goodson (Lebia), Julie Donald (Yuki).

**Consumer Tips:** ☆☆☆ MPAA Rating: Unrated. SF/fantasy anthology. Two separate Japanese featurettes. *Neo-Tokyo* is a SF/fantasy tryptich designed for film-festival audiences, while *Silent Möbius* is a SF/horror thriller.

**Story:** *Neo-Tokyo* consists of three tales: "Labyrinth," in which a little girl and her cat travel into a creepy wonderland where a clown invites them into a sinister circus; "The Running Man," about the last race of a racing driver cybernetically connected to his futuristic racing car; and "The Order to Stop Construction," in which a human superintendent cannot stop robot workers from building a useless city. In *Silent Möbius*, earth is invaded by demonic monsters, and a special police force consisting of women with psychic powers battles against them.

**Comments:** Streamline Pictures, a distributor specializing in importing Japanese animation, combined these two featurettes from Kadokawa Films to make a single feature-length theatrical release. *Neo-Tokyo* (*Manie-Manie* or *Labyrinth Tales*) was produced for international film festivals; it premiered on September 25, 1987, at a Tokyo Fantastic Film Festival. *Silent Möbius* (1991) is based upon a popular SF/horror manga by Kia Asamiya.

*Neo-Tokyo* begins with a slow pan drawing the viewer into the ominous entrance of a cave in a fantastic jungle. In "Labyrinth," by Rin Taro (this pseudonym is usually written as Rintaro), a young girl, Sachi, and her cat, Cicero, go through a mirror into a surrealistic city consisting of back alleys where they encounter invisible children and their dog, a tram of glowing skeletal commuters, and similar fantastic inhabitants. A Pierrot clown invites them into a deserted French circus where they are the only audience for the next two sequences.

"The Running Man," by Yoshiaki Kawajiri, is narrated by a nameless magazine reporter at Le Circus, a futuristic automotive racetrack where the racers are cybernetically connected to their cars. Some signs in the background are in French, and Kawajiri's art style is strongly reminiscent of French SF comic-book artist Möbius (Jean Giraud).

"The Order to Stop Construction," by Katsuhiro Otomo, is a sci-fi dark comedy. Tsutomo Sugioka is a minor bureaucrat at a megacorporation that has been using robots to construct a city in a South American jungle. When the Republic of Arawana's government is overthrown and the rebels order Project 444 shut down, Sugioka is sent to the tropical hellhole to stop the construction and salvage as much equipment as he can. Otomo plays a riff on the subplot with the computer HAL-9000 in *2001: A Space Odyssey*. The pompous Sugioka simply screams orders at the robots to stop, while the robots led by mechanical Project Manager 444-1, which have been programmed to let nothing stop them from building the city, ignore him.

*Neo-Tokyo* ends back in the circus tent as Sachi applauds and grotesque circus performers welcome her and Cicero to join them. The closing circus-scape is reminiscent of both Bosch's medieval vision of Hell and Bozetto's surrealistic "Bolero" landscape in *Allegro Non Troppo*, while the whole "Labyrinth" sequence has the mood of Ray Bradbury's early fantasy-horror short stories.

*Silent Möbius*, released August 17, 1991, in Japan, is a SF adventure in a *Blade Runner*-ish future Tokyo. In A.D. 2028, earth is invaded by transdimensional monsters called Lucifer Hawks, whose main dimensional portal is in Tokyo. A special police force, the A.M.P. (Attacked Mystification Police), is established to fight them. Its members consist of young women with strong psychic powers: Rally Cheyenne, Lebia Maverick, Nami Yamigumo, Yuki Saiko, and Kiddy Phenil. (Despite the high-tech gloss, the setup is clearly ancient Japanese horror with supernatural monsters being combatted by Shinto temple virgin priestesses.) (FP)

**Additional Credits:** *Neo-Tokyo*: Screenplay: Yoshiaki Kawajiri ("The Running Man"), Katsuhiro Ôtomo ("The Order to Cease Construction"), Rintaro ("Labyrinth-Labyrintos"). Sound recordist: Ichiro Tsujii. Animators: Nobumasa Arakawa, Atsuko Fukushima, Kengo Inagaki, Toshio Kawaguchi, Reiko Kurihara, Kôji Morimoto, Takashi Nakamura, Shinji Otsuka, Kunihiko Sakurai, Manabu Ôhashi. *Silent Möbius*: Story: Kia Asamiya.

Music: Kaoru Wada. Original script: Kei Shigema and Michitaka Kikuchi. Art Director: Norihiro Hiraki.

**Nightmare Before Christmas** (10/13/93) Disney. 75 mins. Director: Henry Selick. Producers: Tim Burton, Denise DiNovi. Voices: Chris Sarandon (Jack Skellington), Danny Elfman (Jack Skellington, singing; Barrel; Clown with the Tearaway Face), Catherine O'Hara (Sally, Shock), William Hickey (Evil Scientist), Glenn Shadix (Mayor), Paul Reubens (Lock), Ken Page (Oogie Boogie), Ed Ivory (Santa Claus, Narrator), Susan McBride (Big Witch, Withered Winged Demon), Debi Durst (Corpse Kid, Corpse Mom, Small Witch), Gregory Proops (Harlequin Demon, Devil, Sax Player), Kerry Katz (Man Under the Stairs, Vampire, Corpse Dad), Randy Crenshaw (Mr. Hyde, Behemoth, Vampire), Sherwood Ball (Mummy, Vampire), Carmen Twillie (Undersea Gal, Creature Under the Bed), Glenn Walters (Wolfman).

©Walt Disney Productions

**Consumer Tips:** ☆☆☆½ MPAA Rating: PG.

**Story:** Jack Skellington of Halloween Town takes over Christmas from Santa Claus.

**Comments:** Though darker than a typical Disney feature, and with a comically morbid undercurrent, *Nightmare Before Christmas* proved to be a surprise hit for the studio, and a triumphant return to the limelight for stop-motion animation. The pairing of the individualistic Tim Burton, who originally wrote *Nightmare* as a poem, and Disney initially seemed odd. However, Burton began his career as a Disney animator, toiling

briefly on *Fox and the Hound* and *Black Cauldron*, and producing the oddball stop-motion short "Vincent" (1982). Subsequent features, from *Pee-wee's Big Adventure* to *Beetlejuice*, used stop-motion to varying degrees, but here the technique comes into its own, along with Burton's cheerfully gothic sensibilities, like a more impish, less sedate Edward Gorey. Though the actual director was San Francisco–based animator Henry Selick, Burton's design sensibilities shaped the final product.

The central conceit behind *Nightmare*'s story, told largely through operetta-like snatches of song and spoken verse, is that holidays spring not from the cultural histories and needs of men, but from fantasy lands hidden behind doors. Halloweentown is a black and white world populated by such amiable ghouls as a family of zombies and the Clown with the Tearaway Face. The ruler, Jack Skellington, a magnificently articulated model, all long delicate limbs and detachable skull, feels oddly dissatisfied, and stumbling upon the colorful, sugar-frosted Christmas Town, decides to take on a new holiday, replacing Santa Claus.

From here, the blend of holiday cheer and macabre humor is infectious, intentionally recalling the Rankin-Bass holiday specials and films. Jack's well-meaning hubris adds a layer of complexity, and indeed contradicts the stereotypical "You can do whatever you dream" moral of other Disney films. The only slightly romantic relationship between Jack and the clear-sighted Sally the rag doll is also subtle and muted compared to its cel-animated counterparts. Santa himself, in an extended cameo, functions as a deservedly testy puppet, manipulated by Jack and others. Oogie Boogie, a gleeful bogey who's as close as the film comes to a villain, is a delightful homage to Cab Calloway, as used in Fleischer's Betty Boop cartoons, even quoting Calloway from *Old Man of the Mountain* (1933). The score, by longtime Burton collaborator and former Oingo Boingo bandleader Danny Elfman, creates a unique mood piece, both creepy and lively, and Elfman lends his own rich vocals to Jack's musical monologues (with actor Chris Sarandon filling in for the pure dialogue scenes).

Though Disney initially seemed somewhat uncomfortable with *Nightmare*, it has since gained widespread following, from families and animation buffs to goths, and in recent years, the corporation has seemed more accepting, with *Nightmare*-themed store merchandise, even going so far as to renovate its "Haunted Mansion" for the Christmas season with a *Nightmare Before Christmas* motif. Indeed, *Nightmare* stands as a visually stunning and narratively satisfying piece of work, and has found a place alongside Rankin-Bass's *Rudolph* and Chuck Jones's *Grinch* as a holiday classic. (MG)

**Additional Credits:** Story/characters: Tim Burton. Screenplay: Caroline Thompson. Adaptation: Michael McDowell. Music/songs: Danny Elfman. Animation supervisor: Eric Leighton. Animators: Trey Thomas, Timothy Hittle, Michael Belzer, Anthony Scott, Owen Klatte, Angie Glocka, Justin Kohn, Eric Leighton, Paul, Joel Fletcher, Kim Blanchette, Loyd Price, Richard C. Zimmerman, Stephen A. Buckley. Additional animation: Harry Walton, Paul W. Jessel, Michael W. Johnson, Ken Willard, Daniel Mason. Effects animation: Gordon Baker, Miguel Domingo Cachuela, Chris Green. Snow animation: Dave Bossert. Storyboard supervisor: Joe Ranft. Storyboard artists: Miguel Domingo Cachuela, Jorgen Klubien, Robert Pauley, Steve Moore. Art director: Deane Taylor. Assistant art directors: Kendal Cronkhite, Kelly Adam Asbury, Bill Boes. Additional character designs: David Cutler, Barry Jackson, Jorgen Klubien. Visual consultant: Rick Heinrichs. Background designer/lead scenic artist: B. J. Fredrickson. Scenic artists: Linda Overby, Jennifer Clinnard, Peggy Hrastar, Loren Hillman. Musicians include: Brad Kay, John Reynolds, Tom Marion, Buster Fitzpatrick.

## Nine Lives of Fritz the Cat

**Nine Lives of Fritz the Cat** (6/26/74) American International. 76 mins. Director: Robert Taylor. Producer: Steve Krantz. Voices: Skip Hinnant (Fritz the Cat), Reva Rose (Fritz's Old Lady), Bob Holt (Many Voices), Robert Ridgeley ("Bowery Buddies," "Black New Jersey"), Fred Smoot ("Bowery Buddies"), "Sweet" Dick Whittington (various), Luke Walker (various), Peter Leeds (Juan, various characters), Louise Moritz (Fritz's sister), Sarina C. Grant (The Roach).

**Consumer Tips:** ☆☆ MPAA Rating: R. Based on character created by R. Crumb.

**Story:** Henpecked and pot-smoking Fritz dreams of eight other lives—including exploits at the White House, in Depression-era breadlines, on a rocket to Mars, and as Hitler's aide-de-camp.

**Comments:** In this sequel to the controversial X-rated 1972 animated hit, Fritz is now married and hating

©American International Pictures, Inc.

every minute of it. In order to ease daily tension he suffers from, mainly due to the annoying antics of his pestering wife, he seeks escape by smoking marijuana and experiences what life might have been like if he were Hitler's orderly or blasting off into outer space.

Animator Robert Taylor, one of Ralph Bakshi's chief collaborators going back to his days at Terrytoons, was approched by Steve Krantz to take on the sequel after Bakshi turned it down cold. Unfortunately Taylor and Krantz lacked any vision or point of view, an important ingredient Bakshi brought to the first outing. The X-rated novelty was gone and without a strong story, there was no point making this film—other than the meager profit to be gleaned from it being a sequel. The animation and art design was superb—as a who's who of Hollywood's top animation talent was employed—but to no avail.

The film was, however, selected as an official U.S. entry at the 27th annual Cannes Film Festival—the first time an animated film was in competition at Cannes. (SF)

**Additional Credits:** Executive producer: Samuel Z. Arkoff. Story: Fred Halliday, Eric Monte, Robert Taylor. Based on the comic books by Robert Crumb. Music: Tom Scott and the LA Express. Animators: Robert Taylor, Jim Davis, Don Williams, Herb Johnson, Paul Sommer, Jack Foster, Manny Perez, Volus Jones, Manny Gould, Bob Maxfield, Bob Bachman, Cosmo Anzilotti, Art Vitello, John Gentilella, Milt Gray, Marty Taras, Fred Hellmich, Frank Andrina, Bob Bransford, Bob Bemiller, John Bruno. New character designs: Robert Taylor. Layout artists: Peter Alvarado, Tony Rivera, Ric Gonzales, Alex Ignatiev, Martin Strudler, Marty Murphy, Sam Kirson, Chris Jenkyns. Background design: Matt Golden, Eric Semones. Background artists: Al Gmuer, Bob Schaefer, Al Budnick. A Steve Krantz Production, released by American International Pictures.

**The Nutcracker Prince** (11/23/90) Warner Bros. (Canada). 75 mins. Director: Paul Schibli. Producer: Kevin Gillis. Voices: Kiefer Sutherland (Nutcracker Prince, Hans), Megan Follows (Clara), Mike MacDonald (Mouseking), Peter Boretski (Uncle Drosselmeier), Phyllis Diller (Mousequeen), Peter O'Toole (Pantaloon), Noam Zylberman (Fritz), Diane Stapley (Mrs. Stahlbaum), George Merner (Dr. Stahlbaum), Stephanie Morgenstern (Louise), Christopher Owens (Erik), Lynne Gorman (Trudy), Teresa Sears (Queen), Mona Wasserman (Princess Perlipat).

©Warner Bros., Inc.

**Consumer Tips:** ☆ MPAA Rating: G.

**Story:** Young Clara helps a toy soldier and a nutcracker prince battle a mouse king.

**Comments:** Sheldon Wiseman, the film's executive producer, and owner of both Lacewood Productions and Hinton Animation Studios in Ottawa, had been captivated by *The Nutcracker* ballet all his life. The ballet and book were copyrighted and could not be duplicated without permission. So he did research into the original E. T. A. Hoffman story and commisioned screenwriter Patricia Watson (*Road to Avonlea*) to illuminate certain parts of the story that had not been widely told.

The film was made in Canada, by Canadian animators, and with Canadian funding. The search for well-known Canadian actors to star led to selecting Kiefer Sutherland, Meagan Fellows, and comedian Mike McDonald in leading vocal roles. American Phyllis Diller and Irishman Peter O'Toole rounded out the stunt casting.

Unfortunately, the animation was not up to the current full character animation standards, as established by Disney and Bluth studios. *The Nutcracker Prince* earned a poor $1.8 million at the box office. As a theatrical feature, the film is sadly lacking in Christmas cheer. Sorry to be a Scrooge, but it's bland, lackluster, and not much fun. (SF)

**Additional Credits:** Screenplay: Patricia Watson. Based on *The Nutcracker and the Mouse King,* by E. T. A. Hoffman. Music: Peter Illich Tchaikovsky. Musical arrangements: Victor Davies. Conductor: Boris Brott. Performed by: London Symphony Orchestra.

**Of Stars and Men** (5/13/64) Brandon Films Inc. 53 mins. Director: John Hubley. Producers: John and Faith Hubley. Voices: Dr. Harlow Shapley (Narrator), Mark Hubley (voice), Hampy Hubley (voice).

**Consumer Tips:** ☆☆☆ MPAA Rating: Unrated. Adults may be intrigued—Kids will be bored.

**Story:** Adaptation of astronomer Harlow Shapley's book (Shapley narrates the film) about man and his place in the universe. This is a "think piece," an animated documentary, creatively produced and artistically significant.

The style of the film is very bold—man and the animals are depicted as white, transparent, and simply designed. The characters never speak—all their actions are told visually through actions. Man, the movie's central character, is depicted as a child. Man recalls his place in the universe, which includes space, time, matter and energy, and the meaning of life. The film argues for science and facts over myths of the past. Through clever stylized animation we take a trip through the universe, from electrons and protons to meteorites, planets, and galaxies.

The Hubleys include a few segments similar to their independent shorts "Moonbird" (1959) and "A Windy

Day" (1967), animating to the voices of their children as they explore the periodic table and ponder the meaning of energy. The film was actually quite provocative in its time for its attempt to raise questions about the origins of life. (SF)

**Additional Credits:** Writers: John and Faith Hubley, Harlow Shapley. Based on the book *Of Stars and Men* by Harlow Shapley. Music: Walter Trampler. Animation directors: Bill Littlejohn, Gary Mooney. Animation/backgrounds: John Hubley, Patricia Byron, Faith Hubley, Nina Di Gangi.

**Oliver and Company** (11/18/88) Walt Disney Pictures. 72 mins. Director: George Scribner. Voices: Joey Lawrence (Oliver), Billy Joel (Dodger), Cheech Marin (Tito), Richard Mulligan (Einstein), Roscoe Lee Browne (Francis), Sheryl Lee Ralph (Rita), Dom DeLuise (Fagin), Taurean Blaque (Roscoe), Carl Weintraub (DeSoto), Robert Loggia (Sykes), Natalie Gregory (Jenny Foxworth), William Glover (Winston), Bette Midler (Georgette).

©Walt Disney Productions

**Consumer Tips:** ☆☆☆ MPAA Rating: G. Inspired by the 1838 novel *Oliver Twist* by Charles Dickens.

**Story:** Oliver is a scrappy young kitten taken in by a streetwise dog, Dodger. Dodger is a member of a canine gang of cons working for down-and-out human Fagin. Fagin, in turn, owes crime boss Sykes a lot of money. When the dogs attempt a con to help out their master, Oliver winds up in the limo of rich but lonely Jenny Foxworth. The little girl immediately adopts Oliver (much to the disgust of Jenny's pampered poo-

dle Georgette), but Dodger's gang thinks he is a prisoner and steals him back. This gives Fagin the idea to hold the cat for ransom, but it's Sykes who ends up with both cat and Jenny. It's Fagin, his dogs, Oliver, and Georgette against Sykes and his twin killer Dobermans in a fur-flying finale before all ends happily.

**Comments:** *Oliver and Company* is an entertaining movie that represented the studio's final dress rehearsal for the great successes of the 1990s. Animators Glen Keane, Mark Henn, Ruben Aquino, Andreas Deja, Dave Pruiksma, and Hendel Butoy were now aboard, and Jeffrey Katzenberg was deeply involved in the production. One of the final pieces fell into place when a young songwriter named Howard Ashman submitted a piece for the movie called "Once Upon a Time in New York City." Disney hired Ashman and his songwriting partner Alan Menken, and the rest is animation history.

Peter Schnieder, Disney's senior vice-president of animation, wanted a hipper, more street-smart film if the cast was going to include another bunch of talking cats and dogs. Schnieder got his wish: New York City, from its filthy alleys to Fifth Avenue, is beautifully represented thanks to art director Dan Hansen and his nine-member backgrounds crew. Playing against those backgrounds: a lively crew of likeable dogs. Billy Joel, with no previous animation voice work to his credit, does a nice job with Dodger. Cheech Marin livens up the film as Tito, an oft-electrocuted Chihuahua that actually resembles the manic comedian. Best of all is Bette Midler's haughty characterization of Georgette. Midler was working on some live-action films for Disney at the time, and Katzenberg convinced her to add her talents to the film. Her rendition of "Perfect Isn't Easy" does not really advance the plot or action, but *Oliver and Company* is still a better film for including the number.

Music was vital to the contemporary feel of the movie. Besides Joel and Midler, Huey Lewis, Barry Manilow, and Ruben Blades also contributed songs and themes. There are a few flaws such as occasional weak spots in the drawing and thick lines around the characters in some scenes. It is unclear why we should be all that sympathetic to Fagin, who seems to have set up his own dilemma and at one point holds Oliver hostage. He is good to his dogs, but puts them to criminal use. The writers eventually had to have Fagin giving up Oliver to avoid breaking Penny's heart (and to win the audience's). Penny herself is a rather superficial character although she is crucial to the film's second half. Still, *Oliver and Company* is a winning, lively movie featuring a terrific cast and production crew. It deserves repeat viewings, if only to see Georgette strutting her snooty stuff.

For the record:

- *Oliver and Company* was the first Disney film to have its own computer effects department. Fagin's rattletrap trike, some cars, and parts of the Brooklyn Bridge were done using computers.
- The film's working title was "Oliver and the Dodger." During one scene showing sunrise over the city, the twin towers of the World Trade Center are prominently displayed.
- Peg, Jock, and Trusty from *Lady and the Tramp* have cameos.
- In one version of the script Fagin was going to attempt to steal a rare panda from a zoo but the writers couldn't figure out how to have the dogs get away with it.
- *Oliver and Company* made $53 million and garnered rave reviews, leading Peter Schneider to announce that Disney would release an animated feature every year. (MG)

***Additional Credits:*** Story: Vance Gerry, Mike Gabriel, Joe Ranft, Jim Mitchell, Chris Bailey, Kirk Wise, Dave Michener, Roger Allers, Gary Trousdale, Kevin Lima, Michael Cedeno, Pete Young, Leon Jooson. Based on *Oliver Twist* by Charles Dickens. Animation screenplay: Jim Cox, Timothy J. Disney, James Mangold. Music supervisor: Carol Childs. Music: J. A. C. Redford. Songs: Howard Ashman, Barry Mann, Dan Hartman, Charlie Midnight, Dean Pitchford, Tom Snow, Barry Manilow, Jack Feldman, Bruce Sussman, Rob Minkoff, Ron Rocha. Supervising animators: Mike Gabriel, Glen Keane, Ruben A. Aquino, Hendel Butoy, Mark Henn, Doug Krohn. Animators: Phil Young, Leon Joosen, Russ Edmonds, Will Finn, Barry Temple, Ron Husband, Rick Farmiloe, Dave Pruiksma, Chris Bailey, Viki Anderson, Kevin Lima, Shawn Keller, Tony Fucile, Anthony DeRosa, Jay Jackson, Kathy Zielinski, Kevin Wurzer, Jorgen Klubien, David P. Stephen, Dan Jeup, David Cutler, Jeffrey Lynch. Effects animators: Barry Cook, Ted Kierscey, Jeff Howard, Kelvin Yasuda, Glenn

Chaika, Randy Fullmer, Mark Myers, Dave Bossert, Mark Dindal, Dorse A. Lanoher, Eusibio Torres. Computer animation: Tina Price, Michael Cedeno. Art director: Dan Hansen. Character design: Mike Gabriel, Andreas Deja, Glen Keane. Production stylist: Guy Dell. Layout artists: Rasoul Azadani, Bill Perkins, Fred Cline, James Beihold, Dan McHugh, Alex Mann, Phil Phillipson, Marc Christianson, Fred Craig, Karen Keller, Bob Smith. Background artists: Jim Coleman, Lisa Keene, Brian Sebern, Steve Butz, John Emerson, Tia Kratter, Andy Phillipson, Phil Phillipson, Bob Stanton. Production consultant: Walt Stanchfield.

**Once Upon a Forest** (6/18/93) 20th Century Fox. 80 mins. Directors: Charles Grosvenor, David Michener. Producers: David Kirschner, Jerry Mills. Voices: Michael Crawford (Cornelius), Ben Vereen (Phineas), Ellen Blain (Abigail), Ben Gregory (Edgar), Paige Gosney (Russell), Elizabeth Moss (Michelle), Paul Eiding (Abigail's Father), Janet Waldo (Edgar's Mom), Susan Silo (Russell's Mom), Will Nipper (Willie), Charlie Adler (Waggs), Rickey Collins (Bosworth), Angel Harper (Bosworth's Mom), Don Reed (Marshbird), Robert David Hall (Truck Driver), Benjamin Smith (Russell's Brother), Haven Hartman (Russell's Sister), Florence Warner Jones (Vocalist).

© Twentieth Century Fox Film Corporation

***Consumer Tips:*** ☆☆ MPAA Rating: G. Ecological adventure. A film that wants you to have a guilt trip. Hal Hinson in the *Washington Post*, June 19, 1993, noted, "It's true than human beings are polluting and destroying the planet, but does anyone really think that the way to help children love nature is to teach them to hate mankind?"

**Story:** An accidental spillage of poisonous chemicals threatens the idyllic forest world of Dapplewood, where the civilized animals talk, wear clothes, and learn about flying flapper-wing-a-ma-things. The wise ol' badger, Cornelius, sends his three students on a treacherous quest: find an herbal anecdote to save his stricken niece Michelle. The "furlings"—headstrong Abigail the wood mouse, overweight Russell the hedgehog, and nerdy Edgar the mole—have to contend with a ferocious naked owl, a "yellow dragon" steam shovel, being washed down a sewage drain, rescuing a marsh bird, and building a flapper-wing-a-ma-thing to get the herbs they need. Together they learn about getting along and never giving up. And in a surprising climax, they learn that not all humans are bad.

**Comments:** In 1989 Rae Lambert, head of graphic design for HTV Cymru/Wales, created a group of woodland characters for an ecological tale, *A Furling's Story*, which he and Mike Young, creative head of Booker Entertainment and creator of Superted (who now has his own studio in America), pitched to Hanna-Barbera. Writers Mark Young (no relation to Mike) and Kelly Ward punched up the story, renamed it *The Endangered* as a television production—and then a deal with 20th Century Fox upped the budget to $13 million for a theatrical feature, retitled *Once upon a Forest*.

For star power, producer David Kirschner's wife Liz suggested Michael Crawford, of Broadway's *Phantom of the Opera*, to voice the compassionate badger Cornelius. Ben Vereen voiced Phineas, the gospel-singing grebe preacher. Phineas's chorus came from the First Baptist Church in South Central Los Angeles. According to Kirschner, "We filmed them, and they were thrilled beyond our expectations. They started flipping their arms and moving their tambourines. They became the gospel birds." Glenn Close voiced a character whose part was excised altogether.

Bill Hanna oversaw the production for six months at Cuckoo's Nest Studios in Taipei, Taiwan. He called *Forest* "the finest feature production Hanna-Barbera has ever done. When I stood up and presented it to the studio, my eyes teared up. It is very, very heartwarming," in an interview with Jeffry Scott of the *Atlanta Journal and Constitution*, May 2, 1993.

Producer David Kirschner, chairman and CEO of Hanna-Barbera at the time, told Philip Wuntch of the *Dallas Morning News*, June 19, 1993, "With *Once upon a Forest*, I don't fool myself that we'll get that all-important teen dating crowd. *Aladdin* has been really the only animated film to attract that audience. *Beauty and the Beast* even had trouble getting over the onus of not being cool. But our film speaks to a contemporary audience in the sense of having a very aggressive female character (Abigail the wood mouse) who is the leader of the pack. Disney has great animators, and the studio has them locked up for years and years. We got the best worldwide animators available from Sweden, Asia, Argentina, Spain, and England."

Fox's *Once upon a Forest* opened with $2.2 million on the second weekend of *Jurassic Park*, which grossed $38.5 million. *Forest* would ultimately earn a disappointing $6.6 million. FoxVideo released the film three months later on September 21.

Aside from *Jurassic Park*, *Forest*'s competition included Filmation's *Happily Ever After*, which earned a meager $1.8 million in 1,018 theaters in its opening week (May 28), an average of just $1,725 per screen (*Variety* called it "about $250,000 per dwarf"). Disney reissed *Snow White and the Seven Dwarfs* on July 2, which opened in fifth place at $6.9 million.

*Forest*'s director, Charles Grosvenor, would later become producer-director of *The Land Before Time* video franchise starting with *Land* V. (WRM)

**Additional Credits:** Executive producers: William Hanna, Paul Gertz. Writers: Mark Young, Kelly Ward. Based on a Welsh story. Music: James Horner. Key animators: Joseph Ekers, Cynthia Wells. Animators: Barry Anderson, Frank Andrina, Brenda Banks, Doug Bennett, Roger Chiasson, Mark Christiansen, Zeon Davush, David Feiss, Ralph Fernan, Brad Forbush, Kent Hammerstrom, Ted Hawkins, Dan Hunn, Andre Knutson, Ernesto Lopez, Sean Newton, Mike Nguyen, William Nunes, Dana O'Connor, Kevin Petrilak, Kunio Shumimora, I-Sin Cyndi Tana, Robert Tyler, Kevin Wurzer, John Walker. Art director: Carol Holman Grosvenor. Storyboard artists: Charles Grosvenor, David Michener, Bob Onorato, Chris Otsuki. A Hanna-Barbera production.

## One Hundred and One Dalmatians (1/25/61)

Walt Disney Pictures. 79 mins. Directors: Wolfgang Reitherman, Hamilton Luske, Clyde Geronimi. Voices: Rod Taylor (Pongo), Lisa Daniels, Cate Bauer (Perdita), Ben Wright (Roger Radcliff), Lisa Davis (Anita Rad-

©Walt Disney Productions

cliff), Betty Lou Gerson (Cruella De Vil), Martha Wentworth (Nanny, Queenie, Lucy), J. Pat O'Malley (The Colonel, Jasper Badun), Fred Worlock (Horace Badun, Inspector Craven), Tudor Owen (Towser), Tom Conway (Quizmaster, Collie), George Pelling (Danny), Thurl Ravenscroft (The Captain), Dave Frankham (Sgt. Tibbs), Ramsay Hill (Television Announcer, Labrador), Queenie Leonard (Princess), Marjorie Bennett (Duchess), Barbara Beaird (Rolly), Micky Maga (Patch), Sandra Abbott (Penny), Mimi Gibson (Lucky), Barbara Luddy (Rover), Paul Frees (Dirty Dawson), Lucille Bliss (Television Commercial Singer), Bob Stevens, Max Smith, Sylvia Marriott, Dallas McKennon, Rickie Sorensen, Basil Ruysdael (Additional Voices).

**Consumer Tips:** ☆☆☆ MPAA Rating: Unrated. Adapted from the 1956 book *The One Hundred and One Dalmatians* by Dodie Smith.

**Story:** Bachelor songwriter Roger Radcliff and his dalmatian Pongo meet cute in the park with Anita and her dalmatian Perdita. Soon all four are married and the dogs are due to have puppies. Their happiness is endangered when Anita's old school chum Cruella De Vil shows up. Cruella would like nothing more than some fancy coats . . . made of dalmatian fur. Cruella and her no-good henchmen kidnap the puppies (along with dozens of others) and keep them prisoner at Hell Hall prior to the slaughter. A paramilitary confederation of animals comes to the rescue, Cruella is soundly routed, and all 101 dalmatians find their way to Roger and Anita, who decide to start a dalmatian plantation.

**Comments:** Made on the cheap for only $3.7 million, this winning film outperformed *Sleeping Beauty* at the box office and went on to become one of Disney's most popular features. Many baby boomers recall *101 Dalmatians* with great fondness, and the film still holds up very well today. Under normal circumstances a dalmatian would be very hard to animate; it would be nearly impossible to keep its spots in register from frame to frame. Ub Iwerks solved this problem for Disney using a process called "Xerography." In short, this allowed animators to transfer their drawing directly to cels, reducing the number of steps it took to get their finished art to the screen.

In *101 Dalmatians* the result was a rough, sketchy look that featured dark black lines around characters. By the late 1970s the process would become more refined, but this film was the training ground. Walt Disney himself was not fond of the style, but Xerography did allow the audiences a more authentic look at the animator's original, dynamic work.

Understanding this technique is essential to understanding the appeal of *101 Dalmatians*, because Xerography allowed for a free-swinging approach to character design and encouraged caricature. Nowhere is this more evident than in the animation of the film's villainess, Cruella De Vil. Disney evildoers of the past were merely dastardly, but Cruella was actually psychotic, a bony, volatile bundle of thinly worn nerves and hysterical egomania.

Storyman Bill Peet developed Cruella's traits and animator Marc Davis designed her dramatic appearance. Davis drew on film stars Bette Davis, Rosalind Russell, Tallulah Bankhead, and Cruella's voice artist, Betty Lou Gerson, as inspirations. This was Davis's final animation assignment at the studio and Cruella De Vil was a fitting exit. With her skeletal face contorted in anger beneath her piebald coif, Cruella De Vil is arguably the most memorable character in any Disney film.

Not that Cruella is the whole show; the story, as sketched out by Peet, is tightly constructed and contains some brilliant plot devices such as "the Twilight Bark." This system of communication, used by England's animals to assist one another allows Peet and the animators to build a society of courageous, dutiful animals that hold our interest throughout the final third of the film. Captain Horse, Colonel Sheepdog, and the heroic Sergeant Tibs (a barnyard cat) ensure the rescue of the doomed dalmatians. A stoic Collie and a Labrador also help Pongo, Perdita, and the ninety-nine pilfered puppies escape Cruella and her fumbling assistants. Three kindly cows feed the frozen, hungry puppies and one wishes that the human heroes in this film were half as efficient as the animals.

For the record:

- A dog's world: Peg and the Bulldog from *Lady and the Tramp* show up in a pet shop window.
- There were 6,469,952 spots drawn on the dalmatians in the making of this film; each of the 99 puppies has 32.
- Just curious, but couldn't Cruella De Vil sue Roger for slander after he publishes a disparaging hit song about her? (MG)

**Additional Credits:** Story: Bill Peet (based on *The Hundred and One Dalmatians* by Dodie Smith). Music: George Bruns (songs by Mel Leven). Directing animators: Milt Kahl, Frank Thomas, Marc Davis, John Lounsbery, Ollie Johnston, Eric Larson. Animators: Hal King, Les Clark, Cliff Nordberg, Blaine Gibson, Eric Cleworth, John Sibley, Art Stevens, Julius Svendsen, Hal Ambro, Ted Berman, Bill Keil, Don Lusk, Dick Lucas, Amby Paliwoda. Effects animators: Jack Boyd, Dan McManus, Ed Parks, Jack Buckley. Art director/production design: Ken Anderson. Layout styling: Don Griffith, Collin Campbell, Ernest Nordli. Layout: Basil Davidovich, McLaren Stewart, Vance Gerry, Dale Barnhart, Homer Jonas, Ray Aragon, Al Zinnen, Sammie June Lanham, Victor Haboush, Dick Ung, Joe Hale. Backgrounds: Al Dempster, Ralph Hulett, Anthony Rizzo, Bill Layne. Character styling: Bill Peet, Tom Oreb. Color styling: Walt Peregoy.

**1001 Arabian Nights** (12/1/59) Columbia—UPA. 76 mins. Director: Jack Kinney. Producer: Stephen Bosustow. Voices: Jim Backus (Uncle Abdul Azziz Magoo), Kathryn Grant (Princess Yasminda), Dwayne Hickman (Aladdin), Hans Conried (The Wicked Wazir), Herschel Bernardi (The Jinni of the Lamp), Alan Reed (The Sultan), Daws Butler (Omar the Rugmaker), Clark Sisters (The Three Little Maids from Damascus).

©Columbia Pictures Corp.

**Consumer Tips:** ☆☆½ MPAA Rating: Unrated.

**Story:** Mr. Magoo plays nearsighted lamp dealer in ancient Baghdad, protecting his love-struck nephew Aladdin with his flying carpet and magic lamp.

**Comments:** For UPA's first animated feature, the studio's biggest star, Mr. Magoo, was chosen to headline this surprisingly fun adaptation, which, despite the title, focuses almost entirely on the Aladdin story. Magoo is here cast as eccentric lamp-seller Uncle Abdul Azziz Magoo, who frets continuously about his unmarried nephew Aladdin. At the same time, the kingdom is being pillaged by the Wicked Wazir (which in a gag seemingly borrowed from radio's Bob and Ray, functions as a name rather than a description). The Wazir, anxious to increase his wealth, tries to dupe Aladdin into finding the lamp for him, as predicted, and the tale spins on from there.

However, the film avoids falling prey to pure clichés and tedium through the constant intrusions of Magoo, blindly weaving in and out of the tale. Magoo by now was a far more sentimental character than the bull-headed old man who first appeared in *Ragtime Bear* (1949), but the character still fits remarkably well here. His steady flow of near stream-of-consciousness mutterings, courtesy of Jim Backus, have reached Popeye-esque proportions, from his conviction that his cat is faithful dog Bowser, to his embarrassment at stumbling into a den of peacocks, "Pardon me, ladies. Wandered into the harem!" Though Aladdin and his lovely Princess Yasminda (the latter played by Bing Crosby's second wife Kathryn Grant) are mostly ciphers, in addition to Magoo, the movie benefits from the Wazir, a no-holds-barred pantomime villain. Expertly voiced by Hans Conried, who made something of a career of such roles, the Wazir, with his bug eyes and lanky gestures, is a true personality, and the scenes in which he coos and cuddles his collection of vermin and reptiles are especially noteworthy.

The overall animation and design recall less the earlier UPA theatrical shorts, which used limited animation and stylized designs as aesthetics, than the later television series, or the output of Jay Ward. Indeed, much of the cast and crew, including Conried, editor Skip Craig, and artists Lew Keller, Shirley Silvey, and Pete Burness, went on to work on *The Bullwinkle Show*. Magoo's role as an actor in a fairy-tale adaptation also set a precedent for his subsequent television career, notably *Mr. Magoo's Christmas Carol* and *The Famous Adventures of Mr. Magoo*. With a jazzy score, fun caricatures, outstanding voice work, and amusing dialogue asides, *1001 Arabian Nights*, though hard to find these days, has unexpected pleasures for children and adults. (AL)

**Additional Credits:** Writer: Czenzi Ormonde, Ted Allen. Music: George Duning. Story: Dick Kinney, Pete Burness, Lew Keller, Ed Nofziger, Ted Allen, Leo Salkin, Margaret Schneider, Paul Schneider, Dick Shaw. Animators: Bob Carlson, Casey Onaitis, Clarke Mallery, Ed Friedman, Harvey Toombs, Herman Cohen, Jack Campbell, James Davis, Ken Hultgren, Phil Duncan, Rudy Zamora, Sandy Strother, Stan Wilkins. Animation director: Abe Levitow. Sequence directors: Alan Zaslove, Gil Turner, Osmond Evans, Rudy Larriva, Tom McDonald. Editors: Carl Bennett, Skip Craig. Supervising editor: Joe Siracusa. Layouts: Gene Miller, Shirley Silvey. Backgrounds: Barbara Begg, Boris Gorelick, Rosemary O'Connor. Ink & Paint supervisor: Marion O'Callahan.

**Osmosis Jones** (8/10/01) Warner Bros. 98 mins. Directors: Peter Farrelly, Bobby Farrelly. Animation directors: Piet Kroon, Tom Sito. Producers: Peter Farrelly, Bobby Farrelly, Bradley Thomas, Zak Penn, Den-

nis Edwards. Cast: Bill Murray (Frank), Molly Shannon (Mrs. Boyd), Chris Elliott (Bob), Elena Franklin (Shane), Danny Murphy (Zookeeper Superintendent), Jack McCullough (Zookeeper), Kathy Wege (Volcano Lady), Will Dunn (Oyster Boy), Jackie Flynn (School Janitor). Voices: Chris Rock (Osmosis Jones), Laurence Fishburne (Thrax), David Hyde Pierce (Drix), Brandy Norwood (Leah), William Shatner (The Mayor), Ron Howard (Tom Colonic), Kenny Olson (Kidney Rock), Joel Silver (The Chief).

©Warner Bros.

**Consumer Tips:** ☆☆ MPAA Rating: PG.

**Story:** A slovenly zookeeper, Frank Detorri, consumes a hard-boiled egg discarded by a chimpanzee, ingesting a killer virus named Thrax. Once inside the body, the film becomes an animated spoof of buddy cop movies, with Osmosis Jones, a wisecracking white blood cell, teaming up with Drix, a stuffy 12-hour cold tablet, to take on Thrax.

**Comments:** "The idea that these cells could be trapped in a runny nose was in the original pitch, and there was a scab idea. The vomiting scene wasn't there until we started shooting," Writer Mark Hyman told Gary Dretzka of the *Chicago Tribune* in August 2001, summing up all you really need to know about *Osmosis Jones*.

*Osmosis Jones* had much potential. The animation sequences are wonderful. Casting Bill Murray was genius, and recruiting the Farrelly Brothers (*There's Something About Mary*) was, in theory, perfect chemistry. Sadly, it didn't work out that way.

Not unlike Richard Fleischer's *Fantastic Voyage* and Joe Dante's *Innerspace* (both taking place inside a man's body) in story structure, *Osmosis Jones* shows the body as a world of vibrant colors and breathtaking landscapes. A perfect setting for an animated adventure.

What went wrong? The comedy just didn't click—and the desire of Warner Bros. to protect its investment and keep it family friendly did not allow the Farrellys and screenwriter Hyman to go all the way. However, the way they did go was gross.

Noteworthy artistic contributors included Dean Wellins, directing animator for Thrax, 2-D effects designer Michel Gagné, production designer Steve Pilcher, and William Shatner as the voice of Mayor Phlegmming—all of whom were nominated for an Annie Award.

One lasting cultural benefit of the movie: in the film, Frank mentions participating in a National Chicken Wing Eating Contest in Buffalo, New York—a contest that didn't exist in real life. A local newspaper columnist pointed it out and shortly thereafter Drew Cerzar of RMI promotions created a National Buffalo Wing Festival, which began the following year.

True to its reputation, Warner Bros. did little to publicize its animated/live-action feature. Hyman pointed out to *USA Today* (August 3, 2001) that because the film was about an unhealthy slob named Frank "who doesn't take care of himself, no fast-food company wanted to have anything to do with us."

For a film filled with gross-out humor, the film barely grossed at the box office. Made for a budget of $75 million, the opening weekend for *Osmosis Jones* was a meager $5.2 million; it ended up earning only $13.4 million in the United States. In Britain, cinemas yanked the film due to the anthrax attacks in the United States after 9/11. Warner Home Video rushed *Osmosis* to DVD on November 13, 2001.

A Saturday morning cartoon spinoff, *Ozzy and Drix*, premiered on the Kids WB Network on September 14, 2002, lasting 26 episodes for two seasons. Frank now resembles what he was supposed to look like in the film: a big fat slob. Ozzy (now voiced by Phil LaMarr) and Drix (Jeff Bennett) are transplanted by mosquito from Frank's body to the body of 13-year-old Hector (Justin Cowden), where they help him contend with infectious diseases, head lice, indigestion, cavities, and zits. Scenes from the movie are occasionally integrated into the tele-

vision show. The only artist to work on both productions was Emmy Award-winning story artist Barry Caldwell.

In the end, *Osmosis Jones* is a film only for those who like burps, farts, phlegm, mucus, puke, zit-pus, excrement, and Bill Murray. (WRM)

**Additional Credits:** Writer: Marc Hyman. Music: Randy Edelman. Supervising animators: Richard Bazley, Dave Brewster, Ricardo Curtis, Tony Fucile, Wendy Perdue, Dean Wellins. Lead animators: Stephan Franck, Lennie K. Graves, Duncan Marjoribanks, Mike Nguyen. Animators: Richard Baneham, Michael Chavez, Ruth Daly, Ralph Fernan, T. J. House, Mark Kausler, Jae H. Kim, Holger Leihe, Craig R. Maras, Frank Molieri, Melina Sydney Padua, Barry John O'Donoghue, Shane Prigmore, Eddie Rosas, Andrew Loell Schmidt, Peter Sohn, Craig Valde, Jim VanDerKeyl, Michael Venturini, Christopher Walsh, John D. Williamson, David Alan Zaboski. Animators (Yowza Animation): Line Anderson, Steve Baker, Adam Beck, Samuel Chou, Trevor Deane-Freeman, Joe Giampapa, Morgan Ginsberg, Daryl Graham Gabe Hordos, Daniel LaFrance, Satjit Matharu, Kevin Micallef, Keith Nicholson, Dennis Pena, Shannon Penner, Troy Quane, Tony Tulipano. CGI Animators: Richard Baneham, David M. Bailey, Richard Bazley, Brad Booker, Adam Dotson, Bruce Edwards, Mark Farquar, Lennie K. Graves, Mike Murphy, Henry Sato Jr., Brian Schindler, David Earl Smith, Glenn Storm, Vincent Truitner, Jim Van Der Keyl. Story head: Mark Andrews. Story: Barry Caldwell, Bob Camp, Steven Fonti, Stephan Franck, Daan Jippes, Mark Kausler, Henry Mayo, Wilbert Plymaar, Pergel Reilly, Jeff Siergey, Moroni.

## The Pagemaster (11/24/94) 20th Century Fox. 75 mins. (Partial live action.) Director (live action): Joe Johnston. Director (animation): Maurice Hunt. Producers: David Kirschner, Paul Gertz. Voices: Macauley Culkin (Richard Tyler), Christopher Lloyd (Mr. Dewey, The Pagemaster), Whoopi Goldberg (Fantasy), Patrick Stewart (Adventure), Leonard Nimoy (Dr. Jekyll and Mr. Hyde), Ed Begley Jr. (Alan Tyler), Mel Harris (Claire Tyler), Frank Welker (Horror, Various Creatures), Phil Hartman (Tom Morgan), George Hearn (Captain Ahab).

**Consumer Tips:** ☆☆½ MPAA Rating: G.

**Story:** A frightened boy is transformed into a cartoon and transported into a world of books, led by talking books Horror, Fantasy, and Adventure.

©Twentieth Century Fox

**Comments:** David Kirschner, then executive head of Hanna-Barbera Productions, conceived this fantasy-cum-reader's advocate film, which was also one of Macauley Culkin's last starring roles as a child actor. In live-action sequences, Culkin plays Richard, a rather paranoid boy obsessed with accident statistics, who is stranded in a library during a rainstorm. Knocked unconscious, he soon becomes an animated character, a transition that recalls Chuck Jones' *Phantom Tollbooth* (indeed the whole film resembles a looser, even more pedantic version of that film). The effects sequence here, as a storybook ceiling mural dissolves into a flood of paint, is one of the more engrossing scenes in the film.

Supplied with three book sidekicks, representing the genres fantasy, adventure, and horror, Richard journeys through a literary landscape in yet another episodic animated quest variant. The snatches from classic literature are taken out of context and considerably condensed, essentially a parade of cameos. A staid Dr. Jekyll suddenly transforms into a wonderfully gibbering, slobbering Mr. Hyde for the mere purpose of menacing the quartet, while Captain Ahab receives a scant few seconds of screen time, attempting to harpoon Moby Dick. *Treasure Island* features more prominently, in a lengthy but meandering excursion with Long John Silver and crew, young Richard basically subbing for Jim Hawkins. Incredibly brief snatches from *A Christmas Carol, The Raven, Hound of the Baskervilles, Alice in Wonderland,* and Mother Goose rhymes also surface, culminating in a surprisingly dull dragon battle.

As laudable as the film's aims are, attempting to introduce young audiences to the joys of literature and the privileges of using the library (a library card is presented as a sacred item), the movie has no clear story structure, and the classic cameos generally don't tie well together. The psychological subject of a child tormented by statistical fears is far more interesting, but it too is resolved in a rather "Afterschool Special" manner. The book characters are fun caricatures, though, with good voice work; Patrick Stewart is particularly fine hamming it up as the piratical Adventure. Christopher Lloyd, providing the voice of the mystical, yet ultimately pointless, Pagemaster, is better served as the character's live-action counterpart, wild-eyed librarian Mr. Dewey, adding a touch of off-kilter energy to the frame sequences. In the end, good intentions aside, kids would probably be better served by reading the actual books referenced. (AL)

**Additional Credits:** Animation producers: David J. Staenberg, Barry Weiss. Live-action producer: Michael R. Joyce. Animation director: Maurice Hunt. Live-action director: Joe Johnston. Screenplay: David Casci, David Kirschner, Ernie Contreras. Story: David Kirschner, David Casci. Music: James Horner. Supervising animator: Bruce W. Smith. Sequence director: Glenn Chaika. Supervising animator (Hollywood Cartoon Company): Skip Jones. Animators: Anne Marie Bardwell, Ralph Fernan, Kevin Johnson, Dave Kupczyk, Jason Lethcoe, Mike Nguyen, Matt O'Callaghan, Bob Scott. Hollywood Cartoon Company: Matthew Bates, Jon Hooper, Mark Koetsier, Linda Miller, Mark Pudleiner, Chad Stewart. Additional animation: Brenda Banks, Dan Haskett. Visual effects supervisor: Richard T. Sullivan. Special effects supervising animators: John Allan Armstrong, Kathleen Quaife-Hodge. Effects animators: Margaret Craig-Chang, Al Holter, Jeffrey Howard, Brice Mallier, Peter Matheson, Brian McSweeney, Allen Stovall. Art director: Pixote. Production design/clean-up layout: Gay Lawrence, Valerio Ventura. Story supervisor: Robert Lence. Storyboards: Tom Ellery Jr., Gay Lawrence, Don Morgan, Mike Nguyen, Sue Nichols, Darrell Rooney, Rick Schneider, Valerio Ventura. Layout supervisor: Don Morgan. Rough layout artists: Arlan Jewell, Dan Milles, Simon Varela, David Womersley. Background supervisor: Jim Hickey. Backgrounds: Bill Dely, Jonathan Coley, Jim Hickey, Mi Kung Joung-Raynis, Jane Nussbaum, George Taylor. Additional backgrounds: Mannix Bennett, Ruben Chavez. A Turner Entertainment/David Kirschner Production released through 20th Century Fox.

©Globe Releasing Corporation

**Panda and the Magic Serpent** (7/8/61) Globe Releasing Company. 78 mins. Director: Taiji Yabushita, Kazuhiko Okabe. Producers: Hiroshi Okawa, Hideyuki Takahashi, Sanae Yamamoto. Voices: Marvin Miller (Narrator), Mel Welles (The Wizard).

**Consumer Tips:** ☆☆☆ MPAA Rating: Unrated. Oriental fantasy adventure. An adaptation of the ancient Chinese folktale *The White Snake Enchantress*. The first animated commercial theatrical feature of the Japanese film industry.

**Story:** Hsu Hsien, a young boy, rescues a white snake and makes it his beloved pet, which loves him in return. Years later when Hsu Hsien is a handsome youth, the snake is reincarnated as the maiden Pai Niang to become his bride. But they are attacked by Fa Hai, a pompous and fanatical magician. He believes that Pai Niang is an evil spirit and is determined to kill her to save Hsu Hsien.

**Comments:** The Japanese animation industry arguably began on July 31, 1956, when the live-action Toei Co. founded its Toei Animation Co. subsidiary with the stated goal of becoming "the Disney of the East." *Panda and the Magic Serpent* (actually *Hakuja Den* or *The White Snake Enchantress*, released October 22, 1958) modeled itself upon the Disney theatrical formula of adapting a popular fairy tale and adding songs and cute animal companions to the main human characters. (Note: this was not Japan's first animated theatrical fea-

ture. That was a 1945 propaganda feature commissioned by the Imperial Navy.)

Toei did a straightforward adaptation of the Chinese legend except for the addition of the songs and the cute animals, Panda and Mimi, and the band of waterfront ruffians led by Fagin the pig, Wiley the weasel, and Chiky the mouse. Changes made for the American audience include calling Fa Hai an "evil magician" instead of a well-meaning but bigoted Taoist priest; identifying Mimi as a "raccoon" instead of a red or lesser panda; and ignoring the point that Hsu is being offered both Pai and her maid Hsiao as his number one and number two wives. For an American novelization of the Chinese legend, see *The Devil Wives of Li Fong*, by E. Hoffman Price (Ballantine, 1979).

*Panda and the Magic Serpent* is one of the best animated adaptations of a Chinese folktale to retain its atmosphere of ancient Chinese culture; most more recent features are overly modernized. The drawback is that it is overly stately and slowly paced by American standards. The cute animals steal the show. (FP)

**Additional Credits:** Screenplay: Taiji Yabushita, Soichi Yashiro, Shin Uehara. Design: Akira Okuwara, Yasuji Mori. Music: Chuji Kinoshita, Masayoshi Ikeda. Cinematography: Takamitsu Tsukahara. Film editor: Shintarô Miyamoto. Art direction: Kiyoshi Hashimoto, Kazuhiko Okabe. Backgrounds: Kazuo Kusano. U.S. producer: Alvin Schoncite. Animation: Yasuo Otsuka, Kazuko Nakamura, Reiko Okuyama, Yusaku Sakamoto, Taku Sugiyama, Gisaburo Sugii.

**WXIII: Patlabor the Movie 3** (1/10/03) Pioneer Entertainment. 105 mins. Director: Fumihiko Takayama. Producers: Atsushi Sugita, Masahiro Fukushima. Voices: Richard Epcar (Isao Ota), Steve Kramer (Boat Captain), Julie Maddalena (Hitomi Misaki), Dan Martin (Police Captain), Daran Norris (Kiichi Goto), Tony Oliver (Baseball Player), Simon Prescott (Toshiro Kurisu), Steven Chester Prince (Shizuo Miyanomori), Michelle Ruff (Noa Izumi), Helen Storm (Kieko Misaki), Alfred Thor (Takeshi Kusumi), Kirk Thornton (Col. Goro Ishihara), Kari Wahlgren (Saeko Misaki), Dave Wittenberg (Shinichiro Hata).

**Consumer Tips:** ☆☆☆☆ MPAA Rating: R. SF/detective adventure. Tokyo police detectives investigate a series of apparent sabotages and discover a bio-engineered monster. This is the third theatrical feature in the *Patlabor, the Mobile Police* series.

**Story:** In the near future, a land reclamation project in Tokyo Bay begins to suffer mysterious equipment disasters that include some fatalities. Police detectives Kusumi and Hata at first suspect sabotage by environmental activists, but mounting evidence convinces them that the attacks are being made by a giant sea monster. They must stop the monster and find out what created it.

**Comments:** *WXIII: Patlabor the Movie 3* (aka. *Patlabor 3: WXIII, Patlabor WXIII the Movie*, and *Patlabor: Wasted Thirteen*) is an enjoyable animated theatrical SF/horror thriller in the *Godzilla* genre. However, it exemplifies some of the problems of theatrical movies made to capitalize on old television series. *Mobile Police Patlabor* (based on a manga by Masami Yuki) actually achieved its popularity through two direct-to-video series, a year-long television series, and two theatrical features between 1988 and 1994, all early works of noted anime director Mamoru Oshii animated by the Headgear and Sunrise studios. Set ten years in the future, *Patlabor* brought the giant robot genre into a relatively realistic setting by using robots as heavy-duty labor vehicles for military, industrial, and police work. The focus was upon the latter, specifically the misadventures of the Tokyo police force's Pat(rol) Labor Division 2 while trying to do their jobs in giant robots instead of patrol cars. The mecha immediately took a backseat to the fully characterized human cast: enthusiastic rookie Noa Izumi, sleepy-looking but sharp-witted Captain Goto, excitable and trigger-happy Officer Ota, and eight or ten others. Many episodes dispensed with the mecha altogether in favor of developing the friendships, loves, rivalries, and personal problems of the team. Plots deliberately varied wildly; the audience never knew whether the next episode would be serious or a comedy, a realistic dramatization of police action or a human-interest episode in one of Labor Division 2's member's lives, or a fantasy-parody of a classic Japanese monster movie.

Ten years later. How to bring back *Patlabor* for the big screen in a way to please both old fans and new viewers unfamiliar with the old cast? It was decided to create a side story in which Labor Division 2 is in the background. *WXIII: Patlabor the Movie 3* (animated by the Madhouse studio, released March 30, 2002) is set in a near future in which a controversial land reclamation project is filling in part of Tokyo Bay. The original Labor Division 2 cast appears only for the lengthy climax, called in to support new characters Kusumi and Hata in their trap for the monster. Madhouse's theatrical animation quality is fine, and the story is a plausibly developed techno-thriller blending conspiracy coverups (what government agency or megacorporation created the monster, and how far can it go to suppress the fact?) with fast-paced police vs. monster action scenes. *Patlabor* fans were disappointed that there was so little of *Patlabor* in it, which may be a benefit for American viewers unfamiliar with the Japanese series. (FP)

**Additional Credits:** Animation director: Takuji Endo. Screenplay: Tori Miki. Story: Yuuki Masami. Executive producer: Fumihiko Takayama. Music: Kenji Kawai. Character design: Hiroki Takagi. Key animation supervisor: Kazuchika Kise.

## The Pebble and the Penguin (4/12/95) MGM/UA. 74 mins. Director: (uncredited) Don Bluth. Producers: James Butterworth, Russell Boland. Voices: Martin Short (Hubie), James Belushi (Rocko), Tim Curry (Drake), Annie Golden (Marina), Shani Wallis (Narrator), Scott Bullock (Chubby, Gentoo), Louise Vallance (Priscilla, Chinstrap #2, Vocals), Pat Musick (Pola, Chinstrap #1), Angeline Ball (Gwynne, Chinstrap #3), Will Ryan (Tika).

**Consumer Tips:** ½ (a half star). MPAA Rating: G. Musical fantasy.

**Story:** Hubie, a shy Adelie penguin, falls in love with the most desirable penguin in Antarctica, Marina, and seeks the perfect pebble to complete the mating ritual. But his rival, the evil Drake, forces him into the sea, where the current sweeps him away from the mainland. Captured by humans, Hubie teams up with a feisty Rockhopper penguin, Rocko, who has a desire to fly. Rocko trains Hubie to fight during their trek back to Antarctica. After Hubie survives his showdown with Drake, he presents his pebble to Marina, who tells him, "It's not the pebble; it's the penguin." And they live happily ever after.

**Comments:** Considering the artistic and financial success of Disney's *Beauty and the Beast*, Don Bluth and Gary Goldman decided to cater to the dating crowd, in addition to preschoolers. Like *Beauty*, their love story included six musical numbers from a popular songwriter (Barry Manilow) and featured an egotistical muscle-bound buffoon of a villain who wants to force the beauty to marry him. Unlike *Beauty*, the hero was a stuttering wimp, the songs didn't advance the plot, the dialogue was incessant and superfluous, and the pacing was plodding and dull.

Bluth clothed his penguins, apparently not trusting his animators to give their characters distinctive movements. Additionally, humans wearing penguin costumes were filmed, and used as photostat references for the animators.

"*Penguin* had story problems. We knew it. The crew knew it," Bluth admitted in his magazine, *Toon Talk* (November 2001). Bluth tried to fix it, but when his Irish studio came under new ownership by Media Assets, a Chinese company, "The story and the film were now compromised. Hence, neither of us stayed to complete the motion picture." The directors removed their names from *Pebble's* credits and accepted an offer from 20th Century Fox's president, Bill Mechanic, to start a new animation studio in the United States. Bluth told his Irish crew, "I can't chew with someone else's mouth."

Walter Mirisch of MGM/UA had a higher appraisal of *Pebble and the Penguin*. "I think it's one of Don's best films ever," he said in the January 24, 1995 *Hollywood Reporter*. "There's no issue of our claiming the credit for this. It's his film."

An utter waste of talent and resources. Once again Bluth and company pander to infantile minds. *Pebble's* weak storytelling is insulting, no matter what the viewer's age.

Once again Bluth and Goldman rely on the same old character-is-dead-but-he's-really-alive-after-all routine. Twice! How does Rocko escape the jaws of the killer whale? How does Drake survive his fall from the precipice? They survive because of a cheap cinematic trick. They reappear because the story can't proceed without them.

What are three sparrows doing in Antarctica? They're cheap little devices for exposition, as a sounding board for Hubie talking and talking and singing, and talking and singing some more. When the film becomes mushy we cut to one of the sparrows reacting with a nasty face—which means Bluth/Goldman didn't want to sustain the intimacy of the moment. This raises the question, why bother making a love story if you keep distracting from it?

The end credits number, "Now and Forever," sung by Barry Manilow and Sheena Easton, is a joy to hear. But "The Good Ship Misery" could be used as an instrument of torture.

MGM/UA released *Pebble* with a short, *Driving Mr. Pink*, which introduced the character of Voodoo Man from the 1995 Pink Panther television series. The film earned a tepid $3.9 million in theaters; MGM Home Entertainment quickly released *Pebble* on VHS on August 15, 1995. (WRM)

**Additional Credits:** Screenplay: Rachel Koretsky, Steve Whitestone. Music score: Mark Watters. Songs: Barry Manilow, Bruce Sussman. Directing animators: John Pomeroy, Len Simon, Richard Bazley, Sylvia Hoefnagels, Ralf Palmer, John Hill, John Power. Animation: Sandro Cleuzo, Marcelo De Moura, Alain Costa, Edison Goncalves, Gabor Steisinger, Fernando Mora, Paul Newberry, Roger Goddy, Robert Fox, Celine Cahill, Glen McIntosh, Robert Sprathoff, Stuart Holgate, Konrad Winterlich, Hugo Tykahashi. A Sullivan Bluth Ltd. Production released through MGM/United Artists.

**Perfect Blue** (10/8/99) Manga Entertainment. 80 mins. Director: Satoshi Kon. Producers: Haruyo Kanesaku, Hiroaki Inoue, Masao Maruyama, Yutaka

Maseba. Voices: Ruby Marlowe (Mima Kirigoe), Barry Stigler (Tadakoro), Wendee Lee (Rumi), Bob Marx (Me-Mania), Richard Plantagenet (Director), Jamieson Price (Mureno), Kirk Thornton (Yamashiro), Dylan Tully (Cham Manager).

**Consumer Tips:** ☆☆☆☆ MPAA Rating: R. Psychological murder mystery.

**Story:** Mima Kirigoe, a pop singing idol, is persuaded to leave her singing group and become a television actress. Her self-doubt as to whether she can be an actress is compounded by accusations by her fans of being a traitor for leaving her group, and her distaste over such debasing roles as a rape victim and psychotic murderess. When members of the television crew are actually murdered, Mima is unsure whether she really is an insane murderess.

**Comments:** Most critics enthusiastically agree with Roger Corman's publicity blurb comparing *Perfect Blue* to a blend of the best of Alfred Hitchcock and Walt Disney. This psychological thriller, director Satoshi Kon's first feature, was animated by the Madhouse studio and released in Japan on November 4, 1997. It became an international film festival award winner and established Kon as an auteur.

Superficially *Perfect Blue* could be filmed in live action, but Kon uses animation in subtle ways to enhance the audience's doubt over whether what is on-screen is real or in Mima's and other characters' imaginations. Mima sees her mirror-image double do things that she realizes are physically impossible; therefore she must be going mad. Some scenes are initially unclear whether they are in real life or are part of a *Double Bind* action scene; in a live-action movie the difference between an actual location and a small television set would be overly obvious. Otherwise, Kon shows that he could be an excellent live-action director. Mima's gradual psychological shift from nervous enthusiasm at starting her first television acting role to hidden but terrified doubt of the reality of everything around her is convincing yet not overacted. (FP)

**Additional Credits:** Executive producers: Marvin Gleicher, Laurence Guinness, Koshiro Kanda, Yuichi Tsurumi. Music: Masahiro Ikumi. Cinematography: Hisao Shirai. Film editor:

Harutoshi Ogata. Art Direction: Nobutaka Ike. Character designers: Hisashi Eguchi, Hideki Hamazu, Satoshi Kon. Animators: Koichi Arai, Nobumasa Arakawa, Shigero Fujita, Hitoshi Haga, Shinji Hamasaki, Shinji Hashimoto, Takeshi Honda, Mitsuo Iso, Kumiko Kawana, Yoshihiro Kitano, Makota Koga, Masahiro Kurio, Mamoru Kurosawa, Hidenori Matsubara, Hiroyuki Morita, Morifumi Naka, Katsuichi Nakayama, Toshiya Niidome, Hideki Nimura, Takuo Noda, Michiyo Suzuki, Masaharu Tada, Shin'ya Takahashi, Kunio Takahide, Hikaru Takanashi, Makoto Yamada, Takaaki Yamashita.

**Peter Pan** (2/5/53) Walt Disney Pictures. 77 mins. Directors: Hamilton Luske, Clyde Geronimi, Wilfred Jackson. Voices: Bobby Driscoll (Peter Pan), Kathryn Beaumont (Wendy), Hans Conried (Captain Hook, Mr. Darling), Bill Thompson (Mr. Snee, Pirate Voices), Heather Angel (Mrs. Darling), Paul Collins (John), Tommy Luske (Michael), Margaret Kerry (Michael, Mermaids), Candy Candido (Indian Chief), Tom Conway (Narrator), Stuffy Singer, Johnny McGovern, Robert Ellis, Jeffery Silvers, Karen Kester, Carol Coombs, Norma Jean Nilsson, Anne Whitfield (Additional Voices), the Mitchell Choirboys.

**Consumer Tips:** ☆☆☆ MPAA Rating: G. Based on the stage play written in 1904 by Sir James Barrie and on several book versions written by Barrie thereafter.

**Story:** Young Wendy loves to regale her little brothers with tales of Peter Pan, the boy who never grows up. Her father has had enough of this and decides to banish Wendy from the nursery. On her final night Peter Pan shows up in search of his missing shadow, aided by his faithful fairy Tinker Bell. Peter transports all the children to Neverland by means of Tinker Bell's "flying dust." In Neverland adventure, fun, and eternal childhood rule, but also lurking there is Captain Hook, sworn enemy of Peter. Hook and his pirate crew nearly defeat Peter but the resourceful young sprite wins the day. Wendy and her brothers return to their home in London, having had the experience of their lives.

**Comments:** Walt Disney bought the rights to Barrie's work as far back as 1935 and the film was in development off and on for two decades; in the 1941 film *The Reluctant Dragon* one can see models of Captain Hook in the background of one shot. What Disney finally developed was a hybrid between Barrie's play and Disney's sense of story and design.

Most of the rules dictating Barrie's play were broken for the film. First: a female must play Peter Pan. Second: a human must play Nana the dog. Third: Tinker Bell must only be seen as a beam of light. Fourth: the crocodile must not be seen on stage. Fifth: the audience must be invoked to save the life of Tinker Bell. Disney kept only one convention: the same actor who portrays Mr. Darling must portray Captain Hook (Hans Conried voiced both). Even with all these elements changed, *Peter Pan* is an excellent film on its own merits, a beautifully crafted snapshot of Disney feature animation in full maturity. Only a very confident crew secure in their abilities to adapt a classic on their own terms could have pulled this movie off. Disney's did.

The movie may be named after the boy who never grows up, but it can be argued that the leading character in the film is Wendy Darling. Nothing really changes for Peter; this was simply another adventure for him. It can be reasonably assumed that Peter will soon be at it with Hook and crew again, that he will continue to flirt with mermaids and Tiger Lily, and that he will remain perpetually prepubescent. Wendy, though, is on the verge of young womanhood and must now leave the nursery—and Peter—behind to prepare for her role in later life. She becomes the mother figure that Neverland never had.

Witness Wendy's influence on the Lost Boys (and even the pirates) as she sings the wistful number "Your Mother and Mine." It is no accident that the pirates have Wendy walk the plank, as she is the destabilizing force in a world that never grows up. This also explains, more than mere jealousy, why Tinker Bell despises Wendy so. Tinker seems to have put up with the other girls in Peter's world for quite some time. Wendy, however, threatens not only Tink's relationship with Peter, but Neverland itself.

Of Disney's famed "Nine Old Men," every single one of them served as a supervising animator on this film. Several scenes stand out: Frank Thomas's outstanding animation of Hook as he attempts to charm Tinker Bell into revealing Peter's hideout; Woolie Reitherman's animation of the same character as he fights for his life against the crocodile; Eric Larson's magical flying scene over a starkly detailed London at nighttime. Ollie Johnston's Smee, a jolly self-caricature, provides excellent comic relief each time he appears. Disney has come under attack for literalizing Barrie's play and must plead guilty as charged. However, in this case, the play's not the thing and Disney's film should be viewed as a rich variation on Barrie's wonderful themes.

For the record:

- It has long been rumored that Tinker Bell was modeled on Marilyn Monroe, but this is not so. The character design, by some accounts, may date back to 1943 when Ms. Monroe was still young enough for Neverland. Margaret Kerry actually served as the fairy's live-action reference.
- Disney bought the rights to the play from the Hospital for Sick Children, Great Ormond Street, London (the beneficiaries of Sir Barrie's will).
- This was the last film that master animator Fred Moore ever worked on. The man who defined the Disney style died several years later in an auto accident. (MG)

**Additional Credits:** Story: Ted Sears, Bill Peet, Joe Rinaldi, Erdman Penner, Winston Hibler, Milt Banta, Ralph Wright, Bill Cottrell. Adapted from the play and books by Sir James M. Barrie. Music: Oliver Wallace. Songs: Sammy Fain, Sammy Cahn, Oliver Wallace, Frank Churchill, Erdman Penner, Winston Hibler, Ted Sears. Directing animators: Milt Kahl, Frank

Thomas, Wolfgang Reitherman, Ward Kimball, Eric Larson, Ollie Johnston, Marc Davis, John Lounsbery, Les Clark, Norman Ferguson. Animators: Hal King, Cliff Nordberg, Hal Ambro, Don Lusk, Ken O'Brian, Marvin Woodward, Art Stevens, Eric Cleworth, Fred Moore, Bob Carlson, Harvey Toombs, Judge Whitaker, Bill Justice, Jerry Hathcock, Claire Weeks. Effects animators: George Rowley, Blaine Gibson, Joshua Meador, Dan McManus. Color/styling: Mary Blair, Claude Coats, John Hench, Donald DaGradi. Background artists: Ray Huffine, Art Riley, Albert Dempster, Eyvind Earle, Ralph Hulett, Thelma Witmer, Dick Anthony, Brice Mack. Layout artists: Mac Stewart, Tom Codrick, A. Kendall O'Connor, Charles Philippi, Hygh Hennesy, Ken Anderson, Al Zinnen, Lance Nolley, Thor Putnam, Don Griffith.

**The Phantom Tollbooth** (11/7/70) MGM. 90 mins. Directors (animation): Chuck Jones, Abe Levitow. Director (live action): David Monahan. Producers: Chuck Jones, Abe Levitow, Les Goldman. Cast: Butch Patrick (Milo). Voices: Shep Menken (Tock), Hans Conried (King Azaz, The Mathemagician), Mel Blanc (Officer Short Shrift, Dodecahedron, Word Man, Demon of Insincerity, Lethargians, Ministers), Les Tremayne (Humbug, Poet), June Foray (Faintly Macabre, Princess of Pure Reason), Daws Butler (Whether Man, Senses Taker, Terrible Trivium, Gelatinous Giant), Cliff Norton (Spelling Bee, Chroma the Great, Ministers), Larry Thor (Dr. Kakofanus A. Dischord, Tollbooth Speaker Voice, Lethargians), Candy Candido (Awful DYNN, Lethargians), Patti Gilbert (Princess of Sweet Rhyme, Teacher Voice), Thurl Ravenscroft (Lethargians), Herb Vigran (Overbearing Know-it-all).

©Metro-Goldwyn-Mayer, Inc.

**Consumer Tips:** ☆☆½ MPAA Rating: G. Based on the book by Norton Juster.

**Story:** A boy is led, via a magic car through a phantom tollbooth, to a strange world where letters and numbers are at war.

**Comments:** Director Chuck Jones's first feature bears his distinctive stamp, although at first the general tone and subject of the film seem to come from different sensibilities than those that resulted in the frantic Road Runner cartoons at Warner Bros. Like the Oscar-winning 1965 short *The Dot and the Line*, which Jones had also produced at MGM, the film was based on a book by Norton Juster. The book's original rough illustrations by cartoonist Jules Feiffer have been converted to the later Jones style, losing touches like the clock embedded in Tock's torso, but still quite appealing. The tale of young (live-action) Milo's travels into a fantastic, animated world built around knowledge is punctuated by punning character names and metaphors/slang expressions as living characters.

This story, then, is by nature rather pedagogical, and songs extolling the virtues of words, numbers, time, and sounds add to that feeling. However, the viewer may not really care, as it's carried off with stylish background designs, courtesy of Maurice Noble, and typically expert animation from Jones' crew of veteran animators. The Doldrums sequence, with the fluid Lethargians drowsily singing their anthem and lazily sliding apart and into each other, is a wonderful set piece and features the most memorable and least cloying song in the film. There's some fine character movement in the duel between the Spelling Bee and the Humbug. Even the obvious puns are good-natured and add to the enjoyment. *Munsters* alumnus Butch Patrick, as Milo, seems rather petulant and bored (to some extent, intentionally perhaps), but Jones wisely surrounded him with a stellar cast of vocal veterans, usually seldom to be heard in the same production, in multiple roles: Warner staples Mel Blanc and June Foray, Hanna-Barbera star Daws Butler, radio actor Larry Thor ("Broadway Is My Beat"), the inimitable Hans Conried, and Shep Menken, with his "Clyde Crashcup" Richard Haydn impression. Another Termite Terrace veteran, Dave Monahan, directed the live-action scenes. Definitely recommended for any Chuck

Jones fans, as it stands as his only complete feature, not counting the anthology *Bugs Bunny/Road Runner Movie*. (AL)

***Additional Credits:*** Writers: Chuck Jones, Sam Rosen. Based on the book *The Phantom Tollbooth* by Norton Juster. Music: Dean Elliott. Songs (uncredited): Lee Pockriss. Lyrics (uncredited): Norman Gimbel, Paul Vance. Supervising animators: Ben Washam, Hal Ambro, George Nicholas. Animators: Irv Spence, Bill Littlejohn, Richard Thompson, Tom Ray, Phillip Roman, Alan Zaslove, Edwin Aardal, Ed DeMattia, Xenia, Lloyd Vaughan, Carl Bell. Production design: Maurice Noble. Layout artists: Tony Rivera, Don Morgan, Oscar Dufau, Rosemary O'Connor, Corny Cole, Phyllis Graham. Background artists: Phillip DeGuard, Irving Weaver, Robert McIntosh.

## Piglet's Big Movie (3/21/03) Disney. 75 mins.

Director: Francis Glebas. Producer: Michelle Pappalardo-Robinson. Voices: John Fiedler (Piglet), Jim Cummings (Winnie the Pooh, Tigger), Andre Stojka (Owl), Kath Soucie (Kanga), Nikita Hopkins (Roo), Peter Cullen (Eeyore), Ken Sansom (Rabbit), Tom Wheatley (Christopher Robin).

©Walt Disney Enterprises, Inc.

***Consumer Tips:*** ☆☆ MPAA Rating: G. Adapted from the popular tales by A. A. Milne.

***Story:*** Winnie the Pooh and pals stage a raid on a honey tree but leave tiny Piglet out of the plan. Piglet ends up ensuring the raid's success but is ignored nonetheless. The unhappy Piglet disappears, leaving the Pooh gang to track him down through his hand-drawn scrapbook of memories. Along the way, Pooh, Eeyore, Roo, Rabbit, and Tigger all come to realize that Piglet is an important and special part of their lives, no matter how small he is in stature.

***Comments:*** Winnie the Pooh and pals have been winners for Disney since 1966, both on screen and in the licensing arena. It is perhaps to be expected that individual characters like Tigger, Piglet, and Eeyore would have films dedicated to them. Taken on its own terms—as a movie for very young kids—*Piglet's Big Movie* succeeds much of the time and is far less of an embarrassment than many of Disney's sequels. Considering that Piglet is by far the least interesting of the Pooh cohorts in Disney's films, this is a notable achievement. Piglet, in fact, did not even appear in the original 1966 film *Winnie the Pooh and the Honey Tree*.

The movie itself is a series of episodic flashbacks, each one inspired by a page in Piglet's scrapbook. The tales highlight Piglet's selflessness, bravery, and worthiness as a friend. The more the characters read as they search for their lost comrade, the more they realize how little they have appreciated him. When the book is inadvertently destroyed in a downpour, the searchers adjourn to Piglet's home to ride out the storm. Using crayons and paper, they re-create the book of memories, even adding their own embellishments. During this scene the crude drawings come to life, as if third-grade artists were doing the animation. This has been done before but does add a touch of charm to the film.

The film's biggest problem is the contrived ending in which Piglet rescues Pooh from a violent death in a waterfall. The characters have already come to regret their actions toward Piglet and have expressed their love for him for the past 40 minutes; having him show up unexpectedly like a modern-day action hero to save the day rather belabors the point.

Jim Cummings continues to shine as Tigger, and Cummings also does a fair job of approximating the late Sterling Holloway's voice for Winnie the Pooh. One of the nicest turns is by veteran voice artist Kath Soucie, whose characterization of Kanga is so soothing and maternal that you'll want to jump into her pouch. Art director Fred Warter and illustrator Rick Law do a very nice job with background and layout; it looks as if the characters are animated against the backdrop of a quality children's book. There is nothing outstanding about *Piglet's Big Movie*, but nothing truly terrible either.

For the record:

- *Piglet's Big Movie* was made during the bitter, ongoing legal battle between Disney and the Milne estate. At the time of this writing, the wrangling over some of the rights had not yet been resolved. The Milne estate is nearly as stringent as Disney; it once sued Jefferson Airplane front man Paul Kantner for using lines from a Pooh story in one of his songs. (MG)

*Additional Credits:* Associate producers: Ferrell Barron, Yukari Kiso. Story: Brian Hohlfeld. Additional screenplay material: Ted Henning. Adapted from and inspired by the works of A. A. Milne. Music: Carl Johnson. Songs: Carly Simon, Richard M. Sherman, Robert B. Sherman. Unit director: Masaki Sugiyama. Animation director: Takeshi Atomura. Assistant directors: Fumio Maezono, Yumiko Suzuki. Animation: Alexander Williams, Scott T. Petersen, Andreas Wessel-Therhorn. Lead animators: Hiroshi Kawamata, Kiyomi Miyakawa, Jyunpei Tatenaka, Kenichi Tsuchiya, Hisashi Wada, Yuji Watanabe. Key animators: Chei Arai, Rei Arai, Yoshiharu Ashino, Genta Chiba, Nozomi Fujii, Atsuhiko Hara, Takahiro Ikezoe, Isamitsu Kashima, Hideaki Kurakawa, Don MacKinnon, Masayo Matsumoto, Kazuhiro Murase, Hiroko Minowa, Yufuki Morimoto, Tomokatsu Nagasaku, Hirofumi Nakata, Takayo Nishimura, Sachio Nishiyama, Emi Noguchi, Masaru Ohshiro, Scott Petersen, Masatomo Saito, Kazuko Shibata, Takeo Shuto, Emil Simeonov, Kouichi Suenaga, Kaori Takeuchi, Yasuyo Torii, Yoshihiro Tsuji, Kouji Ukai, Sachiko Wakabayashi, Andreas Wessel-Therhorn, Alexander Williams, Theresa Wiseman. Supervising effects animation director: Madoka Yasuet. CGI effects artists: Kiyoteru Ogawa, Hiroyuki Hatada, Gina Di Bari, Hock-Lian Law, Eric Rosenthal. CGI effects assistants: Tetsuya Hasebe, Mayumi Hiramatsu. Art director: Fred Warter. Storyboard artists: Andrew Austin, Keith Baxter, Ben Gluck, Susan Nichols, Robert Sledge. Additional storyboards: Carin-Anne Greco, Douglas Murphy, Dave Prince, Debra Pugh, Carolyn Gair, Kenny Thompkins. Background stylists: Fred Warter, Paro Hozumi. Layout director: Kazuyoshi Takeuchi. Layout animators: Shinichi Suzuki, Shigeru Yamamoto. Background supervisor: Hiroshi Ohno. Background artists: Kaori Anmi, Yuri Hamaya, Emi Kitahara, Chie Ohkubo, Kumiko Ohno, Yasuyuki Yuzawa.

**Pinocchio** (2/7/40) Walt Disney Productions. 88 mins. Directors: Ben Sharpsteen, Hamilton Luske.

Voices: Dickie Jones (Pinocchio), Cliff Edwards (Jiminy Cricket), Christian Rub (Gepetto), Walter Catlett (J. Worthington Foulfellow), Charles Judels (Stromboli, Coachman), Frankie Darro (Lampwick), Evelyn Venable (Blue Fairy), Mel Blanc (Gideon), Don Brodie (Carnival Barker).

*Consumer Tips:* ☆☆☆☆ MPAA Rating: G. Adapted from the serialized novel by Carlo Lorenzini (aka Collodi) written from 1880 to 1883.

*Story:* Vagabond Jiminy Cricket drops in on Gepetto, a gentle woodcarver, just as he finishes a cute puppet. In his loneliness Gepetto wishes that his Pinocchio were a real boy. The Blue Fairy, noting Gepetto's kindness to others, grants the puppet life and the chance to give Gepetto his wish in full. All the puppet has to do is prove himself brave, unselfish, and truthful. The fairy appoints Jiminy as the puppet's conscience, but this is a harder job than it looks. Pinocchio is naively coopted into terrifying adventures and often fails to learn from his mistakes. But with an act of caring and self-sacrifice he bravely fulfills the Blue Fairy's requirements and becomes a living boy.

*Comments:* *Pinocchio* is undoubtedly one of the greatest achievements in animation. Before one invokes the name of Pixar it should be noted that the most advanced computer available to the Disney studio when animation on the film began in 1938 was a slide rule. After the triumph of *Snow White and the Seven*

*Dwarfs* it seems that Disney's animators and artists pushed to see how far they could stretch the technical boundaries of animation. As a result *Pinocchio* contains scenes using techniques that were never duplicated or even attempted again. The studio was developing *Fantasia* at the same time, and many of the advancements in *Pinocchio* benefited that film as well.

The biggest challenges in *Pinocchio*, however, were not technical. The original story featured an irascible antihero, countless villains, and very few moments of lightness or comedy. It is to Disney's credit that the feel of Collodi's work was retained; much of the film is a dark nightmare punctuated by moments of real horror. *Pinocchio* can be viewed as a perilous journey to responsibility and maturity, but an alternative reading is certainly possible: *Pinocchio* depicts the consequences of failure on such a journey, and the despair, terror, and hopelessness that ensue when a life is ruined and all opportunities are lost. *Pinocchio* takes place in a cruel, exploitative world in which evil goes unpunished. There is not one villain in the movie that gets his comeuppance, and the villains presumably continue to lie in wait for the next sucker—or victim.

Disney realized that these concepts would work best if the main character were a gullible naïf rather than the cocky, abrasive puppet that Collodi created. Pinocchio started out as a stark wooden puppet but animator Milt Kahl eventually redesigned him as a pleasant little boy; there are times one forgets he is actually a puppet. To counteract the many villains and bad influences Pinocchio encounters, Disney brought a minor character from the book—a talking cricket that Pinocchio kills—into the film. Dubbed "Jiminy Cricket," the bug was now to serve as Pinocchio's guide and conscience. Jiminy was redesigned several times by animator Ward Kimball, who eliminated nearly all of Jiminy's insect aspects. Finally, Pinocchio's "father" Gepetto was softened up for both warmth and comic relief. The original voice actor sounded too harsh to Walt and was replaced by a grandfatherly character actor named Christian Rub.

The villains of *Pinocchio* range from comic to satanic, and Monstro the Whale (who swallows Gepetto alive) is simply a brute force of nature. Foulfellow the Fox and Gideon the Cat want to exploit Pinocchio for monetary gain; the volatile puppeteer Stromboli wants to use Pinocchio as his star performer/slave. The coachman (and his terrifying, hooded flock of demons) makes his living by trapping bad little boys on Pleasure Island, where they transmute into donkeys and are then sold for profit.

Pinocchio, despite Jiminy's best efforts, falls for each villainous ploy. Every time he does his ordeal is worse. Pinocchio's courageous attempt to save his father from Monstro the whale finally kills the puppet. If fairy tales are indeed a way for children to deal with the fears of growing up, *Pinocchio* is a fairy tale for the ages. There are also mythic/religious themes present that lend a powerful undercurrent to the film. The boy magically born of no mother, the wanderings and return of the Prodigal Son, the themes of sin, temptation, resurrection, and sacrifice can be found in many cultures, and they find sharp resonance in Disney's film.

These mythic elements are wedded to spectacular animation. There is extensive use of the multiplane camera, which was refined to track horizontal as well as vertical shots for added dimensionality. One scene celebrated by animation fans features Pinocchio caged in Stromboli's wagon; five different levels of camerawork are used, with independent light effects for each level. The opening scene, which panned down into Gepetto's village, required twelve separate planes. Underwater scenes are shot through wavy panes of glass that distort the animation cels. Surface ocean effects were created through photographic cutouts of waves that were treated with blue and black pencil dust. 750 artists, technicians, and effects specialists (including 10 airbrush artists) toiled on the film at a cost of $2.6 million, and their efforts are magnificent indeed. Children's book illustrator Gustaf Tenggren (who left before *Pinocchio* was completed) set the film's detailed style, and the art directors followed suit. It is difficult to find a film with richer visuals, and *Pinocchio* must have looked astounding to audiences in 1940.

Unfortunately, World War II cut off much of Walt Disney's audience base and revenues. The film was not a hit domestically, and *Pinocchio* lost over a million dollars. It took numerous rereleases and the eventual verdict of history to raise *Pinocchio* to its present, well-deserved status. Moments such as Lampwick and Pinocchio's transformations into terrified donkeys, the appearance of the ethereal Blue Fairy, the sight of Monstro charging directly into the camera, and Pinocchio's performance in Stromboli's puppet show represent some of the best work to be found in any animated feature. *Pinocchio* is a triumph on all levels, a wonderful wedding of animation technology and mature narrative.

For the record:

- *Pinocchio* gave the Disney studio its signature song, "When You Wish Upon a Star." The song was written by Leigh Harline and Ned Washington and performed by Cliff Edwards in his role as Jiminy Cricket. It was the 1941 Oscar Winner for Best Song, and the picture won the award for Best Music as well.
- The Disney shop built working models of every clock and toy in Gepetto's shop for the animators to study. The multiplane camera cost close to $30,000 per minute of use.
- Christian Rub, the voice of kindly old Gepetto, was Viennese by birth and a supporter of Adolf Hitler; he frequently annoyed the crew with pro-Nazi rantings.
- Margaret Belcher, who later married animator Art Babbitt, was the live-action model for the Blue Fairy.
- Gepetto's pet cat Figaro became a star of Disney shorts, usually as the pet of Minnie Mouse.
- Jiminy Cricket would make frequent television appearances on Disney shows and starred in two more films.
- Voice artist supreme Mel Blanc recorded an entire voice track for Gideon the cat, just as Walt Disney decided the cat should be mute. All that remains is a single hiccup.
- Leigh Harline also worked on *The Wizard of Oz* (1939) and cowrote "Somewhere over the Rainbow." (MG)

**Additional Credits:** Story adaptation: Ted Sears, Otto Englander, Webb Smith, William Cottrell, Joseph Sabo, Erdman Penner, Aurelius Battaglia. Based on the book *The Adventures of Pinocchio* by Collodi/Carlo Lorenzini. Music/lyrics: Leigh Harline, Ned Washington, Paul J. Smith. Sequence directors: Bill Roberts, Norman Ferguson, Jack Kinney, Wilfred Jackson, T. Hee. Animation directors: Fred Moore, Franklin Thomas, Milton Kahl, Vladimir Tytla, Ward Kimball, Arthur Babbitt, Eric Larson, Wolfgang Reitherman, Shamus Culhane (uncredited). Animators: Jack Campbell, Berny Wolf, Don Towsley, Oliver M. Johnston Jr., Don Lusk, John Lounsbery, Norman

Tate, John Bradbury, Lynn Karp, Charles Nichols, Art Palmer, Joshua Meador, Don Tobin, Robert Martsch, George Rowley, John McManus, Don Patterson, Preston Blair, Les Clark, Marvin Woodward, Hugh Fraser, John Elliotte. Uncredited animators: Ed Aardal, Al Geiss, Mo Gollub, Frank Grundeen, Ralph Heimdahl, Ben Oda, Joe Wehrle. Art directors: Charles Philippi, Hugh Hennesy, Kenneth Anderson, Dick Kelsey, A. Kendall O'Connor, Terrell Stapp, Thor Putnam, John Hubley, McLaren Stewart, Al Zinnen. Character designers: Albert Hurter, Joe Grant, John P. Miller, Campbell Grant, Martin Provenson, John Walbridge. Character sculptures (uncredited): Bob Jones, Charles Christodero, Helen Nervobig. Background artists: Claude Coats, Merle Cox, Ed Starr, Ray Huffine.

### Pinocchio and the Emperor of the Night

(12/25/87) New World. 91 mins. Director: Hal Sutherland. Producer: Lou Scheimer. Voices: Scott Grimes (Pinocchio), Tom Bosley (Gepetto), Edward Asner (Scalawag), Lana Beeson (Twinkle), Linda Gary (Bee-Atrice), Jonathan Harris (Lt. Grumblebee), James Earl Jones (Emperor of the Night), Rickie Lee Jones (Fairy Godmother), Don Knotts (Gee Willikers), Frank Welker (Igor), William Windom (Puppetino).

©Filmation Associates

**Consumer Tips:** ☆☆ MPAA Rating: G.

**Story:** *Pinocchio and the Emperor of the Night* is a sequel to Disney's *Pinocchio*. This film is set a year after Pinocchio's adventures in the Disney classic. In this film, he is celebrating his first year as a real boy. His new sidekick, a glowbug named Gee Wilikers, accompanies Pinocchio on an errand that goes awry as he is returned to being a wooden puppet. Only by confronting the evil Emperor of the Night can he return to normal.

**Comments:** *Pinocchio and the Emperor of the Night* was based on a story by Dennis O. Flaherty, while Disney's *Pinocchio* was based on Collodi's 1883 classic, *The Adventures of Pinocchio*. Although this film was a thin-veiled sequel to Disney's 1940 *Pinocchio*, Filmation tried not to imitate the Disney classic. Instead, it put Pinocchio in a more contemporary setting with a slightly different story.

In this film, Pinocchio has a series of adventures that were similar to the first Pinocchio's. In addition, this film has a subplot involving Gee Willikers and a bumblebee, two characters reminiscent of the Fleischers' 1941 *Mr. Bug Goes to Town*.

Hal Sutherland, Filmation's house director, did the chores on *Pinocchio and the Emperor of the Night*. The impressive voice cast included Edward Asner, Don Knotts, and James Earl Jones (sounding not unlike Darth Vader as the Emperor of the Night), as well as veteran animation television voice actors like Frank Welker and Linda Gray.

*Pinocchio and the Emperor of the Night* received lukewarm reviews. About the music, *Variety* wrote, "the songs are saccharine to the extreme." The film was a failure at the box office: *Pinocchio and the Emperor of the Night* cost $8 million to produce, but grossed only $3.3 million in ticket sales.

Disney sued Filmation Associates for copyright infringement of *Pinocchio*, a character who had now become closely identified with Disney. (Disney simultaneously sued Filmation for attempting to create animated "sequels" to *Alice in Wonderland* and *The Jungle Book*.) Filmation claimed Collodi's Pinocchio character was in public domain and won the lawsuit.

*Pinocchio and the Emperor of the Night* was advertised at the time as the last animated feature to be produced entirely in the United States. Since then, several animated features, mainly CG films, including all the Pixar, PDI-DreamWorks, and Blue Sky productions have been produced entirely in the United States. (SF)

**Additional Credits:** Writers: Robby London, Barry O Brien, Dennis O. Flaherty. Based on a story by Dennis O. Flaherty. Music: Anthony Marinelli, Brian Banks. Music/lyrics: Will Jennings, Barry Mann, Steve Tyrell, Anthony Marinelli. Supervis-

ing animators: John Celestri, Chuck Harvey, Kamoon Song. Animation: Robert Alvarez, Carl Bell, Bob Carlson, Yi-Cheh Chen, Doug Crane, James Dacism, Zeon Davush, Edward DeMattia, Will Finn, Fernando Gonzalez, Steve Gordon, Fred Grable, Lennie K. Graves, Daniel Haskett, Ruth Kissane, Jung Woo Lee, Clarke Logerstrom, Ernesto Lopez, Marcea Manta, Mauro Maressa, Costy Mustatea, Enory Myrick, Bill Nunes, Eduar do Olivares, Jack Ozark, Kevin Petrilak, Young Kyu Rhim, Lenord Robinson, Joe Roman, Mike Sanger, Louis Scarborough, Thomas Sito, Bruce W. Smith, Jason So, Ken Southworth, Leo Sullivan, Bob Tyler, Larry White, Allen Wilzback, Bruce Woodside. A New World Pictures release of a Filmation presentation.

**Pinocchio in Outer Space** (12/22/65) Universal (U.S.-Belgium). 90 mins. Director: Ray Goossens. Producers: Norm Prescott, Fred Ladd. Voices: Arnold Stang (Nurtle the Turtle), Peter Lazer (Pinocchio), Jess Cain (Gepetto), Mavis Mims (Blue Fairy), Conrad Jameson (G. Codline Sharp), Minerva Pious (Blue Fairy's Mother), Cliff Owens (Groovy). Additional voices: Norman Rose, Kevin Kennedy.

©Universal City Studios, Inc.

**Consumer Tips:** ☆☆ MPAA Rating: Unrated.

**Story:** Pinocchio, once again a puppet, looks to do a good deed in order to return to being a real boy. With the help of space-age pal Nurtle the Turtle, Pinocchio battles Astro, a flying whale.

**Comments:** Though *Yellow Submarine* is generally remembered as the trippiest animated feature of the psychedelic 1960s, in its own strange way, *Pinocchio in*

*Outer Space* is a serious challenger to the title. Fred Ladd, who had previously dubbed such Japanese imports as *Kimba the White Lion* and *Gigantor*, first ventured into features with this bizarre offering. Though Ladd produced and wrote (along with Norm Prescott of Filmation), the actual animation was farmed out to Bellvision, a Belgian studio that had previously produced a fairly successful *Tin Tin* series.

Both an update to and a sequel to the original tale, though with little resemblance to Collodi or Disney, Pinocchio, a puppet again due to misbehavior, is bored with studying science, although thrilled by reports of a large "space whale," Astro, an odd creation with sharp visible teeth, a leering eye, and a jet engine tail. Scenes with Gepetto, the Blue Fairy (whose mother bemoans the encroachment of satellites on the fairy's homestead), and the fox and cat (the latter now a beatnik) are dispatched with summarily to focus on a new creation, Nurtle the Twurtle, a secret agent who for some reason is intent on reaching Mars. Pinocchio accompanies him, leading to a visit to an abandoned Mars full of desolate cities, giant sand crabs, and strange breeding experiments, all accompanied by pedantic pseudo-scientific banter, in the best tradition of live-action entries in this genre, which lend a strange tone to the film. Forcedly cheerful songs, with titles like "Goody Good Morning," abound as well, and the descent into sentimentality at the end, while predictable, seems at odds with the rest of the film.

The basic concept and approach of the movie is so bizarre that, while it's difficult to really become involved in the story, it's also hard to dislike it entirely. The New York voice cast does its best with what it has; Arnold Stang as Nurtle elevates the material somewhat, and Minerva Pious, Mrs. Nussbaum on the Fred Allen radio show in the 1940s, is also featured. Such an almost intentionally inaccessible, determinedly off-kilter movie is hard to assess, and perhaps best enjoyed in the company of convivial friends rather than gaping, confused children. (AL)

**Additional Credits:** Writer: Fred Laderman (Fred Ladd). Based on an idea by Norm Prescott from the book *The Adventures of Pinocchio* by Carlo Collodi. Music: F. Leonard, H. Dobelaere, E. Schurmann. Songs: Robert Sharp, Arthur Korb. Animation directors: Willy Lateste, Vivien Miessen. Animation: Bob Zicot, Eddie Lateste, Nic Broca, Luc Maezello. Special effects: Jos Marissen, Danny Provo. Character designs/storyboards/layouts: Ray Goossens, Willy Lateste, Bert Freund, John Bean. Background artsists: Claude Lambert, Eddy Ploegarts, Carl Saldeslachts.

**Pippi Longstocking** (8/22/97) Legacy. 75 mins. Director: Clive Smith. Producers: Waldemar Bergendahl, Hasmi Giakoumis, Merle-Anne Ridley. Voices: Melissa Altro (Pippi Longstocking), Catherine O'Hara (Mrs. Prysselius), Carole Pope (Teacher), Dave Thomas (Thunder-Karlsson), Gordon Pinsent (Capt. Longstocking), Peter Karlsson (Dunder-Karlsson), Jan Sigurd (Constable Kling), Tomas Bolme (Constable Klang), Marika Lindström (Mrs. Settergren), Elin Larsson (Pippi Longstocking), Samuel Fröler (Mr. Settergren), Wallis Grahn (Mrs. Prysselius), Max Wallér-Zandén (Tommy), Börje Ahlstedt (Captain Efraim Longstocking), Pontus Gustafsson (Blom), Jasmine Heikura (Annika), Gunilla Röör.

**Consumer Tips:** ☆½ MPAA Rating: G. Based on the books by Astrid Lindgren.

**Story:** Pippi, awaiting her father's return from the sea, guards her dad's precious gold coins from a pair of bumbling crooks.

**Comments:** A child's ultimate fantasy—that of being able to live one's life on his or her own terms and to be free to be in charge of one's destiny. Pippi Longstocking is a nine-year-old girl who lives that dream in this animated musical motion picture that attempts to be loyal to the famous series of books that it is based on.

Swedish author Astrid Lindgren's Pippi books began appearing in 1944 and have been adapted in many live-action features and television series throughout the years. Canadian-based Nelvana Ltd. bought the rights to the Pippi stories with dreams of multiple movies and television spin-offs. Bankrolling this $10 million project were several international companies (German, Sweden, and French participation is refelcted in the credits).

Loud, noisy, obnoxious—those words not only sum up Pippi's personality, but this film, its direction, and its soundtrack. A lot of effort clearly went into the making of this bland musical motion picture—but it did not pay off. The film was released in the United

States to only 73 theaters and reportedly earned roughly a half-million dollars at the box office, hardly making a profit. No further Pippi features have been made to date. (SF)

*Additional Credits:* Executive producers: Michael Hirsh, Patrick Loubert, Clive A. Smith, Lennart Wilkund. Coexecutive producer: David Ferguson. Story: Catharina Stackelberg. Additional dialogue: Frank Nissen, Ken Sobol. Story consultant: Susan Snooks. Based on the books by Astrid Lindgren. Music: Anders Berglund, Asher Ettinger, Great Big Music, Tony Kosinec, Thinkmusic. Animation directors: Ute V. Minchon-Pohl, Edson Basarin, Robin Budd, Bill Giggle. Art director: Christoph Baum, Clive Powsey. Visual effects: Oliver Arnold. Storyboard supervisors: Frank Nissen, Clive A. Smith. Design supervisors: Paul Riley, Dermot Walshe. An AB Svensk Filmindustry/Iduna Films/TFC Trickcompany and Nelvana Limited Production; released by Legacy Releasing.

**The Plague Dogs** (12/17/83) Self-released. 103 mins. Director/producer: Martin Rosen. Voices: John Hurt (Snitter), Christopher Benjamin (Rowf), James Bolam (The Tod), Nigel Hawthorne (Dr. Boycott), Warren Mitchell (Tyson, Wag), Bernard Hepton (Stephen Powell), Brian Stirner (Laboratory Assistant), Penelope Lee (Lynn Driver), Geoffrey Matthews (Farmer), Barbara Leigh-Hunt (Farmer's Wife), John Bennett (Don), John Franklyn-Robbins (Williamson), Bill Maynard (Editor), Malcolm Terris (Robert Lindsay), Judy Geeson (Pekinese), Phillip Locke (Civil Servant #1), Brian Spink (Civil Servant #2), Tony Church (Civil Servant #3), Anthony Valentine (Civil Servant

#4), William Lucas (Civil Servant #5), Dandy Nichols (Phyllis Dawson), Rosemary Leach (Vera Dawson), Patrick Stewart (Major), Percy Edwards (Animal Vocalizations).

*Consumer Tips:* ☆☆☆ MPAA Rating: PG-13. Based on a book by Richard Adams. Completed in 1981, the date listed above refers to the Seattle test engagement. The New York opening was on January 9, 1985.

*Story:* A pair of dogs escape from an animal experimentation lab and are hunted down like criminals.

*Comments:* *The Plague Dogs* was a follow-up to *Watership Down* (both films based on Richard Adams's books), and with most of the same crew involved. However, this tale of escaped lab dogs, believed to be infected with a deadly virus, is even more grimly realistic and depressing than its predecessor, with a decidedly downbeat outcome. Like Don Bluth's *Secret of NIMH*, one of the film's major themes is the subject of animal experimentation, but here the inherent cruelties are displayed in stark detail (the opening scene depicts one of the lead dogs being subjected to near drowning). Indeed, the good doctors in the laboratory scenes are more reminiscent of the Nazis in Disney's WWII propaganda films than the traditional funny or insane cartoon scientist, callously detached. The barest touches of dark humor occasionally emerge in the pathetic ramblings of Snitter, a deranged terrier who sports a painful head wound (voiced movingly by John Hurt, the lead in *Watership Down*). The general story is bleak, however, focusing on the two dogs (and their occasional companion, a canny fox) as they struggle to escape from their human pursuers and to survive in the wild, and sidelines examining the general ignorance or paranoia by the government and news media in reaction to their escape. While Adams's book offered a nominal happy ending for the characters, going so far as to admit that such an ending was a fantasy (as the dogs are saved and given new owners), no such closure is offered here.

The animation is often more fluid than its predecessor's, with a generally more polished look. In addition to using various British animators such as Arthur Humberstone, Alan Simpson, and Colin White, held over from *Watership Down*, producer Rosen set up a

San Francisco unit, which included Brad Bird, Phil Robinson (later to join *Wild Brain*), and, most interestingly, Retta Scott, the Disney veteran who had animated the vicious hunting dogs in *Bambi* and thus was especially well suited to this material. Rosen had considerable difficulty securing distribution for the film, and though completed in 1982, it did not receive even limited release in the United States until 1984. Probably one of the three most depressing animated films ever made (alongside *When the Wind Blows* and *Grave of the Fireflies*), the film is not for children and is hard going even for adults. Still, the closing theme song, "Time and Tide" sung by Alan Price, is a wonderfully moving gospel-style ballad. (AL)

**Additional Credits:** Writer: Martin Rosen. Based on the novel by Richard Adams. Music: Patrick Gleeson, Antonio Vivaldi, Kronos Quartet. Animation directors: Tony Guy, Colin White. Senior animators: George Jackson, Arthur Humberstone, Colin White, Phil Robinson, Tony Guy, Alan Simpson, Bill Hajee. Animators: Marie Szimachowska, Retta Scott, Mary Carroll Millican, Karen Peterson, Terry Hudson, Brad Bird. Effects animators: John Allen Armstrong, Tony Guy. Senior assistant animators: Nicolas Stern, Randy Hamm, Margot Allen, Kathryn Staats, Lennie K. Graves, Mary Sandberg, Sean Turner, Jodi Shuster, Rob LaDuca, Ellen E. Lichtwardt, Craig Armstrong. Assistant animators: David Sandberg, Trell Yocum, Michael J. Felber, A. Heeney, Nicola Kaftan, Alex Mann, Sam Kai. Production design: Gordon Harrison. Senior background artists: Ian Henderson, Gary Sycamore. Background artists: Paul Shardlow, Michael B. Moore. Layout artists: Gordon Harrison, Peter See. Painters: Peter Albrecht, George Berticevich, Sharron Evans, Ellen Ferguson, Barry Frederick, Adelia Fritts, Alison Gilham, Angela Greene, Ian Henderson, Susan Herzog, Debra Hill-Crivelli, Stacy Rose James, Mitzi Johnson, Christi Lyon, Carol Ann Parlato, Krist-Ann Pehrson, Kevin Richardson, Beth Ann Shannon, Myoung Smith, Suki Stern, Annick Thierrien, Laurie Wyman.

**Pocahontas** (6/23/95) Walt Disney Pictures. 81 mins. Directors: Mike Gabriel, Eric Goldberg. Producer: James Pentecost. Voices: Irene Bedard (Pocahontas, speaking), Judy Kuhn (Pocahontas, singing), Mel Gibson (John Smith), David Ogden Stiers (Governor Ratcliffe, Wiggins), James Apaumut Fall (Kocoum), Russell Means (Powhatan), Michelle St. John (Nakoma), Linda Hunt (Grandmother Willow), John

©Walt Disney Productions

Kassir (Meeko), Frank Welker (Flit), Danny Mann (Percy), Christian Bale (Thomas), Joe Baker (Lon), Gordon Tootoosis (Kekata).

**Consumer Tips:** ☆☆ MPAA Rating: G. Romantic musical film based on historical accounts of Native American princess Pocahontas (1595–1617).

**Story:** Two cultures collide when English settlers bound for the New World encounter a Native American tribe. Captain John Smith did not come to make war, but the loutish Governor Ratcliffe will walk over anyone to exploit the natural resources of this new world. Chief Powhatan's headstrong daughter Pocahontas and Captain Smith fall in love against a background of growing hate and intolerance, as settlers and Indians regard each other as heartless savages. An unfortunate incident finally triggers a war. Pocahontas and Smith must stop the conflict if their love is to survive, but have things gone too far?

**Comments:** *Pocahontas* was Disney's 33rd animated film. Expectations for the picture were high, since it followed on the heels of the critically acclaimed, record-breaking film *The Lion King*. Disney had not truly faltered since 1989, but *Pocahontas* was to be a disappointment. The film, for one thing, tries to do too much. There are themes concerning multiculturalism, environmentalism, feminism, spiritualism, and tolerance for diversity. The film is unprecedented in its preoccupation with political correctness. During one interview codirector Mike Gabriel stated that this was actually a compliment, since that meant the film hadn't offended anybody. Unfortunately, due to its heavy ideological burdens it didn't entertain anybody very much either.

*Pocahontas* does not work on many levels. The villain, Governor Ratcliffe, is little more than a selfish, greedy cad with no real menace to him at all. He commands a toady named Wiggins, and their relationship is a pale reflection of the much richer byplay between Captain Hook and Mr. Smee in *Peter Pan*. There is a surfeit of funny animal sidekicks; where Disney typically features at least one in its films, *Pocahontas* features no less than three, and not one of them is particularly memorable. For the record, Pocahontas has a hummingbird and a raccoon, while Ratcliff owns a stuffy little pug. The animals get to enact and parallel the human storyline of intolerance and reconciliation. The score by Alan Menken and Stephen Schwartz is a good one, but the best number, "If I Never Knew You," is stuck playing over the end credits simply because it could not be wedged into the film without stopping the action.

This was not a film that showcased codirector Eric Goldberg's creative talents. Goldberg had long admired the wilder side of animated comedy and was heavily influenced by Chuck Jones. Goldberg was probably the Disney studio's true heir to Ward Kimball, but with *Pocahontas* he labored on a film that took itself far too seriously. Watching this movie is like reading a dull revisionist history book with great illustrations: in the end only the pictures are recalled.

Still, what pictures! Animator Glen Keane was very enthusiastic about the film, and he spent quite some time refining the appearance of Pocahontas. She is exquisitely beautiful, a blend of strength and grace that only the finest animators could summon. When she is first fully sighted by John Smith, it is animation's answer to Botticelli's "The Birth of Venus." *Pocahontas* is a rich and vivid film to look at, with possibly the best use of color seen in any Disney feature of the 1990s. Art director Michael Giaimo, artistic coordinator Don Hansen, and background supervisor Cristy Maltese give *Pocahontas* far better moments than anything found in its script or story.

The remaining character animation is, on the whole, variable but solid. Ken Duncan does a fine job on a minor character named Thomas, who embodies the

righteousness and resolution that will lead to a declaration of independence someday. John Pomeroy's John Smith is handsome enough, but his sculpted, rigid coif looks as if it belongs on an action figure. The usually reliable Duncan Marjoribanks animates a rather stock villain in Ratcliffe, but he wasn't given much of a character to work with in any case.

*Pocahontas* is worth viewing for its visual beauty, Keane's animation of the lead character, and the superlative "Colors of the Wind" musical sequence that initiates the romance between Smith and the princess. The movie at least gets points for avoiding the traditional pat happy ending. Then, of course, there's that great song playing over the end credits. (MG)

***Additional Credits:*** Screenplay: Carl Binder, Susannah Grant, Philip LaZebnik. Story: Tom Sito, Glen Keane, Joe Grant, Ralph Zondag, Burny Matttinson, Kaan Kalyon, Francis Glebas, Robert Gibbs, Bruce Morris, Todd Kurosawa, Duncan Marjoribanks, Chris Buck. Music: Alan Menken. Songs: Alan Menken, Stephen Schwartz. Supervising animators: Glen Keane, John Pomeroy, Duncan Marjoribanks, Nik Ranieri, Ruben A. Aquino, Ken Duncan, Chris Buck, T. Daniel Hofstedt, Dave Pruiksma, Anthony DeRosa, Michael Cedeno. Animation: Mark Henn, Pres Antonio Romanillos, Randy Haycock, Michael Show, Tom Bancroft, Bob Bryan, Trey Finney, Aaron Blaise, Doug Krohn, Ken Hettig, Brad Kuha, Tom Gately, Gilda Palinginis, John Ripa, Ralf Palmer, Eric Walls, Joe Haidar, Richard Bazley, Ron Husband, Dave Kupczyk, David A. Zaboski, Jean Morel, Gary J. Perkovac, Michael Swofford, William Recinos, Bill Waldman, Philip Morris, Doug Frankel, Teresa Martin, Mark Koetsier, Chris Suave, Ken Boyer, Brian Ferguson, Raul Garcia, Dave Kuhn, Steven P. Gordon, James Young Jackson, Gregory S. Manwaring, Anthony Wayne Michaels, Craig R. Maras, Chris Wahl, Broose Johnson, Larry White, David Burgess, James Lopez, Rejean Bourdages, Barry Temple, Kent Hammerstrom, Tim Allen, Geefwee Boedoe, D. Anthony Wawrzaszek, Sasha Dorogov, Branko Mihanovich, Travis Blaise, Ellen Woodbury. Effects animators: Dorse Lanpher, Ed Coffey, Garrett Wren, Ted C. Kierscey, Tom Hush, Stephen B. Moore, Kathleen Quaife-Hodge, Marlon West, James De V. Mansfield, Allen Blyth, Troy A. Gustafson, Jazno Francoeur. 3-D effects: David A. Bossert, Stephen B. Moore, Daniel E. Wanket, Ed Coffey, Dan Chaika. Story supervisor: Tom Sito. Layout supervisors: Raoul Azadani, Jeff Dickson. Layout artists: Daniel Hu, Allen Tam, Doug Walker, Mac George, Karen Keller, William H. Frake III, Tom

Humber, Peter Bielicki. Background supervisors: Christy Maltese, Robert E. Stanton. Background artists: Allison Belliveau-Proulx, Thomas Cardone, Barry Atkinson, Dominick R. Domingo, Natalie Franscioni-Karp, Barry Kooser, Serge Michaels, Patricia Palmer-Phillipson, Sean Sullivan, Kevin Turcotte, Thomas Woodington, Keith Newton, Justin Brandstater,

Sunny Apinchapong, Brooks Campbell, Debbie Du Bois, Mi Kyung Joung-Raynis, David McCamley, Don Moore, Philip Phillipson, MaryAnn Thomas, Chuck Vollmer, David Wang Ying Guang, Dan Cooper.

**Pogo for President** See *I Go Pogo*.

## Pokémon series

*Pokémon* began in Japan in 1996 as a Nintendo children's video game, *Pocket Monsters*. Designer Satoshi Tajiri based it on his own childhood fascination for exploring in the woods for unusual insects. Players must capture and train exotically cute small (pocket-sized) fantasy animals (monsters) to become their pets. The player with the most pocket monsters wins. The original game came with 150 different monsters and the slogan "Gotta catch 'em all!"

*Pocket Monsters* was fantastically popular, quickly spinning off a comic book (manga) series and a weekly television cartoon series, beginning on April 1, 1997, produced by the O.L.M. (Oriental Light & Magic) animation studio. All were popularly called "Pokémon" in Japanese juvenile shorthand slang, which was adopted as the official title by the American licensees. *Pokémon* is still running in new weekly episodes in Japan (with a title change to *Pokémon Advanced* in 2002), and, as of November 4, 2004, were up to episode number 378. An annual mid-July theatrical double bill began in 1998 of a 20- to 25-minute comedy short featuring Pikachu and his fellow Pokémon, followed by an adventure feature of about 75 minutes. The features often introduce new Pokémon being added to the gaming cast.

The television storyline is set in an imaginary world (in the Japanese version; it's supposedly our own world in the American) in which children throughout the world are encouraged to capture wild Pokémon and train them into loyal semi-intelligent pets. Ash Ketchum, a hyperactive ten-year-old boy, vows to win the title of Master Pokémon Trainer by catching more kinds than anyone else.

The first that he goes after is an electric mouse called Pikachu. Ash's interactions with Pikachu lead to their becoming firm friends more than owner and pet. Pikachu always travels with Ash as he adds more and more Pokémon to his score through the television episodes and movies. Ash has two other close friends among the Pokémon-hunting children; the girl Misty and the boy Brock. The continuing villains are James and Jesse, slightly older arrogant teens who are trying to win the Master Trainer title by sabotaging other hunters and stealing their Pokémon rather than capturing their own. The two call themselves Team Rocket and have a loyal Pokémon who is as dishonest as they are, the greedy, catlike Meowth.

Despite the internationally notorious incident in December 1997 of a strobing-light effect in a television episode that caused epileptic-like seizures in hundreds of children, *Pokémon* debuted in America (the video games and television series simultaneously) in September 1998. By mid-1999 the *Pokémon* phenomenon was garnering national news coverage as the latest juvenile game/comics/television/toy mania. The theatrical features were adapted by the American production company 4Kids Entertainment and released, at first, by Warner Bros., about a year after their Japanese premieres. In general the theatrical movies feature higher-quality animation and a more dramatic story centering upon Pokémon that are especially rare and possess dangerous powers that could destroy the world if they are provoked. The stories are often linked to events in the television storyline at the time of the movies' release in Japan. All are MPAA-rated G. (FP)

**Pokémon the First Movie: Mewtwo Strikes Back** (11/12/99) Warner Bros. 75 mins. Directors: Kunihiko Yuyama, Michael Haigney.

Giovanni, a rich villain, hires scientists to clone Mew, an extinct Pokémon with great powers. They succeed in creating an even more powerful new Pokémon, Mewtwo. But Giovanni's brutal attempt to force it to help him conquer the world backfires. Mewtwo escapes and, believing now that all humans are bad, vows to conquer the world to liberate all Pokémon. He issues a challenge for the world's greatest Pokémon trainers (who he expects will be the cruelest villains) to compete. Ash and his friends are among the finalists who are invited to Mewtwo's lair.

*Pocket Monsters: Mewtwo no Gyakushuu* was released July 18, 1998, in Japan, accompanied by the short "Pikachu's Summer Vacation" about Pikachu playing with his Pokémon friends Squirtle, Togepi, Charizard, Bulbasaur, and over a dozen others. The characters pantomime because none of the Pokémon speak; they just make cute animal noises. (FP)

**Pokémon the Movie 2000** (7/21/00) Warner Bros. 100 mins. Directors: Kunihiko Yuyama, Michael Haigney.

On-screen subtitle: *The Power of One.* Lawrence III, an arrogant, rich man self-styled "The Collector," captures three legendary avian Pokémon with the powers of fire (Moltres), ice (Articuno), and lightning (Zapdos), which together can summon the even mightier "beast of the sea" Pokémon, Lugia. The capture of the three birds alone sets off natural disasters all around

the world; Lugia could destroy the world. Ash (with Pikachu) and his friends Misty, Tracey, and Melody (with their Pokémon), plus the unlikely help of Team Rocket (who do not want to be destroyed either), go on a quest in the Orange Islands to find three orbs, one on each of the three birds' islands, that can placate Lugia.

*Gekijô-ban Pocket Monster: Maboroshi no Pokémon: Lugia Bakutan* (*Pocket Monsters the Movie: The Phantom Pokémon: Lugia's Explosive Birth*) released July 17, 1999 in Japan, accompanied by the short "Pikachu's Rescue Adventure" ($43.7 million U.S. gross as of October 2, 1999). (FP)

**Pokémon the Movie 3** (4/6/01) Warner Bros. 88 mins. Directors: Kunihiko Yuyama, Michael Haigney.

On-screen subtitle: *Spell of the Unown.* Ash, Brock, and Misty, on their way with Ash's mother Delia to the Johto League Championships, come to a mountain town where Molly, an orphaned girl, has found the Unown, a unique group of Pokémon consisting of 26 letter-shaped individuals that "have the power to bring human thoughts and dreams into reality." Molly wishes for a father and the Unown creates Entei, a father-figure Pokémon. Then Molly wishes for a mother, and Entei kidnaps Mrs. Ketchum and hypnotizes her into becoming Molly's mother. Ash and his friends (including Team Rocket again) must break the spell, both to rescue Mrs. Ketchum and to free Molly from her Pokémons' well-intentioned but sterile ice-tower dreamworld prison.

*Pocket Monster: Kesshou To no Teiou* (*Pocket Monsters: Lord of the Unknown Tower*), released July 8, 2000 in Japan, accompanied by the short "Pikachu and Pichu." It grossed $16,622,570 as of May 8, 2001.

The first three Pokémon theatrical features played to steadily decreasing grosses: $85,744,662 in 1999, $43,758,684 in 2000, and $17,052,128 for *Pokémon the Movie 3.* Warner Bros. dropped the distributorship, which was picked up by Miramax Films for the fourth and fifth features. Miramax did not include the 20-minute Pikachu featurettes with the theatrical releases, although they were added as extras to the Buena Vista Home Entertainment DVD releases. (FP)

**Pokémon 4-Ever** (10/11/02) Miramax Films. 79 mins. Directors: Kunihiko Yuyama, Jim Malone.

A prologue 40 years in the past shows Celebi, an extremely rare forest Pokémon with the power to travel through time, being hunted by a brutal adult Pokémon trainer, the Iron Masked Marauder, who comes from the far future in a time machine. The Marauder is actually Vicious, the descendant of James and Jesse, who has been brainwashing Pokémon with his Dark Ball into turning evil to aid him in his plans to conquer the world. After being rescued by a young boy, Sammy, Celebi transports them both to the present, which is Ash Ketchum's world. Ash and Sammy become friends, and Ash and Pikachu join them in fleeing into the forest when the Marauder comes after them. There are similarities between Celebi, the Voice of the Forest, and the Forest God in Miyazaki's *Princess Mononoke.* Celebi briefly succumbs to the Marauder's Dark Ball but is rescued by another rare Pokémon, Suicune the North Wind. Ash and his friends prevail, of course. It is revealed (which young viewers have been prompted to guess by blatant clues) that Sammy is the boyhood version of Professor Samuel Oak, a regular supporting character in the television adventures.

*Pocket Monster: Celebi Toki o Koeta Deai* (*Pocket Monsters: Celebi—Voice of the Forest*) released July 7, 2001 in Japan. The accompanying Pikachu short not included with the American theatrical release is "Pikachu's Pika-Boo." (FP)

**Pokémon Heroes** (05/16/03) Miramax Films. 79 mins. Directors: Kunihiko Yuyama, Jim Malone.

©Pikachu Projects

Ash, Pikachu, Misty, and Brock are in Alto Mare, the water capital of the world, an ancient city of vast canals so close to Venice as to be plagiarized. They help Bianca, a local girl, protect two Pokémon from Annie and Oakley, criminal agents of Giovanni, the villain in the first movie. Latios (brother) and Latias (sister) are Pokémon who can shape-shift into humans, and are the secret guardians of Alto Mare's magical jewel, the Droplet of the Heart, which controls the tides.

*Pocket Monster: Mizu no Miyako no Mamori Gami—Latias to Latios* (*Pocket Monsters: Guardian Spirits of the Water Capital—Latias and Latios*) was released July 13, 2002, in Japan. The accompanying Pikachu short not included with the American theatrical release is "Camp Pikachu."

The box-office grosses of the fourth and fifth Pokémon movies continued to decline; $1,727,447 for *Pokémon 4-Ever* and $746,381 for *Pokémon Heroes.* The sixth (July 19, 2003, in Japan) and seventh (July 17, 2004) movies were direct-to-video releases in America. (FP)

**The Polar Express** (11/10/04) Warner Bros. 132 mins. Director: Robert Zemeckis. Producers: Steve Starkey, Robert Zemeckis, Gary Goetzman, William Teitler. Voices: Tom Hanks (Conductor, Santa Claus, Hobo, Father), Daryl Sabara (Hero Boy), Nona Gaye (Hero Girl), Jimmy Bennet (Lonely Boy), Eddie

©Warner Bros. Entertainment

Deezen (Know-It-All), Charles Fleischer (Elf General), Andre Sogliuzzo (Smokey, Steamer), Isabella Peregrina (Sister Sarah), Steven Tyler (Elf Singer).

**Consumer Tips:** ☆☆ MPAA Rating: G. Based on the book by Chris Van Allsburg.

**Story:** On Christmas Eve, suspecting that Santa Claus might not be real, a boy takes a ride on a magical train bound for the North Pole.

**Comments:** Creepy. That was the word most often used by movie reviewers and critics when describing the actors in *The Polar Express*.

Robert Zemeckis (*Who Framed Roger Rabbit*) and Tom Hanks (*Toy Story*) teamed up to create an epic Christmas fairy tale of Chris Van Allsburg's *The Polar Express*. This book was a 30-page illustrated children's story and was first published in 1985. Tom Hanks fell in love with the story and the artwork, and optioned the property. He partnered with Van Allsburg and recruited Robert Zemeckis (with whom Hanks had made *Forrest Gump* and *Cast Away*); together they developed *The Polar Express* into a full-length feature film.

They decided to try something new by creating the entire film in the computer, using motion capture technology. This enabled Hanks to act eight of the character parts, from the hero boy to Santa Claus. Zemeckis wrote the screenplay with William Broyles Jr. (*Apollo 13*), and raised a budget of $165 million from production partners Warner Bros. and Castle Rock Entertainment.

In a noble effort to recreate each painting in the book, the producers decided to try state-of-the-art motion capture and digital animation, working closely with Sony Imageworks to achieve the look and feel they desired. Zemeckis is quoted in the film's production notes as saying that he "was looking for something more realistically alive" than what was achievable with standard animated cartoons.

Unfortunately, he fell a bit short of his goal. The characters that are supposed to look real end up looking artificial and creepy. On the flip side, the settings, props, landscapes, and the train itself—all created in the computer—look incredibly real.

Though the book did not have a strong story, the screenplay itself is charming, and the film is certainly dazzling visually. However, the lead characters look strange. It's hard to get past the synthetic look of the children, the robotic persona of the conductor and Santa Claus, and the downright scary visualizations of the elves.

As of 2004, creating a believable human being in the computer is still a goal to be attained. Pixar's competing film that year, *The Incredibles*, did a much better job generating real and lifelike emotions using traditional character animators and clever character designers.

Motion capture, or "performance capture," had also been done before, as with Gollum in the *Lord of the Rings* trilogy, or in the dismal SF failure *Final Fantasy* (2001). The technique itself is a high-tech version of Max Fleischer's 1917 rotoscope, which was used most notably by Ralph Bakshi for his features *Lord of the Rings* (1978), *American Pop* (1981), and *Fire and Ice* (1983).

*The Polar Express* was a hit, despite these criticisms, and despite competition with Pixar and Nickelodeon (*SpongeBob*) that year. The film grossed well over $100 million in the United States. It was also the first mainstream film to be simultaneously released as a 3-D IMAX presentation. (JB)

**Additional Credits:** Screenplay: Robert Zemeckis, William Broyles Jr. Executive producer: Tom Hanks, Jack Rapke, Chris Van Allsburg. Coproducer: Steven Boyd. Associate producers: Debbie Denise, Josh McLaglen, Peter M. Tobyansen. Original music: Alan Silvestri. Cinematography: Don Burgess, Robert Presley. Film editors: R. Orlando Duenas, Jeremiah O'Driscoll.

Production design: Rick Carter, Doug Chiang. Art direction: Tony Fanning, Alicia Maccarone, Norman Newberry. Production manager: Josh McLaglen. Executive in charge of production: Mark Scoon. Unit production manager: Peter M. Tobyansen. Storyboard coordinator: Maureen Beatty. Concept Artists: James Clyne, Marc Gabbana. Storyboard artist: Philip Keller. Illustrator: Oliver Scholl. Motion capture tech: Lisa Buono. Animation production director: Robin A. Linn. Visual effects supervisor: Jim Berney. Digital effects artist: Thomas Bland. Motion capture technical director: Vaughn Cato. Visual effects supervisor: Jerome Chen. Character animator: Tom Bruno Jr.

## Pound Puppies and the Legend of Big Paw

(3/18/88) Tri-Star. 76 mins. Director: Pierre DeCelles. Producers: Donald Kushner, Peter Locke. Voices: George Rose (Mr. McNasty), B. J. Ward (Whopper), Cathy Cavadini (Collette), Nancy Cartwright (Bright Eyes), Greg Berg (Beamer), Ruth Buzzi (Nose Marie), Brennan Howard (Cooler), Hal Rayle (Howler), Joey Dedio, Ashley Hall.

©Tonka Corporation and Carolco

**Consumer Tips:** ☆ MPAA Rating: G.

**Story:** The mythical Bone of Scone, which keeps the peace and allows kids and dogs to speak to each other, is broken and stolen by Mr. McNasty. The Pound Puppies come to the rescue and solve the mystery of the lengendary Big Paw.

**Comments:** *Variety* found *Pound Puppies and the Legend of Big Paw* "uninvolving and endlessly derivative." Indeed, only the very young may be entertained by this film, if they don't become confused with the muddled story and disjointed visuals. This film has a feeling of a Saturday morning cartoon, with the story line being sufficient only for a half hour of meaningful action and dialogue. Stretching it out to feature length waters it down considerably, with repetitive dialogue and visual gimmicks used as filler.

The animation is a mixed bag: while the backgrounds are somewhat imaginative and colorful, the character animation is flat and lifeless. Rapid cuts to new angles of the same shot seem to try to cover up limitations of the animation technique. The strongest asset of the film was the music, by Steve Tyrell. He reworked rock 'n' roll hits from the 1950s and changed the lyrics to fit the canine world. The end result is a lively score.

The Pound Puppies were a popular line of stuffed toys by Tonka and were developed into an ABC Saturday morning television show. During the late 1980s, popular toys were being used more and more as the stars of television shows and movies. Tonka and the filmmakers for *Pound Puppies and the Legend of Big Paw* aggressively marketed these toys as a tie-in for the movie, hoping for a payoff despite the poor quality of the film. The end of the movie suggested to the kiddies to adopt Pound Puppies toys, a shameless advertisement to buy their product. (SF)

**Additional Credits:** Coproducer: Diana Dru Bogsford. Screenplay: Jim Carlson, Terrence McDonnell. Original music: Richard Kosinski, Sam Winans. Songs: Steve Tyrell, Ashley Hall, Stephanie Tyrell. A Family Home Entertainment and Tonka Corp. presentation of an Atlantic/Kushner-Locke Production, in association with the Maltese Companies. Released by Tri-Star.

## The Powerpuff Girls

(7/3/02) Warner Bros. 74 mins. Director: Craig McCracken. Producer: Donna Castricone. Voices: Catherine Cavadini (Blossom), Tara Strong (Bubbles), E. G. Daily (Buttercup), Roger L. Jackson (Mojo Jojo), Tom Kane (Professor Utonium), Jennifer Hale (Ms. Keane), Tom Kenny (Narrator, Mayor, Mitch, Punk), Jennifer Hale (Ms. Keane), Jennifer Martin (Sara Bellum), Jeff Glen Bennett (Ace, Big Billy, Grubber, Hotcha Chatcha), Grey DeLisle (Linda, Woman at Zoo), Phil LaMarr (I. P. Host, Local Anchor), Rob Paulsen (Hota Wata, Killa Drilla, Cukor

©Cartoon Network

the Pickle Man), Kevin M. Richardson (Rocko Socko, Ojo Tango), Frank Welker (Whole Lotta Monkeys).

**Consumer Tips:** ☆☆½ MPAA Rating: PG, "for non-stop, frenetic animated action."

**Story:** The kindly Professor Utonium mixes sugar, spice, and everything nice to create his own perfect little girls—but his experimental monkey Jojo bumps him into a vat of Chemical X. The resulting explosion creates the super-powered and fingerless Powerpuff Girls: Blossom (brains), Buttercup (brawn), and Bubbles (beauty/bubbliness). The girls playfully indulge in a game of tag, but in using their powers they nearly destroy Townsville. Rejected as social misfits, the girls seek solace from Mojo Jojo, who unknown to them has mutated into an evil genius. He tricks the girls into helping him create an army of superpowered simians to take over the world. The simians, however, have other plans.

**Comments:** *The Powerpuff Girls* (in "Meat Fuzzy Lumpkins") was the very first creator-driven "World Premiere Toon" short commisioned by Cartoon Network, and had its debut on February 20, 1995. It proved popular and premiered as a full-fledged series on November 18, 1998. After raking in $350 million in Powerpuff merchandise in the year 2000, Cartoon Network decided to make *Powerpuff Girls* its first feature film.

"We didn't have any screenwriters," Craig McCracken told the online IGN Filmforce. "I don't believe in scripts. If you're going to write, then you also have to draw, if you want to work on *Powerpuff*. So it was being written and boarded at the same time—basically like they used to make animated movies."

"One thing I noticed in a lot of (superhero movies) is the arch villain is always threatening to do something bad, but never really does anything," McCracken told the *Buffalo News*. "The superhero's job is to come in and stop him at the last minute, and be like a security guard. So I wanted to do a movie where the villain actually pulls off an evil plan, and the hero has to come and fix it and stop it from getting worse."

Why tell the origin story? "We could've made the movie completely for die-hard fans and included a lot of inside jokes, but I felt that would alienate the people who've never seen the show," McCracken told Fred Shuster of the *Los Angeles Daily News*, July 4, 2002. "We wanted to introduce the idea to a new audience, while at the same time meeting the expectations of the fans. So we had to find a story that would work on two levels."

Budgeted at a mere $10 million, management interference was minimal—until, McCracken points out, "Near the end, as we were finishing it up, there was a little more involvement—just because this is such a big investment from the network's point of view, that they were like, 'We want to make sure that everybody's on board with this movie and there's nothing in it that could be problematic.' There were a few edits that had to be made from Warner Bros.' standpoint, but nothing so disastrous that it affected the final film."

The studio insisted on including a pop song in the film, but McCracken says, "That was one thing that we really fought against. We were like, 'There are not going to be any pop songs in the middle of this.' There're songs during the end credits, but that's okay because there's nothing in the body of the story. We basically said, 'We don't do the show like that, and we're not about to make the movie that way. People have expectations.'"

Because Warner Bros. was the distributor, concerns were raised about the lack of promotion for the film. Its competition, *Lilo and Stitch* and *Men in Black II*, had already been publicized six months in advance. Two weeks before *Powerpuff*'s premiere, McCracken noted, "I don't see any posters, I don't see any billboards, the only commercials I've seen are the ones Cartoon Network's been airing. In theory, Warner Bros. is putting $20 million into promoting this movie."

According to the Tacoma, Washington, *News Tribune,* July 2, 2002, Jim Samples, executive vice president and general manager of Cartoon Network, said ads for the movie didn't start appearing on MTV and WB until the previous week.

While Warner Bros. Pictures marketed the movie to the television show's core audience, children two to eleven, the show's creator told Kate O'Hare of the *Buffalo News,* June 30, 2002, "We've made it for everybody. It's for kids; it's for adults; it's for teenagers and college kids. We've really never set out to say that we're going to make a children's movie."

The film was advertised, on posters and trailers, as "The Powerpuff Girls Movie." It was released with a *Dexter's Laboratory* short, "Chicken Scratch." Playing mostly to matinee audiences, it earned an opening weekend box-office gross of $3.5 million, and ultimately did $11.4 million total in its theatrical release. Warner Home Video gave the film a DVD release on November 5, 2002.

*Powerpuff*'s box-office failure dampered plans for further feature films based on Cartoon Network properties, at least for the foreseeable future. Another competitor, *Hey, Arnold! The Movie,* likewise flopped, but Nickelodeon continues to make animated feature films based on their shows, finding huge success with the *SpongeBob SquarePants Movie* in the winter of 2004.

To sum up, this is a 21-minute episode padded out to 74 minutes, with an overly long "tag" sequence, drab colors, and a depressing vibe throughout. *The Powerpuff Girls* are worthy of better material. (WRM)

***Additional Credits:*** Executive producers: Craig McCracken, Brian A. Miller. Screenplay/story/storyboards: Charlie Bean, Lauren Faust, Craig McCracken, Paul Rudish, Don Shank. Story: Amy Keating Rogers. Music: James L. Venable. Art director: Mike Moon. Animation director: Genndy Tartakovsky. Additional animation direction: Robert Alvarez, Randal L. Myers. Additional animation: Lauren Faust, Dave Kupczyk. Effects animation supervisor: John Dillon. Effects animation: Michel Gagne, Jeff Howard, Kevin O'Neil, Gary Sole, Ryan Woodward. CGI Animators: Wim Bien, Paul Davies, Christopher Grun, Tim Petre, John Savage, Kenneth Sullivan, Tom Sullivan. Development/character design: Craig Kellman. Lead

character design: Carey Yost. Character design: Chris Battle, Andy Bialk, Lauren Faust, Shakeh Hagnazarian, Bob Logan, Craig McCracken, Dexter Smith. "Be an Artist" design: Laura Kramer. Family portrait design: Amber Cushing. Character layout supervisor: Lauren Faust. Character layout: Carrie Buell, Mark Calongelo, Cathlin Hidalgo-Polvani, Dave Kupczyk, Lane Lueras, Craig McCracken, Dexter Smith. Background layout: Steven Avila, Ted Blackman, Edgar Carlos, David Dunnet, Christopher Holt, Robert Kline, Kenneth McGill, John Nevarez, Louis M. Police, Paul Stec, Justin K. Thompson. Overseas layout supervisor: Bill Perkins. Prop design: Chris Battle, Bruce Berkey, Frederick J. Gardner, Timothy L. Hardin, Jason Hulst, Noel Tolentino. Lead background design: David Dunnet. Background design: Bruce Berkey, Frederick J. Gardner, Paul Stec, Justin K. Thompson, Keith Weesner, Jim Worthy. Lead background painter: Chris Roszak. Background painters: Martin Ansolabehere, Timothy Barnes, Kit Boyce, Seonna Hong, Susan Mondt, Jill A. Petrilak, Sy Thomas, Carol Wyatt, Micki Zurcher.

## The Prince of Egypt (12/18/98) DreamWorks. 97 mins. Directors: Brenda Chapman, Steve Hickner, Simon Wells. Producers: Penney Finkelman Cox, Sandra Rabins. Voices: Val Kilmer (Moses, God), Ralph Fiennes (Rameses), Michelle Pfeiffer (Tzipporah), Sandra Bullock (Miriam), Jeff Goldblum (Aaron), Danny Glover (Jethro), Patrick Stewart (Pharaoh Seti I), Helen Mirren (the Queen), Steve Martin (Hotep), Martin Short (Huy), Bobby Motown (Rameses' son), Eden Riegel (Young Miriam), Ofra Haza (Yocheved), Amick Byram (Moses, singing), Brian Stokes Mitchell (Jethro, singing), Sally Dworsky (Miriam, singing), Linda Dee Shayne (the Queen, singing), Mel Brooks (uncredited),

Natalie Portman (uncredited), Shira Roth, Michael Patrician, Christopher Marquette, Justin Timsit (Singing Hebrew Children), Whitney Houston (vocalist), Mariah Carey (vocalist), the Boys Choristers of Salisbury Cathedral (vocalists), Andrew Johnson of St. Paul's Cathedral Choir (vocalist), Boys II Men (vocalists).

**Consumer Tips:** ☆☆☆½ MPAA Rating: PG. An epic of Biblical proportions. For audiences age 8 and older.

**Story:** This animated version of the book of Exodus tells the story of Moses, his encounter with God at the burning bush, his conflict with his Egyptian half-brother Rameses, the deliverance of the Hebrews, and the spectacular parting of the Red Sea.

**Comments:** Four years and over $75 million in the making, utilizing high-profile celebrities as voice actors and over 400 animation artists, DreamWorks SKG's second animated film (after *Antz*) tackled controversial subject matter—faith, slavery, responsibility unto God, genocide—and blasted the boundaries of American animated feature films.

Said executive producer Jeffrey Katzenberg to the *Straits Times*, "Before *Prince of Egypt*, all you get in animation are fairy-tale cartoons for toddlers—although I say this with extreme admiration because Disney has done some sterling work. But at some point, you will need variety. You will scream for a change."

To avoid offending the constituency of the film, Katzenberg sought the advice of some 500 historians, archaeologists, and religious leaders representing Christianity, Judaism, and Islam, including 75 Vatican cardinals, Talmudic scholar Burton Visotzky, religious broadcaster Jerry Falwell, Dr. Paige Patterson of the Southern Baptist Convention, ethicist Richard Land, Jesse Jackson, Billy Graham, and Rabbi Marvin Hier of the Simon Wiesenthal Center. And the film was changed accordingly, though some scenarios—like a chariot race between Moses and Rameses, or Moses' basket traveling down the Nile instead of staying in the papyrus bushes—are not in the text of Exodus. Knowing this, the filmmakers added a disclaimer, "While artistic and historical license has been taken, we believe that this film is true to the essence, values, and integrity of a story that is a cornerstone of faith for millions of people worldwide."

The film established the studio's house style, that of angular human designs, incredibly detailed backgrounds, and moving the camera for the sake of moving the camera.

*Prince of Egypt* was set to premiere November 18, but then Disney scheduled *A Bug's Life* for the same date. DreamWorks moved its film to December 18 (December 16 for France and Belgium), and scheduled its CG film, *Antz*, to October, six weeks ahead of *A Bug's Life*.

According to the *Los Angeles Daily News* (November 20, 1998), *Prince* opened on an unprecedented 8,000 to 10,000 screens in 40 countries and in two dozen languages between December 16 and 26, the widest simultaneous worldwide rollout at the time. In the United States, it earned $14 million on 3,118 screens on its opening weekend—ultimately grossing $101 million—a respectable amount, but not the mega-blockbuster hoped for by the studio. Nevertheless, Jeffrey Katzenberg is to be lauded for his risk-taking, for making such an ambitious project, and for giving the subject matter the lavish treatment it deserves. The artists, animators, and artisans are to be commended for their outstanding achievement.

*Prince of Egypt* won the following accolades:

- 1999 Academy Awards, Best Music, Original Song—Stephen Schwartz for "When You Believe";
- 1999 Broadcast Film Critics Association Awards Best Animated Film (tied with *A Bug's Life*) and Best Song;
- 2000 ASCAP Film and Television Music Award, Most Performed Songs from Motion Pictures.
- The film was nominated in five categories in the 1999 Annie Awards, but was outvoted by those supporting *The Iron Giant*.

For the record:
- DreamWorks made a direct-to-video prequel, *Joseph, King of Dreams*, directed by Rob LaDuca and Robert C. Ramirez, released October 2, 2002.
- Val Kilmer, who voiced Moses and God, reprised Moses in the Los Angeles musical stage play, *The Ten Commandments*, which premiered September 27, 2004. (WRM)

**Additional Credits:** Executive producer: Jeffrey Katzenberg. Associate producer: Ron Rocha. Writer: Philip LaZebnik. Based on the Biblical book of *Exodus*. Additional screenplay: Nicholas Meyer. Music: Hans Zimmer. Songs: Stephen Schwartz. Additional music: Harry Gregson-Williams, Rupert Gregson-Williams. Supervising animators: Kristof Serrand, William Salazar, David Brewster, Sergei Kouchnerov, Rodolphe Guenoden, Gary Perkovac, Patrick Mate, Bob Scott, Fabio Lignini, Rick Farmiloe, Jurgen Gross. Animators: James Baxter, Arnaud Berthier, Dave B. Boudreau, Emmanuela Cozzi, Bruce Ferriz, Lionel Gallat, Maximilian Graenitz, Luis Grane, Steve Horrocks, Jakob Hjort Jensen, Cathy Jones, Fabrice Joubert, Teresa Martin, Simon Otto, Jane Poole, Pedro Ramos, Erik C. Schmidt, Andrea Simonti, Dan Wagner, Eric Walls, Dan Boulos, Paul Jesper, Brad Kuha, Jean-Francois Rey, Philippe LeBrun, Maryann Malcomb, Ken Morrisey, Andy Schmidt, Manuel Almela, Cecile Bender, Antony Grey, Robert Milne, Kent Culotta, Mark Chavez, Ki-han Chen, Michelle Cowart, Wendy Elwell, Ryan Roberts, Michael Spokas, Mike Ullner. Additional animation: Claudio Acciari, Scott Petersen, Cinzia Angelini, Emil Simeonov, Gary Dunn, Sean Springer, Jerome Guillard, Derek Thompson, Ken Hettig, Frans Vischer, Duncan Marjoribanks, Kathy Zielinski, Claire Morrissey, Susan Zytka, Sylvia Muller. Animating assistants: Marc Bascougnano, Oliver Coipel, Catherine Feraday, Richard Kim, Eric Koenig, Kevin O'Hara, Warren O'Neill, Tom Owen, Mariateresa Scarpone, Herman Sharff, Dimos Vrysellas, Robert Weaver, Greg Whittaker, Scott Wright. Art directors: Kathy Altieri, Richard Chavez. Production design: Darek Gogol. Story supervisors: Kelly Asbury, Lorna Cook. Story artists: Ronnie Del Carmen, Tony Leonidis, James Fujii, Mike Ploog, Ken Harsha, Scott Santoro, Todd Kurosawa, Tom Sito. Additional story: David Bowers, Paul Fisher, Randy Cartwright, Carole Holliday, Rebecca Cassady, Frank Tomura.

### The Princess and the Goblin (6/3/94) Hemdale (Hungarian). 82 mins. Director: Jozsef Gemes. Producer: Robin Lyons. Voices: Sally Ann Marsh (Princess Irene), Joss Ackland (The King), Roy Kinnear (Mump), Rik Mayall (Froglip), Peter Murray (Curdi), Claire Bloom (Fairy Godmother), Peggy Mount (Goblin Queen), Victor Spinetti (Glump), Mollie Sugden (Nanny Lootie), Robin Lyons (Goblin King).

**Consumer Tips:** ☆☆ MPAA Rating: G. Based on the 1872 novel by Scottish writer George MacDonald.

**Story:** Princess Irene meets young Curdi, a miner's son, who has learned that underground goblins are

©Hemdale Releasing

plotting to seize the kingdom. She must overcome her fears in order to save her kingdom.

**Comments:** The movie was originally released in Europe in 1993. Limping into U.S. distribution several weeks before Disney's blockbuster, *The Lion King*, this small film did not have a real chance at the U.S. box office.

Made at a cost of $10 million, producer and screenwriter Robin Lyons hired Pannonia Studios Jozsef Gemes to supervise animation artists in Wales and Hungary. Gemes was a widely respected director for his work on the epic paint-on-glass feature, *Heroic Times* (1982).

Given a first-rate director in Gemes, and a charming medieval story, the film had potential. However, the uneven, stiff technique and unimaginative plotting resulted in a bland, unsatisfying film for all but the youngest viewers. Derek Elley of *Variety* wrote, ". . . the look and coloring are solid, but coin-saving lack of detail and of in-betweening results in jerky motion." The screenplay was not well written, with plot points that went unresolved, and with one-dimensional characters. Charles Solomon of the *Los Angeles Times* said, ". . . the characters aren't interesting enough to hold the viewer's attention."

The U.S. distributor, Hemdale, so desperate for some good reviews, used quotes in its newspaper ads from the children of noted movie critics. "I absolutely loved it!" said Sarah Medved, daughter of critic Michael Medved. "It gets 91 stars!" said the four-year-old daughter of Bob Campbell of Newhouse News Service. Hemdale executives said there was a perception in the industry that critics favored Disney-animated films and overlooked non-Disney animated features. Thus, they asked critics to view this film with children, then asked the children to rate the movie by stars.

All was not lost, however. This motion picture was the winner of the Film Advisory Board's Award of Excellence, the Dove Seal of Approval from the Dove Foundation Review Board, and the Best Children's Film Award from the Fort Lauderdale International Film Festival. (SF)

**Additional Credits:** Executive producers: Steve Walsh, Marietta Dardan. Screenplay: Robin Lyons. Based on the novel by George MacDonald. Music: Istvan Lerch. Animation director: Les Orton. Key animators: Katalina Banki, Lloyd Sutton, Dimitre Bakalov, Chris Webster, Zoltan Mardanse, Rick Villeneuve, Edit Szalay, John Miller, Eguenil Linkov, Hugh Workman, Laszio Adam, Stuart Selkirk, Magda Kecskala, Charlie McCrae, Igvor Ganchev, Less Gibbard, Yvette Sesteries, Les Orton, Erzebet Nyiro, Graham Griffiths, Dandor Bakali. Additional animation: Jose Sallis, Jose Xavier, Jack Stokes, Kevin Molloy, Gary McGarver, Errill Johnson, Steve Weston, Jorgen Lerden, Michael Hegmer, Bendt Naillson, Alan Green. Effects: Sosama Balyski, Piroska Martsa. Character designs: Richard Fawdry, Lazlo Adam, Katalyn Banki. Pre-production visualizations: Mike Wall. Storyboard artists: Andrew Offler, Wayne Thomas. Layout artists: Jozsef Gemes, Sue Butterworth, David Elvin, Tony Ely, Peter Ferk, Wayne Thomas, Marek Fitzinger. Background style: Gizeha N, Csatho. Background artists: David Blake, Errol Bryant, Gizelle N. Csatho, Gizella Neuberg, Timea Otaka, Mike Wall.

**Princess Mononoke** (10/29/99) Miramax Films. 133 mins. Director: Hayao Miyazaki. Producer: Toshio Suzuki. Voices: Gillian Anderson (Moro), Billy Crudup (Prince Ashitaka), Claire Danes (San, The Princess Mononoke), Keith David (Okkoto), John DeMita (Kohroku), Minnie Driver (Lady Eboshi), Jada Pinkett Smith (Toki), Tara Strong (Kaya), Billy Bob Thornton (Jigo).

**Consumer Tips:** ☆☆☆☆ MPAA Rating: PG-13. Japanese historical fantasy.

**Story:** In prehistoric Japan the young warrior Ashitaka, on a quest to find a cure for a cursed wound that is

©Studio Ghibli

slowly killing him, comes to a primeval forest where a war is being fought between the ancient nature gods and a village of metalworkers who are trying to cut down the trees for firewood. The gods are led by a giant wolf goddess and her adopted human daughter, San, while the village is led by the aggressive Lady Eboshi who is protective of her people. A third side is led by Jiku, a priest and agent of the emperor who has been sent to get the head of the great god of the forest, and who tries to manipulate Ashitaka or Eboshi into killing it for him.

**Comments:** *Princess Mononoke* is an adventure fantasy steeped in ancient Japanese history, rich enough in detail to be exciting to audiences unfamiliar with the historical background. The undated story is roughly set during the Muromachi period (1336–1573), when Japan was evolving from an animistic culture dominated by belief in thousands of spirits and gods that controlled humans, to a society in which humans dominated and cultivated the land and its resources. This was also the period when the imperial government, which had risen from the Yamato tribe to rule central Japan, began its expansion to occupy all Japan and complete the conquest/absorption of all remaining independent regions.

The small village of the Emishi tribe is attacked by a fearsome monster, a giant boar god driven mad by pain from a mysterious wound. Ashitaka, leader of the Emishis' young warriors, suffers a poisoned wound while killing the Tatarigami ("cursed god"), which he is told will kill him unless he can find a cure in the land of whatever evil wounded the boar god. Ashitaka journeys on his giant stag until he reaches an ancient forest where the nature gods (huge talking boars and wolves led by an awesome shape-changing "god of the forest" known as Shishi by day and Didaribotchi by night) still reign; but they are being pushed back by an encroaching human village of metalworkers who are cutting down the forest for firewood to work their smelters. The Tataraba village is a revolutionary community of free women led by Lady Eboshi, who has rejected the male-dominated central imperial government and gathered oppressed women (mistreated wives, women sold into prostitution) into an independent society that is supporting itself by making primitive firearms and selling them to the empire's feuding warlords.

Ashitaka realizes that the Tatarigami was wounded by Eboshi's warriors while fighting against Tataraba's expansion into the forest. The forest gods are slowly losing; their only effective fighter is "mononoke hime" (the monster princess), a human girl raised by the wolf goddess Moro as her own daughter. This girl, San, is a fierce guerrilla fighter (shown as a representative of Japan's Stone Age culture ca. 2000 B.C.) but she cannot hold off Eboshi's armed villagers by herself.

*Princess Mononoke* (released July 12, 1997 in Japan) is a masterpiece of animation, and became Japan's highest-grossing theatrical release. But it was a surprisingly violent and complex adult drama after Miyazaki's several previous children's and family films. Miramax gave it an art-house release in only 150 American theaters, to the disappointment of America's anime fans. (FP)

***Additional Credits:*** Screenplay: Hayao Miyazaki. English adaptation: Neil Gaiman. Executive producers: Yasuyoshi Tokuma, Bob Weinstein, Harvey Weinstein. Original Music: Joe Hisaishi. Cinematography: Atsushi Okui. Film editing: Hayao Miyazaki, Takeshi Seyama. Animation directors: Masashi Ando, Yoshifumi Kondo, Katsuya Kondô, Kitaro Kosaka. Animators: Tsutomu Awata, Masaaki Endo, Makiko Futaki, Takeshi Imamura, Megumi Kagawa, Yoshinori Kanada, Toshio Kawaguchi, Katsuya Kondô, Ken'ichi Konishi, Ikuo Kuwana, Mariko Matsuo, Masaru Matsuse, Michio Mihara, Hiroko Minowa, Noriko Moritomo, Takehiro Noda, Shinji Otsuka, Hiroshi Shimizu, Masako Shinohara, Sachiko Sugino, Atsuko Tanaka, Ken'ichi Yamada, Hideaki Yoshio, Atsuko Ôtani.

**The Professional: Golgo 13** (10/23/92) Streamline (Japan). 95 mins. Directors: Osamu Dezaki, Shichiro Kobayasahi, Hirokata Takahashi. Voices: Kiyoshi Kobayashi (Gen. T. Jefferson), Tetsurô Sagawa (Golgo 13), Gorô Naya (Leonard Dawson), John Dantona (Bishop Moretti), Carlos Ferro (Thomas Waltham), Michael Forest (E. Young), Eddie Frierson (Gold), Milt Jamin (Albert), Steve Kramer (Paco), Joyce Kurtz (Cindy), Kerrigan Mahan (Pablo, Silver), Edward Mannix (Gen. Jefferson), Michael McConnohie (Leonard Dawson), Diane Michelle (Rita), Karlyn Michelson (Emily), Edie Mirman (Laura), Tony Oliver (Robert Dawson), David Povall (F. Garvin), Mike Reynolds (Lt. Bob Bragen), Gregory Snegoff (Duke "Golgo 13" Togo, Snake), Jeff Winkless (Informant).

©Saito Productions / TMS

***Consumer Tips:*** ☆☆☆ MPAA Rating: Unrated. Violent crime thriller. Based on the Golgo 13 series of graphic novels by Takao Saito.

***Story:*** Golgo 13, a pseudonymous international killer-for-hire who never fails, murders the son and heir of ruthless business tycoon Leonard Dawson. After carrying out two more impossible hits, Golgo 13 finds himself the target of killers hired by Dawson to avenge his son. As Dawson's killers are themselves killed, the tycoon uses political pressure to force the FBI, CIA, and the Pentagon to send its secret government assassins after Golgo 13 in a series of attempted hits of escalating spectacular violence.

***Comments:*** Takao Saito's *Golgo 13* is one of Japan's longest-running (since 1970) and most popular violent action-adventure manga for adult men. The protagonist is a stony-faced professional killer known only by the pseudonyms Duke Togo and Golgo 13, who will kill anyone if his price is met. The series' popularity is due to Saito setting up realistic situations where it is seemingly absolutely impossible for Golgo 13 to succeed, and then showing in plausible detail how he manages to overcome every obstacle. Golgo 13 has been compared to James Bond totally without morals or emotions, interested in nothing but his job of killing.

The movie, titled in Japan as simply *Golgo 13*, was produced by Tokyo Movie Shinsha and released May 28, 1983.

*Golgo 13* was notable as the first Japanese animated feature to contain CGI sequences, notably the helicopter gunship attack. The dramatic action scenes are generally excellent, but the original story by the TMS staff was reportedly publicly criticized by Saito for its lack of realism on such points as having the super-macho Mafia taking orders from a beautiful, sexy female capo, and professional U.S. agencies employing assassins so flamboyant as to practically be costumed super-villains. (FP)

**Additional Credits:** Creator: Takao Saito. Original music: Toshiyuki Omori. Production manager: Jerry Beck. Chief director: Osamu Dezaki. Animation director: Akio Sugino. Key animators: Atsuko Fukushima, Shinji Otsuka. Animator: Kôji Morimoto.

**The Puppetoon Movie** (6/12/87) Expanded Entertainment. 80 mins. Director/producer: Arnold Leibovit. Voices: Paul Frees (Arnie the Dinosaur, Pillsbury Doughboy), Dallas McKennon (Gumby, Gremlin), Art Clokey (Pokey), Dick Beals (Speedy Alka-Seltzer).

**Consumer Tips:** ☆☆☆ MPAA Rating: G.

**Story:** Gumby and Pokey learn from Arnie the dinosaur about the wonderful animated films of George Pal.

**Comments:** Although best remembered today for his many science-fiction films, director George Pal first made his mark with the stop-motion animated *Puppetoons*, originally distributed through Paramount. This loving compilation feature by Pal admirer Arnold Lei-

©Arnold Leibovit

bovit (who also produced the earlier *The Fantasy Film Worlds of George Pal*) spotlights nine shorts, released between 1937 and 1947: "Phillips Broadcast of 1938," "Phillips Cavalcade," "John Henry and the Inky Poo," "Together in the Weather," "Jasper in a Jam," "The Sleeping Beauty," "Southseas Sweethearts," "Tulips Shall Grow," and "Tubby the Tuba."

The standouts include "John Henry," a fine retelling of the legend with narration by Rex Ingram; the sweet fable "Tubby the Tuba," based on the story and record by Paul Tripp; and especially the 1942 wartime allegory "Tulips Shall Grow." Possibly Pal's most personal animated short, based on his own experiences as a refugee from war-torn Europe, the short features early animation by Willis O'Brien and Ray Harryhausen, manipulating the Screwball Army.

The new framing footage has guest stars Gumby and Pokey receiving a quick history of Pal's life and work from Arnie the dinosaur (voiced by frequent Pal collaborator Paul Frees in his final role, essentially standing in for producer Leibovit, as the name suggests). A brief but impressive finale has a host of stop-motion creatures, from the Pillsbury Doughboy to Clokey's Blockheads and Dave Allen's King Kong model used in a successful Volkswagen commercial, pay their respects to George Pal in a scene veering between touching homage and crude product placement. As with all compilation features, the shorts are better served by themselves in small doses, with full credits. At present, however, *The Puppetoon Movie* stands as the most readily available collection of Pal's animated work, and a recent DVD release included several additional shorts. The new framing footage is surprisingly satisfying on its own, representing a collaboration between many of the leading stop-motion filmmakers of the day (Clokey, Pal alums Gene Warren Jr. and Pete Kleinow, and the Chiodos, amongst others). (AL)

**Additional Credits:** Writer: Arnold Leibovit. Script consulting: Peter Kleinow. Music: Buddy Baker. Animation director: Gene Warren Jr. New prologue animation: Peter Kleinow. Gumby consultant: Art Clokey. Art directors: Gene Warren Jr., Michael Minor. Set/miniature construction supervisor: Gary Campsie. Additional construction: Mike Joyce, Gary Rhodaback, Richard Smith, Paul Kassler, Dennis Schultz. Gumby maker: Kurt Hanson. Arnie the Dinosaur artistic finishing: Charlie Chiodo, Steve Chiodo. Main title design/George Pal book refinishing: Ed Garbert. Additional graphics: Ernest D. Farinol. Still photographs: Kurt Hanson, Tony Alderson. Original puppetoons animators: John S. Abbott, Wah Ming Chang, Ray Harryhausen, Phil Kellison, Fred Madison, William Oberlin, Willis O'Brien, Gene Warren.

**Quest for Camelot** (5/15/98) Warner Bros. 85 mins. Director: Frederik Du Chau. Producer: Dalisa Cooper Cohen. Voices: Jessalyn Gilsig (Kayley), Cary Elwes (Garrett), Gary Oldman (Baron Ruber), Eric Idle (Devon), Don Rickles (Cornwall), Jane Seymour (Lady Juliana), Pierce Brosnan (King Arthur), Sir John Gielgud (Merlin), Bronson Pinchot (The Griffin), Jaleel White (Bladebeak), Gabriel Byrne (Sir Lionel), Jessica Hathaway (Lynnit), Frank Welker (Ayden), Al Roker (Knight), Jess Harnell (Minion), Sarah Freeman (Young Kayley), Andrea Corr (Kayley, singing), Bryan

White (Garrett, singing), Celine Dion (Lady Juliana, singing), Steve Perry (King Arthur, singing).

**Consumer Tips:** ☆½ MPAA Rating: G. A meandering medieval musical fairy tale.

**Story:** Ousted knight of the round table, Ruber, plots to steal the legendary sword Excalibur. When the sword is lost in the Forbidden Forest, Ruber begins an all-out search but is foiled by Kayley, daughter of one of the knights; Garrett, a blind warrior; and a goofy two-headed dragon named Devon and Cornwall.

**Comments:** Sniffing the profits from Disney's megahit, *The Lion King*, Warner Bros. decided to enter the high-budget animation arena. Along with DreamWorks SKG, the resulting competition with Disney generated a demand for animation artists and, for awhile, year-round employment. In May 1995, it announced its first project, *The Quest for the Grail*, (later changed to *The Quest for Camelot*), loosely based upon the novel *The King's Damosel* by Vera Chapman.

The studio put the film into production before the story was finalized. Animators spent considerable downtime waiting for management to make up their minds.

Chrystal Klabunde, lead animator for the blind hero Garrett, told Jenny Peters in *Animation Magazine*, May 1998, "It was top heavy. All the executives were happily running around and playing executive, getting their corner offices—but very few of them had any concept about animation at all, about doing an animated film. It never occurred to anybody at the top that they had to start from the bottom and build that up. The problems were really coming from the inexperience of everyone involved. Those were people from Disney that had the idea that you just said, 'Do it,' and it gets done. It never occurred to them that it got done because Disney had an infrastructure in place, working like clockwork. We didn't have that."

Creative differences forced codirector Bill Kroyer and his wife, producer Sue Kroyer, to leave the project in February 1997. Dalisa Cooper Cohen replaced Frank Gladstone, while Warner Bros. entrusted their $120 million-plus enterprise to a novice, Belgian animator Frederick Du Chau, as the sole director.

Said the effects supervisor Michel Gagné, "People were giving up. The head of layout was kicked out, the head of background, the executive producer, the producer, the director, the associate producer—all the heads rolled. It's kind of a hard environment to work in."

While the feature animation division retooled the story, it loaned its artists to the struggling *Space Jam* crew to help meet its deadlines. *The Quest for Camelot* (the "The" was dropped from the final title) premiere was pushed from November 1997 to May 1998, ahead of Disney's *Mulan*, which also featured a headstrong heroine and a comical dragon in a similar storyline.

According to Cohen, "We made this movie in a year, basically. That was a lot of the problem. We worked around the clock." Warner Feature Animation employed 800 artists, using their main facility in Glendale, California, an ad hoc studio in London, Heart of Texas in Austin, Yowza in Toronto, Canada, and A Film in Copenhagen, Denmark.

The songs were written by David Foster and Carole Bayer Sager, wife of Bob Daly, chairman and co-CEO of Warner Bros.

On its opening weekend, May 15–17, *Quest* grossed a meager $6 million. The following Monday, Fox Animation cancelled *Planet Ice*, due to *Quest*'s lackluster box-office performance. Most who had worked on *Ice* (in Fox's Van Nuys studio) were laid off at the end of May, while Fox's studio in Phoenix continued to work on the *Bartok* direct-to-video. Don Bluth revamped *Planet Ice* as *Titan A.E.*

On June 5, executive producer Max Howard left Warner Bros. for DreamWorks, where he became involved with *Spirit: Stallion of the Cimarron*. Warner Bros. closed its London facility, cut its Glendale staff in half, and stop-lighted development on *The Zoo*, *Aquaman*, Jack Kirby's *The New Gods*, and *The Iguana Brothers*. Production continued on Brad Bird's *The Iron Giant*.

*Quest*'s U.S. box-office total was a sad $22.7 million as of August 9, 1998. It was released in Europe as *The Magic Sword* because, apparently, the word "Camelot" is offensive.

This is a schizoid movie, which can't make up its mind what kind of movie it is. *Quest* is a world where knights can be slain—yet has a talking, cliché-spouting chicken with floating eyebrows. It has a terrifying griffin that attacks a castle—and later becomes the victim of a butt joke. It has ferocious fire-breathing dragons—and a double-headed dragon that cracks airplane jokes and sings rock-and-roll. Weak characters, out-of-place music, choppy editing, amateur directing, inconsistent animation, awkward plot, antithetical character designs—all the hallmarks of amateur filmmaking. *Quest*'s greatest asset is the outstanding effects animation helmed by Michel Gagné. Otherwise, the film is a colossal artistic and box-office failure, nearly ending the legacy of Warner Bros. Animation, and encouraging the myth that audiences don't like hand-drawn animated films because they're hand drawn. (WRM)

**Additional Credits:** Screenplay: Kirk DiMicco, William Schifrin, Jacqueline Feather, David Seidler. Based on the novel *The King's Damosel* by Vera Chapman. Music: Patrick Doyle. Songs: David Foster, Carole Bayer-Sager. Lead animators: Nassos Vakalis, Chrystal S. Klabunde, Alexander Williams, Dan Wagner, Cynthia L. Overman, Stephen A. Franck, Mike Nguyen, Lennie K. Graves, Alyson Hamilton. Supervising animator (U.K.): Russell Hall. Animators (U.S): Clare D. Armstrong, Dale Baer, Richard Baneham, David E. Boudreau, Adam Burke, Jennifer Cardon, Michael A. Chavez, Yarrow T. Cheney, Jesse M. Cosio, Alain Costa, Ricardo Curtis, Bob Davies, James A. Davis, Jeffrey D. Etter, Lauren J. Faust, Ralph I. Fernan, Steve Garcia, Heidi Guedel Garafalo, Kent Hammerstrom, Adam Henry, Len Jones, Leon Joosen, Ernest Keen, Ken Keys, Juliana Korsborn, Jacques Muller, Randall T. Myers, Melina Sydney Padua, Scott T. Petersen, Anna Saunders, Sean Springer, Derek L. Thompson, Jim W. Van Der Keyl, Roger L. Vizard, Mark A. Williams, John D. Williamson, Dan N. Boulos, Larry D. Whittaker. Animators (U.K): Cinzia Angelini, Laurent Benhamo, Alberto Campos, Lee Chamberland, Murray Debus, Sean Leaning, Paul Lee, Quentin Miles, Stephen Perry, Thierry Schiel, Michael Schlingman, Sharon Smith, Gerben Steenks, Paul Stone, Vladimir Todorov, Jan Van Buyten, Duncan Varley, Peter Western, Gabrielle Zuchelli. CGI head: Tad A. Gielow.

**Race for Your Life Charlie Brown** (8/24/77) Paramount. 76 mins. Director: Bill Melendez. Producers: Lee Mendelson, Bill Melendez. Voices: Duncan Watson (Charlie Brown), Gregory Felton (Schroeder), Stuart Brotman (Peppermint Patty), Gail Davis (Sally), Liam Martin (Linus), Jimmy Ahrens (Marcie), Melanie Kohn (Lucy), Kirk Jue (Bully), Jordan Warren (Another Bully), Tom Muller (Another Bully), Bill Melendez (Snoopy), Fred Van Amburg (Radio Announcer).

©United Feature Syndicate, Inc.

**Consumer Tips:** ☆☆ MPAA Rating: G.

**Story:** Charlie Brown, Lucy, and the *Peanuts* gang, away at summer camp, are challenged by bullies to a number of sporting activities, topped by a contest that takes them rafting on a wild river. Meanwhile, Snoopy and Woodstock get lost in the woods.

**Comments:** By 1977, the *Peanuts* movie franchise was beginning to run down. This third entry takes yet another running theme from the strip, the annual summer camp trips for Charlie Brown and the gang. Inevitably, Snoopy and Woodstock tag along, riding a motorcycle. The gang adjusts to conditions, camp bullies, and competitions, all of which come across as oddly dull and generic (though the bullies' pet cat, a huge beast in a spiked collar, is a nice touch).

Though once again Charles Schulz scripted the adaptation, the venture is oddly lifeless. Instead of the moments of introspection and complexities of childhood that stood out in the strip and previous animated productions, the dialogue is trite and an inordinate amount of time seems to be spent on rather pointless character squabbles; the entire cast seems to have contracted Lucy's crabbiness. There are still a few genuine character moments, such as Linus brandishing his blanket like a whip to protect his friends, and there's a cute mountain cabin sing-a-long. The central set piece is a lengthy river race between the boys, the girls, and the bullies, but little excitement is generated. Perhaps part of the problem lay in displacing the *Peanuts* gang from

their nameless suburban environment, which with its kite-eating trees and five-cent psychiatry booths, actually offered more wonders and excitement than the bland wilderness of summer camp.

The music score, by former Bakshi composer Ed Bogas, offers some distraction, and marks Bogas's first collaboration with Melendez Productions (he would go on to write scores and songs for numerous *Peanuts* specials and the *Garfield* series for Film Roman). The movie is amiable enough, and there is a nice moral about teamwork and cooperation. In the end, adult *Peanuts* fans may be disappointed, but kids will probably enjoy seeing Snoopy and the gang again. (AL)

**Additional Credits:** Codirector: Phil Roman. Writer/creator of the *Peanuts* characters: Charles M. Schulz. Music: Ed Bogas. Animation: Don Lusk, Bob Matz, Hank Smith, Rod Scribner, Ken O'Brien, Al Pabian, Joe Roman, Jeff Hall, Sam Jaimes, Bob Bachman, George Singer, Bill Littlejohn, Bob Carlson, Patricia Joy, Terry Lennon, Larry Leichliter. Layouts/backgrounds: Evert Brown, Bernard Gruver, Tom Yakutis, Dean Spille, Elle Bogardus.

**Raggedy Ann and Andy** (4/1/77) 20th Century Fox. 84 mins. Director: Richard Williams. Producer: Richard Horner. Voices: Didi Conn (Raggedy Ann), Mark Baker (Raggedy Andy), Fred Stuthman (the Camel with the Wrinkeled Knees), Niki Flacks (Babette), George S. Irving (the Captain), Arnold Stang (Queasy the Parrot), Joe Silver (The Greedy), Alan Sues (the Loony Knight), Marty Brill (King Koo Koo), Paul Dooley (Gazooks), Mason Adams (Grandpa), Allen

©Twentieth Century Fox

Swift (Maxi-Fixit), Claire Williams (Marcella), Hetty Galen (Susie Pincushion), Sheldon Harnick (Barney Beanbag, Socko), Ardyth Kaiser (Topsy), Margery Gray, Lynne Stuart (The Twin Pennies).

**Consumer Tips:** ☆☆½ MPAA Rating: G. Based on the books by Johnny Gruelle.

**Story:** Raggedy Ann and Andy set out to retrieve a pretty French doll, who was captured by a toy pirate. Along the way they meet the camel with the wrinkled knees and get captured by the Greedy, a morphing muck of candy.

**Comments:** Johnny Gruelle's toy characters, first created in 1920, were ideally suited to animation, a medium concerned with bringing things to life, and of course, toys, dishes, food items, and other inanimate objects had been favorite subjects since the 1930s. Both Fleischer Studios and its successor, Famous Studios, had previously animated Raggedy Ann and friends as two-reel short subjects. This production, funded by publisher Bobbs-Merrill, however, was much more ambitious.

Produced by a pair of Broadway backers, the original director, Chuck Jones animator Abe Levitow, succumbed to fatal illness early on and was quickly replaced by Richard Williams. Williams first made a name for himself through acclaimed short subjects (1958's "The Little Island" and 1972's "A Christmas Carol") and a series of striking animated title sequences and commercials. Most of these projects, as well as *Raggedy Ann and Andy*, were undertaken primarily to fund Williams's dream project, *Thief and the Cobbler* (though the director used the opportunity to cast his daughter, Claire, as Marcella in the live-action frame scenes). Williams assembled an impressive team, blending seasoned animators and rising newcomers from both Hollywood and New York studios (with production divided between coasts); the crew, cast by character in the tradition of Disney features, included Hungarian animator Tissa David (Raggedy Ann), Lantz veteran Emery Hawkins (the Greedy), Ward Kimball's son John Kimball (the loony knight), and especially the Disney legend Art Babbitt, handling the forlorn camel with the wrinkled knees. Joe Raposo, veteran of *Sesame Street* and scribe of Kermit's trademark song "It's Not Easy Being Green," was brought in to orchestrate, score, write songs, and he even supplies some unbilled bit voices.

As for the movie itself, it begins well, with elaborate opening titles, in which the artists' names are paired with their characters (the first time animators were credited by character, predating *Beauty and the Beast*). The story that follows is structured like a stage musical, complete with chorus numbers and solo turns for every principal character (mostly voiced by Broadway veterans), as Raggedy Ann and Andy attempt to rescue their owner's new doll Babbette from the love-starved pirate captain. On the one hand, the quest motif, a timeworn favorite in animated features, allowed an excuse for striking set pieces involving the Greedy, an amorphous blob of candy, and the insane loony knight. The musical structure, however, lends an odd self-consciousness to scenes, with characters apparently playing to the balcony; the closing number has the cast facing forward as if about to take bows and accept tossed roses. There are also odd lapses in design, when the "star" animator isn't involved, where the doll characters no longer resemble cartoons but literally animated toys, stiff painted faces and limping along as if tugged by strings.

Ultimately costing $4 million, the movie was considered a box-office failure. Still, the movie is engaging enough for children, and the animators' showpieces are well worth seeing. As assistant/inbetweener Michael Sporn said in a letter to Funnyworld, "The behind-the-scenes story of *Raggedy Ann and Andy* seems more interesting to some people than the story that we had to live with on screen." Indeed, animation historian John Canemaker scored his first success with a book chronicling the feature's development. (AL)

**Additional Credits:** Screenplay: Patricia Thackray, Max Wilk. Based on the stories and characters created by Johnny Gruelle. Music/lyrics: Joe Raposo. Assistant director: Cosmo Anzilotti. Sequence director: Gerald Potterton. Animators: Art Babbitt, Tissa David, Emery Hawkins, Hal Ambro, Charlie Downs, John Kimball, Gerry Chiniquy, Chrystal Spencer, John Bruno, Doug Crane, George Bakes, Art Vitello, Grim Natwick, Corny Cole, Cosmo Anzilotti, Tom Roth, Irv Spence, Warren Batchelder, Willis Pyle, Jack Schnerk, Richard Williams. Assistant animation supervisors: Marlene Robinson, Michael Sporn. Assistant animators: Loren Bowie, David Block, Gian-Franco

Celestri, Jerry Dvorak, Jeffrey Gatrall, John Gaug, Eric Goldberg, Daniell Haskett, Helen Komar, Jim Logan, Mary Carol Millican, Lester Pegues Jr., Karen Peterson, Barney Posner, Michel Rochon, Tom Sito, Duane Ullrich. Production designer: Corny Cole. Production consultant: Shamus Culhane. West Coast coordinator: Carl Bell.

## Rainbow Brite and the Star Stealer (11/15/85)

Warner Bros. 97 mins. Director: Bernard Deyries. Codirector: Kimio Yabuki. Producers: Jean Chalopin, Andy Heyward, Tetsuo Katayama. Voices: Bettina Bush (Rainbow Brite), Patrick Fraley (Lurky, On-X, Buddy Blue, Dog Guard, Spectran, Slurthie, Glitterbot), Peter Cullen (Murky, Castle Monster, Glitterbot, Guard, Skydancer, Slurthie), Robbie Lee (Twin, Shy Violet, Indigo, La La Orange, Spectran, Sprites), Andre Stojka (Starlite, Wizard, Spectran), David Mendenhall (Krys), Rhonda Aldrich (The Princess, The Creature), Les Tremayne (Orin Bombo, Television Announcer), Mona Marshall (Red Butler, Witch, Castle Creature, Spectran, Patty O. Green, Canary Yellow), Jonathan Harris (Count Blogg), Marissa Mendenhall (Stormy), Scott Menville (Brian), Charlie Adler (Popo), David Workman (Sergeant Zombo).

©Hallmark Cards, Inc.

**Consumer Tips:** 0 (no stars). Sorry kids, the star stealer was here. MPAA Rating: G. There are segments that are nighmarish for children.

**Story:** Rainbow Brite, from Rainbow Land, is confronted by a dark princess who plots to steal Spectra, a planet-sized diamond.

**Comments:** Rainbow Brite is a brave little girl who has a very special rainbow-making belt and travels the world by rainbow roads, giving color and joy to all those in need. Oh brother!

This movie is aimed at preschool children. The *New York Post* said, "the picture's plot, dialogue and action are pure kid stuff, but the drawings and scenery are splendidly imaginative." However, *Variety* said the film is "stifflingly sweet . . . too short on character and invention to stir a child's imagination at any age." In addition, Janet Maslin of the *New York Times* said the film has a "suffocating prettiness . . . it isn't a movie, it's a marketing tool."

The creator of Rainbow Brite was Hallmark Properties, the licensing arm of Hallmark Cards. Hallmark worked with D.I.C. Enterprises, which is an independent animation studio run by Jean Chalopin and Andy Heyward, to produce three *Rainbow Brite* animated television specials for the first-run syndication market. These specials did fairly well on television, which prompted D.I.C. and Hallmark to produce a feature-length film.

The art director on the film was Rich Rudish, whose previous experience was as a Hallmark Card designer since 1964. Codirecting was Bernard Deyries of France, who helmed many of D.I.C.'s earliest series, including *The Littles, Mysterious Cities of Gold*, and *The Get Along Gang*. His partner in Japan, Kimio Yabuki, was behind the popular *Ikkyusan* and *Ken the Wolf Boy*.

The film did fairly well, and it created the demand among young girls for more *Rainbow Brite* material. This lead to a television series in 1986 for the first-run syndication market. (SF)

**Additional Credits:** Codirector: Kimio Yabuki. Writer: Howard R. Cohen. Based on a story by Jean Chalopin and Howard R. Cohen, and on characters developed by Hallmark Properties. Music: Haim Saban, Shuki Levy. Animation: Kaoru Hirata, Satoe Nishiyama, Fukuo Yamamoto, Mitsuru Aoyama, Masaki Kajishima, Nobuyuki Haga, Yasunopri Miyazawa, Kazuhiko Miyake, Yasushi Tanizawa, Kinichiroi Suzuki, Masami Shimada, Shinichi Imakuma, Yasayuki Tada, Makoto Shinjou, Junzo Ono, Toshio Kaneko, Tado Katsu Yoshida, Michio Ikeda, Hitomi Kakaburi, Atsumi Hashimoto, Kiyomi Masuda, Katsuo Takasaki, Yoshio Makainkakano, Hiroshi Oikawa, Shigetaka Kiyoyama, Katsuko Kanazawa, Tashashi Hyodo, Akinobia Takahashi, Katsuko Kanazawa, Takashi Hyodo, Takennori Mihara.

**The Real Shlemiel** See *Aaron's Magic Village.*

**Recess: School's Out** (1/16/04) Walt Disney Television Animation. 84 mins. Director: Chuck Sheets. Producers: Paul Germain, Joe Ansolabehere, Toshio Suzuki, Stephen Swafford. Voices: Andrew Lawrence (T. J. Detweiler), Ricky D'Shon Collins (Vince LaSalle), Jason Davis (Mikey Blumberg), Ashley Johnson (Gretchen Grundler), Pamela Segall (Ashley Spinelli), Courtland Mead (Gus Griswald), Dabney Coleman (Principal Prickly), James Woods (Dr. Philliam Benedict), Paul Wilson (Mr. Detweiler), Allyce Beasley (Alordayne Grotky), Robert Goulet (Mikey Blumberg singing), April Winchell (Mrs. Detweilwer, Muriel Finster), Melissa Joan Hart (Becky Detweiler), Peter MacNichol (Fenwick), Anndi McAfee (Ashley "A"), Francesca Smith (Ashley "B"), Rachel Crane (Ashley "Q").

©Disney Enterprises

**Consumer Tips:** ☆☆½ MPAA Rating: G. Adapted from the Disney cable television series *Recess.*

**Story:** The evil ex-principal of Third Street Elementary School, Philliam Benedict, hatches a plot to destroy summer vacation forever by relocating the moon via a powerful tractor beam. Eternal winter (and longer study hours) will be the result. Arrayed against him is T. J. Detweiler's *Recess* gang, the current principal, and eventually every student and teacher in the town. Will they be enough to stop Benedict and his cadre of goons, ninjas, and scientists?

**Comments:** *School's Out* is a continuation of the popular series produced by Walt Disney Television animation, and it very much resembles its televised counterpart. Unlike other movies that have their genesis in television shows, nothing special has been added to the animation, and, until the closing credits, the art direction is less than spectacular. The movie's plot is highly improbable, and even young children will have a hard time swallowing the final showdown between good and evil that takes place in the school's auditorium. When all the other elements are this weak, a film had better compensate with interesting characters and their relationships. This, in fact, is *School's Out*'s saving grace. The *Recess* gang is comprised of six diverse fourth-graders that disrupt authority through clever, low-tech ruses. Leader T. J. Detweiler is a smart little anarchist. His best friend Vince is a jock, science nerd Gretchen is the brains of the outfit, Ashley yearns for pro wrestling fame, and Mikey is a hulking giant of a lad with a gentle heart. Rounding out the group is newbie kid Gus. The group, tighter than a unit of Navy Seals, ultimately saves the day, but the film's most interesting relationship turns out to be between T. J. and his bête noire, Principal Peter Prickly.

When Prickly's old rival Philliam Benedict vows revenge on him for defeating a plot to eradicate recess back in 1969, the principal is forced into an unlikely alliance with T. J. to stop Benedict's mad plan to destroy summer. T. J. finds out (via flashback) that not only was a hip Prickly very supportive of children, the principal also has golden memories of his own summer vacations. As T. J. gains increasing respect for his pedantic antagonist, Prickly shocks T. J. by telling him to enjoy the wondrous, fleeting years of his childhood while he still has them. *Recess: School's Out* is ultimately a film about rapprochement between the generations.

In recognition of this device, directors Germain and Ansolabehere filled the soundtrack with hits from the 1960s and '70s, bringing a touch of Prickly's generation into the children's world. This is the cleverest device in the film, reaching its apogee in the closing credits; the *Recess* kids are recast as hippie musicians playing the Lemon Pipers' 1969 hit *Green Tambourine* in a psychedelic music video. On the drums: Principal Prickly as seen in the 1969 flashback.

The kooky world of Third Street Elementary, in which every female student seems to be named Ashley and the kindergarteners are feral forces of nature, is consistently re-created from the television series. As is the recent custom in animated films there are nearly 50 voice actors and many of them are celebrities. Stand-outs include James Woods as the nefarious Dr. Benedict and Robert Goulet, who is all too beautiful as the singing voice of Mikey. This film marks Goulet's third go-round at toon stardom: he also provided the voices for Jaune Tom, the feline hero of *Gay Purr-ee* (1962) and for Wheezy the Penguin in *Toy Story 2.*

Wearing your politics on your sleeve: Philliam Benedict, who is revealed to be a former Secretary of Education, is a thinly disguised parody of President Reagan's own post holder, William Bennett. (MG)

**Additional Credits:** Production supervisor: Christopher Kracker. Screenplay: Jonathan Greenberg. Story: Paul Germain, Joe Ansolabehere, Jonathan Greenberg. Original music: Denis M. Hannigan. Orchestrator/conductor: Bruce Babcock. Original character design: David Shannon. Art direction: Eric Keyes. Special effects: Raymond C. King.

**The Reluctant Dragon** (6/30/41) Walt Disney Pictures. 72 mins. Director: Alfred L. Werker. Voices: Gerald Mohr (Narrator, "Baby Weems" segment), Leone LeDoux, Raymond Severn (Baby Weems), Ernie Alexander (John Weems), Linda Marwood (Mrs. Weems), Art Gilmore (Franklin Roosevelt), Edward Marr (Walter Winchell), Clarence Nash (Donald Duck), John McLeish (Narrator, "How to Ride a Horse" segment), Pinto Colvig (Goofy), J. Donald Wilson (Narrator, "The Reluctant Dragon" segment), Barnett Parker (Dragon, Father), Claude Allister (Sir Giles), Billy Lee (Boy).

**Consumer Tips:** ☆ MPAA Rating: Unrated. This film is basically a public relations piece for Disney. Kenneth Grahame wrote the story of *The Reluctant Dragon* in 1898.

**Story:** His wife informs humorist Peter Benchley that the story of *The Reluctant Dragon* would make a great film. She sends hubby to the studio to pitch it to Walt

©Walt Disney Productions

Disney. Benchley winds up taking an informal studio tour, meets some of the Disney crew, and gets a look at how cartoons are made. When he finally meets Walt, Mr. Benchley finds he is just in time for a screening of *The Reluctant Dragon.*

**Comments:** *The Reluctant Dragon* is possibly Disney's most forgettable film. It is also the victim of the worst possible timing; the movie was released just a few weeks after the infamous Disney labor strike began. Benchley is shown touring a studio of happy, enthusiastic employees. In the film, some of the Disney staff are actually actors who had never worked a day in the studio. The reality was vastly different, and the film lent fuel to the fire among the angry strikers. The premiere at the Pantages Theater was accompanied by scores of picketers, many of them superb artists who caricatured Walt Disney as a malicious dragon.

As for the animation, the most celebrated segment of the film is "Baby Weems." This is the tale of a baby born so brilliant that he dwarfs every mind on earth, composes musical masterpieces, and holds brilliant discourse with President Roosevelt, Albert Einstein, and George Bernard Shaw. Young Herbert Weems announces that he has the solution to all the world's problems, but on the eve of his address to a breathless planet he takes ill. Baby Weems recovers from his fever, but at the cost of his intellect; he is now a simple, pre-verbal infant. His mom and dad may not have Herbert's head added to Mount Rushmore any longer, but they do have their baby back at last. "Baby Weems" has undeniable charm and is the only segment that stays with the viewer after the film is over.

"Baby Weems" can hardly be called an animated film. Movements are limited and stylized. The short is rather like a storyboard that moves on its own, with characters that look as if they were designed for television commercials. Although "Baby Weems" is hailed as a stylistic breakthrough (for commercial audiences, it certainly was), Disney was already moving towards limited animation. Earlier in 1941 Disney worked with engineers from Lockheed to produce a training film called *Four Methods of Flush Riveting*. The animations in that film made "Baby Weems" appear like *Bambi* in comparison. During the war Disney would turn out hundreds of such films for the military.

Goofy's celebrated series of "How To" (more accurately, "How *Not* To") shorts made their debut in this film. "How to Ride a Horse" has imaginative devices such as showing the audience Goofy's fatal fumblings in slow-motion replay. Best of all is the sonorous voice-over by John McLeish, who describes the action in dead earnest. According to Jack Kinney, McLeish never saw the film and thought that he was reading an educational script. McLeish, upset at first, finally took the deception in good humor.

The animated segments "Casey Jr." and "Old Mac-Donald Duck" are very brief and are used for Mr. Benchley's edification. The showpiece of the film, "The Reluctant Dragon," is an exercise in pure silliness. It's hard to describe the dragon in politically correct terms, but the Disney press release describes him as a "pink tea character." Disney had the dragon modeled on actor Franklin Pangborn, who frequently portrayed comic effeminates. With his fluttery voice and eyelashes, balletic poses, and tendency to recite fey poetry, the dragon might not seem a match for dragon-slayer Sir Giles. It turns out, however, that Sir Giles and the dragon have quite a bit in common (the tea party/poetry recital must be seen to be believed). Rather than fight, the two new friends fake an epic battle in which the dragon takes a dive and then comes to live in the village as a sort of mascot.

*The Reluctant Dragon* does offer some insight into the Disney studio and the animation process, but die-hard animation fans and historians will hardly find themselves sated after watching this film. (MG)

**Additional Credits:** "Goofy" sequence director: Jack Kinney. Assistant live-action director: Jasper Blystone. Screenplay: Ted Sears, Al Perkins, Larry Clemmons, Bill Cottrell, Harry Clark. Animation story: Erdman Penner, T. Hee, Joe Grant, Dick Huemer, John P. Miller. Music: Frank Churchill, Larry Morey. Animation: Ward Kimball, Fred Moore, Milt Neil, Wolfgang Reitherman, Walt Kelly, Jack Campbell, Claude Smith, Harvey Toombs, Bud Swift. Uncredited animator: Tony Strobl. Special effects: Ub Iwerks, Joshua Meador. Cartoon art directors: Ken Anderson, Hugh Hennesy, Charles Phillipi. Background artists: Ray Huffine, Art Riley. Main title caricatures: T. Hee.

**The Rescuers** (6/22/77) Walt Disney Pictures. 77 mins. Directors: Wolfgang Reitherman, John Lounsberry, Art Stevens. Producer: Wolfgang Reitherman. Voices: Eva Gabor (Miss Bianca), Bob Newhart (Bernard), Geraldine Page (Madame Medusa), Joe Flynn (Mr. Snoops), Michelle Stacy (Penny), James Macdonald (Evinrude), Jeanette Nolan (Ellie Mae), Pat Buttram (Luke), Jim Jordan (Orville), John McIntire (Rufus), Bernard Fox (Chairman), Larry Clemons (Gramps), George Lindsey (Deadeye), Dub Taylor (Digger), John Fiedler (Deacon), Bill McMillan (Television Newsman).

**Consumer Tips:** ☆☆½ MPAA Rating: G. Adapted from Margery Sharp's two books, *The Rescuers* (1959) and *Miss Bianca* (1962).

**Story:** The International Rescue Aid Society is comprised of a multinational assembly of mice in the basement of the United Nations. A call for help is found

©Walt Disney Productions

in a bottle, and Hungarian member Miss Bianca takes the assignment. She chooses janitor Bernard to assist her. The message is from Penny, a young girl kidnapped from a New York orphanage and transported to the Southern swamps, a captive of Madame Medusa and her two burly alligators. Medusa and her corpulent partner, Mr. Snoops, have located a pirate cave where the Devil's Eye diamond has been hidden, and only a small girl can fit through the hole to retrieve it. Bianca and Bernard finally reach the swamps via a helpful albatross and soon enlist the local animals against Medusa. A rousing victory ends in Penny's return and adoption.

**Comments:** Walt Disney had a plan for *The Rescuers* in the works since 1960, but it took 15 years to reach the production stage. Venerable veterans Ollie Johnston, Frank Thomas, and Milt Kahl—one-third of Disney's brain trust known as his "Nine Old Men"—all retired after this film. Woolie Reitherman directed for the final time, and John Lounsberry died several months before the film was released. This film saw the dawn of a new generation led by hopefuls like Don Bluth, John Pomeroy, and Gary Goldman; little did Disney know they would stage a walkout only three years later.

The story needed some massaging. It was originally to be set in the Antarctic, because the most recent book in the series took place there. There was to be a polar bear played by Louis Prima (named Louie, no less), and the villain was an evil penguin king. However, the staff balked at animating against the sparse designs a polar setting would require, and it was back to the drawing board. The final version of the film is a pleasant, entertaining diversion. No one scene can really be said to stand out, but nothing much goes wrong, either. *The Rescuers* may be a less-than-fitting farewell to the "Nine Old Men," but by 1977 Disney was no longer capable of turning out features equal to its finest at any rate.

Milt Kahl was determined to go out with a bang, and he animated Madame Medusa virtually without assistance. This frowsy, histrionic witch is a study in greed, and Kahl leaned heavily on actress Geraldine Page for character and mannerisms. Kahl may have done better work in his time, but his Medusa is an inspired creation. Mr. Snoops, Medusa's unappetizing assistant, was actually a caricature of animation trade journalist/historian John Culhane. Culhane was often at the studio doing research and chumming with the animators, and Reitherman though it would be funny to model Snoops on him. Longtime character actor Joe Flynn provided the voice.

Eva Gabor and Bob Newhart actually have very good chemistry as Bianca and Bernard, and they are very well drawn. The Xerography process that had been introduced in 1961 still produced sketchy, dark lines around the characters (and characters the size of mice can suffer considerably as a result), but on the whole the heroes are animated with few problems. *The Rescuers* was not heavily promoted, nor was much merchandise produced. Still, the film did exceptionally well at the box office due to its appealing characters, simple storyline, and exceptional voice work. No one will ever compare the film to *Pinocchio* or even *Cinderella*, but the "Nine Old Men" could still ride off into the sunset with heads held high.

Madame Medusa was nearly portrayed by Cruella De Vil, villainess supreme of *101 Dalmatians*, but Ollie Johnston stated that it felt wrong to attempt what amounted to a sequel. However, *101 Dalmatians* eventually went on to have a live-action remake and live-action sequel, and a sequel to *The Rescuers* was made in 1990. It was originally planned to have Bernard and Bianca as married detectives, but the writers felt that they could develop more romance between the two by having them meet at the U.N. and go off on an adventure together. Rufus the cat is a self-caricature by veteran animator Ollie Johnston. After 42 years of stellar service at Disney, he was certainly entitled to a part in the film. (MG)

**Additional Credits:** Story: Larry Clemmons, Ken Anderson, Vance Gerry, David Michener, Burny Mattinson, Frank Thomas, Fred Lucky, Ted Berman, Dick Sebast. Adapted from *The Rescuers and Miss Bianca* by Margery Sharp. Music: Artie Butler. Songs: Carol Connors, Alyn Robbins, Sammy Fain. Directing animators: Ollie Johnston, Frank Thomas, Milt Kahl, Don Bluth. Animators: John Pomeroy, Andy Gaskill, Art Stevens, Chuck Harvey, Bob McCrea, Cliff Nordberg, Gary Goldman, Dale Baer, Ron Clements, Bill Hajee, Glen Keane. Effects animators: Jack Buckley, Ted Kierscey, Dorse A. Lanpher, James L. George, Dick Lucas. Art director: Don Griffith. Layout artists: Joe Hale, Guy Deel, Tom Lay, Sylvia Roemer. Color styling: Al Dempster. Background artists: Jim Coleman, Ann Guenther, Daniela Bielacka. Preliminary sketches: Ralph Hulett. Titles: Melvin Shaw, Eric Larson, Burny Mattinson.

**The Rescuers Down Under** (11/16/90) Walt Disney Pictures. 74 mins. Directors: Hendel Butoy, Mike Gabriel. Producer: Thomas Schumaker. Voices: Eva Gabor (Miss Bianca), Bob Newhart (Bernard), John Candy (Wilbur), Tristan Rogers (Jake), Adam Ryen (Cody), George C. Scott (McLeach), Wayne Robson (Frank), Douglas Seale (Krebbs), Bernard Fox (Chairmouse, Doctor), Peter Firth (Red), Billy Barty (Baitmouse), Ed Gilbert (Francois), Carla Meyer (Faloo, Mother), Russi Taylor (Nurse Mouse), Frank Welker (Joanna, Various Animals).

©Walt Disney Productions

***Consumer Tips:*** ☆☆½ MPAA Rating: G. The continuing adventures of Bernard and Miss Bianca, now set in Australia.

***Story:*** The International Rescue Aid Society is at it again when young Cody falls into the clutches of poacher Percival McLeach and his voracious lizard Joanna. McLeach is after the rare golden eagle Marahute and will stop at nothing to make Cody reveal the bird's whereabouts. Orville's flighty brother Wilbur and an adventurous kangaroo rat named Jake aid Bernard and Bianca in the rescue, defeating McLeach and ensuring Marahute's freedom forever. Bernard proposes to Miss Bianca, who readily accepts.

***Comments:*** Thirteen years after *The Rescuers*, Disney decided to make its first sequel. The decision was not really a hard one; the original movie made quite a bit of money and the studio needed a film release while the extensive production of *Beauty and the Beast* was taking place. Only a couple of new characters had to be designed, and the basic plot of mice rescuing a human child from a greedy villain did not need much revision. It was not really a cheat; after all, that's what Bernard and Bianca do as an avocation. That they would be transported by an albatross and assisted by other animals is a given and needed no tinkering. Thus, for better or worse, the film virtually wrote itself.

Disney sent a team of artists to Australia under the supervision of art director Maurice Hunt and came back with hundreds of sketches, drawings, and photos of the local terrain, having traversed 4,000 miles in less than three weeks in order to sample a wide variety of landscapes. *The Rescuers Down Under* is an unusually rich-looking film that somehow recalls Walt Disney's *True Life Adventures* series. The film is rather like a nature travelogue with animated characters running around in it. The best sequence in the film is the opening, where Cody scales a dangerous cliff in order to free Marahute from the first of McLeach's traps. The eagle then takes the lad on an exhilarating ride through the outback and into the clouds, perfectly tracked by the camera from multiple angles.

As for Bernard and Bianca, they neither do nor say much that we haven't seen in the first film, and nothing in their characters is further developed. There is a sort of subplot where Jake vies for Miss Bianca's affections, but there's never the sense he's a serious threat to our stolid hero. Duncan Marjoribanks does a nifty job turning George C. Scott into a cartoon villain, and Scott himself turns in a perfectly creepy performance; catch his impromptu singing number as he prepares to lower poor Cody into a swarm of crocodiles. There is some evidence of the still unperfected art of computer animation; McLeach's bizarre vehicle, a combination of truck, army half-track, hoist, and animal cage is prominently featured several times in the film. It looks unreal and out of place against the 2-D animation, but better things were soon to come.

*The Rescuers Down Under* is a serviceable film that has better animation and pacing than its predecessor, but it was clearly out of place coming between *The Little Mermaid* and *Beauty and the Beast*. Jeffrey Katzenberg reportedly loved this film as much as his

Broadway-style blockbusters, but in the final analysis it is a well-animated piece of nostalgia, an homage by the Disney crew to their training days and the final reign of the "Nine Old Men." (MG)

**Additional Credits:** Screenplay: Jim Cox, Karey Kirkpatrick, Byron Simpson, Joe Ranft. Music: Bruce Broughton. Supervising animators: Glen Keane, Mark Henn, Russ Edmonds, David Cutler, Ruben A. Aquino, Nik Ranieri, Ed Gombert, Anthony De Rosa, Kathy Zielinski, Duncan Marjoribanks. Animators: James Baxter, Ron Husband, Will Finn, David Burgess, Alexander S. Kupershmidt, Chris Bailey, Mike Cedeno, Rick Farmiloe, Jacques Muller, Dave Pruiksma, Rejean Bourdages, Roger Chiasson, Ken Duncan, Joe Haidar, Ellen Woodbury, Jorgen Klubien, Geefwee Boedoe, Barry Temple, David P. Stephan, Chris Wahl, Larry White, Brigitte Hartley, Doug Krohn, Phil Young, Tom Roth, Leon Joosen. Computer animation: Tina Price, Andrew Schmitt. Effects supervisor: Randy Fulmer. Effects animators: Ted Kierscey, Dave Bossert, Kelvin Ysuda, Mark Myer, Eusebio Torres, Christine Harding, Barry Cook, Mark Dindal, Glenn Chaika. Art director: Maurice Hunt. Story supervisor: Joe Ranft. Storyboards: Ed Gombert, Christopher Sanders, Roger Allers, Glen Keane, Vance Gerry, Kelly Asbury, Gary Trousdale, Brenda Chapman, Will Finn, Robert Lence, Kirk Wise. Character design/visual development: Christopher Sanders, Bruce Zick, Glen Keane, Chris Buck, Gay Lawrence-Ventura, Gil Hung, Kevin Lima, Kelly Asbury, Duncan Marjoribanks, Kevin Donoghue, Valerio Lawrence-Ventura. Layout supervisor: Dan Hansen. Key layout artists: Rasoul Azadani, Bill Perkins. Layout artists: Karen Keller, Robert Walker. Background supervisor: Lisa L. Keene. Background artists: Jim Coleman, Douglas Ball, Cristy Maltese, Tom Woodington, Robert E. Stanton, Tia Kratter, Donald Towns, Phil Phillipson, Dean Gordon, Diana Wakeman, Michael Humphries.

**Return to Neverland** (2/15/02) Disney. 72 mins. Director: Robin Budd. Producers: Christopher Chase, Michelle Robinson, Dan Rounds. Voices: Harriet Owen (Jane and Young Wendy), Blayne Weaver (Peter Pan), Corey Burton (Captain Hook), Jeff Bennett (Smee and Pirates), Kath Soucie (Wendy), Andrew McDonough (Danny), Roger Rees (Edward), Spencer Breslin (Cubby), Bradley Pierce (Nibs), Quinn Beswick (Slightly).

**Consumer Tips:** ☆☆½ MPAA Rating: G.

©Walt Disney Enterprises, Inc.

**Story:** During the height of World War II, Wendy's daughter Jane was kidnapped by Captain Hook. Peter Pan and the Lost Boys come to the rescue—but they must convince her to believe in fairies, to both save Tinker Bell and allow her the ability to fly home.

**Comments:** Beginning in the mid-1990s, the major studios discovered that considerable profit could be made from lower-budget, typically outsourced sequels to popular animated movies. Disney joined the bandwagon slightly later, but with considerable zest. Though most such entries went straight to video, a few entries had brief theatrical releases. *Return to Neverland* is one of these, and a surprisingly decent entry. The sequel came almost 50 years after Disney's *Peter Pan*, but unlike some stories, there was certain leeway in the original texts, and indeed Barrie himself had written about Peter Pan visiting Wendy's daughter Jane, the basic plot used here. The principal change is that Jane is now a skeptic, abducted by Hook, rather than willingly following Peter. An interesting choice was made to set the action against the London Blitz, a more serious backdrop than one expects from most such sequels, which are more deliberately aimed at children, and an interesting contrast to the fantasy of Neverland.

The work of the "Nine Old Men" on the original is replaced by animation from Disney's Australian studio artists, whose work compares surprisingly well to the original, albeit far more distractingly glossy. In the modern fashion, songs are used more as mood backdrops, reiterating themes in a somewhat heavy-handed fashion. The character voices are generally good, with Corey Burton, as Hook, giving his finest impression of the great Hans Conried. Some gags, such as an inexplicably ravenous octopus replacing the crocodile, fall flat, and in fact scenes depicting Hook's terror of the creature, and Smee's response, are lifted almost verbatim from the original. A nice touch occurs when Hook's CG pirate ship sails to Neverland, the transition represented by kaleidoscopic images straight from *The Wonderful World of Color*. Good-natured if slight, the movie certainly fares better than most such sequels, displaying unexpected reverence for both the source material and the Disney versions of the characters. Though the continued rash of "cheapquels" is dismaying, and one fears *Three Caballeros: Fun with Mexican Water* will surface any day now, *Return to Neverland* is a rare success, at least. (AL)

**Additional Credits:** Screenplay: Temple Matthews. Additional written material: Carter Crocker. Music: Joel McNeely. Additional animation directors: Charlie Bonifacio, Keith Ingham, Ryan O'Loughlin, Larry Whitaker. Supervising animators: Lianne Hughes, Andrew Collins, Pierre Lommerse, Bob Baxter, Ryan O'Loughlin. Senior animators: Simon Ashton, Adam Murphy, Alex Stadermann, Myke Sutherland, Manny Banados, Kevin Wotton, Josef Szekeres. Animators: Kathie O'Rourke, Andrew Brooks, Andries Maritz, Gie Santos, Dan O'Sullivan, Donald Walker, Don Pattenden, Deborah Cameron, Noel Cleary, Jocelyn Sly, Rowena Hamlyn-Aspden, Bernard Derriman, Lily Dell, Sid Ahearne, Alan Lam, Michael Ward, Davide Benvenuti, Manuk Chang, Rizaldy, Valencia, Robert Mason, Warwick Gilbert, Michael Badman, Ramdy Glusac, Marco Zanoni, Charlie Lee, John Power, Tina Burke, Daniel Lafrance, Donna Brockopp, Robert Fox, Tobias Schwartz. Additional animators: Adam Beck, Darren Brereton, Trevor Deane-Freeman, Marvin Estropia, Joe Giampapa, Scott Glynn, Magnus Hjerpe, Danny Kahan, Kevin McDonagh, John Maholovich, Victor Marchetti, Kevin Micallef, Eileen Middleton, Sean Newton, Dennis Pena, Dave Quesnelle, Nilo Santillan, Shawn Sele, Marc Sevier, Nuranee Shaw, Gregory Stainton, Robyne Tsuji, Nick Vallinakis, Marc Wasik.

**The Road to El Dorado** (3/31/00) DreamWorks. 88 mins. Director: Eric "Bibo" Bergeron, Don Paul. Producers: Bonnie Radford, Brooke Breton. Voices: Kevin Kline (Tulio), Kenneth Branagh (Miguel), Rosie Perez (Chel), Armand Assante (Tzekel-Kan), Edward

©DreamWorks L.L.C.

James Olmos (Chief), Jim Cummings (Cortes), Frank Welker (Altivo), Tobin Bell (Zaragosa), Duncan Marjoribanks (Acolyte), Elijah Chang (Kid #1), Cyrus Shaki-Khan (Kid #2), Elton John (Narrator).

**Consumer Tips:** ☆☆☆ MPAA Rating: PG.

**Story:** Two 17th century conmen accidentally stow away on a ship bound for the New World and follow a trail to a legendary city of gold, where they are mistaken for gods.

**Comments:** As pointed out by several critics, the film bears a certain resemblance to the Bob Hope/Bing Crosby/Dorothy Lamour "Road" movies. Apart from the title, the picture focuses on a pair of wisecracking con artists (a la Hope and Crosby) and the lovely lady they meet along the way (the Dorothy Lamour role). There's even a scene that is a variation on the Road pictures' "patty cake" routine. Unlike DreamWorks' previous cel animated effort, *The Road to El Dorado* strives for the comic buddy movie feel. However, it is placed against grandiose backdrops and in the glamorous age of exploration. Still, several of the wisecracks are amusing, and much humor comes from the addition of Altivo, the friendly horse, and a bouncy little armadillo. The armadillo features prominently in one of the film's best set pieces, a traditional Meso-American ball game, with the armadillo serving as the ball. However, the most interesting character in the film is the villain, Tzekel-Kan. The character, as animated by

Kathy Zielinski, is not the usual purely malevolent, scowling plotter, but brings a joyous zest to his work and has a passion for human sacrifices and contact sports. Armand Assante, who voices the character, brings a certain gleeful energy to such lines as "Will you be devouring their essences whole or piece by piece?" The use of genuine Meso-American art symbols and architectural patterns in the backgrounds and set designs brings an air of authenticity to the atmosphere, something that was completely ignored by *The Emperor's New Groove*. These designs and symbols are also utilized in the end titles, but feature most prominently in the opening creation sequence, by Dream-Works' CGI arm, PDI (which is also visually reminiscent in some ways of the prologue to *Watership Down*). (AL)

*Additional Credits:* Screenplay: Ted Elliott, Terry Rosio. Animation story writer: Philip LaZebnik. Additional dialogue: Karey Kirkpatrick. Songs: Elton John, Tim Rice. Music: Hans Zimmer, John Powell. Additional sequence directors: Will Finn, David Silverman. Sequence supervisor (Stardust Pictures): Rob Stevenhagen. Senior supervising animators: James Baxter, David Brewster. Supervising animators: William Salazar, Sergei Kouchnerov, Bob Scott, Rodolphe Guenoden, Kathy Zielinski, Frans Vischer, Kristof Serrand, Sylvain Deboissy, Nicolas Marlet, Patrick Mate, Erik Schmidt. Animators: Claudio Acciari, Cinzia Angelini, Cecile Bender, Arnaud Bauthier, Jennifer Cardon, Rick Farmiloe, Lionel Gallat, Steve Horrocks, Jakob Hjort Jensen, Fabrice Jaubert, Ken Morrisey, Kevin O'Hara, Pedro Ramos, Emil Simeonov, Dan Wagner, Alex Williams, Scott Wright, David B. Boudreau, Adam Burke, Antony Gray, Richard Sanguoon Kim, Brad Kuha, Robert Milne, Claire Morrisey, Anthony Tom Owens, Jean-Francois Rey, Erik C. Schmidt, Andreas Simonti, Dimos Vrysellas, Eric Walls, Manuel Almela, Bruce Ferriz, Bo Johannesson, Dave Kupczyk, Philippe Le Brun, Mike Nguyen, Jane Poole, Robert Bryan, Mike Chavez, Emanuela Cozzi, Ricardo Curtis, Tim Genge, Steve Horrocks, Duncan Marjoribanks, Gary Perkovac, Mark Williams, Dan Boulos, Kent Culotta, Maximillian Graenitz, Teresa Martin, Sylvia Miller, Oliver Coipel, Catherine Fradas, Luis Grane, Fabio Lignini, Mary Ann McKerns, Simon Otto, Pres Romanillos, Paul Jesper, Uriel Mimran, Herman Shanck, Michelle Cowart, Wendy Elwell, Ryan Roberts, Michael Spokas, Mike Ullner. (Stardust Pictures): Dino Athanassiou, Paul Lee, Michael Schlingman, Sharon Smith, Gabrielle Zuccheli. Production designer: Christian Schellewald. Art directors: Raymond Zibach, Paul Lasaine, Wendell Luebbe.

Additional production design: Victoria Jenson. Additional art director: Sam Michlap. Story supervisors: Ronnie DelCarmen, Jeff Snow. Story artists: Rejean Bourdages, David Bowers, Paul Fisher, Edmund Fong, Victoria Jenson, Jennifer Lerew, Ted Mathot, Douglas McCarthy, Donald Morgan, Scott Santoro, Brian Sheesley, David Soren.

**Robin Hood** (11/8/73) Walt Disney Pictures. 83 mins. Director: Wolfgang Reitherman. Producer: Wolfgang Reitherman. Voices: Brian Bedford (Robin Hood), Phil Harris (Little John), Andy Devine (Friar Tuck), Monica Evans (Maid Marian), Peter Ustinov (Prince John, King Richard), Terry-Thomas (Sir Hiss), Roger Miller (Allen-a-Dale), Carole Shelley (Lady Kluck), Pat Buttram (Sheriff of Nottingham), George Lindsey (Trigger), Ken Curtis (Nutsy), Billy Whitaker (Skippy), Dana Laurita (Sis), Dora Whitaker (Tagalong), Richie Sanders (Toby), J. Pat O'Malley (Otto), Candy Candido (Crocodile), Barbara Luddy (Mother Rabbit), John Fiedler (Church Mouse).

©Walt Disney Productions

*Consumer Tips:* ☆ MPAA Rating: G. Adapted from the 12th-century legends of Robin Hood.

*Story:* The film is actually a series of episodes, which pit Robin Hood and Little John against Prince John, Sir Hiss, and the Sheriff of Nottingham. The only segment approaching a plot concerns the rescue of Friar Tuck and the people of Nottingham during the final part of the film.

*Comments:* When considering the entire manifest of Disney features, there must come a judgment that some are better than others and some far worse. *Robin Hood* is a strong and nearly uncontested candidate for last place among the studio's animated features. Given the talent that went into the making of this picture and the funds available, there is no excuse for this shoddy, half-hearted effort. Had things turned out differently in the past, a lot of ink and paint could have been saved for better things.

Disney first toyed with the idea of adapting the 11th-century European poems concerning Reynard the Fox in 1937. As the story developed, Walt Disney began to have reservations about the nature of the character. Reynard was a trickster, swindler, thief, and murderer, and Walt felt that it would be impossible to make him sympathetic enough for audiences. He also feared the Hays Office would prohibit the glorification of a criminal. Story man Otto Englander suggested turning Reynard into a sort of Robin Hood, and Walt relented. Work continued into the 1950s and contained versions of the character designs that were finally used in *Robin Hood*. The Reynard film, which was to be combined with the tale of Chanticleer the Rooster, was ultimately shelved.

It was Ken Anderson who revived the idea in the early 1970s by drawing up some attractive character designs. Reynard became Robin Hood, and the rest of the cast was made up of humanized animals as well. After that idea, nothing went right. To begin with, there is basically no plot to the film, merely vignettes in which Robin Hood outwits the bad guys. Phil Harris again plays Baloo the Bear, who has ended up in Merrie Olde England along with his companion from *The Jungle Book*, Kaa. In this film Baloo is called Little John. Kaa is named Sir Hiss and is voiced by Terry-Thomas rather than Sterling Holloway, but the character and design are virtually the same. Sir Hiss even has Kaa's hypnotic powers, which are never used even once against Robin or his allies. All of the villains, in fact, are so clownish, hapless, and unbelievable that we never accept that Robin Hood is in any danger.

The animation in much of *Robin Hood* is frankly terrible; virtually everything animated in long shot is poorly done. One sequence, in which animal children play in the forest prior to meeting Maid Marian, is so sloppy and careless it is impossible to believe that Disney artists worked on it. Some of the better animation in the film jitters, and for once, the special effects are clumsy and unconvincing. Worst of all, the animators actually retraced scenes from prior Disney films during the "Phony King of England" musical number. Dances and animation from *Snow White and the Seven Dwarfs* and *The Aristocats* are superimposed over new characters, a device seen only in the shoddiest of Saturday morning animation. Some of the characters, notably the Sheriff of Nottingham, are given voices that seem to come from rural Arkansas, and much of the music and score is far more mod than madrigal. The only redeeming morsel in all of *Robin Hood* is Peter Ustinov's funny portrayal of Prince John. Everything else, yea verily, stinketh. Watch thee some better film.

For the record:

- Ken Anderson originally had Friar Tuck portrayed by a pig but was worried that the church would be offended. The good friar wound up as a badger. Fifteen years earlier, however, Chuck Jones made a theatrical short while at Warner Bros. called *Robin Hood Daffy*. Porky Pig portrayed Friar Tuck, but the Vatican never seemed to notice. (MG)

**Additional Credits:** Story: Larry Clemmons. Based on character and story conceptions by Ken Anderson. Music: George Bruns. Songs: Roger Miller, Floyd Huddleston, George Bruns, Johnny Mercer. Directing animators: Milt Kahl, Frank Thomas, Ollie Johnston, John Lounsbery. Animators: Hal King, Art Stevens, Cliff Nordberg, Burny Mattinson, Eric Larson, Don Bluth, Dale Baer, Fred Hellmich. Effects animation: Dan MacManus, Jack Buckley. Color styling: Al Dempster. Art director: Don Griffith. Layout artists: Basil Davidovich, Joe Hale, Sylvia Roemer, Ed Templer Jr. Background artists: Bill Laynem, Ralph Hulett, Ann Guenther.

**Robot Carnival** (1/25/91) Streamline Pictures. 91 mins. Directors: Katsuhiro Otomo, Atsuko Fukushima, Kouji Morimoto, Kiroyuki Kitazume, Mao Lamdo, Hidetoshi Ohmori, Yasuomi Umetsu, Hiroyuki Kitakubo, Takashi Nakamura. Producer: Kazufumi Nomura. Voices: Michael McConnohie (The Man), Lisa Michelson (His Robot, Yayoi), Barbara Goodson (His Wife), Tom Wyner (The Gent), Bob Bergen (Sankichi), Eddie Frierson (Kukusuke), Kerrigan Mahan (Denjiro), Tom Wyner (Daimaru), Steve Kramer (Volkeson).

THE ANIMATION EVENT OF THE YEAR

ROBOT CARNIVAL

NINE ANIMATORS
ONE VISION

*Streamline Pictures* ©1990 A.P.P.P. Co., Ltd.

©A.P.P.P.

**Consumer Tips:** ☆☆☆☆ MPAA Rating: Unrated. SF/fantasy art film. An anthology of nine short films by different directors about robots.

**Story:** Nine of Japan's top anime directors were commissioned to produce short films of about 10 minutes each on the theme of robots. The result, intended for screening at international film festivals and art theaters as a feature or separately, is a high-quality mixture of drama, comedy, and mood pieces in each director's individual style.

**Comments:** Producer Kazufumi Nomura of the A.P.P.P. studio conceived of this art-house anthology and gave each director the freedom to do whatever he or she wanted as long as it was about robots. In the dark-comedy opening and closing that bookends the anthology, by Atsuko Fukushima and Katsuhiro Otomo, a small desert community is crushed beneath a huge "Robot Carnival," which looks like a gigantic child's toy that has been trundling automatically across the world for centuries and is breaking down (which it does in the closing).

"Franken's Gear," by Kouji Morimoto, is a dark-comedy pastiche of the Frankenstein legend. "Dr. Franken" is trying to build an artificial man out of archaic nuts, bolts, and cogwheels. He succeeds, to his regret, in the Shaggy Dog ending.

In "Starlight Angel," by Hiroyuki Kitazume, a teen girl at a futuristic amusement park is menaced by the giant robot monster in a horror ride, then saved by an android entertainer.

"Deprive," by Hideotoshi Ohmori, is a fast-paced mood piece set in a future where humans and androids that look like humans live as equals. When the villain (who resembles a KISS-like demonic rock singer) sends his mechanical minions to kidnap the girl, the hero races to her rescue. It is not clear until the end which of the three leads are human and which are androids.

"Clouds," by Mao Lambdo, is a slower and dreamier mood piece about a robotic young child who marvels at the beauties of nature, especially the clouds drifting overhead.

"Presence," by Yasuomi Umetsu, is set in a future society that has turned against technology and outlawed all robots. A dilettante inventor constructs a robotic beautiful woman in secrecy, but when she falls in love with him and insists on following him, he smashes her to keep her from revealing his crime—then regrets it for the rest of his life. The moody "Presence" and the comedic "A Tale of Two Robots" are the only two films that contain dialogue.

"A Tale of Two Robots," by Hiroyuki Kitakubo, is a slapstick farce mixing the conventions of modern boys' adventure anime with 19th-century Japanese fear of foreigners. A cackling American mad scientist inventor (calling himself the "world's greatest genius" in English) crosses the Pacific in a huge electric-powered robot to conquer Japan. He is opposed by a typical gang of teen heroes (comically melodramatic hero, cute girl, brainy kid with glasses, and beefy muscle guy) in their steam-powered robot.

"Nightmare," by Takashi Nakamura, is a combined pastiche of two Disney classic animated sequences: the "Night on Bald Mountain" in *Fantasia* and the Headless Horseman's pursuit of Ichabod Crane in *The Adventures of Ichabod and Mr. Toad*. A drunk who has passed out in a Tokyo alley wakes up at midnight when the business district is deserted of humans. He sees nightmarish mechanical monsters dancing in the streets and is pursued on his motor scooter by their comically horrific leader.

Aside from film festival screenings, *Robot Carnival* was released in Japan as a direct-to-video feature on July 21, 1987. (FP)

**Additional Credits:** Production supervisors: Toshiharu Umetsu. Music: Joe Hisaishi, Isaku Fujita, Yasunori Honda. Writers/designers: Katsuhiro Otomo, Atsuko Fukushima, Kouji Morimoto, Hiroyuki Kitazume, Mao Lamdo, Hidetoshi Ohmori, Yasuomi Umetsu, Takashi Nakamura, Yoshiyuki Sadamoto. Animators: Kumiko Kawana, Yuji Moriyama, Kazuaki Mori, Hideki Nimura, Shinsuke Terasawa, Namabu Ohashi, Tom Wyner. Inbetween artists: Hatsune Ohashi, Shiho Ohashi. Mechanical designer: Mahiro Maeda. English adaptation producer: Carl Macek. English adaptation associate producers: Jerry Beck, Michael Haller. English adaptation production supervisor: Jerry Beck. English adaptation: Carl Macek.

## Robotech: The Movie

(7/25/86) Cannon. 80 mins. Directors: Carl Macek, Ishiguro Noboru. Producers: Ahmed Agrama, Miura Toru. Voices: Ryan O'Flannigan/Kerrigan Mahan (Mark Landry), Greg Snow/Gregory Snegoff (Col. B. D. Andrews), Brittany Harlow (Becky Michaels), Muriel Fargo (Eve), Guy Garrett (General Leonard), Jeffrey Platt (Rolf Emerson), Penny Sweet/Edie Merman (Kelly), Wendee Swan/Wendee Lee (Stacey), Merle Pearson (Professor Embrey), A. Gregory (Robotech Master), Guy Garrett (Robotech Master), Don Warner (Todd Harris), Anthony Wayne (Nick). Additional voices: Dave Mallow, Colin Philips, Tom Wyner, Drew Thomas, Mike Reynolds, Ray Michaels.

©Harmony Gold

**Consumer Tips:** ☆☆½ MPAA Rating: PG. Science fiction. Combines footage from the Japanese television series *Super Dimensional Cavalry Southern Cross* and a direct-to-video, *Megazone 23, Part One*. Ads boasted that the film's budget was $8 million.

**Story:** In the year 2027, the alien Robotech Masters attempt to retrieve the data within the SDF-1, a bat-

tle fortress that had crashed on the earth years earlier. The united Earth government tries to suppress the alien incursion and keep it a secret from the public. Young Mark Landry, with the help of the MODAT (a transforming motorcycle) and Eve (a holographic television host), exposes the plot and together they fight for the freedom of the world.

**Comments:** In *Animato* #20, Spring 1990, producer Carl Macek described making *Robotech: The Movie* as "the worst experience of my professional career. . . . I was actually glad that it never got a broad release because it was, to me, an abomination. I never look at that though I still have it on tape."

*Robotech: The Movie* was supposed to generate revenue to pay production costs for the second television season, *Robotech: The Sentinels*. But the film lasted only three weeks in north Texas theaters. Of the three major area papers, only the *Fort Worth Star-Telegram* reviewed it, its critic rating it 7 out of 10 stars. Theaters limited show times to afternoon matinees, so there was no way *Robotech* could attract an adult audience except over the weekend.

The *Sherman* (Texas) *Democrat* received no publicity materials. All it knew about the film was it was "a science fiction adventure movie with music by Three Dog Night." The only local advertising Cannon provided was a one-sheet poster and a *Robotech Masters* comic book, issue #8. The ad in the Friday *Sherman Democrat* (July 25) used the comic's masthead, so it looked like the movie was called *Robotech Masters* starring Dana Sterling (who was never in the movie). In the Sunday paper, the ad changed the title to *Robotech Masters of the Universe*.

The following July, the movie played to a sell-out crowd during the Second Los Angeles International Animation Celebration at the Nuart Theater. It was released as a videocassette overseas, but not in the United States.

An overly complicated story and choppy editing mars an otherwise intriguing adventure. As Macek pointed out to his bosses, the print quality is uneven, with the *Southern Cross* scenes being fuzzy and the *Megazone 23* scenes being razor-sharp. The use of realistic sounds greatly enhances the movie's believability, from the crashing of cars to the roar of Veritech fighters. The vocal performances are also first rate. In places where there was no dialogue, the characters don't gasp or go "oh" every time their mouth is open—a significant improvement over the television show. Perhaps *Robotech*'s greatest asset is its music, which is practically nonstop. Much of it comes from the television series, with some selections from *Captain Harlock and the Queen of a Thousand Years*. The end credits number, "The Future Is Now," is especially good. (WRM)

**Additional Credits:** Screenplay: Ardwright Chamberlain. Based on a story by Carl Macek. Production supervisor: Alan Letz. Executive producers: Frank and Jehan Agrama. Orchestral score: Ulpio Minucci, Arlon Ober. Music: Three Dog Night, Joanne Harris, Michael Bradley, Gigi Agrama.

**Rock*A*Doodle** (4/3/92) Samuel Goldwyn. 77 mins. Director: Don Bluth. Producers: Gary Goldman, John Quested, Morris F. Sullivan. Cast: Toby Scott Granger (Edmond), Kathryn Holcomb (Mother), Stan Ivar (Dad), Jason Marin (Mark), Christian Hoff (Scott). Voices: Glen Campbell (Chanticleer), Phil Harris (Patou, Narrator), Christopher Plummer (the Duke), Sandy Duncan (Peepers), Ellen Greene (Goldie), Charles Nelson Reilly (Hunch), Eddie Deezen (Snipes), Sorrell Booke (Pinky), Will Ryan (Stuey Pig), Dee Wallace (Mother), Louise Chamis (Minnie Rabbit), Bob Galaco (Radio Announcer), Jake Steinfeld (Farmyard Bully, Max the Bouncer).

**Consumer Tips:** ☆☆ MPAA Rating: G. Musical fantasy. Aimed at two- to six-year-olds.

©Goldcrest and Sullivan Bluth Ltd.

**Story:** A rock 'n' roll rooster named Chanticleer moves to the city and becomes a big star. Without the rooster to crow up the sun, the farm becomes a rained-out nightmare, controlled by an evil owl, the Grand Duke. A little boy, Edmond, transformed into a cat by the Duke, leads the farm animals to the city to bring the rooster back.

**Comments:** This film is heartbreaking—great layouts, superb animation, dazzling color design on the one hand. A terrible story, badly told, with ugly, unsympathetic characters on the other. Test audiences were so confused by the storytelling that Phil Harris, as the character Patou, provides some tacked-on narration in an attempt to clarify the tale. That narration, however, is so intrusive it ruins the opening song and after awhile becomes annoying.

And it's odd that Patou the dog would even narrate the film. After all, the first sequence is supposed to be read to Edmond by his mother. The rest of the film is a dream the boy is having, so why is the dog narrating it? This sums up the level of incompetence behind this film.

Bluth wanted a live-action/animated movie like *Who Framed Roger Rabbit*. Originally the film opened on Edmond's farm, with Edmond's mother (played by an Irish actress, voiced dubbed by Dee Wallace Stone) reading him the story of Chanticleer. The live-action was to bookend the animation in the same way *The Wizard of Oz* used a black-and-white real world to bookend the colorful land of Oz. Victor French (Agent 44 from *Get Smart!*, Michael Landon's costar in *Highway to Heaven*) was to direct the live action, but when he discovered he had terminal lung cancer, he bowed out of the production, leaving Don Bluth himself—a live-action novice—to direct. Much of that footage was never used.

Goldie the Pheasant was the equivalent of Jessica Rabbit: large "attributes," skimpy dress with lots of glitter, as seen in the *Rock-a-Doodle* trailer on the *All Dogs Go to Heaven* video. But when the studio test-screened the film, mothers were offended by Goldie's outrageous proportions. Goldcrest, Bluth's investor, also didn't want a PG movie, since *All Dogs* bombed at the box office. So Bluth's artists covered her cleavage with feathers (cel overlays) and reduced her feminine proportions. Neither could Chanticleer drink alcohol. In the

"Kiss and Coo" scene, his wine glass was redrawn as a transparent cup; his wine bottle relabeled as King Soda. The Grand Duke, an ominous owl whose breath could transform people into animals, had to have his breath laced with Lucky Charms to make the effect less threatening. The changes forced the editors to work overtime to meet the film's projected Thanksgiving 1990 release. But the studio encountered financial difficulties with the original distributor, MGM-Pathe. Bluth found a new distributor with Samuel Goldwyn. *Rock-a-Doodle* was rescheduled to December 1991, but was moved to April 1992 to avoid competing against *Beauty and the Beast* and *An American Tail II*.

In *Comics Scene* #31, Bluth lamented that "I would probably have made sure that it's clear the little boy is the story's hero. Chanticleer overpowers everything." This statement would horrify those who felt that the sexy, Elvis-styled Chanticleer should have been predominant, and that Bluth should have deep-sixed the wimpy mush-mouthed Edmond.

Ugly character designs basically recycled earlier characters, with Edmond evoking Banjo the Woodpile Cat, Goldie mixed from Princess Daphne and Tinker Bell, and the Grand Duke a cloaked version of the Great Owl from *Secret of NIMH*.

After *Rock-a-Doodle* sank at the box office with a tepid $11.6 million, Don Bluth's Dublin-based studio and its unit in Burbank, California, were forced into liquidation in October 1992. Media Assets, a Hong Kong-based conglomerate, purchased the studio's three unfinished films, *A Troll in Central Park*, *Thumbelina*, and *The Pebble and the Penguin*.

A prime example of a film, lavishly animated, whose story problems should have been solved before it entered production. (WRM)

**Additional Credits:** Codirectors: Gary Goldman, Dan Kuenster. Associate producer: Thad Weinlein. Story: Don Bluth, David N. Weiss, John Pomeroy, T. J. Kuenster, David Steinberg, Gary Goldman. Music/songs: T. J. Kuenster. Directing animators: John Pomeroy, Jeffrey J. Varab, Jean Morel, Linda Miller, T. Daniel Hofstedt, Ken Duncan, Lorna Pomeroy-Cook, Jeff Etter, Dick Zondag, Ralph Zondag. Animators: John Hill, Ralf Palmer, Anne-Marie Bardwell, John Power, Colm Duggan, Alain Costa, Cathy Jones, Dave Kupczyk, Silvia Hoefnagels, Mark Pudleiner, Gary Perkovac, Doug Bennett, Jon Hooper, Jesper Moller, David G. Simmons, Jean-Jacques Prunes, Piet DeRycker, Chris Derochie, Kim Hagen-Jensen, Dan Harder, Rob Koo, Donnachada Daly, Mark Koetsier, Bruce Smith, Dave Brewster, Charlie Bonifacio. Additional animation: Richard Bazley, Paul Newberry, Ben Burgess, Wendy Perdue, Robert Fox, Jens Pindal, Larry Leker, Tom Roth, Fernando Moro, Nasos Vakalis, Brian Mitchell, Shane Zalvin. Storyboard artists: Don Bluth, Dan Kuenster, Ralph Zondag, Dick Zondag.

**Rock and Rule** (8/5/85) MGM/UA. 83 mins. Director: Clive A. Smith. Producers: Patrick Loubert, Michael Hirsh. Voices: Don Francks (Mok), Paul LeMat (Omar), Susan Roman (Angel), Sam Langevin (Mok's Computer), Dan Hennessey (Dizzy), Greg Duffell (Stretch, Zip), Chris Wiggins (Toad), Brent Titcomb (Sleazy), Donny Burns (Quadhole, 1st Radio Announcer), Martin Lavut (Mylar, 2nd Radio Announcer), Catherine Gallant (Cindy), Keith Hampshire (Other Computers), Melleny Brown (Carnegie Hall Groupie), Anna Bourque (Edna), Nick Nichols (Border Guard), John Halfpenny (Uncle Mikey), Maurice LaMarche (Sailor), Catherine O'Hara (Aunt Edith).

©The Canada Trust Company

**Consumer Tips:** ☆☆☆ MPAA Rating: PG.

**Story:** Mok, an aging rock superstar, plans to raise a demon that will give him immense power. He needs a particular voice to finish the job and finds it in Angel, a female singer, whom he lures into his dark world.

**Comments:** *Rock and Rule* involves a post-apocalyptic world where there are no humans; the only survivors are dogs, cats, and rats. Mok, an aging rock star, has dreams of power and seeks a demon that will give him incredible power. The missing element is a voice, which belongs to a female singer named Angel, who is a member of a musical group that lives in the city of Ohmtown.

*Rock and Rule* has attained cult status as an animated science-fiction musical because of its intricate story, stellar animation, and unique sense of humor. The formidable soundtrack includes songs from artists such as Cheap Trick, Debbie Harry, Lou Reed, Iggy Pop, and Earth, Wind and Fire.

This was the first full-length motion picture produced by Nelvana, a Canadian animation studio that later achieved great success in television. Nelvana was founded by Michael Hirsch, Clive A. Smith, and Patrick Loubert in Toronto, Canada. Among their many credits are *Rupert, Babar, The Care Bears,* Maurice Sendak's *Little Bear, Tales of the Cryptkeeper*, and quite a few others.

MGM/UA, who picked up the film, had no idea what to do with this film, and subsequently did nothing with it. Self-produced by Nelvana at a time when animation was getting darker and edgier (e.g., Ralph Bakshi, *Watership Down*, etc.), the film failed to connect to its audience—the comic book/college crowd—but has since become a favorite of animation fans. (SF)

**Additional Credits:** Screenplay: Peter Sauder, John Halfpenny. Story: Patrick Loubert, Pete Sauder. Music: Patrick Cullen. Animators: Anne Marie Bardwell, Dave Brewster, Charles Bonifacio, Robin Budd, Chuck Gammage, Frank Nissen, Bill Speers, Tom Sito, Gian-Franco Cilestri, Roger Allers, Wendy Perdue, John Collins, Devenand Ramsaran, Elaine Despins, Louis Scarborough, Terry Godfrey, Dale Schott, Larry Jacobs, Ken Stephenson, Ralph Palmer.

## Roujin Z (Old Man Z) (1/5/96) Kit Parker Films.

80 mins. Director: Hiroyuki Kitakubo. P: Yasuku Kazama, Yoshiaki Motoya, Kazufumi Nomura, Yasuhito Nomura. Voices: Toni Barry (Haruko), Nicolette McKenzie (Haru), Barbara Barnes (Nobuko), Allan Wenger (Terada), Jana Carpenter (Norie), John Jay Fitzgerald (Hasegawa), Adam Henderson (Maeda), Peter Marinker (Reporter), Ian Thompson (Ian).

**Consumer Tips:** ☆☆☆ MPAA Rating: PG-13. SF sociological satire. An experimental robotic hospital bed that is secretly being used to test military com-

©Central Park Media Corporation

puter programming breaks out of the hospital with its senile patient and runs amok through the city.

**Story:** The Ministry of Public Welfare tries to care for the growing number of elderly by creating an automated bed to care for all their needs. Terada, a ministry bureaucrat, uses senile Mr. Takazawa as the human model in the Z-001 superbed, to the horror of Haruko, a young nurse who objects to the callousness of plugging old people into machines so society can forget about them. But the revolutionary computer programs itself with Takazawa's memories of his dead wife. When he wants to go to the beach, the robotic bed smashes through the city and all obstacles to take him there.

**Comments:** *Roujin Z* (produced by A.P.P.P., released September 14, 1991) is a witty satire advertised as "by the creator of *Akira*." Katsuhiro Otomo created the story, screenplay, and mechanical design, although the primary look of the film is by character designer Hisashi Eguchi. *Roujin Z* is an important early film for several of its main staff, including director Kitakubo, who would later direct *Blood: The Last Vampire*, and art designer Satoshi Kon, who would later direct *Perfect Blue* and *Millennium Actress*.

One of *Roujin Z*'s poster blurbs was "Machines Gone Mad!" continuing a tradition since *2001: A Space Odyssey* of publicity copywriters attributing computer malfunction or malevolence to futuristic computers that are actually accurately following programmed instructions that have unexpected ramifications. The

Z-001 blends public welfare's programming to care for its patient's physical and emotional needs with the secret military programming to make it an agile and unstoppable combat vehicle. Morals seem to be that technological developments that look perfect in theory often turn out to have unexpected results in practice; that those who design technology for the future must not forget about the human element; and that bureaucracies always favor the organization over the individual. Terada is clearly more enthusiastic about the Z-001 because it will enhance the prestige of his ministry than because it will improve the lives of the bedridden. *Roujin Z* is an excellent animated editorial cartoon; funny but with a sharply satirical sting. Its rating would be higher if its animation was not so limited. (FP)

**Additional Credits:** Screenplay: Katsuhiro Ôtomo. Executive producer: Laurence Guinness. Music: Bun Itakura. Cinematography: Hideo Okazaki. Film editing: Eiko Nishide. Assistant directors: Toshiaki Hontani, Sadami Morikawa. Animator: Kouji Morimoto.

**Rover Dangerfield** (8/6/91) Warner Bros. 74 mins. Directors: Jim George, Bob Seeley. Producers: Willard Carroll, Thomas L. Wilhite. Voices: Rodney Dangerfield (Rover Dangerfield), Susan Boyd (Daisy), Ronnie Schell (Eddie), Ned Luke (Raffles), Shawn Southwick (Connie), Dana Hill (Danny), Sal Landi (Rocky), Tom Williams (Coyote, Rooster), Chris Collins (Big Boss, Coyote, Sparky, Wolf, Horse), Bob Bergen (Gangster, Farm Voice), Paxton Whitehead (Count), Ron Taylor (Mugsy, Bruno), Bert Kramer (Max), Eddie Barth (Champ), Ralph Monaco (Truck Driver), Tress MacNeille (Queenie, Chorus Girls, Hen, Chickens, Turkey), Michael Sheehan (Jose, Sheep), Lara Cody (Gigi, Chorus Girl, Sheep), Owen Bush (Fisherman #1), Ken White (Fisherman #2), Gregg Berger (Cal), Heidi Banks (Katie), Dennis Blair (Lem), Don Stuart (Clem), Robert Pine (Duke).

**Consumer Tips:** ☆☆½ MPAA Rating: G.

**Story:** Rover is a wisecracking Las Vegas dog, living the high life as the pet of Connie, a chrous girl. Her jealous boyfriend throws Rover into the Hoover Dam, but he survives, washing up on a farmyard where he tries to fit in, and falls in love.

©Warner Bros., Inc.

**Comments:** Since the days when Felix the Cat encountered William S. Hart (*Felix in Hollywood*, 1923), celebrity caricature has been a standard device in animation. However, Rover Dangerfield takes the concept and builds a feature around it. Comedian Rodney Dangerfield, long a staple of Las Vegas clubs, with his "I don't get no respect" shtick and self-deprecating one-liners, conceived and starred in this fish-out-of-water comedy. In a rather slim plot thread involving his showgirl owner and an abusive, low-life boyfriend, the canine Dangerfield is plucked from the comforts of Vegas, dropped into Hoover Dam, and transplanted to a farm for conflict that seems to have come from the television series *Green Acres*.

As strange as the concept is, and despite a considerably loose structure, Dangerfield's personality and voice hold the movie together. The comedian functioned as executive producer, writer (with Harold Ramis), and even lyricist, coming up with ditties seldom heard in a family animated film. "I'd Never Do It on a Christmas Tree," an ode to canine restraint for the holidays, is a particularly offbeat example. The cockeyed Rover, despite at times giving the impression of needing medical attention to correct his vision, is an oddly endearing if somewhat abrasive personality, like the real Dangerfield. The other characters, all clichés (animal-loving boy, faithful farm dogs, demure canine love interest), function as feeds, foils, and audience to Rover's stand-up. The animation, by Hyperion Studios (who around the same time worked on another feature based on a comedian's routines, *Bebe's Kids*), is crisp and enjoyably caricatural throughout; the soap operatic Vegas humans come complete with slick hair and brick-like chins. The twin settings of gambling mecca and rural pastures don't necessarily mesh well, and in much the same way, Dangerfield's humor seems an odd fit with the funny animal star and sentimental subplots. In addition, many of the seemingly endless array of sidekick characters could have been excised.

Still, the movie is decidedly good natured, and the showbiz in-jokes, if a bit excessive, provide unexpected pleasures (thanks to Warner Bros.' distribution, bits of the *Maverick* theme and the Chuck Jones *Wabbit Season* trilogy blare from apartment televisions).

Dangerfield passed away suddenly in October 2004. Although his live-action films like *Caddyshack* and *Back to School* were much better received, *Rover* is still a lively encapsulation of the man's talent and personality. (AL)

**Additional Credits:** Screenplay: Rodney Dangerfield. Story developed by Rodney Dangerfield and Harold Ramis. Music: David Newman. Songs: Dangerfield, Billy Tragessen. Sequence directors/animators: Steve Moore, Matthew O'Callaghan, Bruce Smith, Dick Sebast, Frans Vischer, Skip Jones. Animation: Jim George, Kevin Petrilak, Mark Koetsier, Jeff Etter, Patrick Gleeson, Kevin Wurzer, Carole Holiday, James Lopez, Joe Ekers, Lenord Robinson, Kelly Halas, Steve Wahl, Bob Seeley, Dan Fausett, Jon Hooper. Animation supervisors (London unit): Christopher O'Hare, Tony Collingwood. (Second unit): Dale L. Baer, Jane M. Baer. Additional animation: Jon Paul Berti, Louis Tate, Kamoon Song, Colm Duggan, Steve Anderson, Natasha Sassic, Carey Yost, David Simmons, Deke Wightman, David Brewster. (London unit): Alvara Gaivato, Duncan Varley, Simon Ward Horner. (Second unit): Tomihiro Yamaguchi, Jay Jackson.

**Rugrats Go Wild** (6/13/03) Paramount. 80 mins. Directors: Norton Virgien, John Eng, Kate Boutilier. Producers: Gabor Csupo, Arlene Klasky. Voices: Elizabeth Daily (Tommy Pickles), Nancy Cartwright (Chuckie Finster), Lacey Chabert (Eliza Thornberry), Tim Curry (Nigel Thornberry), Flea (Donnie), Danielle Harris (Debbie Thornberry), Bruce Willis (Spike), Cheryl Chase (Angelica Pickles), Kath Soucie (Phil, Lil, Betty DeVille), Tom Kane (Darwin), Jodi Carlisle (Marianne Thornberry), Cree Summer (Susie Carmichael), Dionne Quan (Kimi Finster), Joe Alaskey (Grandpa Lou), Tress MacNeille (Charlotte Pickles),

©Paramount Pictures and Viacom International, Inc.

Michael Bell (Drew Pickles, Chas Finster), Melanie Chartoff (Didi Pickles), Julia Kato (Kira Finster), Philip Proctor (Howard DeVille), Jack Riley (Stu Pickles), Tara Strong (Dil Pickles), Chrissie Hynde (Siri), Tony Jay (Dr. Lipschitz), Ethan Phillips (Toa).

**Consumer Tips:** ☆☆☆ MPAA Rating: PG. Based on the *Rugrats* and *The Wild Thornberrys* television shows on Nickelodeon.

**Story:** The Rugrats get shipwrecked and encounter the eccentric Thornberry family.

**Comments:** The last of the Rugrats theatrical trilogy and a follow-up to *The Wild Thornberrys Movie* (2002), *Rugrats Go Wild* is the least of the Klasky Csupo feature films. However, it's still a perfectly enjoyable family flick, especially if you are well-versed in the mythos of the two Nickelodeon series that inspired it.

The Rugrats clan gets shipwrecked on a deserted tropical island (a perfect excuse for the kids to be allowed to run free). The Thornberry family is on the same island, shooting a documentary. In contrast to the Rugrats, they seem to have all the comforts of home, and they come to the Rugrats' rescue.

There are humorous, bifurcated stories, including Angelica idolizing teenage Debbie Thornberry, and

Eliza's conversations with Rugrat pup Spike (voiced by Bruce Willis). These stories barely hold the film together, but are enjoyable because of our familiarity with the characters, and because of the lush, better-than-it-has-any-right-to-be animation and art direction.

In original release engagements of this film, audiences were given "odorama" scratch-and-sniff smell cards, for a true interactive movie-going experience. This allowed the kids to whiff various stinky scents, the worst of which was "bare foot."

The film's gross was a disappointing $39.4 million in the summer of 2003. *Rugrats* was trounced by Pixar's megahit *Finding Nemo*, but bested the soggy $26 million gross of DreamWorks' doomed *Sinbad: Legend of the Seven Seas*. (JB)

**Additional Credits:** Coproducers: Tracy Kramer, Patrick Stapleton, Terry Thoren. Executive producers: Eryk Casemiro, Albie Hecht, Julia Pistor, Hal Waite. Writer: Kate Boutilier. Story: Edmund Fong. Music: George Acogny. Additional music: Kevin Kliesch. Songs: Elizabeth Daily, Greg De Belles, Curtis Hudson, Jeff Lynne, Mark Mothersbaugh, Joe Perry, Lisa Stevens, Steven Tyler. Sequence director: Raymie Muzquiz.

**Rugrats in Paris: The Movie** (11/17/00) Paramount. 78 mins. Directors: Stig Bergqvist, Paul Demeyer. Producers: Arlene Klasky, Gabor Csupo. Voices: E. G. Daily (Tommy Pickles), Tara Charendoff (Dil Pickles), Cheryl Chase (Angelica Pickles), Christine Cavanaugh (Chuckie Finster), Cree Summer (Susie Carmichael), Kath Soucie (Phil and Lil DeVille, Betty DeVille), Michael Bell (Drew Pickles, Chas Finster), Tress MacNeille (Charlotte Pickles), Casey Kasem (Wedding DJ), Joe Alaskey (Grandpa Lou Pickles), Debbie Reynolds (Lulu Pickles), Jack Riley (Stu Pickles), Susan Sarandon (Coco LaBouche), John Lithgow (Jean-Claude), Julia Kato (Kira Watanabe), Dionne Quan (Kimi Watanabe), Melanie Chartoff (Didi Pickles), Phil Proctor (Howard DeVille), Tim Curry (Sumo Singer), Billy West (Sumo Singer).

**Consumer Tips:** ☆☆☆½ MPAA Rating: G. Based on the Nickelodeon television series.

**Story:** In Paris, the Rugrats use a giant Reptar robot to rescue Chuckie's dad from marrying an evil Euro theme park executive.

©Paramount Pictures and Viacom International, Inc.

**Comments:** The success of *The Rugrats Movie* (1998) spawned several feature-length sequels. This second film, *Rugrats in Paris: The Movie*, is the best of the bunch. The difference is a tight, truly funny script, great animation, and something sadly lacking in the first film—heart.

The film ties together several storylines: Chuckie's poignant desire for a new mommy, Stu Pickles's battle with a ruthless international theme park executive, and the Rugrats' exploration of a new universe—a foreign country. It also contains a spectacular action climax, with the kids in control of a runaway "Reptar" (a giant mechanical theme-park robot) that is running amok through the streets of Paris, while all are being chased by a giant mecha-escargot.

Another improvement over the first *Rugrats* movie is the addition of some talented superstar stunt casting: Susan Sarandon as the voice of Coco LaBuche, the villainous manager of EuroReptarland who has eyes for Chuckie's dad; John Lithgow, as Coco's personal assistant; and Debbie Reynolds as Grandpa's new love interest, Lulu.

Clever bits give this movie a bigger scope than the previous and subsequent installments. Some of these bits include an opening scene that parodies *The Godfather*, a manic scene where the kids run loose around the theme park eluding their ninjalike pursuers, and a surreal dream sequence with Chuckie dreaming he's a martial arts expert.

If you're going to see a Rugrats movie, this is the one to see. It grossed a very respectable $76.5 million in its U.S. theatrical run. (JB)

*Additional Credits:* Executive producers: Albie Hecht, Julia Pistor, Eryk Casemiro, Hal Waite. Screenplay: David N. Weiss, J. David Stern, Jill Gorey, Barbare Herndon, Kate Boutiller. Based on characters created by Arlene Klasky, Gabor Csupo, Paul Germain. Music: Mark Mothersbaugh. Sequence directors: John Eng, Raul Garcia, John Holmwuist, Greg Tiernan. Additional sequence directors: Zhenia Deliouissine, Panogiatas Rappas, Toni Vian.

**The Rugrats Movie** (11/25/98) Paramount. 79 mins. Directors: Norton Virgien, Igor Kovalyov. Producers: Arlene Klasky, Gabor Csupo. Voices: E. G. Daily (Tommy Pickles), Christine Cavanaugh (Chuckie Finster), Christine Cavanaugh (Chuckie Finster), Kath Soucie (Phil and Lil DeVille, Betty DeVille), Melanie Chartoff (Didi Pickles, Minka), Phil Proctor (Howard DeVille, Igor), Cree Summer (Susie Carmichael), Andrea Martin (Aunt Miriam), Michael Bell (Chas Finster, Grandpa Boris, Drew Pickles), Tress MacNeille (Charlotte Pickles), Jack Riley (Stu Pickles), Busta Rhymes (Reptar Wagon), Joe Alaskey (Grandpa Lou Pickles), Cheryl Chase (Angelica Pickles), Tony Jay (Dr. Lipschitz), Laurie Anderson, Beck, B Real, Jakob Dylan, Phife, Gordon Gano, Iggy Pop, Lenny Kravitz, Lisa Loeb, Lou Rawls, Patti Smith, Dawn Robinson, Fred Schneider, Kate Pierson, Cindy Wilson (Newborn Babies), Margaret Cho (Lieutenant Klavin), Tim Curry (Rex Pester), Whoopi Goldberg (Ranger Margaret), David Spade (Ranger Frank).

*Consumer Tips:* ☆☆☆ MPAA Rating: G. Based on the Nickelodeon television series.

*Story:* The Rugrats gang, including newly arrived brother Dil, get lost in the woods when they take a ride in the prototype Reptar Wagon, created by toy-inventing papa, Stu Pickles.

*Comments:* The *Rugrats* made its debut on the kids' cable network, Nickelodeon, on August 11, 1991 (as one of the original trio of Nicktoons, which included *Doug* and *The Ren and Stimpy Show*). The premise of the series is about life from the point of view of infant Tommy Pickles and his friends: the fearful, bespectacled Chuckie, zany twins Phil and Lil, and Tommy's bratty older cousin, Angelica. The kids could not communicate with their parents; only Angelica (who could speak to grown-ups) and the home-viewing audience could understand their baby talk.

The witty series plodded along for 65 episodes on a weekly basis, finally exploding as a signature animated hit for Nick in 1994, when the episodes were stripped for daily airing. Nickelodeon had, at that time, established an in-house movie unit to develop feature films for sister Viacom company, Paramount Pictures. *The Rugrats Movie* thus became Nickelodeon Movies' first animated feature.

Klasky-Csupo created the series with producer Paul Germain. Klasky-Csupo had been a very small animation studio, primarily doing television series (anyone remember *Duckman, Santa Bugito,* or *Stressed Eric?*), stylish commercials, and the first several seasons of *The Simpsons*. Animation producer/designer Arlene Klasky came up with the original concept of the Rugrats, observing her own two infants and wondering what they would say if they could speak. Cocreator Gabor Csupo was born in Budapest, Hungary, where he learned the craft of animation. He relocated to Los Angeles and formed a studio with Klasky in 1981, where they created company logos, promotional films, and commercials. One of their earliest jobs was creating animated sequences for *The Tracey Ullman Show*. This led to the start of *The Simpsons*.

To direct the big-screen debut of *Rugrats*, the producers chose to create a team of Norton Virgien, a two-time Emmy winner for his directing work on the series, and Igor Kovalov, an internationally acclaimed designer, animator, and director.

The film's animation and visuals are miles beyond the crude look of the television series. The story has a rather simple plot—basically, the kids get lost in the forest—but the pace is quite fast. The film opened the same Christmas season as DreamWorks' *Prince of Egypt*, and matched its $100 million gross. *The Rugrats Movie*, costing about a fourth of the DreamWorks epic, was highly profitable and led to two theatrical sequels—*Rugrats in Paris* and *Rugrats Go Wild*. (JB and SF)

**Additional Credits:** Executive producers: Alby Hecht, Debby Beece. Screenplay: David N. Weiss, J. David Stern. Based on characters created by Arlene Klasky, Gabor Csupo, Paul Germain. Music: Mark Mothersbaugh. Additional music: Jamshied Sharif, Vladimir Horunzhy. Songs: Elvis Costello, Nigel Harrison, Busta Rhymes, Gwen Stefani. Executives in charge of production: Tracy Kramer, Terry Thoren. Production managaer: Sean Lurie. Sequence directors: Zhenia Delioissine, Paul Demeyer, Raymie Muzquiz, Peter Shin, Andrei Svislotsky. Additional sequence directors: Toni Vian, Vitaly Shafirov. Storyboard artists: Peter Avazino, Peter Chung, Sam Cornell, Vitaly Shaforov, Gyula Szabo, Robert Taylor, Tony Vian, Kang Lin Zhu.

## Sakura Wars: The Movie

**Sakura Wars: The Movie** (7/18/03) Pioneer Entertainment. 85 mins. Director: Mitsuro Hongo. Producer: Toshimichi Otsuki. Voices (English version): Julie Anne Taylor (Lachette Altair), Wendee Lee (Sakura Shinguji), Annie Pastrano (Li Kohran), Carrie Savage (Iris Chateaubriand), Dave Lelyveld (Captain Ichiro Oogami), Jane Alan (Maria Tachibana), Michelle Ruff (Sumire Kanzaki), David Lucas (Yuichi Kayama), David Orozco (Ikki Yoneda), Lia Sargent (Kaeda Fujieda).

**Consumer Tips:** ☆☆ MPAA Rating: PG-13. SF/fantasy adventure. Based on the video game, OAV, and television series. Supernatural monsters threatening Tokyo versus a female defense corps.

**Story:** In 1926, the Imperial Fighting Troupe, Flower Division, has already defended Tokyo against two kouma (demon) attacks using the Koubu-kai battle armor developed in Japan. A lobbyist for an American industrialist pressures the army to adopt the superior American battle armor and put the Flower Division on indefinite stand-by status. But when the American battle armor turns out to be a plot to conquer Japan by American demons, the Flower Division girls sortie against orders to defend the Imperial Capital once again.

**Comments:** *Sakura Wars* (*Sakura Taisen*) began as an extremely popular Sega Saturn video game and manga by Ouji Hiroi in 1996, quickly spinning off numerous additional video games, novels, animation series, and even live stage revues in emulation of those in the story. The animation began with a four-episode *Original Anime Video* series in 1997, which led to two OAV sequels and a 25-episode television series during 2000 that was a revision and expansion of the story in the original OAV series. *Sakura Wars: The Movie*, produced by the Production I.G. studio and released on December 22, 2001, was a true sequel.

The popularity of *Sakura Wars* can be attributed to its combination of supernatural horror, battle action, girls' romance, and nostalgia for Japan's past. It is set in the mid-1920s, a couple of years after the Great Kanto Earthquake that destroyed Tokyo and enabled the whole city to be rebuilt and modernized. In this story, it was the kouma demons that caused the earthquake, and it was the invention of steam-powered battle armor that can only be powered by the mental energy of young women that defeated them. This led to the government's creation of the secret all-girl Imperial Fighting Troupe, Flower Division, to defend Tokyo against future kouma attacks. The cover-identity of the Flower Division is that they are the operetta troupe of the newly built Great Imperial Theater opera house.

This scenario has the allure of combining modern SF/horror action with a romanticized Japanese near-past. Tokyo in the 1920s is freshly built and vigorously expanding to becoming a world metropolis. Even the theme song is in the style of Japanese 1920s pop music. The Flower Divison, composed entirely of young women with mental powers, is an SF modernization of the belief in the demon-exorcising powers of Shinto temple priestesses. Their disguise as an all-girl theatrical troupe is a pastiche of Japan's popular all-woman Takarazuka Revue Company, founded in 1914. For girls, *Sakura Wars* offers the fantasy-action of defending Japan from monsters (usually the prerogative of boys) in giant robot battle armor they get to customize in feminine colors like magenta, chartreuse, and puce. They get colorful uniforms modelled after the ornate costumes of Louis XVI's court at Versailles. Boys get to identify with the handsome young Imperial Army Captain assigned as liaison to the Flower Division, whom all the girls have a crush on. The setting emphasizes the "steampunk" atmosphere of huge gears, powerful pistons, and roaring engines.

A darker aspect, emphasized in the movie, is that this lead to Japan's militaristic imperialism of the 1930s. Japan is the natural leader of all East Asia. The demons trying to destroy Tokyo are the Western modern influences that threaten Japan's historic cultural identity.

The movie is a sequel to the story in the first OAV and television series, and is set simultaneously to the action in the Sakura Wars III video game. It assumes that the viewer is familiar with all this. The mostly adolescent girls of the Flower Division have defeated two kouma attacks on Tokyo by now and are feeling the confidence of working effectively as a team. Captain Oogami, their popular heartthrob liaison, is temporarily on assignment in Paris, and the girls are rehearsing for their next theatrical production, a Las Vegas-style revue. Trouble comes when the powerful American Douglas-Stewart manufacturing company invents its own anti-kouma steam-powered battle armor, the Japhkiel, which is more powerful and cheaper than the Japanese Koubu-kai models and does not require a pilot. Douglas-Stewart's young whiz kid president, Brent Furlong, comes to Japan to market it as a cheap replacement for the Koubu-kai.

The movie's strong points are its colorful costuming and the CGI sequences showing the activation of the Koubu-kai armor and its delivery by underground trains to its launching sites. Its major weakness is the lack of background explanations. The plot allows no time to establish individual personalities for the girls. To viewers who are not already familiar with *Sakura Wars*, the Flower Division is eight mostly interchangeable girls, including a child who goes into battle with her stuffed bear. When Oogami returns from Paris just in time to join the Division during its final battle, he appears as a deus ex machina hero arriving out of thin air. Furlong and Hamilton are blatant anti-American stereotypes who comment to each other about how superior Americans are to Japanese, and who sneeringly use Japanese innocent bystanders to demonstrate the lethality of American weaponry. (Apologists have claimed that this is just an in-character depiction of the Japanese ultra-nationalists' anti-American propaganda of the World War II period. If so, it is out of place as early as the mid-1920s.) There is no explanation as to just what kouma are (there is in

the 36-page booklet that comes with the DVD release), or to the sudden escalation of Furlong from an arrogant American businessmen to either an arch-kouma himself or a black wizard who can control the kouma, or to Patrick Hamilton who is an obviously inhuman sorcerer at all times. *Sakura Wars: The Movie* is for *Sakura Wars* fans only. (FP)

***Additional Credits:*** Screenplay: Mitsuro Hongo, Hiroyuki Nishimura, Nobutoshi Terado, Ohji Hiroi. Story: Ohji Hiroi. ADR Script: Wendee Lee. ADR director: Kaeko Sakamoto. Cinematography: Tanaka Kouji. Editor: Junichi Uematsu. Supervisor: Satoru Akahori. Music: Kohei Tanaka. Original character designs: Losuke Fujishima. Character designs: Hidenori Matsuhara. Animation character designer: Takuya Saito. 3-D Director: Tokumitsu Kifune. Character animation supervisor: Takuya Saito. Color Supervisor: Nobuko Mizuta. Key animation supervisor: Mitsuru Ishihara. Layout: Hiroshi Kato. Sound director: Masafumi Mima.

**Saludos Amigos** (2/6/43) Walt Disney Pictures. 42 mins. Directors: Bill Roberts, Jack Kinney, Hamilton Luske, Wilfred Jackson. Voices: Clarence Nash (Donald Duck), Fred Shields (Narrator), Frank Graham (Narrator), Jose Oliviera (Joe Carioca), Pinto Colvig (Goofy).

***Consumer Tips:*** ☆☆ This is a South American travelogue with four animated sequences.

***Story:*** There is no story; this film details a visit by the Disney crew to South America where they compose a part animated, part live-action feature.

©Walt Disney Productions

**Comments:** *Saludos Amigos* is less interesting than the story behind it. Disney never intended to fly to South America but did so at the behest of the State Department. World War II was in full swing, and it was feared that Axis influence might be taking hold south of the border. It was hoped that a little Disney magic might spread some goodwill among Latin Americans, so the government paid to send Walt and company to make some short films featuring their colorful culture. The U.S. government, coincidentally, did not mind that Walt was out of the country while the bitter strike at his studio was settled. Walt took the strike personally and was incapable of negotiating with any objectivity.

Donald Duck starts in the first and last of *Saludos Amigos* four animated segments, "Lake Titicaca" and "Aquarela do Brasil." In the first, Donald is a tourist who runs afoul of a llama, a terrifying suspension bridge, and a reed boat that treats Donald like most inanimate objects tend to do. The final segment teams Donald with Joe Carioca, a Brazilian parrot who teaches the duck the joys of the samba. Joe has the uncanny ability to turn anything into a musical instrument, including Donald's hat. Before the dancing begins, an unseen artist wielding a magical watercolor brush does some beautiful, surreal animation. Backgrounds, objects, and other details are painted or transformed as Donald and Joe prance their way across the screen. Donald, in fact, starts out as a large red and white flower that swallows a bee, undergoes a flowing transformation, and ends up as the duck. This is by far the finest of *Saludos Amigos* animated segments and is clearly the inspiration for Disney's second South American opus, *The Three Caballeros*, which was made two years later.

"Pedro" is the rather pedestrian tale of a little mail plane that must make a tough, taxing flight over the Andes and back again when Daddy plane comes down with a bad cold. The anthropomorphic planes are nothing special in design, and neither is the story. Almost predictably it turns out that Pedro has risked his wings to deliver a banal postcard. Tex Avery would do almost the same thing 10 years later at MGM with a film called *Little Johnny Jet*. Goofy is the subject of the other animated segment. The Goof is a Texas cowboy transplanted to Uruguay where he becomes a gaucho, or at least gives it his best shot. Goofy deals with a sassy horse much smarter than he is, an unwieldy saddle made of bedding, a speedy ostrich, and a deadly set of bolos that, in Goofy's hands, is much more dangerous to him than to anything else.

*Saludos Amigos* runs a mere 42 minutes. Walt Disney shot some of the live-action himself using his 16mm camera. Jose (Joe) Carioca was based on a Brazilian folk character called "El Papagayo," a lively wiseguy. Joe would find his way into three Disney films and countless Disney comic books, but he never did become one of the studio's stars. (MG)

**Additional Credits:** Production supervisor: Norman Ferguson. Story research: Ted Sears, William Cottrell, Webb Smith. Story: Homer Brightman, Ralph Wright, Roy Williams, Harry Reeves, Dick Huemer, Joe Grant. Music: Ed Plumb, Paul Smith, Ary Baroso. Sequence directors: Bill Roberts, Jack Kinney, Hamilton Luske, Wilfred Jackson. Animation: Fred Moore, Ward Kimball, Milt Kahl, Milt Neil, Wolfgang Wooly Reitherman, Les Clark, Bill Justice, Vladimir Bill Tytla, John Sibley, Hugh Fraser, Paul Allen, John McManus, Andrew Engman, Dan McManus, Joshua Meador. Uncredited animator: Art Palmer.

**Santa and the Three Bears** (11/7/70) Ellman Enterprises. 63 mins. Director/producer: Tony Benedict. Live-action director: Barry Mahon. Cast: Hal Smith (Grandfather), Beth Goldfarb (Beth), Brian Hobbes (Brian). Voices: Hal Smith (Santa, Mr. Ranger), Jean Vander Pyl (Nana), Annette Ferra (Nikomi), Bobby Riha (Chinook). Additional voices: Joyce Taylor, Ken Engels, Lenard Keith, Kathy Lemmon, Roxanne Poole, Michael Rodriguez.

**Consumer Tips:** ☆ MPAA Rating: G.

**Story:** Two bear cubs and their mother learn about Christmas and Santa Claus from a park ranger.

**Comments:** This sweet animated film focuses on two innocent, cute little bear cubs, who decide not to hibernate in Yellowstone National Park. Instead, they decide to wait for the arrival of Santa Claus, who they have always wanted to meet in person.

The movie opens in live action, with a kind-hearted grandfather relating a story to his grandchildren. The grandfather was played by veteran voice actor Hal Smith, who also voiced the animated characters of Ranger and Santa Claus.

Barry Mahon, an exploitation film schlockmeister, expressly created *Santa and the Three Bears* to play Saturday matinee performances. The film is not as bad as it could have been. Mahon had the good sense to hire a Hollywood professional, Hanna-Barbera veteran Tony Benedict, to make the film on a shoestring budget.

*Santa and the Three Bears* has good design work and television-level animation quality, but otherwise you can hibernate through it. This one is a snooze. (SF)

**Additional Credits:** Coproducer: Barry Mahon. Associate producer: James Kernodle. Writer: Tony Benedict. Music: Doug Goodwin, Tony Benedict, Joe Leahy. Animators: Bill Hutton, Tony Love, Volus Jones. Key assistant animators: Eva Scheider, Judy Drake, Sylvia Mattinson. Assistant animators: Cynthia Beck, Janice Stocks, Lenore Wood, Linda Gionet. Effect animator: Stan Green.

**The Secret of NIMH** (7/2/82) United Artists—Aurora Productions. 83 mins. Director: Don Bluth. Producers: Don Bluth, John Pomeroy, Gary Goldman. Voices: Elizabeth Hartman (Mrs. Brisby), Dom DeLuise (Jeremy), Peter Strauss (Justin), Derek Jacobi (Nicodemus), Paul Shenar (Jenner), Arthur Malet (Mr. Ages), John Carradine (The Great Owl), Hermione Baddeley (Auntie Shrew), Shannen Doherty (Teresa), Wil Wheaton (Martin), Jodi Hicks (Cynthia), Ian Fried (Timmy), Tom Hatten (Farmer Fitzgibbons), Lucille Bliss (Mrs. Fitzgibbons), Aldo Ray (Sullivan).

**Consumer Tips:** ☆☆☆☆ MPAA Rating: G. Fantasy Adventure. Based on a Newberry Award-Winning book, *Mrs. Frisby and the Rats of NIMH.*

©Mrs. Brisby Ltd.

**Story:** Mousey Mrs. Brisby needs to move her home and family before a farm tractor destroys it with her sickly son bedridden inside. With the help of Jeremy the crow, she seeks out the rats of NIMH, an advanced breed of intelligent rodent who overcome their own struggles to help her move her home.

**Comments:** *The Secret of NIMH* can be looked at today as the seed that began the animation boom of the 1990s. Though it would be Don Bluth's next feature (*An American Tail*, 1986) that propelled the industry forward, *NIMH* laid the groundwork for the master plan to awaken feature animation from its doldrums.

*The Secret of NIMH* stands as an important animated feature, and it is Bluth's best film to date. Disney turned down the book as a potential cartoon feature in the 1970s, but Don and several storymen liked this slightly darker mouse tale. When Bluth left Disney in 1979 and joined forces with Aurora Productions (a film-producing partnership made up of several ex-Disney executives), he recommended they purchase the movie rights. In adapting the Newberry Award-winning *Mrs. Frisby and the Rats of NIMH* (published in 1971), Bluth had to change the name of his lead character from Frisby to Brisby because of potential conflict in the merchandising of toys (Frisby sounded too much like Wham-O's popular "Frisbee").

*NIMH* was a direct response to the work being produced by Disney's deteriorated animation department of the 1970s. Bluth and company hoped to break the mold by going one step backward (detailed art, full animation, and strong story) and two steps forward (beating Disney at its own game). With *NIMH*, they revived the classic (i.e., 1940s) look and feel, with no cliched musical numbers, and the darker tone and meatier story line they desired.

The budget was set at $7 million, which was a fraction of what Disney usually spent on its animated features. Great liberties were taken with the screen story adaptation from the original novel. The most notable change was in giving Mrs. Brisby a magic amulet, which allowed for a visually powerful climactic sequence.

This was Jerry Goldsmith's first score for an animated film, and he cowrote *NIMH*'s only song, "Flying Dreams," with Paul Williams. The U.S. release of the film was parcelled out regionally over the months of July and August, as opposed to having a broad single date national release. This hurt the grosses, as did some competition from a certain Steven Spielberg film sensation—*E.T.*—that was eating up all family audience business.

The film grossed a mere $14.6 million in domestic release, and caused Aurora Productions to back away from a planned second feature, *East of the Sun, West of the Moon*. Bluth and his studio found interim work on the innovative video games "Dragon's Lair" and "Space Ace."

It was through composer Jerry Goldsmith that Bluth met Spielberg; this meeting hatched *An American Tail*. (JB)

**Additional Credits:** Executive producers: Rich Irvine, James L. Stewart. Based on the novel *Mrs. Frisby and the Rats of NIMH*, by Robert C. O'Brien. Story adaption: Don Bluth, John Pomeroy, Gary Goldman, Will Finn. Music: Jerry Goldsmith. Backgrounds: Don Moore, Ron Dias, David Goetz. Layout artists: Don Bluth, Larry Leker. Color story sketch: William Lorencz. Special effects animation: Dorse Lanpher. Directing animators: John Pomeroy, Gary Goldman, Don Bluth. Animators: Lorna Pomeroy, Skip Jones, Dave Spafford, Will Finn, Linda Miller, Dan Kuenster, Heidi Guedel, David Molina, Emily Jiuliano, Kevin M. Wurzer.

**The Secret of the Sword** (3/29/85) Atlantic. 88 mins. Directors: Ed Friedman, Lou Kachivas, Marsh Lamore, Bill Reed, Gwen Wetzler. Producer: Arthur Nadel. Voices: John Erwin (He-Man), Melindy Britt

©Mattel, Inc.

(She-Ra), George DiCenzo (Hordack). Alan Oppenheimer, Erika Scheimer, Linda Gary, Eric Gunden.

**Consumer Tips:** ☆ MPAA Rating: G.

**Story:** He-Man meets his long-lost sister, Adora, who becomes She-Ra, and together they defeat evil Hordak in a sword-and-scorcery adventure.

**Comments:** He-Man, the hero and champion of good, and She-Ra, princess of power, unite in this movie. Kidnapped shortly after she was born, She-Ra has no idea who her true friends and family are, and He-Man tries to rescue her from her evil stepfather Hordack, and helps her realize who she really is.

He-Man was the central hero in the wildly successful "Masters of the Universe" toy line and syndicated animated television series. Mattel Toys, who had created both He-Man and She-Ra, really went after the boys' action market by making this film. In essence, each time the He-Man doll appears on the screen, it is an advertisement for little boys to buy the Mattel doll. By introducing She-Ra, Mattel cleverly broadened its market to girls. In short, this film is a big, long advertisement.

The *Masters of the Universe* animated series began as a television cartoon in 1983 and immediately became a smash hit. It was the first made-for-syndication animated show. Previous syndicated children's fare was old network television shows, or earlier theatrical cartoons. When *Masters of the Universe* began as a five-day-a-week series in the fall of 1983, it had virtually no competition, and its Nielsen ratings were huge. *Masters of the Universe* enjoyed a long healthy run on afternoon television, and the characters also appeared in a live-action feature in 1987, starring Dolph Lungren, released by Cannon Pictures.

While *The Secret of the Sword* is visually engaging, it is only because of its many optical effects rather than its animation. The big screen *The Secret of the Sword* does not compare favorably with the television series: it does not have the same kind of color, diversity, and depth. Screen it for nostalgic purposes only. (SF)

**Additional Credits:** Executive producer: Lou Scheimer. Writer: Larry Ditillo, Robert Forward. Music: Shuki Levy, Haim Saban. Background artist: Ruben Chavez. Film editor: Joe Gall. A Filmation Associates Production.

**Shame of the Jungle** (9/14/79) International Harmony (Belgium). 73 mins. Director: Picha. Producers: Boris Szulzinger, Michel Gast. Voices: Johnny Weissmuller Jr. (Shame), John Belushi (Perfect Master), Christopher Guest (Chief M'Bulu), Pat Bright (Queen Bazonga), Emily Prager (June), Bill Murray (Speaker), Adolph Caesar (Brutish), Brian Doyle-Murray (Siamese Twin 1), Andrew Duncan (Siamese Twin 2), Judy Graubart (Steffanie Starlet), Guy Sorel (Prof. Cedric Addlepate), Bob Perry (Narrator).

**Consumer Tips:** ☆☆½ MPAA Rating: R. Adults only. Nudity, violence, sex, racism, and profanity. Need we say more?

©Twentieth Century Fox

**Story:** An R-rated spoof of Tarzan. Tarzoon attempts to rescue his mate, June, from the bald-headed Queen Bazonga, who seeks her locks before setting her plan for world domination.

**Comments:** This is a crude, politically incorrect animated feature. It is in bad taste, to be sure, and the violence, penis jokes, and racial stereotypes will, without a doubt, turn some people off. However, *Shame of the Jungle* is surprisingly clever and witty in spots, and is one of the better adult animated features to emerge during the 1970s in the wake of *Fritz the Cat* (1972).

*Shame of the Jungle* was made in Belgium by well-known cartoonist Picha (Jean-Paul Walravens) and rewritten and dubbed by a gaggle of veteran *National Lampoon/Saturday Night Live* writers and performers. The film, made for $1 million, premiered in September 1975 in France under the title *Tarzoon, La Honte de la Jungle*. It immediately ran into trouble from the Edgar Rice Burroughs estate (*Tarzan*), which alleged plagiarism. The film was withdrawn and retitled, dropping the Tarzoon name, and distributed throughout most of Europe by 20th Century Fox.

Fox had the rights to distribute it in the United States but wisely declined. The film was originally rated X, and played a few U.S. markets with this rating and its original title. But before it premiered in New York and Los Angeles, the sex scenes were shortened, all references to Tarzoon were removed, and it was rerated R.

The film is filled with gags of all types, even in-jokes aimed at Disney and Looney Tunes. It also has a cameo by Euro cartoon superstar Tin-Tin. John Belushi's character is specially credited (as "created and performed by" Belushi). His role is a cameo at best, in which he depicts a beer-drinking teenage guru who, at one point, encounters Shame. This scene looks as if it were tacked onto to the U.S. release because the artwork of his character, "The Perfect Master," is drawn in a cruder style than the rest of the movie.

It was an inspired choice for the producers to cast Johnny Weissmuller Jr. as the voice of Shame. Bill Murray, Christopher Guest, and Brian Doyle Murray have all gone on to better things (and have voiced better cartoon characters in later years). They have probably forgotten about the day they spent in a recording booth on this film.

The filmmakers were aiming for nothing more than to create a few laughs, to draw some funny pictures, and to tell a few dirty jokes. There are no lofty political statements here, or greater pretentions of art. You've been suitably warned. (JB)

**Additional Credits:** Executive producers: Michel Gast, Jenny Gérard. Codirector: Boris Szulzinger. Music: Teddy Lasry. Assistant director: Bernard de Vissher. Writers: Pierre Bartier, Picha, Anne Beatts, Michael O'Donoghue. Adaptation: Picha, Boris Szulzinger, Michel Gasté, Jenny Gérard, Pierre Bartier. Dialogue: Pierre Bartier, Christian Dura. Animation directors: Vivian Miessen, Claude Monfort, Kjeld Simonsen, Alan Ball. Animators: Malcom Draper, Jack Stokes, Arthur Button, Richard Cox, Tom Barker, Michael Stuart, Denis Rich.

**Shark Tale** (10/1/04) DreamWorks. 89 mins. Directors: Bibo Bergeron, Vicky Jenson, Rob Letterman. Producers: Bill Damaschke, Janet Healy, Allison Lyon Segan. Voices: Will Smith (Oscar), Robert DeNiro (Don Lino), Renée Zellweger (Angie), Angelina Jolie (Lola), Jack Black (Lenny), Martin Scorsese (Sykes), Ziggy Marley (Ernie), Doug E. Doug (Bernie), Michael Imperioli (Frankie), Vincent Pastore (Luca), Peter Falk (Don Brizzi), Katie Couric (Katie Current), David Soren (Shrimp, Worm, Starfish #1, Killer Whale #2), David P. Smith (Crazy Joe).

©DreamWorks L.L.C.

**Consumer Tips:** ☆☆½ MPAA Rating: PG.

**Story:** A fast-talking big city fish is mistaken for a shark slayer, but his newfound fame gets him mixed up with a shark mob boss and his runaway vegetarian son.

**Comments:** *Shark Tale* was DreamWorks' fourth completely computer-animated feature, though only the first to be produced completely within the studio (the previous three had been made at DreamWorks-owned Pacific Data Images). Though there is a visual difference as a result, like *Antz* and the *Shrek* movies, *Shark Tale* is built largely on pop culture references, celebrity voice talent, and attempts by the filmmakers to be hip. Though the film was initially discussed and promoted mostly in terms of its jabs at Mafia movies, the basic plot is an odd blend of *The Reluctant Dragon* and *The Brave Little Tailor*, as a small-time fish named Oscar takes credit for the death of shark mobster Don Lino's eldest son, and then further uses Lenny, the don's vegetarian offspring and black sheep of the family, to build his image as a celebrity and a protector of his community.

The plot's twisted Horatio Alger qualities can be oddly discomforting, for while the desire to be rich and famous may be almost universal, Oscar's obsession with it, ignoring his faithful girlfriend, and basic lack of other characteristics beyond his whiny selfishness and smooth tongue, makes for a rather unappealing protagonist. This wouldn't be a problem if the movie doesn't seem to want the audience to love its hero, and Will Smith's hammy vocals certainly seem to be trying. Far more appealing is Lenny, the misfit shark, who has a quiet sincerity and good nature, freeing prawns from a shark restaurant. In general, the heavy reliance on celebrity voices overshadows characterization, and the presence of Robert DeNiro, Martin Scorsese, and two regulars of *The Sopranos* as mobsters led to protests from Italian-American groups. (Oddly, the African-American qualities of Oscar and a pair of Rastafarian jellyfish went largely uncriticized.) Like *Shrek 2*, the movie is rife with product references, recast in undersea terms, which feel more like crass commercialism than subversive wit. The blaring pop soundtrack, with undersea caricatures of singers Missy Elliott and Christina Aguilera, is particularly obnoxious.

Still, these calculated attempts to keep the film trendy and popular, though liable to date it considerably in 20 or 30 years, proved successful. Contrary to initial critical skepticism, *Shark Tale* proved to be a surprise hit, grossing over $160 million at the box office. (AL)

**Additional Credits:** Executive producer: Jeffrey Katzenberg. Screenplay: Rob Letterman, Damian Shannon, Mark Swift,

Michael J. Wilson. Music: Hans Zimmer. Additional music: Trevor Morris, Geoff Zanelli, Ryeland Allison, Missy Elliott. Supervising animators: Ken Stuart Duncan, Lionel Gallat, Fabrice Joubert, Fabio Lignini, William Salazar, Bill Diaz. Animators: Ben Rush, Sean McLaughlin, Gavin Moran, Kristof Serrand, Michael Surrey. Senior character animator: Paul Newberry. Production design: Dan St. Peirre. Production supervisors: Brian Behling, Onil Chibas, Fred De Bradeny, Christina DeSilva, Stacey Ernst, Kim Mackey, Dina McLaughlin, Kay Sasatomi, Cameron Stevning, Mark Tarbox. Storyboard artist: Jenny Lerew. Sound: Richard L. Anderson. Assistant animator: Eric Deuel. Story artist: David Bowers, Darryl Kidder. Animation production supervisor: Rene Harnois Jr. Lead character technical directors: Carlos Cabral, Stephen Krauth. Character technical directors: Ben Cheung, T. J. Galda, Annick Harmel-Tourneru, Aaron Holly, James Jacobs, Alisa Loren Klein, Marc Wilhite. CGI animation supervisor: Teddy T. Yang. CGI supervising animator: Fabrice Joubert. Lead CGI supervisor: Kevin Rafferty. CGI supervisor: Mark Wendell, Bert Poole. CGI animators: Paul Newberry, Theodore Ty, Greg Whittaker. CGI character animators: Kevin MacLean, Steve Mason, Joe Oh, Ben Rush, Dimos Vrysellas, Greg Whittaker.

**Shinbone Alley** (6/18/71) Allied Artists. 86 mins. Director: John David Wilson. Producer: Preston M. Fllet. Voices: Carol Channing (Mehitabel), Eddie Bracken (Archy), Alan Reed (Big Bill Sr.), John Carradine (Tyrone T. Tattersall), Byron Kane (The Newspaperman), Hal Smith (Freddie the Rat, Prissy Cat, Mabel, Pool Player), Joan Gerber (Penelope the Fat Cat, Ladybugs of the Evening), Ken Sansom (Rosie the Cat), Sal Delano (Beatnik Spider), The Jackie Ward Singers (Singing Alley Cats, Kittens).

©Fine Arts Films

**Consumer Tips:** ☆☆½ MPAA Rating: G.

**Story:** A poet cockroach falls in love with an alley cat, and convinces her to leave the rough street life to become a house cat.

**Comments:** Archy and Mehitabel, the characters made famous in Don Marquis's narrative poems, were characters that one might say cried out for animation, but the results are mixed. Marquis's short tales, noted for their lack of punctuation, were first published in 1916 in the *New York Sun*, as part of Marquis's "Sun Dial" column. The stories were by (and often about) a cockroach named Archy, who is actually a reincarnated poet, and commented on life among insects and alley animals in New York. The tales, when collected in book form, were accompanied by striking illustrations from George Herriman of *Krazy Kat* fame, and in 1954, certain of the poems were adapted for an LP, with music by George Kleinsinger and lyrics by Joe Darion. The record, which cast Eddie Bracken as Archy and Carol Channing as Mehitabel, was expanded into a short-lived Broadway musical *Shinbone Alley* (with Eartha Kitt replacing Channing). This, more than the original stories, was the source of this animated feature, which adds unnecessary elements such as Archy's reincarnation being the result of suicide, or Archy actually being in love with Mehitabel, rather than merely observing and chronicling her failed romances and other misadventures.

The latter change alters the entire structure of the story and prevents Archy from being a more active character as he passively pines for Mehitabel to reform and be his. Animated in a rather scratchy style, the movie recalls DePatie-Freleng's theatrical output at the time (though British animator John David Wilson is credited as director, DePatie-Freleng veteran David Detiege, supervising director, clearly influenced the look of the film). The style shifts for certain set pieces, veering into *Yellow Submarine*–style psychedelics at one point and into photo manipulations in another. Herriman's original art, though abandoned for the main character designs, surfaces during a fantasy sequence, "Archy Declares War," complete with cameos by Krazy Kat and Ignatz.

Despite the deviations from Marquis's tone, Channing and Bracken make a fine pair, dueting well on such numbers as "Flotsam and Jetsam." Veterans Alan Reed and John Carradine portray Mehitabel's beaus in broad, energetic fashion, but can't handle the demands of their musical numbers. Even the backing chorus sounds oddly high-pitched and shrill in several spots (notably "There's a Dance or Two in the Old Girl Yet," based on Mehitabel's catchphrase). As the original stories were a trifle salty, with occasional mild expletives and constant references to Mehitabel's loose morals, additional elements such as the suicide and a strange encounter by Archy with bug prostitutes kept this from headlining kiddie matinees. However, despite its problems, *Shinbone Alley* has much to offer mature viewers in search of something offbeat that occasionally delves into serious issues, as well as being a must for Broadway enthusiasts and Marquis completists. (AL)

**Additional Credits:** Executive producer: John David Wilson. Screenplay: Joe Darion. Based on the book for the musical play by Darion and Mel Brooks. From the *Archy and Mehitabel* stories by Don Marquis. Story: John David Wilson, David Detiege, Richard Kinney, Marty Murphy. Music: George Kleinsinger. Supervising director: David Detiege. Animators: Frank Andrina, John Sparey, Amby Paliwoda, Gil Rugg, George Waiss, Bob Bransford, Jim Hiltz, Fred Grable, Brad Case, Frank Gonzales, Barrie Nelson, Ken Southworth, Russ Von Neida, Frank Onaitis, Bob Bemiller, Rudy Cataldi, Spencer Peel, Selby Daley. Production design: Gary Lund, John David Wilson, Cornelius Cole, James Bernardi, David Detiege, Jules Engel, Sam Cornell.

**Shrek** (5/16/01) DreamWorks. 89 mins. Directors: Andrew Adamson, Vicky Jenson. Producers: Jeffrey Katzenberg, Aron Warner, John H. Williams. Voices: Mike Myers (Shrek), Eddie Murphy (Donkey), Cameron Diaz (Princess Fiona), John Lithgow (Lord Farquaad), Vincent Cassel (Monsieur Hood), Peter Dennis (Ogre Hunter), Clive Pearse (Ogre Hunter), Jim Cummings (Captain of Guards), Bobby Block (Baby Bear), Chris Miller (Geppetto, Magic Mirror), Cody Cameron (Pinocchio, Three Pigs), Kathleen Freeman (Old Woman), Michael Galasso (Peter Pan), Christopher Knights (Blind Mouse, Thelonious), Simon J. Smith (Blind Mouse), Conrad Vernon (Gingerbread Man), Jacquie Barnbrook (Wrestling Fan), Guillaume Aretos (Merry Man), John Bisom (Merry Man), Matthew Gonder (Merry Man), Calvin Rems-

©DreamWorks L.L.C.

berg (Merry Man), Jean-Paul Vignon (Merry Man), Val Bettin (Bishop).

**Consumer Tips:** ☆☆☆½ MPAA Rating: PG for profanity and crude humor.

**Story:** In a fantasy world that parodies fairy tales and Disneyland, an ogre helps a tyrant by rescuing an imprisoned princess.

**Comments:** Encouraged by the success of *Antz*, DreamWorks continued its focus toward CG animation with Pacific Data Images, based in Palo Alto, California. Its next CG project would be based upon the 1990 children's book by William Steig, *Shrek*, which the studio optioned in November 1995. The film continued the DreamWorks tradition of casting celebrities as voiceover talent, with heavyweight comedian Chris Farley as the title character. Farley died of a drug overdose in December 1997, forcing the studio to scrap development work involving storyboards and six recording sessions, work that *Entertainment Weekly* in its June 22, 2001, issue said cost $34 million alone. Farley's replacement was another *Saturday Night Live* comedian, Mike Myers, who initially voiced Shrek with a thick Canadian accent. But a rough cut screening in February 2000 convinced Myers to rethink his vocal delivery and give Shrek a Scottish brogue. By then a third of Shrek's scenes had already been animated. To match the new line readings, animators would have to redo the character's mouth, expressions, and body movements. Reluctantly, Katzenberg acquiesced. The revisions added three months of production and $4 million to a budget of $60 million.

The story team enlivened *Shrek* with outrageous gags unthinkable at Disney. For example: while singing for a bluebird, Princess Fiona's voice becomes so shrill the bluebird pops. She then makes breakfast with its eggs.

*Shrek* was an immediate success. Its U.S. opening set a record of $42.3 million, the second-biggest opening for any animated film and the biggest-ever opening for DreamWorks, ultimately earning a total U.S. gross of $267.8 million. The DVD release on November 2, 2001, saw worldwide sales of 43 million units. Thus *Shrek* became DreamWorks' first blockbuster franchise that has, as of this writing, spawned three sequels and a spinoff property.

On March 24, 2001, *Shrek* won the first Academy Award given for Best Animated Feature. It was nominated in 2001 for a Golden Palm Award at the Cannes Film Festival—the first for an animated feature since *The Nine Lives of Fritz the Cat* in 1974. It swept the 2001 Asifa-Hollywood Annie Awards as well. The success of *Shrek*, coupled with the success of Disney/Pixar's films and Fox/Blue Sky's *Ice Age*, and the failures of contemporary hand-drawn films (with the exception of *Lilo and Stitch*), led to the corporate mindset that hand-drawn animated features were no longer economically viable.

Storyboard artist Conrad Vernon, who voiced the Gingerbread Man, became the codirector of *Shrek 2*, in which he voiced the Gingerbread Man, Cedric, the Announcer, the Muffin Man, and Mongo. *Shrek* has interesting, likeable characters, and even Donkey surpasses his role of annoying sidekick into being a genuinely entertaining fellow. Ironically, *Shrek* becomes the fairy tale that it parodies. (WRM)

**Additional Credits:** Executive producers: Penney Finkelman Cox, Sandra Rabins, Steven Spielberg (uncredited). Coexecutive producer: David Lipman. Associate producer: Jane Hartwell. Coproducers: Ted Elliott, Terry Rossio. Screenplay: Ted Elliott, Terry Rosio, Joe Stillman, Roger S. H. Schulman. Based upon the book by William Steig. Additional dialogue: Cody Cameron, Chris Miller, Conrad Vernon. Music: Harry Gregson-Williams, John Powell. Supervising animator: Raman Hui. Directing animators: Tim Cheung, Paul Chung, Denis Couchon, Donnachada Daly, James Satoru Straus. Additional animation supervisor: Rex Grignon. Animators: Edip Agi, Chung

Chan, Raffaella Flipponi, Anthony Hodgson, Ethan Hurd, Tim Keon, Ken Keys, Boris Kossmehl, Eric Lessard, Noel McGinn, Michelle R. Meeker, Fredrik Nilsson, David Radder, Jason A. Reisig, Rick Richards, Emmanuel Roth, Tom Roth, David Spivack, Don Venhaus. Story artists: Kelly Asbury, Francisco Avalos, Rejean Bourdages, Ken Harsha, Ken Bruce, Cody Cameron, Becky Cassady, Eric Darnell, Rick Farmiloe, James Fujii, Edmund Fong, Robert Koo, Todd Kurosawa, Robert Lence, Chris Miller, Catherine Yuh Rader, Tom Sito, David Soren, Robert Souza, John Stevenson, Conrad Vernon.

**Shrek 2** (5/19/04) DreamWorks. 88 mins. Directors: Andrew Adamson, Kelly Asbury, Conrad Vernon. Producers: David Lipman, Aron Warner, John H. Williams. Voices: Mike Myers (Shrek), Cameron Diaz (Princess Fiona), Eddie Murphy (Donkey), John Lithgow (Lord Farquaad), John Cleese (King Harold), Julie Andrews (Queen Lillian), Antonio Banderas (Puss in Boots), Rupert Everett (Prince Charming), Jennifer Saunders (Fairy Godmother), Aron Warner (Wolf), Kelly Asbury (Page, Elf, Nobleman, Nobleman's Son), Cody Cameron (Pinocchio, Three Pigs), Conrad Vernon (Gingerbread Man, Cedric, Announcer, Muffin Man, Mongo), Christopher Knights (Blind Mouse), Mark Moseley (Mirror, Dresser), Larry King (Ugly Stepsister), Joan Rivers (Joan Rivers).

**Consumer Tips:** ☆☆☆½ MPAA Rating: PG, for profanity and crude humor. Fractured fairy tale.

**Story:** Shrek and his bride, Princess Fiona, visit her parents in a land Far Far Away, where an evil fairy god-

©DreamWorks L.L.C.

mother and her son, Prince Charming, plot to separate the two. Fiona's father, King Harold, hires the famous swordsman and ogre-killer, Puss in Boots.

**Comments:** DreamWorks allocated the first sequel to *Shrek* with a $70 million budget. Mike Myers, Eddie Murphy, and Cameron Diaz re-signed on August 8, 2001. The studio augmented its star power with Julie Andrews as Queen Lillian, John Cleese as King Harold, and Jennifer Saunders as the fairy godmother. Antonio Banderas signed on in October 2002, parodying his earlier role of Zorro as the charismatic feline, Puss in Boots. Banderas also voiced Puss in both Spanish (but with an Andalusian accent, which sounds funny to the Spanish) and Latin American (with a Castilian accent, which sounds funny to Latin Americans) versions. John Cleese, whose character turns out to be a frog, earlier played a frog who fancied himself to be a prince, in *The Swan Princess*.

In this tale, the story team parodies Hollywood in the land of Far Far Away. Watch for the product placement at the following stores: Farbucks Coffee (Starbucks), Burger Prince (Burger King), Olde Knavery (Old Navy), Saxon Fifth Avenue (Saks Fifth Avenue), Versarchery (Versace), Gap Queen (Gap Kids), Tower of London Records (Tower Records), Friar's Fat Boy (Big Boy), and Baskin Robinhood (Baskin-Robbins ice cream; incidentally, Baskin-Robbins is usually involved in promoting DreamWorks animated films, offering *Shrek* ice cream in its stores).

Production officially began January 27, 2003. On May 15, 2004, it premiered in competition at the Cannes Film Festival.

DreamWorks gave *Shrek 2* the widest release ever at 4,163 theaters, which yielded the biggest single-day gross at $44.8 million. Its opening weekend earned $108 million, topping *Finding Nemo*'s opening at $70.3 million. In less than six months, *Shrek 2* surpassed *Shrek*, *The Lion King*, and *Finding Nemo* and became the highest-grossing animated film. On August 12, 2004, it became the third U.S. domestic box-office champion, behind *Titanic* and *Star Wars*. As of December 2004, it has grossed $441.2 million.

On November 5, 2004, *Shrek 2* became available on DVD, with 12.1 million copies sold in the first three days. On November 19, 2004, DreamWorks announced a direct-to-video CG spinoff starring Puss

in Boots, to be written by Ed Decter and John Strauss (*The Lizzie Maguire Movie*), with Antonio Banderas reprising the role.

Reportedly, *Shrek 3* will have Shrek and Donkey facing King Arthur and the Knights of Camelot, to be released in the year 2007. At the Cannes Film Festival, Jeffrey Katzenberg announced *Shrek 4* will be out in 2008 (now likely 2009), when, "In the last chapter, we will understand how Shrek came to be in that swamp when we met him in the first movie."

Yet another triumph for the cast and crew at DreamWorks. (WRM)

**Additional Credits:** Executive producer: Jeffrey Katzenberg. Story: Andrew Adamson. Writers: Ted Elliott, Terry Rossio. Book: William Steig. Story/screenplay: Andrew Adamson. Screenplay: J. David Stem, Joe Stillman, David N. Weiss. Story supervisor: Latifa Ouaou. Music: Harry Gregson-Williams, Ryeland Allison. Additional Music: James McKee Smith. Songs: Adam Duritz, Mark Everett. Production design: Guillaume Aretos. Art direction: Steve Pilcher. Production manager: Denise Nolan Cascino. Production supervisors: Tony Cosanella, Jennifer Dahlman, Philip R. Garrett. Story supervisor: Latifa Ouaou. Head of story: Chris Miller. Storyboard artists: Steven E. Gordon, John Stevenson, Piet Kroon, Ken Mitchroney. Supervising animators: James Baxter, Rex Grignon, Raman Hui. Animators: Darrin Butts, Lou Dellarosa, Emilio Ghorayeb, Mariko Hoshi, Ethan Hurd, Jeffrey Joe, Heather Knight, Kevin Koch, Marek Kochout, Sean McLaughlin, Mark Pudleiner, David Spivack. Character animators: Carlos M. Rosas, Kevan Shorey, Cassidy Curtis. Supervising character technical director: Lawrence D. Cutler. Character technical directors: Gilbert Davoud, Peter Farson, Mariette Marinus, Rob O'Neill, Nico Scapel, J. Todd Taylor, Marc White. Animation technical director: York N. Schueller.

## Sinbad: Legend of the Seven Seas (7/2/03)

DreamWorks. 86 mins. Directors: Tim Johnson, Patrick Gilmore. Producers: Jeffrey Katzenberg, Mireille Soria. Voices: Brad Pitt (Sinbad), Catherine Zeta-Jones (Marina), Michelle Pfeiffer (Eris), Joseph Fiennes (Proteus), Dennis Haysbert (Kale), Timothy West (Dymas), Adriano Giannini (Rat), Raman Hui (Jin), Chung Chan (Li), Jim Cummings, (Luca, Council Judge, Dignitary, Guard, Others), Conrad Vernon (Jed), Andrew Birch (Grum, Chum), Chris Miller (Tower Guard), Lisbeth Scott (Sirens).

©DreamWorks L.L.C.

**Consumer Tips:** ☆☆☆ MPAA Rating: PG.

**Story:** To save his boyhood friend from death, Sinbad must battle spirits and monsters to rescue the "Book of Peace" from an evil goddess.

**Comments:** *Sinbad* is (presumably) the final 2-D animated feature to come from DreamWorks (for a time, anyway), and, arguably, its best (or at least second to *Prince of Egypt*). It is a definite improvement over *Spirit* in aspirations and concept, in pacing and overall plot. That plot, however, and the writing in general, still had some serious problems: underdeveloped relationship between Sinbad and Proteus; clichéd romance that one could accept in a 1940s MGM musical but may have trouble with here, and that feels even more forced than in those musicals; Proteus being little more than the generic noble friend at every turn; poorly written quips; and a very nagging lack of explanation for Sinbad's escape from Tarterus. All that said, it was still reasonably enjoyable.

The voice cast was moderately better than expected, for while Brad Pitt's performance was hardly outstanding, at least he tried to give some life to a rakish character (who as written, is largely unsympathetic as well). The character animation is as expected. Apart from the aforementioned problem with Proteus's unflinching loyalty to Sinbad, the relationships that work best, due largely to the animation and vocals rather than the actual writing, are between Sinbad and his mate Kale and Proteus and his father Dymas (particularly as the latter, well voiced by stage and BBC radio vet Timothy West, fears for his son's life). The set pieces involving the creature encounters worked best. The sirens' sequence worked very well, due to both the music (score by Gregson-Williams, vocal chanting by Lisbeth Scott) and the animation. The highlight for me, though, was the encounter with the Roc. Here, for one of the few times in the movie, or in most animated films that include CGI monsters, the animators managed to give the creature a semblance of a personality. Perhaps it was just me, but I had the distinct impression that the bird was chasing the crew as much out of playfulness as out of mindless bestial rage, and the CG facial animation (if it was indeed entirely CG) was surprisingly expressive, lacking the stiffness seen in earlier films. Definitely an improvement, with some truly charming moments, and one wonders if the DreamWorks crew might have continued to improve and produce some really fine films, or at least pleasant entertainment (as despite their greater box-office success, the PDI CG films thus far have been far less aesthetically pleasing). U.S. box-office gross was an un-heroic $26 million. (AL)

**Additional Credits:** Associate producer: Jill Hopper. Screenplay: John Logan. Music: Harry Gregson-Williams. Additional music: Stephen Barton. Animation supervisor: Kristoff Serrand. Lead supervising animator: Jacob Hjort Jensen. Supervising animators: James Baxter, Simon Otto, William Salazar, Dan Wagner, Rodolphe Guenoden, Bruce Ferriz, Fabio Lignini, Sergei Kouchnerov, Steve Horrocks, Pres Romanillos, Fabrice Joubert, Michael Spokas, Michelle Cowart. Animators: Allessandro Carloni, Lionel Gallat, Antony Gray, James R. Hull, Jeff Johnson, Jae Kim, Bang Won Lee, Holger Leihe, Kevin O'Hara, Erik C. Schmidt, Oliver Thomas, Dimos Vrysellas, Greg Whittaker, Alexander Williams, Scott Wright, Davide Benvenuti, Arnaud Berthier, Emanuela Cozzi, Cathy Jones, Mary Ann Malcomb, Claire Morrisey, Jean-Francois Rey, Robert Weaver, Kathy Zielinski, Robert Espanto Domingo, John Hill, Yoshimichi Tamura, David Boudreau, Adam Burke, Steve Cunningham, Aaron Kirby, Phillipe LeBrun, Ken Morrisey, Xavier Riffault, Simon Otto, Paul Newberry, Phillip Young. CG character animators: Manuel Almela, Cinzia Angelini, Dave Burgess, Darrin Butts, Paul Chung, Cassidy Curtis, Rex Grignon, Anthony Hodgson, Cameron Hood, Kyle Arthur Jefferson, Richard Sang Uoon Kim, Eric Lessard, Sean McLaughlin, Van Phan, Trey Thomas, Mark A. Williams. Digital supervisor: Craig Ring.

Story: Eric "Bibo" Bergeron, Serguei Kouchnerov, Denise Nagisa Koyama, Jurgen Gross, Rob Porter, Rodolphe Guenoden, Jeff Snow, Simon Wells. Additional story artists: Randy Cartwright, Ronaldo Del Carmen, Bob Logan, Phil A. Keller, Hank Tucker, Catherine Yuh Rader.

**Sky Blue** (12/31/04) Maxmedia/Endgame Entertainment. 86 mins. Director: Moon Sang Kim. Director English version: Park Sunmin. Producer: Kay Hwang. Producers English version: J. Ethan Park, Park Sunmin. Voices: David Naughton, Joon-ho Chung, Hyejin Yu, Ji-tae Yu.

**Consumer Tips:** ☆☆☆ MPAA Rating: Unrated. SF adventure. A futuristic dystopian tragedy combining elements of *Romeo and Juliet* with *Metropolis*.

**Story:** In A.D. 2142 earth has been destroyed by a century of toxic polluted rain except for its last and greatest city, Ecoban, a technological utopia built to preserve humanity. But only a few thousand live in luxury in Ecoban. The descendants of the masses survive in labor camps as abused workers (Diggers) who are on the verge of revolt. Jay, the heroine, is a young captain in Ecoban's security forces who sympathizes with the Diggers. Shua, the hero, reluctantly becomes a leader of the Diggers' revolt. When Jay and Shua meet again after being separated for years, romantic feelings are reborn—to the dismay of Cade, a security commander who wants Jay for himself.

**Comments:** *Sky Blue* is the title of the international cut of this South Korean feature (the Korean domestic cut is titled *Wonderful Days*). It is South Korea's most ambitious animated theatrical feature, produced by Tin House, blending traditional 2-D character animation over 3-D CGI and live-action miniature sets and backgrounds. It is visually stunning, top-quality animation in every respect. However, although the story is well-acted and compelling on a scene-by-scene basis, it is overly derivative of SF dystopian clichés and is fundamentally unconvincing.

As in Fritz Lang's *Metropolis* or the Eloi and Morlocks in H. G. Wells's *The Time Machine*, the entirety of human existence has been compressed into a society divided between a ruling decadent, a parasitic upper class, and a laboring, oppressed underclass. The

extremes are even greater because the technology that supports the mechanized Ecoban is wearing out after a century, and the Diggers are literally being worked to death by Ecoban's brutal security guards. Also, the carbonite deposits necessary to maintain Ecoban's power generators are running out. Yet when the Diggers threaten to strike for better working conditions, Security Commander Locke's proposed solution to all the problems is to kill all the Diggers as mutinous scum. The only dissent is over whether this may be a bit extreme and inhumane. There is never any questioning of how killing the entire labor force is supposed to increase production or prevent catastrophic mechanical breakdown. (FP)

**Additional Credits:** Associate producer: Jeffrey Winter. Coproducer: Kyeong-hak Lee. Screenplay: Moon-saeng Kim, Jun-Young Park, Yong-jun Park. English adaptation: Howard Rabinowitz, Park Sunmin, Jeffrey Winter. Music: Jaell Sim, Il Won. Animation director: Yeong-ki Yoon. 3-D animation supervisor: Young-Min Park. Art directors: Yoon-cheol Jung, Suk-Young Lee. Special effects: Sung-Ho Hong. Editor: Michael McCusker.

**Sleeping Beauty** (1/29/59) Walt Disney Pictures. 75 mins. Directing supervisor: Clyde Geronimi. Voices: Mary Costa (Princess Aurora), Eleanor Audley (Maleficent), Barbara Luddy (Merryweather), Verna Felton (Flora), Barbara Jo Allen (Fauna), Bill Shirley (Prince Philip), Taylor Holmes (King Stefan), Bill Thompson (King Hubert), Marvin Miller (Narrator), Candy Candido, Pinto Colvig, Bob Amsberry (Maleficent's Goons), Dallas McKennon (Owl).

©Walt Disney Productions

**Consumer Tips:** ☆☆ MPAA Rating: Unrated. Based on a folk fairy tale codified by Charles Perrault in 1697.

**Story:** The kingdom rejoices at the birth of Princess Aurora, but the cruel witch Maleficent curses the infant with death to come on her 16th birthday. Three good fairies—Flora, Fauna, and Merryweather—blunt the spell to one of sleep. Only the kiss of true love can break this spell. The fairies spirit Aurora to their cottage hideout in the forest, intending to keep her safe until the fateful birthday passes. The young Aurora meets Prince Philip in the woods (unaware that their fathers have arranged at birth for the two to marry) and they fall in love. Maleficent finds the hideout, fulfills her curse, and imprisons Philip, but the good fairies free him and see him to victory over the evil witch. The requisite kiss sets everything right.

**Comments:** *Sleeping Beauty*, depending on one's point of view, is either Disney's last great classic or an overrated piece of work drowning in style but woefully short on action and story. There are good arguments for both viewpoints, but for those who believe that a film should tell an engrossing story filled with memorable characters, *Sleeping Beauty* falls into the latter camp. Walt Disney began *Sleeping Beauty* in 1953 with the best of intentions, declaring that it would surpass all his other efforts. Disney's efforts, however, were not exclusively animated anymore. Walt was now making live-action features, producing a television show, and building the mecca known as Disneyland. Disney already had a profitable live-action hit with his *Davy Crockett* films, and his many projects were distracting him from his first love. Disney had very little to do with *Sleeping Beauty* and the film was often laid aside in order to have the artists work on the television show or paint murals for Disneyland. It was not finished until 1958.

As a result, *Sleeping Beauty* fell increasingly into the hands of designers and artists, and they soon outstripped every other department including story. Layout designer John Hench visited a medieval art exhibition where he viewed the legendary unicorn tapestries. Hench loved the style and soon he and stylist Eyvind Earle were giving the film the sharp, lineated look found in the art of the Middle Ages. Earle drew not only sketches, but also dozens of finished backgrounds featuring razor-sharp colors, strong vertical lines, and flat perspective. *Sleeping Beauty* is styled like a masterpiece in stained-glass glory. There are few other films in the history of animation with as many backgrounds, and some of them are seen only for a few seconds of screen time.

Meanwhile, the studio was crafting a film with virtually no action until the final 15 minutes, and *Sleeping Beauty* is rather unexciting to watch. We are mostly left with Aurora and Philip sharing one song, the fairies fussing and fumbling to get along without their magic powers, and Maleficent grumbling in her palace along with her gremlin goons. The battle between Philip and Maleficent—now transformed into an enormous dragon—is filmed with verve and excitement, but it is also a cheat. After all, the good fairies have freed Philip, armed him, aided him at every turn, and finally enchanted his sword so that it literally flies into the dragon's dark breast. Virtually all Philip had to do was show up.

None of this would have been problematic if Flora, Fauna, and Merryweather were funnier or more interesting as characters, if Philip was somehow differentiated from a standard cartoon prince, of if Princess Aurora were more than just a pretty blonde waiting around in a forest for the man of her dreams. When the prince's horse, Samson, is a more memorable character than his rider, something is amiss. Of special note: Marc Davis's animation of Maleficent. She would be little more than a variation on Art Babbitt's queen in *Snow White* were it not for Davis's skillful work in animating the female face and form in all of its variegated expressions. *Sleeping Beauty* cost $6 million, making it the most expensive animated film to date. It met with poor reviews and struggled to regain its cost. History has been kinder to the film in recent years. (MG)

**Additional Credits:** Story adaptation: Erdman Penner. Additional story: Joe Rinaldi, Winston Hibler, Bill Peet, Ted Sears, Ralph Wright, Milt Banta. Based on the traditional story as told by Charles Perrault. Music: Fydor Tchaikovsky. Music adaptation/arrangement: George Bruns. Songs: George Bruns, Tom Adair, Winston Hibler, Ted Sears, Erdman Penner, Sammy Fain, Jack Lawrence. Sequence directors: Eric Larson, Wolfgang Reitherman, Les Clark. Directing animators: Milt Kahl, Frank Thomas, Marc Davis, Ollie Johnston, John Lounsbery. Animation: Hal King, Blaine Gibson, Ken Hultgren, George Nicholas,

Henry Tanous, Hal Ambro, John Sibley, Harvey Toombs, Bob Youngquist, John Kennedy, Don Lusk, Bob Carlson, Fred Kopietz, Eric Cleworth, Ken O'Brien. Effects animators: Dan MacManus, Joshua Meador, Jack Boyd, Jack Buckley. Production design: Donald DaGradi, Ken Anderson. Color Styling: Eyvind Earle. Layout: McLaren Stewart, Don Griffith, Basil Davidovich, Joe Hale, Jack Huber, Tom Codrick, Erni Nordli, Victor Haboush, Homer Jonas, Ray Aragon. Backgrounds: Frank Armitage, Al Dempster, Bill Layne, Dick Anthony, Richard H. Thomas, Thelma Witmer, Walt Peregoy, Ralph Hulett, Fil Mottola, Anthony Rizzo.

**The Smurfs and the Magic Flute** (11/25/83) Atlantic (French-Belgium). 74 mins. Directors: Jose Dutillieu. English version: John Rust. Producer: Jose Dutillieu. Voices: Cam Clarke (Pee-Wee), Grant Gottschall, Patty Foley, Mike Reynolds, Ted Lehman, Bill Capizzi, Ron Gans, X. Phifer, Dudly Knight, John Rust, Richard Miller, David Page, Durga McBroom, Robert Axelrod, Michael Sorich.

**Consumer Tips:** ☆☆ MPAA Rating: G. Based on the comic strip by Peyo.

**Story:** Peewee, a court musician, finds an enchanted flute created by the Smurfs. When the flute is stolen, the Smurfs create a new flute to defeat the thief.

**Comments:** Peyo, a Flemish artist and writer of children's books, created the Smurfs in 1960 and had decades of incredible success with the characters in France and Europe. One day in the late 1970s, Fred

Silverman, then the head of NBC, found his daughter reading a Smurfs book. After looking through it himself, Mr. Silverman contacted Hanna-Barbera, recommending they investigate the television rights because it seemed to have potential for a Saturday morning cartoon.

Hanna-Barbera developed the concept and sold the series to NBC for their 1981–82 fall schedule. The television cartoons were instantly popular, and the subsequent merchandising was huge. As reported by the *Wall Street Journal* in the early 1980s, the revenue produced by the Smurfs was larger than the GNP of various foreign nations.

However, several years before the Hanna-Barbera television show, in 1975, Peyo oversaw the production of a Smurfs animated movie, produced by Belvision Studios in Brussels. *La Flûte à Six Schtroumpfs* was released in 1976, with music by Michel LeGrand, Academy Award winner for *The Thomas Crown Affair* (1968) and *The Summer of '42* (1972). This movie was essentially forgotten until the success of the American cartoon series.

Stuart R. Ross (whose First Performance Pictures Corporation gets a presentation credit on the U.S. release), smelling a fast buck to be made, picked up the feature film for U.S. distribution for a million dollars. He quickly made a handsome profit selling the home video rights to Vestron Video, the television rights to Tribune Entertainment, and the theatrical rights to Atlantic Releasing.

Is the film any good? It is passable entertainment for Smurfs completists only. Otherwise, mom and dad will have a tough time sitting through this one. There are no standout sequences, nothing particularly endearing, nor is it artistically interesting. It is a bland television cartoon stretched out to fill 74 minutes. As part of 1980s pop culture, the Smurfs are classic icons, and nostalgia value alone might be worth giving the film a look. But be warned that the Hanna-Barbera voice crew wasn't employed here—no Don Messick as Papa Smurf, no sped-up voices of Frank Welker, Hamilton Camp, or Michael Bell. A non-union voice crew, familiar to those who enjoy dubbed anime, looped the proceedings here.

With 420 prints, a territorial state-by-state release plan, and a $2 million print and marketing budget, Atlantic Releasing grossed over $16 million with the film, which was a record at the time for a non-Disney animated film.

The success of *The Smurfs and the Magic Flute* encouraged Atlantic to pick up further animated features. Atlantic eventually established a distribution label, Clubhouse Pictures, for several 1985–86 animated releases. (JB)

*Additional Credits:* Writers: John Rust, Yvan Delporte. Based on the comic book by Peyo. Music: Michael Legrand. Supervising animator: Eddie Lateste. Animation: Nic Broca, Marcel Colbrant, Louis-Michael Carpentier, Borge Ring, Bjorn Frank Jensen, Per Ulvar Lygum, Brigitta Jansen, Christiane Segers, Jean-Pol Chapelle, John Vander Linden, Christine Schotte, Jean Claude De Ridder, Godelieve Zeghers.

**Snoopy Come Home** (8/9/72) National General. 70 mins. Director: Bill Melendez. Producers: Lee Mendelson, Bill Melendez. Voices: Chad Webber (Charlie Brown), Robin Kohn (Lucy Van Pelt), Stephen Shea (Linus Van Pelt), Stephen Shea (Schroeder), Johanna Baer (Lila), Hilary Momberger (Sally Brown), Chris DeFaria (Peppermint Patty), Linda Ercoli (Clara), Lynda Mendelson (Frieda), Bill Melendez (Snoopy, Woodstock). Featured Vocalists: Shelby Flint, Thurl Ravenscroft, Guy Pohlman, Ray Pohlman, Don Ralke.

*Consumer Tips:* ☆☆ MPAA Rating: G. Based on the *Peanuts* comic strip.

*Story:* Snoopy leaves home to find Lila, his original owner, who writes from the hospital that she needs him.

*Comments:* For the second *Peanuts* film, as the title indicates, Charlie Brown and friends step aside and allow Snoopy, mainly a supporting character in *A Boy Named Charlie Brown*, to take center stage. While Charlie Brown struggles with his own doubts and insecurities, Snoopy blithely skips through life and has lively encounters with Peppermint Patty and the Van Pelts. His enthusiasm is only slightly dampened by the recurring threat of the "No Dogs Allowed" signs (veteran animation vocalist Thurl Ravenscroft blares the censorious warnings in his trademark bass, one of the movie's best gags). However, a greater crisis occurs when Snoopy learns that his original owner, a sweet girl named Lila, is in the hospital and desperate to see him. The beagle and his bird companion Woodstock leave abruptly, and the remainder of the film cuts between the pair's travels, and the increased distress of Charlie Brown over his pet's sudden departure.

The "meanwhile, back at the ranch" cutting allows for some fine introspection by Charlie Brown and the gang, ultimately learning more of Snoopy's background. Schulz's witty writing truly shines, with such lines as "You got a used dog, Charlie Brown!" and "I think that blanket is doing something to you." Outstanding sequences include Snoopy's sudden incarceration by an overly eager child, thrilled to own "a sheepdog and a parrot." The Sherman Brothers, who offer some of their best non-Disney tunes here, write a Mary Poppins–like nonsense word song for the girl, who cheerfully sings about friendship while inadvertently abusing the poor dog. The sobbing farewell party for Snoopy is simply hilarious, and the little character bits between Snoopy and Woodstock, in pantomime, are a joy. Director Bill Melendez again vocalizes for Snoopy (and Woodstock as well), and his steady stream of yelps, guffaws, and whines truly make the beagle come to life. The child performances for the rest of the cast are genuine and warm (coproducer Lee Mendelson's daughter Linda has a small role as Frieda). In some ways more ambitious, and less complex, than *Boy Named Charlie Brown*, *Snoopy, Come Home* is a rousing movie with a universal theme—the longing for absent friends. (AL)

***Additional Credits:*** Screenplay: Charles M. Schulz. Music/lyrics: Richard M. Sherman, Robert B. Sherman. Music arranger: Donald Ralke. Animators: Don Lusk, Phil Roman, Rod Scribner, Bill Littlejohn, Rudy Zamora, Sam Jaimes, Bob Carlson, Jim Pabian, Bob Matz, Al Pabian, Hank Smith. Uncredited animator: Emery Hawkins. Backgrounds: Ed Levitt, Bernard Gruver, Evert Brown, Frank Smith, Dean Spille, Ellie Bogardus, Al Shean, Jacques Vasseu, Ruth Kissane.

**The Snow Queen** (11/20/59) Universal (Russian). 70 mins. Director: Lev Atamanov. Live-action director: Phil Patton. Producer: Robert Farver. Cast: Art Linkletter, Tammy Marihugh, Jennie Lynn, Billy Booth, Rickey Busch. Voices: Sandra Dee (Gerda), Tommy Kirk (Kay), Patty McCormack (Angel), Louise Arthur (Snow Queen), Paul Frees (Ol' Dreamy, The Raven), June Foray (Henretta, Eskimo Woman), Joyce Terry (Princess), Richard Beals (Prince), Lillian Buyeff (Granny), Vladimir Gribkov (Ole Lukoje), Sergei Martinson (Karraks).

©Universal-International

***Consumer Tips:*** ☆☆☆ MPAA Rating: Unrated. Based on the Hans Christian Andersen story.

***Story:*** The evil snow queen kidnaps a boy. His sister sets out to find him, along the way encountering a series of witches, talking animals, and a princess who help her.

***Comments:*** Russia's state controlled Soyuzmultfilm Studios had long been a prolific producer of quality fairy tale adaptations. Veteran director Lev Atamov helmed this particular entry, based on the Hans Christian Andersen tale. Young Kay has his heart chilled by the snow queen, who steals him away to her icy wonderland, and childhood sweetheart Gerda adventures to find him. The film soon becomes episodic, as Gerda has picturesque encounters with a sorceress, a prince and princess, a band of thieves, and numerous talking animals. These sequences are smartly executed, with some particularly excellent rubber-hose style animation of the thieves.

The character designs are charming, and the effects sequences well-handled. However, the unfortunate inclusion of a narrator character, Ol' Dreamy, detracts from the flow of the story. The interruptions by this character, visually reminiscent of Jiminy Cricket, are basically redundant, perhaps indicative of the film's original target audience, Russian children, explaining details that could easily be inferred. Still, the basic story works, despite a deus ex machina ending.

The English dub featured teen stars Tommy Kirk and Sandra Dee as Kay and Gerda, as well as voice pros like Paul Frees and June Foray, plus Frees' wife at the time, Joy Terry; Dave Fleischer was credited as "technical supervisor" for the English version (his only animated feature credit outside of the Fleischer's own output). Though the vocal performances are generally fine, the attempt to precisely match the lip sync leads to some odd line deliveries. When originally released theatrically in the states, *The Snow Queen* was accompanied by a live-action prologue featuring Art Linkletter and a group of kids, an extension of the "Kids Say the Darndest Things" segments of Linkletter's television series.

*The Snow Queen* is a bit choppy in parts, and sentimentality is favored over humor in adapting the classic fairy tale. Though older children may be bored, the movie is well-suited to younger audiences, as well as internationally minded film buffs. (AL)

***Additional Credits:*** Story: Lev Atamanov, Nikolai Erdman. Based on the story by Hans Christian Andersen. English adaptation/live-action story: Alan Lipscott, Bob Fisher. Music: Frank Skinner, Joseph Gershenson. Songs: Diane Lampert, Richard Loring.

**Snow White and the Seven Dwarfs** (12/21/37) Walt Disney Pictures. 83 mins. Director: David Hand. Voices: Adriana Caselotti (Snow White), Harry Stockwell (Prince), Lucille LaVerne (Queen, Witch), Scotty Mattraw (Bashful), Roy Atwell (Doc), Pinto Colvig (Grumpy, Sleepy), Otis Harlan (Happy), Billy Gilbert (Sneezy), Moroni Olson (Magic Mirror), Stuart Buchanan (Huntsman).

**Consumer Tips:** ☆☆☆☆ MPAA Rating: Unrated. A landmark animated film. This version was adapted from the fairy tale told in the Brothers Grimm compilation work (1812–15).

**Story:** A wicked queen despises young Snow White for her youth and beauty, especially after a handsome prince takes notice of the girl. When the Magic Mirror confirms Snow White as the fairest in the land, the queen decides to have her killed. The huntsman assigned to the job allows Snow White to flee deep into the woods. Seven kindly dwarfs take her in. The queen discovers that Snow White still lives and disguises herself as a hideous crone selling lovely (but poisoned) apples. Snow White bites one and appears to instantly die. The furious dwarfs chase the queen, who falls off a cliff to her death. As they grieve Snow White's death, the prince happens by and gives her a farewell kiss. The kiss revives her, and they live happily ever after.

**Comments:** *Snow White* is one of the most significant animated films ever made and certainly among the most famous. It is a major innovation containing countless other innovations, and can be considered the very definition of the Disney style: realism, tight storytelling, strong personality animation, and technical creativity. All of these factors combine in a way that emotionally involves an audience and makes them feel as if they have entered a special world where ink and paint have been transformed into flesh and blood. Had *Snow White* never been made, it is fair to say that the development of American animation may have taken a different course.

None of it was easy. Since Disney had never attempted a full-length feature, nearly everything was learned on the wing. One of the earliest mistakes was underestimating the cost of the film. After announcing the project to his staff in 1934, Disney figured production costs based on what it might cost to make nine or ten animated shorts. What Disney did not count on was expanding his staff to 750 artists or his own perfectionism and insistence on the best, most detailed animation possible. A budget of $250,000 ballooned into a final cost of $1,480,000. Partway through production the studio simply ran out of funds and had to stage a partial showing of completed footage for the Bank of America in order to obtain enough money to complete *Snow White*.

It was well worth it. At Disney's command was one of the greatest animation teams ever to convene in one studio. All of Disney's future "Nine Old Men" put their talents into this film, most of them working under men who were already legends. Norm Ferguson, Fred Moore, Art Babbitt, and Vladimir (Bill) Tytla were already established animators, and Disney also hired

©Walt Disney Productions

stars such as James Culhane and Grim Natwick to augment the talent already on hand. Natwick was the man who created and animated Betty Boop for the rival Fleischer studio, and Disney especially wanted Natwick for his proficiency with the female form.

For several years preceding *Snow White* Disney had established training classes, lectures, and intensive study of animated drawing and action at the studio. Technical advances such as the multiplane camera and full-spectrum Technicolor had been tested out in animated shorts and were now at the service of *Snow White.* Even with such weapons, the film was an enormous gamble; other movie studios called the expensive film "Disney's folly" and doubted that any audience would sit through a 90-minute cartoon.

In the end Disney won perhaps his greatest triumph, but it was proportional to the intensive work that went into *Snow White.* The film featured the most detailed animation ever attempted, right down to the props and backgrounds. Art director and illustrator Gustaf Tenggren gave *Snow White* a classic storybook feel, and the layouts still look amazing today. Story was more important than ever, and one of the most vital decisions made was to give each dwarf a personality; this is not indicated in the original fairy tale. Some 60 different dwarfs were considered before final selections were made. It also took some time before Snow White herself took form: animator Grim Natwick and his supervising ani-

mator Hamilton Luske warred bitterly over the heroine. Natwick, used to the more sensual style at Fleischer, designed a young girl on the brink of sexual awakening and very much aware of it. Luske wanted a sweet little innocent and was eventually backed by Disney.

That put more pressure on animators Bill Tytla and Fred Moore to make the dwarfs more complex, and they succeeded admirably. Tytla's Grumpy is one of the most lifelike and complex animated characters ever portrayed on the screen. A young animator named Frank Thomas made his reputation by drawing the scene where the dwarfs mourn Snow White; countless viewers have wept along with them. Not all the dwarfs share the same amount of screen time and dialogue, but they clearly have distinct personalities, postures, and mannerisms that enrich the film. Since the dwarfs' relationship with Snow White is truly the emotional core of the film, this was especially important.

Walt Disney virtually lived at the studio during production, writing, editing, making suggestions, and revising on the fly. One of the most difficult decisions he made was to cut out two sequences that had been virtually completed. In one of them the dwarfs build Snow White a bed. In the other they sing a song called "There's Music in Your Soup." Walt felt that the scenes slowed the action down too much. There was already a sequence where Snow White has the dwarfs wash for dinner, and another scene where the dwarfs dance with

©Walt Disney Productions

Snow White to "The Dwarfs Yodel Song." These scenes adequately performed the function of bonding the dwarfs with Snow White, so Disney brought the hatchet down. Novice animator Ward Kimball, who animated both deleted scenes, was crushed. So was Roy Disney when he considered what those scenes had already cost. Still, it was the right thing to do in order to make a tighter film.

Walt Disney knew that *Snow White* would be a musical, but at nearly 90 minutes it was difficult to know how many musical numbers should be included. Twenty-four songs were written for the film, and eight of those were actually used. Frank Churchill, Larry Morey, Paul J. Smith, and Leigh Harline all contributed, and their work is a fine compliment to the overall story. The cheerful tune "Whistle While You Work" and the jaunty march "Heigh Ho" became popular hits, as did the wistful "Someday My Prince Will Come." The latter is still used as one of Disney's signature tunes.

It is impossible to write a brief summary of all the unforgettable moments in *Snow White* or the wizardry behind them. Every emotion possible is touched upon in the animated acting, and each time it unerringly resonates in the viewer. Witness Grumpy's gradual realization that Snow White has completely broken down his cantankerous resistance to her. The exact moment that Grumpy is forced to admit he has truly come to care for the girl is visible in his expression, posture, and inner thoughts; not a word of dialogue is needed. Consider the terrifying transformation of the queen into a hideous crone via the talents of Norm Ferguson: This brief but powerful scene, dripping with dark menace, is one of animation's unequalled moments of horror.

*Snow White and the Seven Dwarfs* contains countless laughs, joys, and tears, and its impact remains just as powerful nearly 70 years after it was made. The movie is an emotional and artistic experience rarely equaled in animation's history, and its many accolades are well deserved. "Disney's folly," as it turned out, launched the animated feature as a viable form of American cinema. *Snow White* was a gamble that paid off not only for Walt Disney but also for generations of animation fans and moviegoers who had always yearned to experience a wonderful fairy tale come to life. (MG)

***Additional Credits:*** Story: Ted Sears, Otto Englander, Earl Hurd, Dorothy Ann Blank, Richard Credon, Merrill De Maris,

Dick Rickard, Webb Smith. Based on the story by the Brothers Grimm. Sequence directors: Perce Pearce, William Cottrell, Wilfred Jackson, Larry Morey, Ben Sharpsteen. Music: Frank Churchill, Leigh Harline, Paul Smith. Song: Frank Churchill, Larry Morey. Supervising animators: Hamilton Luske, Vladimir Tytla, Fred Moore, Norman Ferguson. Animators: Frank Thomas, Dick Lundy, Arthur Babbitt, Eric Larson, Milton Kahl, Robert Stokes, James Algar, Al Eugster, Cy Young, Joshua Meador, Ugo D Orsi, George Rowley, Les Clark, Fred Spencer, Bill Roberts, Bernard Garbutt, Grim Natwick, Jack Campbell, Marvin Woodward, James Culhane, Stan Quackenbush, Ward Kimball, Wolfgang Reitherman, Robert Martsch. Uncredited animators: Josh Meador, Cy Young. Art directors: Charles Phillipi, Hugh Hennesy, Terell Stapp, McLaren Stewart, Harold Miles, Tom Codrick, Gustaf Tenggren, Kenneth Anderson, Kendall O'Connor, Hazel Sewell. Character designers: Albert Hurter, Joe Grant. Background artists: Samuel Armstrong, Mique Nelson, Merle Cox, Claude Coats, Phil Dike, Ray Lockrem, Maurice Noble. Inspirational Sketches: Ferdinand Huszti Horvath, Gustaf Tenggren.

**Song of the South** (11/2/46) Walt Disney Pictures. 94 mins. Cartoon director: Wilfred Jackson. Live-action director: Harve Foster. Associate producer: Perce Pierce. Voices: Johnny Lee (Brer Rabbit), James Baskett (Brer Fox), Nicodemus Stewart (Brer Bear).

***Consumer Tips:*** ☆☆ Adapted from *Uncle Remus: His Songs and Sayings* (1850) by Joel Chandler Harris.

***Story:*** Poor little Johnny! Not only is he without a last name, his parents are splitting up and he must now live

©Walt Disney Productions

with mom and grandma on the latter's Southern plantation. Johnny's despair is short-lived, however, when he meets Uncle Remus, the sage old storyteller of the plantation hands. Life gets even better when Johnny becomes acquainted with sweet little Ginny. Uncle Remus teaches Johnny life's lessons through the (animated) tales of Brer Rabbit and ultimately saves the boy's life just in time for dad's return and the happy finale.

**Comments:** Walt Disney felt that the future of his studio lay increasingly with live-action films, and *Song of the South* is an important milepost in Disney's history. This was Disney's first serious attempt at combining animation and live action since his early *Alice Comedies.* Harris had written over 180 short tales featuring Brer Rabbit, Brer Fox, Brer Bear, and many other supporting Brers. Three of the most popular tales were adapted to fill out the animated portions of the movie, and they are much more interesting than anything that goes on in live action. Credit for this goes to story man Bill Peet, whose vivid concept drawings and storyboards helped bring Remus's tales to life.

Milt Kahl was highly enthusiastic about his animation of Brer Rabbit (a task he shared with Ollie Johnston), and rightfully so. The doughty rabbit must triumph over his enemies using his smarts, and the task is a tough one. Brer Fox, a manic schemer, wants to have Brer Rabbit for dinner, while the phlegmatic but brutal Brer Bear simply wants to knock his head off. In the hands of Kahl and Johnston, Brer Rabbit is a fantastic actor. All three vignettes feature Brer Rabbit captured and inches from death before brains conquer brawn; as he hatches his plots his desperate expressions clearly show that even *he* is not sure he'll get out alive. A split second later the rabbit is faking bravado or amusement with such conviction that Brer Fox and Bear are easily suckered by his trickery. It might have been interesting had Disney initiated a series of shorts starring these wonderful characters—after all, he could have made up to 180 of them.

The live action and animation, when it occurs, is seamlessly fused and is still impressive today; one easily senses that the film was technically ahead of its time, and audiences in 1946 must have been deeply impressed. When Uncle Remus enters his imaginary world singing "Zippity-Doo-Dah" and interacts with animated butterflies, moles, possums, and "Mr. Blue-

bird on My Shoulder," the effects are both "nach'ral" and "satisfactual" indeed.

*Song of the South* became a major public relations headache for Disney. The original script was written by Southern novelist Dalton Reymond but his efforts were considered too racially offensive. Maurice Rapf was hired on to coauthor and keep Reymond in check, but the two quarreled and Rapf wound up working on *Cinderella.* Morton Grant was the next coauthor and he finished the script with Reymond. No amount of massaging could disguise the film's stereotypical underpinnings, however, and *Song of the South* came under attack by the NAACP, *Ebony* magazine, the National Negro Congress, and black leaders such as Adam Clayton Powell Jr. The attacks were largely leveled at the live-action sequences; everyone seemed to like the Brer Rabbit vignettes just fine.

For the record:

- James Baskett, who portrayed Uncle Remus, is also remembered as a regular on the radio series *Amos 'n' Andy.* He did win an honorary Oscar in 1948 for his engaging portrayal of Uncle Remus. He died a few months later.
- *Song of the South* was produced for $2 million and made $500,000 more than its cost.
- De tar baby, he say nothin', and Brer Fox, he lay low: The film has not been shown in public since 1986 and to date has never been released to video or DVD in its entirety (although avid collectors were able to purchase Japanese laserdiscs of the film).
- The animated segments in *Song of the South* comprise 25 minutes of the film's 94-minute running time. (MG)

**Additional Credits:** Screenplay: Dalton Reymond, Morton Grant, Maurice Rapf. Story: Dalton Reymond. Based on *The Tales of Uncle Remus* by Joel Chandler Harris. Cartoon story: William Peet, Ralph Wright, George Stallings. Musical director: Charles Wolcott. Cartoon Score: Paul J. Smith. Songs: Ray Gilbert, Sam Coslow, Allie Wrubel, Arthur Johnson, Johnny Lange, Hy Heath, Eliot Daniel, Robert McGimsey, Foster Carling. Directing animators: Milt Kahl, Eric Larson, Oliver M. Johnston Jr., Les Clark, Marc Davis, John Lounsbery. Animators: Don Lusk, Tom Massey, Murray McClellan, Jack Campbell, Hal King, Harvey Toombs, Ken O'Brien, Al Coe, Hal Ambro, Cliff

Nordberg, Rudy Larriva. Effects animators: Joshu Meador, George Rowley. Art directors: Kenneth Anderson, Charles Philippi, Hugh Hennesy, Harold Doughty, Philip Barber. Background/color stylists: Claude Coats, Mary Blair. Background artists: Ralph Hulett, Brice Mack, Ray Huffine, Edgar Starr, Albert Dempster. Special photographic processes: Ub Iwerks.

**South Park: Bigger, Longer and Uncut** (6/30/99) Paramount/Warner Bros. 80 mins. Director: Trey Parker. Producers: Trey Parker, Matt Stone. Voices: Trey Parker (Stan Marsh, Eric Cartman, Mr. Garrison, Mr. Hat, Officer Barbrady), Matt Stone (Kyle Broflovski, Kenny McCormick, Pip, Jesus, Jimbo), Mary Kay Bergman (Mrs. Cartman, Sheila Broflovski, Sharon Marsh, Mrs. McCormick, Wendy Testaburger, Principal Victoria, Mole Child, Female Bodypart), Isaac Hayes (Chef), George Clooney (Dr. Gouache), Brent Spiner (Conan O'Brien), Minnie Driver (Brooke Shields), Dave Foley (the Baldwin Brothers), Eric Idle (Dr. Vosknocker), Stewart Copeland (American Soldier #1), Mike Judge (Kenny's Goodbye).

©Paramount Pictures

**Consumer Tips:** ☆☆☆ MPAA Rating: R. Based on the Comedy Central television show. Adults only.

**Story:** Third graders Stan, Kyle, Cartman, and Kenny attend the R-rated movie version of television favorites Terrance and Philip (in *Asses of Fire*). The bad language gleamed from the movie causes parents of the South Park community to rally and "Blame Canada."

**Comments:** As student filmmakers at the University of Colorado, Trey Parker and Matt Stone outraged their teachers and delighted their friends with a short, crudely made, animated spoof of Christmas television specials. The film, *Frosty vs. Santa Claus* (1994), became an underground hit, and caught the eye of Brian Graden, an executive at Fox.

Graden commissioned Parker and Stone for $2,000 to make another short film that he could send to his friends at Christmastime, as a sort of video Christmas card. That film, *The Spirit of Christmas* (1995), was widely bootlegged and became a cause célèbre. It led to a television series deal with Comedy Central, and that series became *South Park*. The small screen popularity of *South Park* led Comedy Central partners, Paramount Pictures and Warner Bros., to coproduce a big screen version. Thus, *South Park: Bigger, Larger and Uncut* was born.

The feature-length version is just as funny and fresh as any of the 22-minute television episodes. The film never feels forced, and the crudely animated figures never get tiresome to watch. The original short films used crude stop-motion animation of paper cut-outs, while the subsequent television series and feature film were created on the computer.

The film skewers pop culture, politics, patriotism, Disney films, gays, Saddam Hussein, and small-town America. It's also a musical, and the songs by Trey Parker and Marc Shaiman have great melodies and hilarious lyrics. The song "Blame Canada" was nominated for an Oscar for Best Song.

The film grossed $52 million in theatrical release—not bad for an R-rated animated comedy with a social message. Matt Stone, in the film production notes, sums it up this way: "You could say *South Park: Bigger, Longer and Uncut* is about the struggle for basic, inalienable freedoms in the face of oppression, but if you did, you'd sound like a jerk." (JB)

**Additional Credits:** Executive producers: Scott Rudin, Adam Schroeder. Animation producer: Frank C. Agnone II. Coproducers: Anne Garefino, Deborah Liebling. Associate producer: Mark Roybal. Line producer: Gina Shay. Screenplay: Trey Parker, Matt Stone, Pam Brady. Music: James Hetfield. Songs: Trey Parker, Bobby Guy, Ernie Lake, Marc Shairman. Director of animation: Eric Stough. Supervising animators: Martin Cendrada, Toni Nugnes. Animators: Fred Baxter, John Fountain, Neil Ishimine, Charles Keagle, Jason A. Lopez, Scott Oberholtzer, Eric Oliver, Jim Ovelmen, Lorelei Pepi, Ryan Quincy,

Jack Shih, Michael Trull, August Wartenberg, Holly Wenger, Heather R. Wilbur, Amy Winfrey, Dustin Woehrmann. Additional animators: Jennifer M. Allen, Alfonso Alpuerto, Andrew Arett, Chris "Crispy" Brion, Matt Brown, Michelle Burry, Lisa Libuha, Sabrina Mar, Peter M. Merryman, Aglaia Mortcheva, Nate Pacheco, Suzanne Smith, Steve Blackman, Tom Dillon, Sam Gebhardt, Keith Jenson, Kirby Miller.

**Space Adventure Cobra** (8/20/95) Tara Releasing. 109 mins. Director: Osamu Dezaki. Producers: Yutaka Fujioka, Tetsuo Katayama. Voices: Dan Woren (Cobra), Jeff Winkless (Crystal Boy), Kirk Thornton (Professor Topolov), Jane Alan (Catherine), Catherine Battistone (Sandra), Barbara Goodson (Jane), Wendee Lee (Dominique).

©Buichi Terasawa / TMS

*Consumer Tips:* ☆☆ MPAA Rating: Unrated. SF adventure. Based on the manga by Buichi Terasawa.

*Story:* A good-guy space pirate helps three beautiful sisters race the sinister Space Mafia Guild to find the most powerful weapon in the galaxy. Cobra, a charismatically roguish ladies' man, is actually a retired space pirate who spends his time helping beautiful damsels in distress. Bounty hunter Jane Flower has the entire Space Mafia Guild, led by Cobra's old enemy Crystal Boy, after her and her two sisters because they hold the key to a weapon that can destroy the galaxy.

*Comments:* *Space Adventure: Cobra* (the Japanese title has a colon) began as a mildly risqué 1978 SF comedy-adventure manga; roughly like a male Barbarella updating Japan's Lupin III's exploits as the galaxy's greatest thief and would-be ladies' man. Cobra was the most successful space pirate in the Seventh Galaxy; a swashbuckling rogue who never harmed his victims. But the all-powerful Space Mafia Guild did not want competition. Cobra could not fight the whole Guild, so he faked his death, changed his face (to that of France's macho movie star Jean-Paul Belmondo), and retired to become a wealthy galactic tourist; the sort of good-natured wise guy who is a swinger at the space disco and is impossible to take seriously.

*Space Adventure Cobra*, released July 3, 1982, was a condensed adaptation of the novel in the first 12 issues of Terasawa's comic book. The feature was followed by a 31-episode television series, October 1982 through May 1983, which retold the same story in its first 12 episodes in much greater detail. The movie was very popular upon its release, but it has dated badly thanks to its 1970s-style disco music and heavy influences from mildly risqué SF movies of the period such as *Barbarella* and the first *Lupin III* theatrical feature (also by Tokyo Movie Shinsha). There are also too many tributes to the first *Star Wars* movie. Its publicity heavily promised "hyper-dimensional multiplane animation," which gave it 3-D depth, but the animation looks much too limited by today's standards. It makes no pretense at presenting a serious drama, but its constant inconsistencies such as the indiscriminate mixing of the terms "planet," "star," "galaxy," and "nebula" for each other becomes irritating. The story is variously described as set in the 23rd, 24th, or 25th century, but Cobra's tomb from his faked death two years previously is dated 2005–2037. *Space Adventure Cobra* is still good fun, but it seems today to be an even lighter space opera intended for a younger audience. (FP)

*Additional Credits:* Screenplay: Buichi Terasawa, Hauya Yamazaki. Music: Osamu Shoji. English language version screenplay: Michael Charles Hill. English Language voice direction: Carl Macek. Character designer: Shichirô Kobayashi. Animation Director: Akio Sugino. Animators: Yukari Kobayashi, Hayao Miyazaki, Kôji Morimoto, Setsuko Shibuichi.

**Space Jam** (11/15/96) Warner Bros. 87 mins. Live-action director: Joe Pytka. Animation directors: Bruce

W. Smith, Tony Cervone. Producers: Daniel Goldberg, Steven Paul Leiva, Joe Medjuck, Ivan Reitman. Cast: Michael Jordan (Himself), Wayne Knight (Stan Podolak), Theresa Randle (Juanita Jordan), Charles Barkley (Himself), Muggsy Bogues (Himself), Shawn Bradley (Himself), Patrick Ewing (Himself), Larry Johnson (Himself), Bill Murray (Himself). Voices: Billy West (Bugs Bunny, Elmer Fudd), Dee Bradley Baker (Daffy Duck, Tasmanian Devil, Bull), Danny DeVito (Swack Hammer), Bob Bergen (Porky Pig, Tweety, Bertie, Hubie, Marvin the Martian), Bill Farmer (Sylvester, Yosemite Sam, Foghorn Leghorn), June Foray (Granny), Maurice LaMarche (Pepe LePew), Kath Soucie (Lola Bunny).

©Warner Bros.

**Consumer Tips:** ☆☆½ MPAA Rating: PG for profanity. Comedy-adventure.

**Story:** Real-life sports hero Michael Jordan stars as himself as he comes to the rescue of Warner Bros. cartoon characters (Bugs Bunny, Daffy Duck, etc.) who must win a life-or-death basketball game against alien life forms.

**Comments:** Michael Jordan and Bugs Bunny first appeared together in a couple of Nike television commercials, *Hare-O-Space Jordan* and *Hare Jordan*. The director, Joe Pitka, thought the concept could be expanded to feature length. *Space Jam* began development in the fall of 1994. Originally meant to be animated at Warner Classic Animation, executive producer Ivan Reitman instead decided to use his own company, Northern Lights, to manage the project and hire his own crew, helmed by Jerry Rees and Steve Leiva.

When production lagged behind schedule, Ron Tippe from Warner Feature Animation became the third producer. The *Space Jam* crew was augmented with artists from Warners' Glendale unit, which was languishing while story problems were being ironed out on *Quest for Camelot*. Several out-of-town studios helped: Uli Meyer, Premiere, Stardust and Warner Feature Animation in London, Character Builders in Cleveland, Heart of Texas in Austin, Calibash in Illinois, Canuck Productions in Canada, High Horse (Dale Baer) in Palmdale, California, as well as artists from DreamWorks. About 500 animation artists had less than a year to complete the film in time for a locked-down release date of November 11, 1996. The overtime necessary to meet the deadline escalated the budget up to $110 million ($16 million went to Michael Jordan). Ivan Reitman increased the production workload by adding and changing scenes.

A rule of thumb was that the Looney Tunes could not be taller than Michael Jordan, which meant the Crusher and Gossamer had a size reduction. Only the Monstars could be taller than Jordan. Bugs Bunny was used as a yardstick in size relation to the other Looney Tunes; his official height was three feet, three inches. The Tune Squad had 16 players, two cheerleaders, and four runners-up. A total of 83 Looney Tunes were featured in the film; 98 animated characters in all. Most of the Looney Tunes appeared in the bleachers during the basketball game. Warner Legal prevented the use of the Gremlin, Private Snafu, the Clampett Cats, and characters that resembled celebrities.

Clashing with the Looney Tunes' design, the aliens looked more like creatures from a Don Bluth movie, with Swackhammer similar to Gnorga from *A Troll in Central Park*: puffy lips and jowls, beady eyes, skin blotches, and fat. Jack Palance was Swackhammer's original voice; Danny DeVito replaced him for the same reason Bill Murray is in the picture: he's friends with the producer.

When the Looney Tunes assemble in the Town Hall, the paintings display earlier versions of the characters. An idea was proposed to have caricatures or real photos of the classic Looney Tunes directors on the wall, but Reitman refused. He also removed a statue of Leon Schlesinger from the front of the building; all that remains is a platform that says "Leon Schlesinger Plaza."

*Space Jam* introduced Lola Bunny as the female counterpart to Bugs. She later appeared juniorized in the 2003 television series, *Baby Looney Tunes*.

In its opening weekend in the United States, *Space Jam* grossed a respectable $27.5 million on 2,650 screens, aided by a sizable publicity campaign atypical of Warner Bros. The film would reach a U.S. gross of $90.4 million by March 23, 1997. But, since the film didn't gross over $100 million and *Mars Attacks!* was a box-office disaster, Ted Turner ordered staff cutbacks throughout the entire corporation, including Warner TV Animation. New Looney Tunes shorts by Chuck Jones's unit also ceased production. However, worldwide box office reached $230 million, with another $209 million in video sales, according to the June 22, 1998, *Fortune* magazine.

One wonders if Warner Bros. execs were familiar with their own characters. To them, "Looney Tunes Land" is at the end of a tunnel deep underground. In actuality, Bugs could easily outwit the Monstars without the aid of Michael Jordan. It would be Daffy, not Bugs, who would beg for Jordan's help. Bill Murray's presence does little for the film; his character is more annoying than funny. The film's snappy character and effects animation are, sadly, undermined by a weak concept and a weaker script.

Bugs and friends made their next theatrical appearance in *Looney Tunes: Back in Action* in 2003, the same year Michael Jordan retired from basketball for good. (WRM)

**Additional Credits:** Executive producers: David Falk, Ken Ross. Coproducers: Sheldon Kahn, Curtis Polk, Gordon Webb. Animation producers: Dennis Edwards, Jerry Rees, Richard Todd Sullivan. Screenplay: Leonardo Benvenuti, Timothy Harris, Steve Rudnick, Herschel Weingrod. Music: James Newton Howard. Songs: Samuel J. Barnes, Iva Davies, Jay-Z, R. Kelly, Method Man, Jean Claude Olivier, Busta Rhymes, Seal, Diane Warren. Supervising animators: Neil Boyle, Chuck Gammage, Uli Meyer, Jeff Siergey, Dave Spafford, Rob Stevenhagen, Bruce Woodside. Lead animators: Dino Athanoussia, Roberto Casale, Paul Chung, Shane Doyle, Gary, Martin Fuller, Dean Roberts, Dan Root, Brian Smith. Animators: Margot Allen, Claire Armstrong, Stephen Baker, Richard Baneham, Dave Boudreau, Dan Boulos, Spike Brandt, Mark Broecking, Adam Burke, Alberto Campos, Ronaldo Canfora, Claire Cantlie, Jennifer Cardon, Tod Carter, Luc Chamberland, Michael Chavez, Stan Chiu, Jesse Cosio, Alain Costa, Denis Couchon, Greg Court, James Davis, Murray Debus, Jeff Etter, Stuart Evans, Jerry Forder, Stephan Franck, Morgan Ginsberg, Scott Glynn, Heidi Guedel, Chris Hauge, Magnus Hjerpe, Richard Jack, Leon Joosen, Hon-Sik Kim, Sean Leaning, Paul Lee, Holger Leihe, Tom Lock, Lee McCaulla, Kevin McDonagh, Tom McGrath, Quentin Miles, Ken Morrissey, Jacques Muller, Mike Nguyen, Michael S. Nickelson, Cynthia Overman, Clive Pallant, Wendy Parkin, John Perkins, Scott T. Petersen, Marco Piersma, Jan Pindal, Tom Riggin, Mitch Rose, Michael Schlingmann, Andrew Shortt, Andrea Simonti, Sharon Smith, Kevin Spruce, Neal Sternecky, Paul A. Stone, Mike Swindall, Vladimir Todorov, Daniela Topham, Tony Tulipano, John Tynan, Jan Van Buyten, Jim VanderKeyl, Darren Vandenburg, Duncan Varley, Andreas Von Andrian, Daniel Wagner, Simon Ward-Horner, Dave Wasson, J. C. Wegman, Andreas Wesell-Therhorn, Pete Western, Larry D. Whittaker Jr., Mark Williams, John D. Williamson, Vincent Woodcock, Chris York, Shane Zalvin.

**Spirit: Stallion of the Cimarron** (5/24/02) DreamWorks. 83 mins. Directors: Kelly Asbury, Lorna Cook. Producers: Jeffery Katzenberg, Mireille Soria. Voices: Matt Damon (Spirit), Daniel Studi (Little Creek), James Cromwell (The Colonel), Chopper Bernet (Sgt. Adams), Jeff LeBeau (Murphy, Railroad Foreman), John Rubano (Soldier), Richard McGonagle (Bill), Matthew Levin (Joe), Adam Paul (Pete), Robert Cait (Jake), Charles Napier (Roy), Meredith Wells (Little Indian Girl), Zahn McClarnon (Little Creek's Friend, ADR Voice), Michael Horse (Little Creek's Friend, ADR Voice), Don Fullilove (Train Pull Foreman, ADR Voice).

**Consumer Tips:** ☆☆☆ MPAA Rating: G. Nominated for Academy Award—Best Animated Feature.

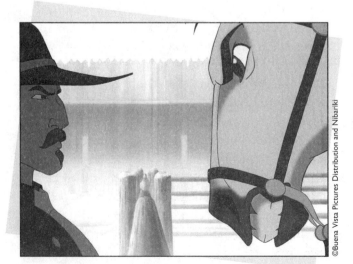

**Story:** Free, untamed stallion leaves its herd and is captured by soldiers, is befriended by American natives, escapes forest fires, rides wild rivers, and makes spectacular jumps in an effort to return to its homeland with its lady love.

**Comments:** While *Spirit: Stallion of the Cimarron* is one of the few animated features to use horses as the principal characters (when used at all, they're usually in bit parts, as in *Sleeping Beauty* or *Beauty and the Beast*) and is the first animated Western since *The Man From Button Willow*, it doesn't take a naysayer to spot certain story problems. The plot, such as it is, depicts events in the life of the titular mustang (actually unnamed until the last few minutes in the film), as told by the horse himself through first person narration. Spirit is raised since his birth as part of a sizable herd of wild horses living in an unspecified region of the American West. Spirit grows up to lead the herd, but wanders off to explore a campsite one night, and after a long chase is captured, having first steered his capturers away from his mother and herd. Brought to a U.S. cavalry fort, the horse refuses to submit, leading the hard-nosed colonel to submit him to starvation. Still unbroken, the horse manages to escape, with a friendly Indian prisoner named Little Creek on his back. Spirit befriends Little Creek's mare, Rain, but still refuses to allow anyone to ride him, even the patient Indian. Further conflict arises when the cavalry clears out the Indian village to make way for the railroad and once again pursues the horse.

The narration, by Matt Damon, is kept to a minimum, as the horses communicate and display emotion through whinnies and through the expressive character animation. Eyebrows and eyelashes, not features normally associated with the equine set, are grafted on, the former to help give the horses personality and the latter to do the same while also signifying which horses are female. The use of the horse's perspective and minimal anthropomorphization are among the film's strengths. The plot is oddly slight, perhaps due to the minute principal cast and minimal dialogue, with the major conflict being quite broad and simple: the horse against those who seek to tame him. Spirit's rapid gallops, either free in the wild plains or while attempting to evade capture or peril, seem to almost replace the narrative. In this way, it is like a silent film, using visuals instead of words. Considering how many recent features suffer from too much plot, however, this benefits the film most of the time.

Bryan Adams's songs, presumably intended to complement the animation in expressing the character's emotions, are actually more distracting than anything else—particularly one cacophonous ditty, while the cavalrymen attempt to ride Spirit, called "Get Off of My Back." The score, too, by the usually reliable Hans Zimmer, has a would-be majestic quality to it that succeeds on occasion but too often blares against the ears with its piercing percussion. The backgrounds in several scenes have a murky quality to them, the supporting horses and humans often seem to fade into the backgrounds themselves, often seeming rather undistinguishable, and there was something oddly jarring about the wing movements of an eagle. The effects animation almost outshines the character work in some scenes, particularly the rustling of grass during Spirit's birth scene, and the use of shadows.

Apart from the music, the film is quiet and unassuming in many ways, which is probably its strongest point, and an antidote to the frenetically paced, overly plotted, action-packed summer blockbusters. Amongst the artists, it's worth noting that background artist Paul Shardlow also worked on *Watership Down* and the "Den" sequence of *Heavy Metal*, while James Baxter is a former Disney animator who supervised Belle in *Beauty and the Beast* and Rafiki in *The Lion King*. Alex Williams is another Disney alum and also the son of famed animator and *Who Framed Roger Rabbit* animation director Richrad Williams, and CGI animators Angie Glocka and Owen Klatte began in stop motion, working on the 1980s *Gumby* revival and Tim Burton's *The Nightmare Before Christmas*. (AL)

**Additional Credits:** Screenplay: John Fusco. Additional story: Henry Mayo, Tom Sito. Music: Hans Zimmer, Steve Jablonsky. Songs: Bryan Adams. Animation supervisor: Kristoff Serrand. Senior supervising animator: James Baxter. Supervising animators: Steve Horrocks, Jakob Hjort Jensen, Dan Wagner, Bruce Ferriz, Pres Antonio Romanillos, William Salazar, Fabio Lignini, Sylvain Deboissy, Lionel Gallat, Erik C. Schmidt, Alex Williams, Phillipe LeBrun, Mary Ann Malcomb, Simon Otto, Patrick Mate. Animators: Cinzia Angelini, Davide Benevenuti, Adam Burke, Kent Culotta, Antony Gray, Cameron Hood, James R. Hull, Bo Johannesson, Dave Kupczyk, Sylvia Muller, Kevin O'Hara, Simon Otto, Mariateresa Scarpone, Dimos Vrysellas, Greg Whittaker, Mark A. Williams, Scott Wright, Kathy Zielinski, Xavier Riffault, David Boudrea, Sergei Kouchnerov, Claire Morrissey, Jane Poole, Jean-Francois Rey, Robert Weaver, Cecile Bender, Arnaud Berthier, Emanuela Cozzi, Cathy Jones, Fabrice Joubert, Richard Sang Uoon Kim, John Hill, Paul Newberry, Luis Grané, Erik Kuska, Bang Wong Lee, Robert Milne, Tom Owens, Paul Jesper, Emil Simeonov. Digital supervisor: Doug Cooper. CG animators: Manuel Almela, Cinzia Angelini, Michelle Cowart, Angie Glocka, Luis Grané, Fabrice Joubert, Owen Klatte, Luci Napier, Christopher Oakley, Jane Poole, Ryan Roberts, Michael Spokas, Mark A. Williams. Production design: Kathy Altieri. Art directors: Luc Desmarchelier, Ronald W. Lukas. Story supervisor: Del Carmen. Story: Sharon Bridgeman, Jurgen Gross, Denise Nagisa Koyama, Larry Leker, Bob Logan, Duncan Marjoribanks, Don Morgan, Jennifer Yuh Nelson, Nassos Vakalis, Simon Wells. Additional story artists: Viki Anderson, Francisco Avalos, Don Hall, Tom Sito.

**Spirited Away** (9/20/02) Walt Disney Studios. 125 mins. Director: Hayao Miyazaki. Producer: Toshio Suzuki. Voices: Daveigh Chase (Chihiro), Suzanne Pleshette (Yubaba, Zeniba), Jason Marsden (Haku), Susan Egan (Lin), David Ogden Stiers (Kamaji), Lauren Holly (Chihiro's Mother), Michael Chiklis (Chihiro's Father), John Ratzenberger (Assistant Manager), Tara Strong (Boh—Baby), Mickie McGowan (Bath House Woman), Jack Angel (Radish Spirit), Bob Bergen (No-Face, The Frog), Rodger Bumpass (Bouncing Heads), Phil Proctor (Frog-Like Chef).

**Consumer Tips:** ☆☆☆☆ MPAA Rating: PG. Fantasy adventure. A young girl and her parents enter what

they think is an abandoned theme park but is actually a bathhouse for Japan's traditional nature spirits and gods.

**Story:** Chihiro, a 10-year-old girl, and her parents are materialistic modern Japanese with no interest in their cultural past. They accidentally wander into an old-fashioned community of Japan's supernatural creatures, dominated by a huge bathhouse managed by the witch Yubaba. When Chihiro's parents are turned into pigs, she must work at the bathhouse in order to stay in the fantasy world long enough to save them.

**Comments:** *Spirited Away* (formally titled *Miyazaki's Spirited Away*), written, designed, and directed by Hayao Miyazaki, was inspired by Miyazaki's realization that modern Japanese children (as represented by his young granddaughters and their friends) cared only about the latest pop culture and had no knowledge of or interest in their cultural past. He made *Spirited Away* to teach them about that past, in a fantasy community of traditional gods and minor demons centered around a bathhouse, which were the communal social centers of 19th-century Japan.

*Spirited Away* (*Sen to Chihiro no Kamikakushi*, which literally translates to "The Spiriting Away of Sen and Chihiro") is a delightful film for all ages. Because Miyazaki designed it to introduce traditional Japanese lifestyles and beliefs to modern children who are unaware of them, it is just as accessible to foreign audiences who are equally unfamiliar with them. It was produced by Miyazaki's Studio Ghibli and released on July 27, 2001. It almost immediately became Japan's highest box-office-earning film ever, and soon became the highest-earning non-American theatrical feature in world history. It also won numerous awards, including the Berlin International Film Festival's Golden Bear Award and the U.S. Academy Award for Best Animated Feature Film. However, its U.S. box-office gross barely reached $10 million. (FP)

**Additional Credits:** Executive producers: Yasuyoshi Tokuma, Takeyoshi Matsushita, Seiichiro Ujiie, Yutaka Narita, Koji Hoshino, Banjiro Uemura, Hironori Aihara, John Lasseter (U.S. release). U.S. production director: Kirk Wise. Producer: Donald W. Ernst. English language adaptation: Cindy Davis Hewitt, Donald H. Hewitt. Translation: Linda Hoaglund, Jim Hubbert. Music: Joe Hisaishi. Songs: Wakako Kaku, Youmi Kimura. Supervising animators: Masashi Ando, Kitaro Kosaka, Megumi Kagawa. Key animators: Takeshi Inamura, Kenichi Yamada, Masaru Matsuse, Hideaki Yoshio, Eiji Yamamori, Katsutoshi Nakamura, Kazuyoshi Onoda, Makiko Suzuki, Mariko Matsuo, Atsushi Tamura, Hiromasa Yonebayashi, Kaori Fujii, Tamami Yamada, Makiko Futaki, Yoshiyuki Momose, Akihiko Yamashita, Nobuyuki Takeuchi, Shogo Furuya, Misuzu Kurata, Atsushi Yamagata, Shigeru Kimishima, Kiroomi Yamakawa, Nobuhiro Osugi, Yuichi Tanaka, Shizue Kaneko, Hideki Hamasu, Hisaki Furukawa, Kenichi Konishi, Masaru Oshiro, Shinya Ohira, Shinji Hashimoto, Hisashi Nakayama, Noboru Takano, Masako Shinohara, Kuniyuki Ishii, Shojuro Yamauchi.

**The SpongeBob SquarePants Movie** (11/19/04) Paramount. 99 mins. Director: Stephen Hillenburg. Producer: Stephen Hillenburg, Julia Pistor. Voices: Tom Kenny (SpongeBob), Bill Fagerbakke (Patrick Star), Clancy Brown (Mr. Krabs), Rodger Bumpass (Squidward), Mr. Lawrence (Plankton), Alec Baldwin (Dennis), David Hasselhoff (Himself), Scarlett Johansson (Mindy), Jeffrey Tambor (King Neptune), Jill Talley (Karen The Computer Wife), Carolyn Lawrence (Sandy), Mary Jo Catlett (Mrs. Puff).

©Paramount Pictures and Viacom International

**Consumer Tips:** ☆☆☆ MPAA Rating: G.

**Story:** When evil Plankton finally hatches a successful plan to lure customers away from the Krusty Krab, SpongeBob and Patrick go on a quest to retrieve the stolen crown of King Neptune. Along the way they face untold perils presented by scary sea monsters, a determined hit man, and a live-action David Hasselhoff.

**Comments:** *SpongeBob*, while continuing the tradition of adapting popular television cartoons for the big screen, is certainly one of the oddest entries in this category. The original series, starring a talking sponge that resembles a cleaning implement more than the actual aquatic counterpart, is cheerfully bizarre in itself. The movie version takes this even further, with moments that alternate between amusing and disturbing. The surprisingly complex plot begins with SpongeBob's excitement and then disappointment over a promotion at his fast-food job, and soon resembles an off-kilter Greek myth, as our hero and pal Patrick undertake a quest to save boss Mr. Krabs from the wrath of King Neptune, an insecure monarch who resembles a Fleischer refugee (boomingly voiced by Jeffrey Tambor). Additional elements include a world-domination plot by Krab's archrival Plankton (voiced by the superb Mr. Lawrence, one of the show's head writers) and a biker hitman (voiced by Alec Baldwin) straight from the Coen brothers' *Raising Arizona*.

While most television-to-film productions attempt to add a certain gloss, *SpongeBob*'s animation is still purely television quality, and rather than worrying about computer shading and intricate, breathtaking backgrounds, director/creator Stephen Hillenburg and crew instead incorporate bits of clay animation, live props, and, most notably, human performers. Indeed, the opening sequence in which a merry pirate crew lustily belts out the theme song, reminiscent of Gilbert and Sullivan, is wonderfully ingratiating. However, there's also a certain amount of jarring John Kricfalusi—esque elements, from loving photography of live-action guest star David Hasselhoff's rotating pectorals and a recurring bloodshot-eyeball motif to mindless displays of huge-eyed rapture by SpongeBob and Patrick.

Actually, the characters' juvenile joy in simple pleasures such as bubbles and costumed peanuts becomes the film's moral, which no doubt resonates with both children and every cartoon/comic-loving adult whose hobby has ever been looked on as infantile. The heavy dialogue is expertly delivered by the original cast and guest stars, highlighted by Tom Kenny's helium vocalization of the star (though Scarlett Johannson, as sweet Mindy the mermaid, sounds too normal and bland in comparison). Inventive sea monster designs and a lengthy encounter with a live-action deep-sea diver are additional highlights, though the recurrent "Goofy Goober" song is frustratingly infectious. Comic buffs should look closely for framed *Krazy Kat* and *Popeye* strips in the background of the ice cream parlor, and the end titles dedicate the film to the memory of the late UPA and Disney designer Jules Engel, Hillenburg's CalArts instructor. Relentlessly silly and strange, and proud of it, *The SpongeBob SquarePants Movie* is far from forgettable. (AL)

**Additional Credits:** Executive producers: Albie Hecht, Gina Shay, Derek Drymon. Associate producer: Ramsey Naito. Screenplay/storyboard: Derek Drymon, Tim Hill, Stephen Hillenburg, Kent Osborne, Aaron Springer, Paul Tibbitt. Based on a story and the series created by Stephen Hillenburg. Line producer: Aaron Parry. Editor: Lynn Hobson. Music: Gregor Nabholz. Executive music producer: Karyn Rachtman. Production designer: Nick Jennings. Sequence directors: Derek Drymon, Kent Osborne. Supervising animation director: Alan Smart. Lead storyboard artist: Sherm Cohen. Animation directors: Dong Kun Won, Yu Mun Jeong, Hoon Choi, Hee Man Yang, Sang Kyun Shin. Supervising sound editor: Timothy J. Borquez. Supervising sound designer: Jeff Hutchins. Camera: Jerzy Zielinski. A Paramount release of a Nickelodeon Movies production in association with United Plankton Pictures.

**Spriggan** (10/12/01) A.D.V. Films. 90 mins. Director: Hirotsugu Kawasaki. Producers: Ayao Ueda, Kazuhiko Ikeguchi, Kazuya Hamana, Haruo Sai, Eiko Tanaka. Voices: Chris Patton (Yu Ominae), Kevin Corn (Colonel MacDougall), Ted Pfister (Dr. Meisel), Andy McAvin (Jean-Jacques Mondo), Kelly Manison (Margaret), Mike Kleinhenz (Fattman), Spike Spencer (Little Boy), John Paul Shephard (Yamamoto), John Swasey (Mr. Smith).

**Consumer Tips:** ☆☆½ MPAA Rating: R. SF adventure. Based on the manga by Hiroshi Takashige (story) and Ryoji Minagawa (art).

**Story:** Yu Ominae is a Spriggan, a secret agent working for ARCAM, an international organization that seeks to keep the superior technology of lost civilizations and aliens from being misused. Noah's Ark is discovered to be an ancient spaceship containing technology that could rule—or destroy—the world. Yu is sent to Mount Ararat to protect ARCAM's research

team from the sadistic cyborg super-soldiers of the Pentagon's secret "U.S. Machine Corps."

**Comments:** A well-directed but poorly plotted superhero action feature, *Spriggan* was highly hyped upon its Japanese release on September 5, 1998. It was by the new high-quality animation Studio 4°C. Despite Kawasaki's direction and character designs credited to Hisashi Eguchi, it looked so much like the work of General Supervisor Katsuhiro Otomo (who scripted it) that some fans mistook it for a sequel to Otomo's megapopular *Akira*. It was promoted as in the action/sci-fi tradition of *Raiders of the Lost Ark* and the James Bond movies. It delivered that, but not much else.

*Spriggan* was adapted from the manga serial by Hiroshi Takashige (story) and Ryoji Minagawa (art), which ran in Japan's Shonen Sunday from 1989 through 1996. It was one of the first manga chosen to be translated into English (retitled *Striker*) because it was so similar to the popular American movie, television, and comic-book formula of battles between good and evil international organizations for world domination: television's live-action *U.N.C.L.E. vs. Thrush* and animated *G.I. Joe vs. Cobra*, or Marvel Comics' *S.H.I.E.L.D. vs. Hydra*. ARCAM is an international archaeological organization with an implied connection to the United Nations. Its secret mission is to search for superior technology in the ruins of ancient civilizations and keep it from being misused by would-be world conquerors. ARCAM's top field agents are adolescents with superhuman battle skills due to either cyber-enhancement or psionic talents. These agents are called Spriggans, from the Celtic word for sprites (as in Shakespeare's Puck/Robin Goodfellow; mischievous imps with supernatural powers.

An ARCAM team searching for Noah's Ark on Mount Ararat in Turkey finds a buried ancient spaceship that generates a magnetic field that destroys a satellite passing overhead. Yu Ominae, a 17-year-old Japanese Spriggan posing as a normal high-school student, is confronted by a fellow student who has been turned into a walking bomb and kills himself after delivering the message, "Noah will be your grave!" Yu demands an explanation from the head of ARCAM's Japanese office and is told about ARCAM's Project Noah to excavate the spaceship. However, the secret has gotten out and the dig is under attack by a powerful enemy that is also issuing challenges to Yu. Although he is ordered to stay away, he immediately leaves for the dig to learn who is threatening him.

At the dig he meets old ARCAM acquaintances Dr. Meisel (elderly scientist), Margaret (Meisel's young assistant), and Jean-Jacques Mondo, the Spriggan (from ARCAM's French office) in charge of Project Noah's defense. A Black Ops commando team slaughters most of the ARCAM scientists. Yu and Jean singlehandedly kill most of the enemy but are stopped by their half-mechanical cyborg commanders Major Fat Man (a hulking armored giant studded with deadly weapons) and Little Boy (a scrawny but superfast garrotte artist). These supervillains are officers in the U.S. Machine Corps, a top-secret team of killers bioengineered by Pentagon generals to ensure America's military superiority.

*Spriggan* is 90 minutes of constant excellently directed frenetic battle action full of bodies flying into gory pieces, against a mega-conspiracy plot of the world secretly under the control of two mysterious warring groups, leading to the suspenseful mystery of what will be found within the alien spaceship. ARCAM acts benevolently to protect humanity from playing with superscientific forces that would run wild and destroy civilization. The Pentagon and its U.S. Machine Corps are out to control the world in the name of American Patriotism, and they will arrogantly slaughter any dissenters. (Fat Man and Little Boy are well-known as the U.S. military's code names for the atomic bombs that destroyed Hiroshima and Nagasaki in 1945.) The action scenes are well worth watching, but most viewers feel cheated at the end by all of the questions raised that are never answered. There are no explanations of what ARCAM stands for or who runs it, how its Spriggan agents (besides Yu, who is a special case) get their superpowers, how the Pentagon expects to secretly control the world by bioengineering supervillains who are shown to be more interested in personal power than in supporting U.S. policy, where the spaceship came from and how its destruction of earth's previous civilization came to be mythologized as Noah's Ark and the flood, what previous items of dangerous lost technology ARCAM may have hidden away, or anything else. (FP)

**Additional Credits:** Screenplay: Yasutaka Itô, Hirotsugu Kawasaki. Music: Kuniaki Haishima. Sound rerecording mixer: Keith Arem. Supervising sound editor: Mike Draghi.

**Star Quest** See *Wings of Honneamise: Royal Space Force.*

**Starchaser: The Legend of Orin** (11/22/85) Atlantic. 98 mins. Director/producer: Steven Hahn. Voices: Joe Colligan (Orin), Carmen Argenziano (Dagg), Noelle North (Elan Aviana), Anthony DeLongis (Zygon), Les Tremayne (Arthur), Tyke Caravelli (Silica), Ken Sansom (Magreb), John Moschitta Jr. (Auctioneer, Z. Gork), Mickey Morton (Minemaster), Herb Vigran (Pung, Hopps), Dennis Alwood (Shooter), Mona Marshall (Kallie), Tina Romanus (Aunt Bella).

**Consumer Tips:** ☆☆ MPAA Rating: PG for profanity, sexual innuendo, and fantasy violence. Looks great in 3-D but in standard viewing sits flat in more ways than one.

**Story:** In the mining world of Trinian, young Orin uses a magical sword to free his enslaved people.

**Comments:** *Starchaser* came at a time when Hollywood tried to revive 3-D with live-action films such as *Jaws 3-D*, *Comin' at Ya*, and *Metalstorm: The Destruction of Jared-Syn*. It was made by Westar Productions, Inc., Los Angeles, in conjunction with a Korean studio, Hanho Heung-Up Co., Ltd., in Seoul, for a budget of $10 million.

Aside from its allusions to *Star Wars*, the film is notable for its American talent, who would play key roles in action-adventure cartoons of the 1990s, such as *Batman: The Animated Series* and *X-Men: Evolution*. Layout supervisor and background designer Roy Allen Smith would produce the first three sequels to *The Land Before Time*. Key animator and computer animation planner Bill Kroyer would start his own studio, and animator Tom Sito would head The Motion Picture Screen Cartoonists Union, Local 839, and codirect *Osmosis Jones*. Sound designer Don Ernst would later coproduce Disney's *Aladdin*, and produce *Fantasia 2000* and the English version of Miyazaki's *Spirited Away*.

The screenwriter, Jeffrey Scott, is a prolific writer of television cartoons, with 120 episodes of *Superfriends* and 29 *Dragon Tales* to his credit, plus three Emmies and one Humanitas Prize for his work on *Jim Henson's Muppet Babies*. His father was Norman Maurer, a story editor at Hanna-Barbera and creator of the world's first 3-D comic book. His mother was Joan Howard Maurer, daughter of Moe Howard of the Three Stooges.

The film was distributed by Atlantic Releasing, which had imported *The Smurfs and the Magic Flute*. *Starchaser* grossed a disappointing $1.6 million on its opening day at 1,020 theaters, with a cumulative U.S. gross at $3.4 million. As of this writing, it is the ninth (out of twelve) highest-grossing 3-D film.

An interesting but primitive film, this is easily outclassed by the Japanese space dramas *The Final Yamato* (1983), *Super Dimension Fortress Macross: Do You Remember Love?* (1984), and *Lensman* (1984). The most memorable line in the film is spoken by a "fembot" named Silica to the mercenary Dagg: "You look awfully good for a meat body." (WRM)

**Additional Credits:** Associate director: John Sparey. Executive producers: Thomas Coleman, Michael Rosenblatt. Writer: Jeffrey Scott. Editor: Don Ernst. Music: Andrew Belling. Animation directors: Mitch Rochon, Jang-Gil Kim. Storyboard artists: Boyd Kirkland, Mario Piluo, Paul Gruwell, Ronald Harris, Dick Sebast. Layout supervisor: Roy Allen Smith. Background designers: Roy Allen Smith, Tim Callahan. Layout: Frank Paur, Gray Graham, Boyd Kirkland, Mario Piluso. Animators: John J. Norton, Gary Payn, Steve Gordon, Thomas Sito, Lenord Robinson, James Stribling, Marlene Robinson May, Bill Kroyer.

**Street Fight** See *Coonskin*.

**The Swan Princess** (11/18/94) New Line. 90 mins. Director: Richard Rich. Producers: Richard Rich, Jared F. Brown. Voices: Jack Palance (Rothbart), Michelle Nicastro (Princess Odette), Howard McGillin (Prince Derek), John Cleese (Jean-Bob), Steven Wright (Speed), Steve Vinovich (Puffin), Mark Harelik (Lord Rogers), James Arrington (Chamberlain), Joel McKinnon Miller (Bromley), Dakin Matthews (King William), Sandy Duncan (Queen Uberta), Brian Nissen (Narrator), Liz Callaway (Princess Odette—singing), Davis Gaines (Chamberlain—singing), Adam Wylie (Young Derek), Adrian Zahiri (Young Odette).

**Consumer Tips:** ☆☆☆ MPAA Rating: G. An engaging, wholesome musical love story/fairy tale. Highly recommended for family audiences.

©Nest Entertainment, Inc.

**Story:** Prince Derek and Princess Odette, destined to marry, are separated by an evil enchanter, Rothbart, who turns Odette into a swan.

**Comments:** After codirecting *The Black Cauldron*, Richard Rich left Disney to form his own company, Rich Animation, hooking up with Jared Brown of Nest Entertainment in Utah. Together they made a series of half-hour direct-to-videos about Mormonism, stories from the Bible, and heroes from American history.

"I had some real good artists—Steve Gordon, Mike Hodgson, and Jim Coleman—and these people who had worked with me on *The Black Cauldron*," Rich told Henry Sheehan of the *Orange Country Register*, November 17, 1994.

"Our goal once we left Disney was to do an animated feature. Brian Nissen, the writer who was writing these half-hours, and I started writing *The Swan Lake*, as it was called to begin with. We shopped it around town and continued to do the half-hours, and they got more and more successful. Then Jared decided they would risk everything they owned and said, 'Let's back Rick and do a feature.' At that point, Don Bluth was closing down his local operations, so we were able to take a lot of his people. Bill Kroyer had just finished directing *FernGully*, so they were dropping people from there, and there were people from Disney who came over."

The company swelled from a staff of 25 to 275 animation artists working out of two stories in their offices in Burbank, California. Animation desks from Spumco were rented to accommodate the newcomers. Character Builders in Ohio would also pitch in on the production. This was one of the last cel-painted animated films.

Rich and Nissen endowed their romantic tale with themes of faith (the song "Far Longer than Forever"), coping with crises ("No Fear") and ethics ("Practice, Practice, Practice"). They also gave their heroes flaws: Prince Derek is brave, handsome, but a bit of a dolt, wondering "What else is there?" besides Odette's beauty, and he neglects to return home from a hunting expedition with his best friend, Bromley. Princess Odette claims that a turtle and a frog were her "best friends in the whole world."

John Cleese and Jack Palance served as the film's star power, but their voices were substituted when it came time for their characters to sing. Cleese played Jean-Bob, a frog with a phony French accent, who believed he was royalty. In *Shrek 2*, Cleese played King Harold, who was, in reality, a frog. Liz Calloway, who sang as Princess Odette, was also the singing voices of Princess Jasmine in *Aladdin II* and *III*, Anastasia in *Anastasia*, and Adult Kiara in *The Lion King II*.

Production assistant Bernie Van De Yacht, who managed the supply room, served as live-action reference for Prince Derek, and made appearances as Derek at Cannes and at Macy's Thanksgiving Day Parade. He would become Rich's casting director in later projects.

Nest Entertainment provided *Swan* with a combined marketing and production budget of $35 million. Promotions included a float at the Macy's Thanksgiving Day Parade. The 32-foot long, 22-foot wide and over 40-foot high motor-powered *Swan Princess* float depicted Prince Derek's castle, featuring a front balcony in the shape of an eight-foot fiberglass swan with a wingspan of 16 feet. There were over 60 *Swan Princess* licensees representing hundreds of licensed retail products. In their first movie tie-in, Sizzler Restaurants offered more than $3 million of advertising and in-store marketing.

Competing with *Swan* for the family dollar: a reissue of *The Lion King*, after a two-month hiatus from its summer release. Its three-day take was $5.5 million (at 1,400 theaters).

"Is that an amazing coincidence?" executive producer Matt Mazer told the *Boston Herald* on November 22, 1994. "And Disney said there were no films for families coming out for the holiday season. What are we, chopped liver?"

*The Swan Princess* earned half of *Lion King*'s take at $2.5 million, eventually earning $9,771,658 at the U.S. box office. *Swan*'s dive forced Rich—with great reluctance—to drastically downsize his crew, and postpone production on *Feathertop*, meant to be a high-quality theatrical feature. (*Feathertop* was retitled *The Scarecrow,* produced on a lower budget, and released on home video in 2000.)

Turner Home Entertainment gave *Swan* a $20 million promotional campaign for its video release on August 1, 1995, which paid off in sales of six million units worldwide. This prompted the production of two sequels: *The Swan Princess II: Escape from Castle Mountain* and *The Swan Princess III: The Mystery of the Enchanted Treasure*. All three *Swan* stories were eventually broadcast on The Disney Channel.

Though one of the best American non-Disney animated features, alas, it suffers the schizoid movie syndrome. On one hand, it's a compelling drama involving eternal love, the death of a king, an exciting hunt for a shape-changer, and a climactic battle between man and beast. On the other hand, it has a chatterbox Puffin who can float in air without flapping his wings, who's stripped naked of his feathers in one shot and reappears fully feathered instants later. Is this a classic fairy tale or a Looney Tune? All too often, *Swan* crosses the line between childlike and childish. The score is wonderful and the songs are engaging, particularly "Far Longer than Forever." But the showstoppers "No More Mr. Nice Guy" and "Princesses on Parade" do just that—they completely stop the show. The hand-drawn special effects, helmed by Bob Simmons and Michel Gagné, outclass even *The Lion King*. Overall, because of its story, quality animation, gorgeous backgrounds, vocal performances, and appealing characters, the film is a worthy challenger to the Disney dynasty. (WRM)

**Additional Credits:** Executive producers: Jared F. Brown, Sheldon Young. Coexecutive producers: Thomas J. Tobin, Matt Mazer. Coproducer: Terry L. Noss. Screenplay: Brian Nissen. Story: Richard Rich, Brian Nissen. Based on *Swan Lake*. Music: Lex de Azevedo. Songs: David Zippel, Lex De Azevedo. Animation director: Steven E. Gordon. Supervising animators: Chrystal S. Klabunde, Steven E. Gordon, Bruce Woodside, Daniel Boulos, Rick Farmiloe, Donnachada Daly. Key animators: Dan

Haskett, Gary Perkovac, Steven E. Gordon, Dan Wagner, Todd Waterman, Colm Duggan, Nassos Vakalis, Juliana Korsborn. Animators: Nassos Vakalis, Jesse Cosio, Steven E. Gordon, Juliana Korsborn, Cynthia Overman, Leon Joosen, Todd Waterman, Gary Perkovac, Jamie Davis, Kevin Petrilak, Mark Fisher, David Block, Jeff Etter, Larry Whitaker, Jay Jackson, Colm Duggan, Eric Schmidt, John Sparey, Dan Wagner, Doug Gregoire, Donnachada Daly, Chuck Harvey, David Simmons, Steve Garcia. Additional Animators: Adam Burke, Scott Sackett, Ken McDonald, Jennifer Marie Stillwell, Silvia Pompei, Kevin O'Neil. Lead keys: Dori Littell-Herrick, Vicki Woodside, Sylvia Fitzpatrick.

**The Sword in the Stone** (12/25/63) Walt Disney Pictures. 75 mins. Director: Wolfgang Reitherman. Voices: Rickie Sorensen, Richard Reitherman (Wart), Karl Swenson (Merlin), Junius C. Matthews (Archimedes), Sebastian Cabot (Narrator, Sir Ector), Martha Wentworth (Madam Mim, Granny Squirrel, Scullery Maid), Norman Alden (Sir Kay), Ginny Tyler (Girl Squirrel), Alan Napier (Sir Pelinore), Barbara Jo Allen (Scullery Maid), Thurl Ravenscroft, Jim Macdonald, Tudor Owen (Additional Voices).

©Walt Disney Productions

**Consumer Tips:** ☆ MPAA Rating: Unrated. Based on the 1939 book *The Sword in the Stone* by T. H. White.

**Story:** England is without a king, but Providence has placed a sword in an anvil; who so pulleth it out is the rightborn king. Since no one can seem to do this, Sir Ector's boorish son Sir Kay can't wait to compete in a tournament that is to decide the issue instead. His hapless young squire, Wart (aka Arthur), encounters the great Merlin, who takes the boy under his wing for training. Arthur survives many lessons, including capture by the demented wizard Madam Mim. Merlin defeats the sorceress but in a fit of pique at Wart, flies off to vacation in Bermuda. While he is gone Arthur unwittingly pulls the sword from the anvil and becomes king of the Britons.

**Comments:** *The Sword in the Stone* is one of Disney's most forgettable features, a mild entertainment that bears little relation to the studio's classic era. This was the first film of several directed solely by Wolfgang "Woolie" Reitherman, and it features many of his future trademarks: episodic set pieces take the place of coherent narrative; gags and humor are mainly broad and slapstick; anachronism passes for wit; and the story (such as it is) is forced along too fast for personalities to emerge in full.

According to some accounts, none of the animators really wanted to make this film. Several of the "Nine Old Men" of Disney's brain trust wanted to revive the long dormant "Chanticleer the Rooster" project, but story man/concept artist Bill Peet was able to convince Walt to go with *The Sword in the Stone* instead. Having greatly enjoyed the 1960 Broadway production of *Camelot*, Walt was easily sold. Resigned, the team settled down to make this rather uninspired film. After the film's completion Walt considered it an especially weak effort and harped on his staff not to make *The Jungle Book* look anything like it.

Foremost among the problems was the character of Merlin, whom Bill Peet based on Walt Disney himself. Far from an all-powerful sorcerer, Merlin comes off as a crotchety pedant prone to tomfoolery more befitting the Three Stooges. Merlin has a pet named Archimedes. This owl evidences the same traits as his master, so the wizard's character is essentially replicated. Giving Archimedes a different personality might have added some depth to the film, but perhaps depth was never the point. Sir Kay and Sir Ector are also one-note characters, and one must dig deep to find anything interesting about Wart or any foreshadowing that he is England's rightful king. Peet decided to forego any hints that Wart was the late king Uther's son, and since personality was not Reitherman's strong suit, Wart is reduced to a spindly waif who is largely manipulated by the other characters in the film.

The Sherman brothers were to write many memorable tunes for future features, but fell flat on their first assignment. There are no memorable songs that might have covered some of the weaknesses that bedeviled *The Sword in the Stone*. There are two sequences that do stand out from the general tedium, however. Wart, transformed into a squirrel by Merlin, is romanced most ardently by a chipper female squirrel who doesn't take no for an answer. When Merlin's spell ends and Wart becomes a boy, she is completely brokenhearted and is last seen in medium shot, tearfully perched on a splintered limb before a fadeout. The distaff squirrel displays more personality than Wart and Merlin combined.

The wizard's duel between Merlin and Madam Mim is the most imaginative sequence in the movie. Both magicians transform themselves into increasingly deadly animal adversaries until Mim breaks the rules and becomes a dragon. Merlin beats her by becoming a virus, making her too sick to continue. Merlin's victory reinforces his constant theme that education is vital and that brains always defeat brawn. Unfortunately, it also exposes a major plot weakness: Wart doesn't need either brains or brawn. He is already the future king and has only to yank the sword from its resting place anyhow. Merlin should have told him five minutes into the film and then gone to Bermuda; we would all have been spared this silliness. (MG)

**Additional Credits:** Story: Bill Peet. Based on the book by T. H. White. Music: George Bruns. Songs: Richard M. Sherman, Robert B. Sherman. Directing animators: Frank Thomas, Milt Kahl, Ollie Johnston, John Lounsbery. Animators: Hal King, Eric Cleworth, Eric Larson, Cliff Nordberg, John Sibley, Hal Ambro, Dick Lucas. Effects animators: Dan MacManus, Jack Boyd, Jack Buckley. Character design: Milt Kahl, Bill Peet. Background artists: Walt Peregoy, Bill Layne, Albert Dempster, Anthony Rizzo, Ralph Hulett, Fil Mottola. Layout artists: Don Griffith, Basil Davidovich, Vance Gerry, Sylvia Cobb, Dale Barnahrt, Homer Jonas.

**Tamala 2010** (12/19/03) Vitagraph Films. 92 mins. Director: trees of Life (t.o.L.). Producers: Seiichi Tsukada, Kazuko Mio, t.o.L. Voices: Hisayo Mochizuki (Tamala), Shinji Takeda (Michelangelo), Béatrice Dalle (Tatla the Machine God), Takeshi Kato (Zombie Cat).

**Consumer Tips:** ☆☆☆ MPAA Rating: Unrated. Surrealistic SF adventure.

**Story:** Tamala, a naively innocent young cat, becomes involved in a civil war between cats and dogs on Planet Q, as the sinister super-corporation Catty & Co. attempts to use her in the expansion of its economic empire. Tamala is a carefree, lusty kitten in the futuristic Feline Galaxy. She is oblivious to the fact that she is the promotional mascot of corporate giant Catty & Co. When Tamala's spaceship is diverted to Planet Q, she goes shopping and picks up a boyfriend, Michelangelo, ignoring the gang warfare between dogs and cats around her. She is killed and then reincarnated, as part of Catty & Co.'s plans to gain economic control of the Feline Galaxy.

**Comments:** *Tamala 2010* (which sometimes adds the subtitle *A Punk Cat in Space*) was released in Japan on October 19, 2002, and became an international film festival favorite for over a year before its U.S. release. It won the Best Animation popular award at the Montréal Fant-Asia Film Festival in August 2003. Supporters praise it as an imaginative and totally original psychedelic masterpiece, while detractors revile it as a tossed-together incoherent hodgepodge of visual elements. It was written/animated/scored by the artistic collective "t.o.L.," producers of animated television commercials and music videos.

At its screening at the American Cinematheque's Los Angeles Anime Festival in May 2003, t.o.L.'s directors/founders/representatives, identified only as Kuno and Kazuka, told the audience that they call themselves t.o.L when working as an animation studio (but they insist on the term "Post Modern Pop Art" rather than "animation") and "trees of Life" when performing as a punk rock band. They named as some of their influences Thomas Pynchon (but not Philip K. Dick as everyone assumes), Franz Kafka, Betty Boop, Oscar Wilde, and lots of conspiracy-theory and chainsaw-slasher horror movies. Other influences/similarities cited in film reviews from various cities include: the robot Maria from *Metropolis*, Ralph Bakshi, a giant mechanical Colonel Sanders (with an axe in its skull) striding across cities with a platter of fried chicken, Sylvain Chomet, all the cats walking with Astro Boy's distinctive electronic squeak sound effect, Andy Warhol, Clint Eastwood's spaghetti Westerns, M. C. Escher, and the Richard Elfman cult film *Forbidden Zone*.

*Tamala* has been described as both an exaggerated feline pastiche of the original sexy Betty Boop, and a lewd parody of *Hello Kitty.* She is a cute, cheerfully foul-mouthed, cigarette-smoking party girl who speaks in uninhibited baby-talk such as, "Me gotta pee-pee," and (when bowling), "A fucking strike!" She lives in Gonnosukezaka Ward, Meguro City, Tokyo on the planet CatEarth in the Feline Galaxy in the futuristic year 2010; near to but separate from her adoptive mother, a dissolute human woman constantly entwined by her pet giant snake. (Tamala calls her "you anaconda bitch.") She is unaware of the fact that her image appears everywhere as the advertising mascot of Catty & Co., the "colossal conglomerate [which] controls 95.725 percent of the total world GDP" and is expanding its control throughout the Feline Galaxy.

Tamala wants to go to the Orion System to search for her birth mother, despite being forbidden by her human mother. While en route in her spaceship, Tamala is knocked off course by a Catty-controlled asteroid and ends up at Planet Q instead. She is just as happy to play tourist there, not caring that its capital, Hate City, is a slum that has fallen into gang warfare between cats and dogs, the latter led by sadistically snarling police dog/chief Kentauros who keeps the mouse Penelope as an S&M sex slave. Tamala picks up the city's last intellectual, Michelangelo, as her boyfriend to take her shopping and partying. She is bored when he takes her to a museum, until she is strangely attracted by a 4,000-year-old statue of Tatla, a symbol of the ancient religious cult of Minerva that practiced live sacrifice and was suppressed around the year 100 B.C. (Before Cats). Tamala has a vision of a new statue of Tatla as a gigantic robot (the *Metropolis* reference) constantly ascending an escalator to heaven.

Michelangelo notices that Tamala's inane non sequiturs become increasingly self-abusive, such as, "Me very tasty. Wanna eat me?" Kentauros takes her literally, attacking during a picnic and devouring her while Michelangelo flees. Michelangelo is still traumatized when Tamala is resurrected (three days later?) and happily leaves (with Penelope, who has escaped Kentauros) to continue her journey to Orion. In 2032 in Shanghai, Michelangelo as the now middle-aged Professor Nominos delivers a lecture on "Antitheology in Capitalism." He demonstrates that Catty & Co. is secretly the disguised Minerva cult that went underground in 100 B.C., first emerged in 1436 in Verona as a commercial mail-delivery service, and began expanding in the 19th century by mergers with other industries. It took the name Catty & Co. and adopted the promotional image of Tamala on April 19, 1869, her real birthday. Tamala is the living incarnation of Tatla, "a goddess destroyed and reborn in infinite succession," which is why she must be eaten as a sacrifice once a year. Catty & Co. bioengineered Tamala from a newborn kitten selected from among 200,000 on the planet Edessa in the Orion System in 1869.

In the final scene Tamala's human mother, revealed as a Catty & Co. high executive, berates another of their immortal agents, the Mysterious Postal Cat, for letting Tamala escape Planet Q. She must never be allowed to reach Orion and find her birth mother.

*Tamala 2010* has been publicized as the first in a theatrical feature trilogy and a television series, although there has been no word since on the others. Its visual style mostly replicates the late 1920s Fleisher Studios black-and-white look through both Flash and full 2-D animation, but with frequent segues into color and/or mechanistic CGI sequences. Notable aspects praised in reviews include t.o.L.'s electro-techno-metal pop score, which ranges from pulsing rave dance music to funereal dirges, and the parodies of famous advertising art, from early 20th-century Alfons Mucha to 1930s Soviet heroic-worker posters to Calvin Klein jeans labels, all featuring Tamala (you have to see the movie at least twice to spot them all). (FP)

**Additional Credits:** Camera (color), t.o.L. editor: Kensuke Kawamura. Animation: t.o.L., Kentaro Nemoto. Music: t.o.L., performed by trees of Life. Character design: t.o.L., Nemoto. A Kinetique production.

**Tarzan** (6/18/99) Walt Disney Pictures. 88 mins. Directors: Chris Buck, Kevin Lima. Producer: Bonnie Arnold. Voices: Tony Goldwyn (Tarzan), Alex D. Linz (Young Tarzan), Minnie Driver (Jane Porter), Lance Henriksen (Kerchak), Glenn Close (Kala), Nigel Hawthorne (Porter), Brian Blessed (Clayton), Rosie O'Donnell (Terk), Wayne Knight (Tantor), Taylor Dempsey (Young Tantor), Aria Noelle Curzon (Baby Apes).

©Burroughs and Disney

**Consumer Tips:** ☆☆☆☆ MPAA Rating: G. Based on the popular book series *Tarzan of the Apes* by Edgar Rice Burroughs.

**Story:** A young orphan is found in the African jungles by a motherly ape named Kala. She brings it back to her tribe of apes as a son, much to the consternation of her husband Kerchak, the tribe's leader. The child, called Tarzan, is soon friends with young ape Turk, elephant Tantor, and other jungle creatures. Tarzan meets no humans until an expedition under Professor Porter shows up to study the great apes. Porter's comely daughter fascinates Tarzan, but the evil guide Clayton only has his eyes on capturing wild gorillas. Tarzan's growing feelings for Jane lead him to unwittingly betray the ape tribe to Clayton, but Tarzan and his animal army defeat the guide and his poachers. It's a bittersweet victory: Kerchak is killed but Jane decides to stay in Africa as Tarzan's mate.

**Comments:** After almost 50 film adventures it might seem that not much else could have been done with Tarzan, but the Disney studio managed to come up with a new take backed by one of the most startling visual processes created for animation. Tarzan had been considered for animation as far back as 1936. The Disney project started in 1995 and was a collaboration between Disney's Burbank studio and its Paris studio, where lead animator Glen Keane and his crew worked on the character of Tarzan.

Directors Chris Buck and Kevin Lima were hard pressed to find a new take on a character that had been

filmed and written about numerous times. They decided to play up the deep relationship Tarzan has to his ape family. There is considerable story and character development devoted to this aspect, and it is well into the film before Professor Porter and his expedition actually arrive. Tarzan becomes a man trapped between two worlds after he finds out there are other creatures like him, especially Jane Porter.

Keane's conception of the character was helped by Edgar Rice Burrough's depiction of Tarzan as a man who had animal-like abilities; it was very difficult for live actors to portray such a role. In the unfettered world of animation, however, Tarzan is an acrobatic marvel, superhuman in his own way. Keane studied films of skateboarders, snowboarders, and bungee jumpers and came up with an extreme athlete capable of traversing a jungle like an ape-man born. Watching Tarzan surf the trees at breakneck speed is one of the treats in the film. Had Burroughs seen the film, he likely would have enjoyed it immensely.

Art director Dan St. Pierre and background supervisor Doug Ball traveled to Africa and shot 150 rolls of film and 60 hours of video to capture the landscape. Computer imaging expert Eric Daniels and 3-D special effects artist Michael Koschalk took it from there using an amazing software program called Deep Canvas. In short, this process enabled a camera to move through three-dimensional painted environments. The effect is one of moving 3-D backgrounds, and the process is much better experienced than explained. Never before has an audience so emphatically been put into the picture. Viewing the animated characters cavorting through the scenes in which Deep Canvas is used is like seeing a 3-D film without the use of special glasses.

Disney broke with its recent musical tradition by having an offstage singer perform the film's musical numbers. Pop artist Phil Collins, who would do a few films with Disney, wrote, arranged, and sang the numbers. Mention must be made of the excellent work by animator Ken Duncan and actress Minnie Driver in creating the character of Jane Porter. Duncan was fast becoming Disney's next Marc Davis by dint of his knack for animating attractive women. At first he drew Jane as a rather proper English type, but Minnie Driver's loose, improvisational approach affected Duncan's conception of the character, much for the better. Jane is an immensely appealing, fully developed character that represents a perfect synergy between animator and voice artist.

*Tarzan* was a major hit for Disney, grossing $172 million. Toon Disney developed a series for cable programming, and a direct-to-video sequel, *Tarzan and Jane,* was released in 2004.

For the record:

- Mrs. Potts and Chip from *Beauty and the Beast* can be seen in Professor Porter's camp.
- Glen Keane's son, an ardent skateboarder, helped his dad out with some of Tarzan's moves.
- No actor who ever portrayed Tarzan wore dreadlocks but, as Chris Buck and Kevin Lima explained, Tarzan would most likely have long hair, which was probably not often washed and groomed. (MG)

***Additional Credits:*** Screenplay: Tab Murphy, Bob Tzudiker, Noni White. Additional screenplay material: David Reynolds, Jeffrey Stepakoff. Music: Mark Mancina. Songs: Phil Collins. Supervising animators: Glen Keane, Ken Stuart Duncan, Russ Edmonds, John Ripa, Michael Surrey, Randy Haycock, David Burgess, Bruce W. Smith, Sergio Fabios, Dominique Monferey, Jay Jackson, T. Daniel Hofstedt, Chris Wahl. Animators: Georges Abolin, Pierre Alart, Marco Allard, David Berthier, Bolheim Bouchier, Patrick Delage, Eric Delbacque, Thierry Goullard, Bobja Montoro Cavero, Enis Tahzin Ozgur, Stephane Sainte-Foi, Tran Quan-Thievjic, Kristoff Verne, Jared Beckstrand, Doug Bennett, Caroline Cruikshank, Mark Koetsier, Doug Krohn, Mario J. Menjkar, Dougg Williams, Andreas Wessell-Therhorn, Steven Pierre Gordon, Jeff Johnson, Yoshimichi Tamura, Adam Dykstra, Danny Galieote, David Moses Pimental, Chad Stewart, Tim George, Richard Hoppe, Michael Stocker, David Block, Theresa Wiseman, Robb Pratt, Marc Smith, James Hull, Mike Kunkel, Jean Morel, Stevan Wahl, Marc Eoche Duval, Juanjo Guarnido, Zoltan Maros, Catherine Poulain, Ruben A. Aquino, Jean-Luc Ballester, Dale Baer, James Baker, Travis Blaise, Tom Bancroft, Richard Bazley, Roger Chiasson, Wayne Carlisli, Michael Cedeno, Robert Espanto Domingo, Jerry Yu Ching, Sandro Cleuzo, Brian Ferguson, Tom Gately, Raul Garcia, David Hancock, Christopher Hubbard, James Young Jackson, Sang Jin Kim, Bert Klein, Sam Levine, Mark Alan Mitchell, Joe Oh, Jamie Oliff, Ralph Palmer, Mark Pudleiner, William Recinos, Michael Show, Bill Waldman, Anthony Ho Wong, Phil Young, Ellen Woodbury. Story

supervisor: Brian Pimental. Story: Stephen Anderson, Mark D. Kennedy, Carole Holliday, Gaeton Brizzi, Paul Brizzi, Don Dougherty, Ed Gombert, Randy Haycock, Don Hall, Kevin L. Harker, Glen Keane, Burny Mattinson, Frank Nissen, John Norton, Jeff Snow, Michael Surrey, Christopher J. Ure, Mark Walton, Stevie Wermers, Kelly Wightman, John Ramirez.

**Tarzoon, Shame of the Jungle** See *Shame of the Jungle.*

**Teacher's Pet** (1/16/04) Walt Disney Pictures. 74 min. Director: Timothy Björklund. Producer: Stephen Swafford. Voices: Nathan Lane (Spot Helperman, Scott Leadready II, Scott Manly-Manning), Shaun Fleming (Leonard Helperman), Kelsey Grammer (Dr. Ivan Krank), Debra Jo Rupp (Mary Lou Helperman), Jerry Stiller (Pretty Boy), David Ogden Stiers (Mr. Jolly), Paul Reubens (Dennis), Megan Mullally (Adele), Rob Paulsen (Ian Wazselewski), Estelle Harris (Mrs. Boogin), Wallace Shawn (Principal Strickler), Jaty Thomas (Barry Anger), Genie Francis (Marcia, Marcia), Anthony Geary (John, Juan), David Maples (Beefeater), Pamela Segall (Trevor, Taylor, Tyler), Timothy Stack (Daddy), Emma Steinkeller (Little Girl), Ken Swafford (Officer White), Lauren Tom (Younghee), Kevin Michael Richardson (Conductor).

©Walt Disney Enterprises, Inc.

***Consumer Tips:*** ☆☆☆ MPAA Rating: G. Big-screen version of one of Disney television's most acclaimed animated series.

***Story:*** Spot Helperman is Leonard's beloved dog but he is obsessed with a dream: to be a real human boy.

The long-suffering pooch sees his chance when mad scientist Ivan Krank announces that he has perfected a genetic transfer process that turns animals into human beings. The Helperman family and their pets are all dragged into a wild adventure as Spot discovers that the deal is far more than he bargained for.

**Comments:** OK, the basics: Spot Helperman is a highly intelligent, small, blue dog with aspirations of being a human. So fervid is this wish that Spot attends school disguised as a little boy named Scott Leadready II. One of Spot's classmates is his owner, Leonard, whose single mom also happens to be the teacher (hence the series' title). Naturally, mom has not a clue, especially since her camouflaged canine is the star pupil of the class. The movie expands on this theme, sending the Helpermans to Florida where mom is competing for a major teaching award. Spot is aboard as a stowaway, hoping to hook up with an insane quack that may be able to grant his dearest wish. Also involved are the Helperman's other pets, a dyspeptic, unshaven parrot named Pretty Boy and Mr. Jolly, a phobic cat.

*Teacher's Pet* is a completely postmodern experience that treats its plot like a trampoline. Inside jokes and sight gags (many of them aimed at Disney) abound, and characters frequently break through the fourth wall to cue the musical numbers, comment on the action, or push a gag just a tad further. Perhaps with a voice cast that included Nathan Lane, Jerry Stiller, Paul Reubens, Kelsey Grammer, and Megan Mullally, the opportunities were too good for director Tim Björklund to pass up. In the best example, a humanized Spot attempts to win reward money by using the "Twilight Bark" (a famous device from *101 Dalmatians*) to locate a lost dog. When Leonard asks what that is, Spot tells him that he needs to watch more animated movies.

References to other films, animated and otherwise, pop up at lightning speed. Starting with the opening scene there is a recurring homage to *Pinocchio* to the point where the Blue Fairy practically becomes a character in *Teacher's Pet*. The animation and color are a high point. By the early 2000s nearly all television animation style seemed to be influenced by two studios, Klasky-Csupo and John Kricfalusi's Spumco outfit. *Teacher's Pet* artist Gary Baseman broke the mold and developed a look that suggests demented greeting card characters with a touch of Max Fleischer thrown in. This approach gives *Teacher's Pet* a very unique look. Music arranger Carl Johnson seems to have taken a page from Jon Kull's arrangements for *South Park: Bigger, Longer, and Uncut* (1999), using grand, faux-Broadway styling for the movie's musical numbers.

Director Björklund never allows *Teacher's Pet* to stand still; characters are perpetually talking, singing, emoting, joking, or fooling about, and nobody stays quiet for very long. Björklund enjoys using unusual camera angles and at times split or multiple screens. *Teacher's Pet* is a hyperkinetic film, a cheerful case of attention deficit disorder in digital color. It is also smart, entertaining, and unusual enough to deserve repeated viewings.

The movie was one of 11 considered for the 2004 Oscar (Best Animated Film). *Teacher's Pet* may not exactly be Oscar material, but it's still doggone good.

For the record:

- Pinocchio, the Seven Dwarfs, Mickey Mouse, and several other Disney mainstays have cameos in the film.
- Nathan Lane also voiced Timon the meerkat in Disney's *Lion King* films.
- There is a very funny reference to *The Jetsons* late in the film for sharp listeners.
- Animation aficionado Kelsey Grammer was last heard as the voice of Gary the Rat on Spike TV's animation block. (MG)

**Additional Credits:** Executive producers: Gary Baseman, Bill Steinkellner, Cheri Steinkellner. Line producer: Michael Karafilis. Associate producer: Melinda Carrillo. Screenplay: Bill Steinkellner, Cheri Steinkellner. Punch up writers: Billiam Coronel, Jim Fisher, David Maples, Jim Staahl, Jess Winfield. Music: Stephen James Taylor. Songs: Randy Peterson, Kevin Quinn, Cheri Steinkellner, Brian Woodbury, Peter Lurye. Art director: Gary Baseman. Assistant art director: Christina Long. Unit animation director: Dante Clemente. Assistant animation supervisor: Nowell Villano. Animators: Delfin Abad, Chris Anacin, Glenn Arriola, Joseph Balderas, Anthony Benitez, Ric Bernardo, Antonio Bugas, Edgar Bugas, Arnold Collao, Arnold Coniconde, Noel De Leon, Agnes De Vera, Noel Domingo, Roody Erenio, Romeo Fabian, Bienifer Flores, Akiblas Flores, Gilbert Francisco, Donato Gallon, Boy Lacampuenga, Wilfredo Leonardo, Alexander Lorena, Manuel Magsaysay, Mark Malonjao, Salvador Marcos, Robert Ocon, Joel Pangilinan, Rowen Pingkian, Ruel Ramos, Oliver Regoniel, Alan Reyes, Warren Romero, Edwin Santiago, Rommel Santiago, Lorna Sun, William Sy, Francis Tan, David Temperante, Joseph Villanueva, Danilo Wabe, Rolando Angelo, Jebbie Barrios, Ricardo Borja, Florencio Concepcion, Dennis Coniconde, James Diores, Edelson Eugenio, Ma. Dina Fabian, Allan Fernando, Alexander Ferrarez, Cynthia Javier, Don Juan, Nonoy Lustria, Maciste Natividad, Vladimir Naval, Larry Pagcaliwangan, Nomer Panlaqui, Edmond Plantilla, Emmanuel Plantilla, Roger Quilatan, Jojo Reynon, Arthur Tolentino, Richmond Zunio.

**Tenchi Muyo in Love!** (8/16/96) Pioneer Entertainment. 95 mins. Director: Hiroshi Negishi. Producers: Tak W. Abe, Naoju Nakamura, Hidemi Satani. Voices: Masami Kikuchi (Tenchi Masaki), Ai Orikasa (Ryoko), Megumi Hayashibara (Achika), Yumi Takada (Ayeka), Chisa Yokoyama (Sasami), Etsuko Kozakura (Ryo-Ohki), Ryûzaburô Ôtomo (Kain), Toshiyuki Morikawa (young Nobuyuki Masaki), Yuko Kobayashi (Washu), Yuko Mizutani (Mihoshi), Yuri Amano (Kiyone).

**Consumer Tips:** ☆☆☆ MPAA Rating: PG-13. SF romance-adventure. Based upon the Tenchi Muyo! video and television series.

**Story:** Teenage Tenchi Masaki is the heir to a royal family. When a criminal alien, Kain, escapes from prison, he ensures that the police will not stop him by traveling back to 1970 to eliminate Tenchi's mother, killing Tenchi before he is even born. Tenchi, and his bevy of galactic girlfriends, travel back in time to when his parents were high-school students to protect them.

**Comments:** *Tenchi Muyo!* (a pun that can mean several things from "This Side Up" to "We don't have time for this!"; since Tenchi is also the hero's name, it is often translated "No Time for Tenchi!") was one of anime's most popular series of the 1990s. It took the sci-fi teenage angst comedy formula of the 1980s, of a normal high-school boy confronted by a girlfriend with either magical or SF superscientific powers, and escalated it by giving Tenchi Masaki a whole harem of galactic girlfriends. The series (all produced by the Anime International Company/A.I.C.) began with a six-episode direct-to-video series from September 1992 through March 1993, followed by several stand-alone

OAV specials and a 26-episode television series, April through September 1995. *Tenchi Muyo in Love!*, released April 20, 1996, was the first of three theatrical features. Numerous additional OAV and television series have followed.

Tenchi Masaki is a shy adolescent living with his grandfather Yosho, a Shinto priest maintaining a family shrine in rural Japan. The shrine is supposed to imprison an ancient evil spirit. Tenchi accidentally releases the spirit, who turns out to be a space pirate from a galactic civilization; actually a hell-raising juvenile delinquent, Ryoko. Ryoko's release triggers alarms in the Galaxy Police, and Tenchi's family shrine is visited by a quickly piling-up series of galactic detectives, princesses, and scientists, each of whom is a teenage cutie (except for Sasami, the tagalong little sister of Princess Ayeka) who gets a crush on the embarrassed Tenchi and stays as a houseguest to complicate his life. Tenchi turns out to be a secret heir to the Jurai royal family of the galactic empire, but decides he prefers the quiet, pastoral life in Japan.

*Tenchi Muyo in Love!* is considerably more dramatic and seriously romantic than the comedic videos and television series. While it has many of the flaws of a theatrical feature made for the fans of the series, they are not as serious because the series is more personality- than plot-driven. The background of the girls' alien origins and the details of the galactic empire are not necessary as long as the audience understands the basic SF setup that Tenchi is the host of several attractive young girls with superscientific powers from a galactic civilization. The space menace created for this story is new and self-explanatory, and the personalities and relationships between the teenagers are amusingly universal.

*Tenchi Muyo in Love!* was produced just as Pioneer Entertainment's U.S. division was beginning to market the whole *Tenchi Muyo!* franchise in America. The movie was designed with an American theatrical release in mind, including getting *Babylon 5* composer Christopher Franke to write its score. (FP)

**Additional Credits:** Screenplay: Hiroshi Negishi, Ryoe Tsukimura. ADR director: Doug Stone. Music: Christopher Franke. Animation producer: Toru Miura. Line producers: Hiroaki Inoue, Kazuaki Morijiri. Design: Masaki Kajishima, Hiroyuki Horiuchi. Art director: Torao Arai. Animation director: Kazuya Kuroda, Michiyo Suzuki, Takahiro Kishida. Assistant directors: Makoto Fuchigami, Pisuo Suetani, Ryuji Asami, Toshi Saga. Director of photography: Hitoshi Sato. Coanimation director: Koji Watanabe, Nobuyuki Kitajima, Takuya Saito, Toshiyuki Tsuru. Art styling: Chitose Asakura, Toshihisa Koyama.

**The Thief and the Cobbler** See *Arabian Knight.*

**The Three Caballeros** (2/3/45) Walt Disney Pictures. 71 mins. Directors: Clyde Geronimi, Jack Kinney, Bill Roberts, Harold Young. Voices: Clarence Nash (Donald Duck), Jose Oliviera (Jose Carioca, Aracuan Bird), Joaquin Garay (Panchito), Frank Graham, Fred Shields, Sterling Holloway (Narrators). Live actors: Carmen Molina, Dora Luz, Aurora Miranda.

**Consumer Tips:** ☆☆ Disney's second Latin-American feature of the 1940s.

**Story:** Donald Duck receives a huge box on his birthday, sent by his Latin-American amigos Jose Carioca and Panchito. Inside the box is an instant tour of South America and other unforgettable treats.

**Comments:** *The Three Caballeros* is the wildest, most surrealistic film ever produced by the Disney studio. At times it resembles a Latino version of *Fantasia*, at other times a weak *Silly Symphony*, and in still other moments a psychedelic head trip where reality warps at a moments notice. The film actually seems to speed up as it progresses; by the last number, "You Belong to My Heart," it seems to be running at five times normal speed, especially when the number is intercut with unexpected, bizarre renditions of the title song. One may be amazed that the "Cold-Blooded Penguin" and "Flying Gauchito" sequences are in the same movie. These two segments about a penguin yearning for a warm place to live and a flying donkey that wins a big race are throwbacks to Disney's animated shorts and are rather conventional (although the penguin short has some literal sight gags that Tex Avery might have loved).

Once Jose Carioca and the *pistolero* rooster Panchito enter the picture, however, the tempo changes and imagination runs wild. Both birds seem to transport Donald to locales where the local women are beautiful dancers and singers, and Donald spends nearly every scene he is in literally throbbing with lust. Much of

the time Panchito and Jose must physically restrain him, and if Donald was supposed to be representative of our citizens or tourists, our neighbors south of the border might have thought twice about adopting a good neighbor policy.

Donald is enthralled by singer Aurora Miranda in Baia; is the star of a large, scantily clad beach party in Acapulco; vainly tries to impress lovely señoritas dancing the Lilongo; and later falls hard for Carmen Molina as she dances the Jesusita. Some of Donald's fantasies are presented in a fever-dream of color and abstraction, a testimony to either his imagination or his hormones.

The film's high point is the "Three Caballeros" number sung by Donald, Jose, and Panchito. Animator Ward Kimball plowed into this scene at full speed without restraint, breaking the laws of physical reality. Objects appear and disappear as the birds need them, but not always according to the rules: when Jose and Panchito call for guitars, Donald gets first a saxophone, then a trumpet, and finally a bass fiddle twice his size. Characters enter and exit from the top, bottom, and sides of the frame, and the song ends with Panchito holding a note for so long that Donald and Jose unleash everything but weapons of mass destruction in order to shut him up.

Stylist Mary Blair, until recently one of the most underrated artistic figures at Disney, hit a high point with this film. Her gorgeous, colorful work can be seen in the "Baia" train sequence, and there is a limited animation sequence in which Panchito explains Mexican Christmas traditions using very simple design to charming effect. Other strange but interesting moments include the depiction of a soundtrack that pulses and distorts in time to the musical instruments that are superimposed over it. The soundtrack grabs Donald and turns him into kaleidoscopic images of himself. *The Three Caballeros* is very much a special-effects feature, and the combination of live action and animation is often stunning. Art supervisor Ken Anderson and special-effects wizard Ub Iwerks underwent countless headaches lining up the timing and perspective of these scenes, which take up more than a third of the film.

Between the hyperkinetic animated characters, the constant dancing, and the surrealistic interludes, *The Three Caballeros* is a head-spinning experience best enjoyed by Disney fans who want an alternative to the sedate symphonies of *Snow White and the Seven Dwarfs* or *Bambi*. This is what it looks like when the studio cut loose, circa 1945.

The Three Caballeros was originally titled *Surprise Package*. It premiered in Mexico City in December of 1944. The film lost money in the United States, and Disney cancelled plans for a third Latin American feature, *Cuban Carnival*. Jose Carioca smokes a cigar throughout nearly the entire picture, but home video and DVD releases left him untouched. The songs "Baia" and "You Belong to My Heart" both became hits in the United States. Some unused 16mm footage from *Saludos Amigos* (1943) appears in this film. Daisy Duck, Donald's longtime squeeze, first appeared as a Mexican beauty named Donna in the 1937 short *Don Donald*. That explains everything. (MG)

**Additional Credits:** Sequence directors: Clyde Geronimi, Jack Kinney, Bill Roberts. Director: Harold Young. Story: Homer Brightman, Ernest Terrazzas, Bill Peet, Ralph Wright, Elmer Plummer, Roy Williams, William Cottrell, Del Connell, James Brodrero. Music: Charles Wolcott, Paul J. Smith, Edward H. Plumb. Animators: Ward Kimball, Eric Larson, Fred Moore, John Lounsbery, Les Clark, Milt Kahl, Hal King, Franklin Thomas, Harvey Toombs, Bob Carlson, John Sibley, Bill Justice, Oliver M. Johnston Jr., Milt Neil, Marvin Woodward, Don Patterson. Special effects animation: Joshua Meador, George Rowley, Edwin Aardal, John McManus. Background artists: Albert Dempster, Art Riley, Don Douglass, Claude Coats. Layout artists: Donald Da Gradi, Hugh Hennesy, McLaren Stewart, Yale Gracey, Herbert Ryman, John Hench, Charles Phillipi. Art supervisors: Mary Blair, Kenneth Anderson, Robert Cormack.

**Thumbelina** (3/30/94) Warner Bros. 94 mins. Directors: Don Bluth, Gary Goldman. Producers: Don Bluth, Gary Goldman, John Pomeroy. Voices: Jodi Benson (Thumbelina), Gino Conforti (Jaquimo), Barbara Cook (Mother), Will Ryan (Hero, Reverend Rat), June Foray (Queen Tabitha), Kenneth Mars (King Colbert), Gary Imhoff (Prince Cornelius), Joe Lynch (Grundel), Charo (Mrs. "Ma" Toad), Danny Mann (Mozo), Loren Michaels (Gringo), Kendall Cunningham (Baby Bug), Tawny Sunshine Glover (Gnatty), Michael Nunes (Li'l Bee), Gilbert Gottfried (Mr. Berkeley Beetle), Carol Channing (Ms. Fieldmouse), John Hurt (Mr. Mole), Pat Musick (Mrs. Rabbit), Neil Ross (Mr. Fox, Mr. Bear).

©Don Bluth Limited

**Consumer Tips:** ☆½ MPAA Rating: G. Wimpy fairy tale, made for ages two to six and for dating couples.

**Story:** Little Thumbelina tries to find others her size, but encounters many odd creatures including Grundel, a love-sick toad, the obnoxious Berkeley Beetle, spinster Ms. Fieldmouse, and the wealthy Mr. Mole, who wants to marry her.

**Comments:** "You can do impossible things if you follow your heart." So sings Jacquimo the swallow. It seems to be a recurring goal for Don Bluth, both in his movies and in real life.

"It's like the beginning of *Pinocchio*," he explains, "When Jiminy Cricket actually sings 'When You Wish Upon a Star' and says, 'That's a nice piece of philosophy, but I bet you don't think it's really true.' Then he proceeds to tell the story to help you understand that it is true," Bluth said in the *Orange Country Register*, April 3, 1994. "I think Jacquimo singing 'Follow Your Heart' is basically the same thing: Here's the philosophy, and we're about to tell you a story to illustrate the philosophy." Bluth grinned and admitted, "It wasn't conscious. There is a lot of our situation that is built into this movie."

Bluth hired a screenwriter, Carol Lynn Pearson, to adapt Hans Christian Andersen's fairy tale. But, he told film critic Philip Wuntch, "In the first screenplay, Thumbelina was so assured and so wise, you wondered why she would want to marry this wimpy prince." Rather than making the prince a stronger character,

Bluth said, "We rewrote it to make her innocent. Still, at one point in her journey, she actually considers marrying Mr. Mole. Winter is coming, and she's completely alone, and Mr. Mole is very wealthy. So she considers marrying just for security, which is a very realistic outlook. A lot of women would do it," he said in the *Dallas Morning News*, April 2, 1994.

"Children just don't want to watch love scenes at all, and they run the risk of being corny. In the love-at-first-sight meeting between Thumbelina and the Prince, we never mention love. Although their eyes indicate they're in love, they talk about everything else. Subtext, rather than the text, is the most important thing in a scene like this."

For the music, Bluth tracked down Barry Manilow, who scored the film with William Ross, and wrote the songs in partnership with lyricists Jack Feldman and Bruce Sussman, one of which was the soaring melody "Let Me Be Your Wings," which exemplified the romance between Thumbelina and Prince Cornelius.

For two years and $28 million, over 200 animators toiled on the film at Bluth's studios in Burbank, California, Dublin, Ireland, and Budapest, Hungary. Although it finished production after *A Troll in Central Park*, *Thumbelina* was considered to be more commercial, so it was released to theaters first. "I think it's our best to date," Bluth told Michael H. Price of the *Fort Worth Star-Telegram*, April 1, 1994.

According to John Horn in the *Los Angeles Times*, June 1, 1997, Warner Bros. held two test screenings. In the first screening, the audience reaction was flat. In the second screening, Warner Bros. prefaced the film with the Disney logo. The audience's response was more favorable.

The film was retitled *Hans Christian Andersen's Thumbelina*, and paired with an *Animaniacs* short, "I'm Mad." It opened with $2.3 million at 1,502 theaters, eventually grossing a meager $11.4 million in the United States. Bluth blamed the film's failure on inadequate marketing on the part of Warner Bros.

*Thumbelina* won the dubious honor of a 1995 Razzie Award for the Worst Original Song, music by Barry Manilow and lyrics by Jack Feldman, for the song "Marry the Mole!"

Perhaps referring to his box-office failures and the low morale at his studio, Bluth told the *Dallas Morning News* that an animator "must be passionate and yet forgiving of all the people he will work with. Animation is very personal, and no one else may see things his way. And he should be financially independent because he may not make a dime. But animation is not about making money. It's not an industry. It's about making life more beautiful."

On May 3, 1994, five weeks before Disney released *The Lion King*, 20th Century Fox announced that it was investing $100 million in an animation division to be headed by Bluth and Goldman, leaving the Irish studio they had run for eight years. Bluth told the *Los Angeles Times* that he and Goldman looked to Fox for the sophisticated scriptwriting and marketing lacked by his company. With Fox, he said, "I think we have a shot at being competitive." (WRM)

**Additional Credits:** Screenplay: Don Bluth. Music: Barry Manilow. Supervising animation director: John Pomeroy. Directing animators: John Hill, Richard Bazley, Jean Morel, Len Simon, Piet Dreycker, Dave Kupczyk. Sequence animation directors: Cathy Jones, Ralf Palmer. Animators: Nassos Vakalis, John Power, Kevin Johnson, Bill Waldman, Marcelo Moura, Chris Derochie, Oliver Wade, Tom Steisinger, Frank Gabriel, Robert Fox, Sam Fleming, Paul J. Kelly, Sandro Cleuzo, Sylvia Hoefnagels, Shane Zalvin, Edison Goncalves, Ben Burgess, Paul Newberry, Troy Saliba, Rusty Stoll, Sung Kwon, Jackie Corley, Robert Jurgen Sprathoff, Konrad Winterlich. Art director: Barry Atkinson. Live action reference cast: Angeline Ball, Penny Dormer (Thumbelina), Chris DeRochie (Prince Cornelius), Kevin Galagher (Mr. Beetle), Brenda Galagher (Ms. Fieldmouse), Moya Mackle (Queen Tabitha), Rowland Wilson (King Colbert), Pat Leavy (Mother).

## The Tigger Movie (2/11/00) Walt Disney Pictures.

77 mins. Director: Jun Falkenstein. Producer: Cheryl Abood. Voices: Jim Cummings (Tigger, Winnie the Pooh), Nikita Hopkins (Roo), Ken Sansom (Rabbit), John Fiedler (Piglet), Peter Cullen (Eeyore), Andre Stojka (Owl), Kath Soucie (Kanga), Tom Attenborough (Christopher Robin), John Hurt (Narrator), Frank Welker (Additional Voices).

**Consumer Tips:** ☆☆ MPAA Rating: G. Adapted from the stories by A. A. Milne.

**Story:** Tigger's frenetic bouncing leads to much irritation in the Hundred Acre Wood and the destruction

©Walt Disney Enterprises, Inc.

of Eeyore's lean-to. The Pooh crew asks Tigger to find someone else to bounce with. Little Roo suggests that Tigger find his family, and after a consultation with Owl, Tigger takes the term "family tree" literally. No kin are to be found up in the trees, so Tigger's well-meaning friends forge a letter from fictitious family members and as a result are forced to masquerade as Tiggers. The deception is discovered, Tigger stalks out in anger, and in a danger-filled finale Tigger discovers that his family has always been there in the form of his companions.

**Comments:** This movie is not adult fare, and it is doubtful that older children will be engrossed. Even for those who are aficionados of Winnie the Pooh and company, *The Tigger Movie* is no exceptional treat. It is a serviceable film spotlighting one of the more rambunctious of Milne's characters; perhaps the most heavily merchandised one. The lesson that anyone who truly loves you is family is rather nice, but any experienced viewer (or sophisticated kid) can see it coming from a Hundred Acres away. The animation is very simple and none too slick either; there are several scenes in which Winnie the Pooh slides noticeably off-model.

There is one interesting, if somewhat incongruous, moment in the picture, the musical number "Round My Family Tree." There are some cute in-jokes for lovers of high art and Busby Berkely musicals. Disney's old songwriting warhorses, Richard and Robert Sherman, wrote the number and it is easily the most energetic sequence in a rather slow-moving film. Another scene that brings a smile is the one in which Pooh and

his cohort arrives at Tigger's house in rumpled, cheesy tiger costumes, pretending to be his family. Even though their most prominent features are poking out of the disguises, it takes Tigger quite some time to catch on. One plot device in *The Tigger Movie* is recycled in a later theatrical release, *Piglet's Big Movie* (2003): the maligned lead character proves his value to the group by saving the other character's lives in a thrilling action-adventure finish. Is this just audience manipulation, or can't Christopher Robin take better care of his toys?

*The Tigger Movie* made $45.5 million on a $20 million budget. Some of the animation was done at the Disney studio in Japan. This was voice artist Jim Cumming's first theatrical turn as Tigger, although he had done the voice for Disney's Winnie the Pooh cable television series. Cummings replaced 76-year-old Paul Winchell. (MG)

**Additional Credits:** Associate producers: Jennifer Blohm, Richmond Horine. Music: Harry Gregson-Williams, Kenny Loggins. Additional music: Klaus Badelt, Steve Jablonsky. Songs: Richard M. Sherman, Robert B. Sherman. Music arranger/orchestrator: Martin Erskine. Orchestrators: Bruce Fowler, Walt Fowler. Art director: Toby Bluth, William Dely. Production manager: Jennifer Blohm. Production supervisors: Ferrell Barron, Christopher Kracker, Jennifer Lopez, Marilyn Munro, Kristin Rawnsley. Supervising animation director: Kenichi Tsuchiya. Animation director: Chris Otsuki, Larry Whitaker. Animators: Ernie Gilbert, Craig R. Maras, Larry Whitaker, Ron Friedman, Ingin Kim. Character animator: Greg Manwaring. Key animator: David Kuhn.

**Titan A.E.** (6/16/00) 20th Century Fox. 95 mins. Directors: Don Bluth, Gary Goldman. Producers: David Kirschner, Gary Goldman, Don Bluth. Voices: Matt Damon (Cale), Bill Pullman (Korso), Drew Barrymore (Akima), John Leguizamo (Gune), Janeane Garofalo (Stith), Nathan Lane (Preed), Ron Perlman (Professor Sam Tucker), Alex D. Linz (Young Cale), Tone Loc (Tek), Jim Breuer (The Cook), Christopher Scarabosio (Queen Drei), Jim Cummings (Chowquin), Charles Rocket (Firrikash, Slave Trader Guard), Ken Campbell (Po), Tsai Chin (Old Woman), Crystal Scales (Drifter Girl), David L. Lander (The Mayor), Thomas A. Chantler (Male Announcer), Elaine A. Clark (Citizen), Roy Conrad (Second Human), Leslie Hedger

©Twentieth Century Fox Film Co.

(First Human, additional voices), Roger L. Jackson (First Alien), Shannon Orrock (Female Announcer), Alex Pels (Soldier), Eric Schniewind (Alien), Stephen W. Stanton (Colonist).

**Consumer Tips:** ☆☆½ MPAA Rating: PG.

**Story:** In the year 3033, 15 years after earth has been destroyed by ruthless aliens called the Drej, a group of surviving humans and aliens led by Cale, a rebellious young man, search for the Titan spacecraft, the only hope to restore the human race.

**Comments:** If there's one thing Don Bluth's films have in common, it's orphans. Pete in *Pete's Dragon* is an orphan. Penny in *The Rescuers* is an orphan. *An American Tail* has Fievel in Orphan's Alley. Littlefoot and Spike are orphans in *The Land Before Time*. Anne-Marie in *All Dogs Go to Heaven*. Anya in *Anastasia*. In *Titan A.E.*, with earth destroyed, Cale and the entire human race have been orphaned. For Don Bluth, *Titan A.E.* is the ultimate orphan film.

The project was originally conceived in 1994 as *Treasure Planet*, developed separately from the John Musker/Ron Clements version at Disney, with Mel Gibson considered in the role of Long John Silver. Then it evolved into *Planet Ice*, fluctuating between CG or hand-drawn/CG hybrid, to be directed by Art Vitello (*Gummi Bears*, *Taz-Mania*). Fox purchased Blue Sky, a feature film effects and commercial studio based in Harrison, New York, to produce the all-CG version. After

*Quest for Camelot* bombed at the box office, Fox scuttled its project and $30 million in development costs. Then, Fox's president, Bill Mechanic, presented it to Don Bluth, who—despite his discomfort with the science-fiction genre—seized the opportunity to direct a project that was edgier and aimed at the same audience that had embraced Fox's smash hit, *Independence Day*.

"Right now, we're pigeonholed as Disney wannabe's," Bluth acknowledged in the *Orange County Register*, June 18, 2000. "Let's try and build a movie that isn't aimed at just the family audience."

With the release delayed from 1999 to summer 2000, Mechanic gave Bluth 19 months to complete the film (Bluth and Goldman preferred two years). The budget: $75 million (inclusive of its earlier costs). The title changed to *Titan A.E.* (After Earth), the rationale being that it was a hip title the way *Independence Day* was marketed as "ID4" or *Terminator 2* as "T2."

According to Gary Goldman, the filmmakers had planned for 40 percent of the film to be CG-animated; the amount rose to 87 percent. Blue Sky Studios produced the creation of the New World sequence.

For their hero, the filmmakers thought the audience would identify with Cale, a cynical young man, whose emotions ran the gamut from grim to grimmer to grimmest. "In some ways, this is a hero who is not easy to like. One thing is for certain—a hero is the last thing he wants to be. He's mercenary, and he's got a real attitude," Gary Goldman admitted to Peter Stack of the *San Francisco Chronicle*, June 4, 2000.

For teen appeal, music supervisor Glen Ballard jammed the film with 11 songs by bands like Powerman 5000, Electrasy, Splashdown, the Urge, and Luscious Jackson, while composer Graeme Revell used electronic music for his score.

Four months prior to *Titan*'s release, in February 2000, Fox Animation laid off 255 of its 320 employees, with no projects greenlit for the future.

*Titan* premiered Wednesday, June 16. It grossed $9.4 million on 2,734 screens in its opening weekend. Disney countered two days later, June 18, with *Fantasia 2000*, which on its opening day grossed $2,911,485 on 1,313 screens. Its gross reached $60.5 million as of January 1, 2001. *Titan* totaled $22.8 million by September 3, 2000.

On June 23, a week after *Titan*'s premiere, Bill Mechanic left Fox. On June 28, Fox closed its Phoenix facility after six years of production, two movies, a direct-to-video production, and $100 million in start-up costs. The corporation had considered withdrawing from animation altogether, but the CG *Ice Age* proved to be so profitable that Fox commissioned more CG animation from Blue Sky, beginning with *Robots*.

Bluth later opened his own office in Phoenix, established a Web site (www.donbluth.com), and produced a third installment of his *Dragon's Lair* video game franchise, *Dragon's Lair 3D: Return to the Lair*, released in 2002.

"Computer-generated animation, it's the flavor of the month," Bluth told Rick Lyman of the *New York Times*, July 24, 2000. "I will never draw another character and give the rights to someone else. And I think that pretty much puts me out of the movie business."

*Titan A.E.* is a poor blend of CG and hand-drawn animation, particularly in scenes where the 2-D characters moved "on twos" (every other frame) in CG environments that panned "on ones" (every frame), causing a strobing effect. Bluth and Goldman failed to learn from Brad Bird's *The Iron Giant*, in which he applied techniques that seamlessly blended hand-drawn animation with CG. And who cares about an unlikable jerk for a hero? The most appealing character is Preed—and he's a villain! The CG visual effects dazzle, but the noisy technopop drowns the dialogue, the gloom-and-doom mood is relentless, and the remaining characters are either bland or annoying. No wonder *Titan* crashed at the box office. (WRM)

**Additional Credits:** Screenplay: Ben Edlund, John August, Joss Whedon. Story: Hans Bauer, Randall McCormick. Music: Graeme Revell. Director of animation: Len Simon. Directing animators: Troy Saliba, John Hill, Robert Fox, Renato Dos Anjos, Edison Goncalves, Paul Newberry. Supervising animator: Paul J. Kelly. Animators: Kelly Baigent, Tobias Schwarz, Rafael Diaz Canales, Marco Plantilla, Maximillan Nepomuceno, Allan Fernado, Steve Cunningham, Michael Tweedle, Jean Kalilie, Helio Takahashi, Melvin Silao, Manuel Galiana, Joey Paraiso, Salvador "JoJo" Young, Hugo M. Takahashi, John Power, Dimitri Tenev, Robert Sprathoff. Additional animation: Sandra R. Keely, Debbie Gold, Ryan McElhinney, Nasos Vakalis, Michael Lahay, Jeff Varab, Barry Iremonger. Effects supervisor: Peter Matheson. Effects directing animators: Deidre Reynolds-Behan, Julian Hynes, Declan Walsh. Effects animators: Leslie Aust, Edwin Bocalan, John Costello, Stephen Deane, Earl A. Hibbert,

Sonnie Lagonera, Paul Morris, Raquel V. Omana, Angelita Ramos, Gorio Vicuna.

**Tokyo Godfathers** (12/5/03) Goldwyn (Japan). 92 mins. Director: Satoshi Kon. Producer: Masao Maruyama. Voices: Toru Emori (Gin), Aya Okamoto (Miyuki), Yoshiaki Umegaki (Hana), Shozo Izuka (Oota), Seizo Kato (Mother).

**Consumer Tips:** ☆☆☆☆ MPAA Rating: PG-13. Christmas melodrama.

**Story:** Gin (a 40ish alcoholic), Hana (a transvestite who longs to be a real woman), and Miyuki, a teenage runaway, are three cynical homeless people thrown together during a freezing, snowy Christmas season in Tokyo. When they find an abandoned baby in a dumpster, their search for its parents gets them involved with a gangland wedding and attempted assassination, the rescue of an old derelict, a transvestite's holiday party, and saving the life of a mentally disturbed woman.

**Comments:** *Tokyo Godfathers*, like Satoshi Kon's previous *Perfect Blue* and *Millennium Actress*, was made more for international film festivals and competition for awards than for its general release. This was Kon's first attempt at a fantasy-comedy rather than a psychological drama in which the fantasy elements are understood by the audience to be in the minds of the characters.

Kon acknowledged that *Tokyo Godfathers* was based upon John Ford's 1948 Christmas Western movie *Three Godfathers*, in which three outlaws find a dying mother and promise to save her baby. Kon updated this melodrama into a sociological commentary on modern urban society's abandonment of homeless street people.

*Tokyo Godfathers* is Kon's first feature to swing all the way from straight drama and tragedy through gentle humor to blatant comedy, emphasized by a visual shift from realistic character design to an exaggerated super-deformed grotesqueness. The physical action is secondary to the emotional state of and relationship between the three godfathers. Gen, a middle-aged drunkard, is despondent about his lost family and dreams of his youth, which he blames on others. Hana is bitterly aware that she is too ugly and masculine to ever pass as a real woman. Miyuki refuses to reveal her past; she is a stereotypical sullen teenager positive that all adults are her enemy. When they find the well-dressed abandoned baby, Hana is frantic to adopt it while Miyuki fears that turning it over to any authorities will get them into trouble. They compromise on finding the baby's parents and learning why such an apparently well-cared-for baby was left in a dumpster.

During their adventures (which skillfully blend comedy and drama into the same scenes rather than alternating between the two), the three constantly argue and hold introspective monologues that reveal personal secrets they had never admitted to each other or to themselves before. The movie begins realistically, but subtle coincidences begin to occur and escalate until, by the movie's end, there is no doubt that Gen, Hana, and Miyuki are being watched over by heavenly forces. *Tokyo Godfathers* is Kon's version of the American traditional Christmas fantasy in which the protagonists have their faith restored by God, angels, Santa Claus, or all of the above.

*Tokyo Godfathers* had its world premiere at the 2003 Big Apple Anime Fest in New York in August, at which Kon was guest of honor. It played at other international film festivals before its Japanese general release or its American art-theater release in December 2003. (FP)

**Additional Credits:** Executive producer: Shinichi Kobayashi, Taro Maki, Masao Takiyama. Screenplay: Satoshi Kon, Keiko Nobumoto. Story: Satoshi Kon. Music: Moonriders, Keiichi Suzuki. Animation director: Ken'ichi Konishi. Character designers: Satoshi Kon, Ken'ichi Konishi. Color designer: Satoshi Hashimoto. Art director: Nobutaka Ike. Codirector: Shogo Furuya. Cinematography: Katsutoshi Sugai. Editor: Takeshi Seyama, Kashiko Kimura. Sound director: Masafumi Mima.

**Tom and Jerry: The Movie** (5/28/93) Miramax. 80 mins. Director/producer: Phil Roman. Voices: Richard Kind (Tom), Dana Hill (Jerry), Anndi McAffee (Robyn Starling), Charlotte Rae (Aunt Figg), Tony Jay (Lickboot), Rip Taylor (Captain Kiddie), Henry Gibson (Dr. Applecheek), Michael Bell (Ferdinand, Straycatcher #1), Ed Gilbert (Puggsy, Daddy Starling), David L. Lander (Frankie da Flea), Howard Morris (Squawk), Sydney Lassick (Straycatcher #2), Raymond McLeod (Alleycat, Bulldog), Mitchell D. Moore (Alleycat), Scott Wojahn (Alleycat), Tino Insana (Patrol-

©Turner Entertainment and Telefilm-Essen GMBH

man), Don Messick (Droopy), B. J. Ward (Woman's Voice), Greg Burson (Man's Voice).

**Consumer Tips:** ☆ MPAA Rating: G.

**Story:** Tom and Jerry end their feud when they meet Robyn, a runaway girl in search of her father, who's being chased by her evil Aunt Figg.

**Comments:** Tom and Jerry had been absent from movie screens for over 25 years when they resurfaced in this saccharine movie. Though cocreator Joe Barbera was credited as a consultant, *Tom and Jerry: The Movie*, released through Turner, was produced by Film Roman, which was then working on such television series as *Garfield and Friends, Bobby's World*, and *The Simpsons*. Film Roman founder Phil Roman directed, having previously worked on the Chuck Jones's Tom and Jerry revival in the 1960s. The most notable aspect of the movie was the fact that both Tom and Jerry spoke. Despite publicity to the contrary, this was not a first by any means. Tom had frequently vocalized, usually an isolated line or occasional singing (1946's *Solid Serenade*), and Jerry narrated *Blue Cat Blues* (1956).

Though the opening credits feature the cat and mouse violence of old, in pantomime, this soon gives way to a rather mawkish story. Tom and Jerry, now homeless, band together and wind up helping a young girl, Robyn, kept under the thumb of her greedy aunt and her lawyer. Dialogue in general, and from Tom and Jerry in particular, weighs down most of the movie, and slapstick chases are given short shrift in favor of musical numbers and bonding moments. In the course of the film, cat, mouse, and girl encounter an increasingly strange parade of antagonists, including a group of pet thieves, a fiendish veterinarian who experiments on animals, and a cheerfully insane carnival proprietor, Captain Kiddie (in one of the more inventive touches, the latter's hand-puppet Squawk has a mind of its own).

The entire caper, though entertaining enough for some kids, resembles a demented remake of John Huston's *Annie*. Other odd character name choices include Lickboot the lawyer, Dr. Applecheeks (for the evil vet), Daddy Starling, and Aunt Pristine Figg. The voices are mostly decent enough, highlighted by Charlotte Rae as Aunt Figg and Rip Taylor as the bizarre Captain Kiddie; both Tom and Jerry sound miscast, but then any sustained voice for the characters would automatically feel unfamiliar and strange to most. Some fun in-jokes lighten things a bit for animation buffs: Tex Avery's Droopy has a cameo (voiced by HB stalwart Don Messick), and at one point Tom passes a butcher shop called Bill and Joe's. Still, as with most character revivals, Tom and Jerry are better enjoyed in the original shorts than in this outing. (AL)

*Additional Credits:* Executive producers: Roger Mayer, Jack Petrik, Hans Brockerman, Justin Ackerman. Coproducer: Bill Schultz. Screenplay: Dennis Marks. Based on characters created by William Hanna, Joseph Barbera. Music: Henry Mancini. Lyrics: Leslie Bricusse. Sequence directors: John Sparey, Monte Young, Bob Nesler, Adam Kuhlman, Eric Daniels, Jay Jackson, Skip Jones. Supervising directors (Taiwan): James Miko, Aundre Knutson. Animation director: Dale L. Baer. Key animators: J. K. Kim, Adam Dykstra, Dan Haskett, Adam Kuhlman, Kevin Petrilak, Kamoon Song, Kevin Wurzer. Animators: Eric Thomas, Art Roman, Doug Frankel, Tony Fucile, Steve Gordon, Leslie Gorin, Brian Robert Hogan, Gabi Payn, Irv Spence, Arnie Wong, David Courtland, Frederick DuChau, Darin Hilton, Sadao Miyamoto, David Nethery, Michael Polvani, Alejandro Reyes, Michael Toth, Larry Whitaker, Tomikiro Yamaguchi, Matthew Bates, Jon Hooper, Mark Koetsier, Dan Kuenster, Linda Miller, Mark Pudleiner, Chad Stewart, Bonita Versh. Effects animation supervisor: Jeff Howard. Effects animators: Sean Applegate, George S. Chialtas, Corny Cole, Mark Dindal, Brett Hisey, John Huey, Craig Littell-Herrick, Gary

McCarver, Mary Mullen, January Nordman. Art Directors: Michael Peraza Jr., Michael Humphries.

**Tom Thumb** See *King Dick*.

**Toy Story** (11/22/95) Disney. 81 mins. Director: John Lasseter. Producers: Ralph Guggenheim, Bonnie Arnold. Voices: Tom Hanks (Woody), Tim Allen (Buzz Lightyear), Don Rickles (Mr. Potato Head), Jim Varney (Slinky Dog), Wallace Shawn (Rex), John Ratzenberger (Hamm), Annie Potts (Bo Peep), John Morris (Andy Davis), Erik von Detten (Sid Phillips), Laurie Metcalf (Andy's Mom), R. Lee Ermey (Sarge), Sarah Freeman (Hannah Phillips), Penn Jillette (Television Announcer).

©Disney / Pixar

*Consumer Tips:* ☆☆☆☆ MPAA Rating: G. Fantasy-adventure. A landmark film and a modern masterpiece.

*Story:* The toys in Andy's room are fearful of being replaced when the boy receieves a Buzz Lightyear action figure. Woody's plan to get rid of Buzz backfires, and they find themselves lost in the world outside of Andy's room.

*Comments:* If *Snow White and the Seven Dwarfs* brought forth the Golden Age of Animation, *Toy Story* ushered in the Silicon Age.

In 1979 George Lucas hired a team of computer graphics specialists to develop a state-of-the-art computer imaging system, resulting in the $100,000 Pixar computer. Their work produced the spectacular "Genesis Effect" sequence in *Star Trek II: The Wrath of*

*Khan* and the hologram of the Death Star II in *Return of the Jedi*. In 1984 Disney animator John Lasseter joined the team, creating the first CG short, "Andre and Wally B." Apple Computer chairman Steve Jobs purchased Lucasfilm's computer graphics division for $10 million, which became an independent company, Pixar. The studio developed its technical capabilities and proprietary software as it produced commercials and short films. "Luxo Jr.," released in 1986, received an Academy Award nomination for Best Animated Short Film. The character became the company icon in later films. "Red's Dream" came next in 1987, followed by "Tin Toy" in 1988—which also received an Academy Award for Best Animated Short Film—and "Knick Knack" in 1989. Pixar also developed the Computer Assisted Production System (CAPS) used by Disney as a digital ink-and-paint system, first applied on *The Rescuers Down Under* in 1990. Pixar's CAPS development team would not be recognized until two years later, winning the Scientific and Engineering Academy Award.

In May 1991, Pixar entered into an agreement with Walt Disney Pictures to develop and produce three animated features to be marketed and distributed by Disney. Their first project: *Toy Story*.

Made for an estimated budget of $30 million, the film ultimately grossed $191 million in the United States, accumulating $361 million worldwide.

Director John Lasseter received a Special Achievement Academy Award for his "inspired leadership of the Pixar *Toy Story* team resulting in the first feature-length computer animated film." *Toy Story*'s additional honors include winning eight ASIFA-Hollywood Annie Awards for Best Animated Feature and an ASCAP Film and Television Music Award. Edwin Catmull, Alvy Ray Smith, Thomas Porter, and Tom Duff received the Scientific and Engineering Academy Award for Digital Image Compositing.

Such was the success of *Toy Story* that in February 1997, Pixar entered a five-picture coproduction agreement with Disney, superceding the first agreement, in which both companies would cofinance, co-own, and cobrand each picture. Both would share equally in the profits after recovery of all marketing and distribution costs, a distribution fee paid to Disney, and other fees and costs. *Toy Story 2* was covered under the agreement but, as a sequel, did not count toward the five original pictures. The five films produced would be *A Bug's Life* (1998), *Monsters, Inc.* (2001), *Finding Nemo* (May 2003), *The Incredibles* (2004), and *Cars* (2006).

*Toy Story* is the kind of film animators dream of working on, with full creative autonomy, a director who knows what he's doing, first-class production values, appealing characters, and a solid, entertaining story that doesn't pander to the audience. Pixar's achievement will serve as inspiration to filmmakers for generations to come. (WRM)

***Additional Credits:*** Screenplay: Joss Whedon, Andrew Stanton, Joel Cohen, Alec Sokolow. Story: John Lasseter, Pete Docter, Andrew Stanton, Joe Ranft. Music/songs: Randy Newman. Supervising animator: Pete Docter. Directing animators: Rich Quade, Ash Brannon. Animation: Michael Berenstein, Kim Blanchette, Colin Brady, Davy Crockett Felten, Angie Glocka, Rex Grignon, Tom K. Gurney, Jimmy Hayward, Hal T. Hickel, Karen Kiser, Shawn P. Krause, Anthony P. Lamolinara, Guionne Leroy, Bud Luckey, Matt Luhn, Les Major, Glenn McQueen, Mark Oftedal, Bob Peterson, Jeff Pidgeon, Jeff Pratt, Steve Rabatich, Roger Rose, Andrew Schmidt, Steve Segal, Doug Sheppeck, Alan Sperling, Doug Sweetland, David Tart, Ken Willard. Additional animation: Shawn P. Krause, Matt Luhn, Bob Peterson, Andrew Schmidt. Art director: Ralph Eggleston.

## Toy Story 2 (11/24/99) Disney-Pixar. 92 mins.

Directors: John Lasseter, Ash Brannon, Lee Unkrich. Producers: Helene Plotkin, Karen Robert Jackson. Voices: Tom Hanks (Woody), Tim Allen (Buzz Lightyear), Joan Cusak (Jessie), Kelsey Grammer (Prospector Pete), Don Rickles (Mr. Potato Head), Jim Varney (Slinky Dog), Wallace Shawn (Rex the Green Dinosaur), John Ratzenberger (Hamm the Piggy Bank), Annie Potts (Bo Peep), Wayne Knight (Al), John Morris (Andy Davis), Laurie Metcalf (Andy's Mom), Estelle Harris (Mrs. Potato Head), Andrew Stanton (Evil Emperor Zurg), Joe Ranft (Wheezy the Penguin).

***Consumer Tips:*** ☆☆☆☆ MPAA Rating: G. A modern-day fantasy-adventure. For everyone who loves toys.

***Story:*** When Woody is accidentally sold in a garage sale, Buzz Lightyear and the toys attempt to rescue him

©Disney / Pixar

from toy collector Big Al, who plans to ship him to Japan.

**Comments:** Another triumph for Pixar, setting standards of excellence at nearly every level.

*Toy Story 2* was initially conceived as a direct-to-video feature. It also suffered from story problems, but after revisions by the crew, the film was given a higher budget and made a theatrical feature.

The introduction of cowgirl Jessie, her story, and the heightened sense of danger brought a new level of demension, drama, and heart to the film. As good as the first film was, this sequel topped it in every way.

Throughout the 1990s Pixar had used shorts (as Walt Disney did in the 1930s) to advance its technical capabilities. In 1997 it released "Geri's Game," which marked new improvements in animating skin and cloth. The following year it would earn the Academy Award for Best Animated Short Film and ASIFA-Hollywood's Annie Award for Outstanding Achievement in an Animated Short Subject. Geri appeared in *Toy Story 2* as a repairman, voiced by Jonathan Harris, who fixes Woody's severed arm.

*Toy Story 2* became the first film to be entirely created, mastered, and exhibited digitally. It also cost more, and earned more, than the original. Made for $90 million, the film's total domestic gross was $245 million, grossing $485 million worldwide.

*Toy Story 2* swept the 2000 Annie Awards in seven categories, including Outstanding Achievement in an Animated Theatrical Feature. It received an Oscar nomination for Best Original Song, and in 2000, Jessie the yodeling cowgirl received the Patsy Montana Entertainer Award from the National Cowgirl Museum and Hall of Fame. (WRM)

**Additional Credits:** Executive producer: Sarah McArthur. Story: John Lasseter, Pete Docter, Ash Brannon, Andrew Stanton. Additional story material: Dan Jeup, Joe Ranft, Lee Unkrich, Jim Capobianco, Colin Brady, Jimmy Hayward, Steve Boyett, Elias Davis, David Reynolds, David Pollock. Screenplay: Andrew Stanton, Rita Hsiao, Doug Chamberlin, Chris Webb. Music: Randy Newman. Supervising animator: Glenn McQueen. Directing animators: Kyle Balda, Dylan Brown. Animation: Nicolas Alan Barillaro, Stephen Barnes, Bobby Beck, Michael Berenstein, Ash Brannon, Jennifer Cha, Scott Clark, Bret Codere, Melanie Cordan, Tim Crawfurd, David Devan, Mark Farquhar, Ike Feldman, Andrew Gordon, Steven Gregory, Jimmy Hayward, Tim Hittle, Steven Hunter, Ethan Hurd, John Kahrs, Nancy Kato, Patty Kihm, Karen Kiser, Shawn Krause, Bob Koch, Wendell Lee, Peter Lepeniotis, Angus MacLane, Dan Mason, Jon Mead, Billy Meritt, Karyn Metler, Valerie Mih, James Ford Murphy, Peter Nash, Mark Oftedal, Bret Parker, Michael Parks, Sanjay Patel, Bobby Padesta, Jeff Pratt, Karen Prell, Brett Pulliam, Rich Quade, Mike Quinn, Roger Rose, Robert H. Ross, Gini Cruz Santos, Anthony Scott, Doug Sheppeck, Alan Sperling, Ross Stevenson, Doug Sweetland, David Tart, J. Warren Trezevant, Mark A. Walsh, Tasha Weeden, Adam Wood, Christina Yim, Kurena Yokoo. Fix animation: Paul Mendoza, Andrea Schultz. Production design: William Cone, Jim Pearson. Story supervisors: Joe Ranft, Dan Jeup. Story artists: Jim Capobianco, David Fulp, Matthew Luhn, Ken Mitchroney, Max Brace, Jill Culton, Rob Gibbs, Jason Katz, Bud Luckey, Ricky Nieva, Sanjay Patel, Bob Peterson, Jeff Pidgeon, Jan Pinkava, Bobby Podesta, David Skelly, Nathan Stanton, Mark A. Walsh.

**Transformers: The Movie** (8/8/86) DEG. 86 mins. Director: Nelson Shin. Producers: Joe Bacal, Tom Griffin. Voices: Orson Welles (Unicron), Robert Stack (Ultra Magnus), Leonard Nimoy (Galvatron), Eric Idle (Wreck-Gar), Judd Nelson (Hot Rod, Rodimus Prime), Lionel Stander (Kup), John Moschitta Jr. (Blurr), Norman Alden (Kranix, Orbilus), Jack Angel (Astrotrain), Michael Bell (Prowl, Scrapper, Swoop, Junkion, Bombshell), Gregg Berger (Grimlock), Susan Blu (Arcee), Arthur Burghardt (Devastator), Corey Burton (Spike, Brawn, Shockwave), Roger C. Carmel (Cyclonus, Quintesson Leader), Regis Cordic (Quintesson Judge),

Scatman Crothers (Jazz), Peter Cullen (Optimus Prime, Ironhide), Bud Davis (Dirge), Walker Edmiston (Inferno), Paul Eiding (Perceptor), Ed Gilbert (Blitzwing), Dan Gilvezan (Bumblebee), Buster Jones (Blaster), Stan Jones (Scourge), Casey Kasem (Cliffjumper), Chris Latta (Starscream, Wheeljack), David Mendenhall (Daniel), Don Messick (Scavenger, Ratchet), Hal Rayle (Shrapnel), Clive Revill (Kickback), Neil Ross (Bonecrusher, Hook, Springer, Slag), Frank Welker (Megatron, Soundwave, Rumble, Frenzy, Laserbeak, Wheelie, Junkion), Victor Caroli (Narrator).

©DeLaurentis Entertainment

**Consumer Tips:** ☆½ MPAA Rating: PG for profanity. A feature-length high-tech toy commercial. Not "user-friendly." For fans only.

**Story:** In the year 2005, transforming robots, led by good guy Ultra Magnus, fight to save the universe from evil Planet Unicron.

**Comments:** Though giant, transforming robot shows were already a yen-a-dozen in Japan, *Transformers* was the first robot show hugely popular with the American public, cross-promoted by the top-selling Hasbro toys. In the year 1985, Earth became the battleground between two sentient robot forces: the virtuous Autobots and the evil Decepticons. Hailing from the planet Cybertron, these automatons could transform into various vehicles and other objects.

Marvel Productions made an initial 13 episodes for weekend syndication, followed by 49 episodes the following season for weekday showings. The series became very popular in Japan, known as *Fight! Super Robot Lifeform Transformers* (*Tatakae! Chô robot seimeitai Transformers*) for Season 1 and *Fight! Super Robot Lifeform Transformers: 2010* for Season 2. Japanese production companies Takara and Tôei Dôga made an OVA called *Transformers: Scramble City Hatsudôden*, released in 1986 but not in the United States.

So popular was the franchise that Marvel made *Transformers: The Movie*, in which the Decepticons take over the home world of Galvatron. To enhance crossover appeal to older audiences, the following celebrities were used: Judd Nelson as Hot Rod/Rodimus Prime, Leonard Nimoy as Galvatron, Robert Stack as Ultra Magnus, Eric Idle as the comical Wreck Gar, and Orson Welles, in his final role, as the devillike planet Unicron.

Several major characters were killed, including Optimus Prime. Why kill the leader of the Autobots? Lane Crockett in the *Shreveport Times*, March 28, 1987, reported that the philosophy of Hasbro is to turn its entire line every two years and introduce new toys. The company thought killing Optimus in the movie justified his disappearance from the toy market.

But, according to Alfred C. Carosi, corporate vice president of marketing services with Hasbro, "We got a lot of phone calls and letters from kids. We were frankly surprised at the number of letters. When we killed off Optimus Prime, I thought they might be a little bit upset, but we had new heroes for them in the movie. That didn't seem to matter. We didn't get any letters about any of the other characters. Based on that, we took a look at bringing Optimus back. If Bobby Ewing can come back, why not Optimus Prime?"

So, Optimus was restored to life in a two-part episode, "The Return of Optimus Prime," in the show's third season.

"Well, we've done it and we learned. The key is to be responsive to the kids, not upset them. We did that inadvertently. By definition, what we do should be fun," Carosi said.

*Transformers: The Movie* had a total domestic gross of $5 million. As a result, "Hasbro probably won't do another film," Carosi said. "They are very expensive to produce. We lost money on *Transformers* and *My Little Pony*, which we also created."(WRM)

**Additional Credits:** Codirector: Kozo Morishita. Executive producers: Margaret Loesch, Lee Gunther. Coproducer: Nelson Shin. Supervising producer: Jay Bacal. Associate producers: Masaharu Etô, Tomo Fukamoto. Writer: Ron Friedman. Story consultant: Flint Dille. Based on the Hasbro toy, The Transformers. Music: Vince DiCola, Spencer Proffer, Robert J. Walsh. Songs: "Weird Al" Yankovic, Anne Bryant, Ford Kinder, Lenny Macaluso. Animation directors: John Patrick Freeman, Norm McCabe, Gerald L. Moeller, Bob Matz, Margaret Nichols. Assistant animation directors: Shigeyasu Yamauchi, Masao Ito, Baik Seung Kyun. Key animators: Nobuyoshi Sasakado, Shigemitsu Fujitaka, Koichi Fukuda, Yoshitaka Koyama, Yoshinori Kanamori, Yoshinobu Inano, Baik Nam Yeoul, Kiyomitsu Tsuji, Masanori Shino, Toshio Mori, Shigenobu Nagasaki, Yasuyoshi Uwai, Shigeo Matoba, Satoshi Yamaguchi, Yoichi Mitsui, Shigeru Murakami, Yoshito Miki, Takahiro Kagami. Special effects: Masayuki Kawachi, Shoji Sato.

**Treasure Planet** (11/27/02) Walt Disney Pictures. 95 mins. Directors: Ron Clements, John Musker. Producers: Ron Clements, Roy Conli, John Musker. Voices: Joseph Gordon-Levitt (Jim Hawkins), Austin Majors (Young Jim), Brian Murray (John Silver), David Hyde Pierce (Dr. Doppler), Emma Thompson (Captain Amelia), Roscoe Lee Browne (Mr. Arrow), Martin Short (B.E.N.), Laurie Metcalf (Sarah Hawkins), Dane A. Davis (Morph), Corey Burton (Onus), Patrick McGoohan (Billy Bones), Michael McShane (Hands), Michael Wilcott (Scroop), Tony Jay (Narrator).

©Walt Disney Enterprises, Inc.

**Consumer Tips:** ☆☆☆ MPAA Rating: PG. Based on the book by Robert Louis Stevenson, first published in 1883.

**Story:** Young Jim Hawkins gets possession of a spherical treasure map and goes off on a spacefaring expedition with Dr. Doppler in search of the legendary Treasure Planet. Also aboard ship are the pirate cyborg Long John Silver and his scurvy crew posing as shipmates. After many close shaves and reversals of fortune, Silver and Hawkins both reach the fabled planet, where they discover that they have forged a bond far more valuable than any treasure.

**Comments:** Whatever its strengths and weaknesses may be, *Treasure Planet* will be remembered for two infamous reasons: it was the biggest financial disaster in the history of Disney animation, and it played a key role in the decision to close the 2-D animation studio that had flourished for 65 years. The film reportedly carried a budget of $140–$180 million (according to which reports one believes), and the final domestic gross was $38 million, a figure so pitiful that *Treasure Planet* did not recoup even its advertising budget.

Ron Clements and John Musker wanted to make the film since 1985, when both were tyros at Disney. Even after the success of *The Little Mermaid* management was loath to touch it. After all, Disney had done the *Treasure Island* story in live action (1950), and it was hard to fit a film based on the novel into the then-popular Broadway extravaganza formula favored by the studio. It was finally agreed to allow Clements and Musker to do the film if they agreed to helm *Hercules*. The directors reworked Stevenson's novel into a galactic fantasy filled with cosmic pirates, exotic aliens, and, yes, a treasure planet.

Jim Hawkins became an unruly, jetboarding teen, Long John Silver a cyborg, and Treasure Island itself an awesome, world-sized construct containing the plunder of a galaxy. There is no reason this picture should have failed as miserably as it did. Repeated viewings prove it to be filled with great special effects and plenty of action. Fantastic backgrounds, layouts, and futuristic styling offer both sci-fi and adventure fans a surfeit of wonders, yet *Treasure Planet* failed to find an audience. It is possible that much of the problem came in the form of timing. The movie features considerable computer-generated effects, but is mostly 2-D. *Monsters, Inc.* and a slew of other computer-generated features had already wowed audiences. *Treasure Planet* was a solid film that floundered in a tidal wave of change, and nothing demonstrates this more emphatically than the movies it opened against: *Harry Potter and the Chamber of Secrets* and *Lord of the Rings: The Two Towers.*

In order to beat this kind of competition, *Treasure Planet* would have to be nearly perfect; but a good-looking, well-made film is not necessarily a great one. At 95 minutes, the movie was on the long side, and some of the time is spent on scenes that do not advance the plot. Jim Hawkins's initial encounter with the irritating robot B.E.N. serves mostly to allow Martin Short to give an over-the-top performance during a slow stretch of the film. Alliances shift one too many times, and after a bit it becomes difficult to accept John Silver's reversals in attitude and Jim's facile forgiveness of his many perfidies.

John Silver is problematic in more ways than one; this is probably animator Glen Keane's least satisfying character. Keane seems to be at his best animating the beautiful and the graceful; creations such as Aladdin, Pocahontas, and Tarzan come naturally to Keane, and even the feral title character featured in *Beauty and the Beast* is, in truth, a very handsome animal; witness the ballroom scene. Called upon to animate an ugly, obese freak, Keane clearly struggles.

Some of the follow-through on the character's movements suggests a water balloon being heaved about, and at other times Silver's expressions are lost in the fleshy folds of his face. Animating the character could not have been easy, as the decision was made to have Silver comprised of both 2-D *and* computer-generated animation. Some of it was quite difficult, such as placing a constantly revolving flywheel on one of Silver's temples. The composite work between Keane and CGI animator Eric Daniels is seamless, but one has to wonder how it affected Keane's depiction of the character and his movements.

Still, there is much that does work in *Treasure Planet.* Most of the highlights are courtesy of art director Andy Gaskill and production designer Steve Olds, who give the film a very striking look. There is a marvelous, three-dimensional traveling shot of a crescent-shaped space station, and the various ships are beautiful to behold. It is ridiculous to think that starships would look like 17th-century schooners, but the designs in service of this fantasy are so good that the idea is readily acceptable. One scene featuring a pod of galactic whales following alongside a star schooner is particularly thrilling.

Had *Treasure Planet* been produced at Clements and Musker's earlier behests, the film may have been much more successful. Faced with the rising tide of movies powered by computer-generated effects, *Treasure Planet* broke apart on the shoals of audience indifference. (MG)

***Additional Credits:*** Screenplay: Ron Clements, John Musker, Rob Edwards. Animation story: Ron Clements, John Musker, Ted Elliott, Terry Rossio. Screenplay: Ron Clements, John Musker, Rob Edwards. Based on the novel *Treasure Island* by Robert Louis Stevenson. Music: James Newton Howard. Song: John Rzenik. Supervising animators: John Ripa, Glen Keane, Ken Duncan, Sergio Pablos, Oskar Urretabizkaia, Michael Show, Jared Beckstrand, T. Daniel Hofstedt, Nancy Beiman, Adam Dykstra, Ellen Woodbury, Brian Ferguson, Marc Smith, John Pomeroy. Animators: James Baker, Michael Cedeno, Jerry Yu Ching, Danny Galieote, Randy Haycock, Richard Hopper, Shawn Keller, Sang-Jin Kim, Doug Krohn, Mario J. Menjivar, Bobby Alcid Rubio, Michael Stocker, Oliver Thomas, Bill Waldman, Dean Wellins, Dougg Williams, Anthony Wong, Anthony DeRosa, Tom Gately, Chris Hubbard, Ron Husband, Bert Klein, Marc Smith, Mark Alan Mitchell, Joe Oh, Dale Baer, David Block, Robert Espanto Domingo, David Moses Pimental, Nik Ranieri, Andrea Simonti, Mark Anthony Austin, Doug Bennett, Jay Jackson, Clay Kaytis, Mike D'Isa, Larry White. CGI lead animator: Eric Daniels. CGI animator: Rebecca Wilson Bresee. Visual effects supervisor: Dave Tidgwell. CGI supervisor: Kyle Odermatt. Visual effects animators: Sean Applegate, Dan Chaika, Ian J. Coony, Peter DeMund, Colbert Fennelly, James Menehune Goss, Bruce Heller, Craig L. Hoffman, Michael Cadwallader Jones, Bill Konersman, Kevin Lee, Brian Lutge, James DelaVera Mansfield, Mark Myer, Masa Oshiro, Kee Nam Suong, Phillip Vigil.

## The Triplets of Belleville (11/26/03) Sony Pictures Classics. 81 mins. Director: Sylvain Chomet. Producers: Didier Brunner, Paul Cadieux. Voices: Béatrice Bonifassi (Triplets singing voices), Jean-Claude Donda, Charles Prevost Linton, Michel Robin, Monica Viegas.

**Consumer Tips:** ☆☆☆☆ MPAA Rating: PG-13. Adventure.

©Les Armateurs / Production / Vivi Film / France 3 Cinema / RGP France / Sylvain Chomet

**Story:** Tour de France cyclist Champion is kidnapped by wine-mafia thugs in the late 1950s and brought overseas to Belleville to ride in captivity for the mobsters' betting games. Champion's grandmother, Madame Souza, and dog, Bruno, cross the Atlantic to rescue him from his captors, joining forces with a trio of singing women that was famous in the 1930s.

**Comments:** Director Sylvain Chomet won the Academy Award for Best Animated Short Film in 1997 for *La Vieille Dame et les Pigeons* (*The Old Lady and the Pigeons*), the story of a poor, starving gendarme who hatches an idea to take advantage of an old woman overfeeding pigeons in a park, not realizing that she has plans for him as well. The film stood out for its wonderful comic timing and twisted sense of humor; in *The Triplets of Belleville* that sense of humor takes us on a wonderful journey from France to North America.

The opening of *Triplets* pays tribute to its animated forebears: the film begins with a cartoon, a cross between a 1930s newsreel and a black-and-white Fleischer cartoon, of the famous singing trio the Triplets of Belleville, who perform onstage with Josephine Baker, Fred Astaire, and Django Reinhardt to a sold-out crowd. With this, we get a perfect sense of how the film will unfold, as we've met the title characters and learned how important music will be for the entire story.

Chomet describes his style as being based on mime and character acting, and being influenced by live camerawork to animation. This explains the almost complete lack of dialogue in this film—not that it needs it.

We have references to character actors and masters of timing from Jacques Tati to Buster Keaton to Tex Avery. Visual humor dominates *Triplets*; the almost complete lack of dialogue in the film makes you focus on the visual components of the plot. The main characters, Madame Souza, her grandson, Champion, and the dog, Bruno, all tell the story with simple expressions that seem to speak volumes.

The film combines traditional animation techniques with computer graphics and 3-D animation, particularly for the crowd shots during the Tour de France, the crossing of the ocean with remarkably realistic water, and some renderings of household items that become the focal points of certain scenes. Chomet's attention to detail is also apparent in the color schemes: the first half of the film, which takes place in France and is quite nostalgic, is dominated by warm colors, but the less hospitable Belleville is shot in cooler grays, blues, and blacks.

*Triplets* was an official selection at the Cannes, Telluride, and Toronto film festivals in 2003, and was nominated for two Academy Awards: Best Animated Feature Film and Best Music, and Original Song for "Belleville Rendez-vous."

What sets this film apart is the remarkable attention to detail: it helps create the humor and gives true personality to the characters and places we see. We get a wonderful view of the fanaticism surrounding the Tour de France, both from the cyclists and their grotesquely muscular calves, to the die-hard fans that chase after the athletes. Food and eating are a recurring theme, particularly the Triplets' diet of nothing but frogs. And Bruno's recurring, black-and-white dreams (the logical palette for a colorblind animal) and lifelong hatred of trains and are just two reasons why he is perhaps the most brilliantly animated and personality-laden non-anthropomorphic cartoon dog since Disney's Pluto—Bruno just about runs off with the film. (Daniel Goldmark)

**Additional Credits:** Screenplay: Sylvain Chomet. Music: Ben Charest. Associate producers: Viviane Vanfleteren, Regis Ghezelbash, Colin Rose. Music: Benoît Charest. Production design: Evgeni Tomov. Film editor: Chantal Colibert Brunner. Color design: Thierry Million. Character color research: Carole Roy. Supervising animator: Jean-Christophe Lie. Production manager: Francios Bernard. End credit song: "M" (Mathieu Chedid). Visual effects: Pieter Van Houte. Animators: Nicolas Quere, Emmanuel Guille, Julie Kuchlein, Rouja Koleva, Antoine Dartige, Laurent Kircher, Florian Fiebig, Yann Tremblay, Jean-Christophe Lie, Hugues Martel, Wang Zhigang, Paul Dutton, Xavier Dujardin, Philippe Lockerby, Sylvain Chomet, Panayot Panayotov, Dan Filippin, Corinne Khuyl, Olivier Goka, Marie Laure Guisset, Dirk de Loose, Joke Eycken, Taiga Zile, Inga Praulina, Ivete Hincenberga, Ieva Smite, Ilga Vevere, Valentina Lietuviete, Dace Darzniece, Roberts Cinkuss, Nelda Karpenska, Elita Kanepe, Zane Kozuhovska, Ilze Ruska.

**A Troll in Central Park** (10/7/94) Warner Bros. 76 mins. Directors: Don Bluth, Gary Goldman. Producers: Don Bluth, Gary Goldman, John Pomeroy. Voices: Dom DeLuise (Stanley), Phillip Glasser (Gus), Tawny Sunshine Glover (Rosie), Cloris Leachman (Queen Gnorga), Hayley Mills (Hilary), Jonathan Pryce (Alan), Charles Nelson Reilly (King Llort).

©Don Bluth Limited

**Consumer Tips:** ☆½ MPAA Rating: G. A musical fairy tale set in New York. Not recommended.

**Story:** An insecure troll named Stanley, banished to New York's Central Park, befriends two lonely children. Their work to beautify the park angers evil Queen Gnorga.

**Comments:** "As it is never a good thing that a child is born prematurely, so it is with producing a film. Development of a script is like the development of a child in the womb: It takes time and must be done right. Building the movie, *A Troll in Central Park*, taught us this lesson, but indeed, the hard way." So

said Don Bluth in his magazine, *Toon Talk*, July 2001, in which he virtually apologized for the production.

"I tell you all this in the hope that you might benefit from our foolish mistakes. Scrutinizing your own work is so important, but let's face it, we all are afraid of not measuring up, so we stubbornly cling to our own opinions, shutting out all others."

The troll was Stanley, banished from the troll kingdom because of his niceness. His voice came from Dom DeLuise, who replaced Buddy Hackett in the role. Bluth endowed his hero with long eyelashes, large bulbous lips, and a cute little bow on his tail. The director later admitted, "Stanley could have been a richer character with more levels to his personality. Maybe he could have had a dark side, a troll side that he struggled with."

Impressed by Ursula the sea witch from Disney's *The Little Mermaid*, Bluth passed along her attributes to Gnorga, the conceited queen of the trolls, complete with her own production number. Cloris Leachman voiced and sang the role. Gnorga's husband, King Llort, was played by Charles Nelson Reilly, replacing Robert Morley early in production.

While management tried to iron out story problems and contend with a fiscal crisis, the artists at Sullivan Bluth's Special Projects unit in Burbank animated footage for MCA/Universal's "Funtastic World of Hanna-Barbera" simulation ride for their new Florida theme park, plus "Princess of the Moon," a multimedia attraction for Oita's Harmony Land in Japan. This work provided welcome income for the studio, allowing it to keep its artists employed until feature funding could be secured.

*Troll* was actually completed before *Thumbelina*, but it was believed the latter film had more box-office potential, so it was released first. Both were distributed by Warner Bros.; both received the usual lack of publicity by Warner Bros.—frequently used as an excuse by Bluth for the failure of his films.

Joe Baltake in the October 11, 1994 *Sacramento Bee* pointed out, "There's nothing intrinsically wrong with Bluth's tale of Stanley, a gentle little troll, except that it evokes the response, 'Who cares?' Warners, the releasing company, doesn't seem to care. The studio opened the film with as little fanfare as ever. (There have been no advance screenings and no TV ads, and only meager print ads for it.) *A Troll in Central Park* may be too personal—so personal that it limits interest in itself."

*Troll's* theatrical intake was a pitiful $71,368 in the United States. By the time *Troll* was released, Bluth and Gary Goldman had already migrated from their studio in Ireland to 20th Century Fox's huge animation facility in Phoenix, Arizona, to work on *Anastasia*. Warner Home Video released the film to stores on January 4, 1995.

In 1990, before *Troll* began production, Bluth told his crew to do their best on the project because "life is very precious." If one didn't feel like investing their life in the project, they should "plant themselves in another garden." After that, several artists planted themselves at Disney, where they contributed to *Beauty and the Beast*.

*Troll* represents another example where talented filmmakers had an opportunity to make an outstanding animated film—and then squandered it. If nothing else, Bluth is to be credited for keeping his animation artists employed, and training them in the principles of classic animation. If only he could come up with worthy stories to tell. (WRM)

**Additional Credits:** Writer: Stu Krieger. Story: Don Bluth, Gary Goldman, John Pomeroy, T. J. Kuenster, Stu Krieger. Music: Robert Folk, Barry Mann. Additional music: Peter Tomashek. Songs: Barry Mann, Cynthia Weil, Norman Gimbel, Robert Folk. Animation superviser: John Pomeroy. Animators: Richard Bazley, Doug Bennett, Robert Fox, Frank Gabriel, Craig R. Maras, Brian Mitchell, Paul Newberry, Hans Perk, Mark Pudleiner, Jeffrey James Varab. Assistant animators: Paul J. Kelly, Ando Tammik. Special effects director: Peter Matheson. Special effects: Dave Tidgwell. Computer animation director: Jan Carlee. Senior computer animator: Greg Maguire.

**The Trumpet of the Swan** (5/11/01) TriStar Pictures. 75 mins. Directors: Richard Rich, Terry L. Noss. Producers: Paul J. Newman, Lin Oliver. Voices: Jason Alexander (Father), Mary Steenburgen (Mother), Reese Witherspoon (Serena), Seth Green (Boyd), Carol Burnett (Mrs. Hammerbotham), Joe Mantegna (Monty), Dee Bradley Baker (Louie), Sam Gifaldi (Sam), Melissa Disney (Billie), Little Richard (Song Performer).

**Consumer Tips:** 0 (zero stars) MPAA Rating: G. Based on an E. B. White novel.

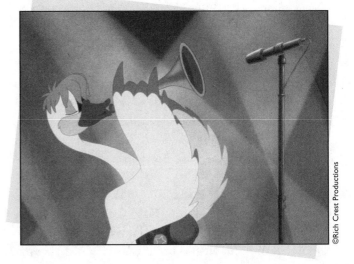

©Rich Crest Productions

**Story:** The adventures of a mute swan who learns to read and write and finds success with a trumpet.

**Comments:** This is a very poor animated feature, especially considering the talents involved. Though based on the classic E. B. White children's novel, codirectors Richard Rich and Terry L. Noss failed to create a satisfying film. Rich (like Don Bluth) is another Disney veteran who simply doesn't get it. He is so in love with the medium of animation that he forgets how to connect with a modern audience.

Rich and his production team previously brought us three other swan movies—a *Swan Princess* trilogy. The first of this trilogy was the best of this team's four feathered flicks. Unfortunately for the viewers, *Trumpet* never develops from an ugly duckling into a graceful bird.

E. B. White's book was far better than this pallid screen adaption. The film is episodic and might be hard for youngsters to follow. In terms of the animation, the characters look similar and do not have different gestures and expressions to give them contrasting personalities. The musical numbers in this film are uneven and forgettable. The only exciting music in the soundtrack comes from Louis, the mute swan, who learns to play jazz trumpet. His jazz riffs are reminiscent of the fabulous Louis Armstrong's, and who can go wrong sounding like Satchmo?

An amazing voice cast was recruited to do the track—Reese Witherspoon, Jason Alexander, Carol Burnett, and Joe Mantegna, to name a few. However, the whole production feels like a third-rate television movie. This is strictly for kids, though kids would more likely be interested in the doings of *SpongeBob, Kim Possible,* or *The Incredibles.*

All in all, this film is noisy, dull, and uninspired. The character animation is mediocre and the storytelling is weak. It is one of those family films that give the medium a bad rap. Traditional animation doesn't need a swan song like this. Avoid at all costs. (JB)

**Additional Credits:** Executive producer: Seldon O. Young. Coproducers: Terry L. Noss, Richard Rich, Thomas J. Tobin. Based on the novel *The Trumpet of the Swan* by E. B. White. Writer: Judy Rothman Rofe. Music: Marcus Miller. Orchestrator/songs: Charles Harrison. Songs: Pamela Phillips Oland. Storyboard: Flora Dery, Steven E. Gordon, Larry Scholl, Mark Sonntag. Character designer: Bronwen Barry, Elena Kravets. Computer animator: Mrian McSweeney. Layout design supervisor: Mike Hodgson. Background supervisor: Jeff Richards.

**Tubby the Tuba** (4/1/75) Avco-Embassy. 81 mins. Director: Alexander Schure. Producers: Barry B. Yellin, Steven R. Carlin, Alexander Schure. Voices: Dick Van Dyke (Tubby the Tuba), David Wayne (Pee-Wee the Piccolo), Paul Tripp (Narrator), Pearl Bailey (Mrs. Elephant), Jack Gilford (The Herald), Ray Middleton (The Great Pepperino), Jane Powell (Celeste), Cyril Ritchard (The Frog), Ruth Enders (The Haughty Violin), Hermione Gingold (Miss Squeek).

**Consumer Tips:** ☆☆ MPAA Rating: G. Based on the original story by Paul Tripp.

**Story:** Tubby leaves the orchestra to find a melody of his own. His travels take him to the circus, the forest, and a fabled Singing City.

**Comments:** Musician, songwriter, actor, and kiddy-show host Paul Tripp (1911–2002) created the musical story *Tubby the Tuba* in 1945. It made its debut that year as a Decca children's record recorded by Danny Kaye and was a tremendous commercial success. George Pal subsequently made a stop-motion animated short film (a Puppetoon) based on the material in 1947, which was nominated for an Academy Award.

Meanwhile, Tripp worked on pioneering television programs with his children's shows *Mr. I. Magination*

in the 1950s and *Birthday House* in the 1960s. In 1974, Alexander Schure, founder of the New York Institute of Technology (NYIT) and an eccentric millionaire, decided to revive *Tubby the Tuba* as a full-length animated film.

NYIT's Animation Department, Visual Arts Center, and Tech Sound Lab on the Westbury, Long Island, campus was set up as the the the base of operations for the production. Schure wanted to make a film to compete with Disney, so he hired Tripp, an all-star voice cast, and distinguished Broadway composer Lehman Engel (1910–1982) to supervise the various aspects of the soundtrack.

Schure wanted to be cutting edge but knew nothing about animation. He rounded up all the available East Coast animation talent he could find. His first mistake, however, was in hiring the notorious television cartoonist Sam Singer (*Courageous Cat, Bucky and Pepito*) to direct the film. At first, Singer recruited art students at NYIT to help, as well as several local, but talented, animation novices. Ultimately, Singer and Schure had no choice but to hire a whole crew of veteran East Coast animators to take over the production, most of whom dated back to the Fleischer Studios heyday. Famed Popeye animator John Gentilella receives animation supervision credit.

Schure, however, found traditional, hand-drawn animation both slow and technically limited. Frustrated with the progress of the *Tubby* project, he soon became interested in the emerging field of computer-generated graphics. Schure went out and brought consultants and scientists in to NYIT to push the field forward. Two of his early recruits were Ed Catmull and Alvy Ray Smith, who were the future founders of Pixar.

"We realized then that he really didn't have what it takes to make a movie," explained Smith, who, along with Catmull, was repulsed by what he saw of *Tubby the Tuba.* Catmull agreed, "It was awful, it was terrible, half the audience fell asleep at the screening. We walked out of the screening room thinking 'Thank God we didn't have anything to do with it, that computers were not used for anything in that movie!'

"NYIT in itself was a significant event in the history of computer graphics" explains Smith. "Here we had this wealthy man, having plenty of money and getting us whatever we needed, we didn't have a budget, we had no goals, we just stretched the envelope. It was such an incredible opportunity, every day someone was creating something new. None of us slept, it was common to work 22-hour days. Everything you saw was something new. We blasted computer graphics into the world. It was like exploring a new continent."

Looking back at NYIT, Catmull reflects "Alex Schure funded five years of great research work, and he deserves credit for that." Instead, he took credit for *Tubby the Tuba*—removing Sam Singer's name from the final print after the first disasterous test screenings.

Visually the film is a mess—but a relatively pleasant one. The soundtrack, with Dick Van Dyke, David Wayne, Pearl Bailey, and others, is delightful.

Avco Embassy picked up the worldwide distribution rights in 1974, and the film was released in several markets for Easter 1975. The film has since drifted into deserved obscurity. But behind the scenes, the CGI as we know it today was being born—and that's something to "toot" about. (JB)

*Additional Credits:* Story and dialogue direction: Paul Tripp. Music: George Kleinsinger. Film editing: Phillip Schopper. Additional music and music direction: Lehman Engel. Director of post-production: George Vales. Layouts: Wayne Boring, Dan Danglo. Storyboards: Roman Arabula, Frank Dorso, Herb Johnson, George Singer. Backgrounds: Nino Carbe, Bob Owens, Gary Selvaggio, John Vita. Supervising animator: John Gentilella. Animators: Cliff Auguston, Dante Barbetta, Jack Dazzo, Ed DeMattia, Ben Farish, Chuck Harriton, Bill Hudson, Earl James, Walt Kubiak, Jack Ozark, Bill Pratt, Morey Reden, Jack Schnerk, Paul Sparagano, Milton Stein, Nick Tafuri, Martin Taras, Gordon Whitier. Assistant animators: Victor Barvetta, John Celestri, James Davis, Lance Gershenoff, Joan LaPallo, Jim Logan, Roger Mejia, Duane Ullrich, Karen Warren.

**The Tune** (9/13/92) October. 69 mins. Director/producer: Bill Plympton. Voices: Daniel Neiden (Del), Maureen McElheron (Didi), Marty Nelson (Mayor, Mr. Mega, Mrs. Mega), Emily Bindiger (Dot), Chris Hoffman (Wiseone, Surfer, Tango Dancer, Note), Jimmy Ceribello (Cabbie), Ned Reynolds (Hound Dog), Jeff Knight (Bellhop), Jennifer Senko (Surfer, Note).

**Consumer Tips:** ☆☆☆ MPAA Rating: Unrated.

**Story:** Del, a forlorn songwriter, is given 47 minutes to write a hit tune, or else.

©Bill Plympton

**Comments:** Independent animator Bill Plympton, having made his mark with shorts and commercials, began the first of several feature film entries with this sprightly epic. Compared to the increasingly explicit comic sex and mayhem that dominated his subsequent movies, *The Tune* presents Plympton at his most whimsical, with a loose plot centering on a young songwriter out to impress a music exec. His desperation to find the perfect excuse leads him to the town of Flooby Nooby, which provides an excuse for Plympton and collaborator Maureen McElheron to play with a host of musical styles and rather odd song themes. A cab driver sings a blues melody about his missing nose, a dog imitates Elvis and lyricizes about his hair, and a country-western ballad about love reunited is illustrated by food items embracing.

This is typical ground for Plympton to pump out gags and wacky set pieces one after another. Some of these segments are rather gratuitous, but still enjoyable—particularly a strange scene in which two men mutilate each other's faces in a variety of ways. This segment, "Push Comes to Shove," highlights Plympton's trademark penchant for transmutation, as does an encounter with "The Wise One," backed by bluegrass guitar (both sequences were released as standalone shorts to help fund the film's completion).

*The Tune* has a simplicity to it that subsequent features lack, and the use of shaded pencils to color the cels adds a unique visual texture and charm. Despite an odd sudden plot hole in the film's last few minutes, the central romantic relationship, if somewhat thin, is sweet and well conveyed through the songs (continuing the penchant for incongruity, the bittersweet "Home" is accompanied by images of an American family barbecuing in space). The songs are lively, with a particular standout being music mogul Mr. Mega's desktop tap number, "Love is My Bottom Line," with such lyrics as "You can keep all the power/I'm a low voltage guy." McElheron, in addition to cowriting the film and penning all of the songs, provides the voice of Didi, the romantic lead. The top-flight musicians, who for once received credit, included Blues Brothers band member Tom "Bones" Malone. Plympton continues his unique, one-man approach to feature films, but this first outing has an Avery-esque blend of innocence and mania that has seldom been matched. (AL)

*Additional Credits:* Story: Bill Plympton, Maureen McElheron, P. C. Vey. Music: Maureen McElheron. Animator: Bill Plympton. Artistic supervisor: Jessica Wolk-Stanley. Additional backgrounds: Tom Cushwa. Lovesick design: Rick Geary.

**Twice Upon a Time** (8/5/83) Warner Bros. 75 mins. Directors: John Korty, Charles Swenson. Producer: Bill Couturié. Voices: Lorenzo Music (Ralph), Marshall Efron (Synonamess Botch), James Cranna (Rod Rescueman, Scuzzbopper, Frivoli Foreman), Julie Payne (Flora Fauna), Hamilton Camp (Greensleeves), Paul Frees (Narrator, Chief of State, Judges, Bailiff), Gillian Gould (Sleeper), Geraldine Green (Sleeper),

©Korty Films and the Ladd Company

Larry Green (Sleeper), William Hall (Sleeper), David Korty (Sleeper), Elma Barry Robertson (Sleeper), Clyde E. Robertson (Sleeper), William Browder (Office Executive), Geoff Hoyle (Man in Elevator), J. E. Freeman (Pool Player), Elizabeth Saxon (Woman on Beach), Sue Murphy (File Clerk), Nancy Fish (Woman Under Dryer), Charles Dorsett (Man at Amusement Park), Judith Kahan Kampmann (The Fairy Godmother).

*Consumer Tips:* ☆☆☆ MPAA Rating: G.

*Story:* Evil Synonamess Botch, maniacal ruler of Murkworks Nightmare Factory, tricks dim-witted Ralph and Mum into freezing time by releasing the magic mainspring from the Cosmic Clock.

*Comments:* The early 1980s were mostly stagnant for theatrical animation, and truly unique, original features were hard to find. *Twice Upon a Time* is one of the exceptions. It is a visually distinctive feature that stays within bounds of a PG rating and has rather adult sensibilities, but was clearly not pandering to kids. The film is codirected by Charles Swenson, veteran of *Dirty Duck* (of all things), and John Korty. Korty is better known as a live-action director, notably helming the television movie *The Autobiography of Miss Jane Pittman*. However, he also had his own Bay-area animation studio, which specialized in cutout animation. Korty and crew had created a number of segments for *Sesame Street*, and the technique, labeled Lumage, made its big-screen debut with the backing of George Lucas (who subsequently hired Korty to helm *The Ewok Adventure*). The characters appear to have been made from loose pieces of construction paper, giving them an interesting layered texture.

The frothy tale, beginning with mock "March of Time" narration courtesy of Paul Frees, focuses on the plots of the evil Synonamess Botch, master of nightmares, to flood the waking world, known as Din, with continual bad dreams by means of the cosmic mainspring. Ralph the All-Purpose Animal, a creature who continually changes species as the occasion demands, and Mum, his mute Chaplin-esque sidekick, are first used by Botch, and then attempt to stop him. Other players in this offbeat excursion include a kibitzing, New York fairy godmother; incompetent superhero Rod Rescueman; and Ibor the video gorilla, a creature with ape arms, tractor wheels, and a television head that plays appropriate clips from *The Muppet Show*, *Abbott and Costello*, *Happy Days*, or *Star Wars*, as the occasion demands.

This setup is mainly an excuse for odd film references, frenetic dialogue, and excursions into the photo-collage world of Din. According to a 1983 *American Cinematography* article, much of the dialogue was improvised, and it shows in the freewheeling structure. One standout set piece has Ralph and Mum, against live-action backdrops, fending off attacks from office furniture, using photographic cutouts and actual props rather than humanized caricatures. The voice cast is superbly funny, from Lorenzo Music's deadpan Ralph to Hamilton Camp's crotchety Scottish Greensleeves, an aging sandman-type character. But the true standout is comedian/writer Marshall Efron as Synonamess Botch, particularly when chortling evilly, praising his minions, or showing off his dried salami collection. This looseness, while liberating, can also be disorienting at times; former *Animato!* editor Harry McCracken recalled it as being "incomprehensible but good-looking." However, the film proved to be a starting ground for a number of fine talents, including Henry Selick, who handled the office nightmare and would go on to direct *The Nightmare Before Christmas*, and special photographic effects man David Fincher, now known as the director of *Fight Club*. (AL)

***Additional Credits:*** Executive producer: George Lucas. Associate producers: Barbara Wright, Suella Kennedy. Writers: John Korty, Charles Swenson, Suella Kennedy. Story: Bill Couturié, Suella Kennedy, John Korty. Music: Ken Melville, Dawn Atkinson, David Moordigian. Songs: Bruce Hornsby, John Hornsby, Tom Ferguson, Maureen McDonald, Michael McDonald. Sequence directors: Brian Narelle, Carl Willat, Henry Selick, Willat. Sequence animator: John Allan Armstrong, Peter Crosman, George Evelyn, Kris Moser, Will Noble, Peggy Okeya, David Pettigrew, Kai Pindal, Deborah Short. Scene animators: Chuck Eyler, Randy Hamm, Doug Haynes, Carol Millican, Mark West. Additional animators: Chris R. Green, Nick Hale, Bruce Heller, Brad Jones, Nancy Morita, John T. Van Vliet.

## Twilight of the Cockroaches (5/5/89) Streamline Pictures. 105 mins. Director: Hiroaki Yoshida. Producers: Hiroaki Yoshida, Hidenori Taga. Voices: Michael Forest, Gregory Snegoff.

©TYO Productions

***Consumer Tips:*** ☆☆☆☆ MPAA Rating: Unrated. Fantasy/political allegory. Partial live action. Animated roaches and live-action humans fight to the death as a bewildered roach girl tries to understand what is happening.

***Story:*** A large community of cockroaches in the apartment of a man living alone is convinced that he is their friend, always leaving out food for them. But he is just a slob who isn't bothered about a few bugs crawling around his dirty dishes. When he brings home a new girlfriend who hates roaches and demands that he get rid of them, it is the end of their world.

***Comments:*** This combination of animation (the cockroaches and their society) and live action (the humans and their apartment building) was frequently compared upon its release (November 21, 1987, in Japan; May 1989 in America) with the recent *Who Framed Roger Rabbit*. The combination of live action and animation is much more crude; more on the level of Warner Bros.' 1940 short, *You Ought to Be in Pictures*. The quality of the animation (by the Madhouse studio), the live-action cinematography, and the art design is adequate but seldom more than that. What makes *Twilight of the Cockroaches* (*Gokiburi-tachi no Tasogare*) so memorable is its bizarre and unique plot, and the bite of its allegorical message.

All the action is seen from the viewpoint of a community of anthropomorphized cockroaches living in a human's apartment. The roaches are drawn with antennaed human heads and four arms. When they are shown seated from the waist up they look relatively human; but when they move about they scuttle on all six legs like regular insects. Their community is animated over live-action backgrounds of floors, underneath furniture, on dirty dishes, and in toilet bowls. Humans are towering giants, seen in extreme upward shots (from the POV of roaches on the floor) or in downward shots (from the POV of roaches scuttling along the tops of walls).

Naomi is a carefree adolescent cockroach girl, a member of an affluent community sharing living space with a friendly human. She and her friends have been partying for what seems like forever. The teen roaches take the easy life, such as pool parties in the toilet bowl, for granted. They are uninterested in the reminiscences of their elders about how tough life used to be before this community developed. Many reviewers cited Naomi's stopping to ask directions from a friendly talking dog turd as the most memorable scene of the movie.

Writer-director Yoshida claimed that *Twilight of the Cockroaches* was a parable of how the Japanese were viewed by the world economic community during their bubble prosperity of the 1980s; as arrogant parasites unaware of how unpopular they were making themselves with their trading partners. But the film can be taken as a parable in much broader ways, such as of organized religion: how many faiths have church leaders who assure their parishioners—and truly believe—that they have a special relationship with God, and know what God's intentions toward us are? The cinematic quality may grow increasingly dated, but the message remains bleakly humorous and disturbing. (FP)

**Additional Credits:** Executive producers: Tatsumi Eatanabe, Mayumi Izumi. Screenplay: Hiroaki Yoshida. Music: Morgan Fisher. Art director: Kiichi Ichida. Animation directors: Toshio Hirata, Yoshinori Kamemori, Kin'ichiro Suzuki. Assistant animation directors: Kunihiko Matsui, Hiroyuki Ebata, Hiroyuki Fukushima, Tatsuhiko Urahata. Animators: Nobumasa Arakawa, Ken Ikuta, Kengo Inagaki, Tashiyuki Inoue, Akio Sakai, Jun'ichi Seki, Makoto Itô, Nobuyuki Kitajima, Reiko Kurihara, Yoshiyuki Momose, Seiji Muta, Hiroshi Oikawa, Kôichi Tsuchida, Hajime Shin. Character design: Hiroshi Kurogane. Cockroach designer: Yoshitaka Amano. Cinematography: Iwao Yamaki. Sound: Susumu Aketagawa. Lighting: Masaaki Uchida.

**Vampire Hunter D** (3/26/93) Streamline Pictures. 80 mins. Director: Toyoo Ashida. Producers: Hiroshi Kato, Mitsuhisa Koeda, Yukio Nagasaki. Voices: Michael McConnohie (D), Lara Cody (Lamika), Barbara Goodson (Doris Rumm), John Rafter Lee (Meier Link), Kerrigan Mahan (Reiganse), Dwight Schutz (Benge), Pamela Segall (Leila Markus), Karen Prell (Dan Rumm).

©Epic / Sony Inc. / Movie, Inc. CBS / Sony Group Inc.

**Consumer Tips:** ☆☆☆ MPAA Rating: Unrated. Fantasy/horror adventure. Based on the Japanese novel by Hideyuki Kikuchi. In a distant future, earth has evolved into a medieval society of vampire nobility preying upon human peasants. "D" is a solitary wanderer, a mercenary who helps humans who are rebelling against their vampire overlords.

**Story:** In a community resembling 18th-century Transylvania, a human town is resigned to being preyed upon once every 50 years by its mostly absentee immortal vampire overlord, Count Lee. When Lee demands beautiful Doris as his latest tribute and her friends and neighbors abandon her, the feisty girl calls in the mysterious vampire hunter known only as "D" to save her. The decadent count is excited by the prospect of a real opponent to fight after centuries of boredom.

**Comments:** This movie is loosely based upon the 1983 first novel in a popular series now running over 15 volumes. *Vampire Hunter D* puts a science-fiction veneer over the classic Gothic fantasy-horror stereotype.

*Vampire Hunter D* (*Kyûketsuki Hunter D*) was one of the mid-1980s productions made primarily for the new home-video market but given a limited theatrical release first (December 21, 1985, made by Ashi Production Co.). Although well-directed, its limited animation is painfully evident. Considerable publicity was released about the character design by noted fantasy artist Yoshitaka Amano (who was the artist of the novels' dust jackets), but in fact Amano only designed D and painted the movie's posters. The character design of the rest of the cast was by director Ashida, and his distinctly different art style really stands out. The story's heavy reliance on a combination of vampire movie and Western clichés (especially *Dracula* and *Shane*, with "Count Lee" a clear tribute to Hammer Films' star vampire Christopher Lee) is also impossible to miss. But the plot moves fast and holds together, the characters act intelligently, and the visual mixture of modern fantasy and ancient technological elements (recently built medieval fortresses nearby the crumbling remains of futuristic buildings; D as a 17th- or 18th-century swordsman riding a cyborg horse; Doris hunting werewolves with a laser rifle and an electronic whip) is unique. *Vampire Hunter D* is popular enough that it has been generally kept in print on home video in Japan and America. It was one of the anime releases of the early 1990s that extended the reputation of anime beyond the fan cult to the art-theater circuit, and on television as more than children's cartoons by appearing as a feature on the Sci-Fi Channel. (FP)

**Additional Credits:** Executive producers: Shigeo Maruyama, Yutaka Takahashi. Screenplay: Yasushi Hirano, Tom Wyner. Based on the novel by Hideyuki Kikuchi. Character design: Yoshitaka Amano. Art director: Toyoo Ashida. Music: Tetsuya Komuro. Music director: Noriyoshi Matsuura. English adaptation producer: Carl Macek. English adaptation production manager: Jerry Beck. Marketing and promotions: Fred Patten, Svea Macek.

**Vampire Hunter D: Bloodlust** (10/5/01) Urban Vision Entertainment. 103 mins. Director: Yoshiaki Kawajiri. Producers: Mata Yamamoto, Masao Muruyama, Taka Nagasawa, Mataichiro Yamamoto. Voices: Andrew Philpot (D), John Rafter Lee (Meier Link), Pamela Segall (Leila), Wendee Lee (Charlotte), Michael McShane (Left Hand), Julia Fletcher (Carmila), Matt McKenzie (Borgoff), John Di Maggio (John Elbourne, Nolt, Mashira), Alex Fernández (Kyle), Jack Fletcher (Grove).

**Consumer Tips:** ☆☆☆☆ MPAA Rating: R. Fantasy/horror adventure. Based on the Japanese novel *D: Demon Deathchase*, by Hideyuki Kikuchi, and the earlier *Vampire Hunter D* feature. When a rich man offers a huge reward for the rescue of his daughter who has been kidnapped by a powerful vampire lord, D and a gang of ruthless bounty hunters fight each other as well as numerous monsters to get it.

**Story:** In the world of A.D. 12,090, vampire lord Meier Link kidnaps Charlotte Elbourne, the daughter of the wealthy boss of a human town and flees with her into unknown lands. Her father and son offer a huge reward for her rescue, or her clean death if she has already been turned into a vampire. The reward is offered to both D and to the Markus family of bounty hunters, a ruthless gang who will try to sabotage or kill D to eliminate his competition. The pursuit takes the hunters across a variety of lands that each have different dangers. A complication is that the girl may have eloped willingly rather than been kidnapped. If she did, how should D treat them?

**Comments:** The 1985 *Vampire Hunter D* was so popular that fans quickly requested a sequel based upon one of the other novels in Kikuchi's series. But Kikuchi detested the movie for its drastic changes to his novel and for the cheapness of its production. However, Kikuchi did like the anime adaptation of his *Wicked City* by the Madhouse studio and director Yoshiaki Kawajiri. In the late 1990s, American distributor Urban Vision Entertainment obtained the licenses for both *Wicked City* and *Vampire Hunter D* and was interested in cofinancing a brand-new sequel. An agreement was reached to make a second *Vampire Hunter D* feature based upon Kikuchi's third D novel, giving him script approval and higher-quality animation by Madhouse with Kawajiri as director.

The coproduction (a pet project of producer Mataichiro Yamamoto, Urban Vision's president) was intended for an art-theater release in both Japan and America, but primarily for American video release. The English language voice track was recorded in Hollywood in 1999 and the feature was animated in Tokyo to match it. Kawajiri came to California to direct the sound effects at the studio of the American composers of the music. Yoshitaka Amano was commissioned to design all the main characters, and more care was taken to match his art style in the design of the minor characters by animation director Yutaka Minowa.

It was decided to make *Vampire Hunter D: Bloodlust* strikingly visually different from the first movie (a major reason that *D: Demon Deathchase* was chosen over other D novels). Instead of a plot that confines its characters to one town and the nearby vampire's castle, Bloodlust features a frantic chase across a countryside that changes from forest to desert to mountains to lakeside; from a half-ruined old European town filled with monsters (supposedly SF mutants but with clearly fantasy/supernatural powers) to a lively American Wild West frontier town. Most of the action is in broad daylight (the vampire Meier Link travels in a beautiful rococo coach whose windows are draped in velvet), amidst settings of tourist-poster beauty. When a vampire's castle is shown, it is a brightly lit Italian-Renaissance palace without a cobweb or lurching undead corpse in sight. D's mystic Left Hand with a face in it, which is mostly ignored in the first movie, has a major role in *Bloodlust* as a querulously sardonic old man who constantly nags and banters; a good emotional counterpart to the grimly silent D.

The action for most of the first two-thirds of *Bloodlust* is centered upon D, the Markus gang, and the three supernatural bodyguards from the monster town of Barbaroi whom Meier Link has hired to kill his pursuers. The Markus family consists of four brothers and an adopted sister: Borgoff, the beefy, falsely jovial leader; Kyle, the wiry, ninja-like knife artist; Nolt, the hulking brute; Grove, the frail invalid who can project his aura outside his body; and Leila, the hard-bitten, cynical tomboy with a soft heart. Borgoff, Kyle, and Nolt just want the reward and have no hesitation to kill D to get it. It is implied that they are equally ready to kill Charlotte and claim she had been turned into a vampire if she will not go with them willingly. Grove is gentle by nature but too weak to go against his brothers' orders. Leila was orphaned by vampires and hates all supernatural creatures including D since he is a dunpeal, but she is protective of Kyle. She clearly wishes that the world was not so filled with danger and misery that she dare not

let her guard down. As a result, she is receptive to being slowly convinced that D is a monster who is genuinely a friend of humans and can be trusted.

Bengo (shadow-ninja), Caroline (plant-ninja), and Mashira (wolf-ninja), the three Barbaroi bodyguards, are exotic monsters who provide some excellent battles with the Markus gang, but they are no match for D. The long climax starts when Meier Link and Charlotte reach the castle of Carmila, one of the greatest vampires remaining on earth who has promised to help them escape to the stars. Although there is a long duel between Meier and D, the main point of the final confrontation is to show D and Leila (and the audience) whether either Meier or Carmila are honorable by the supposed standards of vampire nobility, and what fate Charlotte will meet.

*Vampire Hunter D: Bloodlust* was promoted in the American anime fan community for over two years before its release. It premiered at film festivals in Sydney, Pusan, and Hong Kong during 2000 before its Japanese release on April 17, 2001, and in America on October 5, 2001. (FP)

***Additional Credits:*** Coproducer: Meileen Choo. Screenplay: Yoshiaki Kawajiri. Based on the novel by Kideyuki Kikuchi. Music: Maro D'Ambrosio. Art direction: Yuji Ikehata. Animation director: Yutaka Minowa. Animators: Lily Hung, Shi Nansun, Kai-Li Ng, Charlie Pu, Tsuneo Leo Sato, Sean Shang. Character designer: Yutaka Minowa. Illustrator (original characters): Yoshitaka Amano. Conceptual designer: Yasushi Nirasawa. Singer: Dai Nagao.

## Victory Through Air Power (7/17/43) United Artists—Disney. 65 mins. Live-action director: H. C. Potter. Supervising animation director: David Hand. Producer: Walt Disney. Voices: Alexander de Seversky (Himself), Art Baker (Narrator).

***Consumer Tips:*** ☆☆☆ Animated documentary. Dated historical references.

***Story:*** Timely World War II propaganda about how the war can end sooner with strategic air power. Animated sequences include "The History of Aviation."

***Comments:*** *Victory Through Air Power* is one of the most unique films Walt Disney ever produced. It

©Walt Disney Productions

stands alone among his feature output. It is the product of a man who was a visionary, a cinema innovator, and a patriot.

Like *Steamboat Willie, Flowers and Trees, Three Little Pigs, Snow White,* and *Fantasia, Victory Through Air Power* was something new for Walt and a risk for the studio. The film is a serious documentary, something we don't usually associate with Disney. It is also propaganda, intended to persuade the public, the president, and allied leaders around the world of a faster way to end the war using strategic aviation.

After Pearl Harbor, things changed dramatically for the Disney company. Production was severely affected. The U.S. military took over part of the Burbank studio; animators were drafted. Walt was forced to stall production of *Peter Pan* and was enlisted by the army, navy, and National Film Board of Canada to make training films, public service announcements, and bond-selling shorts. Disney films lost a source of revenue when their European distribution was cut off. Seeking to make the best of the situation, he embarked on his South American "Good Neighbor" tour, which resulted in the package films, *Saludos Amigos* and *The Three Caballeros.* The studio was doing its bit for the war effort, but Walt wanted to do more.

Major Alexander de Seversky was a military aeronautic pioneer and inventor. At a time when air travel was still new and its use as a military tool was evolving, de Seversky had a clear vision on how aviation strategy could end the worldwide conflict. But the military, steeped in its methods of traditional land-based warfare, was not listening. Seversky put his ideas in print with articles in *Look, Coronet,* and *Reader's Digest* (among others), and became a familiar voice on radio making many broadcast appearances to discuss them. He collected his thoughts in a bestselling book published in 1942, called *Victory Through Air Power.*

Walt Disney had an interest in aviation and wanted to produce feature films relevant to the war effort. A movie based on Roald Dahls's imaginary wartime air devils, *The Gremlins,* was announced, but was ultimately abandoned.

Disney was clearly struck with the progressive ideas of Seversky and optioned his book in July 1942. It was, as they say today, "fast-tracked" into production. The film was produced by Disney, independent of the studio's affiliation with RKO, and subsequently the picture was released by United Artists.

H. C. Potter was hired to direct the scenes with Major de Seversky. Potter was a top stage and film director, recently completing Olsen and Johnson's screen version of *Hellzapoppin'.* Potter would go on to direct *The Farmer's Daughter* and *Mr. Blandings Builds His Dream House,* among others. He was also an aviator, and he and Seversky were acquainted.

Walt told the *Hollywood Citizen News* in 1942, "We have a chance to project the future in filming Seversky's book." The ideas in *Victory Through Air Power* weren't fantasy, but scientific fact. Thus, *Victory Through Air Power* was the first public display of Disney's interest in the wonders of modern science and technology, something he'd revisit again in developing Tomorrowland, the Tomorrowland television segments, and Epcot. (Of additional interest: the basic format of this film uses Major de Seversky speaking directly to us from his office, using books, charts, and the globe, to illustrate his points. Is it just a coincidence that this is nearly the exact format of the weekly *Disneyland* and *Wonderful World of Color* television shows—with Walt in Seversky's place?)

Disney also used this film, as he would every feature, to improve and stretch the skills of his staff. One goal of his was to turn a feature film around in less than a year. This required using limited animation creatively in many scenes, but not skimping one bit on production values.

This would be the last Disney project for animation legends David Hand and Bill Tytla. Hand was animation supervisor on this film and had been the supervising director of *Snow White* and *Bambi*. Tytla was well known for his powerful animation of Stromboli in *Pinocchio* and *Fantasia's* "Night on Bald Mountain" sequence.

*Victory Through Air Power* is a powerful piece of filmmaking. The *New York Times* film critic, Thomas M. Pryor, wrote: "On purely cinematic terms, *Victory Through Air Power* is an extraordinary accomplishment, marking it, as it were, a new milestone in the screen's recently accelerated march toward maturity. Mr. Disney has adroitly blended the documentary techniques of the presentation with his own highly skilled cartoon form of infectious humor. The result is a delightful and stimulating combination entertainment-information film. If *Victory Through Air Power* is propaganda, it is at least the most encouraging and inspiring propaganda that the screen has afforded us in a long time. Mr. Disney and his staff can be proud of their accomplishment." (JB)

**Additional Credits:** Story director: Perce Peerce. Adapted from the book by Alexander P. de Seversky. Story adaptors: T. Hee, Erdman Penner, William Cottrell, James Brodrero, George Stallings, Jose Rodriguez. Music: Edward Plumb, Paul J. Smith, Oliver Wallace. Sequence directors: Clyde Geronimi, Jack Kinney, James Algar. Animators: Ward Kimball, Josh Meador, John Lounsbery, Carleton Boyd, Hugh Fraser, Bill Justice, George Rowley, Ed Aardal, John Sibley, John McManus, Norm Tate, Oliver M. Johnston Jr., Vladimir Tytla, Marvin Woodward, Harvey Toombs.

## The Wacky World of Mother Goose (12/2/67)

Embassy Pictures. 77 mins. Director: Jules Bass. Producer: Arthur Rankin. Voices: Margaret Rutherford (Mother Goose), Robert McFadden, Bradley Bolke, Laura Leslie, James Dougherty, Craig Sechler, Susan Melvin, Kevin Gavin, Bryna Raeburn, Robert Harter, William Marine.

**Consumer Tips:** ☆ MPAA Rating: Unrated.

**Story:** Mother Goose leaves Mother Goose Land and it falls prey to evil Count Walktwist and his crooked knights. Jack Horner, with Mary and her little lamb, restore the kingdom.

**Comments:** Rankin-Bass' first cel-animated feature was built around Mother Goose rhymes, which had

©Embassy Pictures

long been fodder for short subjects. The thin storyline is built around Mother Goose's going on vacation, during which time the land falls prey to the evil Count Walktwist, the Crooked Man who, since Victor Herbert's original *Babes in Toyland,* has always been the favored villain for such productions. The plot is essentially an excuse to use as many nursery characters as possible, as well as indulge in some very dated musical numbers.

As the voice and model for Mother Goose, Rankin-Bass cast the venerable British stage and screen actress Margaret Rutherford. Though a staple of Ealing Studio comedies in the 40s, she was best known to American audiences for her portrayal of Miss Marple, and a recent Oscar winner for her supporting role in *The VIPs* (1963). With her compact frame, heavy-lidded eyes, and bulldog chin, Rutherford was an ideal subject for caricature, and her voice adds warmth and distinction to the enterprise. Unfortunately, despite the title and Rutherford's star billing, Mother Goose's role is limited; she's absent for most of the film, functioning largely as narrator, plot device, and deus ex machina, rather than a character in her own right.

The efforts of Jack Horner, Mary Quite Contrary, and Humpty Dumpty to alert Mother Goose take up much of the running time, as does a romantic subplot involving King Cole's daughter that even kiddie audiences would likely find tedious. At times the continual nursery rhyme references become wearying, though the depiction of Georgie Porgie as a prepubescent letch is priceless. For older viewers, the chief enjoyment, apart from Rutherford, comes from the moustache-twirling villainy of the green-skinned Count Walktwist. The lisping midget King Cole is also fun, as are the eccentric voice characterizations (mostly courtesy of perennial television voice Robert McFadden) for the nursery cameos (i.e., the baker man's Irish brogue, a dog who sounds like the Pepperidge Farm spokesman). The limited, linear animation lends the movie a comic strip feel, rather than a storybook one. Overall a good-natured effort, but generally less distinctive than Rankin-Bass' stop-motion productions. (AL)

**Additional Credits:** Executive producer: Joseph E. Levine. Associate producer: Larry Roemer. Writer: Romeo Muller. Story: Arthur Rankin Jr. Based on characters created by Charles Perrault in the book *Mother Goose Tales*. Music/lyrics: George Wilkins, Jules Bass. Assistant director: Kizo Nagashima.

**Waking Life** (10/19/01) Fox Searchlight. 99 mins. Directors: Richard Linklater, Bob Sabiston. Producers: Anne Walker-McBay, Tommy Pallotta, Palmer West, Jonah Smith. Voices: Peter Atherton (Hit-and-Run Driver), Wiley Wiggins (Main Character), Louis Black (Kierkegaard Disciple), Ken Webster (Bartender), Trevor Jack Brooks (Young Boy Playing Paper Game), Julie Delpy (Celine), Ethan Hawke (Jesse), Charles Gunning (Angry Man in Jail), Alex Jones (Man in Car with P.A.), Mona Lee (Quiet Woman), Lorelie Linklater (Young Girl), Edith Mannix (Artist), Caveh Zahedi (Himself), Timothy "Speed" Levitch (Himself), Steven Soderbergh (Himself), Louis Mackey (Himself), Robert C. Solomon (Himself), Richard Linklater, Bill Wise, Steven Prince, Steve Brudniak, John Christensen, Nicky Katt, Kim Krizan.

**Consumer Tips:** ☆☆☆ MPAA Rating: R.

**Story:** An unnamed teenager drifts through a dreamlike existence in an anonymous city, encountering people who randomly spout philosophy and social theory.

**Comments:** *Waking Life* is an intellectually daring and curiously abstract narrated film, in some ways the closest animation has come to fitting into the "indy film" scene. Though animation has always been a proven way to depict dream and fantasy sequences, here live-action director Richard Linklater takes a stream-of-consciousness approach, while building the animation over live-reference footage. The entire film was shot and edited, through handheld digital camera, beforehand. Whereas features such as Bakshi's *American Pop* used the rotoscope to merely paint over characters, *Waking Life*'s approach, using a special digital animation/painting software created by art director Bob Sabiston, is quite different.

The film's narrative, such as it is, follows an unnamed young man (played by Wiley Wiggins) through a dream landscape, as he encounters a parade of different individuals with different views on life, death, and reality, among other topics. The characters range from a boy who transforms into an alien and the captain of a "boat car" to a lecturing monkey. However, the majority of the cast members are composed of academics, performance artists, friends and neighbors of the crew, and actors who had appeared in Linklater's previous films. Ethan Hawke and Julie Delpy reprise their roles from *Before Sunrise*, sharing a bedroom discussion. Due to this approach, while the general events were plotted and much of the dialogue was scripted, the individuals themselves often improvised monologues or lectures, usually based on their own interests and perceptions of reality. This method, while decidedly unique, and a welcome inclusion of stimulating, adult ideas, prevents one from truly engaging with the movie, as the actors/characters are mouthpieces rather than individuals. The constant stream of intellectual discourse becomes a bit overwhelming as well.

The animation style shifts considerably throughout the film, partially by intent to reflect the flux of the

©Twentieth Century Fox Film Corp.

dream landscape and partially due to the approaches of the different animators, most of whom came from fine art backgrounds. Many of the scenes are straight rotoscope, basically just painting the real actors and backdrops (this is particularly evident in most of the shots of the dreamer), while at other times creative exaggeration is used to highlight a character's ideas or personality. The latter is particularly evident in a monologue by Speed Levitch, an encounter with a woman on the stairs, in which both dreamer and speaker resemble Colorform pieces stuck together, and a monkey lecturing to a film collage. The string-heavy score, by group Tasco Tango (who also appear in the film), offers low-key yet distinct accompaniment.

Alternately viewed as innovative or pretentious, the movie generally received limited distribution outside of art house and campus theaters, grossing a little over $2 million in the United States. However, subsequent DVD sales and word of mouth allowed the film to gain more of a cult following, especially among the college crowd—both students and professors were intrigued by the subject matter almost more than the approach. (AL)

**Additional Credits:** Executive producers: Jonathan Sehring, Caroline Kaplan, John Sloss. Screenplay: Richard Linklater. Music: Glover Gill. Art director/animation software: Bob Sabiston. Animators: Jason Archer, Paul Beck, John Bruch, Jean Caffeine, Zoe Charlton, Randy Cole, Kate Dollenmayer, Jennifer Drummond, Rahab El Ewaly, Pat Falconer, Holly Louise Fisher, Dan Gillotte, Nathan Jensen, Matthew Langland, Michael Layne, Travis C. Lindquist, Chris Minley, Katy O'Connor, John Paul, Shannon Pearson, Eric Power, Bob Sabiston, Susan Sabiston, Katie Salen, Divya Srinivasan, Patrick Thornton, Penny Van Horn, Mary Varn, Rosie Q. Weaver, Wiley Wiggins, Constance Wood.

**Warriors of the Wind** (4/15/86) New World Pictures. 95 mins. Director: Hayao Miyazaki. Producer: Isao Takahata. Voices: Emily Bauer (Princess Lastelle), Cam Clarke (Prince Milo), Mark Hamill (Mayor of Pejite), Shia LaBeouf (Asbel), Alison Lohman (Nausicaa), Chris Sarandon (Kurotawa), Patrick Stewart (Lord Yupa), Uma Thurman (Kushana).

**Consumer Tips:** ☆☆☆ MPAA Rating: PG. SF adventure. A thousand years after cataclysmic warfare

has almost destroyed the world, a young warrior princess tries to keep renewed warfare from completing the extinction of humanity. A severely edited and rewritten version of Hayao Miyazaki's classic *Nausicaä of the Valley of the Wind(s)*.

©New World Pictures

**Story:** An apocalyptic war a thousand years earlier destroyed civilization and reduced humanity to small feudal communities amidst jungles of poisonous fungus inhabited by giant insects. Princess Zandra of the Valley of the Wind realizes that continued violence by humans will result in the insects swarming and destroying mankind. Zandra must stop two warring kingdoms from creating this violence.

**Comments:** *The Warriors of the Wind* edit of *Nausicaä* is one of the most controversial animated features in existence. Twenty-three minutes were cut from the original 118 minutes, and the story was rewritten to change a complex science-fiction tale about ecological balance and the evolution of new life forms into a simplistic fantasy of good versus evil. Miyazaki's almost totally original story (although he named many influences ranging from Japanese and Greek mythology to American and British SF, notably Brian Aldiss's *Hothouse* stories and Ursula LeGuin's *Earthsea* novels) is made to look, especially on the *Warriors of the Wind* movie poster with its tagline proclaiming "A band of young warriors on the wings of their greatest challenge!", like a hodgepodge of fantasy movie clichés ripped off from *Star Wars*, *Dune*, and *Clash of the Titans*. *Nausicaä* is definitely worth four (if not five) stars, but while *Warriors of the Wind* has deservedly been described as butchered, it is still good enough to rate three stars.

A far-future earth has drastically evolved during a thousand years since an apocalyptic "Seven Days of Fire" war destroyed civilization. (A flashback showing armies of huge "Fire Demon" artificial warriors ("God Warriors" in *Nausicaä*) blasting fire from their mouths implies that this was either several hundred years after the 20th century, or the setting is not our earth at all.) Small pockets of humanity that survived the devastation have slowly rebuilt themselves to the level of feudal kingdoms. However, "Toxic Jungles" of strange new fungal plants have spread even more quickly. Although beautiful, their deadly gas (spores in *Nausicaä*) is fatal to humans, and they are filled with huge fierce insects that attack in large swarms when disturbed.

The Valley of the Wind(s) is a small kingdom in a valley surrounded by mountains. Winds blowing over the mountains keep it free from the gas of the nearby Toxic Jungle. Princess Zandra (Nausicaä), the young daughter of the dying king (a victim of the gas), is an enthusiastic amateur scientist who ventures into the Toxic Jungle to explore it and search for a cure for its spores. She learns that the insects, dominated by the Giant Gorgons (Ohmu), are more intelligent and better organized than humans had realized.

A primitive airplane of the empire of Tolmekia is attacked by flying insects and crashes in the valley. The plane is carrying a captive princess of Placeda (Pejitei) who is killed, and a mysterious large, throbbing, egg-like object that Zandra's advisor Lord Yuppa (Yupa with a long "u") fears is an embryonic legendary fire demon. The next day, an air fleet from Tolmekia commanded by Queen Salena (Princess Kushana) occupies the valley and kills the king. Salena tells Zandra, as the valley's new ruler, that Tolmekia is conscripting their country as an ally in its war against Placeda, whose daring Prince Milo (Asbel) is harrying their transport craft.

*Warriors of the Wind* turns this SF parable of the importance of ecological balance into a juvenile fantasy "voyage through time and space to the magical and dreamlike Valley of the Wind where good battles evil for the future of the human race." Most of the missing 23 minutes includes character development and background that enrichens the story. Zandra seems to rush into action without any forethought, just trusting to luck, while Nausicaä is shown carefully examining,

thinking, and planning. Queen Salena is a shallowly arrogant conqueror, while Princess Kushana is an ambitious minor commander, the younger sister of several higher-ranking princes; and her plan to burn back the Toxic Jungle is a desperate attempt to win favorable attention from her royal father and Tolmekia's lords. The carefully composed music by Jo Hisaishi is chopped up into abrupt, unconnected melodic passages. *Warriors of the Wind* is better than many children's fantasy adventure movies, but it is seriously inferior to the original Japanese feature in every respect.

*Nausicaä* (*Kaze no Tani no Nausicaä*) was the first feature made by Miyazaki at what was intended to be a temporary studio financed by Tokuma Publishing, which Tokuma established permanently under Miyazaki as Studio Ghibli. It was released on March 11, 1984. Miyazaki was so disgusted by New World's *Warriors of the Wind* edit that he has refused to license any more of his features without a contractual requirement that not one frame of them will be altered, which the Disney studio agreed to in 1996. Walt Disney Home Entertainment released a redubbed *Nausicaä of the Valley of the Wind* to the home-video market on February 22, 2005. (FP)

**Additional Credits:** Executive producers: Tohru Hara, Michio Kondo, Yasuyoshi Tokuma. Screenplay/comic: Hayao, Miyazaki. Music: Joe Hisaishi. Art direction: Mitsuki Nakamura. Animation director/character design: Kazuo Komatsubara. Animators: Hideaki Anno, Tadashi Fukuda, Yoshiyuki Hane, Takanori Hayashi, Junko Ikeda, Megumi Kagawa, Yoshinori Kanada, Kazuyuki Kobayashi, Yôichi Kotabe, Osamu Nabeshima, Shuichi Obara, Shunji Saida, Kitarou Takasaka, Tsukasa Tannai, Shôji Tomiyama, Takashi Watanabe, Tadakatsu Yoshida, Noboru Takano. Assistant animators: Tomihilo Okubo, Masahiro Yoshida.

**Watership Down** (11/1/78) Avco-Embassy. 92 mins. Director/producer: Martin Rosen. Voices: John Hurt (Hazel), Richard Briers (Fiver), Michael Graham-Cox (Bigwig), John Bennett (Captain Holly), Ralph Richardson (Chief Rabbit), Simon Cadell (Blackberry), Terence Rigby (Silver), Roy Kinnear (Pipkin), Richard O'Callaghan (Dandelion), Denholm Elliott (Cowslip), Lynn Farleigh (Cat), Mary Maddox (Clover), Zero Mostel (Kehaar), Harry Andrews (General Woundwort), Hannah Gordon (Hyzenthlay), Nigel Hawthorne (Captain Campion), Clifton Jones (Blackavar), Derek Griffiths (Vervain), Michael Hordern (Frith), Joss Ackland (Black Rabbit), Michelle Price (Lucy), Art Garfunkel (Vocalist).

©Nepenthe Productions, Ltd.

**Consumer Tips:** ☆☆☆ MPAA Rating: PG.

**Story:** A rabbit named Fiver has bizarre visions of impending doom. The rabbits, led by Hazel, attempt to find a new place to burrow, but encounter danger in the forms of a farm dog, a killer cat, and a dictatorial hare, General Woundwart.

**Comments:** *Watership Down* is one of the earliest, significant fully animated British films not produced by Halas and Batchelor studios. Based on the celebrated book by Richard Adams, the film focuses on the inner lives and complex society of a group of rabbits. The original warren near Sandleford is threatened by man's encroachment, though only clairvoyant Fiver is aware of it. His noble brother Hazel believes Fiver, and, though unable to persuade the entire warren, an intrepid group, notably the blustery warrior Bigwig and the inventive Blackberry, ventures out. Both film and book focus on the group's escape from the original warren and their struggles to survive, including encounters with a farm cat and the quest to find female mates. This quest leads them first to seek the assistance of Kehaar the seagull, and ultimately to conflict with the military, totalitarian warren Efrafa, run by the large and despotic General Woundwort.

The film is a surprisingly faithful adaptation, retaining most of the book's plot and mostly cutting a few supporting characters and the many folktales of El-hair-airah, the rabbit prince, which peppered the book and explained much about the rabbit culture and religion. This is more than a minor loss, but the decision was made presumably to allow for a smoother, less episodic and dense cinematic narrative. Only the tale of El-hair-airah's origin is retained, through a colorful, stylized prologue. This prologue clearly bears the stamp of John Hubley, who was initially slated to direct but fell into conflict with Martin Rosen, who then took over directorial duties in addition to producing and directing.

The film is brutal at times, as is the book, not skimping on blood, and actually inserting two additional (and largely unnecessary) deaths not included in the original text. Still, the pacing is fairly even. Though the realistic animation and rather earthen color tones sometimes lead to difficulties distinguishing one rabbit from another (with a few exceptions, such as the smaller, more visibly high-strung Fiver, the doddering and slow-moving Chief Rabbit, and the enormous, foaming Woundwort). This is compensated, however, by a top-notch cast of British thespians, including John Hurt as Hazel, Richard Briers as Bigwig, and Harry Andrews as Woundwort. American comedian Zero Mostel provides the only real comic relief through his Teutonic-accented, pidgin English-speaking Kehaar, and this is accentuated by both the animation and the bouncy background score by Angela Morley. Far less successful than Morley and Williamson's score is the ballad by Art Garfunkel, a tune called "Bright Eyes" that is not necessarily bad, but has little in the way of a clear connection to the film and seems largely irrelevant.

Ultimately, though naturally less dense than the book, and somewhat hard going for those who prefer brighter films (in terms of both visuals and content), *Watership Down* is well worth viewing, and its success led to an even gloomier follow up, an adaptation of Adams's *Plague Dogs*, and a somewhat bowdlerized television series, with Hurt and Briers now voicing the Efrafan villains. (AL)

**Additional Credits:** Coproducer: Philip Alton. Writer: Martin Rosen. Based on the novel by Richard Adams. Uncredited prologue direction/design: John Hubley. Music: Angela Morley, Malcolm Williamson. Songs: Mike Batt. Supervising animator: Philip Duncan. Animation director: Tony Guy. Senior animators: Arthur Humberstone, George Jackson, Tony Guy, Philip Duncan. Animators: Edric Radage, Bill Littlejohn, Ruth Kissane, John Perkins, Ralph Ayres, Brian Foster, Chris Evans, Marie Szimichowska, Alan Simpson, Colin White, Doug Jensen, Bill Geach, Spud [Kathleen] Houston, Barrie Nelson. Special sequence design: Liciana Arighini. Assistant animators: Ray Kelly, Bobby Clennell, Alistair Byrt, Chris Caunter, Malcolm Bourne, Steve Woods, April Spencer, Carol Slader.

**We're Back! A Dinosaur's Story** (11/24/93) Universal. 72 mins. Directors: Dick Zondag, Ralph Zondag, Phil Nibbelink, Simon Wells. Producer: Steve Hickner. Voices: John Goodman (Rex), Blaze Berdahl (Buster), Julia Child (Dr. Bleeb), Walter Cronkite (Captain Neweyes), Charles Fleischer (Dweeb), Felicity Kendal (Elsa), René Le Vant (Woog), Jay Leno (Vorb), Kenneth Mars (Professor Screweyes), Rhea Perlman (Mother Bird), Joe Shea (Louie), Martin Short (Stubbs the Clown), Larry King (Radio Voice), Yeardley Smith (Cecilia).

©Universal City Studios and Amblin Entertainment

**Consumer Tips:** ☆ MPAA Rating: G. Children's fantasy tale in New York. Pure pabulum for infantile minds.

**Story:** Four prehistoric dinosaurs are force-fed "Brain Gain" and transported to modern-day Manhattan where they get mixed up in the plight of Louie, a runaway boy, and Cecilia, a poor little rich girl.

**Comments:** *We're Back! A Dinosaur's Story,* by Hudson Talbott, was named Children's Book of the Year by the Library of Congress in 1987. *Little Mermaid* directors John Musker and Ron Clements wanted to option the story for Disney, but Spielberg beat them to it. It became the second film produced by Amblimation in London after *An American Tail II: Fievel Goes West.* The film was a dismal failure from the get-go.

However, the film did set a historical precedent: it marked the first use of American Film Technologies' digital ink-and-paint system in a feature film.

MCA/Universal moved *We're Back!* from a November 12 release to November 24 to take advantage of national promotions planned for the picture with Pizza Hut and Macy's (in the story, the dinosaurs enter New York by means of the Macy's Thanksgiving Day Parade).

The film boasted John Goodman, Jay Leno, Rhea Perlman, Walter Cronkite, Martin Short, Felicity Kendal, and Julia Child in the cast. But not even the name of Steven Spielberg on the marquee could save this dodo from extinction. Its total U.S. domestic gross: $9 million. MCA/Universal Home Video released the film on March 15, 1994. An embarrassing waste of time and talent.

For the record:

- Codirector Ralph Zondag would later codirect Disney's *Dinosaur.*
- John Goodman, the voice of Rex, later voiced better roles as Pacha in *The Emperor's New Groove,* Sully in *Monsters, Inc.,* Baloo in *The Jungle Book 2,* and Larry in *Father of the Pride,* and played Fred Flintstone in the live-action film *The Flintstones.* (WRM)

**Additional Credits:** Screenplay: John Patrick Shanley. Based on the book by Hudson Talbott. Music: James Horner. Songs: James Horner, Thomas Dolby. Supervising animators: Jeffrey J. Varab, Bibo Bergeron, Kristof Serrand, Rob Stevenhagen, Thierry Schiel, Sahin Ersoz, Borge Ring. Animation: Rodolphe Guenoden, Nicolas Marlet, David Bowers, Patrick Mate, Daniel Jeanette, William Salazar, Andreas Van Andrian, Fabio Lignini, Jan Van Buyten, Quentin Miles, Miguel A. Fuertes, Denis Couchon, Jurgen Richter, Glenn Sylvester, Todd Waterman, Michael Eames, Frank Vibert, Johnny Zeuthen, Olivier Pont, George S. Abola, Jacques Muller, Phil Morris, Eric Bouillette, Arnaud Berthier, Alain Costa, Oskar Urretabizkaia, Rudi Bloss.

**When the Wind Blows** (3/11/88) Kings Road Entertainment. 85 mins. Director: Jimmy T. Murakami. Producer: John Coates. Voices: Peggy Ashcroft (Hilda), John Mills (Jim), Robin Houston (Announcer).

©National Film Finance Corp. / Film Four International / TVC London / Penguin Books

**Consumer Tips:** ☆☆☆ MPAA Rating: PG. Adults only.

**Story:** An elderly British couple survives a nuclear bombing. Assuming the government will soon arrive with supplies, they wait and slowly begin to get sick. Days go by with no relief, no food, and conditions getting worse. Sores develop, their hair falls out, and as the film ends, the dying couple begins to pray.

**Comments:** This film was based on the best-selling cartoon book, *When the Wind Blows*, by Raymond Briggs. The *Sunday Telegraph* wrote that everyone should read this "grimly humorous and horribly honest book." Although the film of *When the Wind Blows* is basically a running dialogue between two characters, it is engaging partly because its source material was so well written.

Much has been done to liven it up visually, given its modest $3 million budget. Conversations are occasionally illustrated with fantasy sequences utilizing various animation techniques. Animators for these special sequences are: Dianne Jackson (Hilda's Dream), Richard Fawdry, Lorraine Marshall, Milly McMillan (Wedding Sequence), Michael Sakled, Venessa Cleg (Blitz Sequence), the well-known animator Jimmy Murakami, and Taylor Grant (Military Command Sequence). Cartoonist Raymond Briggs provides the main character designs, which are animated against three-dimensional background sets.

All in all, the story is powerful, the visuals are good, and the film is effective. This was reflected in *Variety's* review, which said, "*When the Wind Blows* is a classy animated feature that looks seriously at the horrors of a nuclear holocaust . . . its strength and impact are undeniable. . . . The makers of the acclaimed animated pic *The Snowman* have produced a remarkable nonpolitical film that is both funny and touching." (JB)

*Additional Credits:* Executive producer: Iain Harvey. Screenplay/novel: Raymond Briggs. Music: Roger Waters. Song: David Bowie. Key sequence animators: Tony Guy, Bill Speers, Dave Varwin, Malcolm Draper, Joe Ekers, John McGuire, Hilary Audus, Joanna Harrison, Gary McCarver, Roger Mainwood. Additional key animators: Richard Fawdry, Paul Stone, Jean Pierre Jacquet, John Bennett, Alan Green, Keith Greig, Kevin Malloy, Dave Parvin, Robin White, Alan Simpson, Harold Whitaker. Special effects sequence animation: Stephen Weston. Special sequence animators: Dianne Jackson, Richard Fawdry, Lorraine Marshall, Milly McMillan, Michael Salkeld, Vanessa Clegg, Jimmy T. Murakami, Taylor Grant. Assistant animators: Margot Allen, Stella Benson, P. John Collier, Paul Donnellon, James Farrington, Francesca Freeman, Julian Gibbs, Malcolm Hartley, Pam Johnson, Giorgio P. Mardesan, Dave Parrin, Terry Piker, Dexter Reed, Michael Salkeld, Joey Shepherd, Lucy Snyder, Karen Stephenson, Paul Stone, Glen Whiting, Bob Angelina, Caroline Cole, Wendo Van Essen, Lys Flowerday, Joan Frestone, Brigitte Hartley, Wendy Russell, Patrick Savage, Alan Simpson, Liz Spencer, Simon Ward-Horner, Boguslaw Wilk, Hugh Workman, Jonathan Webber, Theresa Wiseman. Special effects assistant: Shelly McIntosh. A Meltdown Production in association with National Film Finance Corp./Film Four International/TVC London/Penguin Books.

**Who Framed Roger Rabbit** (6/22/98) Walt Disney Pictures. 103 mins. Director: Robert Zemeckis. Producers: Frank Marshall, Robert Watts. Voices: Charles Fleischer (Roger Rabbit, Benny, Greasy, Psycho), Lou Hirsch (Baby Herman), April Winchell (Mrs. Herman), Mae Questel (Betty Boop), Mel Blanc (Daffy Duck, Bugs Bunny, Tweety Bird, Sylvester, Porky Pig), Morgan Deare (Bongo the Gorilla), Tony Anselmo (Donald Duck), Joe Alaskey (Yosemite Sam), Richard Williams (Droopy), Mary T. Radford (Hippo), Tony Pope (Goofy, Wolf), David Lander (Smart Ass), June

Foray (Wheezy, Lena Hyena), Fred Newman (Stupid), Russi Taylor (Minnie Mouse, Birds), Wayne Allwine (Mickey Mouse), Les Perkins (Toad), Peter Westy (Pinocchio), Pat Buttram, Jim Gallant, Jim Cummings (Bullets), Cherry Davis (Woody Woodpecker), Frank Sinatra (Singing Sword), Kathleen Turner (Jessica Rabbit speaking—uncredited), Amy Irving (Jessica Rabbit singing). Live actors: Bob Hoskins, Christopher Lloyd, Joanna Cassidy, Stubby Kaye, Alan Tilvern, Richard Le Parmentier, Joel Silver, Morgan Deare, Laura Frances.

©Touchstone Pictures and Amblin Entertainment

***Consumer Tips:*** ☆☆☆☆ MPAA Rating: PG. Based on the book, *Who Censored Roger Rabbit* (1981) by Gary K. Wolf.

***Story:*** 1940s Hollywood, where cartoon characters are actually alive, is shaken when toon star Roger Rabbit is accused of murdering a human. Roger begs embittered, toon-hating private detective Eddie Valiant to clear his name. Valiant's investigation takes him from encounters with the sinister Judge Doom to Toontown, an animated environment where the toons live. Also involved is a mysterious will left behind by Roger's alleged victim, Marvin Acme. Who is behind Cloverleaf Industries' plot to buy up all the trolley cars in Los Angeles? What part does Roger's voluptuous wife play in all of this? Can Eddie Valiant rescue Toontown from Judge Doom's nefarious plans? Never fear: Roger is vindicated, Doom is defeated, and all ends happily for the celebrating inhabitants of Toontown.

***Comments:*** *Who Framed Roger Rabbit* must be considered one of the most influential animated features ever produced, even though much of the action is shared with live actors. The popularity of this landmark movie almost singlehandedly fueled a renewed interest in animation by the public and established animation as legitimate entertainment for adults. *Roger Rabbit* also changed the face and style of animated television fare; Steven Spielberg made a full-fledged commitment to the genre and produced some of the zaniest, most sophisticated programs in decades as a result of his experience with the film.

The story, in fact, begins with Spielberg and two other rather famous men named Michael Eisner and George Lucas. All three were once at Paramount, where Eisner was head of production. He was of immense help to Spielberg and Lucas in producing *Raiders of the Lost Ark* (1982). After Eisner moved on to Disney, Spielberg returned the favor by partnering with Eisner on the *Roger Rabbit* project. George Lucas lent Disney the services of his special-effects arsenal, Industrial Light and Magic. Spielberg was a fan of classic cartoons and used his great influence to secure appearances from other studios' animated characters. Some, like Heckle and Jeckle, could not be had but many others could be. By the time Spielberg was done, *Roger Rabbit* boasted an unprecedented cast of cartoon characters from every studio and era of animation. There are, by final count, 90 of them featured in the film.

Both toons and humans were then placed in a tongue-in-cheek tribute to American film noir circa 1945. This unlikely combination turned out to be irresistible. Although the animated action is frenetic at times, *Roger Rabbit* never once spins out of control because the story is contained within the rules and boundaries of the noir formula. The rules of cartoondom get equal respect: when Roger Rabbit, in the throes of a jealous rage, runs through an actual office wall, the resultant hole is shaped exactly like him.

Sharp-eyed animation fans picked up an anachronism or two, but *Roger Rabbit* is a marvelous period piece featuring nods to classic Hollywood animation and the hard-boiled detective genre respectively. Director Robert Zemeckis had a good appreciation of both styles; sometimes it's the humans, such as Marvin Acme, who are cartoony while toons like Jessica Rabbit display surprising emotional depth. One scene in which Betty Boop (the only toon still animated in black and white) believes her fading charms are equal to Jessica's is both funny and poignant.

The film opens with a Roger Rabbit/Baby Herman opus titled *Somethin's Cookin'*, a rapid-fire homage to the MGM cartoons of Hanna-Barbera and Tex Avery. Animation director Richard Williams, one of the genre's most esteemed figures, designed Roger using features from characters seen in MGM, Warner Bros., and Disney cartoons. Charles Fleischer's voice completes what must be considered an archetypal cartoon character, one easily strong enough to carry the rather tough demands of a starring role against human actors. Jessica Rabbit is the direct descendant of Tex Avery's famous "Red" character, a scarlet-tressed bombshell who ignited the hormones of an eponymous wolf in some of Avery's wilder offerings of the 1940s.

Perhaps the greatest treat is watching an all-star collection of cartoon characters interacting with each other for the first—and only—time. Bugs Bunny and Mickey Mouse have a brief but very funny scene together, and the dueling piano performance featuring Daffy and Donald Duck is a must-see. Video and DVD aficionados have worn out their pause buttons during scenes set in Toontown in order to catch the animated characters that rush by or appear during group shots.

Equally marvelous is the painstaking pairing of live action and animation. *Roger Rabbit* was made well before significant advances in computer-generated imagery, and the film was made the old-fashioned way. Much of this involved meticulous manipulation of props, superimposing animation onto photostatic blowups, shading characters by careful estimation rather than with digital paint software programs, and dealing with the constant movement of cameras. Animators who worked on Benny the cab, for example, could not create him or turn him in three dimensions on a computer for at least another decade. Instead, they animated Benny's actions over filmed footage of a careening go-cart.

Despite the daunting technical challenges, Zemeckis, cast, and crew made everything work, and they exceeded everyone's wildest expectations. By the end of the film—set to a song from an obscure 1931 Warner Bros. short—our hearts are solidly in Toontown, where both justice and hilarity have triumphed forever.

For the record:

- Well-known comedians such as Dan Aykroyd were originally considered for Eddie Valiant, but Zemeckis saw them as being too close to human cartoons. He decided to cast a down-to-earth, lesser-known actor named Bob Hoskins rather than have Eddie Valiant compete against the film's toon stars.
- Mae Questel, the voice of Betty Boop, held the job from 1931 to 1939. She made a comeback appearance 50 years later for this film.
- Roger and Jessica Rabbit went on to star in three theatrical shorts that also featured Baby Herman and Droopy Dog.
- Felix the Cat could not be used in the film, but there is a likeness of him over the entrance to Toontown.
- This is possibly the only film ever to gross $328 million worldwide and not get a sequel.
- *Roger Rabbit* created a stir after it was released on laserdisc: viewers who were handy at freezing frames focused on a scene where Jessica Rabbit was thrown from Benny the cab during a smash-up. For one frame it was revealed that Jessica had left her panties back in Toontown that day. Once this was discovered, Disney ensured that future copies were more modest. (MG)

**Additional Credits:** Executive producers: Steven Spielberg, Kathleen Kennedy. Associate producers: Don Hahn, Steve Starkey. Based on the novel *Who Censored Roger Rabbit* by Gary K. Wolf. Writers: Jeffrey Price, Peter S. Seaman. Original music: Alan Silvestri. Songs: Joe McCoy, Dave Franklin, and Cliff Friend. Chief executive and supervising animator: Dale Baer. Animators: Gordon Baker, James Baxter, Ted Berglund, David Byers-Brown, Roger Chiasson, Alain Costa, Caron Creed, Al Gaivoto, Chuck Gammage, Raul Garcia, Chris R. Green, Joe Haidar, Alyson Hamilton, Bridgitte Hartley, Mark Kausler, Greg Manwaring, Gary Mudd, Jacques Muller, Matthew O'Callaghan, Brent Odell, Dave Pacheco, Mik Ranieri, Alan Simpson, Tom Sito, Dave Spafford, Nick Stern, Mike Swindall, Robert Stevenhagen, Bruce W. Smith. Assistant animators: Margot Allen, Carl Bell, Rejean Bourdages, Neil Boyle, Bella Bremner, Brenda Chat-McKie, Paul Chung, Christopher Clarke, Irene Coulouris, Annie Dubois, Helga Egilson, Margaret Flores Nichols, Martyn Jones, Renee Holt-Bird, Helen Kincaid,

Calvin Le Duc, Denise Meara-Hahn, David Nethery, Robert Newman, Brett Newton, Dave Pacheco, Vera Pacheco, Andrew Painter, Gilda Palinginis, Garry French Powell, Isabel Radage, Philippe Rejaudry, Philip Scarrold.

**Wicked City** (8/20/93) Streamline Pictures. 90 mins. Director: Yoshiaki Kawajiri. Producers: Yoshio Masumizu, Koohei Kuri. Voices: Greg Snegoff (Taki Renzaburo), Edie Mirman (Spider Woman), Robert V. Barron (Black Guard's Japan Section Chief), Gaye Kruger (Makie), Mike Reynolds (Giuseppe Mayart), David Povall (Teito Hotel Manager), Kerrigan Mahan (Jin), Jeff Winkless (Mr. Shadow, Head Black World Terrorist).

©Japan Home Video

**Consumer Tips:** ☆☆☆☆ MPAA Rating: Unrated. Fantasy/horror drama. Based on the horror novel *Yoju Toshi* by Hideyuki Kikuchi.

**Story:** Earth and hell (the "Dark Realm") have diplomatic relations. When renegade demons come to earth to prey on humans despite a peace treaty, a human secret agent and a succubus demon secret agent are teamed up to hunt them down. Secret agent Renzaburo Taki is assigned to protect humanity's diplomat until a new treaty is signed. His partner assigned by the Dark Realm government is Makie, a female demon. Despite their natural antipathy, a romance develops.

**Comments:** Japanese animated pornography is almost as old as its 1980s direct-to-video industry. *Yoju Toshi* ("Supernatural Beast City"), based on a popular horror literary novel, was the first since Osamu Tezuka's

attempts with *1,001 Nights* and *Cleopatra* to elevate it to a respectably intellectual level, on a par with the literary fiction in *Playboy* magazine. Although made primarily for the home-video market, *Wicked City* featured theatrical quality animation and had a theatrical release on April 25, 1987.

Its sophisticatedly erotic nature is established in the prologue where Renzaburo Taki, a suavely handsome electronics salesman, visits a high-class bar to meet an expensive call girl. They are relaxing in her penthouse bed after having sex when she transforms into a spider-woman, revealing her demonic nature, and scurries down the side of the building after taunting him that she has learned what she wanted to know about him. Taki comments ruefully that it looks like his cover has been blown.

Taki is the top agent of the Japanese division of the Black Guard, the international secret organization to monitor that the treaty establishing a strict separation between the human and Dark Realm dimensions is enforced. Long ago, before the treaty, demons often crossed to our world to hunt humans for sport; and there are still many, analogous to arrogant big-game hunters, who continue to poach in the human world when they can get away with it. The most recent treaty, signed in the 19th century, is about to expire and the renewal ceremony is scheduled in Tokyo. The Black Guard has just been informed by its colleagues in the Dark World that demons who want to resume preying upon humans are uniting into a militant rebel organization that has already sent agents to our world to make sure that the treaty is not renewed. Taki is assigned as a bodyguard to the human delegate who will sign the treaty, the wizard Giuseppe Mayart; the same representative who signed the current treaty over a century ago. Due to the severity of the threat (with the enemy openly mocking him), the Dark World's division of the Black Guard will send one of its own top agents to be Taki's partner.

At Tokyo Airport, Mayart's plane is destroyed as it is landing. Taki battles two Dark World terrorists, "Men in Black," who can transform into amorphous monsters reminiscent of those in John Carpenter's *The Thing*. The battle is turning desperate when Taki's Dark World partner arrives to quickly annihilate the demons. The partner is Makie, a female demon who has taken the form of a sultry supermodel. Their initial relationship is mildly antagonistic, with Taki asserting that he could have won without her help while she patronizingly dismisses this as macho posturing.

*Wicked City* mixes eroticism with an intelligent plot and well-choreographed action scenes. It inspired numerous poorer-quality imitations and a 1993 Hong Kong live-action remake directed by Tsui Hark. It was the second production (after *Lensman*) to bring public recognition to the Madhouse studio and to director Yoshiaki Kawajiri, who employed an art and color design reminiscent of the sophisticated American commercial artist Patrick Nagel, emphasizing stylishly moody blues and blacks. (FP)

**Additional Credits:** Screenplay: Kisei Choo. Based on the novel by Hideyuki Kikuchi. Music: Osamu Shooji. Editor: Harutoshi Ogata. Director of photography: Kinichi Ishikawa. English adaptation writer/producer: Carl Macek. English dialogue/direction: Greg Snegoff.

**The Wild Thornberrys Movie** (12/20/02) Paramount Pictures. 85 min. Directors: Cathy Malkasean, Jeff McGrath. Producers: Arlene Klasky, Gabor Csupo. Voices: Lacey Chabert (Eliza Thornberry), Tom Kane (Darwin), Tim Curry (Nigel Thornberry, Colonel Radcliffe Thornberry), Jodi Carlisle (Marianne Thornberry), Danielle Harris (Debbie Thornberry), Flea (Donnie Thornberry), Lynn Redgrave (Cordelia Thornberry), Marisa Tomei (Bree Blackburn), Rupert Everett (Sloan Blackburn), Obba Babatunde (Boko), Kevin Michael Richardson (Shaman Mnyambo), Alfre Woodward (Akela), Kimberly Brooks

©Paramount Pictures and Nickelodeon Movies

(Tally), Melissa Greenspan (Sarah Wellington), Crystal Scales (Cheetah Cubs), Cree Summer (Phaedra), Brock Peters (Jomo).

**Consumer Tips:** ☆☆ MPAA Rating: PG. Lukewarm film based on the Nickelodeon television series.

**Story:** The Thornberry family lives in the wild, since dad Nigel is the host of a nature show and his wife Marianne is the entire camera crew. Sisters Debbie and Eliza share this life, but little Eliza is special; after freeing an ancient shaman from a curse, she has been granted the gift to freely converse with animals. She'll need all her power to save a herd of elephants from a husband-wife team of poachers, but what can Eliza and her faithful chimp Darwin do when the girl tragically loses her magical abilities?

**Comments:** *The Wild Thornberrys* first appeared on the Nickelodeon cable network in 1998, drawing good ratings and generally good reviews. The show's theme of understanding other species and cultures went over well with both adults and kids, and there was generally some adventure and education that went along with the humor and fun. When one of Nickelodeon's first original series, *Rugrats*, was made into a feature film the same year the *Thornberrys* appeared, the cable channel discovered that it had been sitting on a gold mine. *The Rugrats Movie* grossed over $100 million, and a sequel two years later garnered another $76 million. It's no surprise that Nick went to the well again with *The Wild Thornberrys Movie* in 2002.

Working from a $35 million budget, the film did no more than make back its cost, with modest profit. Part of the problem was that the writers had to punch the story up in order to stretch a half-hour concept into a feature; this entailed putting Eliza into several thrilling but perilous situations that hiked the rating up to PG. Another problem was a thin, less-than-interesting plot that grinds to a halt twice in order to inflate the running time. In one long sequence Eliza is sent from Africa to a boarding school in London because she has been cutting up dangerously with the local wildlife (her parents are unaware of her powers). This diversion makes for some foolery with Darwin the chimp, who has stowed away in Eliza's suitcase, among the *veddy* proper English girls. This sequence does nothing to advance the plot and is irrelevant to the rest of the film; it seems to be a stand-alone episode.

A second subplot concerns Eliza's sister Debbie, who lights out into the jungle on an ATV to find her missing sister. The main joke is that this airheaded überteen has to endure mud, baboon butts, and a friendly tribe that knows neither English nor mall rat dialect. The main plot, pitting Eliza against the poachers as she struggles to rescue a kidnapped cheetah cub, gets less time than these sideshows. At the climax, everybody manages to come together to thwart the poacher's ultimate plot (electrocuting a herd of elephants) but there is no life to the film until that late point.

The characters are intended to be kooky, but most of them are a major annoyance. Darwin the chimp has the standard British tone and vocabulary seen in countless Ronald Coleman–type animated sidekicks. The Thornberrys have adopted a feral child named Donnie; his only function in this film is to chatter in an unintelligible manner and bounce around in hyperactive spasms while giving out wedgies. A (very) little bit of Debbie's sulky, pouty attitude goes a long way, and Nigel's parents are all-too-typical, paint-by-the-numbers eccentrics. This series has always had a problem with unappealing character design; the humans are among the homeliest ever generated for an animated series, and their quirky design does not grow more endearing over a feature-length viewing. Conversely, the wild animals are animated in a realistic style, almost as a thematic counterpoint to the humans. There may be a point intended, but that would be going far too deep for a movie such as this. (MG)

**Additional Credits:** Executive producers: Eryk Casemiro, Albie Hecht, Julia Pistor, Hal Waite. Coproducers: Tracy Kramer, Sean Lurie, Terry Thoren, Norton Virgien. Writer: Kate Boutilier. Character writers: Arlene Klasky, Gabor Csupo, Steve Pepoon, David Silverman, Stephen Sustarsic. Music: Randy Kerber, Drew Neumann, Paul Simon. Songs: Brandy Norwood, J. Peter Robinson. Production designer: Dima Malanitchev. Production supervisor: Nicholisa Contis. Storyboard artists: Jennifer Coyle, Rick Farmiloe, Edmund Fong, Eric Lara, Jean Morel, Toni Vian. Additional storyboards: Igor Kovalyov. Lead character designer: Patrick Dene. Character designers: Steve Fellner, Bill Schwab. Animator: Craig R. Maras. CGI animators: Nadja Bonacina, Leonard F.W. Green, Jim Ovelmen, Joe Tseng. Sequence directors: Paul Demeyer, Raul Garcia, John Holmquist, Sylvia Keulen, Frank Marino, Mark Risley, Greg Tiernan.

**Willy McBean and His Magic Machine** (6/23/65) Mangna Dist. Corp. 94 mins. Director/producer: Arthur Rankin Jr. Voices: Billie Richards (Willie McBean), Larry Mann (Professor Von Rotten), Alfie Scopp, Paul Kligman, Claude Ray, Corrine Connely, James Doohan, Pegi Loder, Paul Soles.

©Rankin-Bass

**Consumer Tips:** ☆☆½ MPAA Rating: Unrated.

**Story:** A young boy and his monkey companion foil a mad scientist's scheme by traveling back in time to meet Buffalo Bill, Christopher Columbus, King Arthur, King Tut, and the caveman who invented the wheel.

**Comments:** *Willy McBean* was the first full-length, stop-motion animated theatrical movie by the team of Arthur Rankin Jr. and Jules Bass. They were known for their popular television specials, *Rudolph, the Red-Nosed Reindeer* and *Frosty, the Snowman*.

*Willy McBean* was put into production right after the completion of the famed *Rudolph* special. Rankin and Bass began a business relationship with Tadahito Mochinaga, who was considered to be the father of puppet animation in Japan. In 1960, they had produced a syndicated puppet-animated *Pinocchio* series and were persuaded to try making feature films for a growing family movie market that developed in the 1960s. The film took three years to complete.

*Willy* is a fairly entertaining little film. The time travel motif allows for many different characters and settings that show off the models and miniatures to their best advantage. The songs are fun too.

The Rankin-Bass films of this era have been parodied for their low-budget look, but the storylines and character animation have great appeal to baby boomers who grew up with them. This film is not great art, but is quite satisfying as an example of disposable pop culture.

Nerd alert: James Doohan, who had a small voice part in *Willy McBean*, later became a regular on television's *Star Trek*, as Scotty. (SF)

**Additional Credits:** Associate producers: Jules Bass, Larry Roemer. Writers: Antony Peters, Arthur Rankin Jr. Additional dialogue: Len Korobkin. Production designer: Antony Peters. Music: Edward Thomas. Songs: Jim Plack, Edward Thomas, Gene Forrell. Continuity design: Anthony Peters. Music: Edward Thomas, Gene Forrell, James Polack. Animation supervision: Tad Mochinaga. Associate director: Kizo Nagashima. A Rankin/Bass /Videocraft International/Dentsu Motion Picture Production; released by Magna Pictures Distribution Corporation.

**Winds of Change** See *Metamorphoses*.

## The Wings of Honneamise: Royal Space Force (3/10/95) Tara Releasing. 125 mins. Director: Hiroyuki Yamaga. Producers: Hiroaki Inoue, Hirohiko Suekichi. Voices: Leo Morimoto (Shiro Lhadatt), Mitsuki Yayoi (Leiqunni Nondelaiko), Masahiro Anzai (Majaho), Chikao Ôtsuka (Dr. Gnomm), Bin Shimada (Yanaran), Kazuyuki Sogabe (Marty), Hirotaka Suzuoki (Domorhot), Kôji Totani (Tchallichammi), Yoshito Yasuhara (Nekkerout).

**Consumer Tips:** ☆☆☆½ MPAA Rating: Unrated. SF adventure. A dramatization of a fictional world's realistic first manned space flight amidst political tensions and war.

**Story:** Shirotsugh Lhadatt is a cadet in the Kingdom of Honneamise's Royal Space Force, a collection of rocketry and astronautical enthusiasts that nobody takes seriously. They are overjoyed when the government funds a serious space program. When they learn that they are really dupes in a political and military hoax, they must struggle against disillusion and an enemy attack to complete their first manned launch.

**Comments:** This amazing feature is a rough parable of the animators who created it. They began as a club of young animation enthusiasts who made two short cartoons for Japan's National SF Convention in 1981 and 1983. These were so popular with fans that they promoted themselves as a new studio, Gainax Ltd., to Bandai and obtained an $800 million budget, the largest at that time for a Japanese animated production, to make a theatrical feature. *Ôritsu Uchûgun: Oneamisu no Tsubasa*, released on March 14, 1987, was so intellectual and slow-paced that it was rejected by a public that had expected lighter entertainment. But it won critical acclaim as an ambitiously promising "flawed masterpiece." Gainax has since become a major animation studio. Members of the *Honneamise* production crew such as special effects artist Hideaki Anno and character designer Yoshiyuki Sadamoto became influential Japanese animation-industry creators during the 1990s.

*Honneamise*'s original intention was to retell the U.S.-Soviet space race of the 1960s, transferred to a mythical planet to maintain the suspense of which rival nation would be successful. The creators got carried away into designing a whole new world that would look realistic yet different: strikingly new architecture, clothing styles blending Central Asiatic and Polynesian motifs, vehicles, names—everything! The story was told through the eyes of an emotionally complex semi-outsider rather than a simplistic hero. The result is a dialogue-heavy story in which exotic background details constantly distract from the action, featuring characters with weird names and a protagonist who seems less complex than shallow and easily swayed. These serious flaws are balanced by an intelligent plot, beautiful art design, smooth animation, and a score by Oscar-winning composer Ryuichi Sakamoto.

Shiro Lhadatt is an adolescent who wants to become a naval fighter pilot. But his grades are not good enough, so he ends up in Honneamise's Royal Space Force, his government's almost-comic-relief space program—a dumping grounds for academic and military rocketry and space-program enthusiasts too influential to be completely ignored—commanded by General Khaidenn, an obsessive Billy Mitchell-type. Morale is dismal, until the government unexpectedly announces its intention to launch the first astronaut into space. Khaidenn is told privately that this is really for Honneamise's international prestige over that of its rival, "the Republic"; but he does not care as long as the space program is activated.

Shiro is chosen as the pilot. He is elated, yet confused when this brings him into conflict with his new girlfriend, Leiqunni Nondelaiko, a religious and social activist who believes that the government should support social welfare rather than "shooting its money into space." Matters turn alarming when attempts are made to sabotage the project, and Shiro barely escapes a professional assassin. As political tensions worsen between the Kingdom and the Republic, the space program team realizes that its launch site is dangerously close to the Republic's border.

When Khaidenn requests some defense, he learns the real truth. Honneamise's intelligence agency has been putting out false clues that its space rocket is really a super-weapon aimed at the Republic. Its goal is to provoke the Republic into destroying the launch site, to justify a war against the Republic "in justified self defense." The Space Force is bitterly disillusioned, but resolves to advance its planned launch date to get Shiro into space before the Republic attacks. Everyone moves up their schedules, and the climax is a tense race to complete the countdown and blastoff as the military fighting sweeps toward the launch site.

One of the strongest criticisms is Shiro's attempted rape of Leiqunni. This is supposed to show how easily he is manipulated by others before he develops self-reliance. At first he wants to be a fighter pilot because everyone thinks they are heroic. When he is assigned to the Space Force, he succumbs to the other cadets' cynical apathy. Leiqunni's inspirational urging to do something great results in his stepping up when Khaidenn calls for pilot volunteers. It is the government's PR campaign to present him as a national hero, and his buddies' macho banter about how a real man doesn't let his woman say no that inspires him to force himself upon Leiqunni. It is his own shock at his out-of-character action that causes Shiro to consciously examine himself and begin to develop his own opinions and ideals. But it still comes across as crass and inappropriate, and for many viewers it is too late in the film for Shiro to start winning their sympathy.

Bandai planned for *Honneamise* to be released in America at the same time as in Japan. An American version, *Star Quest*, was given a Hollywood gala premiere at Mann's Chinese Theater on February 19, 1987. Anime fans filled the theater, some coming from as far as Atlanta. It was almost unanimously reviled for having been camped up. Serious dialogue was replaced with inane one-liner jokes wherever possible. Reportedly Bandai charged the American producer with breach of contract for failing to produce an accurate translation as specified. As far as is known, *Star Quest* was never publicly shown again. An accurate translation was released theatrically in March 1995 and on video by Manga Entertainment in June 1995. (FP)

***Additional Credits:*** Screenplay: Mason Hiroshi Ônogi, Hiroyuki Yamaga. English adaptation: Quint Lancaster, Mary Mason. Executive producers: Toshio Okada, Shigeru Watanabe. Original music: Ryuichi Sakamoto. Cinematography: Hiroshi Isagawa. Film editing: Harutoshi Ogata. Art direction: Hiromasa Ogura. Assistant directors: Takami Akai, Shinji Higuchi, Shôichi Masuo. Sound recording: Shohei Hayashi. Digital tracking: Joe Romersa. Production/layout designers: Takami Akai, Hideaki Anno, Kamui Fujiwara, Shinji Higuchi, Fumio Iida, Harutora Inaba, Jirô Kanai, Mahiro Maeda, Kenichi Sonoda, Hiroshi Sugiura, Masayuki Takano, Yôichi Takizawa, Emi Tanaka, Seiki Tanaka, Takeshi Urabe, Akira Watanabe, Kazuyoshi Yaginuma, Ley Yumeno. Anime directors: Fumio Iida, Hideaki Anno, Yûji Moriyama, Yoshiyuki Sadamoto. Animators: Tatsuya Egawa, Masaaki Endou, Makiko Futaki, Chihiro Hayashi, Michiyasu Hiraga, Toshiaki Hontani, Yoshinobu Ineno, Atsuko Inoue, Tashiyuki Inoue, Yoshiyuki Ishikawa, Ichirô Itano, Yoko Kadokami, Jirô Kanai, Toshio Kawaguchi, Kumiko Kawana, Nobuyuki Kitajima, Katsuya Kondô, Toshiyuki Kubooka, Mahiro Maeda, Masayuki, Tôru Misaka, Sadami Morikawa, Akiko Nakano, Shuichi Obara, Hiroshi Oikawa, Yutaka Okamura, Shinji Otsuka, Kunihiko Sakurai, Teiichi Shintani, Mika Sugai, Yasuko Tachiki, Takao Takano, Kitarou Takasaka, Kazuyoshi Takeuchi, Tomokazu Tokoro, Akiko Tsukui, Kazuyoshi Yaginuma, Satoshi Yamamoto, Noriyasu Yamauchi, Kinji Yoshimoto, Nobuteru Yuuki, Ken'ichi Ônuki, Tomoko Ôtaki.

**Wizards** (3/2/77) 20th Century Fox. 81 mins. Director/producer: Ralph Bakshi. Voices: Bob Holt (Avatar), Jesse Welles (Elinore), Richard Romanus (Weehawk), David Proval (Peace), Jim Connell (President), Steve Gravers (Blackwolf), Barbara Sloane (Fairy), Angelo Grisanti (Frog), Hyman Wien (Priest), Christopher Tayback (Peewhittle), Mark Hamill (Sean), Peter

Hobbs (General), Tina Bowman (Prostitute), Ralph Bakshi (Various Characters), Susan Tyrrell (Narrator, Various Characters).

©Twentieth Century Fox Film Corp.

**Consumer Tips:** ☆☆ MPAA Rating: PG.

**Story:** Set millions of years after a nuclear holocaust, the world is divided between the Badlands, the kingdom of evil wizard Blackwolf, and the Goodlands, the realm of fairies and elves and the domain of Blackwolf's twin brother, the good wizard Avatar. Avatar is joined by Elinor (a sexy fairy), Weehawk (an elfin scout), and Peace (one of Blackwolf's assassins converted to good) on a mission to destroy Blackwolf's abuse of high technology.

**Comments:** Ralph Bakshi's *Wizards,* the fourth movie released but the fifth he made (*Hey Good Lookin'* would be delayed for over five years), also marked his first foray into fantasy. Whereas Bakshi's earliest films had been gritty, urban tales of sex, drugs, crime, and misery in the big city, *Wizards* signals the shift into "sword and sorcery." Unlike the subsequent *Lord of the Rings* and *Fire and Ice*, mingled with attempts to create a stirring saga, Bakshi's own odd sense of humor and personal influences still surface. This creates an uneasy blend.

The central figure, Avatar, is a crusty old wizard who sounds a great deal like Peter Falk, and clearly owes much to cartoonist Vaughn Bode's Cheech Wizard character. The conflict between Avatar and his evil brother Blackwolf is both clichéd and mostly dealt with at a distance, as the opposing sides gradually grow

nearer. The film is a hodgepodge of strange but intriguing concepts. Despite the fantasy elements, the story is supposed to take place in the distant future, with fairies and mutants replacing humans. Thus Blackwolf, unable to motivate his armies, dredges up old Nazi footage of Hitler, galvanizing his campaign, even going so far as to use the swastika as a throw rug. While the imagery is striking, it's unclear as to why this footage, when shown to loyal minions and opposing armies, instills both awe and fear, apart from Hitler's sheer presence, as the characters have no knowledge of WWII and other events in human history. Similarly, in a throwaway gag, two priests, who behave like stereotyped Jewish comedians, work beneath the CBS eye logo as their shrine.

In addition to Avatar, who mutters and grumbles and wonders if he packed his scotch, the cast includes a brazen giggly fairy, an earnest but uninteresting elf warrior, and a slew of fairy creatures who show up only to be slaughtered. Only Peace, a robot assassin turned weary pacifist, is fairly interesting, and he is soon dispatched with little fanfare. The poster for the film, by artist William Stout, depicted Peace astride a two-legged horse creature, and is arguably more interesting than the actual film. Worst of all, Bakshi's dalliance with live action continues, as strange tinted rotoscope footage is used to flesh out Blackwolf's armies. This technique further distances and confuses the audience, and would be overused again in *Lord of the Rings*. The constant shift between one-liners and shots of comically whining minions and more serious fantasy battles is wearying. The film has a few interesting moments, particularly in a series of still illustrations by Marvel comic artist Mike Ploog, but is perhaps most notable as a turning point, not necessarily a positive one, in Bakshi's film career. As a footnote, *Wizards* featured Mark Hamill's first theatrical role, in a bit as the voice of an unfortunate fairy, just before *Star Wars* became a hit. (AL)

**Additional Credits:** Story: Ralph Bakshi. Original music/musical director: Andrew Belling. Animators: Brenda Banks, Irven Spence, Martin Taras, Robert Taylor, Arthur Vitello. Sequence animation: Irv Spence. Layout: John Sparey. Illustrated histories: Mike Ploog. Background designs: Ian Miller. Backgrounds: Johnnie Vita, David Jonas, Ian Miller, Martin Strudler, Ira Turek. Background supervisor: Martin

Strudler. Editor: Donald W. Ernst. A Bakshi Production released by 20th Century Fox.

**Wonderbird** See *The Adventures of Mr. Wonderbird.*

**The World of Hans Christian Andersen** (3/1/71) United Artists (Japan). 80 mins. Directors/producers: Al Kilgore, Chuck McCann. Original Japanese director: Kimio Yabuki. Voices: Chuck McCann (Uncle Oley), Hetty Galen (Hans), Corinne Orr (Elisa), Jim MacGeorge (Kaspar Kat), Lionel G. Wilson (Hannibal Mouse), Linda November (Lullaby vocal), Ruth Bailew, Sidney Filson, Earl Hammond.

©United Artists Corp.

***Consumer Tips:*** ☆☆☆ MPAA Rating: G. Fantasy musical. A fantasy based on the life and tales of famous storyteller Hans Christian Andersen.

***Story:*** A young boy in early 19th-century Denmark has magical adventures that will become the inspirations of his later wonderful tales. Hans is the son of a talented but poor cobbler. A friendly old man, Uncle Oley (actually the Sandman), encourages Hans to use his imagination. When the mayor orders the city's cobblers to make their best pair of shoes for the princess to wear to the opera, Uncle Oley gives Hans's father a superb piece of red leather. But the mayor refuses to pay the prize money. When Hans goes to the opera, he sees his poor friend Elisa selling matches and he spends his ticket money on her matches instead. Stuck outside the theater, Hans tells a young boy fantasies based upon Elisa's matches. He does not notice that the crowd leaving the opera has stopped to also listen

to his tales, becoming the first of his lifelong admiring audiences.

***Comments:*** *The World of Hans Christian Andersen* (*Andersen Monogatari*; literally *Andersen Stories*), released March 19, 1968, was Toei Animation Company's closest production to the classic Disney theatrical feature formula it had chosen as its earliest model. It is set in a fairy-tale version of northern Europe, with anthropomorphized cute animals gamboling around Hans, the Sandman acting as his fairy godfather, and lots of happy songs as he has magical experiences that the audience will recognize as the inspirations for his famous tales. One wonders whether Samuel Goldwyn's 1952 film *Hans Christian Andersen*, a similar musical extravaganza starring Danny Kaye as the young Hans, similarly inspired this feature.

Hans, a boy about 10 years old, is the cheerfully imaginative son of a cobbler in a fantasy version of an early 19th-century Danish village. He has anthropomorphized animal friends similar to Cinderella's mice in that Disney feature, although unlike Gus and Jaq, Hans's companions, including Hannibal Mouse (Keke in the Japanese version) and his three look-alike sons, and the cat lovers Kaspar and Kitty (Goro and Mimi), never do much more than stand around looking cute.

*The World of Hans Christian Andersen* is pleasant children's fare; a stereotypical and clichéd "fun for the whole family" animated feature. By the late 1960s the Japanese animation industry was actively designing productions to have international marketing potential, and Hans Christian Andersen and his tales were considered a particularly rich raw resource—popular throughout Europe and the Americas, and in the public domain. In addition to Toei's 1968 feature, Zuiyo/Nippon Animation produced an identically titled 52-episode television series during 1971, and Toei made animated features of Andersen's *The Little Mermaid* and *Thumbelina* during the 1970s, over a decade before the Disney and Don Bluth versions.

The English-language dub was the last film personally presented by legendary producer Hal Roach (*Laurel and Hardy, Our Gang*). Roach hired actor, comedian, and New York City television host Chuck McCann (himself a wonderful Oliver Hardy impersonator) and cartoonist Al Kilgore (both loyal members and officers of Sons of the Desert, the official Laurel and Hardy fan club) to oversee the film's translation into English. (FP)

**Additional Credits:** Executive producers: Herbert Gelbspan, Bill Yellin. Original music: Ronald Frangiapane, Seiichiro Uno. Lyricist: Al Kilgore. Editors: Eli Haviv, Emil Haviv. Sound: Dick Vorisek.

**X** (3/24/00) Manga Entertainment. 98 mins. Director: Rintaro. Producers: Kazuhiko Ikeguchi, Kazuo Kokoyama, Masanori Maruyama. Voices: Toni Barry (Karen Kasumi), David Lucas (Seiichirou Aoki), Rupert Degas (Shuogo Asagi), Denica Fairman (Kanoe), Mike Fitzpatrick (Sorata Arisugawa), Teresa Gallagher (Arashi Kishu), Jeff Harding (Kusangi), Adam Henderson (Fuma Summit), Stacey Jefferson (Hinoto), Annemarie Lawless (Yuzuriha Nekoi), Alan Marriott (Kamui Shirou), Larissa Murray (Kotari Summit), Liza Ross (Toshiu).

**Consumer Tips:** ☆☆ MPAA Rating: R. Fantasy adventure. Two groups of psychic warriors, the Seven Dragons of Heaven and the Seven Dragons of Earth, battle for the fate of the world. Based upon the *X/1999* manga novel by CLAMP.

**Story:** Tokyo has become the battleground of two mystic groups combining ancient supernatural powers and modern technology. The Seven Dragons of Earth want to protect the earth from man's waste and pollution by destroying humanity. The Seven Dragons of Heaven believe that mankind represents the earth and must be saved. Both teams believe that fate has already predetermined which will win, except for the teenager Kamui Shiro, who is so psychically powerful that he can control his own future. Both sides try to win Kamui to their cause.

**Comments:** The movie begins as Kamui watches in horror as his nude mother pulls a sword from within her body, hands it to him, and bids him to go to Tokyo. A disparate group of individuals throughout Tokyo—a high-school student, a temple acolyte, a computer technician, a bar girl, a mystic priestess, a businessman, a soldier, and others—abruptly react and say, "Kamui has returned!" The last adds, "For the final battle to decide the fate of this planet." Nonstop supernatural battles ensue.

*X/1999*, the long-running manga serial by CLAMP (an all-woman team of four cartoonists) beginning in 1992, quickly became one of Japan's most popular manga hits of the 1990s. It was announced from the beginning that this would lead up to the story of the end of the world—the Apocalypse in 1999, the Year of Destiny predicted by Nostradamus. It was a moody "shojo" (women's) fantasy emphasizing tragedy, betrayal, the despair of childhood friends fated to become deadly enemies, and lots of mystic action such as mid-air sword battles between handsome winged youths against backgrounds filled with ominous portents such as tarot cards and pentagrams. A large cast was slowly introduced and developed into distinctive characters who gradually joined one or the other of the opposing teams of supernatural warriors.

Kadokawa Publishing, the Japanese media giant publishing the manga, is also a theatrical distributor. It commissioned the Madhouse animation studio to produce a theatrical feature to be released during 1996 (August 3). Since the manga serial still had several years to run before its planned conclusion, and it was desirable to film a story that would be popular with the general public who was not familiar with the almost 20 major characters, it was decided to make the movie a synthetic preview of the long-anticipated grand climactic Tokyo-destroying battle; a self-contained story cutting out all the subplots and character development that was in the manga.

The result is a feature-length arcane war or a series of individual sorcerous battles that is spectacular to look at, well directed, drawn in CLAMP's attractively distinct art style, and with such memorable individual concepts as the temple hidden beneath the Diet (Japanese Parliament) Building where Princess Hinoto, a beautiful, blind, deaf-mute priestess, telepathically advises leading government officials. But the story is confusing and shallow. There are Seven Dragons of Earth who want to protect the planet from violent, polluting humanity by destroying civilization. There are Seven Dragons of Heaven who believe in the basic goodness of humanity and vow to fight to protect civilization. There are three Dreamwatchers who are powerful Oriental priestesses who get the story going and recruit the two Dragon groups. The 14 psychic warriors are mostly mid-teens, although some are as young as 14 and some as old as their early 30s. In the manga each character is developed into a distinct personality, but in the movie they are barely introduced before being thrown into deadly battles. Character development is reduced to giving all the Dragons of Heaven noble expressions and body-language while the Dragons of Earth sneer arrogantly. Antagonists cry despairingly, "Why must we fight?" just before rushing into battle against each other. Buildings, including some famous Tokyo landmarks, crumble, the skies are filled with demonic crows, people dissolve into clouds of cherry blossoms, the earth is circled by fiery dragons, and eventually it ends. Five years later Madhouse redeveloped *X* as a 24-episode anime television series (October 3, 2001, to March 27, 2002; directed by Yoshiaki Kawajiri), and its publicity essentially promised, "See the *X* story presented in enough depth that it makes sense this time!"

If the movie has a central character, it is 16-year-old Kamui Shiro. As a child, his playmates were Fuma Monou and his sister Kotori. Kamui moved away from Tokyo with his mother when he was 10 years old, and he has missed them ever since. As the movie opens, Kamui's mother bewilders him with mystic prophecies about him being the Promised One who must return to Tokyo to save it and the world from destruction. Kamui does return, but he is not interested in protecting Tokyo or the world; only his old friends Fuma and Kotori. (How safe they will be if the rest of the world is destroyed is a question that never occurs to him.)

The 1999 date was dropped from the title and plot once that real year passed. The feature was titled simply *X* for its 2000 American theatrical release (although it is often referred to as *X: The Movie*).

The DVD includes a lengthy interview with the director, who specifies that his professional name, "Rintaro," is a single word. It is a pun on his real name, Shigeyuki Hayashi, though you have to understand Japanese to realize how the pun works. (FP)

**Additional Credits:** Executive producer: Tsuguhiko Kadokawa. Screenplay: Nanase Okawa, Asami Watanabe. Story: Mokona Apapa, Satsuki Igarashi, Mick Nekoi. Music: Yasuaki Shimizu, X-Japan. Animation director/character designer: Nobuteru Yuuki. Animator: Yoshinori Kanada. Draughtsmen (manga drawings): Mokona Apapa, Satsuki Igarashi. Sound director: Yasunori Honda. Cinematography: Hitoshi Yamaguchi.

**Yellow Submarine** (11/13/68) United Artists. 85 mins. Director: George Dunning. Producer: Al Broadax. Voices: Paul Angelis (Ringo, Chief Blue Meanie), John Clive (John), Paul Batten (George), Geoff Hughes (Paul), Lance Percival (Old Fred).

©Subafilms, Ltd.

**Consumer Tips:** ☆☆☆☆ MPAA Rating: G. Based on the song by John Lennon and Paul McCartney.

**Story:** The Beatles are recruited to join the battle to save peaceful Pepperland and its people from the horrific Blue Meanies.

**Comments:** *Yellow Submarine* began life as the solution to two contractual obligations. By 1967 the Beatles still owed United Artists one more movie in their original three-picture deal. Having made *A Hard Day's Night* in 1964, and *Help!* in 1965, they were no longer interested in the tedious process of moviemaking, and were too busy experimenting in the recording studio to take the time for another extracurricular project.

Enter Al Brodax, who for the previous three years had been enjoying success producing the Beatles' Saturday morning cartoon series through a London animation studio called *TVCartoons*. Brodax reminded the Beatles' manager, Brian Epstein, that Epstein had promised him the chance to make a Beatles theatrical feature if the series had been a hit. So, to fulfill this verbal agreement, satisfy United Artists, and free up the Beatles to travel to India to study meditation with the Maharishi, the deal was made.

With a working budget of just under $1 million, a deadline less than 11 months away, and spurred on by the music of the Beatles, an animation crew was assembled, comprised of many artists who worked on the series, including producer John Coates, director George Dunning, animation director Jack Stokes, as well as artists who would make names for themselves later as independent animators like Paul Driessen, Diane Jackson, and Alison de Vere.

As one of the two animation directors, Stokes would divide chores with Bob Balzer, Stokes dealing with the more narrative Pepperland sequences, Balzer the sections depicting the submarine's journey to get there, and all of the strange lands visited along the way. Charlie Jenkins handled special photographic sequences like the "Eleanor Rigby" section, director Dunning pulled the whole thing together.

Because the Beatles did not like the cheapness of the Saturday morning series, they initially didn't imagine that the feature would be of any artistic merit so they kept their distance, becoming unavailable to voice their own characters in the film, and only contributing songs that were deemed subpar for inclusion on *Sgt. Pepper* and *The White Album*.

But they needn't have worried. Coates and Dunning were granted enviable permission to listen to recordings of the then-unreleased *Sgt. Pepper* album and agreed that the style of the television series would not complement the Beatles' new sound. A new look would be needed. Several designers were considered to create the right feel for the film, among them Alan Aldridge and

Milton Glaser, before German-born Heinz Edelmann was chosen. His flat, illustrative style that he utilized to design the characters of John, Paul, George, and Ringo, as well as all of the other creatures and locations in the film, was the perfect visual counterpart to the Beatles' psychedelic music. Edelmann ended up staying in London and overseeing the design aspects of the film for the entire 11 months of production.

Midway through the production the Beatles did visit the cartoon studio to view the work-in-progress and found, to their astonishment, that their little contractual obligation had developed into an exciting artistic achievement; a monument to both the Beatles' music and the progressive attitudes of the 1960s generation. So they asked to be included in a live-action scene at the film's conclusion.

The only element still missing was a finished script. Several drafts were written and rewritten as production continued to move forward. If a solid story arc seems to be lacking, it's due to writing and artwork carrying on simultaneously. It didn't help that the Beatles were late with their song contributions. "Hey Bulldog" arrived too late to be used as anything except in the final battle scene.

After the film's London premiere on July 17, 1968, Brodax decided that the "Hey Bulldog" sequence was anticlimactic, had it cut out, and commissioned a new ending with a more straightforward battle scene. For 30 years, that is the version everyone knew until the film's restoration and DVD release in 1999 in which the "Hey Bulldog" sequence was added back in.

Because the schedule was so tight, certain scenes seem animated with less care than others. Indeed, the entire film could be described as top-heavy with design. But the look and feel of the entire movie never ceases to be interesting visually. Eye-popping, inspiring, and thoroughly modern in a way that most traditionally animated features are not, it really is the rare case of something being both a product of its time and timeless. (David Bastian)

©Subafilms, Ltd.

**Additional Credits:** Line producer: John Coates. Production coordinator: Abe Goodman. Production based at TVC, Ltd. London. Music: The Beatles. Musical director: George Martin. Original story: Lee Minoff. Screenplay: Lee Minoff, Al Brodax, Jack Mendelsohn, Erich Segal. Designer: Heinz Edelmann. Animation directors: Jack Stokes, Bob Balser. Additional sequence director: Edrich Radage. Special effects: Charles Jenkins. Associate producer: Mary Ellen Stewart. Background supervisors: Alison deVere, Millicent McMillian. Animators: Alan Ball, Reg Lodge, Tom Halley, Dave Livesey, Duane Crowther, Cam Ford, Mike Pocock, Geoff Loynes, Mike Stuart, Malcolm Draper, Ted Percival, Lawrence Morrcroft, Dennis Hunt, Arthur Humberstone, Anne Jolliffe, Tony Cuthbert, Paul Driessen, Hester Coblentz, Dick Horn, John Challis, Diane Jackson, Geoff Collins, Gerry Potterton.

## Yu-Gi-Oh!: The Movie

**Yu-Gi-Oh!: The Movie** (8/13/04) Warner Bros. 88 mins. Director: Hatsuki Tsuji. Producers: Noriko Kobayashi, Naoki Sasada, Lloyd Goldfine, Katia Milani, Michael Pecoriello. Voices: Dan Green, Eric Stuart, Scottie Ray, Wayne Grayson, John Campbell, Amy Birnbaum, Tara Jayne, Maddie Blaustein, Darren Dunstan, Ben Baron, Mike Pollock, Andrew Paull, Ed Paul, Lisa Ortiz, Marc Thompson, Sebastian Arcelus.

©Kazuki Takahashi

**Consumer Tips:** ☆☆ MPAA Rating: PG. Based upon the television animated series, which is based upon the *Japanese Yu-Gi-Oh!: Duel Monsters* collectible card games and comic books by Kazuki Takahashi.

**Story:** Five thousand years ago in Egypt, the mighty wizards Pharaoh (good) and Anubis (evil) fought a mystic Shadow Games battle to control the world. Pharaoh won and sealed the powerful magic away for the good of mankind. But today the magic has been revived as Duel Monsters, a juvenile card game. Yugi Moto is the world champion player, but rich brat Seto Kaiba is determined to win the championship fairly or foully. Kaiba is counting on using the Pyramid of

Light, a card so powerful no player has used it in 5,000 years—not realizing that the spirit of Anubis is using him as a pawn to destroy the world.

**Comments:** *Yu-Gi-Oh!: The Movie* is a typical animated theatrical feature made to cash in on the transient popularity of a juvenile television series at its peak. Its only distinction is that, unlike similar imported Japanese animated television series and subsequent features, there was no theatrical feature to import. Warner Bros., the American distributor of the television series on Kids' WB!, commissioned the theatrical feature from the Japanese television producer, Studio Gallop, especially for its American release.

*Yu-Gi-Oh!* (*King of Games*) began as a Japanese weekly comic book serial in 1996. Its fictional Duel Monsters mystic card game was developed into a real merchandising spinoff in 1999, and then a *Yu-Gi-Oh!: Duel Monsters* television animated series in 2000. It debuted on America's Kids' WB! network in September 2001.

Yugi Moto is a courageous high-school student in a frail body. He is also the reincarnation of the Pharaoh, the ancient wizard whose name inspired the title of the later Egyptian rulers. When Yugi's grandfather, who owns a gaming shop, gives him a complicated Millennium Puzzle found in the Pyramids, Yugi solves it and awakens the spirit of the Pharaoh, Dark Yugi (Yami Yugi) within him. The mystically powerful Shadow Games that the Pharaoh had thought hidden from humanity for eternity have just been rediscovered ("Even eternity doesn't last forever!") in the form of a modern internationally popular collectible card game, Duel Monsters. Its players do not realize that a supernatural warrior or monster is sealed within each card and that they are playing with genuine sorcery. To protect the world, Yugi and the Pharaoh must team up (two personalities in the same body; Dark Yugi has a deeper voice and more dynamic personality) to make Yugi the game's world-champion player so he can control its magic.

A secondary tagline of the movie is, "Can This Be the Final Duel?" Since it was publicized that the movie adventure would take place between television episodes #144 and #145, and the television series was already far past that point, obviously it could not be. This did not keep the fans of the television series and the games from enjoying it; *Yu-Gi-Oh!: The Movie*'s U.S. box-office gross topped out at $19.7 million. But the movie was strictly designed for only those fans. For anyone else it is simplistically one-dimensional and lacking any real suspense. (FP)

**Additional Credits:** Executive producers: Hideyuki Nagai, Tamizo Suzuki, Hideki Yamashita, Alfred R. Kahn, Norman J. Grossfeld. Animation directors: Nak Soo Choi, Hee Nam Cho, Koung Tae Kim. Screenplay: Matthew Drdek, Lloyd Goldfine, Norman J. Grossfeld, Michael Pecioriello. Based on characters created by Kazuki Takahashi, Studio Dice. Story: Junki Takegami, Masahiro Hikokubo. Camera: Hiroaki Edamitsu, Duk Gyu Choi, Tae Hee Heo, Kang Ok Kim. Editor: Masao Nakagawa. Music: Elik Alvarez, John Angier, Joel Douek, Ralph Schuckett, Wayne Sharpe, Freddy Sheinfeld, Gil Talmi. Sound: Mike Patrick, Robert Olari. Supervising sound editor: A. Maddy Shirazi. Animation production: Studio Gallop. Character designer: Hatsuki Tsuji. Monster designer: Hidekazu Shimamura. Story and gameplay adviser: Arthur "Sam" Murakami. Associate producers: Shane Guenego, Chris Guido. Assistant directors: Yoshiaki Tsutsui, Woo Hyun Park, Sung Woon Ko, Chi Man Park. A 4Kids Entertainment production.

# Appendix I

# Limited Release Animated Features

The following animated features had limited runs, played locked art house engagements and festivals, or were screened exclusively at midnight showings or children's Saturday matinees.

**Sinbad, the Sailor** (7/21/62) Signal International. 81 mins. D: Taiji Yabushita. ExP: Okawa Hiroshi. Sinbad and his young friend Ali join a pirate ship where he frees an imprisoned princess and, after many adventures, discovers a secret treasure. Aka *The Adventures of Sinbad* (*Shindbad No Baden*, 1962).

**Marco Polo Jr.** (4/12/73) Premore. 85 mins. D & P: Eric Porter. ExP: Sheldon Moldoff. Voices: Bobby Rydell (Marco Polo Junior), Arnold Stang (The Delicate Dragon). Marco Polo Jr. sets sail for Xanadu to reunite two halves of a magical medallion, but is thwarted by evil ruler Red Dragon, who has imprisoned the princess, the rightful heir to Xanadu's throne. Also known as *Marco Polo*, *Marco Polo and the Red Dragon*, and *The Red, Red Dragon*. This film was remade 28 years later as *Marco Polo: Return to Xanadu* (2001).

**Once Upon a Girl** (6/20/76) Producers Releasing Organization. 77 mins. D: Don Jurwich. P: Joel Siebel. Voice: Richmond Johnson. Live-action wraparound of Mother Goose (actor Hal Smith in drag) in court, on the witness stand, recounting an X-rated retelling of famous fairy tales: Jack and the Beanstalk, Cinderella, and Little Red Riding Hood told in XXX animation.

**Once Upon a Time** (10/1/76) G.G. Communications. 83 mins. D: Rolf Kauka, Roberto Gavioli. P: Rolf Kauka. Voices: Dolphy, Chuckie Dreyfuss, Richard

Gomez, Tessie Tomas. Maria, a beautiful girl from a poor family, outwits her wicked stepmother and stepsister to reunite with a handsome prince. Also known as *Maria d'Oro* and *Bello Blue*.

**Rudolph and Frosty's Christmas in July** (7/1/79) Avco-Embassy. 97 mins. D: Arthur Rankin Jr., Jules Bass. Voices: Red Buttons (Milton), Ethel Merman, (Lilly Loraine), Mickey Rooney (Santa Claus). Rudolph the red-nosed reindeer teams up with Frosty the snowman to save a circus and defeat evil King Winterbolt.

**Nutcracker Fantasy** (7/7/79) Sanrio (Japan). 82 mins. D: Takeo Nakamura. P: Walt deFaria, Mark L. Rosen, Arthur Tomioka. Voices: Michele Lee (Narrator), Melissa Gilbert (Clara), Lurene Tuttle (Aunt Gerda), Christopher Lee (Uncle Drosselmeyer, Street Singer, Puppeteer, Watchmaker). Based on *The Nutcracker* and *The Mouse King* by E. T. A. Hoffman.

**King Dick** (7/3/82) Aquarius Releasing. 65 mins. D: Gioacchino Libratti. P: Claudio Monti. A midget servant must fall in love with a haggard witch to break a spell and return the pair to prince and princess. Aka *Little Dick, The Mighty Midget*, an X-rated feature, and *Il Nano e la strega*.

**Mighty Mouse in the Great Space Chase** (12/10/82) Filmation. 88 mins. D: Ed Friedman, Lou Kachivas, Marsh Lamore, Gwen Wetzler, Kay Wright, Lou Zukor. P: Don Christensen, Norm Prescott, Lou Scheimer. Voices: Alan Oppenheimer (Mighty Mouse), Diane Pershing (Pearl Pureheart). Space Queen Pearl Pureheart, in her spacecraft, is pursued by evil Harry the Heartless who has captured a Doomsday Machine.

Mighty Mouse faces many perils in his effort to vanquish the villain. Played Saturday matinees only.

**Swan Princess II: Escape from Castle Mountain** (7/18/97) Legacy. 71 mins. D: Rich Rich. P: Jared F. Brown, Richard Rich. Voices: Michelle Nicastro (Odette), Douglas Sills (Derek). Princess Odette returns as a swan to save her prince, when evil Clavius, who plots to rule the world with a globe-sized Orb, gains the powers of the Forbidden Arts.

**The Mighty Kong** (5/29/98) Legacy. 78 mins. D: Art Scott. P: Lyn Henderson, Denis deVallance. Voices: Dudley Moore (Carl Denham, King Kong), Jodi Benson (Ann Darrow). Animated musical version of King Kong story with Jodi Benson as Ann Darrow and songs by the Sherman brothers.

**Rudolph, the Red-Nosed Reindeer** (11/15/98) Legacy. 83 mins. D: Bill Kowalchuck. P: William R. Kowalchuk. Voices: John Goodman (Santa Claus), Whoopi Goldberg (Stormella, the Evil Ice Queen), Debbie Reynolds (Mrs. Claus). Cruel villainess Stormella unleashes severe weather to disrupt Santa's yearly trip. Rudolph arrives to save the day.

**Sinbad: Beyond the Veil of Mists** (1/28/00) Trimark Pictures. 85 mins. D: Evan Ricks, Alan Jacobs. P: Sriram Rajan. Voices: Brendan Fraser (Sinbad), Mark Hamill (Captain of the Guard), Leonard Nimoy (Akron, Baraka, King Chandra). When an evil wizard exchanges bodies with the king, the princess joins Sinbad to find a way to reverse the spell.

**Kirikou and the Sorceress** (2/18/00) Artmattan Productions. 70 mins. D: Michael Ocelot. P: Didier Brunner, Paul Thiltges, Jacques Vercruyssen. Voices: Theo Sebeko (Kirikou), Antoinette Kellermann (Karaba). Based on an African folktale, baby Kirikou is born to challenge evil sorceress Karaba and save his village.

**Marco Polo: Return to Xanadu** (12/28/01) Tooniversal Co. 86 mins. D: Ron Merk. P: Chris Holter, Igor Meglic, Ron Merk. Voices: Nicholas Gonzalez (Young Marco), John Matthew (the Delicate Dinosaur), Tony Pope (Foo-Ling). A young descendant of Marco Polo sets sail for Xanadu to reunite two halves of a magical medallion. He is thwarted by evil ruler Foo-Ling, who has imprisoned the princess Ming-Yu, the rightful heir to Xanadu's throne. L.A. release date to qualify for Oscar. A remake of Marco Polo Jr. (1973), the film recycles animation from the original with additional new animation sequences and songs.

**Rescue Heroes: The Movie** (10/24/03) Artisan/Family Home Entertainment (Nelvana). 78 mins. D: Ron Pitts. P: Pamela Lehn. Voices: Norm Spencer (Billy Blazes), Joe Motiki (Rocky Canyon), Lenore Zann (Wendy Waters). A series of mysterious lightning storms wreaking havoc worldwide spiral through the atmosphere toward Greenland. When they collide, it will create one massive storm that will result in cataclysmic destruction. The Rescue Heroes race to the scene. Chicago release date.

**Kaena: The Prophecy** (6/25/04) Goldwyn/Destination. 91 mins. D: Chris Delaporte. P: Marc Du Pontavice. Voices: Kirsten Dunst (Kaena), Richard Harris (Opaz), Anjelica Huston (Queen of the Selenites). Sci-fi adventure, set in another universe, about an orphan girl who sets off on a mission to save her people from an imperious queen, who has brought their village to the brink of extinction. (New York release date above; L.A. release date July 9, 2004.) U.S. box-office gross: $8,593.

**The Legend of Buddha** (10/22/04) Blazeway/Pentamedia (India). 88 mins. D: Shamboo Falke. P: Pentamedia Graphics Limited. The life of Prince Gautama, who leaves behind his kingdom and wealth to take a journey seeking truth, to attain Nirvana and become Buddha—The Enlightened One. Los Angeles release date for Academy consideration.

**Muhammad: The Last Prophet** (11/14/04) Fine Media Group. 90 mins. D: Richard Rich. P: Mowafak El-Harthy. Voice: Eli Allem (Abu Talib). The story of a man of humble origins who became a spiritual leader.

# Appendix 2

# Top 60 Animated Features Never Theatrically Released in the United States

The following represents a mere handful of the hundreds of animated features produced around the world that have never been released theatrically in the United States. We have listed 20 significant films in each category.

## Top 20 (U.S.-Produced) Direct-to-Video Animated Films

**Tiny Toon Adventures: How I Spent My Vacation** (1992) Warner Bros. 73 mins. Directors: Rich Arons, Ken Boyer, Kent Butterworth, Barry Caldwell, Alfred Gimeno, Art Leonardi, Byron Vaughns. Screenplay: Paul Dini, Nicholas Hollander, Tom Ruegger, Sherri Stoner. Voices: Charles Adler (Buster Bunny), Tress MacNeille (Babs Bunny), Joe Alaskey (Plucky Duck). The Tiny Toon characters attending Acme Looniversity look forward to a summer vacation, which includes Buster and Babs Bunny taking a white-water rafting trip through the Deep South; and Plucky Duck and Hamton Pig sharing an awful car journey to HappyWorldLand.

**Aladdin and the King of Thieves** (1996) Disney. 80 mins. Director: Tad Stones. Screenplay: Mark McCorkle, Robert Schooley. Voices: Robin Williams (Genie), Scott Weinger (Aladdin), Linda Larkin (Princess Jasmine). Aladdin is about to marry Princess Jasmine. When the 40 thieves disrupt the wedding trying to steal a magical talisman, Aladdin is drawn into a dangerous quest to stop the thieves . . . and find his long-lost father.

**Pooh's Grand Adventure: The Search for Christopher Robin** (1997) Disney. 70 mins. Direc-

tor: Karl Geurs. Screenplay: Carter Crocker, Karl Geurs. Voices: Jim Cummings (Winnie the Pooh), Brady Bluhm (Christopher Robin), Peter Cullen (Eeyore). Christopher Robin is off to school, but Pooh misunderstands his note and believes he has gone to "Skull" and needs his help. Pooh launches a rescue mission with the help of Rabbit, Tigger, and Piglet.

**The Lion King II: Simba's Pride** (1998) Disney. 81 mins. Directors: Darrell Rooney, Rob LaDuca. Screenplay: Flip Kobler, Cindy Marcus. Voices: Matthew Broderick (Simba), Moira Kelly (Nala), Neve Campbell (Adult Kiara). Simba's daughter is the key to a resolution of a bitter feud between Simba's pride and the outcast pride led by the mate of Scar.

**Hercules and Xena the Animated Movie: The Battle for Mount Olympus** (1998) 86 mins. Universal. Director: Lynne Naylor. Screenplay: John Loy. Voices: Kevin Sorbo (Hercules), Lucy Lawless (Xena), Renée O'Connor (Gabrielle). Hera decides that it should be her time to rule the universe, steals the Chronos Stone, the source of the God's power, and unleashes the four Titans from eons of imprisonment. With these angry behemoths on the loose, only the combined forces of Hercules and Xena can save Mount Olympus.

**Batman: Sub-Zero** (1998) Warner Bros. 70 mins. Director: Boyd Kirkland. Screenplay: Boyd Kirkland and Randy Rogel. Voices: Kevin Conroy (Bruce Wayne, Batman), Michael Ansara (Dr. Victor Fries, Mr. Freeze), Loren Lester (Robin). Mr. Freeze, to save his dying wife, kidnaps Barbara (Batgirl) Gordan as an involuntary organ donor. Batman and Robin must find her before the operation can begin.

**Pocahontas II: Journey to a New World** (1998) Disney. 72 mins. Directors: Tom Ellery, Bradley Raymond. Screenplay: Allen Estrin, Cindy Marcus, Flip Kobler. Voices: Irene Bedard (Pocahontas), Jim Cummings (King James), Donal Gibson (John Smith). When news of John Smith's death reaches America, Pocahontas sets off to London to meet with the king of England on a diplomatic mission to create peace and respect between the two great lands.

**Wakko's Wish** (1999) Warner Bros. 80 mins. Directors: Liz Holzman, Rusty Mills, Tom Ruegger. Screenplay: Nick Dubois, Kevin Hopps, Charles M. Howell IV, Earl Kress, Randy Rogel, Tom Ruegger. Voices: Jess Harnell (Wakko), Rob Paulsen (Yakko, Pinky), Tress MacNeille (Dot). One night, Wakko Warner wishes on a falling star and surprisingly finds he'll actually get a wish, so long as he gets to the fallen star first. Yakko, Wakko, and Dot head to the fallen star, but then so does everyone else who wants a wish.

**Bartok the Magnificent** (1999) 20th Century Fox. 67 mins. Directors: Don Bluth, Gary Goldman. Screenplay: Jay Lacopo. Voices: Hank Azaria (Bartok), Kelsey Grammer (Zozi), Andrea Martin (Baba Yaga). Bartok the bat must save the young heir to the Russian throne, Prince Ivan. However, he must face a series of tasks and adventures set for him by the crazy witch of the Iron Forest, Baba Yaga.

**An Extremely Goofy Movie** (2000) Disney. 76 mins. Directors; Ian Harrowell, Douglas McCarthy. Screenplay: Scott Gorden. Voices: Bill Farmer (Goofy), Jason Marsden (Max), Jim Cummings (Peter Pete). Goofy's son Max enrolls in college, finally free of his embarrassing father. Unfortunately, Goofy loses his job and learns that he cannot get another job without a college degree. To his son's horror, Goofy decides to join him on campus to get that degree. There Goofy meets a wonderful librarian who shares his nostalgic love for 1970s pastimes.

**Tweety's High Flying Adventure** (2000) Warner Bros. 72 mins. Directors: Karl Toerge, Charles Visser, James T. Walker. Screenplay: Tom Minton, Tim Cahill, Julie McNally. Voices: Joe Alaskey (Sylvester, Tweety), June Foray (Granny). Granny wagers Colonel Rimfire that Tweety can make it around the world in 80 days, despite the attempts of Sylvester to stop him.

**Joseph: King of Dreams** (2000) DreamWorks Animation. 75 mins. Director: Rob LaDuca, Robert C. Ramirez. Screenplay: Eugenia Bostwick-Singer, Raymond Singer. Voices: Ben Affleck (Joseph), Mark Hamill (Judah), Richard Herd (Jacob). The life of Joseph, a miracle child with the gift of interpreting dreams. He becomes the favorite of his father, Jacob, who gives Joseph a beautiful coat, much to the envy of his 10 older brothers.

**Lady and the Tramp II: Scamp's Adventure** (2001) Disney. 69 mins. Director: Darrell Rooney and Jeannine Roussel. Screenplay: Bill Motz and Bob Roth. Voices: Scott Wolf (Scamp), Alyssa Milano (Angel), Chazz Palminteri (Buster). Seeking the freedom to be a wild dog, the son of Lady and the Tramp runs away to join a gang of junkyard dogs.

**Batman Beyond: Return of the Joker** (2001) Warner Bros. Director: Curt Geda. Screenplay: Paul Dini. Story: Paul Dini, Glen Murakami, Bruce W. Timm. Voices: Will Friedle (Terry McGinnis, Batman), Kevin Conroy (Bruce Wayne, Batman), Mark Hamill (the Joker). The best of the Batman animated movies finds the caped crusader, 40 years from now, facing the mystery of the reappearance of his deadliest foe and unraveling his murderous plot.

**Tom and Jerry: The Magic Ring** (2002) Warner Bros. 62 mins. Director: James T. Walker. Screenplay: Tim Cahill, Julie McNally. Voices: Jeff Bennett (Tom), Frank Welker (Jerry), Jim Cummings (Butch). Tom is left in charge of a priceless magical ring by his young wizard master. He is then horrified when the ring gets stuck on Jerry's head, who then runs off into the city.

**The Animatrix** (2003) Warner Bros. Directors: Peter Chung, Andy Jones, Yoshiaki Kawajiri, Takeshi Koike, Mahiro Maeda, Kôji Morimoto, Shinichirô Watanabe. Screenplay: the Wachowski Brothers, Peter Chung, Yoshiaki Kawajiri, Kôji Morimoto, Shinichirô Watanabe. Voices: Carrie-Anne Moss (Trinity), Olivia d'Abo (Rox), Clayton Watson (The Kid). Anthology of nine state-of-the-art short anime films tied in to the 1999 blockbuster *The Matrix* and its sequels.

## 101 Dalmations II: Patch's London Adventure

(2003) Disney. 70 mins. Directors: Jim Kammerud, Brian Smith. Screenplay: Brian Smith, Jim Kammerud. Voices: Barry Bostwick (Thunderbolt), Jason Alexander (Lightning), Martin Short (Lars). In order to save his job, television superdog Thunderbolt decides he will go into the real world and perform an act of true heroism to prove himself. Patch, an expert on Thunderbolt's many adventures, provides the perfect guide for the superstar in his attempts at real-life heroics.

**Lion King** 1½ (2004) Disney. 77 mins. Director: Bradley Raymond. Screenplay: Tom Rogers. Voices: Nathan Lane (Timon), Ernie Sabella (Pumbaa), Matthew Broderick (Simba). Timon and Pumbaa retell the story of *The Lion King*, from their own warped perspectives.

## Mickey, Donald, Goofy: The Three Musketeers

(2004) Disney. 68 mins. Director: Donovan Cook. Screenplay: David M. Evans, Evan Spiliotopoulos. Voices: Wayne Allwine (Mickey Mouse), Tony Anselmo (Donald Duck), Bill Farmer (Goofy). Castle janitors Mickey, Donald, and Goofy have their dream of becoming Musketeers come true when Peg-Leg Pete hires them as Princess Minnie's personal bodyguards.

**L'il Pimp** (2005) Revolution Studios. 80 mins. Directors: Mark Brooks, Peter Gilstrap. Screenplay: Mark Brooks, Peter Gilstrap. Voices: Mark Brooks (Lil Pimp), Carmen Electra (Honeysack), Bernie Mac (Fruit Juice). Originally planned for theatrical release, this R-rated production, based on an Internet cartoon, was released direct to video. It's the first mainstream animated feature produced using Flash animation.

# Top 20 (U.S.-Aired) Made-for-TV Animated Features

## A Connecticut Yankee in King Arthur's Court

(1970) Syndicated by D.L. Taffner Limited. 75 mins. Director: Zoran Janjic. Screenplay: Michael Robinson. Broadcast in the United States on November 26, 1970,

Thanksgiving Day, this feature, produced by Air Programs International in Sydney, Australia, was the first full-length animated feature produced exclusively for television showing.

**The Point** (1971) ABC. Murakami Wolf. 74 mins. Director: Fred Wolf. Screenplay: Norm Lenzer. Voices: Mike Lookinland (Oblio), Ringo Starr (Narrator— home video release), Paul Frees (Oblio's father). Dustin Hoffman originally narrated the television version of songwriter Harry Nilsson's fable about a boy born with a round head in the land of the pointy-headed. This was the first network (ABC) prime-time made-for-television feature film.

**Everybody Rides the Carousel** (1976) CBS. Hubley Studio. 72 mins. Director: John Hubley. Screenplay: Faith Hubley, John Hubley. Voices: Alvin Epstein (Narrator), Lou Jacobi (Relative), Meryl Streep (Lover). The eight stages of human development, as seen through psychiatrist Erik Erikson's theories and unique Hubley animation.

**The Hobbit** (1977) NBC. Rankin-Bass. 77 mins. Directors: Jules Bass, Arthur Rankin Jr. Screenplay: Romeo Muller (based on the novel by J. R. R. Tolkien). Voices: Orson Bean (Bilbo Baggins), John Huston (Gandalf the Grey), Hans Conreid (Thorin Oakenshield). Bilbo Baggins, a Hobbit, assists Gandalf the Wizard and 13 dwarves in their mission to reclaim their kingdom. In his adventures through Middle Earth, Bilbo encounters many creatures and demons, but with his cleverness, and the use of his magic ring, Baggins reclaims the Dwarf King's gold, and escapes with his life. This is a musical with an antiwar message.

**The Lion, the Witch, and the Wardrobe** (1979) CBS. Children's Television Workshop. 95 mins. Director: Bill Melendez. Screenplay: David D. Connell, Bill Melendez (based on the novel by C. S. Lewis, *The Chronicles of Narnia*). Voices: Rachel Warren (Lucy), Susan Sokol (Susan), Reg Williams (Peter). During World War II, four children pass into an old wardrobe closet and discover the magical kingdom of Narnia, which is under a witch's spell, and where it is "always winter but never Christmas." With the help of Aslan (the Lion), the children successfully challenge the witch's tyrannical rule. An Emmy award winner for Best Animated Special. The three parts of the story were each animated by a different studio.

**Animalympics** (1980) NBC. Lisberger Productions. 78 mins. Director: Steven Lisberger. Screenplay: Steven Lisberger, Michael Fremer. Voices: Gilda Radner (Barbara Warblers, Brenda Springer), Harry Shearer (Keen Hacksaw), Billy Crystal (Rugs Turkell). In this lampoon of the Olympics, the animal kingdom stages the first Animalia Winter Games. Four announcers tie together the athletic episodes that are often built around songs in the score. A sequel was made but not aired because of America's boycott of the 1980 Moscow Olympic Games. The two films were later combined, with some added scenes, and released in 1983 as a video movie.

**Yogi's First Christmas** (1980) Syndicated. Hanna-Barbera Productions. 98 mins. Director: Ray Patterson. Screenplay: Willie Gilbert. Voices: Daws Butler (Yogi Bear, Huckleberry Hound, Augi Doggie, Snagglepuss), Don Messick (Boo Boo, Ranger Smith, Herman the Hermit), Janet Waldo (Cindy Bear, Mrs. Throckmorton). Yogi Bear and his sidekick Boo Boo awaken from hibernation just in time to save the Jellystone Lodge from being sold. The first of many Hanna-Barbera made-for-television feature films.

**Return of the King** (1980) ABC. Rankin-Bass Productions in association with Toei Animation. 98 mins. Directors: Arthur Rankin Jr., Jules Bass. Screenplay: Romeo Muller, based on J. R. R. Tolkien's final book of the *Lord of the Rings* trilogy. Voices: Orson Bean (Frodo), Roddy McDowall (Samwise), John Huston (Gandalf). Adaptation of the third book of the *Lord of the Rings* trilogy. Frodo and Samwise struggle through the barren land of Mordor to destroy the Ruling Ring in Mount Doom.

**The Soldier's Tale** (1981) PBS (Great Performances). 60 mins. Director: R. O. Blechman. Screenplay: R. O. Blechman. Voices: Andre Gregory (Narrator), Max von Sydow (The Devil), Galina Panova (Princess). Based upon the theater piece by the composer Igor Stravinsky and the playwright C. F. Ramuz, concerning a soldier who, returning home from war, chances upon a stranger who offers to buy his violin. The stranger turns out to be the devil, and the violin is the soldier's soul.

**Flash Gordon—The Greatest Adventure of Them All** (1982) NBC. Filmation. 95 mins. Director: Gwen Wetzler. Screenplay: Samuel A. Peeples. Robert Ridgely (Flash Gordon), Diane Pershing (Dale Arden), Bob Holt (Ming the Merciless). Considered one of the best things Filmation ever produced, this feature-length adaptation of Alex Raymond's classic comic strip served as an elaborate pilot to a Saturday morning television series.

**Flight of the Dragons** (1986) ABC. Rankin-Bass. 96 mins. Directors: Jules Bass, Arthur Rankin Jr., Fumihiko Takayama, Katsuhisa Yamada. Screenplay: Jeffery Walker, Romeo Muller. Voices: John Ritter (Peter Dickenson), Harry Morgan (Carolinus), James Earl Jones (Ommadon). Based on novels by Peter Dickenson and Gordon R. Dickson, about a young writer who travels back in time to the Age of Magic.

**Disney's Fluppy Dogs** (1986) ABC. 60 mins. Director: Fred Wolf. Screenplay: Haskell Barkin. Voices: Marshall Efron (Stanley), Carl Stevens (Jamie Bingham), Hal Smith (Dink, Haimish). A band of dimension-hopping canines need the help of two kids to return home. Disney's first made-for-television movie.

**The Wind and the Willows** (1987) ABC. Rankin-Bass. 96 mins. Directors: Jules Bass, Arthur Rankin Jr. Screenplay: Romeo Muller. Voices: Charles Nelson Reilly (Mr. Toad), Eddie Bracken (Moley), Roddy McDowall (Ratty).

**Jonny's Golden Quest** (1993) 95 mins. USA Network. Hanna-Barbera. Director: Mario Piluso. Screenplay: Mark Young. Voices: Will Estes (Jonny), Don Messick (Dr. Quest), Granville Van Dusen (Race Bannon). *Jonny's Golden Quest* aired first on USA Network, making it the first made-for-cable animated feature. The film deals with the death of Jonny's mother, Mrs. Quest.

**Drawn from Memory** (1995) PBS. American Playhouse. 60 mins. Writer and director: Paul Fierlinger. Autobiographical film by independent animator Fierlinger about his life in various countries.

**Superman: Last Son of Krypton** (1996) WB Network, Warner Bros. Animation. 64 mins. Director: Curt Geda, Scott Jeralds, Dan Riba, Bruce W. Timm. Screenplay: Alan Burnett, Paul Dini. Voices: Tim Daly (Clark Kent, Kal-El, Superman), Dana Delany (Lois Lane), Clancy Brown (Lex Luthor). The origin of Superman, this movie served as an introduction to a new Superman animated series.

**Dexter's Laboratory Ego Trip** (1999) Cartoon Network. 64 mins. Director: Genndy Tartakovsky. Voices: Christine Cavanaugh (Dexter), Kathryn Cressida (Deedee), Eddie Deezen (Mandark). After Dexter is confronted with robots who wish to "destroy the one who saved the future," he uses his time machine to see how he saved it.

**Daria: Is It Fall Yet?** (2000) MTV. 75 mins. Directors: Karen Disher, Guy Moore. Screenplay: Glenn Eichler, Peggy Nicoll. Voices: Tracy Grandstaff (Daria), Wendy Hoopes (Jane), Russell Hankin (Tom). Based on MTV's *Daria*, explores the summer vacation of Daria and her classmates from Lawndale High.

**The Flintstones on the Rocks** (2001) Cartoon Network. 85 mins. Directors: Chris Savino, David Smith. Screenplay: Cindy Morrow, Clay Morrow, Chris Savino, David Smith. Voices: Jeff Bergman (Fred), Tress MacNeille (Wilma), Kevin Michael Richardson (Barney). The Flintstone marriage is crumbling and is not helped by an exotic vacation anniversary gift from the Rubbles.

**Star Wars: Clone Wars** (2003) Cartoon Network/Lucasfilm. 69 mins. Director: Genndy Tartakovsky. Screenplay: Bryan Andrews, Mark Andrews, Darrick Bachman, Paul Rudish, Genndy Tartakovsky. Voices: Mat Lucas (Annakin), Anthony Daniels (C-3PO), Grey DeLisle (Asajj Ventress). This film bridges the *Star Wars* story line between Episodes 2 (*Attack of the Clones*) and 3 (*Revenge of the Sith*). It was originally aired as a 20-part serial (as three-minute chapters) on Cartoon Network in 2003 and 2004 and was compiled into a legitimate feature-length version released in 2005.

## Top 20 Foreign Theatrical Features That Never Opened in the United States

*Note: Most of these are now available for home-video purchase.*

**The Tinderbox** (1946) A/S Palladium. Denmark. 68 mins. Director: Svend Methling. Screenplay: Peter Toubro, Henning Pade. Voices: Neville Williams (Soldier), Charlotte Vittmer (Princess), Watcyn Watcyns (Watchman). Hans Christian Andersen's classic tale.

**Rose of Bagdad** (1948) Italy. 76 mins. Director: Anton Gino Domenighini. Screenplay: Nina Maguire, Tony Maguire. Voices: Julie Andrews (Princess), Howard Marion-Crawford (Narrator). Also known as "The Singing Princess."

**Havoc in Heaven** (1961–64) China. 106 mins. Director: Wan Laiming. Screenplay: Li Kuero, Wan Laiming. Also known under the titles "Uproar in Heaven" or "Confusion in the Sky," was produced by the Shanghai Film Factory of Fine Arts. The definitive animated film of the Monkey King legend. First part was released in 1961, the second half came out in 1965.

**Ruddigore** (1966) 54 mins. (Great Britain) Director: Joy Batchelor. Voices: John Reed (Robin, Sir Ruthven), David Palmer (Richard Dauntless), Ann Hood (Rose Maybud). Adapted from the operetta by Gilbert and Sullivan.

**Jack and the Witch** (1967) Japan. 80 mins. Director: Gisaburo Sugii. Screenplay: Shinichi Sekizawa, Shinsaku Takahisa. Voice: Meiko Nakamura (Jack). Surreal anime fairy tale has a cult following today.

**The Little Norse Prince** (1968) Japan. 82 mins. Director: Isao Takahata. Screenplay: Kazuo Fukazawa. Voices: Hisako Ôkata (Hols), Mikijiro Hira (Ice Demon), Etsuko Ichihara (Hilda). One of Miyazaki's first animation assignments was assisting on this film—and his influence shows throughout.

**The Wonderful World of Puss in Boots** (1969) Japan. 80 mins. Director: Kimio Yabuki. Screenplay: Hisashi Inoue, Morihisa Yamamoto. Toei Doga's first foray into animation and a significant early credit for animator Hayao Miyazaki. Dubbed into English by Fred Ladd, and shown only on U.S. television.

**One Thousand and One Arabian Nights** (1969) Japan. 128 mins. Director: Eiichi Yamamoto. Screenplay: Kazuo Fukazawa, Hiroyuki Kumai, Osamu Tezuka. One of the first "adult" anime films—features graphic sexual sequences, psychedelic images, and a groovy rock score.

**Dick Deadeye, or, Duty Done** (1975) Great Britain. 81 mins. Director: Bill Melendez. Screenplay: Robin Miller, Leo Rost. Voices: Victor Spinetti, Peter Reeves, George A. Cooper. Another British animated feature adapting Gilbert and Sullivan, with stylish design by Ronald Searle.

**Son of the White Mare** (1980) Hungary. 81 mins. Director: Marcell Jankovics. Screenplay: Laszlo Gyorgy, Marcell Janovics. Based on Hungarian folktales, a humanoid son of a magical white horse goes on a quest to a netherworld to rescue three princesses. Outstanding art direction.

**Time Masters** (1981) France. 78 mins. Director: René Laloux. Screenplay: Jean Giraud (Moebius), René Laloux. Voices: Jean Valmont (Jaffar), Michel Elias (Silbad), Frédéric Legros (Piel). Laloux's (Fantastic Planet, Light Years) best film was never released in the United States—an ambitious attempt to bring Mobius comic art style to the screen.

**The Sea Prince and the Fire Child** (1981) Japan. 108 mins. Director: Masami Hata. Screenplay: Masami Hata, Chiho Katsura. Years after a war between the Children of Water and the Children of Fire, a sea prince named Sirius encounters a beautiful fire princess named Malta. Beautiful animation.

**Vuk (The Little Fox)** (1981) Hungary. 76 mins. Director: Attila Dargay. Screenplay: Attila Dargay, Ede Tarbay, István Imre, Ede Tarbay. Voices: Tibor Bitskey (Storyteller), József Gyabronka (Vuk), Judit Pogány (Young Vuk). An orphaned fox learns about the rules of the forest and the animal kingdom's feared enemy, man.

**Heroic Times** (1982) Hungary. 80 mins. Director and screenplay: Jozef Gémes. Legends of medieval knighthood in Hungary, told through a series of animated oil paintings.

**Samson and Sally: Song of the Whales** (1984) Denmark. 63 mins. Director: Jannik Hastrup. Screenplay: Bent Haller, Jannik Hastrup. Voices: Jesper Klein (Samson), Helle Hertz (Sally), Per Pallesen (Seagull). A whale searching for Moby Dick swims through polluted waters in this poignant comedy drama.

**Grave of the Fireflies** (1988) Japan. 85 mins. Director and screenplay: Isao Takahata. Voices: Tsutomu Tatsumi (Seita), Ayano Shiraishi (Setsuko), Yoshiko Shinohara (Mother). A young boy and his little sister struggle to survive in Japan during World War II.

**Kiki's Delivery Service** (1989) Japan. 105 mins. Director and screenplay: Hayao Miyazaki. Voices (Disney dub): Kirsten Dunst (Kiki), Debbie Reynolds (Miss Dora), Phil Hartman (Jiji). A young witch finds fitting into a new community difficult while she supports herself by running an air courier service.

**Porco Rosso** (1992) Japan. 94 mins. Director and screenplay: Hayao Miyazaki. Voices (Disney dub): Michael Keaton (Porco Rosso), Susan Egan (Gina), Cary Elwes (Curtis). Miyazaki aviation melodrama with spectacular arial battle sequence.

**Catnapped!** (1998) Japan. 90 mins. Director: Takashi Nakamura. Screenplay: Chiaki Konaka, Takashi Nakamura. A boy and his sister discover their dog has been abducted by anthropomorphic cats who plan to bring him to another world that will evolve the canine into a bizarre giant monster.

**The Cat Returns** (2002) Japan. 75 mins. Director: Hiroyuki Morita. Voices (Disney dub): Anne Hathaway (Haru), Rene Auberjonois (Natori), Peter Boyle (Muta). A girl rescues a cat from being hit by a truck. The cat turns out to be a prince from a cat kingdom.

# Appendix 3

# Top 20 Live-Action Films Featuring Great Animation

**King of Jazz** (1930) Universal. 105 mins. Director: John Murray Anderson. Screenplay: Charles MacArthur, Harry Ruskin. Animators: Walter Lantz, William Nolan. Cast: Paul Whiteman (Himself), Laura La Plante (The Editor, The Secretary), Bing Crosby (Himself). The opening animation sequence was the first ever to be produced in Technicolor.

**King Kong** (1933) RKO. 100 mins. Director: Merian C. Cooper, Ernest B. Schoedsack. Screenplay: James Ashmore Creelman, Ruth Rose. Cast: Fay Wray (Ann Darrow), Robert Armstrong (Carl Denham), Bruce Cabot (Jack Driscoll). Classic Willis O'Brien character animation of Kong—a stop-motion tour de force.

**Hollywood Party** (1934) MGM. 70 mins. Directors: Richard Boleslawski, Allan Dwan, Roy Rowland. Screenplay: Howard Dietz, Arthur Kober. Cast: Laurel and Hardy (Themselves), Jimmy Durante (Himself), Lupe Velez (Herself). Disney contributes a great sequence, "Hot Chocolate Soldiers," which is practically a Silly Symphony cartoon . . . and Mickey Mouse makes a cameo appearance with Jimmy Durante.

**Anchors Aweigh** (1945) MGM. 143 mins. Director: George Sidney. Screenplay: Isobel Lennart. Animators: Bill Hanna and Joe Barbera. Cast: Frank Sinatra (Clarence Doolittle), Gene Kelly (Joseph Brady), Kathryn Grayson (Susan Abbott). This film contains the classic "Worry Song" dance sequence with Gene Kelly and Jerry Mouse.

**Alice in Wonderland** (1951) Souvaine Selective Pictures, Inc. 96 mins. Producer: Lou Bunin. Director: Dallas Bower. Screenplay: Henry Meyers, Albert Lewin, Edward Eliscu. Production designers: Eugene Fleury, Bernyce Polifka. Cast: Carol Marsh (Alice), Steven Murray (Lewis Carroll), Pamela Brown (Queen Victoria). Released by Souvaine Selective Pictures, Inc. in 1951 despite Disney's best efforts to suppress it. This combination live-action/stop-motion film contains outstanding Lou Bunin puppet animation.

**Dangerous When Wet** (1953) MGM. 95 mins. Director: Charles Walters. Screenplay: Dorothy Kingsley. Cast: Esther Williams (Katie Higgins), Charlotte Greenwood (Ma Higgins), Fernando Lamas (Andre Lanet). Hanna & Barbera contribute a delightful animation sequence featuring Tom & Jerry swimming with Esther Williams.

**Invitation to the Dance** (1954) MGM. 93 mins. Director, screenplay: Gene Kelly. Cast: Gene Kelly (Host, Pierrot, The Marine, Sinbad), Igor Youskevitch (The Lover, The Artist), Tamara Toumanova (The Streetwalker). Hanna and Barbera team again with Gene Kelly in a tour-de-force 20-minute "Sinbad The Sailor" sequence that finds Kelly dancing in an enchanted animated world.

**Pink Panther** (1964) United Artists. 113 mins. Director: Blake Edwards. Screenplay: Blake Edwards, Maurice Richlin. Cast: Peter Sellers (Inspector Jacques Clouseau), David Niven (Sir Charles Lytton), Capucine (Simone Clouseau). The DePatie-Freleng title sequence almost stole the show (Sellers's Clouseau character shares the honor). It was a sensation and spawned the last great cartoon star from the golden age of animation.

**Mary Poppins** (1964) Disney. 140 mins. Director: Robert Stevenson. Screenplay: Bill Walsh, Don DaGradi, based on the novel by P. L Travers. Cast: Julie

Andrews (Mary Poppins), Dick Van Dyke (Bert, Mr. Dawes Sr.), David Tomlinson (Mr. George W. Banks). The animated "Jolly Holiday" sequence is one of the greatest moments in Disney history.

**Bedknobs and Broomsticks** (1971) Disney. 117 mins. Director: Robert Stevenson. Screenplay: Bill Walsh, Don DaGradi. Cast: Angela Lansbury (Eglantine Price), David Tomlinson (Mr. Emelius Browne), Roddy McDowall (Mr. Jelk). Similar to Mary Poppins, a 20-minute excursion to the animated storybook island of Naboombu steals the show in this elaborate musical fairy tale.

**The War Between Men and Women** (1972) National General Pictures. 110 mins. Director: Melville Shavelson. Screenplay: Melville Shavelson, Danny Arnold, based on the writings of James Thurber. Cast: Jack Lemmon (Peter Edward Wilson), Barbara Harris (Theresa Alice Kozlenko), Jason Robards (Stephen Kozlenko). DePatie Freleng provided the James Thurber-styled animated sequences in this comedy feature.

**Return of the Pink Panther** (1975) United Artists. 113 mins. Director: Blake Edwards. Screenplay: Frank Waldman, Blake Edwards. Cast: Peter Sellers (Inspector Jacques Clouseau), Christopher Plummer (Sir Charles Litton), Catherine Schell (Lady Claudine Litton). Richard Williams's title sequence is a spectacular display of character animation.

**Pink Floyd: The Wall** (1983) MGM/Tin Blue/ Goldcrest. 95 mins. Director: Alan Parker. Screenplay: Roger Waters. Cast: Bob Geldof (Pink), Christine Hargreaves (Pink's Mother), James Laurenson (Pink's Father). Gerald Scarfe's surreal animated sequences add to the outrageous visuals in this rock musical drama.

**Volere Volare** (1993) Fine Line Features. 98 mins. Directors: Guido Manuli, Maurizio Nichetti. Screenplay: Guido Manuli, Maurizio Nichetti. Cast: Maurizio Nichetti (Maurizio), Angela Finocchiaro (Martina), Mariella Valentini (Loredana). An Italian, R-rated live-action/animated comedy about a cartoon sound effects editor who becomes an animated character himself when aroused by a sexy new girlfriend.

**Alice** (1988) First Run Features. 86 mins. Director and screenplay: Jan Svankmajer. Cast: Kristyna Kohoutová (Alice). Surrealist Czech puppet animator Svankmajer adds his unique flavor to Lewis Carroll's world in this live-action/animation production.

**The Secret Adventures of Tom Thumb** (1994) Tara Releasing. 60 mins. Director and screenplay: Dave Borthwick. Cast: Nick Upton (Pa Thumb), Deborah Collar (Ma Thumb), Frank Passingham (Man). Poignant, provocative, and disturbing stop-motion animation combined with live action.

**Stuart Little** (1999) Columbia Pictures. 84 mins. Director: Rob Minkoff. Screenplay: M. Night Shyamalan and Gregory J. Brooker. Cast: Geena Davis (Mrs. Eleanor Little), Hugh Laurie (Mr. Fredrick Little), Jonathan Lipnicki (George Little). Live-action and computer-generated characters combine in this wonderful adaptation of E. B. White's classic novel. Michael J. Fox voices mousey Stuart Little, and Nathan Lane vocalizes Snowbell, the Littles' housecat.

**Monkey Bone** (2001) 20th Century Fox. 92 mins. Directed by Henry Selick. Screenplay: Sam Hamm. Cast: Brendan Fraser (Stu Miley), Bridget Fonda (Dr. Julie McElroy), Chris Kattan (Organ Donor Stu). Henry Selick (*Nightmare Before Christmas*) made this highly imaginative live-action/stop-motion feature film that was killed by the critics and tanked at the box office. In a coma, a cartoonist finds himself trapped within his own underground creation.

**Stuart Little 2** (2002) Columbia Pictures. 78 mins. Director: Rob Minkoff. Screenplay: Bruce Joel Rubin. Cast: Geena Davis (Mrs. Eleanor Little), Hugh Laurie (Mr. Fredrick Little), Jonathan Lipnicki (George Little). Even better character animation highlights this sequel based on E. B. White's book.

**Scooby Doo** (2002) Warner Bros. 86 mins. Director: Raja Gosnell. Screenplay: James Gunn. Cast: Freddie Prinze Jr. (Fred), Sarah Michelle Gellar (Daphne), Matthew Lillard (Shaggy). Live-action comedy mystery based on the Hanna-Barbera cartoon with surprisingly effective CG of Scooby Doo—a cartoonish, buffoonish Great Dane.

# Index